THE PATRISTIC UNDERSTANDING OF CREATION

THE PATRISTIC UNDERSTANDING OF CREATION

An Anthology of Writings from the Church Fathers on Creation and Design

Edited by William A. Dembski, Wayne J. Downs,
& Fr. Justin B. A. Frederick

Erasmus
PRESS

The Patristic Understanding of Creation: An Anthology of Writings from the Church Fathers on Creation and Design
Edited by William A. Dembski, Wayne J. Downs, and Fr. Justin B. A. Fredericks

Copyright 2008 by Erasmus Press

Published by Erasmus Press, an imprint of Influence Press, Nashville, TN

All rights reserved.

No part of this publication may be used or reproduced in any manner whatsoever without written permission, except in the case of brief quotations in critical articles and reviews. For permissions contact Influence Press at http://www.influence-press.com.

Since this page cannot legibly accommodate all the copyright notices, the following page constitutes an extension of the copyright page.

Designed by Erasmus Press

Printed in the United States of America.

ISBN: 978-1645-427-001 (print) 978-1645-427-018 (digital)

Library of Congress Control Number: 2008930284

Subject: REL106000 RELIGION / Religion & Science

PERMISSION ACKNOWLEDGEMENTS

Origen *Homilies on Genesis and Exodus*. In vol. 71 of *The Fathers of the Church*. Edited by Hermigild Dressler, O.F.M. Translated by Ronald E. Heine. Copyright © 1982 by The Catholic University of America Press. Used with permission: The Catholic University of America Press. Washington, DC.

Ephrem the Syrian *Selected Prose Works: Commentary on Genesis, Commentary on Exodus, Homily on Our Lord, Letter to Publius*. In vol. 91 of *The Fathers of the Church*. Edited by Kathleen McVey. Translated by Edward G. Matthews, Jr. and Joseph P. Amar. Copyright © 1994 by The Catholic University of America Press. Used with permission: The Catholic University of America Press. Washington, DC.

John Chrysostom *Homilies on Genesis (1 – 17)*. In vol. 74 of *The Fathers of the Church*. Edited by Thomas P. Halton. Translated by Robert C. Hill. Copyright © 1986 by The Catholic University of America Press. Used with permission: The Catholic University of America Press. Washington, DC.

Excerpts from *St. Augustine: The Literal Meaning of Genesis*, translated and annotated by John Hammond Taylor, SJ. Copyright © 1982 by Johannes Quasten, Rev. Walter J. Burghardt, SJ, and Thomas Comerford Lawler. Paulist Press. New York/Mahwah, NJ. Reprinted by permission of Paulist Press, Inc. www.paulistpress.com.

Excerpts from *Maximus Confessor: Select Writings*, translated and annotated by George C. Berthold. Copyright © 1985 George Berthold Paulist Press, Inc., New York/Mahwah, NJ. Reprinted by permission of Paulist Press, Inc. www.paulistpress.com

Maximus the Confessor: The Early Church Fathers series, by Andrew Louth, Copyright © 1996 by Routledge. Reproduced by permission of Taylor & Francis Books UK.

Florovsky, Georges. "Creation and Creaturehood." In *Creation and Redemption: Collected Works of Georges Florovsky, Vol. 3*. Copyright © 1976 by Nordland Publishing Company. The copyright owner is missing.

All other rights are registered as Public Domain. We are grateful to the Christian Classics Ethereal Library for their dedication to making the writings of the Church Fathers widely accessible at www.ccel.org.

Cover illustration: *The Big Bang*, by Alfred J. Smuskiewicz. Copyright © Alfred J. Smuskiewicz. Used by permission of Alfred J. Smuskiewicz.

CONTENTS

Foreword	i
Justin Martyr	1
Hortatory Appeal to the Greeks	2
The First Apology	15
The Second Apology	17
Athenagoras	18
A Plea for the Christians	18
Irenæus	28
Against Heresies, Book II	28
Against Heresies, Book IV	53
Clement of Alexandria	57
The Instructor, Book I	57
Stromata	58
Tertullian	59
Against Hermogenes	59
On the Resurrection of the Flesh	85
Theophilus of Antioch	90
To Autolycus, Book I	90
To Autolycus, Book II	92
Origen	103
Homilies on Genesis and Exodus	103
De Principiis, Book II	122
Contra Celsum, Book I	136
Contra Celsum, Book VI	139
Commentary on the Gospel of John	150
Lactantius	157
The Divine Institutes, Book II	158
The Divine Institutes, Book VII	175
Athanasius	190
Contra Gentes	191
On the Incarnation of the Word	206
Contra Arianos	220

Ephrem the Syrian	225
Commentary on Genesis	225
Methodius of Olympus	246
Concerning Free Will	246
Extracts from the Work on Things Created	261
Cyril of Jerusalem	268
Catechetical Lectures	268
Gregory Nazianzen	277
Orations	277
Basil the Great	284
Hexæmeron	284
Gregory of Nyssa	340
On the Making of Man	340
Against Eunomius, Book I	357
John Chrysostom	359
Homilies on John	359
Homilies on Romans	363
Homilies on Hebrews	364
Homilies on Genesis	366
Augustine of Hippo	418
The Literal Meaning of Genesis, Book I	419
The Literal Meaning of Genesis, Book II	425
The Literal Meaning of Genesis, Book IV	427
The Literal Meaning of Genesis, Book V	434
The Literal Meaning of Genesis, Book VI	443
City of God, Book XI	456
City of God, Book XII	481
Maximus	505
The Four Hundred Chapters on Love	505
Chapters on Knowledge	508
Difficulty 10	510

John of Damascus	516
An Exact Exposition of the	
Orthodox Faith, Book II	517
An Afterword by Georges Florovsky	536
"Creation and Creaturehood"	536
Florovsky Notes & References	566
List of Abbreviations	577
Bibliographic Information	578
Specific Locations of Cited Texts	580
Index	581

FOREWORD

All of the major theological themes that define Christian orthodoxy were first articulated and refined in the early centuries of Christianity and preserved in the ecumenical creeds and writings of the Church Fathers. Most of the early councils, such as the council at Nicaea in 325 AD, were convened to resolve disputes involving Christ's humanity and divinity. The Nicene Creed in its final form reflects the outcome of these disputes, bequeathing to the Church a wordy section describing the Father's only Son our Lord as: "God from God, Light from Light, True God from True God, Begotten, not made, one in being with the Father, through him all things were made...."

In contrast, the doctrine of creation, to judge from the creed, might seem to have gotten short shrift. All we have (in both the Nicene and Apostles' Creeds) is a simple, unadorned profession of belief in God as "Creator of heaven and earth." But this brevity does not imply that the doctrine of creation was unimportant to the Church Fathers. In reality, the doctrine of creation was fundamental; it simply was not the subject of intense debate *within* the Church, whereas Christology was. So in the Creeds we affirm the doctrine of creation in the very first sentence, and its truth is presupposed in all the claims that follow it.

But beyond that brief affirmation of God as Creator of "heaven and earth" – that is, of everything other than God – what did the Fathers teach about creation? Alas, answering that question is a bit daunting since their extant writings fill several bookshelves. The easiest way to provide an answer is to compile an anthology of their writings on the subject. That is the purpose of this volume.

This anthology is not, however, merely an exercise in historical nostalgia. In recent years, Christian leaders such as Pope Benedict XVI have called for renewed attention to the doctrine of creation. In the early 1980s, then Cardinal Joseph Ratzinger – now Pope Benedict XVI – observed that the creation itself is the subject of constant attention due to heightening environmental concerns, and yet, paradoxically, "the creation account is noticeably and nearly completely absent from catechesis, preaching, and even theology." Thus, in response to what he called "the practical abandonment of the doctrine of creation on influential modern theology," he wrote a series of homilies on the biblical creation account, which were later published as *'In the Beginning...'* (Eerdmans, 1995, pp. ix – x). These writings were intended to move the doctrine to the forefront of theological discussion; and accordingly, he has continued to emphasize the doctrine of creation in the years since he first wrote those homilies.

Pope Benedict's *'In the Beginning...'* is part of a book series intended, in part, as a *ressourcement* – a rediscovery of the Church's tradition, and especially its patristic and medieval sources – "for the purpose of drawing out the meaning and significance of these sources for the critical questions of our time" (inside page). This anthology represents the same desire for recovery and return.

A return to the original Christian reflection on a subject means, first of all, to read the primary sources directly. This is especially important when the primary sources have been widely misrepresented. It was just such a misrepresentation that led William Dembski to propose this anthology in the late 1990s. With Dembski's encouragement, Brian Frederick (now Eastern Orthodox priest Fr. Justin Frederick) began putting together a volume that encapsulated what the Church Fathers had to say, *in their own words*, on the topic of creation. Frederick made tremendous progress on the project, but it was only finally completed, a decade later, with the help of a third editor, Wayne Downs.

The need for this anthology has persisted – and indeed grown more urgent – in the years since it was first conceived. Process theology, open theism, and other efforts to revise the traditional concept of creation continue to gain ground within Christian circles. And certainly, the contemporary debate over intelligent design (ID) has done much to awaken the interest in this subject among a greater, more secular population.

In fact, Dembski first saw the need for this volume as a result of responding to an ID critic, physicist Howard Van Till. Van Till, at the time a physics professor at Calvin College, claimed that ID violated the creation's functional integrity, or what he later called the "robust formational economy principle." According to this principle, in creation God endowed nature with *all* the creative capacities it would ever need. Thus, once nature and its laws were in place, nature's productions would never require any further additions by God (such as supernatural interventions).

In hindsight, it is clear that Van Till's principle was an attempt to square Christian theology with "methodological naturalism" (the view that scientific inquiry may proceed only by invoking material forces governed by unbroken natural laws). But that was never his argument. Instead, he argued that his robust formational economy principle was rooted in the thought of two prominent Church Fathers, St. Basil the Great and St. Augustine of Hippo. Insofar as ID contradicted this putative principle, Van Till claimed that it was contrary to the Christian tradition.

In the intervening years, certain Christian academics – both Protestant and Catholic – have tried their hand at similar arguments. They claim that intelligent design is not only misguided but also contrary to traditional Christian theology. At times, ID proponents have been accused of promoting a "mechanistic" philosophy contrary to the Christian tradition; that is, of advocating a crude interventionism in which God, like a clockmaker, has to "fix up" a creation that he did not get right the first time. ID, it is said, also posits a God who is just another member of the universe – a mere Artificer rather than its transcendent Creator. Lapsed Catholic priest Francisco Ayala has gone so far as to charge ID proponents with blasphemy. ID proponents with theological training have argued, in response, that these accusations misrepresent not only ID but the Christian tradition as well.

The Patristic Understanding of Creation is intended to provide a representative cross-section of what the Church Fathers actually wrote about creation, design, and related topics. It begins with the early Church Father Justin Martyr (c. 100 – c. 165 AD) and ends with John of Damascus (c. 650 – c. 749 AD). Since all the sources precede by centuries the Great Schism between the Eastern and Western Christians in 1054 and the Reformation in 1517, this anthology thus draws on resources that are the common inheritance of Catholic, Eastern Orthodox, and Protestant Christians. Lastly, this volume includes an afterword by Russian Orthodox theologian Georges Florovsky, whose essay, "Creation and Creaturehood," situates the Church Fathers' understanding of creation within the current theological conversation in a way that is historically accurate and theologically sound.

While the Fathers show some diversity in their understanding of the doctrine of creation, the careful reader can glean from their writings an emerging "patristic consensus." The Fathers, in general, were committed to creation ex nihilo, to a beginning not only of the creation but of time itself, to the transcendence and immanence of God in creation, to "the absolute creatureliness and non-self-sufficiency of the world" (to use a phrase of Florovsky), to the original goodness of creation, and to the openness of the world to divine action. Moreover, contrary to many modern-day critics of intelligent design, the Fathers affirmed that God is free to act in a variety of ways within the created order.

Though the full-blown Christian doctrine of creation emerged from their reflection on God's special revelation, the Fathers believed that reason alone should lead everyone to acknowledge a Creator. As St. Athanasius puts it in this anthology: "The rationality and order of the universe proves that it is the work of reason or Word of God." St. Gregory Nazianzen, one of the so-called Cappadocian Fathers, says much the same thing: "Now our very eyes and the Law of Nature teach us that God exists and that He is the Efficient and Maintaining Cause of all things."

Design also makes a frequent appearance in these patristic texts. Gregory Nazianzen presents an argument of design much like William Paley's – with one important difference. Rather than comparing the creation to a watch, Gregory compares it to a lute:

> For every one who sees a beautifully made lute, and considers the skill with which it has been fitted together and arranged, or who hears its melody, would think of none but the lutemaker, or the luteplayer, and would recur to him in mind, though he might not know him by sight. And thus to us also is manifested That which made and moves and preserves all created things, even though He be not comprehended by the mind. And very wanting in sense is he who will not willingly go thus far in following natural proofs.... For what is it which ordered things in heaven and things in earth?... Is it not the Artificer of them Who implanted reason in them all, in accordance with which the Universe is moved and controlled?

As Dembski has noted, the lute is a much more fitting theological metaphor than a watch, since it suggests not only that God is the Creator, but also that God interacts continually with his creation (see William Dembski's *The Design Revolution*, p. 149 as well as chs. 7 and 20).

This project was supported financially by Discovery Institute's Center for Science & Culture, and falls within its mandate for cultural engagement. Modern ID arguments are an attempt to establish design on the basis of public scientific evidence and natural reason apart from special revelation. For that reason, they can be properly considered within natural science and philosophy. At the same time, ID has obvious cultural and theological implications. In recent years, critics of ID have made much of ID's supposed incompatibility with Christian theology. Our hope is that this volume will allow open-minded observers and participants to evaluate that charge for themselves.

Much of the modern case for intelligent design is based on evidence unknown to Justin Martyr, Athanasius, Augustine, and the like. Nevertheless, a careful reading of the texts in this anthology should make clear that while intelligent design does not, by itself, provide a theology of nature or a doctrine of creation, its theological implications are quite at home in the orthodox Christian tradition.

- *Jay W. Richards, Ph.D. is a Senior Fellow and Director of Research at the Discovery Institute.*

Justin Martyr

St. Justin Martyr (c. 100 – c. 165) was a philosopher who later in life converted to Christianity. Putting his philosophical training to work, he became an apologist, defending the Christian faith from attacks by pagans and Jews. He was martyred with several companions under Emperor Marcus Aurelius for refusing to offer sacrifice to the Roman gods.

Hortatory Appeal to the Greeks is not Justin's best-known work, and many scholars now doubt that he wrote it, though it is widely attributed to him. If it is not his, it probably dates to the third century. *The Appeal* treats the Christian doctrine of Creation in response to Greek philosophical and poetical conceptions of the world's origin. The author responds to various prevailing opinions of his day concerning the origin of the world by arguing that vestiges of the truth are to be found in the philosophers and poets but that the full truth about creation is to be found in the Hebrew prophets.

The author thus argues that whatever Plato and Homer correctly expressed about the origin of the world resulted from their familiarity with the writings of Moses, a view held by other early Fathers. He points out disagreements among the philosophers as evidence that they do not know the truth; moreover, he argues that Christians do know the truth through God's revelation to Moses. He also affirms the creation of time.

In his two *Apologies*, Justin speaks of God creating the world out of unformed matter, as taught by Plato. This idea, though at odds with other Fathers, is in keeping with Justin's apologetic purpose of showing the extent to which Christian teaching is also found in Greek philosophy, thereby highlighting similarities between Christians and pagans. For Justin, Christian distinctiveness consists in Christians being more virtuous and knowing the truth more completely than their pagan counterparts. A lesson he wanted his pagan readers to draw is that Christians are persecuted unjustly and innocent of any crime.

Justin Martyr *Hortatory Appeal to the Greeks*

Chapter III – Opinions of the School of Thales

And if you decline citing the poets, because you say it is allowable for them to frame myths, and to relate in a mythical way many things about the gods which are far from true, do you suppose you have some others for your religious teachers, or how do you say that they themselves have learned this religion of yours? For it is impossible that any should know matters so great and divine, who have not themselves learned them first from the initiated. You will no doubt say, "The sages and philosophers." For to them, as to a fortified wall, you are wont to flee, when any one quotes the opinions of your poets about the gods.

Therefore, since it is fit that we commence with the ancients and the earliest, beginning thence I will produce the opinion of each, much more ridiculous as it is than the theology of the poets. For Thales of Miletus, who took the lead in the study of natural philosophy, declared that water was the first principle of all things; for from water he says that all things are, and that into water all are resolved. And after him Anaximander, who came from the same Miletus, said that the infinite was the first principle of all things; for that from this indeed all things are produced, and into this do all decay. Thirdly, Anaximenes – and he too was from Miletus – says that air is the first principle of all things; for he says that from this all things are produced, and into this all are resolved. Heraclitus and Hippasus, from Metapontus, say that fire is the first principle of all things; for from fire all things proceed, and in fire do all things terminate. Anaxagoras of Clazomenae said that the homogeneous parts are the first principles of all things. Archelaus, the son of Apollodorus, an Athenian, says that the infinite air and its density and rarity are the first principle of all things. All these, forming a succession from Thales, followed the philosophy called by themselves physical.

Chapter IV – Opinions of Pythagoras and Epicurus

Then, in regular succession from another starting-point, Pythagoras the Samian, son of Mnesarchus, calls numbers, with their proportions and harmonies, and the elements composed of both, the first principles; and he includes also unity and the indefinite binary. Epicurus, an Athenian, the son of Neocles, says that the first principles of the things that exist are bodies perceptible by reason, admitting no vacuity, unbegotten, indestructible, which can neither be broken, nor admit of any formation of their parts, nor alteration, and are therefore perceptible by reason. Empedocles of Agrigentum, son of Meton, maintained that there were four elements – fire, air, water, earth; and two elementary powers – love and hate, of which the former is a power of union, the latter of separation.

You see, then, the confusion of those who are considered by you to have been wise men, whom you assert to be your teachers of religion: some of them declaring that water is the first principle of all things; others, air others, fire; and others, some other of these fore-mentioned elements; and all of them employing persuasive arguments for the establishment of their own errors, and attempting to prove their own peculiar dogma to be the most valuable.

These things were said by them. How then, ye men of Greece, can it be safe for those who desire to be saved, to fancy that they can learn the true religion from these philosophers, who were neither able so to convince themselves as to prevent sectarian wrangling with one another, and not to appear definitely opposed to one another's opinions?

Chapter V – Opinions of Plato and Aristotle

But possibly those who are unwilling to give up the ancient and inveterate error, maintain that they have received the doctrine of their religion not from those who have now been mentioned, but from those who are esteemed among them as the most renowned and finished philosophers, Plato and Aristotle. For these, they say, have learned the perfect and true religion. But I would be glad to ask, first of all, from those who say so, from whom they say that these men have learned this knowledge; for it is impossible that men who have not learned these so great and divine matters from some who knew them, should either themselves know them, or be able correctly to teach others; and, in the second place, I think we ought to examine the opinions even of these sages. For we shall see whether each of these does not manifestly contradict the other. But if we find that even they do not agree with each other, I think it is easy to see clearly that they too are ignorant.

For Plato, with the air of one that has descended from above, and has accurately ascertained and seen all that is in heaven, says that the most high God exists in a fiery substance. But Aristotle, in a book addressed to Alexander of Macedon, giving a compendious explanation of his own philosophy, clearly and manifestly overthrows the opinion of Plato, saying that God does not exist in a fiery substance: but inventing, as a fifth substance, some kind of ætherial and unchangeable body, says that God exists in it. Thus, at least, he wrote: "Not, as some of those who have erred regarding the Deity say, that God exists in a fiery substance." Then, as if he were not satisfied with this blasphemy against Plato, he further, for the sake of proving what he says about the ætherial body, cites as a witness him whom Plato had banished from his republic as a liar, and as being an imitator of the images of truth at three removes, for so Plato calls Homer; for he wrote: "Thus at least did Homer speak, 'And Zeus obtained the wide heaven in the air and the clouds,'" wishing to make his own opinion appear more worthy of credit by the testimony of Homer; not being aware that if he used Homer as a witness to prove that he spoke truth, many of his tenets would be proved untrue.

For Thales of Miletus, who was the founder of philosophy among them, taking occasion from him, will contradict his first opinions about first principles. For Aristotle himself, having said that God and matter are the first principles of all things, Thales, the eldest of all their sages, says that water is the first principle of the things that exist; for he says that all things are from water, and that all things are resolved into water. And he conjectures this, first, from the fact that the seed of all living creatures, which is their first principle, is moist; and secondly, because all plants grow and bear fruit in moisture, but when deprived of moisture, wither. Then, as if not satisfied with his conjectures, he cites Homer as a most trustworthy testimony, who speaks thus: "Ocean, who is the origin of all."

May not Thales, then, very fairly say to him, "What is the reason, Aristotle, why you give heed to Homer, as if he spoke truth, when you wish to demolish the opinions of Plato; but when you promulgate an opinion contrary to ours, you think Homer untruthful?"

Chapter VI – Further Disagreements between Plato and Aristotle

And that these very wonderful sages of yours do not even agree in other respects, can be easily learned from this. For while Plato says that there are three first principles of all things, God, and matter, and form – God, the maker of all; and matter, which is the subject of the first production of all that is produced, and affords to God opportunity for His workmanship; and form, which is the type of each of the things produced – Aristotle makes no mention at all of form as a first principle, but says that there are two, God and matter. And again, while Plato says that the highest God and the ideas exist in the first place of the highest heavens, and in fixed sphere, Aristotle says that, next to the most high God, there are, not ideas, but certain gods, who can be perceived by the mind. Thus, then, do they differ concerning things heavenly?

So that one can see that they not only are unable to understand our earthly matters, but also, being at variance among themselves regarding these things, they will appear unworthy of credit when they treat of things heavenly. And that even their doctrine regarding the human soul as it now is does not harmonize, is manifest from what has been said by each of them concerning it. For Plato says that it is of three parts, having the faculty of reason, of affection, and of appetite. But Aristotle says that the soul is not so comprehensive as to include also corruptible parts, but only reason. And Plato loudly maintains that "the whole soul is immortal." But Aristotle, naming it "the actuality," would have it to be mortal, not immortal. And the former says it is always in motion; but Aristotle says that it is immoveable, since it must itself precede all motion.

Chapter VII – Inconsistencies of Plato's Doctrine

But in these things they are convicted of thinking in contradiction to each other. And if any one will accurately criticise their writings, they have chosen to abide in harmony not even with their own opinions.

Plato, at any rate, at one time says that there are three first principles of the universe – God, and matter, and form; but at another time four, for he adds the universal soul. And again, when he has already said that matter is eternal, he afterwards says that it is produced; and when he has first given to form its peculiar rank as a first principle, and has asserted for its self-subsistence, he afterwards says that this same thing is among the things perceived by the understanding. Moreover, having first declared that everything that is made is mortal he afterwards states that some of the things that are made are indestructible and immortal.

What, then, is the cause why those who have been esteemed wise among you disagree not only with one another but also with themselves? Manifestly, their unwillingness to learn from those who know, and their desire to attain accurate knowledge of things heavenly by their own human excess of wisdom though they were able to understand not even earthly matters.

Certainly some of your philosophers say that the human soul is in us; others, that it is around us. For not even in this did they choose to agree with one another, but, distributing, as it were, ignorance in various ways among themselves, they thought fit to wrangle and dispute with one another even about the soul. For some of them say that the soul is fire, and some that it is the air; and others, the mind; and others, motion; and others, an exhalation; and certain others say that it is a power flowing from the stars; and others, number capable of motion; and others, a generating water. And a wholly confused and inharmonious opinion has prevailed among them, which only in this one respect appears praiseworthy to those who can form a right judgment, that they have been anxious to convict one another of error and falsehood.

Chapter VIII – Antiquity, Inspiration, and Harmony of Christian Teachers

Since therefore it is impossible to learn anything true concerning religion from your teachers, who by their mutual disagreement have furnished you with sufficient proof of their own ignorance, I consider it reasonable to recur to our progenitors, who both in point of time have by a great way the precedence of your teachers, and who have taught us nothing from their own private fancy, nor differed with one another, nor attempted to overturn one another's positions, but without wrangling and contention received from God the knowledge which also they taught to us. For neither by nature nor by human conception is it possible for men to know things so great and divine, but by the gift which then descended from above upon the holy men, who had no need of rhetorical art, nor of uttering anything in a contentious or quarrelsome manner, but to present themselves pure to the energy of the Divine Spirit, in order that the divine plectrum itself, descending from heaven, and using righteous men as an instrument like a harp or lyre, might reveal to us the knowledge of things divine and heavenly. Wherefore, as if with one mouth and one tongue, they have in succession, and in harmony with one another, taught us both concerning God, and the creation of the world, and the formation of man, and concerning the immortality of the human soul, and the judgment which is to be after this life, and concerning all things which it is needful for us to know, and thus in divers times and places have afforded us the divine instruction.

Chapter XIII – History of the Septuagint

But if any one says that the writings of Moses and of the rest of the prophets were also written in the Greek character, let him read profane histories, and know that Ptolemy, king of Egypt, when he had built the library in Alexandria, and by gathering books from every quarter had filled it, then learnt that very ancient histories written in Hebrew happened to be carefully preserved; and wishing to know their contents, he sent for seventy wise men from Jerusalem, who were acquainted with both the Greek and Hebrew language, and appointed them to translate the books; and that in freedom from all disturbance they might the more speedily complete the translation, he ordered that there should be constructed, not in the city itself, but seven stadia off (where the Pharos was built), as many little cots as there were translators, so that each by himself might complete his own translation; and enjoined upon those officers who were appointed to this duty, to afford them all attendance, but to prevent communication with one another, in order that the accuracy of the translation might be discernible even by their agreement. And when he ascertained that the seventy men had not only given the same meaning, but had employed the same words, and had failed in agreement with one another not even to the extent of one word; but had written the same things, and concerning the same things, he was struck with amazement, and believed that the translation had been written by divine power, and perceived that the men were worthy of all honour, as beloved of God; and with many gifts ordered them to return to their own country. And having, as was natural, marvelled at the books, and concluded them to be divine, he consecrated them in that library.

These things, ye men of Greece, are no fable, nor do we narrate fictions; but we ourselves having been in Alexandria, saw the remains of the little cots at the Pharos still preserved, and having heard these things from the inhabitants, who had received them as part of their country's tradition, we now tell to you what you can also learn from others, and specially from those wise and esteemed men who have written of these things, Philo and Josephus, and many others. But if any of those who are wont to be forward in contradiction should say that these books do not belong to us, but to the Jews, and should assert that we in vain profess to have learnt our religion froth them, let him know, as he may from those very things which are written in these books, that not to them, but to us, does the doctrine of them refer.

That the books relating to our religion are to this day preserved among the Jews, has been a work of Divine Providence on our behalf; for lest, by producing them out of the Church, we should give occasion to those who wish to slander us to charge us with fraud, we demand that they be produced from the synagogue of the Jews, that from the very books still preserved among them it might clearly and evidently appear, that the laws which were written by holy men for instruction pertain to us.

Chapter XX – Testimony of Plato

But Plato, though he accepted, as is likely, the doctrine of Moses and the other prophets regarding one only God, which he learned while in Egypt, yet fearing, on account of what had befallen Socrates, lest he also should raise up some Anytus or Meletus against himself, who should accuse him before the Athenians, and say, "Plato is doing harm, and making himself mischievously busy, not acknowledging the gods recognised by the state; "in fear of the hemlock-juice, contrives an elaborate and ambiguous discourse concerning the gods, furnishing by his treatise gods to those who wish them, and none for those who are differently disposed, as may readily be seen from his own statements. For when he has laid down that everything that is made is mortal, he afterwards says that the gods were made.

If, then, he would have God and matter to be the origin of all things, manifestly it is inevitably necessary to say that the gods were made of matter; but if of matter, out of which he said that evil also had its origin, he leaves right-thinking persons to consider what kind of beings the gods should be thought who are produced out of matter. For, for this very reason did he say that matter was eternal, that he might not seem to say that God is the creator of evil.

And regarding the gods who were made by God, there is no doubt he said this: "Gods of gods, of whom I am the creator." And he manifestly held the correct opinion concerning the really existing God. For having heard in Egypt that God had said to Moses, when He was about to send him to the Hebrews, "I am that I am," he understood that God had not mentioned to him His own proper name.

Chapter XXI – The Namelessness of God

For God cannot be called by any proper name, for names are given to mark out and distinguish their subject-matters, because these are many and diverse; but neither did any one exist before God who could give Him a name, nor did He Himself think it right to name Himself, seeing that He is one and unique, as He Himself also by His own prophets testifies, when He says, "I God am the first," and after this, "And beside me there is no other God." On this account, then, as I before said, God did not, when He sent Moses to the Hebrews, mention any name, but by a participle He mystically teaches them that He is the one and only God. "For," says He; "I am the Being;" manifestly contrasting Himself, "the Being," with those who are not, that those who had hitherto been deceived might see that they were attaching themselves, not to beings, but to those who had no being.

Since, therefore, God knew that the first men remembered the old delusion of their forefathers, whereby the misanthropic demon contrived to deceive them when he said to them, "If ye obey me in transgressing the commandment of God, ye shall be as gods," calling those gods which had no being, in order that men, supposing that there were other gods in existence, might believe that they themselves could become gods. On this account He said to Moses, "I am the

Being," that by the participle "being" He might teach the difference between God who is and those who are not.

Men, therefore, having been duped by the deceiving demon, and having dared to disobey God, were cast out of Paradise, remembering the name of gods, but no longer being taught by God that there are no other gods. For it was not just that they who did not keep the first commandment, which it was easy to keep, should any longer be taught, but should rather be driven to just punishment. Being therefore banished from Paradise, and thinking that they were expelled on account of their disobedience only, not knowing that it was also because they had believed in the existence of gods which did not exist, they gave the name of gods even to the men who were afterwards born of themselves.

This first false fancy, therefore, concerning gods, had its origin with the father of lies. God, therefore, knowing that the false opinion about the plurality of gods was burdening the soul of man like some disease, and wishing to remove and eradicate it, appeared first to Moses, and said to him, "I am He who is." For it was necessary, I think, that he who was to be the ruler and leader of the Hebrew people should first of all know the living God. Wherefore, having appeared to him first, as it was possible for God to appear to a man, He said to him, "I am He who is;" then, being about to send him to the Hebrews, He further orders him to say, "He who is hath sent me to you."

Chapter XXII – Studied Ambiguity Plato

Plato accordingly having learned this in Egypt, and being greatly taken with what was said about one God, did indeed consider it unsafe to mention the name of Moses, on account of his teaching the doctrine of one only God, for he dreaded the Areopagus; but what is very well expressed by him in his elaborate treatise, the Timaeus, he has written in exact correspondence with what Moses said regarding God, though he has done so, not as if he had learned it from him, but as if he were expressing his own opinion. For he said, "In my opinion, then, we must first define what that is which exists eternally, and has no generation, and what that is which is always being generated, but never really is."

Does not this, ye men of Greece, seem to those who are able to understand the matter to be one and the same thing, saving only the difference of the article? For Moses said, "He who is," and Plato,

"That which is." But either of the expressions seems to apply to the ever-existent God. For He is the only one who eternally exists, and has no generation. What, then, that other thing is which is contrasted with the ever-existent, and of which he said, "And what that is which is always being generated, but never really is," we must attentively consider. For we shall find him clearly and evidently saying that He who is unbegotten is eternal, but that those that are begotten and made are generated and perish – as he said of the same class, "gods of gods, of whom I am maker" – for he speaks in the following words: "In my opinion, then, we must first define what that is which is always existent and has no birth, and what that is which is always being generated but never really is. The former, indeed, which is apprehended by reflection combined with reason, always exists in the same way; while the latter, on the other hand, is conjectured by opinion formed by the perception of the senses unaided by reason, since it never really is, but is coming into being and perishing."

These expressions declare to those who can rightly understand them the death and destruction of the gods that have been brought into being. And I think it necessary to attend to this also, that Plato never names him the creator, but the fashioner of the gods, although, in the opinion of Plato, there is considerable difference between these two. For the creator creates the creature by his own capability and power, being in need of nothing else; but the fashioner frames his production when he has received from matter the capability for his work.

Chapter XXIII – Plato's Self-Contradiction

But, perhaps, some who are unwilling to abandon the doctrines of polytheism, will say that to these fashioned gods the maker said, "Since ye have been produced, ye are not immortal, nor at all, imperishable; yet shall ye not perish nor succumb to the fatality of death, because you have obtained my will, which is a still greater and mightier bond." Here Plato, through fear of the adherents of polytheism, introduces his "maker" uttering words which contradict himself. For having formerly stated that he said that everything which is produced is perishable, he now introduces him saying the very opposite; and he does not see that it is thus absolutely impossible for him to escape the charge of falsehood. For he either at first uttered what is false when he said that everything which is produced is perishable, or now, when he propounds the very opposite to what he had formerly said. For if, according to his former definition, it is absolutely necessary that every created thing be perishable, how can he consistently make that possible which is absolutely impossible? So that Plato seems to grant an empty and impossible prerogative to his "maker," when he propounds that those who were once perishable because made from matter should again, by his intervention, become imperishable and enduring. For it is quite natural that the power of matter, which, according to Plato's opinion, is uncreated, and contemporary and coaeval with the maker, should resist his will. For he who has not created has no power, in respect of that which is uncreated, so that it is not possible that it (matter), being free, can be controlled by any external necessity. Wherefore Plato himself, in consideration of this, has written thus: "It is necessary to affirm that God cannot suffer violence."

Chapter XXVI – Plato Indebted to the Prophets

And let no one wonder that Plato should believe Moses regarding the eternity of God. For you will find him mystically referring the true knowledge of realities to the prophets, next in order after the really existent God. For, discoursing in the Timaeus about certain first principles, he wrote thus: "This we lay down as the first principle of fire and the other bodies, proceeding according to probability and necessity. But the first principles of these again God above knows, and whosoever among men is beloved of Him." And what men does he think beloved of God, but Moses and the rest of the prophets? For their prophecies he read, and, having learned from them the doctrine of the judgment, he thus proclaims it in the first book of the Republic....

Chapter XXX – Homer's Knowledge of Man's Origin

And he was obviously deceived in the same way regarding the earth and heaven and man; for he supposes that there are "ideas" of these. For as Moses wrote thus, "In the beginning God created the heaven and the earth," and then subjoins this sentence, "And the earth was invisible and unfashioned," he thought that it was the pre-existent earth which was spoken of in the words, "The earth was," because Moses said, "And the earth was invisible and unfashioned;" and he thought that the earth, concerning which he says, "God created the heaven and the earth," was that earth which we perceive by the senses, and which God made according to the pre-existent form. And so also, of the heaven which was created, he thought that the heaven which was created – and which he also called the firmament – was that creation which the senses perceive; and that the heaven which the intellect perceives is that other of which the prophet said, "The heaven of heavens is the Lord's, but the earth hath He given to the children of men." And so also concerning man: Moses first mentions the name of man, and then after many other creations he makes mention of the formation of man, saying, "And God made man, taking dust from the earth."

He thought, accordingly, that the man first so named existed before the man who was made, and that he who was formed of the earth was afterwards made according to the pre-existent form. And that man was formed of earth, Homer, too, having discovered from the ancient and divine history which says, "Dust thou art, and unto dust shalt thou return," calls the lifeless body of Hector dumb clay. For in condemnation of Achilles dragging the corpse of Hector after death, he says somewhere: "On the dumb clay he cast indignity, Blinded with rage." And again, somewhere else, he introduces Menelaus, thus addressing those who were not accepting Hector's challenge to single combat with becoming alacrity – "To earth and water may you all return," – resolving them in his violent rage into their original and pristine formation from earth. These things Homer and Plato, having learned in Egypt from the ancient histories, wrote in their own words.

Chapter XXXIII – Plato's Idea of the Beginning of Time Drawn from Moses

And from what source did Plato draw the information that time was created along with the heavens? For he wrote thus: "Time, accordingly, was created along with the heavens; in order that, coming into being together, they might also be together dissolved, if ever their dissolution should take place." Had he not learned this from the divine history of Moses? For he knew that the creation of time had received its original constitution from days and months and years.

Since, then, the first day which was created along with the heavens constituted the beginning of all time (for thus Moses wrote, "In the beginning God created the heavens and the earth," and then immediately subjoins, "And one day was made," as if he would designate the whole of time by one part of it), Plato names the day "time," lest, if he mentioned the "day," he should seem to lay himself open to the accusation of the Athenians, that he was completely adopting the expressions of Moses. And from what source did he derive what he has written regarding the dissolution of the heavens? Had he not learned this, too, from the sacred prophets, and did he not think that this was their doctrine?

Chapter XXXVI – True Knowledge Not Held by the Philosophers

And if "the discovery of the truth" be given among them as one definition of philosophy, how are they who are not in possession of the true knowledge worthy of the name of philosophy? For if Socrates, the wisest of your wise men, to whom even your oracle, as you yourselves say, bears witness, saying, "Of all men Socrates is the wisest" – if he confesses that he knows nothing, how did those who came after him profess to know even things heavenly? For Socrates said that he was on this account called wise, because, while other men pretended to know what they were ignorant of, he himself did not shrink from confessing that he knew nothing. For he said, "I seem to myself to be wisest by this little particular, that what I do not know, I do not suppose I know."

Let no one fancy that Socrates ironically feigned ignorance, because he often used to do so in his dialogues. For the last expression of his apology which he uttered as he was being led away to the prison, proves that in seriousness and truth he was confessing his ignorance: "But now it is time to go away, I indeed to die, but you to live. And which of us goes to the better state, is hidden to all but God." Socrates, indeed, having uttered this last sentence in the Areopagus, departed to the prison, ascribing to God alone the knowledge of those things which are hidden from us; but those who came after him, though they are unable to comprehend even earthly things, profess to understand things heavenly as if they had seen them.

Aristotle at least – as if he had seen things heavenly with greater accuracy than Plato – declared that God did not exist, as Plato said, in the fiery substance (for this was Plato's doctrine) but in the fifth element, air. And while he demanded that concerning these matters he should be believed on account of the excellence of his language, he yet departed this life because he was overwhelmed with the infamy and disgrace of being unable to discover even the nature of the Euripus in Chalcis.

Let not any one, therefore, of sound judgment prefer the elegant diction of these men to his own salvation, but let him, according to that old story, stop his ears with wax, and flee the sweet hurt which these sirens would inflict upon him. For the above-mentioned men, presenting their elegant language as a kind of bait, have sought to seduce many from the right religion, in imitation of him who dared to teach the first men polytheism.

Be not persuaded by these persons, I entreat you, but read the prophecies of the sacred writers. And if any slothfulness or old hereditary superstition prevents you from reading the prophecies of the holy men through which you can be instructed regarding the one only God, which is the first article of the true religion, yet believe him who, though at first he taught you polytheism, yet afterwards preferred to sing a useful and necessary recantation – I mean Orpheus, who said what I quoted a little before; and believe the others who wrote the same things concerning one God. For it was the work of Divine Providence on your behalf, that they, though unwillingly, bore testimony that what the prophets said regarding one God was true, in order that, the doctrine of a plurality of gods being rejected by all, occasion might be afforded you of knowing the truth.

Justin Martyr *The First Apology*

Chapter X – How God is to be Served

But we have received by tradition that God does not need the material offerings which men can give, seeing, indeed, that He Himself is the provider of all things... And we have been taught that He in the beginning did of His goodness, for man's sake, create all things out of unformed matter... For as in the beginning He created us when we were not, so do we consider that, in like manner, those who choose what unpleasing to Him are, on account of their choice, deemed worthy of incorruption and of fellowship with Him. For the coming into being at first was not in our own power...

Chapter XX – Heathen Analogies to Christian Doctrine

And the Sibyl and Hystaspes said that there should be a dissolution by God of things corruptible. And the philosophers called Stoics teach that even God Himself shall be resolved into fire, and they say that the world is to be formed anew by this revolution; but we understand that God, the Creator of all things, is superior to the things that are to be changed. If, therefore, on some points we teach the same things as the poets and philosophers whom you honour, and on other points are fuller and more divine in our teaching, and if we alone afford proof of what we assert, why are we unjustly hated more than all others? For while we say that all things have been produced and arranged into a world by God, we shall seem to utter the doctrine of Plato; and while we say that there will be a burning up of all, we shall seem to utter the doctrine of the Stoics: and while we affirm that the souls for the wicked, being endowed with sensation even after death, are punished, and that those of the good being delivered from punishment spent a blessed existence, we shall seem to say the same things as the poets and philosophers; and while we maintain that men ought not to worship the works of their hands, we say the very same things which have been said by the comic poet Menander, and other similar writers, for they have declared that the workman is greater than the work.

Chapter LIX – Plato's Obligation to Moses

And that you may learn that it was from our teachers – we mean the account given through the prophets – that Plato borrowed his statement that God, having altered matter which was shapeless, made the world, hear the very words spoken by Moses, who, as above shown, was the first prophet, and of greater antiquity than the Greek writers; and through whom the Spirit of prophecy, signifying how and from what materials God at first formed the world, spake thus: "In the beginning God created the heaven and the earth. And the earth was invisible and unfurnished, and darkness was upon the face of the deep; and the Spirit of God moved over the waters. And God said, 'Let there be light;' and it was so." So that both Plato and they who agree with him, and we ourselves, have learned, and you also can be convinced, that by the word of God the whole world was made out of the substance spoken of before by Moses. And that which the poets call Erebus, we know was spoken of formerly by Moses.

Justin Martyr *The Second Apology*

Chapter IV – Why the Christians do not Kill Themselves

But lest some one say to us, "Go then all of you and kill yourselves, and pass even now to God, and do not trouble us," I will tell you why we do not so, but why, when examined, we fearlessly confess. We have been taught that God did not make the world aimlessly, but for the sake of the human race; and we have before stated that He takes pleasure in those who imitate His properties, and is displeased with those that embrace what is worthless either in word or deed. If, then, we all kill ourselves we shall become the cause, as far as in us lies, why no one should be born, or instructed in the divine doctrines, or even why the human race should not exist; and we shall, if we so act, be ourselves acting in opposition to the will of God.

Athenagoras

> Athenagoras of Athens (second century) was, in the judgment of many, the most eloquent of the early Christian apologists. Little is known about him. His *Apology* (also known as *A Plea for the Christians*), written about 177, is addressed to the Emperor and Stoic philosopher Marcus Aurelius.
>
> Described as "the Christian Philosopher of Athens," he had a well-developed doctrine of the Trinity and upheld the eternal permanence of marriage. His main project was to refute the charge that Christians are atheists. In making this defense, he has occasion to write on creation, engaging Greek thinking on the topic.
>
> Athenagoras makes a vital ontological distinction between Creator and created things. The earth is created as a sphere. The universe reflects reason (*logos*) because God created all things through His Son, the *Logos*. Having created the universe, God continues to preserve it in existence and to exercise providential care over all aspects of it.
>
> Athenagoras uses a striking image for the relation of God to the universe, one used by other Fathers who followed him: the universe is like a well-tuned instrument, and God is the One who has made it, tuned it, plays it, and sings to its accompaniment. The instrument without the musician is dull and silent; so, too, the universe without God.
>
> This image and others from the Fathers clash with more recent conceptions of the universe that view it as a machine. Machines, unlike musical instruments, run on their own according to fixed natural laws. The machine metaphor for the universe gave rise, historically, to deism and materialism – both of which contradict the Fathers' understanding of creation.

Athenagoras *A Plea for the Christians*

Chapter IV – The Christians are Not Atheists, But Acknowledge Only One God

As regards, first of all, the allegation that we are atheists – for I will meet the charges one by one, that we may not be ridiculed for having no answer to give to those who make them – with reason did the Athenians adjudge Diagoras guilty of atheism, in that he not only divulged the Orphic doctrine, and published the mysteries of Eleusis and of the Cabiri, and chopped up the wooden statue of Hercules to boil his turnips, but openly declared that there was no God at all. But to us, who distinguish God from matter, and teach that matter is one thing and God another, and that they are separated by a wide interval (for that the Deity is uncreated and eternal, to be beheld by the understanding and reason alone, while matter is created and perishable), is it not absurd to apply the name of atheism?

If our sentiments were like those of Diagoras, while we have such incentives to piety – in the established order, the universal harmony, the magnitude, the colour, the form, the arrangement of the world – with reason might our reputation for impiety, as well as the cause of our being thus harassed, be charged on ourselves. But, since our doctrine acknowledges one God, the Maker of this universe, who is Himself uncreated (for that which is does not come to be, but that which is not) but has made all things by the Logos which is from Him, we are treated unreasonably in both respects, in that we are both defamed and persecuted.

Chapter VI – Opinions of the Philosophers as to the One God

Philolaus, too, when he says that all things are included in God as in a stronghold, teaches that He is one, and that He is superior to matter. Lysis and Opsimus thus define God: the one says that He is an ineffable number, the other that He is the excess of the greatest number beyond that which comes nearest to it. So that since ten is the greatest number according to the Pythagoreans, being the Tetractys, and containing all the arithmetic and harmonic principles, and the Nine stands next to it, God is a unit – that is, one. For the greatest number exceeds the next least by one.

Then there are Plato and Aristotle – not that I am about to go through all that the philosophers have said about God, as if I wished to exhibit a complete summary of their opinions; for I know that, as you excel all men in intelligence and in the power of your rule, in the same proportion do you surpass them all in an accurate acquaintance with all learning, cultivating as you do each several branch with more success than even those who have devoted themselves exclusively to any one. But, in as much as it is impossible to demonstrate without the citation of names that we are not alone in confining the notion of God to unity, I have ventured on an enumeration of opinions.

Plato, then, says, "To find out the Maker and Father of this universe is difficult; and, when found, it is impossible to declare Him to all," conceiving of one uncreated and eternal God. And if he recognises others as well, such as the sun, moon, and stars, yet he recognises them as created: "gods, offspring of gods, of whom I am the Maker, and the Father of works which are indissoluble apart from my will; but whatever is compounded can be dissolved." If, therefore, Plato is not an atheist for conceiving of one uncreated God, the Framer of the universe, neither are we atheists who acknowledge and firmly hold that He is God who has framed all things by the Logos, and holds them in being by His Spirit.

Aristotle, again, and his followers, recognising the existence of one whom they regard as a sort of compound living creature, speak of God as consisting of soul and body, thinking His body to be the etherial space and the planetary stars and the sphere of the fixed stars, moving in circles; but His soul, the reason which presides over the motion of the body, itself not subject to motion, but becoming the cause of motion to the other.

The Stoics also, although by the appellations they employ to suit the changes of matter, which they say is permeated by the Spirit of God, they multiply the Deity in name, yet in reality they consider God to be one. For, if God is an artistic fire advancing methodically to the production of the several things in the world, embracing in Himself all the seminal principles by which each thing is produced in accordance with fate, and if His Spirit pervades the whole world, then God is one according to them, being named Zeus in respect of the fervid part of matter, and Hera in respect of the air, and called by other names in respect of that particular part of matter which He pervades.

Chapter VIII – Absurdities of Polytheism

As regards, then, the doctrine that there was from the beginning one God, the Maker of this universe, consider it in this wise, that you may be acquainted with the argumentative grounds also of our faith. If there were from the beginning two or more gods, they were either in one and the same place, or each of them separately in his own. In one and the same place they could not be. For, if they are gods, they are not alike; but because they are uncreated they are unlike: for created things are like their patterns; but the uncreated are unlike, being neither produced from any one, nor formed after the pattern of any one. Hand and eye and foot are parts of one body, making up together one man: is God in this sense one? And indeed Socrates was compounded and divided into parts, just because he was created and perishable; but God is uncreated, and, impassible, and indivisible – does not, therefore, consist of parts.

But if, on the contrary, each of them exists separately, since He that made the world is above the things created, and about the things He has made and set in order, where can the other or the rest be? For if the world, being made spherical, is confined within the circles of heaven, and the Creator of the world is above the things created, managing that by His providential care of these, what place is there for the second god, or for the other gods? For he is not in the world, because it belongs to the other; nor about the world, for God the Maker of the world is above it. But if he is neither in the world nor about the world (for all that surrounds it is occupied by this one), where is he? Is he above the world and [the first] God? In another world, or about another? But if he is in another or about another, then he is not about us, for he does not govern the world; nor is his power great, for he exists in a circumscribed space. But if he is neither in another world (for all things are filled by the other), nor about another (for all things are occupied by the other), he clearly does not exist at all, for there is no place in which he can be.

Or what does he do, seeing there is another to whom the world belongs, and he is above the Maker of the world, and yet is neither in the world nor about the world? Is there, then, some other place where he can stand? But God, and what belongs to God, are above him. And what, too, shall be the place, seeing that the other fills the regions which are above the world? Perhaps he exerts a providential care? [By no means.] And yet, unless he does so, he has done nothing. If, then, he neither does anything nor exercises providential care, and if there is not another place in which he is, then this Being of whom we speak is the one God from the beginning, and the sole Maker of the world.

Chapter X – The Christians Worship the Father, Son, and Holy Ghost

That we are not atheists, therefore, seeing that we acknowledge one God, uncreated, eternal, invisible, impassible, incomprehensible, illimitable, who is apprehended by the understanding only and the reason, who is encompassed by light, and beauty, and spirit, and power ineffable, by whom the universe has been created through His Logos, and set in order, and is kept in being – I have sufficiently demonstrated. [I say "His Logos"], for we acknowledge also a Son of God. Nor let any one think it ridiculous that God should have a Son. For though the poets, in their fictions, represent the gods as no better than men, our mode of thinking is not the same as theirs, concerning either God the Father or the Son.

But the Son of God is the Logos of the Father, in idea and in operation; for after the pattern of Him and by Him were all things made, the Father and the Son being one. And, the Son being in the Father and the Father in the Son, in oneness and power of spirit, the understanding and reason (*nous kia logos*) of the Father is the Son of God. But if, in your surpassing intelligence, it occurs to you to inquire what is meant by the Son, I will state briefly that He is the first product of the Father, not as having been brought into existence (for from the beginning, God, who is the eternal mind [*nous*], had the Logos in Himself, being from eternity instinct with Logos [*logikos*]; but in as much as He came forth to be the idea and energizing power of all material things, which lay like a nature without attributes, and an inactive earth, the grosser particles being mixed up with the lighter.

The prophetic Spirit also agrees with our statements. "The Lord," it says, "made me, the beginning of His ways to His works." The Holy Spirit Himself also, which operates in the prophets, we assert to be an effluence of God, flowing from Him, and returning back again like a beam of the sun. Who, then, would not be astonished to hear men who speak of God the Father, and of God the Son, and of the Holy Spirit, and who declare both their power in union and their distinction in order, called atheists? Nor is our teaching in what relates to the divine nature confined to these points; but we recognise also a multitude of angels and ministers, whom God the Maker and Framer of the world distributed and appointed to their several posts by His Logos, to occupy themselves about the elements, and the heavens, and the world, and the things in it, and the goodly ordering of them all.

Chapter XIII – Why the Christians Do Not Offer Sacrifices

But, as most of those who charge us with atheism, and that because they have not even the dreamiest conception of what God is, and are doltish and utterly unacquainted with natural and divine things, and such as measure piety by the rule of sacrifices, charges us with not acknowledging the same gods as the cities, be pleased to attend to the following considerations, O emperors, on both points. And first, as to our not sacrificing: the Framer and Father of this universe does not need blood, nor the odour of burnt offerings, nor the fragrance of flowers and incense, for as much as He is Himself perfect fragrance, needing nothing either within or without; but the noblest sacrifice to Him is for us to know who stretched out and vaulted the heavens, and fixed the earth in its place like a centre, who gathered the water into seas and divided the light from the darkness, who adorned the sky with stars and made the earth to bring forth seed of every kind, who made animals and fashioned man. When, holding God to be this Framer of all things, who preserves them in being and superintends them all by knowledge and administrative skill, we "lift up holy hands" to Him, what need has He further of a hecatomb?...

Chapter XV – The Christians Distinguish God from Matter

But grant that they acknowledge the same. What then? Because the multitude, who cannot distinguish between matter and God, or see how great is the interval which lies between them, pray to idols made of matter, are we therefore, who do distinguish and separate the uncreated and the created, that which is and that which is not, that which is apprehended by the understanding and that which is perceived by the senses, and who give the fitting name to each of them – are we to come and worship images?

If, indeed, matter and God are the same, two names for one thing, then certainly, in not regarding stocks and stones, gold and silver, as gods, we are guilty of impiety. But if they are at the greatest possible remove from one another – as far asunder as the artist and the materials of his art – why are we called to account? For as is the potter and the clay (matter being the clay, and the artist the potter), so is God, the Framer of the world, and matter, which is subservient to Him for the purposes of His art.

But as the clay cannot become vessels of itself without art, so neither did matter, which is capable of taking all forms, receive, apart from God the Framer, distinction and shape and order. And as we do not hold the pottery of more worth than him who made it, nor the vessels or glass and gold than him who wrought them; but if there is anything about them elegant in art we praise the artificer, and it is he who reaps the glory of the vessels: even so with matter and God – the glory and honour of the orderly arrangement of the world belongs of right not to matter, but to God, the Framer of matter. So that, if we were to regard the various forms of matter as gods, we should seem to be without any sense of the true God, because we should be putting the things which are dissoluble and perishable on a level with that which is eternal.

Chapter XVI – The Christians Do Not Worship the Universe

Beautiful without doubt is the world, excelling, as well in its magnitude as in the arrangement of its parts, both those in the oblique circle and those about the north, and also in its spherical form. Yet it is not this, but its Artificer, that we must worship. For when any of your subjects come to you, they do not neglect to pay their homage to you, their rulers and lords, from whom they will obtain whatever they need, and address themselves to the magnificence of your palace; but, if they chance to come upon the royal residence, they bestow a passing glance of admiration on its beautiful structure: but it is to you yourselves that they show honour, as being "all in all." You sovereigns, indeed, rear and adorn your palaces for yourselves; but the world was not created because God needed it; for God is Himself everything to Himself – light unapproachable, a perfect world, spirit, power, reason.

If, therefore, the world is an instrument in tune, and moving in well-measured time, I adore the Being who gave its harmony, and strikes its notes, and sings the accordant strain, and not the instrument. For at the musical contests the adjudicators do not pass by the lute players and crown the lutes. Whether, then, as Plato says, the world be a product of divine art, I admire its beauty, and adore the

Artificer; or whether it be His essence and body, as the Peripatetics affirm, we do not neglect to adore God, who is the cause of the motion of the body, and descend "to the poor and weak elements," adoring in the impassible air (as they term it), passible matter; or, if any one apprehends the several parts of the world to be powers of God, we do not approach and do homage to the powers, but their Maker and Lord.

I do not ask of matter what it has not to give, nor passing God by do I pay homage to the elements, which can do nothing more than what they were bidden; for, although they are beautiful to look upon, by reason of the art of their Framer, yet they still have the nature of matter. And to this view Plato also bears testimony; "for," says he, "that which is called heaven and earth has received many blessings from the Father, but yet partakes of body; hence it cannot possibly be free from' change." If, therefore, while I admire the heavens and the elements in respect of their art, I do not worship them as gods, knowing that the law of dissolution is upon them, how can I call those objects gods of which I know the makers to be men? Attend, I beg, to a few words on this subject.

Chapter XIX – The Philosophers Agree with the Poets Respecting the Gods

Such was the beginning of the existence both of their gods and of the universe. Now what are we to make of this? For each of those things to which divinity is ascribed is conceived of as having existed from the first. For, if they have come into being, having previously had no existence, as those say who treat of the gods, they do not exist. For, a thing is either uncreated and eternal, or created and perishable. Nor do I think one thing and the philosophers another. "What is that which always is, and has no origin; or what is that which has been originated, yet never is?"

Discoursing of the intelligible and the sensible, Plato teaches that that which always is, the intelligible, is unoriginated, but that which is not, the sensible, is originated, beginning to be and ceasing to exist. In like manner, the Stoics also say that all things will be burnt up and will again exist, the world receiving another beginning. But if, although there is, according to them, a twofold cause, one active and governing, namely providence, the other passive and changeable, namely matter, it is nevertheless impossible for the world, even though under the care of Providence, to remain in the same state, because it is created – how can the constitution of these gods remain, who are not self-existent, but have been originated? And in what are the gods superior to matter, since they derive their constitution from water? But not even water, according to them, is the beginning of all things.

From simple and homogeneous elements what could be constituted? Moreover, matter requires an artificer, and the artificer requires matter. For how could figures be made without matter or an artificer? Neither, again, is it reasonable that matter should be older than God; for the efficient cause must of necessity exist before the things that are made.

Chapter XXV – The Poets and Philosophers Have Denied a Divine Providence

These angels, then, who have fallen from heaven, and haunt the air and the earth, and are no longer able to rise to heavenly things, and the souls of the giants, which are the demons who wander about the world, perform actions similar, the one (that is, the demons) to the natures they have received, the other (that is, the angels) to the appetites they have indulged. But the prince of matter, as may be seen merely from what transpires, exercises a control and management contrary to the good that is in God:

> "Ofttimes this anxious thought has crossed my mind,
> Whether 'tis chance or deity that rules
> The small affairs of men; and, spite of hope
> As well as justice, drives to exile some
> Stripped of all means of life, while others still
> Continue to enjoy prosperity."

Prosperity and adversity, contrary to hope and justice, made it impossible for Euripides to say to whom belongs the administration of earthly affairs, which is of such a kind that one might say of it:

> "How then, while seeing these things, can we say There is a race of gods, or yield to laws?"

The same thing led Aristotle to say that the things below the heaven are not under the care of Providence, although the eternal providence of God concerns itself equally with us below:

"The earth, let willingness move her or not,
Must herbs produce, and thus sustain my flocks,"

and addresses itself to the deserving individually, according to truth and not according to opinion; and all other things, according to the general constitution of nature, are provided for by the law of reason.

But because the demoniac movements and operations proceeding from the adverse spirit produce these disorderly sallies, and moreover move men, some in one way and some in another, as individuals and as nations, separately and in common, in accordance with the tendency of matter on the one hand, and of the affinity for divine things on the other, from within and from without – some who are of no mean reputation have therefore thought that this universe is constituted without any definite order, and is driven hither and thither by an irrational chance.

But they do not understand, that of those things which belong to the constitution of the whole world there is nothing out of order or neglected, but that each one of them has been produced by reason, and that, therefore, they do not transgress the order prescribed to them; and that man himself, too, so far as He that made him is concerned, is well ordered, both by his original nature, which has one common character for all, and by the constitution of his body, which does not transgress the law imposed upon it, and by the termination of his life, which remains equal and common to all alike; but that, according to the character peculiar to himself and the operation of the ruling prince and of the demons his followers, he is impelled and moved in this direction or in that, notwithstanding that all possess in common the same original constitution of mind.

Irenæus of Lyons

> St. Irenæus (115 – 202) was the most important theologian of the second century. From Smyrna in Asia Minor, he sat at the feet of Bishop Polycarp, who had known the Apostle John. Irenæus ended up in Lyon as bishop of the church there. Though he served in the West, he wrote in Greek. His primary surviving work, *Against Heresies*, is a long refutation of the Gnostic heresies and an exposition of Christian doctrine. Johannes Quasten regards him as the founder of Christian theology.
>
> According to Irenæus, God created all things by His Word, not by angels or intermediary deities. He has no need of anything, and did not need to create. Creation reveals that God has created it. God's power is demonstrated in that He created matter, which prior to creation had no existence. Just as a lyre, composed of different strings, may produce harmonious sounds, so the universe, though composed of different parts, constitutes a harmonious whole. Other Fathers also use this image.

Irenæus *Against Heresies*, Book II

Chapter II – The World Was Not Formed by Angels, or by Any Other Being, Contrary to the Will of the Most High God, But Was Made by the Father Through the Word

1. Those, moreover, who say that the world was formed by angels, or by any other maker of it, contrary to the will of Him who is the Supreme Father, err first of all in this very point, that they maintain that angels formed such and so mighty a creation, contrary to the will of the Most High God. This would imply that angels were more powerful than God; or if not so, that He was either careless, or inferior, or paid no regard to those things which took place among His own possessions, whether they turned out ill or well, so that He might drive away and prevent the one, while He praised and rejoiced over the other. But if one would not ascribe such conduct even to a man of any ability, how much less to God.

2. Next let them tell us whether these things have been formed within the limits which are contained by Him, and in His proper ter-

ritory, or in regions belonging to others, and lying beyond Him? But if they say [that these things were done] beyond Him, then all the absurdities already mentioned will face them, and the Supreme God will be enclosed by that which is beyond Him, in which also it will be necessary that He should find His end. If, on the other hand, [these things were done] within His own proper territory, it will be very idle to say that the world was thus formed within His proper territory against His will by angels who are themselves under His power, or by any other being, as if either He Himself did not behold all things which take place among His own possessions, or was not aware of the things to be done by angels.

3. If, however, [the things referred to were done] not against His will, but with His concurrence and knowledge, as some [of these men] think, the angels, or the Former of the world [whoever that may have been], will no longer be the causes of that formation, but the will of God. For if He is the Former of the world, He too made the angels, or at least was the cause of their creation; and He will be regarded as having made the world who prepared the causes of its formation. Although they maintain that the angels were made by a long succession downwards, or that the Former of the world [sprang] from the Supreme Father, as Basilides asserts; nevertheless that which is the cause of those things which have been made will still be traced to Him who was the Author of such a succession.

[The case stands] just as regards success in war, which is ascribed to the king who prepared those things which are the cause of victory; and, in like manner, the creation of any state, or of any work, is referred to him who prepared materials for the accomplishment of those results which were afterwards brought about. Wherefore, we do not say that it was the axe which cut the wood, or the saw which divided it; but one would very properly say that the man cut and divided it who formed the axe and the saw for this purpose, and [who also formed] at a much earlier date all the tools by which the axe and the saw themselves were formed.

With justice, therefore, according to an analogous process of reasoning, the Father of all will be declared the Former of this world, and not the angels, nor any other [so-called] former of the world, other than He who was its Author, and had formerly been the cause of the preparation for a creation of this kind.

4. This manner of speech may perhaps be plausible or persuasive to those who know not God, and who liken Him to needy human beings, and to those who cannot immediately and without assistance form anything, but require many instrumentalities to produce what they intend. But it will not be regarded as at all probable by those who know that God stands in need of nothing, and that He created and made all things by His Word, while He neither required angels to assist Him in the production of those things which are made, nor of any power greatly inferior to Himself, and ignorant of the Father, nor of any defect or ignorance, in order that he who should know Him might become man. But He Himself in Himself, after a fashion which we can neither describe nor conceive, predestinating all things, formed them as He pleased, bestowing harmony on all things, and assigning them their own place, and the beginning of their creation. In this way He conferred on spiritual things a spiritual and invisible nature, on super-celestial things a celestial, on angels an angelical, on animals an animal, on beings that swim a nature suited to the water, and on those that live on the land one fitted for the land – on all, in short, a nature suitable to the character of the life assigned them – while He formed all things that were made by His Word that never wearies.

5. For this is a peculiarity of the pre-eminence of God, not to stand in need of other instruments for the creation of those things which are summoned into existence. His own Word is both suitable and sufficient for the formation of all things, even as John, the disciple of the Lord, declares regarding Him: "All things were made by Him, and without Him was nothing made." Now, among the "all things" our world must be embraced. It too, therefore, was made by His Word, as Scripture tells us in the book of Genesis that He made all things connected with our world by His Word. David also expresses the same truth [when he says] "For He spake, and they were made; He commanded, and they were created."

Whom, therefore, shall we believe as to the creation of the world – these heretics who have been mentioned that prate so foolishly and inconsistently on the subject, or the disciples of the Lord, and Moses, who was both a faithful servant of God and a prophet? He at first narrated the formation of the world in these words: "In the beginning God created the heaven and the earth," and all other things in succession; but neither gods nor angels [had any share in the work].

Now, that this God is the Father of our Lord Jesus Christ, Paul the apostle also has declared, [saying,] "There is one God, the Father, who is above all, and through all things, and in us all." I have indeed proved already that there is only one God; but I shall further demonstrate this from the apostles themselves, and from the discourses of the Lord. For what sort of conduct would it be, were we to forsake the utterances of the prophets, of the Lord, and of the apostles, that we might give heed to these persons, who speak not a word of sense?

Chapter III – The Bythus and Pleroma of the Valentinians, as Well as the God of Marcion, Shown to Be Absurd; The World Was Actually Created by the Same Being Who Had Conceived the Idea of It, and Was Not the Fruit of Defect or Ignorance

1. The Bythus, therefore, whom they conceive of with his Pleroma, and the God of Marcion, are inconsistent. If indeed, as they affirm, he has something subjacent and beyond himself, which they style vacuity and shadow, this vacuum is then proved to be greater than their Pleroma. But it is inconsistent even to make this statement, that while he contains all things within himself, the creation was formed by some other. For it is absolutely necessary that they acknowledge a certain void and chaotic kind of existence (below the spiritual Pleroma) in which this universe was formed, and that the Propator purposely left this chaos as it was, either knowing beforehand what things were to happen in it, or being ignorant of them. If he was really ignorant, then God will not be prescient of all things. But they will not even [in that case] be able to assign a reason on what account He thus left this place void during so long a period of time. If, again, He is prescient, and contemplated mentally that creation which was about to have a being in that place, then He Himself created it who also formed it beforehand [ideally] in Himself.

2. Let them cease, therefore, to affirm that the world was made by any other; for as soon as God formed a conception in His mind, that was also done which He had thus mentally conceived. For it was not possible that one Being should mentally form the conception, and

another actually produce the things which had been conceived by Him in His mind. But God, according to these heretics, mentally conceived either an eternal world or a temporal one, both of which suppositions cannot be true. Yet if He had mentally conceived of it as eternal, spiritual, and visible, it would also have been formed such. But if it was formed such as it really is, then He made it such who had mentally conceived of it as such; or He willed it to exist in the ideality of the Father, according to the conception of His mind, such as it now is, compound, mutable, and transient. Since, then, it is just such as the Father had [ideally] formed in counsel with Himself, it must be worthy of the Father. But to affirm that what was mentally conceived and pre-created by the Father of all, just as it has been actually formed, is the fruit of defect, and the production of ignorance, is to be guilty of great blasphemy. For, according to them, the Father of all will thus be [regarded as] generating in His breast, according to His own mental conception, the emanations of defect and the fruits of ignorance, since the things which He had conceived in His mind have actually been produced.

Chapter IX – There is But One Creator of the World, God the Father: This is the Constant Belief of the Church

1. That God is the Creator of the world is accepted even by those very persons who in many ways speak against Him, and yet acknowledge Him, styling Him the Creator, and an angel, not to mention that all the Scriptures call out [to the same effect], and the Lord teaches us of this Father who is in heaven, and no other, as I shall show in the sequel of this work. For the present, however, that proof which is derived from those who allege doctrines opposite to ours, is of itself sufficient – all men, in fact, consenting to this truth: the ancients on their part preserving with special care, from the tradition of the first-formed man, this persuasion, while they celebrate the praises of one God, the Maker of heaven and earth; others, again, after them, being reminded of this fact by the prophets of God, while the very heathen learned it from creation itself. For even creation reveals Him who formed it, and the very work made suggests Him who made it, and the world manifests Him who ordered it. The Universal Church, moreover, through the whole world, has received this tradition from the apostles.

2. This God, then, being acknowledged, as I have said, and receiving testimony from all to the fact of His existence, that Father whom they conjure into existence is beyond doubt untenable, and has no witnesses [to his existence]. Simon Magus was the first who said that he himself was God over all, and that the world was formed by his angels. Then those who succeeded him, as I have shown in the first book, by their several opinions, still further depraved [his teaching] through their impious and irreligious doctrines against the Creator. These [heretics now referred to], being the disciples of those mentioned, render such as assent to them worse than the heathen. For the former "serve the creature rather than the Creator," and "those which are not gods," notwithstanding that they ascribe the first place in Deity to that God who was the Maker of this universe. But the latter maintain that He, [i.e., the Creator of this world], is the fruit of a defect, and describe Him as being of an animal nature, and as not knowing that Power which is above Him, while He also exclaims, "I am God, and besides Me there is no other God."

Affirming that He lies, they are themselves liars, attributing all sorts of wickedness to Him; and conceiving of one who is not above this Being as really having an existence, they are thus convicted by their own views of blasphemy against that God who really exists, while they conjure into existence a god who has no existence, to their own condemnation. And thus those who declare themselves "perfect," and as being possessed of the knowledge of all things, are found to be worse than the heathen, and to entertain more blasphemous opinions even against their own Creator.

Chapter X – Perverse Interpretations of Scripture by the Heretics: God Created All Things Out of Nothing, and Not from Pre-Existent Matter

1. It is therefore in the highest degree irrational, that we should take no account of Him who is truly God, and who receives testimony from all, while we inquire whether there is above Him that [other being] who really has no existence, and has never been proclaimed by any one. For that nothing has been clearly spoken regarding Him, they themselves furnish testimony; for since they, with wretched success, transfer to that being who has been conceived of by them, those

parables [of Scripture] which, whatever the form in which they have been spoken, are sought after [for this purpose], it is manifest that they now generate another [god], who was never previously sought after. For by the fact that they thus endeavour to explain ambiguous passages of Scripture (ambiguous, however, not as if referring to another god, but as regards the dispensations of [the true] God), they have constructed another god, weaving, as I said before, ropes of sand, and affixing a more important to a less important question. For no question can be solved by means of another which itself awaits solution; nor, in the opinion of those possessed of sense, can an ambiguity be explained by means of another ambiguity, or enigmas by means of another greater enigma, but things of such character receive their solution from those which are manifest, and consistent and clear.

2. But these [heretics], while striving to explain passages of Scripture and parables, bring forward another more important, and indeed impious question, to this effect, "Whether there be really another god above that God who was the Creator of the world?" They are not in the way of solving the questions [which they propose]; for how could they find means of doing so? But they append an important question to one of less consequence, and thus insert [in their speculations] a difficulty incapable of solution. For in order that they may know "knowledge" itself (yet not learning this fact, that the Lord, when thirty years old, came to the baptism of truth), they do impiously despise that God who was the Creator, and who sent Him for the salvation of men. And that they may be deemed capable of informing us whence is the substance of matter, while they believe not that God, according to His pleasure, in the exercise of His own will and power, formed all things (so that those things which now are should have an existence) out of what did not previously exist, they have collected [a multitude of] vain discourses. They thus truly reveal their infidelity; they do not believe in that which really exists, and they have fallen away into [the belief of] that which has, in fact, no existence.

3. For, when they tell us that all moist substance proceeded from the tears of Achamoth, all lucid substance from her smile, all solid substance from her sadness, all mobile substance from her terror, and that thus they have sublime knowledge on account of which they are

superior to others – how can these things fail to be regarded as worthy of contempt, and truly ridiculous?

They do not believe that God (being powerful, and rich in all resources) created matter itself, inasmuch as they know not how much a spiritual and divine essence can accomplish. But they do believe that their Mother, whom they style a female from a female, produced from her passions aforesaid the so vast material substance of creation. They inquire, too, whence the substance of creation was supplied to the Creator; but they do not inquire whence [were supplied] to their Mother (whom they call the Enthymesis and impulse of the Aeon that went astray) so great an amount of tears, or perspiration, or sadness, or that which produced the remainder of matter.

4. For, to attribute the substance of created things to the power and will of Him who is God of all, is worthy both of credit and acceptance. It is also agreeable [to reason], and there may be well said regarding such a belief, that "the things which are impossible with men are possible with God." While men, indeed, cannot make anything out of nothing, but only out of matter already existing, yet God is in this point pre-eminently superior to men, that He Himself called into being the substance of His creation, when previously it had no existence. But the assertion that matter was produced from the Enthymesis of an Aeon going astray, and that the Aeon [referred to] was far separated from her Enthymesis, and that, again, her passion and feeling, apart from herself, became matter – is incredible, infatuated, impossible, and untenable.

Chapter XIV – Valentinus and His Followers Derived the Principles of Their System from the Heathen; The Names Only are Changed

1. Much more like the truth, and more pleasing, is the account which Antiphanes, one of the ancient comic poets, gives in his Theogony as to the origin of all things. For he speaks Chaos as being produced from Night and Silence; relates that then Love sprang from Chaos and Night; from this again, Light; and that from this, in his opinion, were derived all the rest of the first generation of the gods. After these he next introduces a second generation of gods, and the

creation of the world; then he narrates the formation of mankind by the second order of the gods.

These men (the heretics), adopting this fable as their own, have ranged their opinions round it, as if by a sort of natural process, changing only the names of the things referred to, and setting forth the very same beginning of the generation of all things, and their production. In place of Night and Silence they substitute Bythus and Sige; instead of Chaos, they put Nous; and for Love (by whom, says the comic poet, all other things were set in order) they have brought forward the Word; while for the primary and greatest gods they have formed the Aeons; and in place of the secondary gods, they tell us of that creation by their mother which is outside of the Pleroma, calling it the second Ogdoad.

They proclaim to us, like the writer referred to, that from this (Ogdoad) came the creation of the world and the formation of man, maintaining that they alone are acquainted with these ineffable and unknown mysteries. Those things which are everywhere acted in the theatres by comedians with the clearest voices they transfer to their own system, teaching them undoubtedly through means of the same arguments, and merely changing the names.

2. And not only are they convicted of bringing forward, as if their own [original ideas], those things which are to be found among the comic poets, but they also bring together the things which have been said by all those who were ignorant of God, and who are termed philosophers; and sewing together, as it were, a motley garment out of a heap of miserable rags, they have, by their subtle manner of expression, furnished themselves with a cloak which is really not their own.

They do, it is true, introduce a new kind of doctrine, inasmuch as by a new sort of art it has been substituted [for the old]. Yet it is in reality both old and useless, since these very opinions have been sewed together out of ancient dogmas redolent of ignorance and irreligion. For instance, Thales of Miletus affirmed that water was the generative and initial principle of all things. Now it is just the same thing whether we say water or Bythus. The poet Homer, again, held the opinion that Oceanus, along with mother Tethys, was the origin of the gods: this idea these men have transferred to Bythus and Sige. Anaximander laid it down that infinite is the first principle of all things, having seminally in itself the generation of them all, and from this he declares the immense worlds [which exist] were formed: this, too, they have dressed up anew, and referred to Bythus and their Aeons. Anaxagoras, again, who has also been surnamed "Atheist," gave it as his opinion that animals were formed from seeds falling down from heaven upon earth. This thought, too, these men have transferred to "the seed" of their Mother, which they maintain to be themselves; thus acknowledging at once, in the judgment of such as are possessed of sense, that they themselves are the offspring of the irreligious Anaxagoras.

3. Again, adopting the [ideas of] shade and vacuity from Democritus and Epicurus, they have fitted these to their own views, following upon those [teachers] who had already talked a great deal about a vacuum and atoms, the one of which they called that which is, and the other that which is not. In like manner, these men call those things which are within the Pleroma real existences, just as those philosophers did the atoms; while they maintain that those which are without the Pleroma have no true existence, even as those did respecting the vacuum.

They have thus banished themselves in this world (since they are here outside of the Pleroma) into a place which has no existence. Again, when they maintain that these things [below] are images of those which have a true existence [above], they again most manifestly rehearse the doctrine of Democritus and Plato. For Democritus was the first who maintained that numerous and diverse figures were stamped, as it were, with the forms [of things above], and descended from universal space into this world. But Plato, for his part, speaks of matter, and exemplar, and God. These men, following those distinctions, have styled what he calls ideas, and exemplar, the images of those things which are above; while, through a mere change of name, they boast themselves as being discoverers and contrivers of this kind of imaginary fiction.

4. This opinion, too, that they hold the Creator formed the world out of previously existing matter, both Anaxagoras, Empedocles, and Plato expressed before them; as, forsooth, we learn they also do under the inspiration of their Mother. Then again, as to the opinion that everything of necessity passes away to those things out of which they

maintain it was also formed, and that God is the slave of this necessity, so that He cannot impart immortality to what is mortal, or bestow incorruption on what is corruptible, but every one passes into a substance similar in nature to itself, both those who are named Stoics from the portico (*stoa*), and indeed all that are ignorant of God, poets and historians alike, make the same affirmation.

Those [heretics] who hold the same [system of] infidelity have ascribed, no doubt, their own proper region to spiritual beings – that, namely, which is within the Pleroma, but to animal beings the intermediate space, while to corporeal they assign that which is material. And they assert that God Himself can do no otherwise, but that every one of the [different kinds of substance] mentioned passes away to those things which are of the same nature [with itself].

5. Moreover, as to their saying that the Saviour was formed out of all the Aeons, by every one of them depositing, so to speak, in Him his own special flower, they bring forward nothing new that may not be found in the Pandora of Hesiod. For what he says respecting her, these men insinuate concerning the Saviour, bringing Him before us as Pandoros (All-gifted), as if each of the Aeons had bestowed on Him what He possessed in the greatest perfection.

Again, their opinion as to the indifference of [eating of] meats and other actions, and as to their thinking that, from the nobility of their nature, they can in no degree at all contract pollution, whatever they eat or perform, they have derived it from the Cynics, since they do in fact belong to the same society as do these [philosophers]. They also strive to transfer to [the treatment of matters of] faith that hairsplitting and subtle mode of handling questions which is, in fact, a copying of Aristotle.

6. Again, as to the desire they exhibit to refer this whole universe to numbers, they have learned it from the Pythagoreans. For these were the first who set forth numbers as the initial principle of all things, and [described] that initial principle of theirs as being both equal and unequal, out of which [two properties] they conceived that both things sensible and immaterial derived their origin. And [they held] that one set of first principles gave rise to the matter [of things], and another to their form. They affirm that from these first principles all things have been made, just as a statue is of its metal and its

special form. Now, the heretics have adapted this to the things which are outside of the Pleroma.

The [Pythagoreans] maintained that the principle of intellect is proportionate to the energy wherewith mind, as a recipient of the comprehensible, pursues its inquiries, until, worn out, it is resolved at length in the Indivisible and One. They further affirm that Hen – that is, One – is the first principle of all things, and the substance of all that has been formed. From this again proceeded the Dyad, the Tetrad, the Pentad, and the manifold generation of the others. These things the heretics repeat, word for word, with a reference to their Pleroma and Bythus. From the same source, too, they strive to bring into vogue those conjunctions which proceed from unity. Marcus boasts of such views as if they were his own, and as if he were seen to have discovered something more novel than others, while he simply sets forth the Tetrad of Pythagoras as the originating principle and mother of all things.

7. But I will merely say, in opposition to these men – Did all those who have been mentioned, with whom you have been proved to coincide in expression, know, or not know, the truth? If they knew it, then the descent of the Saviour into this world was superfluous. For why [in that case] did He descend? Was it that He might bring that truth which was [already] known to the knowledge of those who knew it? If, on the other hand, these men did not know it, then how is it that, while you express yourselves in the same terms as do those who knew not the truth, ye boast that yourselves alone possess that knowledge which is above all things, although they who are ignorant of God [likewise] possess it?

Thus, then, by a complete perversion of language, they style ignorance of the truth knowledge: and Paul well says [of them], that [they make use of] "novelties of words of false knowledge." For that knowledge of theirs is truly found to be false. If, however, taking an impudent course with respect to these points, they declare that men indeed did not know the truth, but that their Mother, the seed of the Father, proclaimed the mysteries of truth through such men, even as also through the prophets, while the Demiurge was ignorant [of the proceeding], then I answer, in the first place, that the things which were predicted were not of such a nature as to be intelligible to no one; for the men themselves knew what they were saying, as did also their disciples, and those again succeeded these. And, in the next place, if either the Mother or her seed knew and proclaimed those things which were of the truth (and the Father is truth), then on their theory the Saviour spoke falsely when He said, "No one knoweth the Father but the Son," unless indeed they maintain that their seed or Mother is No-one.

Chapter XXV – God is Not to Be Sought After by Means of Letters, Syllables, and Numbers; Necessity of Humility in Such Investigations

1. If any one, however, say in reply to these things, What then? Is it a meaningless and accidental thing, that the positions of names, and the election of the apostles, and the working of the Lord, and the arrangement of created things, are what they are? – we answer them: Certainly not; but with great wisdom and diligence, all things have clearly been made by God, fitted and prepared [for their special purposes]; and His word formed both things ancient and those belonging to the latest times; and men ought not to connect those things with the number thirty, but to harmonize them with what actually exists, or with fight reason.

Nor should they seek to prosecute inquiries respecting God by means of numbers, syllables, and letters. For this is an uncertain mode of proceeding, on account of their varied and diverse systems, and because every sort of hypothesis may at the present day be, in like manner, devised by any one; so that they can derive arguments against the truth from these very theories, inasmuch as they may be turned in many different directions. But, on the contrary, they ought to adapt the numbers themselves, and those things which have been formed, to the true theory lying before them. For system does not spring out of numbers, but numbers from a system; nor does God derive His being from things made, but things made from God. For all things originate from one and the same God.

2. But since created things are various and numerous, they are indeed well fitted and adapted to the whole creation; yet, when viewed individually, are mutually opposite and inharmonious, just as the sound of the lyre, which consists of many and opposite notes, gives rise to one unbroken melody, through means of the interval

which separates each one from the others. The lover of truth therefore ought not to be deceived by the interval between each note, nor should he imagine that one was due to one artist and author, and another to another, nor that one person fitted the treble, another the bass, and yet another the tenor strings; but he should hold that one and the same person [formed the whole], so as to prove the judgment, goodness, and skill exhibited in the whole work and [specimen of] wisdom.

Those, too, who listen to the melody, ought to praise and extol the artist, to admire the tension of some notes, to attend to the softness of others, to catch the sound of others between both these extremes, and to consider the special character of others, so as to inquire at what each one aims, and what is the cause of their variety, never failing to apply our rule, neither giving up the [one] artist, nor casting off faith in the one God who formed all things, nor blaspheming our Creator.

3. If, however, any one do not discover the cause of all those things which become objects of investigation, let him reflect that man is infinitely inferior to God; that he has received grace only in part, and is not yet equal or similar to his Maker; and, moreover, that he cannot have experience or form a conception of all things like God; but in the same proportion as he who was formed but today, and received the beginning of his creation, is inferior to Him who is uncreated, and who is always the same, in that proportion is he, as respects knowledge and the faculty of investigating the causes of all things, inferior to Him who made him. For thou, O man, art not an uncreated being, nor didst thou always co-exist with God, as did His own Word; but now, through His pre-eminent goodness, receiving the beginning of thy creation, thou dost gradually learn from the Word the dispensations of God who made thee.

4. Preserve therefore the proper order of thy knowledge, and do not, as being ignorant of things really good, seek to rise above God Himself, for He cannot be surpassed; nor do thou seek after any one above the Creator, for thou wilt not discover such, For thy Former cannot be contained within limits; nor, although thou shouldst measure all this [universe], and pass through all His creation, and consider it in all its depth, and height, and length, wouldst thou be able to conceive of any other above the Father Himself. For thou wilt not be

able to think Him fully out, but, indulging in trains of reflection opposed to thy nature, thou wilt prove thyself foolish; and if thou persevere in such a course, thou wilt fall into utter madness, whilst thou deemest thyself loftier and greater than thy Creator, and imaginest that thou canst penetrate beyond His dominions.

Chapter XXVI – "Knowledge Puffeth Up, But Love Edifieth"

1. It is therefore better and more profitable to belong to the simple and unlettered class, and by means of love to attain to nearness to God, than, by imagining ourselves learned and skilful, to be found [among those who are] blasphemous against their own God, inasmuch as they conjure up another God as the Father. And for this reason Paul exclaimed, "Knowledge puffeth up, but love edifieth:" not that he meant to inveigh against a true knowledge of God, for in that case he would have accused himself; but, because he knew that some, puffed up by the pretence of knowledge, fall away from the love of God, and imagine that they themselves are perfect, for this reason that they set forth an imperfect Creator, with the view of putting an end to the pride which they feel on account of knowledge of this kind, he says, "Knowledge puffeth up, but love edifieth."

Now there can be no greater conceit than this, that any one should imagine he is better and more perfect than He who made and fashioned him, and imparted to him the breath of life, and commanded this very thing into existence. It is therefore better, as I have said, that one should have no knowledge whatever of any one reason why a single thing in creation has been made, but should believe in God, and continue in His love, than that, puffed up through knowledge of this kind, he should fall away from that love which is the life of man; and that he should search after no other knowledge except [the knowledge of] Jesus Christ the Son of God, who was crucified for us, than that by subtle questions and hair-splitting expressions he should fall into impiety.

2. For how would it be, if any one, gradually elated by attempts of the kind referred to, should, because the Lord said that "even the hairs of your head are all numbered," set about inquiring into the number of hairs on each one's head, and endeavour to search out the reason on account of which one man has so many, and another so many, since all have not an equal number, but many thousands upon thousands are

to be found with still varying numbers, on this account that some have larger and others smaller heads, some have bushy heads of hair, others thin, and others scarcely any hair at all – and then those who imagine that they have discovered the number of the hairs, should endeavour to apply that for the commendation of their own sect which they have conceived?

Or again, if any one should, because of this expression which occurs in the Gospel, "Are not two sparrows sold for a farthing? and not one of them falls to the ground without the will of your Father," take occasion to reckon up the number of sparrows caught daily, whether over all the world or in some particular district, and to make inquiry as to the reason of so many having been captured yesterday, so many the day before, and so many again on this day, and should then join on the number of sparrows to his [particular] hypothesis, would he not in that case mislead himself altogether, and drive into absolute insanity those that agreed with him, since men are always eager in such matters to be thought to have discovered something more extraordinary than their masters?

3. But if any one should ask us whether every number of all the things which have been made, and which are made, is known to God, and whether every one of these [numbers] has, according to His providence, received that special amount which it contains; and on our agreeing that such is the case, and acknowledging that not one of the things which have been, or are, or shall be made, escapes the knowledge of God, but that through His providence every one of them has obtained its nature, and rank, and number, and special quantity, and that nothing whatever either has been or is produced in vain or accidentally, but with exceeding suitability [to the purpose intended], and in the exercise of transcendent knowledge, and that it was an admirable and truly divine intellect which could both distinguish and bring forth the proper causes of such a system: if, [I say,] any one, on obtaining our adherence and consent to this, should proceed to reckon up the sand and pebbles of the earth, yea also the waves of the sea and the stars of heaven, and should endeavour to think out the causes of the number which he imagines himself to have discovered, would not his labour be in vain, and would not such a man be justly declared mad, and destitute of reason, by all possessed of common sense?

And the more he occupied himself beyond others in questions of this kind, and the more he imagines himself to find out beyond others, styling them unskilful, ignorant, and animal beings, because they do not enter into his so useless labour, the more is he [in reality] insane, foolish, struck as it were with a thunderbolt, since indeed he does in no one point own himself inferior to God; but, by the knowledge which he imagines himself to have discovered, he changes God Himself, and exalts his own opinion above the greatness of the Creator.

Chapter XXVII – Proper Mode of Interpreting Parables and Obscure Passages of Scripture

1. A sound mind, and one which does not expose its possessor to danger, and is devoted to piety and the love of truth, will eagerly meditate upon those things which God has placed within the power of mankind, and has subjected to our knowledge, and will make advancement in [acquaintance with] them, rendering the knowledge of them easy to him by means of daily study. These things are such as fall [plainly] under our observation, and are clearly and unambiguously in express terms set forth in the Sacred Scriptures. And therefore the parables ought not to be adapted to ambiguous expressions. For, if this be not done, both he who explains them will do so without danger, and the parables will receive a like interpretation from all, and the body of truth remains entire, with a harmonious adaptation of its members, and without any collision [of its several parts]. But to apply expressions which are not clear or evident to interpretations of the parables, such as every one discovers for himself as inclination leads him, [is absurd.] For in this way no one will possess the rule of truth; but in accordance with the number of persons who explain the parables will be found the various systems of truth, in mutual opposition to each other, and setting forth antagonistic doctrines, like the questions current among the Gentile philosophers.

2. According to this course of procedure, therefore, man would always be inquiring but never finding, because he has rejected the very method of discovery. And when the Bridegroom comes, he who has his lamp untrimmed, and not burning with the brightness of a steady light, is classed among those who obscure the interpretations of the parables, forsaking Him who by His plain announcements

freely imparts gifts to all who come to Him, and is excluded from His marriage chamber.

Since, therefore, the entire Scriptures, the prophets, and the Gospels, can be clearly, unambiguously, and harmoniously understood by all, although all do not believe them; and since they proclaim that one only God, to the exclusion of all others, formed all things by His word, whether visible or invisible, heavenly or earthly, in the water or under the earth, as I have shown from the very words of Scripture; and since the very system of creation to which we belong testifies, by what falls under our notice, that one Being made and governs it – those persons will seem truly foolish who blind their eyes to such a clear demonstration, and will not behold the light of the announcement [made to them]; but they put fetters upon themselves, and every one of them imagines, by means of their obscure interpretations of the parables, that he has found out a God of his own. For that there is nothing whatever openly, expressly, and without controversy said in any part of Scripture respecting the Father conceived of by those who hold a contrary opinion, they themselves testify, when they maintain that the Saviour privately taught these same things not to all, but to certain only of His disciples who could comprehend them, and who understood what was intended by Him through means of arguments, enigmas, and parables. They come, [in fine,] to this, that they maintain there is one Being who is proclaimed as God, and another as Father, He who is set forth as such through means of parables and enigmas.

3. But since parables admit of many interpretations, what lover of truth will not acknowledge, that for them to assert God is to be searched out from these, while they desert what is certain, indubitable, and true, is the part of men who eagerly throw themselves into danger, and act as if destitute of reason? And is not such a course of conduct not to build one's house upon a rock which is firm, strong, and placed in an open position, but upon the shifting sand? Hence the overthrow of such a building is a matter of ease.

Chapter XXVIII – Perfect Knowledge Cannot Be Attained in the Present Life: Many Questions Must Be Submissively Left in the Hands of God

1. Having therefore the truth itself as our rule and the testimony concerning God set clearly before us, we ought not, by running after numerous and diverse answers to questions, to cast away the firm and true knowledge of God. But it is much more suitable that we, directing our inquiries after this fashion, should exercise ourselves in the investigation of the mystery and administration of the living God, and should increase in the love of Him who has done, and still does, so great things for us; but never should fall from the belief by which it is most clearly proclaimed that this Being alone is truly God and Father, who both formed this world, fashioned man, and bestowed the faculty of increase on His own creation, and called him upwards from lesser things to those greater ones which are in His own presence, just as He brings an infant which has been conceived in the womb into the light of the sun, and lays up wheat in the barn after He has given it full strength on the stalk. But it is one and the same Creator who both fashioned the womb and created the sun; and one and the same Lord who both reared the stalk of corn, increased and multiplied the wheat, and prepared the barn.

2. If, however, we cannot discover explanations of all those things in Scripture which are made the subject of investigation, yet let us not on that account seek after any other God besides Him who really exists. For this is the very greatest impiety. We should leave things of that nature to God who created us, being most properly assured that the Scriptures are indeed perfect, since they were spoken by the Word of God and His Spirit; but we, inasmuch as we are inferior to, and later in existence than, the Word of God and His Spirit, are on that very account destitute of the knowledge of His mysteries. And there is no cause for wonder if this is the case with us as respects things spiritual and heavenly, and such as require to be made known to us by revelation, since many even of those things which lie at our very feet (I mean such as belong to this world, which we handle, and see, and are in close contact with) transcend out knowledge, so that even these we must leave to God.

For it is fitting that He should excel all [in knowledge]. For how stands the case, for instance, if we endeavour to explain the cause of the rising of the Nile? We may say a great deal, plausible or otherwise, on the subject; but what is true, sure, and incontrovertible regarding it, belongs only to God. Then, again, the dwelling-place of birds – of those, I mean, which come to us in spring, but fly away again on the approach of autumn – though it is a matter connected with this world, escapes our knowledge. What explanation, again, can we give of the flow and ebb of the ocean, although every one admits there must be a certain cause [for these phenomena]? Or what can we say as to the nature of those things which lie beyond it? What, moreover, can we say as to the formation of rain, lightning, thunder, gatherings of clouds, vapours, the bursting forth of winds, and such like things; of tell as to the storehouses of snow, hail, and other like things? [What do we know respecting] the conditions requisite for the preparation of clouds, or what is the real nature of the vapours in the sky? What as to the reason why the moon waxes and wanes, or what as to the cause of the difference of nature among various waters, metals, stones, and such like things? On all these points we may indeed say a great deal while we search into their causes, but God alone who made them can declare the truth regarding them.

3. If, therefore, even with respect to creation, there are some things [the knowledge of] Which belongs only to God, and others which come with in the range of our own knowledge, what ground is there for complaint, if, in regard to those things which we investigate in the Scriptures (which are throughout spiritual), we are able by the grace of God to explain some of them, while we must leave others in the hands of God, and that not only in the present world, but also in that which is to come, so that God should for ever teach, and man should for ever learn the things taught him by God? As the apostle has said on this point, that, when other things have been done away, then these three, "faith, hope, and charity, shall endure."

For faith, which has respect to our Master, endures unchangeably, assuring us that there is but one true God, and that we should truly love Him for ever, seeing that He alone is our Father; while we hope ever to be receiving more and more from God, and to learn from Him, because He is good, and possesses boundless riches, a kingdom without end, and instruction that can never be exhausted. If, therefore, according to the rule which I have stated, we leave some questions in the hands of God, we shall both preserve our faith uninjured, and shall continue without danger; and all Scripture, which has been given to us by God, shall be found by us perfectly consistent; and the parables shall harmonize with those passages which are perfectly plain; and those statements the meaning of which is clear, shall serve to explain the parables; and through the many diversified utterances [of Scripture] there shall be heard one harmonious melody in us, praising in hymns that God who created all things.

If, for instance, any one asks, "What was God doing before He made the world?" we reply that the answer to such a question lies with God Himself. For that this world was formed perfect by God, receiving a beginning in time, the Scriptures teach us; but no Scripture reveals to us what God was employed about before this event. The answer therefore to that question remains with God, and it is not proper for us to aim at bringing forward foolish, rash, and blasphemous suppositions [in reply to it]; so, as by one's imagining that he has discovered the origin of matter, he should in reality set aside God Himself who made all things.

4. For consider, all ye who invent such opinions, since the Father Himself is alone called God, who has a real existence, but whom ye style the Demiurge; since, moreover, the Scriptures acknowledge Him alone as God; and yet again, since the Lord confesses Him alone as His own Father, and knows no other, as I shall show from His very words – when ye style this very Being the fruit of defect, and the offspring of ignorance, and describe Him as being ignorant of those things which are above Him, with the various other allegations which you make regarding Him – consider the terrible blasphemy [ye are thus guilty of] against Him who truly is God. Ye seem to affirm gravely and honestly enough that ye believe in God; but then, as ye are utterly unable to reveal any other God, ye declare this very Being in whom ye profess to believe, the fruit of defect and the offspring of ignorance.

Now this blindness and foolish talking flow to you from the fact that ye reserve nothing for God, but ye wish to proclaim the nativity and production both of God Himself, of His Ennoea, of His Logos, and Life, and Christ; and ye form the idea of these from no other than a mere human experience; not understanding, as I said before, that it is possible, in the case of man, who is a compound being, to speak in this way of the mind of man and the thought of man; and to say that thought (ennoea) springs from mind (sensus), intention (enthymesis) again from thought, and word (logos) from intention (but which logos? for there is among the Greeks one logos which is the principle that thinks, and another which is the instrument by means of which thought is expressed); and [to say] that a man sometimes is at rest and silent, while at other times he speaks and is active.

But since God is all mind, all reason, all active spirit, all light, and always exists one and the same, as it is both beneficial for us to think of God, and as we learn regarding Him from the Scriptures, such feelings and divisions [of operation] cannot fittingly be ascribed to Him. For our tongue, as being carnal, is not sufficient to minister to the rapidity of the human mind, inasmuch as that is of a spiritual nature, for which reason our word is restrained within us, and is not at once expressed as it has been conceived by the mind, but is uttered by successive efforts, just as the tongue is able to serve it.

5. But God being all Mind, and all Logos, both speaks exactly what He thinks, and thinks exactly what He speaks. For His thought is Logos, and Logos is Mind, and Mind comprehending all things is the Father Himself. He, therefore, who speaks of the mind of God, and ascribes to it a special origin of its own, declares Him a compound Being, as if God were one thing, and the original Mind another. So, again, with respect to Logos, when one attributes to him the third place of production from the Father; on which supposition he is ignorant of His greatness; and thus Logos has been far separated from God. As for the prophet, he declares respecting Him, "Who shall describe His generation?" But ye pretend to set forth His generation from the Father, and ye transfer the production of the word of men which takes place by means of a tongue to the Word of God, and thus are righteously exposed by your own selves as knowing neither things human nor divine.

6. But, beyond reason inflated [with your own wisdom], ye presumptuously maintain that ye are acquainted with the unspeakable mysteries of God; while even the Lord, the very Son of God, allowed that the Father alone knows the very day and hour of judgment, when He plainly declares, "But of that day and that hour knoweth no man, neither the Son, but the Father only." If, then, the Son was not

ashamed to ascribe the knowledge of that day to the Father only, but declared what was true regarding the matter, neither let us be ashamed to reserve for God those greater questions which may occur to us. For no man is superior to his master.

If any one, therefore, says to us, "How then was the Son produced by the Father?" we reply to him, that no man understands that production, or generation, or calling, or revelation, or by whatever name one may describe His generation, which is in fact altogether indescribable. Neither Valentinus, nor Marcion, nor Saturninus, nor Basilides, nor angels, nor archangels, nor principalities, nor powers [possess this knowledge], but the Father only who begat, and the Son who was begotten. Since therefore His generation is unspeakable, those who strive to set forth generations and productions cannot be in their right mind, inasmuch as they undertake to describe things which are indescribable. For that a word is uttered at the bidding of thought and mind, all men indeed well understand.

Those, therefore, who have excogitated [the theory of] emissions have not discovered anything great, or revealed any abstruse mystery, when they have simply transferred what all understand to the only-begotten Word of God; and while they style Him unspeakable and unnameable, they nevertheless set forth the production and formation of His first generation, as if they themselves had assisted at His birth, thus assimilating Him to the word of mankind formed by emissions.

7. But we shall not be wrong if we affirm the same thing also concerning the substance of matter, that God produced it. For we have learned from the Scriptures that God holds the supremacy over all things. But whence or in what way He produced it, neither has Scripture anywhere declared; nor does it become us to conjecture, so as, in accordance with our own opinions, to form endless conjectures concerning God, but we should leave such knowledge in the hands of God Himself.

In like manner, also, we must leave the cause why, while all things were made by God, certain of His creatures sinned and revolted from a state of submission to God, and others, indeed the great majority, persevered, and do still persevere, in [willing] subjection to Him who formed them, and also of what nature those are who sinned, and of what nature those who persevere – [we must, I say, leave the cause of these things] to God and His Word, to whom alone He said,

"Sit at my right hand, until I make Thine enemies Thy footstool." But as for us, we still dwell upon the earth, and have not yet sat down upon His throne. For although the Spirit of the Saviour that is in Him "searcheth all things, even the deep things of God," yet as to us "there are diversities of gifts, differences of administrations, and diversities of operations;" and we, while upon the earth, as Paul also declares, "know in part, and prophesy in part."

Since, therefore, we know but in part, we ought to leave all sorts of [difficult] questions in the hands of Him who in some measure, [and that only,] bestows grace on us. That eternal fire, [for instance,] is prepared for sinners, both the Lord has plainly declared, and the rest of the Scriptures demonstrate. And that God foreknew that this would happen, the Scriptures do in like manner demonstrate, since He prepared eternal fire from the beginning for those who were [afterwards] to transgress [His commandments]; but the cause itself of the nature of such transgressors neither has any Scripture informed us, nor has an apostle told us, nor has the Lord taught us.

It becomes us, therefore, to leave the knowledge of this matter to God, even as the Lord does of the day and hour [of judgment], and not to rush to such an extreme of danger, that we will leave nothing in the hands of God, even though we have received only a measure of grace [from Him in this world]. But when we investigate points which are above us, and with respect to which we cannot reach satisfaction, [it is absurd] that we should display such an extreme of presumption as to lay open God, and things which are not yet discovered, as if already we had found out, by the vain talk about emissions, God Himself, the Creator of all things, and to assert that He derived His substance from apostasy and ignorance, so as to frame an impious hypothesis in opposition to God.

8. Moreover, they possess no proof of their system, which has but recently been invented by them, sometimes resting upon certain numbers, sometimes on syllables, and sometimes, again, on names; and there are occasions, too, when, by means of those letters which are contained in letters, by parables not properly interpreted, or by certain [baseless] conjectures, they strive to establish that fabulous account which they have devised. For if any one should inquire the reason why the Father, who has fellowship with the Son in all things, has

been declared by the Lord alone to know the hour and the day [of judgment], he will find at present no more suitable, or becoming, or safe reason than this (since, indeed, the Lord is the only true Master), that we may learn through Him that the Father is above all things. For "the Father," says He, "is greater than I."

The Father, therefore, has been declared by our Lord to excel with respect to knowledge; for this reason, that we, too, as long as we are connected with the scheme of things in this world, should leave perfect knowledge, and such questions [as have been mentioned], to God, and should not by any chance, while we seek to investigate the sublime nature of the Father, fall into the danger of starting the question whether there is another God above God.

9. But if any lover of strife contradict what I have said, and also what the apostle affirms, that "we know in part, and prophesy in part," and imagine that he has acquired not a partial, but a universal, knowledge of all that exists – being such an one as Valentinus, or Ptolemaeus, or Basilides, or any other of those who maintain that they have searched out the deep things of God – let him not (arraying himself in vainglory) boast that he has acquired greater knowledge than others with respect to those things which are invisible, or cannot be placed under our observation; but let him, by making diligent inquiry, and obtaining information from the Father, tell us the reasons (which we know not) of those things which are in this world – as, for instance, the number of hairs on his own head, and the sparrows which are captured day by day, and such other points with which we are not previously acquainted – so that we may credit him also with respect to more important points.

But if those who are perfect do not yet understand the very things in their hands, and at their feet, and before their eyes, and on the earth, and especially the rule followed with respect to the hairs of their head, how can we believe them regarding things spiritual, and super-celestial, and those which, with a vain confidence, they assert to be above God? So much, then, I have said concerning numbers, and names, and syllables, and questions respecting such things as are above our comprehension, and concerning their improper expositions of the parables: [I add no more on these points,] since thou thyself mayest enlarge upon them.

Irenæus *Against Heresies*, Book IV

Chapter XIV – If God Demands Obedience from Man, If He Formed Man, Called Him and Placed Him Under Laws, It Was Merely for Man's Welfare; Not that God Stood in Need of Man, But that He Graciously Conferred Upon Man His Favours in Every Possible Manner

1. In the beginning, therefore, did God form Adam, not as if He stood in need of man, but that He might have [some one] upon whom to confer His benefits. For not alone antecedently to Adam, but also before all creation, the Word glorified His Father, remaining in Him; and was Himself glorified by the Father, as He did Himself declare, "Father, glorify Thou Me with the glory which I had with Thee before the world was." Nor did He stand in need of our service when He ordered us to follow Him; but He thus bestowed salvation upon ourselves. For to follow the Saviour is to be a partaker of salvation, and to follow light is to receive light.

2. Thus it was, too, that God formed man at the first, because of His munificence; but chose the patriarchs for the sake of their salvation; and prepared a people beforehand, teaching the headstrong to follow God; and raised up prophets upon earth, accustoming man to bear His Spirit [within him], and to hold communion with God: He Himself, indeed, having need of nothing, but granting communion with Himself to those who stood in need of it, and sketching out, like an architect, the plan of salvation to those that pleased Him…

Chapter XX – That One God Formed All Things in the World, by Means of the Word and the Holy Spirit: and that Although He is to Us in This Life Invisible and Incomprehensible, Nevertheless He is Not Unknown; Inasmuch as His Works Do Declare Him, and His Word Has Shown that in Many Modes He May Be Seen and Known

1. As regards His greatness, therefore, it is not possible to know God, for it is impossible that the Father can be measured; but as regards His love (for this it is which leads us to God by His Word), when we obey Him, we do always learn that there is so great a God,

and that it is He who by Himself has established, and selected, and adorned, and contains all things; and among the all things, both ourselves and this our world.

We also then were made, along with those things which are contained by Him. And this is He of whom the Scripture says, "And God formed man, taking clay of the earth, and breathed into his face the breath of life." It was not angels, therefore, who made us, nor who formed us, neither had angels power to make an image of God, nor any one else, except the Word of the Lord, nor any Power remotely distant from the Father of all things. For God did not stand in need of these [beings], in order to the accomplishing of what He had Himself determined with Himself beforehand should be done, as if He did not possess His own hands. For with Him were always present the Word and Wisdom, the Son and the Spirit, by whom and in whom, freely and spontaneously, He made all things, to whom also He speaks, saying, "Let Us make man after Our image and likeness;" He taking from Himself the substance of the creatures [formed], and the pattern of things made, and the type of all the adornments in the world.

2. Truly, then, the Scripture declared, which says, "first of all believe that there is one God, who has established all things, and completed them, and having caused that from what had no being, all things should come into existence:" He who contains all things, and is Himself contained by no one. Rightly also has Malachi said among the prophets: "Is it not one God who hath established us? Have we not all one Father?" In accordance with this, too, does the apostle say, "There is one God, the Father, who is above all, and in us all." Likewise does the Lord also say: "All things are delivered to Me by My Father;" manifestly by Him who made all things; for He did not deliver to Him the things of another, but His own. But in all things [it is implied that] nothing has been kept back [from Him], and for this reason the same person is the Judge of the living and the dead; "having the key of David: He shall Open, and no man shall shut: He shall shut, and no man shall open."

For no one was able, either in heaven or in earth, or under the earth, to open the book of the Father, or to behold Him, with the exception of the Lamb who was slain, and who redeemed us with His own blood, receiving power over all things from the same God who made all things by the Word, and adorned them by [His] Wisdom, when "the Word was made flesh;" that even as the Word of God had the sovereignty in the heavens, so also might He have the sovereignty in earth, inasmuch as [He was] a righteous man, "who did no sin, neither was there found guile in His mouth;" and that He might have the pre-eminence over those things which are under the earth, He Himself being made "the first-begotten of the dead;" and that all things, as I have already said, might behold their King; and that the paternal light might meet with and rest upon the flesh of our Lord, and come to us from His resplendent flesh, and that thus man might attain to immortality, having been invested with the paternal light.

3. I have also largely demonstrated, that the Word, namely the Son, was always with the Father; and that Wisdom also, which is the Spirit, was present with Him, anterior to all creation, He declares by Solomon: "God by Wisdom founded the earth, and by understanding hath He established the heaven. By His knowledge the depths burst forth, and the clouds dropped down the dew." And again: "The Lord created me the beginning of His ways in His work: He set me up from everlasting, in the beginning, before He made the earth, before He established the depths, and before the fountains of waters gushed forth; before the mountains were made strong, and before all the hills, He brought me forth." And again: "When He prepared the heaven, I was with Him, and when He established the fountains of the deep; when He made the foundations of the earth strong, I was with Him preparing [them]. I was He in whom He rejoiced, and throughout all time I was daily glad before His face, when He rejoiced at the completion of the world, and was delighted in the sons of men."

4. There is therefore one God, who by the Word and Wisdom created and arranged all things; but this is the Creator (Demiurge) who has granted this world to the human race, and who, as regards His greatness, is indeed unknown to all who have been made by Him (for no man has searched out His height, either among the ancients who have gone to their rest, or any of those who are now alive); but as regards His love, He is always known through Him by whose means He ordained all things. Now this is His Word, our Lord Jesus Christ, who in the last times was made a man among men, that He might join the end to the beginning, that is, man to God. Wherefore the prophets, receiving the prophetic gift from the same Word, announced His

advent according to the flesh, by which the blending and communion of God and man took place according to the good pleasure of the Father, the Word of God foretelling from the beginning that God should be seen by men, and hold converse with them upon earth, should confer with them, and should be present with His own creation, saving it, and becoming capable of being perceived by it, and freeing us from the hands of all that hate us, that is, from every spirit of wickedness; and causing us to serve Him in holiness and righteousness all our days, in order that man, having embraced the Spirit of God, might pass into the glory of the Father.

Clement of Alexandria

> St. Clement of Alexandria (c. 150 – c. 215) believed in taking truth wherever he found it. He was therefore open to secular sources and to drawing connections between Christianity and pagan Greek culture. In these short excerpts, he teaches that time was created along with the rest of creation and therefore that creation did not take place in time. He also teaches that God's will orders the creation and that God's hand directly formed humanity (in contrast with the rest of creation, which was produced by God's command alone). Clement explains God's rest on the seventh day as God's way of preserving the order of creation.

Clement of Alexandria *The Instructor*, Book I

Chapter III – The Philanthropy of the Instructor

The Lord ministers all good and all help, both as man and as God: as God, forgiving our sins; and as man, training us not to sin. Man is therefore justly dear to God, since he is His workmanship. The other works of creation He made by the word of command alone, but man He framed by Himself, by His own hand, and breathed into him what was peculiar to Himself. What, then, was fashioned by Him, and after He likeness, either was created by God Himself as being desirable on its own account, or was formed as being desirable on account of something else.

If, then, man is an object desirable for itself, then He who is good loved what is good, and the love-charm is within even in man, and is that very thing which is called the inspiration [or breath of God]; but if man was a desirable object on account of something else, God had no other reason for creating him, than that unless he came into being, it was not possible for God to be a good Creator, or for man to arrive at the knowledge of God. For God would not have accomplished that on account of which man was created otherwise than by the creation of man; and what hidden power in willing God possessed, He carried fully out by the forth-putting of His might externally in the act of creating, receiving from man what He made man; and whom He had He saw, and what He wished that came to pass; and there is nothing which God cannot do.

Man, then, whom God made, is desirable for himself, and that which is desirable on his account is allied to him to whom it is desirable on his account; and this, too, is acceptable and liked.

Clement of Alexandria *Stromata*, Book VI

Chapter 16 – Gnostic Exposition of the Decalogue

The sensible types of these, then, are the sounds we pronounce. Thus the Lord Himself is called "Alpha and Omega, the beginning and the end," "by whom all things were made, and without whom not even one thing was made." God's resting is not, then, as some conceive, that God ceased from doing. For, being good, if He should ever cease from doing good, then would He cease from being God, which it is sacrilege even to say. The resting is, therefore, the ordering that the order of created things should be preserved inviolate, and that each of the creatures should cease from the ancient disorder. For the creations on the different days followed in a most important succession; so that all things brought into existence might have honour from priority, created together in thought, but not being of equal worth. Nor was the creation of each signified by the voice, in as much as the creative work is said to have made them at once. For something must needs have been named first. Wherefore those things were announced first, from which came those that were second, all things being originated together from one essence by one power. For the will of God was one, in one identity. And how could creation take place in time, seeing time was born along with things which exist.

Tertullian

> Tertullian of Carthage (155 – c. 220) was a lawyer who converted to Christianity in 193 and then became a priest. In 207, he went over to the Montanist sect, thereby leaving the established Church. Even so, Christians of all stripes have always greatly valued his writings.
>
> The work excerpted here, *Against Hermogenes*, was written some time after 200. Hermogenes was a painter and Gnostic from Carthage. His views were so influential that Theophilus of Antioch also wrote a work to refute them. Hermogenes held that matter was eternal and that God had created all things out of this pre-existing matter. Explaining the existence of evil appears to have been his primary motivation for holding this view, for by it he could attribute evil to the fault of matter and not to God.
>
> In writing against Hermogenes, Tertullian strongly affirmed the Christian doctrine of creation out of nothing. Tertullian's refutation of Hermogenes is elaborate; in it one sees a lawyer trying to address every possible angle in his opponent's position.
>
> Though theologically sound on creation, *Against Hermogenes* displays a flawed Trinitarian theology: Tertullian writes that there was a time before the Son was begotten (ch. 3) and therefore a time when God was not Father.

Tertullian *Against Hermogenes*

Containing an Argument Against His Opinion that Matter is Eternal.

Chapter I – The Opinions of Hermogenes, by the Prescriptive Rule of Antiquity Shown to Be Heretical. Not Derived from Christianity, But from Heathen Philosophy. Some of the Tenets Mentioned

We are accustomed, for the purpose of shortening argument, to lay down the rule against heretics of the lateness of their date. For in as far as by our rule, priority is given to the truth, which also foretold that there would be heresies, in so far must all later opinions be prejudged as heresies, being such as were, by the more ancient rule of truth, predicted as (one day) to happen.

Now, the doctrine of Hermogenes has this taint of novelty... However, never mind the man, when it is his doctrine which I question. He does not appear to acknowledge any other Christ as Lord, though he holds Him in a different way; but by this difference in his faith he really makes Him another being – nay, he takes from Him everything which is God, since he will not have it that He made all things of nothing. For, turning away from Christians to the philosophers, from the Church to the Academy and the Porch, he learned there from the Stoics how to place Matter (on the same level) with the Lord, just as if it too had existed ever both unborn and unmade, having no beginning at all nor end, out of which, according to him, the Lord afterwards created all things.

Chapter II – Hermogenes, After a Perverse Induction from Mere Heretical Assumptions, Concludes that God Created All Things Out of Pre-Existing Matter

Our very bad painter has coloured this his primary shade absolutely without any light, with such arguments as these: He begins with laying down the premiss, that the Lord made all things either out of Himself, or out of nothing, or out of something; in order that, after he has shown that it was impossible for Him to have made them either out of Himself or out of nothing, he might thence affirm the residuary proposition that He made them out of something, and therefore that that something was Matter. He could not have made all things, he says, of Himself; because whatever things the Lord made of Himself would have been parts of Himself; but He is not dissoluble into parts, because, being the Lord, He is indivisible, and unchangeable, and always the same. Besides, if He had made anything out of Himself, it would have been something of Himself.

Everything, however, both which was made and which He made must be accounted imperfect, because it was made of a part, and He made it of a part; or if, again, it was a whole which He made, who is a whole Himself, He must in that case have been at once both a whole, and yet not a whole; because it behaved Him to be a whole, that He might produce Himself, and yet not a whole, that He might be produced out of Himself. But this is a most difficult position. For if He were in existence, He could not be made, for He was in existence already; if, however, he were not in existence He could not make, because He was a nonentity.

He maintains, moreover, that He who always exists, does not come into existence, but exists for ever and ever. He accordingly concludes that He made nothing out of Himself, since He never passed into such a condition as made it possible for Him to make anything out of Himself. In like manner, he contends that He could not have made all things out of nothing – thus, He defines the Lord as a being who is good, nay, very good, who must will to make things as good and excellent as He is Himself; indeed it were impossible for Him either to will or to make anything which was not good, nay, very good itself.

Therefore all things ought to have been made good and excellent by Him, after His own condition. Experience shows, however, that things which are even evil were made by Him: not, of course, of His own will and pleasure; because, if it had been of His own will and pleasure, He would be sure to have made nothing unfitting or unworthy of Himself. That, therefore, which He made not of His own will must be understood to have been made from the fault of something, and that is from Matter, without a doubt.

Chapter III – An Argument of Hermogenes. The Answer: While God is a Title Eternally Applicable to the Divine Being, Lord and Father are Only Relative Appellations, Not Eternally Applicable. An Inconsistency in the Argument of Hermogenes Pointed Out

He adds also another point: that as God was always God, there was never a time when God was not also Lord. But it was in no way possible for Him to be regarded as always Lord, in the same manner as He had been always God, if there had not been always, in the previous eternity, a something of which He could be regarded as evermore the Lord. So he concludes that God always had Matter co-existent with Himself as the Lord thereof.

Now, this tissue of his I shall at once hasten to pull abroad. I have been willing to set it out in form to this length, for the information of those who are unacquainted with the subject, that they may know that his other arguments likewise need only be understood to be refuted.

We affirm, then, that the name of God always existed with Himself and in Himself – but not eternally so the Lord. Because the condition of the one is not the same as that of the other. God is the designation of the substance itself, that is, of the Divinity; but Lord is (the name) not of substance, but of power. I maintain that the substance existed always with its own name, which is God; the title Lord was afterwards added, as the indication indeed of something accruing. For from the moment when those things began to exist, over which the power of a Lord was to act, God, by the accession of that power, both became Lord and received the name thereof...

Chapter VIII – On His Own Principles, Hermogenes Makes Matter, on the Whole, Superior to God

[Do you suppose, therefore, that he has not made Matter equal with God, although, forsooth, he pretends it to be inferior to Him? (from end ¶7, ed.)] Nay more, he even prefers Matter to God, and rather subjects God to it, when he will have it that God made all things out of Matter. For if He drew His resources from it for the creation of the world, Matter is already found to be the superior, inasmuch as it furnished Him with the means of effecting His works; and God is thereby clearly subjected to Matter, of which the substance was indispensable to Him. For there is no one but requires that which he makes use of; no one but is subject to the thing which he requires, for the very purpose of being able to make use of it. So, again, there is no one who, from using what belongs to another, is not inferior to him of whose property he makes use; and there is no one who imparts of his own for another's use, who is not in this respect superior to him to whose use he lends his property.

On this principle, Matter self, no doubt, was not in want of God, but rather lent itself to God, who was in want of it – rich and abundant and liberal as it was – to one who was, I suppose, too small, and too weak, and too unskilful, to form what He willed out of nothing. A grand service, verily, did it confer on God in giving Him means at the present time whereby He might be known to be God, and be called Almighty – only that He is no longer Almighty, since He is not powerful enough for this, to produce all things out of nothing.

To be sure, Matter bestowed somewhat on itself also – even to get its own self acknowledged with God as God's co-equal, nay more, as His helper; only there is this drawback, that Hermogenes is the only man that has found out this fact, besides the philosophers – those patriarchs of all heresy. For the prophets knew nothing about it, nor the apostles thus far, nor, I suppose, even Christ.

Chapter IX – Sundry Inevitable But Intolerable Conclusions from the Principles of Hermogenes

He cannot say that it was as its Lord that God employed Matter for His creative works, for He could not have been the Lord of a substance which was co-equal with Himself. Well, but perhaps it was a title derived from the will of another, which he enjoyed – a precarious holding, and not a lordship, and that to such a degree, that although Matter was evil, He yet endured to make use of an evil substance, owing, of course, to the restraint of His own limited power, which made Him impotent to create out of nothing, not in consequence of His power; for if, as God, He had at all possessed power over Matter which He knew to be evil, He would first have converted it into good – as its Lord and the good God – that so He might have a good thing to make use of, instead of a bad one. But being undoubtedly good, only not the Lord withal, He, by using such power as He possessed, showed the necessity He was under of yielding to the condition of Matter, which He would have amended if He had been its Lord.

Now this is the answer which must be given to Hermogenes when he maintains that it was by virtue of His Lordship that God used Matter – even of His non-possession of any right to it, on the ground, of course, of His not having Himself made it. Evil then, on your terms, must proceed from God Himself, since He is – I will not say the Author of evil, because He did not form it, but – the permitter thereof, as having dominion over it.

If indeed Matter shall prove not even to belong to God at all, as being evil, it follows, that when He made use of what belonged to another, He used it either on a precarious title because He was in need of it, or else by violent possession because He was stronger than it. For by three methods is the property of others obtained – by right, by permission, by violence; in other words, by lordship, by a title derived from the will of another, by force. Now, as lordship is out of the question, Hermogenes must choose which (of the other methods) is suitable to God. Did He, then, make all things out of Matter, by permission, or by force? But, in truth, would not God have more wisely determined that nothing at all should be created, than that it should be created by the mere sufferance of another, or by violence, and that, too, with a substance which was evil?

Chapter X – To What Straits Hermogenes Absurdly Reduces the Divine Being; He Does Nothing Short of Making Him the Author of Evil

Even if Matter had been the perfection of good, would it not have been equally indecorous in Him to have thought of the property of another, however good, (to effect His purpose by the help of it)? It was, therefore, absurd enough for Him, in the interest of His own glory, to have created the world in such a way as to betray His own obligation to a substance which belonged to another – and that even not good. Was He then, asks (Hermogenes), to make all things out of nothing, that so evil things themselves might be attributed to His will?

Great, in all conscience, must be the blindness of our heretics which leaves them to argue in such a way that they either insist on the belief of another God supremely good, on the ground of their thinking the Creator to be the author of evil, or else they set up Matter with the Creator, in order that they may derive evil from Matter, not from the Creator. And yet there is absolutely no god at all that is free from such a doubtful plight, so as to be able to avoid the appearance even of being the author of evil, whosoever he is that – I will not say, indeed, has made, but still – has permitted evil to be made by some author or other, and from some source or other.

Hermogenes, therefore, ought to be told at once, although we postpone to another place our distinction concerning the mode of evil, that even he has effected no result by this device of his. For observe how God is found to be, if not the Author of, yet at any rate the conniver at, evil, inasmuch as He, with all His extreme goodness, endured evil in Matter before He created the world, although, as being good, and the enemy of evil, He ought to have corrected it. For He either was able to correct it, but was unwilling; or else was willing, but being a weak God, was not able. If He was able and yet unwilling, He was Himself evil, as having favoured evil; and thus He now opens Himself to the charge of evil, because even if He did not create it yet still, since it would not be existing if He had been against its existence, He must Himself have then caused it to exist, when He refused to will its non-existence.

And what is more shameful than this? When He willed that to be which He was Himself unwilling to create, He acted in fact against His very self, inasmuch as He was both willing that that should exist which He was unwilling to make, and unwilling to make that which He was willing should exist. As if what He willed was good, and at the same time what he refused to be the Maker of was evil. What He judged to be evil by not creating it, He also proclaimed to be good by permitting it to exist. By bearing with evil as a good instead of rather extirpating it, He proved Himself to be the promoter thereof; criminally, if through His own will – disgracefully, if through necessity. God must either be the servant of evil or the friend thereof, since He held converse with evil in Matter – nay, more, effected His works out of the evil thereof.

Chapter XI – Hermogenes Makes Great Efforts to Remove Evil from God to Matter; How He Fails to Do This Consistently with His Own Argument

...But, as the argument now stands, since what is eternal can be deemed evil, the evil must prove to be invincible and insuperable, as being eternal; and in that case it will be in vain that we labour "to put away evil from the midst of us;" in that case, moreover, God vainly gives us such a command and precept; nay more, in vain has God appointed any judgment at all, when He means, indeed, to inflict punishment with injustice. But if, on the other hand, there is to be an end of evil...if in this way an end is compatible with evil, it must follow of necessary that a beginning is also compatible with it; and Matter will turn out to have a beginning, by virtue of its having also an end. For whatever things are set to the account of evil, have a compatibility with the condition of evil.

Chapter XII – The Mode of Controversy Changed; The Premises of Hermogenes Accepted, in Order to Show into What Confusion They Lead Him

Come now, let us suppose Matter to be evil, nay, very evil, by nature of course, just as we believe God to be good, even very good, in like manner by nature. Now nature must be regarded as sure and fixed, just as persistently fixed in evil in the case of Matter, as immoveable and unchangeable in good in the case of God. Because, as is evident, if nature admits of change from evil to good in Matter, it can be changed from good to evil in God... But bear in mind that Matter has once for all been determined to be eternal, as being unmade, unborn, and therefore supposably of an unchangeable and incorruptible nature; and this from the very opinion of Hermogenes himself, which he alleges against us when he denies that God was able to make (anything) of Himself, on the ground that what is eternal is incapable of change, because it would lose – so the opinion runs – what it once was, in becoming by the change that which it was not, if it were not eternal. But as for the Lord, who is also eternal, (he maintained) that He could not be anything else than what He always is.

Well, then, I will adopt this definite opinion of his, and by means thereof refute him. I blame Matter with a like censure, because out of it, evil though it be – nay, very evil – good things have been created, nay, "very good" ones: "And God saw that they were good, and God blessed them" – because, of course, of their very great goodness; certainly not because they were evil, or very evil. Change is therefore admissible in Matter; and this being the case, it has lost its condition of eternity; in short, its beauty is decayed in death. Eternity, however, cannot be lost, because it cannot be eternity, except by reason of its immunity from loss. For the same reason also it is incapable of change, inasmuch as, since it is eternity, it can by no means be changed.

Chapter XIV – Tertullian Pushes His Opponent into a Dilemma

Now, if it be also argued, that although Matter may have afforded Him the opportunity, it was still His own will which led Him to the creation of good creatures, as having detected what was good in matter – although this, too, be a discreditable supposition – yet, at any rate, when He produces evil likewise out of the same (Matter), He is a servant to Matter, since, of course, it is not of His own accord that He produces this too, having nothing else that He can do than to effect creation out of an evil stock – unwillingly, no doubt, as being good; of necessity, too, as being unwilling; and as an act of servitude, because from necessity.

Which, then, is the worthier thought, that He created evil things of necessity, or of His own accord? Because it was indeed of necessity that He created them, if out of Matter; of His own accord, if out of nothing. For you are now labouring in vain when you try to avoid making God the Author of evil things; because, since He made all things of Matter, they will have to be ascribed to Himself, who made them, just because He made them. Plainly the interest of the question, whence He made all things, identifies itself with (the question), whether He made all things out of nothing; and it matters not whence He made all things, so that He made all things thence, whence most glory accrued to Him.

Now, more glory accrued to Him from a creation of His own will than from one of necessity; in other words, from a creation out of nothing, than from one out of Matter. It is more worthy to believe that God is free, even as the Author of evil, than that He is a slave. Power, whatever it be, is more suited to Him than infirmity.

If we thus even admit that matter had nothing good in it, but that the Lord produced whatever good He did produce of His own power, then some other questions will with equal reason arise. first, since there was no good at all in Matter, it is clear that good was not made of Matter, on the express ground indeed that Matter did not possess it. Next, if good was not made of Matter, it must then have been made of God; if not of God, then it must have been made of nothing. For this is the alternative, on Hermogenes' own showing.

Chapter XV – The Truth, that God Made All Things from Nothing, Rescued from the Opponent's Flounderings

Now, if good was neither produced out of matter, since it was not in it, evil as it was, nor out of God, since, according to the position of Hermogenes, nothing could have been produced out of God, it will be found that good was created out of nothing, inasmuch as it was formed of none – neither of Matter nor of God. And if good was formed out of nothing, why not evil too? Nay, if anything was formed out of nothing, why not all things? Unless indeed it be that the divine might was insufficient for the production of all things, though it produced a something out of nothing. Or else if good proceeded from evil matter, since it issued neither from nothing nor from God, it will follow that it must have proceeded from the conversion of Matter contrary to that unchangeable attribute which has been claimed for it, as an eternal being. Thus, in regard to the source whence good derived its existence, Hermogenes will now have to deny the possibility of such. But still it is necessary that (good) should proceed from some one of those sources from which he has denied the very possibility of its having been derived.

Now if evil be denied to be of nothing for the purpose of denying it to be the work of God, from whose will there would be too much appearance of its being derived, and be alleged to proceed from Matter, that it may be the property of that very thing of whose substance it is assumed to be made, even here also, as I have said, God will have to be regarded as the Author of evil; because, whereas it had been His duty to produce all good things out of Matter, or rather good things simply, by His identical attribute of power and will, He did yet not only not produce all good things, but even (some) evil things – of course, either willing that the evil should exist if He was able to cause their non-existence, or not being strong enough to effect that all things should be good, if being desirous of that result, He failed in the accomplishment thereof; since there can be no difference whether it were by weakness or by will, that the Lord proved to be the Author of evil. Else what was the reason that, after creating good things, as if Himself good, He should have also produced evil things, as if He failed in His goodness, since He did not confine Himself to the production of things which were simply consistent with Himself?

What necessity was there, after the production of His proper work, for His troubling Himself about Matter also by producing evil likewise, in order to secure His being alone acknowledged as good from His good, and at the same time to prevent Matter being regarded as evil from (created) evil? Good would have flourished much better if evil had not blown upon it. For Hermogenes himself explodes the arguments of sundry persons who contend that evil things were necessary to impart lustre to the good, which must be understood from their contrasts.

This, therefore, was not the ground for the production of evil; but if some other reason must be sought for the introduction thereof, why could it not have been introduced even from nothing, since the very same reason would exculpate the Lord from the reproach of being thought the author of evil, which now excuses the existence of evil things, when He produces them out of Matter? And if there is this excuse, then the question is completely shut up in a corner, where they are unwilling to find it, who, without examining into the reason itself of evil, or distinguishing how they should either attribute it to God or separate it from God, do in fact expose God to many most unworthy calumnies.

Chapter XVI – A Series of Dilemmas; They Show that Hermogenes Cannot Escape from the Orthodox Conclusion

On the very threshold, then, of this doctrine, which I shall probably have to treat of elsewhere, I distinctly lay it down as my position, that both good and evil must be ascribed either to God, who made them out of Matter; or to Matter itself, out of which He made them; or both one and the other to both of them together, because they are bound together – both He who created, and that out of which He created; or (lastly) one to One and the other to the Other, because after Matter and God there is not a third.

Now if both should prove to belong to God, God evidently will be the author of evil; but God, as being good, cannot be the author of evil. Again, if both are ascribed to Matter, Matter will evidently be the very mother of good, but inasmuch as Matter is wholly evil, it cannot be the mother of good. But if both one and the other should be thought to belong to Both together, then in this case also Matter will be comparable with God; and both will be equal, being on equal terms allied to evil as well as to good. Matter, however, ought not to be compared with God, in order that it may not make two gods.

If, (lastly), one be ascribed to One, and the other to the Other – that is to say, let the good be God's, and the evil belong to Matter – then, on the one hand, evil must not be ascribed to God, nor, on the other hand, good to Matter. And God, moreover, by making both good things and evil things out of Matter, creates them along with it. This being the case, I cannot tell how Hermogenes is to escape from my conclusion; for he supposes that God cannot be the author of evil, in what way soever He created evil out of Matter, whether it was of His own will, or of necessity, or from the reason (of the case).

If, however, He is the author of evil, who was the actual Creator, Matter being simply associated with Him by reason of its furnishing

Him with substance, you now do away with the cause of your introducing Matter. For it is not the less true, that it is by means of Matter that God shows Himself the author of evil, although Matter has been assumed by you expressly to prevent God's seeming to be the author of evil. Matter being therefore excluded, since the cause of it is excluded, it remains that God without doubt, must have made all things out of nothing. Whether evil things were amongst them we shall see, when it shall be made clear what are evil things, and whether those things are evil which you at present deem to be so. For it is more worthy of God that He produced even these of His own will, by producing them out of nothing, than from the predetermination of another, (which must have been the case) if He had produced them out of Matter. It is liberty, not necessity, which suits the character of God. I would much rather that He should have even willed to create evil of Himself, than that He should have lacked ability to hinder its creation.

Chapter XVII – The Truth of God's Work in Creation; You Cannot Depart in the Least from It, Without Landing Yourself in an Absurdity

This rule is required by the nature of the One – only God, who is One – only in no other way than as the sole God; and in no other way sole, than as having nothing else (co-existent) with Him. So also He will be first, because all things are after Him; and all things are after Him, because all things are by Him; and all things are by Him, because they are of nothing: so that reason coincides with the Scripture, which says: "Who hath known the mind of the Lord? Or, who hath been His counsellor? Or, with whom took He counsel? Or, who hath shown to Him the way of wisdom and knowledge? Who hath first given to Him, and it shall be recompensed to him again?" Surely none! Because there was present with Him no power, no material, no nature which belonged to any other than Himself. But if it was with some (portion of Matter) that He effected His creation, He must have received from that (Matter) itself both the design and the treatment of its order as being "the way of wisdom and knowledge." For He had to operate conformably with the quality of the thing, and according to the nature of Matter, not according to His own will in consequence of which He must have made even evil things suitably to the nature not of Himself, but of Matter.

Chapter XIX – An Appeal to the History of Creation; True Meaning of the Term Beginning, Which the Heretic Curiously Wrests to an Absurd Sense

But I shall appeal to the original document of Moses, by help of which they on the other side vainly endeavour to prop up their conjectures, with the view, of course, of appearing to have the support of that authority which is indispensable in such an inquiry. They have found their opportunity, as is usual with heretics, in wresting the plain meaning of certain words. For instance the very beginning, when God made the heaven and the earth, they will construe as if it meant something substantial and embodied, to be regarded as Matter. We, however, insist on the proper signification of every word, and say that *principium* means beginning – being a term which is suitable to represent things which begin to exist. For nothing which has come into being is without a beginning, nor can this its commencement be at any other moment than when it begins to have existence. Thus *principium* or beginning, is simply a term of inception, not the name of a substance.

Now, inasmuch as the heaven and the earth are the principal works of God, and since, by His making them first, He constituted them in an especial manner the beginning of His creation, before all things else, with good reason does the Scripture preface (its record of creation) with the words, "In the beginning God made the heaven and the earth;" just as it would have said, "At last God made the heaven and the earth," if God had created these after all the rest.

Now, if the beginning is a substance, the end must also be material. No doubt, a substantial thing may be the beginning of some other thing which may be formed out of it thus the clay is the beginning of the vessel and the seed is the beginning of the plant. But when we employ the word beginning in this sense of origin, and not in that of order, we do not omit to mention also the name of that particular thing which we regard as the origin of the other. On the other hand, if we were to make such a statement as this, for example, "In the beginning the potter made a basin or a water-jug," the word beginning will not here indicate a material substance for I have not mentioned the clay, which is the beginning in this sense, but only the order of the work, meaning that the potter made the basin and the jug first, before anything else – intending afterwards to make the rest.

It is, then, to the order of the works that the word beginning has reference, not to the origin of their substances. I might also explain this word beginning in another way, which would not, however, be inapposite. The Greek term for beginning, which is *archç*, admits the sense not only of priority of order, but of power as well; whence princes and magistrates are called *archontes*. Therefore in this sense too, beginning may be taken for princely authority and power. It was, indeed, in His transcendent authority and power, that God made the heaven and the earth.

Chapter XX – Meaning of the Phrase – "In the Beginning;" Tertullian Connects It with the Wisdom of God, and Elicits from It the Truth that the Creation Was Not Out of Pre-Existent Matter

But in proof that the Greek word means nothing else than beginning, and that beginning admits of no other sense than the initial one, we have that (Being) even acknowledging such a beginning, who says: "The Lord possessed me, the beginning of His ways for the creation of His works." For since all things were made by the Wisdom of God, it follows that, when God made both the heaven and the earth *in principio* – that is to say, in the beginning – He made them in His Wisdom. If, indeed, beginning had a material signification, the Scripture would not have informed us that God made so and so in principio, at the beginning, but rather *ex principio*, of the beginning; for He would not have created in, but of, matter.

When Wisdom, however, was referred to, it was quite right to say, in the beginning. For it was in Wisdom that He made all things at first, because by meditating and arranging His plans therein, He had in fact already done (the work of creation); and if He had even intended to create out of matter, He would yet have effected His creation when He previously meditated on it and arranged it in His Wisdom, since It was in fact the beginning of His ways: this meditation and arrangement being the primal operation of Wisdom, opening as it does the way to the works by the act of meditation and thought.

This authority of Scripture I claim for myself even from this circumstance, that whilst it shows me the God who created, and the works He created, it does not in like manner reveal to me the source from which He created. For since in every operation there are three principal things, He who makes, and that which is made, and that of which it is made, there must be three names mentioned in a correct narrative of the operation – the person of the maker the sort of thing which is made, and the material of which it is formed. If the material is not mentioned, while the work and the maker of the work are both mentioned, it is manifest that He made the work out of nothing. For if He had had anything to operate upon, it would have been mentioned as well as (the other two particulars).

In conclusion, I will apply the Gospel as a supplementary testimony to the Old Testament. Now in this there is all the greater reason why there should be shown the material (if there were any) out of which God made all things, inasmuch as it is therein plainly revealed by whom He made all things. "In the beginning was the Word" – that is, the same beginning, of course, in which God made the heaven and the earth – "and the Word was with God, and the Word was God. All things were made by Him, and without Him nothing was made."

Now, since we have here clearly told us who the Maker was, that is, God, and what He made, even all things, and through whom He made them, even His Word, would not the order of the narrative have required that the source out of which all things were made by God through the Word should likewise be declared, if they had been in fact made out of anything? What, therefore, did not exist, the Scripture was unable to mention; and by not mentioning it, it has given us a clear proof that there was no such thing: for if there had been, the Scripture would have mentioned it.

Chapter XXI – A Retort of Heresy Answered; That Scripture Should in So Many Words Tell Us that the World Was Made of Nothing is Superfluous

But, you will say to me, if you determine that all things were made of nothing, on the ground that it is not told us that anything was made out of pre-existent Matter, take care that it be not contended on the opposite side, that on the same ground all things were made out of

Matter, because it is not likewise expressly said that anything was made out of nothing.

Some arguments may, of course, be thus retorted easily enough; but it does not follow that they are on that account fairly admissible, where there is a diversity in the cause. For I maintain that, even if the Scripture has not expressly declared that all things were made out of nothing – just as it abstains (from saying that they were formed) out of Matter – there was no such pressing need for expressly indicating the creation of all things out of nothing, as there was of their creation out of Matter, if that had been their origin. Because, in the case of what is made out of nothing, the very fact of its not being indicated that it was made of any particular thing shows that it was made of nothing; and there is no danger of its being supposed that it was made of anything, when there is no indication at all of what it was made of.

In the case, however, of that which is made out of something, unless the very fact be plainly declared, that it was made out of something, there will be danger, until it is shown of what it was made, first of its appearing to be made of nothing, because it is not said of what it was made; and then, should it be of such a nature as to have the appearance of having certainly been made of something, there will be a similar risk of its seeming to have been made of afar different material from the proper one, so long as there is an absence of statement of what it was made of.

Then, if God had been unable to make all things of nothing, the Scripture could not possibly have added that He had made all things of nothing: (there could have been no room for such a statement), but it must by all means have informed us that He had made all things out of Matter, since Matter must have been the source; because the one case was quite to be understood, if it were not actually stated, whereas the other case would be left in doubt unless it were stated.

Chapter XXII – This Conclusion Confirmed by the Usage of Holy Scripture in Its History of the Creation; Hermogenes in Danger of the Woe Pronounced Against Adding to Scripture

And to such a degree has the Holy Ghost made this the rule of His Scripture, that whenever anything is made out of anything, He mentions both the thing that is made and the thing of which it is made. "Let the earth," says He, "bring forth grass, the herb yielding seed, and the fruit tree yielding fruit after its kind, whose seed is in itself, after its kind. And it was so. And the earth brought forth grass, and herb yielding seed after its kind, and the tree yielding fruit, whose seed was in itself, after its kind." And again: "And God said, Let the waters bring forth abundantly the moving creatures that have life, and fowl that may fly above the earth through the firmament of heaven. And it was so. And God created great whales, and every living creature that moveth, which the waters brought forth abundantly, after their kind." Again afterwards: "And God said, Let the earth bring forth the living creature after his kind, cattle, and creeping thing, and beasts of the earth after their kind."

If therefore God, when producing other things out of things which had been already made, indicates them by the prophet, and tells us what He has produced from such and such a source (although we might ourselves suppose them to be derived from some source or other, short of nothing; since there had already been created certain things, from which they might easily seem to have been made); if the Holy Ghost took upon Himself so great a concern for our instruction, that we might know from what everything was produced, would He not in like manner have kept us well informed about both the heaven and the earth, by indicating to us what it was that He made them of, if their original consisted of any material substance, so that the more He seemed to have made them of nothing, the less in fact was there as yet made, from which He could appear to have made them?

Therefore, just as He shows us the original out of which He drew such things as were derived from a given source, so also with regard to those things of which He does not point out whence He produced them, He confirms (by that silence our assertion) that they were produced out of nothing. "In the beginning," then, "God made the heaven and the earth."

I revere the fulness of His Scripture, in which He manifests to me both the Creator and the creation. In the gospel, moreover, I discover a Minister and Witness of the Creator, even His Word. But whether all things were made out of any underlying Matter, I have as yet failed anywhere to find. Where such a statement is written, Hermogenes' shop must tell us. If it is nowhere written, then let it fear the woe which impends on all who add to or take away from the written word.

Chapter XXVI – The Method Observed in the History of the Creation, in Reply to the Perverse Interpretation of Hermogenes

We, however, have but one God, and but one earth too, which in the beginning God made. The Scripture, which at its very outset proposes to run through the order thereof tells us as its first information that it was created; it next proceeds to set forth what sort of earth it was. In like manner with respect to the heaven, it informs us first of its creation – "In the beginning God made the heaven:" it then goes on to introduce its arrangement; how that God both separated "the water which was below the firmament from that which was above the firmament," and called the firmament heaven – the very thing He had created in the beginning. Similarly it (afterwards) treats of man: "And God created man, in the image of God made He him." It next reveals how He made him: "And (the Lord) God formed man of the dust of the ground, and breathed into his nostrils the breath of life; and man became a living soul."

Now this is undoubtedly the correct and fitting mode for the narrative. first comes a prefatory statement, then follow the details in full; first the subject is named, then it is described. How absurd is the other view of the account, when even before he had premised any mention of his subject, i.e. Matter, without even giving us its name, he all on a sudden promulged its form and condition, describing to us its quality before mentioning its existence – pointing out the figure of the thing formed, but concealing its name! But how much more credible is our opinion, which holds that Scripture has only subjoined the arrangement of the subject after it has first duly described its formation and mentioned its name!

Indeed, how full and complete is the meaning of these words: "In the beginning God created the heaven and the earth; but the earth was without form, and void," – the very same earth, no doubt, which God made, and of which the Scripture had been speaking at that very moment. For that very "but" is inserted into the narrative like a clasp, (in its function) of a conjunctive particle, to connect the two sentences indissolubly together: "But the earth." This word carries back the mind to that earth of which mention had just been made, and binds the sense thereunto. Take away this "but," and the tie is loosened; so much so that the passage, "But the earth was without form, and void," may then seem to have been meant for any other earth.

Chapter XXIX – The Gradual Development of Cosmical Order Out of Chaos in the Creation, Beautifully Stated

God, indeed, consummated all His works in a due order; at first He paled them out, as it were, in their unformed elements, and then He arranged them in their finished beauty. For He did not all at once inundate light with the splendour of the sun, nor all at once temper darkness with the moon's assuaging ray. The heaven He did not all at once bedeck with constellations and stars, nor did He at once fill the seas with their teeming monsters. The earth itself He did not endow with its varied fruitfulness all at once; but at first He bestowed upon it being, and then He filled it, that it might not be made in vain. For thus says Isaiah: "He created it not in vain; He formed it to be inhabited."

Therefore after it was made, and while awaiting its perfect state, it was "without form, and void:" "void" indeed, from the very fact that it was without form (as being not yet perfect to the sight, and at the same time unfurnished as yet with its other qualities); and "without form," because it was still covered with waters, as if with the rampart of its fecundating moisture, by which is produced our flesh, in a form allied with its own. For to this purport does David say: "The earth is the Lord's, and the fulness thereof; the world, and all that dwell therein: He hath founded it upon the seas, and on the streams hath He established it."

It was when the waters were withdrawn into their hollow abysses that the dry land became conspicuous, which was hitherto covered with its watery envelope. Then it forthwith becomes "visible," God saying, "Let the water be gathered together into one mass, and let the dry land appear." "Appear," says He, not "be made." It had been already made, only in its invisible condition it was then waiting to appear. "Dry," because it was about to become such by its severance from the moisture, but yet "land." "And God called the dry land Earth," not Matter. And so, when it afterwards attains its perfection, it ceases to be accounted void, when God declares, "Let the earth bring forth grass, the herb yielding seed after its kind, and [ac]cording to its likeness, and the fruit tree yielding fruit, whose seed is in itself, after its kind." Again: "Let the earth bring forth the living creature after his kind, cattle, and creeping things, and beasts of the earth, after their kind." Thus the divine Scripture accomplished its full order. For to that, which it had at first described as "without form (invisible) and void," it gave both visibility and completion.

Now no other Matter was "without form (invisible) and void." Henceforth, then, Matter will have to be visible and complete. So that I must see Matter, since it has become visible. I must likewise recognize it as a completed thing, so as to be able to gather from it the herb bearing seed, and the tree yielding fruit, and that living creatures, made out of it, may minister to my need.

Matter, however, is nowhere, but the Earth is here, confessed to my view. I see it, I enjoy it, ever since it ceased to be "without form (invisible), and void." Concerning it most certainly did Isaiah speak when he said, "Thus saith the Lord that created the heavens, He was the God that formed the earth, and made it." The same earth for certain did He form, which He also made. Now how did He form it? Of course by saying, "Let the dry land appear." Why does He command it to appear, if it were not previously invisible? His purpose was also, that He might thus prevent His having made it in vain, by rendering it visible, and so fit for use. And thus, throughout, proofs arise to us that this earth which we inhabit is the very same which was both created and formed by God, and that none other was "Without form, and void," than that which had been created and formed. It therefore follows that the sentence, "Now the earth was without form, and void," applies to that same earth which God mentioned separately along with the heaven.

Chapter XXXI – A Further Vindication of the Scripture Narrative of the Creation, Against a Futile View of Hermogenes

But this circumstance, too, will be caught at, that Scripture meant to indicate of the heaven only, and this earth of yours, that God made it in the beginning, while nothing of the kind is said of the above – mentioned specific parts; and therefore that these, which are not described as having been made, appertain to unformed Matter. To this point also we must give an answer.

Holy Scripture would be sufficiently explicit, if it had declared that the heaven and the earth, as the very highest works of creation, were made by God, possessing of course their own special appurtenances, which might be understood to be implied in these highest works themselves. Now the appurtenances of the heaven and the earth, made then in the beginning, were the darkness and the deep, and the spirit, and the waters. For the depth and the darkness underlay the earth. Since the deep was under the earth, and the darkness was over the deep, undoubtedly both the darkness and the deep were under the earth. Below the heaven, too, lay the spirit and the waters. For since the waters were over the earth, which they covered, whilst the spirit was over the waters, both the spirit and the waters were alike over the earth. Now that which is over the earth, is of course under the heaven. And even as the earth brooded over the deep and the darkness, so also did the heaven brood over the spirit and the waters, and embrace them. Nor, indeed, is there any novelty in mentioning only that which contains, as pertaining to the whole, and understanding that which is contained as included in it, in its character of a portion.

Suppose now I should say the city built a theatre and a circus, but the stage was of such and such a kind, and the statues were on the canal, and the obelisk was reared above them all, would it follow that, because I did not distinctly state that these specific things were made by the city, they were therefore not made by it along with the circus and the theatre? Did I not, indeed, refrain from specially mentioning the formation of these particular things because they were implied in the things which I had already said were made, and might be understood to be inherent in the things in which they were contained?

But this example may be an idle one as being derived from a human circumstance; I will take another, which has the authority of Scripture itself. It says that "God made man of the dust of the ground and breathed into his nostrils the breath of life, and man became a living soul." Now, although it here mentions the nostrils, it does not say that they were made by God; so again it speaks of skin and bones, and flesh and eyes, and sweat and blood, in subsequent passages, and yet it never intimated that they had been created by God.

What will Hermogenes have to answer? That the human limbs must belong to Matter, because they are not specially mentioned as objects of creation? Or are they included in the formation of man? In like manner, the deep and the darkness, and the spirit and the waters, were as members of the heaven and the earth. For in the bodies the limbs were made, in the bodies the limbs too were mentioned. No element but what is a member of that element in which it is contained. But all elements are contained in the heaven and the earth.

Chapter XXXII – The Account of the Creation in Genesis a General One; Corroborated, However, by Many Other Passages of the Old Testament, Which Give Account of Specific Creations; Further Cavillings Confuted

This is the answer I should give in defence of the Scripture before us, for seeming here to set forth the formation of the heaven and the earth, as if (they were) the sole bodies made. It could not but know that there were those who would at once in the bodies understand their several members also, and therefore it employed this concise mode of speech. But, at the same time, it foresaw that there would be stupid and crafty men, who, after paltering with the virtual meaning, would require for the several members a word descriptive of their formation too. It is therefore because of such persons, that Scripture in other passages teaches us of the creation of the individual parts. You have Wisdom saying, "But before the depths was I brought forth," in order that you may believe that the depths were also "brought forth" – that is, created – just as we create sons also, though we "bring them forth."

It matters not whether the depth was made or born, so that a beginning be accorded to it, which however would not be, if it were subjoined to matter. Of darkness, indeed, the Lord Himself by Isaiah says, "I formed the light, and I created darkness." Of the wind also Amos says, "He that strengtheneth the thunder, and createth the wind, and declareth His Christ unto men;" thus showing that that wind was created which was reckoned with the formation of the earth, which was wafted over the waters, balancing and refreshing and animating all things: not (as some suppose) meaning God Himself by the spirit, on the ground that "God is a Spirit," because the waters would not be able to bear up their Lord; but He speaks of that spirit of which the winds consist, as He says by Isaiah, "Because my spirit went forth from me, and I made every blast." In like manner the same Wisdom says of the waters, "Also when He made the fountains strong, things which are under the sky, I was fashioning them along with Him."

Now, when we prove that these particular things were created by God, although they are only mentioned in Genesis, without any intimation of their having been made, we shall perhaps receive from the other side the reply, that these were made, it is true, but out of Matter, since the very statement of Moses, "And darkness was on the face of the deep, and the spirit of God moved on the face of the waters," refers to Matter, as indeed do all those other Scriptures here and there, which demonstrate that the separate parts were made out of Matter.

It must follow, then, that as earth consisted of earth, so also depth consisted of depth, and darkness of darkness, and the wind and waters of wind and waters. And, as we said above, Matter could not have been without form, since it had specific parts, which were formed out of it – although as separate things – unless, indeed, they were not separate, but were the very same with those out of which they came. For it is really impossible that those specific things, which are set forth under the same names, should have been diverse; because in that case the operation of God might seem to be useless, if it made things which existed already; since that alone would be a creation, when things came into being, which had not been (previously) made.

Therefore, to conclude, either Moses then pointed to Matter when he wrote the words: "And darkness was on the face of the deep, and the spirit of God moved on the face of the waters; "or else, inasmuch as these specific parts of creation are afterwards shown in other passages to have been made by God, they ought to have been with equal explicitness shown to have been made out of the Matter which, according to you, Moses had previously mentioned; or else, finally, if Moses pointed to those specific parts, and not to Matter, I want to know where Matter has been pointed out at all.

Chapter XXXIII – Statement of the True Doctrine Concerning Matter; Its Relation to God's Creation of the World

But although Hermogenes finds it amongst his own colourable pretences (for it was not in his power to discover it in the Scriptures of God), it is enough for us, both that it is certain that all things were made by God, and that there is no certainty whatever that they were made out of Matter. And even if Matter had previously existed, we must have believed that it had been really made by God, since we maintained (no less) when we held the rule of faith to be, that nothing except God was uncreated. Up to this point there is room for controversy, until Matter is brought to the test of the Scriptures, and fails to make good its case.

The conclusion of the whole is this: I find that there was nothing made, except out of nothing; because that which I find was made, I know did not once exist. Whatever was made out of something, has its origin in something made: for instance, out of the ground was made the grass, and the fruit, and the cattle, and the form of man himself; so from the waters were produced the animals which swim and fly. The original fabrics out of which such creatures were produced I may call their materials, but then even these were created by God.

Chapter XXXIV – A Presumption that All Things Were Created by God Out of Nothing Afforded by the Ultimate Reduction of All Things to Nothing; Scriptures Proving This Reduction Vindicated from Hermogenes' Charge of Being Merely Figurative

Besides, the belief that everything was made from nothing will be impressed upon us by that ultimate dispensation of God which will bring back all things to nothing. For "the very heaven shall be rolled together as a scroll;" nay, it shall come to nothing along with the earth itself, with which it was made in the beginning. "Heaven and earth shall pass away," says He. "The first heaven and the first earth passed away," "and there was found no place for them," because, of course, that which comes to an end loses locality. In like manner David says, "The heavens, the works of Thine hands, shall themselves perish. For even as a vesture shall He change them, and they shall be changed." Now to be changed is to fall from that primitive state which they lose whilst undergoing the change. "And the stars too shall fall from heaven, even as a fig tree casteth her green figs when she is shaken of a mighty wind." "The mountains shall melt like wax at the presence of the Lord;" that is, "when He riseth to shake terribly the earth." "But I will dry up the pools;" and "they shall seek water, and they shall find none." Even, "the sea shall be no more."

Now if any person should go so far as to suppose that all these passages ought to be spiritually interpreted, he will yet be unable to deprive them of the true accomplishment of those issues which must come to pass just as they have been written For all figures of speech necessarily arise out of real things, not out of chimerical ones; because nothing is capable of imparting anything of its own for a similitude, except it actually be that very thing which it imparts in the similitude. I return therefore to the principle which defines that all things which have come from nothing shall return at last to nothing. For God would not have made any perishable thing out of what was eternal, that is to say, out of Matter; neither out of greater things would He have created inferior ones, to whose character it would be more agreeable to produce greater things out of inferior ones – in other words, what is eternal out of what is perishable.

This is the promise He makes even to our flesh, and it has been His will to deposit within us this pledge of His own virtue and power, in order that we may believe that He has actually awakened the universe out of nothing, as if it had been stepped in death, in the sense, of course, of its previous non-existence for the purpose of its coming into existence.

Chapter XLIV – Curious Views Respecting God's Method of Working with Matter Exposed; Discrepancies in the Heretic's Opinion About God's Local Relation to Matter

But it remains that I should show also how you make God work. You are plainly enough at variance with the philosophers; but neither are you in accord with the prophets. The Stoics maintain that God pervaded Matter, just as honey the honeycomb. You, however, affirm that it is not by pervading Matter that God makes the world, but simply by appearing, and approaching it, just as beauty affects a thing by simply appearing, and a loadstone by approaching it. Now what similarity is there in God forming the world, and beauty wounding a soul, or a magnet attracting iron?...

Chapter XLV – Conclusion. Contrast Between the Statements of Hermogenes and the Testimony of Holy Scripture Respecting the Creation. Creation Out of Nothing, Not Out of Matter

But it is not thus that the prophets and the apostles have told us that the world was made by God merely appearing and approaching Matter. They did not even mention any Matter, but (said) that

Wisdom was first set up, the beginning of His ways, for His works. Then that the Word was produced, "through whom all things were made, and without whom nothing was made." Indeed, "by the Word of the Lord were the heavens made, and all their hosts by the breath of His mouth." He is the Lord's right hand, indeed His two bands, by which He worked and constructed the universe. "For," says He, "the heavens are the works of Thine hands," wherewith "He hath meted out the heaven, and the earth with a span."

Do not be willing so to cover God with flattery, as to contend that He produced by His mere appearance and simple approach so many vast substances, instead of rather forming them by His own energies. For this is proved by Jeremiah when he says, "God hath made the earth by His power, He hath established the world by His wisdom, and hath stretched out the heaven by His understanding." These are the energies by the stress of which He made this universe. His glory is greater if He laboured. At length on the seventh day He rested from His works. Both one and the other were after His manner. If, on the contrary, He made this world simply by appearing and approaching it, did He, on the completion of His work, cease to appear and approach it any more. Nay rather, God began to appear more conspicuously and to be everywhere accessible from the time when the world was made.

You see, therefore, how all things consist by the operation of that God who "made the earth by His power, who established the world by His wisdom, and stretched out the heaven by His understanding;" not appearing merely, nor approaching, but applying the almighty efforts of His mind, His wisdom, His power, His understanding, His word, His Spirit, His might. Now these things were not necessary to Him, if He had been perfect by simply appearing and approaching. They are, however, His "invisible things," which, according to the apostle, "are from the creation of the world clearly seen by the things that are made; they are no parts of a nondescript Matter, but they are the sensible evidences of Himself. "For who hath known the mind of the Lord," of which (the apostle) exclaims: "O the depth of the riches both of His wisdom and knowledge! How unsearchable are His judgments, and His ways past finding out!"

Now what clearer truth do these words indicate, than that all things were made out of nothing? They are incapable of being found out or investigated, except by God alone. Otherwise, if they were traceable or discoverable in Matter, they would be capable of investigation. Therefore, in as far as it has become evident that Matter had no prior existence (even from this circumstance, that it is impossible for it to have had such an existence as is assigned to it), in so far is it proved that all things were made by God out of nothing. It must be admitted, however, that Hermogenes, by describing for Matter a condition like his own – irregular, confused, turbulent, of a doubtful and precipate and fervid impulse – has displayed a specimen of his own art, and painted his own portrait.

Tertullian *On the Resurrection of the Flesh*

Chapter V – Some Considerations in Reply Eulogistic of the flesh; It Was Created by God; The Body of Man Was, in Fact, Previous to His Soul

...In the first place, because all things were made by the Word of God, and without Him was nothing made. Now the flesh, too, had its existence from the Word of God, because of the principle, that here should be nothing without that Word. "Let us make man," said He, before He created him, and added, "with our hand," for the sake of his pre-eminence, that so he might not be compared with the rest of creation. And "God," says (the Scripture), "formed man."

There is undoubtedly a great difference in the procedure, springing of course from the nature of the case. For the creatures which were made were inferior to him for whom they were made; and they were made for man, to whom they were afterwards made subject by God. Rightly, therefore, had the creatures which were thus intended for subjection, come forth into being at the bidding and command and sole power of the divine voice; whilst man, on the contrary, destined to be their lord, was formed by God Himself, to the intent that he might be able to exercise his mastery, being created by the Master the Lord Himself. Remember, too, that man is properly called flesh, which had a prior occupation in man's designation: "And God formed man the clay of the ground." He now became man, who was hitherto clay. "And He breathed upon his face the breath of life, and man (that is, the clay) became a living soul; and God placed the man whom He had formed in the garden."

So that man was clay at first, and only afterwards man entire. I wish to impress this on your attention, with a view to your knowing, that whatever God has at all purposed or promised to man, is due not to the soul simply, but to the flesh also; if not arising out of any community in their origin, yet at all events by the privilege possessed by the latter in its name.

Chapter VI – Not the Lowliness of the Material, But the Dignity and Skill of the Maker, Must Be Remembered, in Gauging the Excellence of the Flesh; Christ Partook of Our Flesh

Let me therefore pursue the subject before me – if I can but succeed in vindicating for the flesh as much as was conferred on it by Him who made it, glorying as it even then was, because that poor paltry material, clay, found its way into the hands of God, whatever these were, happy enough at merely being touched by them. But why this glorying? Was it that, without any further labour, the clay had instantly assumed its form at the touch of God? The truth is, a great matter was in progress, out of which the creature under consideration was being fashioned. So often then does it receive honour, as often as it experiences the hands of God, when it is touched by them, and pulled, and drawn out, and moulded into shape.

Imagine God wholly employed and absorbed in it – in His hand, His eye, His labour, His purpose, His wisdom, His providence, and above all, in His love, which was dictating the lineaments (of this creature). For, whatever was the form and expression which was then given to the clay (by the Creator) Christ was in His thoughts as one day to become man, because the Word, too, was to be both clay and flesh, even as the earth was then. For so did the Father previously say to the Son: "Let us make man in our own image, after our likeness." And God made man, that is to say, the creature which He moulded and fashioned; after the image of God (in other words, of Christ) did He make him And the Word was God also, who being in the image of God, "thought it not robbery to be equal to God." Thus, that clay which was even then putting on the image of Christ, who was to come in the flesh, was not only the work, but also the pledge and surety, of God.

To what purpose is it to bandy about the name earth, as that of a sordid and grovelling element, with the view of tarnishing the origin of the flesh, when, even if any other material had been available for forming man, it would be requisite that the dignity of the Maker should be taken into consideration, who even by His selection of His material deemed it, and by His management made it, worthy? The hand of Phidias forms the Olympian Jupiter of ivory; worship is given to the statue, and it is no longer regarded as a god formed out of a most silly animal, but as the world's supreme Deity – not because of the bulk of the elephant, but on account of the renown of Phidias. Could not therefore the living God, the true God, purge away by His own operation whatever vileness might have accrued to His material, and heal it of all infirmity? Or must this remain to show how much more nobly man could fabricate a god, than God could form a man?

Now, although the clay is offensive (for its poorness), it is now something else. What I possess is flesh, not earth, even although of the flesh it is said: "Dust thou art, and unto dust shall thou return," In these words there is the mention of the origin, not a recalling of the substance. The privilege has been granted to the flesh to be nobler than its origin, and to have happiness aggrandized by the change wrought in it. Now, even gold is earth, because of the earth; but it remains earth no longer after it becomes gold, but is a far different substance, more splendid and more noble, though coming from a source which is comparatively faded and obscure. In like manner, it was quite allowable for God that He should dear the gold of our flesh from all the taints, as you deem them, of its native clay, by purging the original substance of its dross.

Chapter VII – The Earthy Material of Which Flesh is Created Wonderfully Improved by God's Manipulation; By the Addition of the Soul in Man's Constitution It Became the Chief Work in the Creation

But perhaps the dignity of the flesh may seem to be diminished, because it has not been actually manipulated by the hand of God, as the clay was at first. Now, when God handled the clay for the express purpose of the growth of flesh out of it afterwards, it was for the flesh that He took all the trouble. But I want you, moreover, to know at what time and in what manner the flesh flourished into beauty out of its clay. For it cannot be, as some will have it, that those "coats of skins" which Adam and Eve put on when they were stripped of paradise, were really themselves the forming of the flesh out of clay, because long before that Adam had already recognised the flesh which was in the woman as the propagation of his own substance ("This is now bone of my bone, and flesh of my flesh"), and the very taking of the woman out of the man was supplemented with flesh; but it ought, I should suppose, to have been made good with clay, if Adam was still clay.

The clay, therefore, was obliterated and absorbed into flesh. When did this happen? At the time that man became a living soul by the inbreathing of God – by the breath indeed which was capable of hardening clay into another substance, as into some earthenware, so now into flesh. In the same way the potter, too, has it in his power, by tempering the blast of his fire, to modify his clayey material into a stiffer one, and to mould one form after another more beautiful than the original substance, and now possessing both a kind and name of its own. For although the Scripture says, "Shall the clay say to the potter?" That is, Shall man contend with God? Although the apostle speaks of "earthen vessels" he refers to man, who was originally clay. And the vessel is the flesh, because this was made of clay by the breath of the divine afflatus; and it was afterwards clothed with "the coats of skins," that is, with the cutaneous covering which was placed over it.

So truly is this the fact, that if you withdraw the skin, you lay bare the flesh. Thus, that which becomes a spoil when stripped off, was a vestment as long as it remained laid over. Hence the apostle, when he call circumcision "a putting off (or spoliation) of the flesh," affirmed the skin to be a coat or tunic. Now this being the case, you have both the clay made glorious by the hand of God, and the flesh more glorious still by His breathing upon it, by virtue of which the flesh not only laid aside its clayey rudiments, but also took on itself the ornaments of the soul.

You surely are not more careful than God, that you indeed should refuse to mount the gems of Scythia and India and the pearls of the Red Sea in lead, or brass, or iron, or even in silver, but should set them in the most precious and most highly-wrought gold; or, again, that you should provide for your finest wines and most costly unguents the most fitting vessels; or, on the same principle, should find for your swords of finished temper scabbards of equal worth; whilst

God must consign to some vilest sheath the shadow of His own soul, the breath of His own Spirit, the operation of His own mouth, and by so ignominious a consignment secure, of course, its condemnation.

Well, then, has He placed, or rather inserted and commingled, it with the flesh? Yes; and so intimate is the union, that it may be deemed to be uncertain whether the flesh bears about the soul, or the soul the flesh; or whether the flesh acts as apparitor to the soul, or the soul to the flesh. It is, However, more credible that the soul has service rendered to it, and has the mastery, as being more proximate in character to God. This circumstance even redounds to the glory of the flesh, inasmuch as it both contains an essence nearest to God's, and renders itself a partake of (the soul's) actual sovereignty. For what enjoyment of nature is there, what produce of the world, what relish of the elements, which is not imparted to the soul by means of the body? How can it be otherwise? Is it not by its means that the soul is supported by the entire apparatus of the senses – the sight, the hearing, the taste, the smell, the touch? Is it not by its means that it has a sprinkling of the divine power, there being nothing which it does not effect by its faculty of speech, even when it is only tacitly indicated? And speech is the result of a fleshly organ.

The arts come through the flesh; through the flesh also effect is given to the mind's pursuits and powers; all work, too, and business and offices of life, are accomplished by the flesh; and so utterly, are the living acts of the soul the work of the flesh, that for the soul to cease to do living acts, would be nothing else than sundering itself from the flesh. So also the very act of dying is a function of the flesh, even as the process of life is.

Now, if all things are subject to the soul through the flesh, their subjection is equally due to the flesh. That which is the means and agent of your enjoyment, must needs be also the partaker and sharer of your enjoyment. So that the flesh, which is accounted the minister and servant of the soul, turns out to be also its associate and co-heir. And if all this in temporal things, why not also in things eternal?

Theophilus of Antioch

> St. Theophilus (d. c. 185), the sixth Bishop of Antioch, was one of the early Christian apologists. Born to pagan parents near the Euphrates and given a Hellenistic education, Theophilus converted to Christianity as an adult. Only his work *To Autolycus* survives (written c. 180), but he also wrote treatises against Marcion and Hermogenes. He was the first Christian writer to use explicitly Trinitarian language in referring to God.
>
> *To Autolycus* is a general work of apologetics for Christians, but in it Theophilus treats extensively the biblical account of creation. God cannot be seen, but humanity can know Him through His works and providence. He created the world out of nothing for humanity, and made humanity in order to know Him. The uncreated God stands in need of nothing, but the creature is needy. Thus creation is not by necessity, but by God's will.
>
> Plants were created on the third day before the sun on the fourth so that humans might not attribute life to the sun and thereby exclude God. Humanity is created in God's image by God's own hands, the only work of creation worthy of being made in this way (the ordinary mode of creation being divine command).
>
> At the end of the work (bk. III.28), Theophilus examines the genealogies in the Greek translation of the Old Testament (the Septuagint) and calculates 5698 years from creation to the death of the Emperor Aurelius Verus (d. 169). That would put the creation of the world in 5529 B.C. Julius Africanus (d. 245) made a similar calculation and determined that there were 5531 years from the creation of Adam to Christ's birth.

Theophilus *To Autolycus*, Book I

Chapter IV – Attributes of God

And He is without beginning, because He is unbegotten; and He is unchangeable, because He is immortal. And he is called God [*Theos*] on account of His having placed [*tethekeinai*] all things on security afforded by Himself; and on account of [*theein*], for *theein* means running, and moving, and being active, and nourishing, and foreseeing, and governing, and making all things alive. But he is Lord, because He rules over the universe; Father, because he is before all things; Fashioner and Maker, because He is creator and maker of the universe; the Highest, because of His being above all; and Almighty, because He Himself rules and embraces all. For the heights of heaven, and the depths of the abysses, and the ends of the earth, are in His hand, and there is no place of His rest. For the heavens are His work, the earth is His creation, the sea is His handiwork; man is His formation and His image; sun, moon, and stars are His elements, made for signs, and seasons, and days, and years, that they may serve and be slaves to man; and all things God has made out of things that were not into things that are, in order that through His works His greatness may be known and understood.

Chapter V – The Invisible God Perceived Through His Works

For as the soul in man is not seen, being invisible to men, but is perceived through the motion of the body, so God cannot indeed be seen by human eyes, but is beheld and perceived through His providence and works. For, in like manner, as any person, when he sees a ship on the sea rigged and in sail, and making for the harbour, will no doubt infer that there is a pilot in her who is steering her; so we must perceive that God is the governor [pilot] of the whole universe, though He be not visible to the eyes of the flesh, since He is incomprehensible. For if a man cannot look upon the sun, though it be a very small heavenly body, on account of its exceeding heat and power, how shall not a mortal man be much more unable to face the glory of God, which is unutterable? For as the pomegranate, with the rind containing it, has within it many cells and compartments which are separated by tissues, and has also many seeds dwelling in it, so the whole creation is contained by the spirit of God, and the containing spirit is along with the creation contained by the hand of God. As, therefore, the seed of the pomegranate, dwelling inside, cannot see what is outside the rind, itself being within; so neither can man, who along with the whole creation is enclosed by the hand of God, behold God. Then again, an earthly king is believed to exist, even though he be not seen by all; for he is recognised by his laws and ordinances, and authorities, and forces, and statues; and are you unwilling that God should be recognised by His works and mighty deeds?

Chapter VI – God is Known by His Works

Consider, O man, His works – the timely rotation of the seasons, and the changes of temperature; the regular march of the stars; the well-ordered course of days and nights, and months, and years; the various beauty of seeds, and plants, and fruits; and the divers species of quadrupeds, and birds, and reptiles, and fishes, both of the rivers and of the sea; or consider the instinct implanted in these animals to beget and rear offspring, not for their own profit, but for the use of man; and the providence with which God provides nourishment for all flesh, or the subjection in which He has ordained that all things subserve mankind. Consider, too, the flowing of sweet fountains and never-failing rivers, and the seasonable supply of dews, and showers, and rains; the manifold movement of the heavenly bodies, the morning star rising and heralding the approach of the perfect luminary; and the constellation of Pleiades, and Orion, and Arcturus, and the orbit of the other stars that circle through the heavens, all of which the manifold wisdom of God has called by names of their own.

He is God alone who made light out of darkness, and brought forth light from His treasures, and formed the chambers of the south wind, and the treasure houses of the deep, and the bounds of the seas, and the treasuries of snows and hail storms, collecting the waters in the storehouses of the deep, and the darkness in His treasures, and bringing forth the sweet, and desirable, and pleasant light out of His treasures; "who causeth the vapours to ascend from the ends of the earth: He maketh lightnings for the rain;" who sends forth His thunder to terrify, and foretells by the lightning the peal of the thunder, that no soul may faint with the sudden shock; and who so moderates the violence of the lightning as it flashes out of heaven, that it does not consume the earth; for, if the lightning were allowed all its power, it would burn up the earth; and were the thunder allowed all its power, it would overthrow all the works that are therein.

Theophilus *To Autolycus*, Book II

Chapter X – The World Created by God Through the Word

And first, they taught us with one consent that God made all things out of nothing; for nothing was coeval with God: but He being His own place, and wanting nothing, and existing before the ages, willed to make man by whom He might be known; for him, therefore, He prepared the world. For he that is created is also needy; but he that is uncreated stands in need of nothing. God, then, having His own Word internal within His own bowels, begat Him, emitting Him along with His own wisdom before all things. He had this Word as a helper in the things that were created by Him, and by Him He made all things. He is called "governing principle" [archç], because He rules, and is Lord of all things fashioned by Him. He, then, being Spirit of God, and governing principle, and wisdom, and power of the highest, came down upon the prophets, and through them spoke of the creation of the world and of all other things. For the prophets were not when the world came into existence, but the wisdom of God which was in Him, and His holy Word which was always present with Him.

Wherefore He speaks thus by the prophet Solomon: "When He prepared the heavens I was there, and when He appointed the foundations of the earth I was by Him as one brought up with Him." And Moses, who lived many years before Solomon, or, rather, the Word of God by him as by an instrument, says, "In the beginning God created the heaven and the earth." first he named the "beginning," and "creation," then he thus introduced God; for not lightly and on slight occasion is it right to name God. For the divine wisdom foreknew that some would trifle and name a multitude of gods that do not exist.

In order, therefore, that the living God might be known by His works, and that [it might be known that] by His Word God created the heavens and the earth, and all that is therein, he said, "In the beginning God created the heavens and the earth." Then having spoken of their creation, he explains to us: "And the earth was without form, and void, and darkness was upon the face of the deep; and the Spirit of God moved upon the water." This, sacred Scripture teaches at the outset, to show that matter, from which God made and fashioned the world, was in some manner created, being produced by God.

Chapter XI – The Six Days' Work Described

Now, the beginning of the creation is light; since light manifests the things that are created. Wherefore it is said: "And God said, Let light be, and light was; and God saw the light, that it was good," manifestly made good for man. [Theophilus goes on to quote the rest of Genesis 1, deleted here.]

Chapter XII – The Glory of the Six Days' Work

Of this six days' work no man can give a worthy explanation and description of all its parts, not though he had ten thousand tongues and ten thousand mouths; nay, though he were to live ten thousand years, sojourning in this life, not even so could he utter anything worthy of these things, on account of the exceeding greatness and riches of the wisdom of God which there is in the six days' work above narrated. Many writers indeed have imitated [the narration], and essayed to give an explanation of these things; yet, though they thence derived some suggestions, both concerning the creation of the world and the nature of man, they have emitted no slightest spark of truth. And the utterances of the philosophers, and writers, and poets have an appearance of trustworthiness, on account of the beauty of their diction; but their discourse is proved to be foolish and idle, because the multitude of their nonsensical frivolities is very great; and not a stray morsel of truth is found in them.

For even if any truth seems to have been uttered by them, it has a mixture of error. And as a deleterious drug, when mixed with honey or wine, or some other thing, makes the whole [mixture] hurtful and profitless; so also eloquence is in their case found to be labour in vain; yea, rather an injurious thing to those who credit it. Moreover, [they spoke] concerning the seventh day, which all men acknowledge; but the most know not that what among the Hebrews is called the "Sabbath," is translated into Greek the "Seventh" (*ebdomas*), a name which is adopted by every nation, although they know not the reason of the appellation. And as for what the poet Hesiod says of Erebus being produced from chaos, as well as the earth and love which lords it over his [Hesiod's] gods and men, his dictum is shown to be idle and frigid, and quite foreign to the truth. For it is not meet that God be conquered by pleasure; since even men of temperance abstain from all base pleasure and wicked lust.

Chapter XIII – Remarks on the Creation of the World

Moreover, his [Hesiod's] human, and mean, and very weak conception, so far as regards God, is discovered in his beginning to relate the creation of all things from the earthly things here below. For man, being below, begins to build from the earth, and cannot in order make the roof, unless he has first laid the foundation. But the power of God is shown in this, that, first of all, He creates out of nothing, according to His will, the things that are made. "For the things which are impossible with men are possible with God." Wherefore, also, the prophet mentioned that the creation of the heavens first of all took place, as a kind of roof, saying: "At the first God created the heavens" – that is, that by means of the "first" principle the heavens were made, as we have already shown. And by "earth" he means the ground and foundation, as by "the deep" he means the multitude of waters; and "darkness" he speaks of, on account of the heaven which God made coveting the waters and the earth like a lid.

And by the Spirit which is borne above the waters, he means that which God gave for animating the creation, as he gave life to man, mixing what is fine with what is fine. For the Spirit is fine, and the water is fine, that the Spirit may nourish the water, and the water penetrating everywhere along with the Spirit, may nourish creation. For the Spirit being one, and holding the place of light, was between the water and the heaven, in order that the darkness might not in any way communicate with the heaven, which was nearer God, before God said, "Let there be light." The heaven, therefore, being like a dome-shaped covering, comprehended matter which was like a clod. And so another prophet, Isaiah by name, spoke in these words: "It is God who made the heavens as a vault, and stretched them as a tent to dwell in." The command, then, of God, that is, His Word, shining as a lamp in an enclosed chamber, lit up all that was under heaven, when He had made light apart from the world. And the light God called Day, and the darkness Night. Since man would not have been able to call the light Day, or the darkness Night, nor, indeed, to have given names to the other things, had not he received the nomenclature from God, who made the things themselves.

In the very beginning, therefore, of the history and genesis of the world, the holy Scripture spoke not concerning this firmament [which we see], but concerning another heaven, which is to us invisible, after which this heaven which we see has been called "firmament," and to which half the water was taken up that it might serve for rains, and showers, and dews to mankind. And half the water was left on earth for rivers, and fountains, and seas. The water, then, covering all the earth, and specially its hollow places, God, through His Word, next caused the waters to be collected into one collection, and the dry land to become visible, which formerly had been invisible. The earth thus becoming visible, was yet without form. God therefore formed and adorned it with all kinds of herbs, and seeds and plants.

Chapter XV – Of the Fourth Day

On the fourth day the luminaries were made; because God, who possesses foreknowledge, knew the follies of the vain philosophers, that they were going to say, that the things which grow on the earth are produced from the heavenly bodies, so as to exclude God. In order, therefore, that the truth might be obvious, the plants and seeds were produced prior to the heavenly bodies, for what is posterior cannot produce that which is prior.

And these contain the pattern and type of a great mystery. For the sun is a type of God, and the moon of man. And as the sun far surpasses the moon in power and glory, so far does God surpass man. And as the sun remains ever full, never becoming less, so does God always abide perfect, being full of all power, and understanding, and wisdom, and immortality, and all good. But the moon wanes monthly, and in a manner dies, being a type of man; then it is born again, and is crescent, for a pattern of the future resurrection.

In like manner also the three days which were before the luminaries, are types of the Trinity, of God, and His Word, and His wisdom. And the fourth is the type of man, who needs light, that so there may be God, the Word, wisdom, man. Wherefore also on the fourth day the lights were made. The disposition of the stars, too, contains a type of the arrangement and order of the righteous and pious, and of those who keep the law and commandments of God. For the brilliant and bright stars are an imitation of the prophets, and therefore they remain fixed, not declining, nor passing from place to place. And those which hold the second place in brightness, are types of the people of the righteous. And those, again, which change their position, and flee from place to place, which also are called planets, they too are a type of the men who have wandered from God, abandoning His law and commandments.

Chapter XVI – Of the Fifth Day

On the fifth day the living creatures which proceed from the waters were produced, through: which also is revealed the manifold wisdom of God in these things; for who could count their multitude and very various kinds? Moreover, the things proceeding from the waters were blessed by God, that this also might be a sign of men's being destined to receive repentance and remission of sins, through the water and laver of regeneration – as many as come to the truth, and are born again, and receive blessing from God. But the monsters of the deep and the birds of prey are a similitude of covetous men and transgressors. For as the fish and the fowls are of one nature – some indeed abide in their natural state, and do no harm to those weaker than themselves, but keep the law of God, and eat of the seeds of the earth; others of them, again, transgress the law of God, and eat flesh, and injure those weaker than themselves: thus, too, the righteous, keeping the law of God, bite and injure none, but live holily and righteously. But robbers, and murderers, and godless persons are like monsters of the deep, and wild beasts, and birds of prey; for they virtually devour those weaker than themselves. The race, then, of fishes and of creeping things, though partaking of God's blessing, received no very distinguishing property.

Chapter XVII – Of the Sixth Day

And on the sixth day, God having made the quadrupeds, and wild beasts, and the land reptiles, pronounced no blessing upon them, reserving His blessing for man, whom He was about to create on the sixth day. The quadrupeds, too, and wild beasts, were made for a type of some men, who neither know nor worship God, but mind earthly things, and repent not. For those who turn from their iniquities and live righteously, in spirit fly upwards like birds, and mind the things that are above, and are well-pleasing to the will of God. But those who do not know nor worship God, are like birds which have wings, but cannot fly nor soar to the high things of God. Thus, too, though such persons are called men, yet being pressed down with sins, they mind grovelling and earthly things.

And the animals are named wild beasts [*thçria*], from their being hunted [*thçreuesthai*], not as if they had been made evil or venomous from the first – for nothing was made evil by God, but all things good, yea, very good – but the sin in which man was concerned brought evil upon them. For when man transgressed, they also transgressed with him. For as, if the master of the house himself acts rightly, the domestics also of necessity conduct themselves well; but if the master sins, the servants also sin with him; so in like manner it came to pass, that in the case of man's sin, he being master, all that was subject to him sinned with him. When, therefore, man again shall have made his way back to his natural condition, and no longer does evil, those also shall be restored to their original gentleness.

Chapter XVIII – The Creation of Man

But as to what relates to the creation of man, his own creation cannot be explained by man, though it is a succinct account of it which holy Scripture gives. For when God said, "Let Us make man in Our image, after Our likeness," He first intimates the dignity of man. For God having made all things by His Word, and having reckoned them all mere by-works, reckons the creation of man to be the only work worthy of His own hands.

Moreover, God is found, as if needing help, to say, "Let Us make man in Our image, after Our likeness." But to no one else than to His own Word and wisdom did He say, "Let Us make." And when He had made and blessed him, that he might increase and replenish the earth, He put all things under his dominion, and at his service; and He appointed from the first that he should find nutriment from the fruits of the earth, and from seeds, and herbs, and acorns, having at the same time appointed that the animals be of habits similar to man's, that they also might eat of an the seeds of the earth.

Chapter XIX – Man is Placed in Paradise

God having thus completed the heavens, and the earth, and the sea, and all that are in them, on the sixth day, rested on the seventh day from all His works which He made. Then holy Scripture gives a summary in these words: "This is the book of the generation of the heavens and the earth, when they were created, in the day that the Lord made the heavens and the earth, and every green thing of the field, before it was made, and every herb of the field before it grew. For God had not caused it to rain upon the earth, and there was not a man to till the ground." By this He signifies to us, that the whole earth was at that time watered by a divine fountain, and had no need that man should till it; but the earth produced all things spontaneously by the command of God, that man might not be wearied by tilling it. But that the creation of man might be made plain, so that there should not seem to be an insoluble problem existing among men, since God had said, "Let Us make man; "and since His creation was not yet plainly related, Scripture teaches us, saying: "And a fountain went up out of the earth, and watered the face of the whole earth; and God made man of the dust of the earth, and breathed into his face the breath of life, and man became a living soul. Whence also by most persons the soul is called immortal. And after the formation of man, God chose out for him a region among the places of the East, excellent for light, brilliant with a very bright atmosphere, [abundant] in the finest plants; and in this He placed man.

Chapter XX – The Scriptural Account of Paradise

Scripture thus relates the words of the sacred history: [Theophilus quotes the rest of Genesis 2, here omitted].

Chapter XXI – Of the Fall of Man

[Theophilus quotes Genesis 3 regarding temptation, fall, and curse, here omitted.]

Chapter XXII – Why God is Said to Have Walked

You will say, then, to me: "You said that God ought not to be contained in a place, and how do you now say that He walked in Paradise? "Hear what I say. The God and Father, indeed, of all cannot be contained, and is not found in a place, for there is no place of His rest; but His Word, through whom He made all things, being His power and His wisdom, assuming the person of the Father and Lord of all, went to the garden in the person of God, and conversed with Adam. For the divine writing itself teaches us that Adam said that he had heard the voice. But what else is this voice but the Word of God, who is also His Son? Not as the poets and writers of myths talk of the sons of gods begotten from intercourse [with women], but as truth expounds, the Word, that always exists, residing within the heart of God. For before anything came into being He had Him as a counsellor, being His own mind and thought. But when God wished to make all that He determined on, He begot this Word, uttered, the first-born of all creation, not Himself being emptied of the Word [Reason], but having begotten Reason, and always conversing with His Reason. And hence the holy writings teach us, and all the spirit-bearing [inspired] men, one of whom, John, says, "In the beginning was the Word, and the Word was with God," showing that at first God was alone, and the Word in Him. Then he says, "The Word was God; all things came into existence through Him; and apart from Him not one thing came into existence." The Word, then, being God, and being naturally produced from God, whenever the Father of the universe wills, He sends Him to any place; and He, coming, is both heard and seen, being sent by Him, and is found in a place.

Chapter XXIV – The Beauty of Paradise

[concerning Paradise deleted till this point] And God having placed man in Paradise, as has been said, to till and keep it, commanded him to eat of all the trees – manifestly of the tree of life also; but only of the tree of knowledge He commanded him not to taste. And God transferred him from the earth, out of which he had been produced, into Paradise, giving him means of advancement, in order that, maturing and becoming perfect, and being even declared a god, he might thus ascend into heaven in possession of immortality. For man had been made a middle nature, neither wholly mortal, nor altogether immortal, but capable of either; so also the place, Paradise, was made in respect of beauty intermediate between earth and heaven. And by the expression, "till it," no other kind of labour is implied than the observance of God's command, lest, disobeying, he should destroy himself, as indeed he did destroy himself, by sin.

Chapter XXV – God Was Justified in Forbidding Man to Eat of the Tree of Knowledge

The tree of knowledge itself was good, and its fruit was good. For it was not the tree, as some think, but the disobedience, which had death in it. For there was nothing else in the fruit than only knowledge; but knowledge is good when one uses it discreetly. But Adam, being yet an infant in age, was on this account as yet unable to receive knowledge worthily. For now, also, when a child is born it is not at once able to eat bread, but is nourished first with milk, and then, with the increment of years, it advances to solid food. Thus, too, would it have been with Adam; for not as one who grudged him, as some suppose, did God command him not to eat of knowledge. But He wished also to make proof of him, whether he was submissive to His commandment. And at the same time He wished man, infant as he was, to remain for some time longer simple and sincere. For this is holy, not only with God, but also with men, that in simplicity and guilelessness subjection be yielded to parents. But if it is right that children be subject to parents, how much more to the God and Father of all things? Besides, it is unseemly that children in infancy be wise beyond their years; for as in stature one increases in an orderly progress, so also in wisdom.

But as when a law has commanded abstinence from anything, and some one has not obeyed, it is obviously not the law which causes punishment, but the disobedience and transgression – for a father sometimes enjoins on his own child abstinence from certain things, and when he does not obey the paternal order, he is flogged and punished on account of the disobedience; and in this case the actions themselves are not the [cause of] stripes, but the disobedience procures punishment for him who disobeys – so also for the first man, disobedience procured his expulsion from Paradise. Not, therefore, as if there were any evil in the tree of knowledge; but from his disobedience did man draw, as from a fountain, labour, pain, grief, and at last fall a prey to death.

Chapter XXVII – The Nature of Man

But some one will say to us, Was man made by nature mortal? Certainly not. Was he, then, immortal? Neither do we affirm this. But one will say, Was he, then, nothing? Not even this hits the mark. He was by nature neither mortal nor immortal. For if He had made him immortal from the beginning, He would have made him God. Again, if He had made him mortal, God would seem to be the cause of his death. Neither, then, immortal nor yet mortal did He make him, but, as we have said above, capable of both; so that if he should incline to the things of immortality, keeping the commandment of God, he should receive as reward from Him immortality, and should become God; but if, on the other hand, he should turn to the things of death, disobeying God, he should himself be the cause of death to himself.

For God made man free, and with power over himself. That, then, which man brought upon himself through carelessness and disobedience, this God now vouchsafes to him as a gift through His own philanthropy and pity, when men obey Him. For as man, disobeying, drew death upon himself; so, obeying the will of God, he who desires is able to procure for himself life everlasting. For God has given us a law and holy commandments; and every one who keeps these can be saved, and, obtaining the resurrection, can inherit incorruption.

Chapter XXVIII – Why Eve Was Formed of Adam's Rib

And Adam having been cast out of Paradise, in this condition knew Eve his wife, whom God had formed into a wife for him out of his rib. And this He did, not as if He were unable to make his wife separately, but God foreknew that man would call upon a number of gods. And having this prescience, and knowing that through the serpent error would introduce a number of gods which had no existence – for there being but one God, even then error was striving to disseminate a multitude of gods, saying, "Ye shall be as gods;" – lest, then, it should be supposed that one God made the man and another the woman, therefore He made them both; and God made the woman together with the man, not only that thus the mystery of God's sole government might be exhibited, but also that their mutual affection might be greater.

Therefore said Adam to Eve, "This is now bone of my bones, and flesh of my flesh." And besides, he prophesied, saying, "For this cause shall a man leave his father and his mother, and shall cleave unto his wife; and they two shall be one flesh;" which also itself has its fulfilment in ourselves. For who that marries lawfully does not despise mother and father, and his whole family connection, and all his household, cleaving to and becoming one with his own wife, fondly preferring her? So that often, for the sake of their wives, some submit even to death. This Eve, on account of her having been in the beginning deceived by the serpent, and become the author of sin, the wicked demon, who also is called Satan, who then spoke to her through the serpent, and who works even to this day in those men that are possessed by him, invokes as Eve. And he is called "demon" and "dragon," on account of his [*apodedrakenai*] revolting from God. For at first he was an angel. And concerning his history there is a great deal to be said; wherefore I at present omit the relation of it, for I have also given an account of him in another place.

Origen

> Origen (185 – 253), though denied sainthood and even condemned for some of his teachings, is universally acknowledged as a Father of the Church. Charged by some as the "hydra of all heresies," he can also be viewed as the "hydra of all orthodoxy," so profound was his influence on those who succeeded him. The later Fathers can scarcely be understood without him, for in one way or another they had to contend with his legacy.
>
> Origen is known for his allegorical interpretation of Scripture, but he never denied the validity of literal interpretation. Indeed, in his first homily on Genesis, he takes for granted the literal meaning of the text – that God created the world as described in Genesis. In *Contra Celsum* he reads the genealogies in Genesis as showing that the earth is less than 10,000 years in age.
>
> Nevertheless, Origen's primary interest was to elaborate Scripture's spiritual meaning. His first homily therefore treats Genesis allegorically. Origen's emphasis on allegorical interpretation reflects his concern (and that of many other Fathers) that Scripture is to be applied to a believer's life to help effect salvation and not merely to be a matter of speculation or to satisfy vain curiosity.
>
> Even with its emphasis on allegory, the first homily throws some light on the question of physical creation. For instance, Origen points out that time itself is created and did not exist before the creation of the world. Notwithstanding, the physical creation is for him a springboard into the spiritual realm and its reality.

Origen *Homilies on Genesis and Exodus*

Homily 1 – On Genesis

IN THE BEGINNING GOD MADE HEAVEN AND EARTH. What is the beginning of all things except our Lord and "Savior of all," Jesus Christ "the firstborn of every creature"? In this beginning, therefore, that is, in his Word, "God made heaven and earth" as the evangelist John also says in the beginning of his Gospel: "In the beginning was the Word, and the Word was with God, and the Word was God. The same was in the beginning with God. All things were made by him and without him nothing was made." Scripture is not speaking here of any temporal beginning, but it says that the heaven and the earth and all things which were made were made "in the beginning," that is, in the Savior.

"And the earth was invisible and disordered and darkness was upon the abyss, and the spirit of God moved over the waters.", "The earth was invisible and disordered" before God said: "Let there be light," and before he divided the light from the darkness, as the order of the account shows. But since in the words which follow he orders the firmament to come into existence and calls this heaven, when we come to that place the reason for the difference between heaven and the firmament will be explained there and also why the firmament was called heaven. But now the text says: "Darkness was upon the abyss." What is "the abyss"? That place, of course, where "the devil and his angels" will be. This indeed is most clearly designated also in the Gospel when it is said of the Savior: "And the demons which he was casting out were asking him that he not command them to go into the abyss."

For this reason, therefore, God dissolved the darkness as the Scripture says: "And God said, 'Let there be light,' and there was light. And God saw that the light was good; and God divided between the light and the darkness. And God called the light day and he called the darkness night. And there was evening and there was morning, one day."

According to the letter God calls both the light day and the darkness night. But let us see according to the spiritual meaning why it is that when God, in that beginning which we discussed above, "made heaven and earth," and said, "let there be light" and "divided between the light and the darkness and called the light day and the darkness night," and the text said that "there was evening and there was morning," it did not say: "the first day," but said, "one day." It is because there was not yet time before the world existed." But time begins to exist with the following days. For the second day and the third and fourth and all the rest begin to designate time.

(2)"And God said: 'Let there be a firmament in the midst of the water and let it divide water from water.' And it was so done. And God made the firmament."

Although God had already previously made heaven, now he makes the firmament. For he made heaven first, about which he says, "heaven is my throne." But after that he makes the firmament, that is, the corporeal heaven. For every corporeal object is, without doubt, firm and solid; and it is this which "divides the water which is above heaven from the water which is below heaven."

For since everything which God was to make would consist of spirit and body, for that reason heaven, that is, all spiritual substance upon which God rests as on a kind of throne or seat, is said to be made "in the beginning" and before everything. But this heaven, that is, the firmament, is corporeal. And, therefore, that first heaven indeed, which we said is spiritual, is our mind, which is also itself spirit, that is, our spiritual man which sees and perceives God. But that corporeal heaven, which is called the firmament, is our outer man which looks at things in a corporeal way.

As, therefore, heaven is called the firmament because it divides between those waters which are above it and those which are below it, so also man, who has been placed in a body, will also himself be called heaven, that is, heavenly man, in the opinion of the apostle Paul who says: "But our citizenship is in heaven," if he can divide and discern what the waters are which are higher, "above the firmament," and what those are which are below the firmament.

The very words of Scripture, therefore, contain it thus: "And God made the firmament, and divided the water which is under the firmament from the water which is above the firmament. And God called the firmament heaven. And God saw that it was good; and there was evening and there was morning, the second day." Let each of you, therefore, be zealous to become a divider of that water which is above and that which is below. The purpose, of course, is that, attaining an understanding and participation in that spiritual water which is above the firmament one may draw forth "from within himself rivers of living water springing up into life eternal," removed without doubt and separated from that water which is below, that is, the water of the abyss in which darkness is said to be, in which "the prince of this world" and the adversary, "the dragon and his angels" dwell, as was indicated above.

Therefore, by participation in that celestial water which is said to be above the heavens, each of the faithful becomes heavenly, that is, when he applies his mind to lofty and exalted things, thinking nothing about the earth but totally about heavenly things, "seeking the things which are above, where Christ is at the right hand of the Father." For then he also will be considered worthy of that praise from God which is written here when the text says: "And God saw that it was good."

And then also those things which are described in the following statements about the third day signify this same meaning. For the text says: "And God said, 'Let the water which is under heaven be gathered into one gathering, and let the dry land appear.' And it was so done."

Let us labor, therefore, to gather "the water which is under heaven" and cast it from us that "the dry land," which is our deeds done in the flesh, might appear when this has been done so that, of course, "men seeing our good works may glorify our Father who is in heaven." For if we have not separated from us those waters which are under heaven, that is, the sins and vices of our body, our dry land will not be able to appear nor have the courage to advance to the light. "For everyone who does evil hates the light and does not come to the light [lest his works be reproved. But he that does truth comes to the light that] his works may be made manifest" and appear, if "they are done in God." This courage certainly will not be given unless like the waters, we cast off from us and remove the vices of the body which are the materials of sins. Once this has been done our dry land will not remain "dry land" as is shown from what follows.

For the text says: "And the water which is under heaven was gathered into its gatherings and the dry land appeared. And God called the dry land earth, and the gathering together of the waters he called seas." As, therefore, this dry land, after the water was removed from it, as we said above, did not continue further as "dry land," but is now named "earth," in this manner also our bodies, if this separation from them takes place, will no longer remain "dry land." They will, on the contrary, be called "earth" because they can now bear fruit for God.

Whereas indeed "in the beginning God made heaven and earth," but later made "the firmament" and "the dry land"; and "the firmament" indeed "he called heaven" giving it the name of that heaven which he had created earlier, but he called "the dry land" "earth" because he bestowed on it the capability of bearing fruits. If, therefore, anyone by his failure still remains dry and offers no fruit but "thorns and thistles," producing, as it were, fuel for the fire, in accordance with those things which he brought forth from himself, he also himself becomes "fuel for the fire." But if, after the waters of the abyss, which are the thoughts of demons, have been separated from himself, he has shown himself fruitful earth by his zeal and diligence, he ought to expect similar things because he also is led by God into "a land flowing with milk and honey."

(3) But let us see from the following words what those fruits are which God orders the earth, on which he himself bestowed this name, to produce. "And God saw," the text says, "that it was good, and God said: 'Let the earth bring forth vegetation producing seed according to its kind and likeness, and the fruit tree bearing fruit whose seed is within it according to its likeness on the earth.' And it was so done."

According to the letter, the fruits are clearly those which "the earth," not "the dry land" produces. But again let us also relate the meaning to ourselves. If we have already been made "earth," if we are no longer "dry land," let us offer copious and diverse fruits to God, that we also may be blessed by the Father who says: "Behold the smell of my son is as the smell of a plentiful field which the Lord has blessed," and that that which the Apostle said might be fulfilled in us: "For the earth that receives the rain which comes frequently upon it and brings forth vegetation fit for those by whom it is cultivated will receive blessings from God. But that which brings forth thorns and briars is reprobate and very near a curse, whose end is to be burned."

(4) "And the earth brought forth green vegetation producing seed according to its kind and likeness and the fruit tree bearing fruit containing seed producing fruit according to its kind on the earth. And God saw that it was good. And there was evening and there was morning, the third day."

Not only does God order the earth to bring forth "green vegetation," but also to bring forth "seed" that it can always bear fruit. And not only does God order that there be "the fruit tree," but also that it "produce fruit containing seed according to its kind," that is, that it can always bear fruit from these seeds which it contains.

And we, therefore, ought thus both to bear fruit and to have seeds within ourselves, that is, to contain in our heart the seeds of all good works and virtues, that, having these fixed in our minds, from them now we might justly perform all the acts which occur to us. For those are the fruits of that seed, namely our acts, which are brought forth "from the good treasure of our heart."

But if, on the one hand, we hear "the word" and from the hearing "immediately" our earth produces vegetation, and this vegetation "wither" before it should come to maturity or fruit, our earth will be called "rocky." But if those things which are said should press forward in our hearts with deepest roots so that they both "bear fruit" of works and contain the seeds of future works, then truly the earth of each of us will bear fruit in accordance with its potential, some "a hundred fold," some "sixty," other "thirty." But also we have considered it necessary to admonish that our fruit have no "darnel," that is, no tares,:" that it not be "beside the way," but be sown in the way itself, in that way which says, "I am the way," that the birds of heaven may not eat our fruits nor our vine. If, however, any of us should deserve to be a vine, let him beware lest he bear thorns for grapes, and for this reason "will no longer be pruned or digged" nor will "the clouds" be ordered "to rain upon it," but on the contrary it will be left "deserted" that "thorns" may overgrow it.

(5) But now, after this, the firmament deserves also to be adorned with lights. For God says: "Let there be lights in the firmament of heaven, that they may give light on the earth and divide between day and night."

As in that firmament which had already been called heaven God orders lights to come into existence that "they might divide between day and night," so also it can happen in us if only we also are zealous to be called and made heaven. We shall have lights in us which illuminate us, namely Christ and his Church. For he himself is "the light of the world" who also illuminates the Church by his light. For just as the moon is said to receive light from the sun so that the night likewise can be illuminated by it, so also the Church, when the light of Christ has been received, illuminates all those who live in the night of ignorance.

But if someone progresses in this so that he is already made a "child of the day," so that "he walks honestly in the day," as "a child of the day and a child of light," this person is illuminated by Christ himself just as the clay is illuminated by the sun.

(6) "'And let them be for signs and seasons, and for days and years; and let them be for illumination in the firmament of heaven, to give light on the earth.' And it was so done."

As those lights of heaven which we see have been set "for signs and seasons and days and years," that they might give light from the firmament of heaven for those who are on the earth, so also Christ, illuminating his Church, gives signs by his precepts, that one might know how, when the sign has been received, to escape "the wrath to come," lest "that day overtake him like a thief," but that rather he can reach "the acceptable year of the Lord."

Christ, therefore, is "the true light which enlightens every man coming into this world." From his light the Church itself also having been enlightened is made "the light of the world" enlightening those "who are in darkness," as also Christ himself testifies to his disciples saying: "You are the light of the world." From this it is shown that Christ indeed is the light of the apostles, but the apostles are "the light of the world." For they, "not having spot or wrinkle or anything of this kind," are the true Church, as also the Apostle says: " That he might present it to himself a glorious Church not having spot or wrinkle or any such thing."

(7) "And God made two great lights, a greater light to rule the day and a lesser light to rule the night, and the stars. And God set them in the firmament of heaven to shine upon the earth and to have authority over the day and the night and to divide between the light and the darkness. And God saw that it was good. And there was evening and there was morning, the fourth day."

Just as the sun and the moon are said to be the great lights in the firmament of heaven, so also are Christ and the Church in us. But since God also placed stars in the firmament, let us see what are also stars in us, that is, in the heaven of our heart.

Moses is a star in us, which shines and enlightens us by his acts. And Abraham, Isaac, Jacob, Isaias, Jeremias, Ezechiel, David, Daniel, and all to whom the Holy Scriptures testify that they pleased God. For just as "star differs from star in glory," so also each of the saints, according to his own greatness, sheds his light upon us.

Moreover, just as the sun and the moon enlighten our bodies so also our minds are enlightened by Christ and the Church. We are enlightened in this way, however, if we are not blind in our minds. For although the sun and moon shine on those who are blind in their bodily eyes they, nevertheless, cannot receive the light. In the same way also Christ offers his light to our minds, but it will so enlighten us only if blindness of mind impede in no way. But even if this happen, those who are blind must follow Christ saying and crying out: "Have mercy on us, son of David," that also receiving sight from him they can then also be radiant in the splendor of his light.

But all who see are not equally enlightened by Christ, but individuals are enlightened according to the measure in which they are able to receive the power of the light. And just as the eyes of our body are not equally enlightened by the sun, but to the extent that one shall have ascended to higher places and contemplated its risings with a gaze from a higher vantage point, to such an extent will he perceive more of both its splendor and its heat. So also to the extent that our mind shall have approached Christ in a more exalted and lofty manner and shall have presented itself nearer the splendor of his light, to such an extent will it be made to shine more magnificently and clearly in his light as also he himself says through the prophet: "'Draw near to me and I shall draw near to you,' says the Lord," And again he says: "I am a God who draws near, and not a God afar off."

We do not, however, all come to him in the same way, but each one "according to his own proper ability." For either we come to him with the crowds and he refreshes us by parables to this end only, lest we faint "in the way" from many fasts, or, of course, we sit always and incessantly at his feet, being free for this alone, that we might hear "his word," not at all disturbed about "much serving," but choosing "the best part which shall not be taken away" from us. And certainly those who thus approach him obtain much more of his light. But if, as the apostles, we should be moved from him in no way at all, but should always remain with him in all his tribulations, then he expounds and solves for us in secret those things which he has spoken to the crowds and enlightens us much more clearly. But if in addition someone should be such as can also ascend the mountain with him, as Peter, James, and John, he will be enlightened not only by the light of Christ, but also by the voice of the Father himself.

(8) "And God said: 'Let the waters bring forth creeping creatures having life and birds flying over the earth in the firmament of heaven.' And it was so done."

According to the letter "creeping creatures" and "birds" are brought forth by the waters at the command of God and we recognize by whom these things which we see have been made. But let us see how also these same things come to be in our firmament of heaven, that is, in the firmness of our mind or heart.

I think that if our mind has been enlightened by Christ, our sun, it is ordered afterwards to bring forth from these waters which are in it "creeping creatures" and "birds which fly," that is, to bring out into the open good or evil thoughts that there might be a distinction of the good thoughts from the evil, which certainly both proceed from the heart. For both good and evil thoughts are brought forth from our heart as from the waters. But by the word and precept of God let us offer both to God's view and judgment that, with his enlightenment we may be able to distinguish what is evil from the good, that is, that we may separate from ourselves those things which creep upon the earth and bear earthly cares.

But let us permit those things which are better. that is, the "birds," to fly not only "above the earth," but also "in the region of the firmament of heaven," that is, let us explore in ourselves the meaning and plan of heavenly things as well as earthly, that we can also understand which of the creeping creatures in us may be harmful. If we should see "a woman to lust after her," that is a poisonous reptile in us. But if we have the disposition of continence, even if an Egyptian mistress love us deeply, we become birds and, leaving the Egyptian garments in her hands, will fly away from the indecent snare. If we should have an inclination inciting us to steal that is a most evil reptile. But it we have an inclination that even if we should have "two mites we would offer these very mites out of mercy as a "gift of God," that inclination is a bird thinking nothing about earthly things, but striving for the firmament of heaven in its flights. If an inclination should come to us persuading us that we ought not bear the tortures of martyrdom, that will be a poisonous reptile. But it an inclination and thought such as this should spring up in us that we struggle for the truth even to death, this will be a bird straining from earthly things to the things above. In the same manner also we should perceive and distinguish concerning other forms of either sins or virtues, which are "creeping creatures" and which are "birds" which our waters are commanded to bring forth for separation before God.

(9) "And God made the great whales, and every creeping creature having life which the waters brought forth according to their kind, and every winged bird according to its kind."

And we should observe concerning these words in the same way as those which we discussed above, that we too ought to bring forth "great whales" and "creeping creatures having life according to their kind." I think impious thoughts and abominable understandings which are against God are indicated in those great whales. All of these, nevertheless, are to be brought forth in the sight of God and placed before him that we may divide and separate the good from the evil, that the Lord might allot to each its place, as is shown from these words which follow.

(10) "And God saw that they were good, and he blessed them saying: 'Increase and multiply and fill the waters which are in the sea and let the birds be multiplied upon the earth.' And there was evening and there was morning, the fifth day."

God commands "the great whales and every creeping creature having life which the waters brought forth to remain in the sea where also "that dragon which God formed to sport with" dwells. But he orders the birds to multiply upon the earth which once was "the dry land," but now already is called "earth" as we explained above.

But someone asks how the great whales and creeping creatures are interpreted as evil and the birds as good when Scripture said about all together, "And God saw that they were good."

Those things which are opposed to the saints are good for them because they can overcome them and when they have overcome them they become more glorious with God. Indeed when the devil requested that power be given to him against Job, the adversary, by attacking him, was the cause of double glory for Job after his victory. What is shown from the fact that he received double those things which he lost in the present is that he will, without doubt, also receive in the same manner in the heavenly places. And the Apostle says that "No one is crowned except the one who has striven lawfully." And indeed, how will there be a contest if there not be one who resists?

How great the beauty and splendor is of light would not be discerned unless the darkness of night intervened. Why are some praised for purity unless because others are condemned for immodesty? Why are strong men magnified unless weak and cowardly men exist? If you use what is bitter then what is sweet is rendered more praiseworthy. If you consider what is dark, the things which are bright will appear more pleasing to you. And, to put it briefly, from the consideration of evil things the glory of good things is indicated more brilliantly. For this reason, therefore, the Scripture says this about everything: "And God saw that they were good."

Why, nevertheless, is it not written: "And God said that they were good," instead of: "God saw that they were good"? That is, God saw the usefulness of those things and that way by which, although in themselves they are as they are, nevertheless, they could perfect good men. For this reason, therefore, he said: "Increase and multiply and fill the waters which are in the sea, and let the birds be multiplied upon the earth," that is, that the great whales indeed and the creeping creatures be in the sea, as we explained above, and the birds upon the earth.

(11) "And God said: 'Let the earth bring forth the living creature according to its kind, four-footed creatures and creeping creatures and beasts of the earth according to their kind.' And it was so done. And God made the beasts of the earth according to their kind and all the creeping creatures of the earth according to their kind. And God saw that they were good."

There is certainly no question about the literal meaning. For they are clearly said to have been created by God, whether animals or four-footed creatures or beasts or serpents upon the earth. But it is not unprofitable to relate these words to those which we explained above in a spiritual sense.

There, for example, it is said: "Let the waters bring forth creeping creatures having life and birds flying above the earth in the region of the firmament of heaven," but here the text says: "Let the earth bring forth the living creature according to its kind, four-footed creatures, creeping creatures, and beasts of the earth according to their kind." And we said that those things certainly, which are brought forth from the waters, ought to be understood as the impulses and thoughts of our mind which are brought forth from the depth of the heart. But in the present text, I think the impulses of our outer man, that is, of our carnal and earthly man, are indicated by this which is said: "Let the earth bring forth the living creature according to its kind, four-footed creatures, creeping creatures, and beasts on the earth according to their kind." In brief. the text indicated nothing winged in these things which are said about the flesh, but only "four-footed creatures, creeping creatures, and beasts of the earth." According to that, to be sure, which is said by the Apostle, that "no good dwells in my flesh" and that "the wisdom of the flesh is hostile to God," those are certainly things which the earth, that is, our flesh, produces, about which the Apostle again admonishes saying: "Put to death your members which are upon the earth, fornication, uncleanness, lewdness, covetousness, idolatry," etc.

When, therefore, all these things which are seen came into existence by the command of God through his Word and that immense visible world was prepared (but at the same time also the allegorical figure showed what those things were which could adorn the lesser world, that is, man), then at that time man himself was created according to those things which are declared subsequently.

(12) "And God said: 'Let us make man according to our image and likeness, and let him have dominion over the fish of the sea and the birds of heaven and the animals and the whole earth and everything which creeps upon the earth.'"

Consequently, in accordance with those things which we explained above, God wishes such a man as we described to have dominion over the previously mentioned beasts, birds, creeping creatures. Four-footed creatures, and all the rest. We explained how these ought to be understood allegorically when we said that the water, that is, man's mind, is ordered to bring forth the spiritual sense and the earth to bring forth the carnal sense, that the mind might rule them and not they rule the mind. For God wishes that man, that great "work" of God on account of whom also the whole world has been created, not only be unstained by these things which we mentioned above and free from them, but also that he might rule them. But now let us consider what sort of living being man is from these same words of Scripture.

All the rest of creation comes into being at the command of God as Scripture says: "And God said, 'Let there be a firmament.'" "And God said, 'Let the water which is under heaven be gathered into one gathering and let the dry land appear.' "And God said: 'Let the earth bring forth vegetation.'" So also Scripture speaks about the remaining things.

But let us see what those things are which God himself made, and in this way let us give attention to what greatness belongs to man. "In the beginning God made heaven and earth." Likewise Scripture says: "And God made two great lights." And now again: "Let us make man." 'The work of God himself is attributed to these alone, but to none of the others. Only heaven and earth, the sun, moon, and stars, and now man have been made by God, but all the rest is said to be made by his command. From this, therefore, consider how great is man's greatness, who is made equal to such great and distinguished elements, who has the honor of heaven for which reason also "the kingdom of heaven" is promised to him. And he has the honor of the earth since indeed he hopes to enter a good land and "a land of the living flowing with milk and honey." He has the honor of the sun and moon having the promise of shining "as the sun in the kingdom of God."

(13) I see, however, something indeed even more distinguished in the condition of man, which I do not find said elsewhere: "And God made man, according to the image of God he made him." We find this attributed neither to heaven nor earth nor the sun or moon.

We do not understand, however, this man indeed whom Scripture says was made "according to the image of God" to be corporeal. For the form of the body does not contain the image of God, nor is the corporeal man said to be "made," but "formed," as is written in the words which follow. For the text says: "And God formed man," that is fashioned," "from the slime of the earth."

But it is our inner man, invisible, incorporeal, incorruptible, and immortal which is made "according to the image of God." For it is in such qualities as these that the image of God is more correctly understood. But if anyone suppose that this man who is made "according to the image and likeness of God" is made of flesh, he will appear to represent God himself as made of flesh and in human form. It is most clearly impious to think this about God. In brief, those carnal men who have no understanding of the meaning of divinity suppose, if they read anywhere in the Scriptures of God that "heaven is my throne, and the earth my footstool," that God has so large a body that they think he sits in heaven and stretches out his feet to the earth. But they think this because they do not have those ears which can worthily hear the words of God about God which are related by the Scripture. For the statement, "Heaven is my throne," is worthily understood of God as follows, that we might know that God rests and resides in these whose "citizenship is in heaven." But in these who are still involved in earthly details, the most remote part of his providence is found, which is figuratively indicated in the mention of feet. If any perchance of this latter group lay hold of a zeal and desire to become heavenly by perfection of life and loftiness of understanding, they also become thrones of God themselves, having first been made heavenly by their warfare and manner of life. These also say: "He raised us up with Christ and at the same time made us sit in the heavenly places." But also those whose "treasure is in heaven" can be said to be heavenly and thrones of God, since "where their treasure is, there is their heart." And not only does God rest upon them, but he also dwells in them.

But if someone can become so great that he can say: "Or do you seek a proof of Christ who speaks in me?" God not only dwells in this man but also walks in him. And for this reason any who are perfect, who have been made heavenly or have become of heaven, "declare the glory of God" as it says in the Psalm. For this reason in brief also the apostles who were of heaven were sent to declare the glory of God and received the name of "Boanerges," "which is the sons of thunder," that by the power of thunder we might believe them truly to be heavens.

Therefore, "God made man, according to the image of God he made him." We must see what that image of God is and inquire diligently in the likeness of what image man is made. For the text did not say that "God made man according to the image or likeness," but "according to the image of God he made him." Therefore, what other image of God is there according to the likeness of whose image man is made, except our Savior who is "the firstborn of every creature," about whom it is written that he is "the brightness of the eternal light and the express figure of God's substance," who also says about himself: "I am in the Father, and the Father in me," and "He who has seen me has also seen the Father"? For just as one who sees an image of someone sees him whose image it is, so also one sees God through the Word of God which is the image of God. And thus what he said will be true: "He who has seen me has also seen the Father."

Man, therefore, is made according to the likeness of his image and for this reason our Savior, who is the image of God, moved with compassion for man who had been made according to his likeness, seeing him, his own image having been laid aside, to have put on the image of the evil one, he himself moved with compassion, assumed the image of man and came to him, as also the Apostle attests saying: "Since he was in the form of God, he did not think it robbery to be equal with God, but emptied himself taking the form of a servant, and in appearance found as a man, he humbled himself even to death."

All therefore, who come to him and desire to become participants in the spiritual image by their progress "are renewed daily in the inner man" according to the image of him who made them, so that they can be made "similar to the body of his glory," but each one in proportion to his own powers. The apostles transformed themselves to his likeness to such an extent that he could say of them, "I go to my Father and your Father, to my God and your God." For he had already petitioned the Father for his disciples that the original likeness might he restored in them when he says: "Father," grant "that just as you and I are one so also they may be one in us."

Let us always, therefore, contemplate that image of God that we can be transformed to his likeness. For if man, made according to the image of God, contrary to nature by beholding the image of the devil has been made like him by sin, much more by beholding the image of God, according to whose likeness he has been made by God, he will receive that form, which was given to him by nature, through the Word and his power. And let no one, seeing his image to be more with the devil than with God, despair that he can again regain the form of the image of God, because the Savior came not "to call the just, but sinners to repentance." Matthew was a publican and undoubtedly his image was like the devil, but when he comes to the image of God, our Lord and Savior, and follows that image he is transformed to the likeness of the image of God. "James, the son of

Zebedee, and John his brother" were fishermen and "uneducated men," who undoubtedly then bore a likeness more to the image of the devil, but they also, by following the image of God, are made like him, as also the other apostles. Paul was a persecutor of the very image of God; but as he was able to behold his grace and beauty, after these were seen he was remade in his likeness to such an extent that he said: "Or do you seek a proof of Christ who speaks in me?"

(14) "Male and female he made them, and God blessed them saying: 'Increase and multiply and fill the earth and have dominion over it.'"

It seems to be worth inquiring in this passage according to the letter how, when the woman was not yet made, the Scripture says, "Male and female he made them." Perhaps, as I think, it is because of the blessing with which he blessed them saying, "Increase and multiply and fill the earth." Anticipating what was to be, the text says, "Male and female he made them," since, indeed, man could not otherwise increase and multiply except with the female. Therefore, that there might be no doubt about his blessing that is to come, the text says, "Male and female he made them." For in this manner man, seeing the consequence of increasing and multiplying to be from the fact that the female was joined to him, could cherish a more certain hope in the divine blessing. For if the Scripture had said: "Increase and multiply and fill the earth and have dominion over it," not adding this, "Male and female he made them," doubtless he would have disbelieved the divine blessing, as also Mary said in response to that blessing which was pronounced by the angel, "How shall I know this, since I know not a man?"

Or perhaps, because all things which have been made by God are said to be united and joined together, as heaven and earth, as sun and moon, so, therefore, that it might be shown that man also is a work of God and has not been brought forth without harmony or the appropriate conjunction, therefore, the text says in anticipation: "Male and female he made them."

These things have been said on that question, which can be raised about the literal meaning.

(15) But let us see also allegorically how man, made in the image of God, is male and female.

Our inner man consists of spirit and soul. The spirit is said to be male; the soul can be called female. If these have concord and agreement among themselves, they increase and multiply by the very accord among themselves and they produce sons, good inclinations and understandings or useful thoughts, by which they fill the earth and have dominion over it. This means they turn the inclination of the flesh, which has been subjected to themselves, to better purposes and have dominion over it while the flesh, of course, becomes insolent in nothing against the will of the spirit. But now if the soul, which has been united with the spirit and, so to speak, joined in wedlock, turn aside at some time to bodily pleasures and turn back its inclination to the delight of the flesh and at one time indeed appear to obey the salutary warnings of the spirit, but at another time yield to carnal vices, such a soul, as if defiled by adultery of the body, is said properly neither to increase nor multiply, since indeed Scripture designates the sons of adulterers as imperfect. Such a soul, to be sure, which prostrates itself totally to the inclination of the flesh and bodily desires, having forsaken conjunction with the spirit, as if turned away from God will shamelessly hear, "You have the face of a harlot; you have made yourself shameless to all." She will be punished, therefore, like a harlot and her sons will be ordered to be prepared for slaughter.

(16) "And have dominion over the fish of the sea and the birds of heaven and the beasts and everything which is upon the earth and the creeping creatures which creep upon the earth "

These words have already been interpreted in their literal meaning, when we discussed that which God said: "Let us make man" and the rest, where he says, "And let them have dominion over the fish of the sea and the birds of heaven," etc.' But allegorically those things no less of which we spoke above seem to me to be indicated in the fish and birds or animals and creeping things of the earth. I mean, either the things which proceed from the inclination of the soul and the thought of the heart, or those which are brought forth from bodily desires and the impulses of the flesh. The saints and all who preserve the blessing of God in themselves exercise dominion over these things guiding the total man by the will of the spirit. But on the other hand, the same things which are brought forth by the vices of the flesh and pleasures of the body hold dominion over sinners.

(17) "And God said, 'Behold I have given to you all vegetation having seed, which produces seed which is upon all the earth, and every tree which has in itself fruit-producing seed. It shall be for food for you and for all the beasts of the earth and for all the birds of heaven and for all the creeping creatures which creep upon the earth, which have in themselves a living soul'"

The historical meaning, at least, of this sentence indicates clearly that originally God permitted the use of foods from vegetation, that is, vegetables and the fruits of trees. But the opportunity of eating flesh is given to men later when a covenant was made with Noah after the flood. The reasons for this, of course, will be explained more appropriately in their own places.

But allegorically the vegetation of the earth and its fruit which is granted to men for food can be understood of the bodily affections. For example, anger and concupiscence are offshoots of the body. The fruit of this offshoot, that is, the work, is common to us who are rational and to the beasts of the earth. For when we become angry justly, that is, for the reproach of one who is transgressing and for correction for his salvation, we eat of that fruit of the earth and the corporeal wrath with which we restrain sin, with which we restore justice, becomes our food.

And lest we appear to you to bring these things forth from our own understanding rather than from the authority of the divine Scriptures, go back to the book of Numbers and recall what Phineas the priest did when he saw a harlot of the Midianite people with an Israelite man clinging in impure embraces in the eyes of all. filled with the wrath of divine jealousy, he drove a sword, which he had seized, through the breast of both. This work was imputed to him by God for righteousness when the Lord says: "Phineas appeased my rage and it shall be imputed to him for righteousness." That earthly food of anger, therefore, becomes our food when we use it rationally for righteousness.

But if anger is agitated irrationally so that it punishes the innocent, so that it rages against those who do nothing wrong, it will be the food of the beasts of the field and the serpents of the earth and the birds of heaven. For the demons also, who both feed on and promote our evil deeds, are nurtured on these foods. For Cain is a sign of this work, who deceived his innocent brother in the anger of envy.

We must think likewise also about concupiscence and the individual affections of this kind. For when "our soul longs for the living God and faints," concupiscence is our food. But when we either see another's wife to lust after her or we lust after something that belongs to a "neighbor," concupiscence becomes a beast – like food, as the lust of Ahab can be an example and the deed of Jezebel concerning the vineyard of Naboth of Jezrahel.

The caution of Holy Scripture certainly must be observed also in the matter of the words. Although Scripture had said of men that God said: "Behold I have given to you all the seedbearing vegetation which is upon the earth, and every tree which is upon the earth; they shall be food for you," it did not say of the beasts that I have given all these things to them for food, but "it shall be for food for them," so that, according to the spiritual understanding which we explained, those affections are understood to have been given to man, indeed, by God, but it is announced by God that they will also be for food for the beasts of the earth. For that reason, therefore, the divine Scripture has made use of the most cautious language. It says that God says to men, indeed: "I have given you these things for food," but when it comes to the beasts, not with the import of a command, but as it were, an announcement, he says that these things will be for food also for the beasts, the birds, and the serpents.

But in accordance with the view of the apostle Paul, let us give attention to the text that we can, as he himself says, receive "the mind of Christ" and know "the things that are given us from God." And let us not make what has been given to us for food the food of pigs or dogs, but let us prepare such food in ourselves, by which he may think it fit that the Word and Son of God be received in the inn of our heart, who comes with his Father and wills to make his dwelling with us in the Holy Spirit whose temple we ought to be first of all by our holiness.

To him be glory forever and ever. Amen.

Origen *De Principiis*, Book II

Chapter I – On the World

1. Although all the discussions in the preceding book have had reference to the world and its arrangements, it now seems to follow that we should specially re-discuss a few points respecting the world itself, i.e., its beginning and end, or those dispensations of Divine Providence which have taken place between the beginning and the end, or those events which are supposed to have occurred before the creation of the world, or are to take place after the end.

In this investigation, the first point which clearly appears is, that the world in all its diversified and varying conditions is composed not only of rational and diviner natures, and of a diversity of bodies, but of dumb animals, wild and tame beasts, of birds, and of all things which live in the waters; then, secondly, of places, i.e., of the heaven or heavens, and of the earth or water, as well as of the air, which is intermediate, and which they term æther, and of everything which proceeds from the earth or is born in it. Seeing, then, there is so great a variety in the world, and so great a diversity among rational beings themselves, on account of which every other variety and diversity also is supposed to have come into existence, what other cause than this ought to be assigned for the existence of the world, especially if we have regard to that end by means of which it was shown in the preceding book that all things are to be restored to their original condition? And if this should seem to be logically stated, what other cause, as we have already said, are we to imagine for so great a diversity in the world, save the diversity and variety in the movements and declensions of those who fell from that primeval unity and harmony in which they were at first created by God, and who, being driven from that state of goodness, and drawn in various directions by the harassing influence of different motives and desires, have changed, according to their different tendencies, the single and undivided goodness of their nature into minds of various sorts?

2. But God, by the ineffable skill of His wisdom, transforming and restoring all things, in whatever manner they are made, to some useful aim, and to the common advantage of all, recalls those very creatures which differed so much from each other in mental conformation to one agreement of labour and purpose; so that, although they

are under the influence of different motives, they nevertheless complete the fulness and perfection of one world, and the very variety of minds tends to one end of perfection. For it is one power which grasps and holds together all the diversity of the world, and leads the different movements towards one work, lest so immense an undertaking as that of the world should be dissolved by the dissensions of souls. And for this reason we think that God, the Father of all things, in order to ensure the salvation of all His creatures through the ineffable plan of His word and wisdom, so arranged each of these, that every spirit, whether soul or rational existence, however called, should not be compelled by force, against the liberty of his own will, to any other course than that to which the motives of his own mind led him (lest by so doing the power of exercising free will should seem to be taken away, which certainly would produce a change in the nature of the being itself); and that the varying purposes of these would be suitably and usefully adapted to the harmony of one world, by some of them requiring help, and others being able to give it, and others again being the cause of struggle and contest to those who are making progress, amongst whom their diligence would be deemed more worthy of approval, and the place of rank obtained after victory be held with greater certainty, which should be established by the difficulties of the contest.

3. Although the whole world is arranged into offices of different kinds, its condition, nevertheless, is not to be supposed as one of internal discrepancies and discordances; but as our one body is provided with many members, and is held together by one soul, so I am of opinion that the whole world also ought to be regarded as some huge and immense animal, which is kept together by the power and reason of God as by one soul. This also, I think, is indicated in sacred Scripture by the declaration of the prophet, "Do not I fill heaven and earth? saith the Lord;" and again, "The heaven is My throne, and the earth is My footstool;" and by the Saviour's words, when He says that we are to swear "neither by heaven, for it is God's throne; nor by the earth, for it is His footstool:" To the same effect also are the words of Paul, in his address to the Athenians, when he says, "In Him we live, and move, and have our being." For how do we live, and move, and have our being in God, except by His comprehending and holding

together the whole world by His power? And how is heaven the throne of God, and the earth His footstool, as the Saviour Himself declares, save by His power filling all things both in heaven and earth, according to the Lord's own words? And that God, the Father of all things, fills and holds together the world with the fulness of His power, according to those passages which we have quoted, no one, I think, will have any difficulty in admitting.

And now, since the course of the preceding discussion has shown that the different movements of rational beings, and their varying opinions, have brought about the diversity that is in the world, we must see whether it may not be appropriate that this world should have a termination like its beginning. For there is no doubt that its end must be sought amid much diversity and variety; which variety, being found to exist in the termination of the world, will again furnish ground and occasion for the diversities of the other world which is to succeed the present.

4. If now, in the course of our discussion, it has been ascertained that these things are so, it seems to follow that we next consider the nature of corporeal being, seeing the diversity in the world cannot exist without bodies. It is evident from the nature of things themselves, that bodily nature admits of diversity and variety of change, so that it is capable of undergoing all possible transformations, as, e.g., the conversion of wood into fire, of fire into smoke, of smoke into air, of oil into fire. Does not food itself, whether of man or of animals, exhibit the same ground of change? For whatever we take as food, is converted into the substance of our body. But how water is changed into earth or into air, and air again into fire, or fire into air, or air into water, although not difficult to explain, yet on the present occasion it is enough merely to mention them, as our object is to discuss the nature of bodily matter.

By matter, therefore, we understand that which is placed under bodies, viz., that by which, through the bestowing and implanting of qualities, bodies exist; and we mention four qualities – heat, cold, dryness, humidity. These four qualities being implanted in the *hulç*, or matter (for matter is found to exist in its own nature without those qualities before mentioned), produce the different kinds of bodies. Although this matter is, as we have said above, according to its own proper nature without qualities, it is never found to exist without a quality. And I cannot understand how so many distinguished men have been of opinion that this matter, which is so great, and possesses such properties as to enable it to be sufficient for all the bodies in the world which God willed to exist, and to be the attendant and slave of the Creator for whatever forms and species He wished in all things, receiving into itself whatever qualities He desired to bestow upon it, was uncreated, i.e., not formed by God Himself, who is the Creator of all things, but that its nature and power were the result of chance. And I am astonished that they should find fault with those who deny either God's creative power or His providential administration of the world, and accuse them of impiety for thinking that so great a work as the world could exist without an architect or overseer; while they themselves incur a similar charge of impiety in saying that matter is un-created, and co-eternal with the uncreated God.

According to this view, then, if we suppose for the sake of argument that matter did not exist, as these maintain, saying that God could not create anything when nothing existed, without doubt He would have been idle, not having matter on which to operate, which matter they say was furnished Him not by His own arrangement, but by accident; and they think that this, which was discovered by chance, was able to suffice Him for an undertaking of so vast an extent, and for the manifestation of the power of His might, and by admitting the plan of all His wisdom, might be distinguished and formed into a world. Now this appears to me to be very absurd, and to be the opinion of those men who are altogether ignorant of the power and intelligence of un-crested nature.

But that we may see the nature of things a little more clearly, let it be granted that for a little time matter did not exist, and that God, when nothing formerly existed, caused those things to come into existence which He desired, why are we to suppose that God would create matter either better or greater, or of another kind, than that which He did produce from His own power and wisdom, in order that that might exist which formerly did not? Would He create a worse and inferior matter, or one the same as that which they call uncreated? Now I think it will very easily appear to any one, that neither a better nor inferior matter could have assumed the forms and species of the world, if it had not been such as that which actually did assume them.

And does it not then seem impious to call that uncreated, which, if believed to be formed by God, would doubtless be found to be such as that which they call uncreated?

5. But that we may believe on the authority of holy Scripture that such is the case, hear how in the book of Maccabees, where the mother of seven martyrs exhorts her son to endure torture, this truth is confirmed; for she says, "I ask of thee, my son, to look at the heaven and the earth, and at all things which are in them, and beholding these, to know that God made all these things when they did not exist." In the book of the Shepherd also, in the first commandment, he speaks as follows: "first of all believe that there is one God who created and arranged all things, and made all things to come into existence, and out of a state of nothingness." Perhaps also the expression in the Psalms has reference to this: "He spake, and they were made; He commanded, and they were created." For the words, "He spake, and they were made," appear to show that the substance of those things which exist is meant; while the others, "He commanded, and they were created," seem spoken of the qualities by which the substance itself has been moulded.

Chapter II – On the Perpetuity of Bodily Nature

1. On this topic some are wont to inquire whether, as the Father generates an uncreated Son, and brings forth a Holy Spirit, not as if He had no previous existence, but because the Father is the origin and source of the Son or Holy Spirit, and no anteriority or posteriority can be understood as existing in them; so also a similar kind of union or relationship can be understood as subsisting between rational natures and bodily matter. And that this point may be more fully and thoroughly examined, the commencement of the discussion is generally directed to the inquiry whether this very bodily nature, which bears the lives and contains the movements of spiritual and rational minds, will be equally eternal with them, or will altogether perish and be destroyed. And that the question may be determined with greater precision, we have, in the first place, to inquire if it is possible for rational natures to remain altogether incorporeal after they have reached the summit of holiness and happiness (which seems to me a most difficult and almost impossible attainment), or whether they must always of necessity be united to bodies. If, then, any one could

show a reason why it was possible for them to dispense wholly with bodies, it will appear to follow, that as a bodily nature, created out of nothing after intervals of time, was produced when it did not exist, so also it must cease to be when the purposes which it served had no longer an existence.

2. If, however, it is impossible for this point to be at all maintained, viz., that any other nature than the Father, Son, and Holy Spirit can live without a body, the necessity of logical reasoning compels us to understand that rational natures were indeed created at the beginning, but that material substance was separated from them only in thought and understanding, and appears to have been formed for them, or after them, and that they never have lived nor do live without it; for an incorporeal life will rightly be considered a prerogative of the Trinity alone.

As we have remarked above, therefore, that material substance of this world, possessing a nature admitting of all possible transformations, is, when dragged down to beings of a lower order, moulded into the crasser and more solid condition of a body, so as to distinguish those visible and varying forms of the world; but when it becomes the servant of more perfect and more blessed beings, it shines in the splendour of celestial bodies, and adorns either the angels of God or the sons of the resurrection with the clothing of a spiritual body, out of all which will be filled up the diverse and varying state of the one world. But if any one should desire to discuss these matters more fully, it will be necessary, with all reverence and fear of God, to examine the sacred Scriptures with greater attention and diligence, to ascertain whether the secret and hidden sense within them may perhaps reveal anything regarding these matters; and something may be discovered in their abstruse and mysterious language, through the demonstration of the Holy Spirit to those who are worthy, after many testimonies have been collected on this very point.

Chapter III – On the Beginning of the World, and Its Causes

1. The next subject of inquiry is, whether there was any other world before the one which now exists; and if so, whether it was such as the present, or somewhat different, or inferior; or whether there was no world at all, but something like that which we understand will

be after the end of all things, when the kingdom shall be delivered up to God, even the Father; which nevertheless may have been the end of another world – of that, namely, after which this world took its beginning; and whether the various lapses of intellectual natures provoked God to produce this diverse and varying condition of the world. This point also, I think, must be investigated in a similar way, viz., whether after this world there will be any (system of) preservation and amendment, severe indeed, and attended with much pain to those who were unwilling to obey the word of God, but a process through which, by means of instruction and rational training, those may arrive at a fuller understanding of the truth who have devoted themselves in the present life to these pursuits, and who, after having had their minds purified, have advanced onwards so as to become capable of attaining divine wisdom; and after this the end of all things will immediately follow, and there will be again, for the correction and improvement of those who stand in need of it, another world, either resembling that which now exists, or better than it, or greatly inferior; and how long that world, whatever it be that is to come after this, shall continue; and if there will be a time when no world shall anywhere exist, or if there has been a time when there was no world at all; or if there have been, or will be several; or if it shall ever come to pass that there will be one resembling another, like it in every respect, and indistinguishable from it.

2. That it may appear more clearly, then, whether bodily matter can exist during intervals of time, and whether, as it did not exist before it was made, so it may again be resolved into non-existence, let us see, first of all, whether it is possible for any one to live without a body. For if one person can live without a body, all things also may dispense with them; seeing our former treatise has shown that all things tend towards one end.

Now, if all things may exist without bodies, there will undoubtedly be no bodily substance, seeing there will be no use for it. But how shall we understand the words of the apostle in those passages, in which, discussing the resurrection of the dead, he says, "This corruptible must put on incorruption, and this mortal must put on immortality. When this corruptible shall have put on incorruption, and this mortal shall have put on immortality, then shall be brought to pass the saying which is written, Death is swallowed up in victory!

Where, O death, is thy victory? O death, thy sting has been swallowed up: the sting of death is sin, and the strength of sin is the law." Some such meaning, then, as this, seems to be suggested by the apostle. For can the expression which he employs, "this corruptible," and "this mortal," with the gesture, as it were, of one who touches or points out, apply to anything else than to bodily matter?

This matter of the body, then, which is now corruptible shall put on incorruption when a perfect soul, and one furnished with the marks of incorruption, shall have begun to inhabit it. And do not be surprised if we speak of a perfect soul as the clothing of the body (which, on account of the Word of God and His wisdom, is now named incorruption), when Jesus Christ Himself, who is the Lord and Creator of the soul, is said to be the clothing of the saints, according to the language of the apostle, "Put ye on the Lord Jesus Christ." As Christ, then, is the clothing of the soul, so for a kind of reason sufficiently intelligible is the soul said to be the clothing of the body, seeing it is an ornament to it, covering and concealing its mortal nature. The expression, then, "This corruptible must put on incorruption," is as if the apostle had said, "This corruptible nature of the body must receive the clothing of incorruption – a soul possessing in itself incorruptibility," because it has been clothed with Christ, who is the Wisdom and Word of God.

But when this body, which at some future period we shall possess in a more glorious state, shall have become a partaker of life, it will then, in addition to being immortal, become also incorruptible. For whatever is mortal is necessarily also corruptible; but whatever is corruptible cannot also be said to be mortal. We say of a stone or a piece of wood that it is corruptible, but we do not say that it follows that it is also mortal. But as the body partakes of life, then because life may be, and is, separated from it, we consequently name it mortal, and according to another sense also we speak of it as corruptible. The holy apostle therefore, with remarkable insight, referring to the general first cause of bodily matter, of which (matter), whatever be the qualities with which it is endowed (now indeed carnal, but by and by more refined and pure, which are termed spiritual), the soul makes constant use, says, "This corruptible must put on incorruption." And in the second place, looking to the special cause of the body, he says, "This mortal must put on immortality."

Now, what else will incorruption and immortality be, save the wisdom, and the word, and the righteousness of God, which mould; and clothe, and adorn the soul? And hence it happens that it is said, "The corruptible will put on incorruption, and the mortal immortality." For although we may now make great proficiency, yet as we only know in part, and prophesy in part, and see through a glass, darkly, those very things which we seem to understand, this corruptible does not yet put on incorruption, nor is this mortal yet clothed with immorality; and as this training of ours in the body is protracted doubtless to a longer period, up to the time, viz., when those very bodies of ours with which we are enveloped may, on account of the word of God, and His wisdom and perfect righteousness, earn incorruptibility and immortality, therefore is it said, "This corruptible must put on incorruption, and this mortal must put on immortality."

3. But, nevertheless, those who think that rational creatures can at any time lead an existence out of the body, may here raise such questions as the following. If it is true that this corruptible shall put on incorruption, and this mortal put on immortality, and that death is swallowed up at the end; this shows that nothing else than a material nature is to be destroyed, on which death could operate, while the mental acumen of those who are in the body seems to be blunted by the nature of corporeal matter.

If, however, they are out of the body, then they will altogether escape the annoyance arising from a disturbance of that kind. But as they will not be able immediately to escape all bodily clothing, they are just to be considered as inhabiting more refined and purer bodies, which possess the property of being no longer overcome by death, or of being wounded by its sting; so that at last, by the gradual disappearance of the material nature, death is both swallowed up, and even at the end exterminated, and all its sting completely blunted by the divine grace which the soul has been rendered capable of receiving, and has thus deserved to obtain incorruptibility and immortality. And then it will be deservedly said by all, "O death, where is thy victory? O death, where is thy sting? The sting of death is sin."

If these conclusions, then, seem to hold good, it follows that we must believe our condition at some future time to be incorporeal; and if this is admitted, and all are said to be subjected to Christ, this (incorporeity) also must necessarily be bestowed on all to whom the subjection to Christ extends; since all who are subject to Christ will be in the end subject to God the Father, to whom Christ is said to deliver up the kingdom; and thus it appears that then also the need of bodies will cease. And if it ceases, bodily matter returns to nothing, as formerly also it did not exist.

Now let us see what can be said in answer to those who make these assertions. For it will appear to be a necessary consequence that, if bodily nature be annihilated, it must be again restored and created; since it seems a possible thing that rational natures, from whom the faculty of free will is never taken away, may be again subjected to movements of some kind, through the special act of the Lord Himself, lest perhaps, if they were always to occupy a condition that was unchangeable, they should be ignorant that it is by the grace of God and not by their own merit that they have been placed in that final state of happiness; and these movements will undoubtedly again be attended by variety and diversity of bodies, by which the world is always adorned; nor will it ever be composed (of anything) save of variety and diversity – an effect which cannot be produced without a bodily matter.

4. And now I do not understand by what proofs they can maintain their position, who assert that worlds sometimes come into existence which are not dissimilar to each other, but in all respects equal. For if there is said to be a world similar in all respects (to the present), then it will come to pass that Adam and Eve will do the same things which they did before: there will be a second time the same deluge, and the same Moses will again lead a nation numbering nearly six hundred thousand out of Egypt; Judas will also a second time betray the Lord; Paul will a second time keep the garments of those who stoned Stephen; and everything which has been done in this life will be said to be repeated – a state of things which I think cannot be established by any reasoning, if souls are actuated by freedom of will, and maintain either their advance or retrogression according to the power of their will.

For souls are not driven on in a cycle which returns after many ages to the same round, so as either to do or desire this or that; but at whatever point the freedom of their own will aims, thither do they direct the course of their actions. For what these persons say is much the same as if one were to assert that if a medimnus of grain were to be poured out on the ground, the fall of the grain would be on the second occasion identically the same as on the first, so that every individual grain would lie for the second time close beside that grain where it had been thrown before, and so the medimnus would be scattered in the same order, and with the same marks as formerly; which certainly is an impossible result with the countless grains of a medimnus, even if they were to be poured out without ceasing for many ages.

So therefore it seems to me impossible for a world to be restored for the second time, with the same order and with the same amount of births, and deaths, and actions; but that a diversity of worlds may exist with changes of no unimportant kind, so that the state of another world may be for some unmistakeable reasons better (than this), and for others worse, and for others again intermediate. But what may be the number or measure of this I confess myself ignorant, although, if any one can tell it, I would gladly learn.

5. But this world, which is itself called an age, is said to be the conclusion of many ages. Now the holy apostle teaches that in that age which preceded this, Christ did not suffer, nor even in the age which preceded that again; and I know not that I am able to enumerate the number of anterior ages in which He did not suffer. I will show, however, from what statements of Paul I have arrived at this understanding. He says, "But now once in the consummation of ages, He was manifested to take away sin by the sacrifice of Himself." For He says that He was once made a victim, and in the consummation of ages was manifested to take away sin. Now that after this age, which is said to be formed for the consummation of other ages, there will be other ages again to follow, we have clearly learned from Paul himself, who says, "That in the ages to come He might show the exceeding riches of His grace in His kindness towards us." He has not said, "in the age to come," nor "in the two ages to come," whence I infer that by his language many ages are indicated.

Now if there is something greater than ages, so that among created beings certain ages may be understood, but among other beings which exceed and surpass visible creatures, (ages still greater) (which perhaps will be the case at the restitution of all things, when the whole universe will come to a perfect termination), perhaps that period in which the consummation of all things will take place is to be understood as something more than an age. But here the authority of holy Scripture moves me, which says, "For an age and more." Now this word "more" undoubtedly means something greater than an age; and see if that expression of the Saviour, "I will that where I am, these also may be with Me; and as I and Thou are one, these also may be one in Us," may not seem to convey something more than an age and ages, perhaps even more than ages of ages – that period, viz., when all things are now no longer in an age, but when God is in all.

6. Having discussed these points regarding the nature of the world to the best of our ability, it does not seem out of place to inquire what is the meaning of the term world, which in holy Scripture is shown frequently to have different significations. For what we call in Latin *mundus*, is termed in Greek *kosmos*, and *kosmos* signifies not only a world, but also an ornament. finally, in Isaiah, where the language of reproof is directed to the chief daughters of Sion, and where he says, "Instead of an ornament of a golden head, thou wilt have baldness on account of thy works," he employs the same term to denote ornament as to denote the world, viz., *kosmos*. For the plan of the world is said to be contained in the clothing of the high priest, as we find in the Wisdom of Solomon, where he says, "For in the long garment was the whole world." That earth of ours, with its inhabitants, is also termed the world, as when Scripture says, "The whole world lieth in wickedness."

Clement indeed, a disciple of the apostles, makes mention of those whom the Greeks called *antichthones*, and other parts of the earth, to which no one of our people can approach, nor can any one of those who are there cross over to us, which he also termed worlds, saying, "The ocean is impassable to men; and those are words which are on the other side of it, which are governed by these same arrangements of the ruling God." That universe which is bounded by heaven and earth is also called a world, as Paul declares: "For the fashion of this world will pass away." Our Lord and Saviour also points out a certain other world besides this visible one, which it would indeed be difficult to describe and make known. He says, "I am not of this world." For, as if He were of a certain other world, He says, "I am not of this world."

Now, of this world we have said beforehand, that the explanation was difficult; and for this reason, that there might not be afforded to any an occasion of entertaining the supposition that we maintain the existence of certain images which the Greeks call "ideas:" for it is certainly alien to our (writers) to speak of an incorporeal world existing in the imagination alone, or in the fleeting world of thoughts; and how they can assert either that the Saviour comes from thence, or that the saints will go thither, I do not see. There is no doubt, however, that something more illustrious and excellent than this present world is pointed out by the Saviour, at which He incites and encourages believers to aim. But whether that world to which He desires to allude be far separated and divided from this either by situation, or nature, or glory; or whether it be superior in glory and quality, but confined within the limits of this world (which seems to me more probable), is nevertheless uncertain, and in my opinion an unsuitable subject for human thought.

But from what Clement seems to indicate when he says, "The ocean is impassable to men, and those worlds which are behind it," speaking in the plural number of the worlds which are behind it, which he intimates are administered and governed by the same providence of the Most High God, he appears to throw out to us some germs of that view by which the whole universe of existing things, celestial and super-celestial, earthly and infernal, is generally called one perfect world, within which, or by which, other worlds, if any there are, must be supposed to be contained. For which reason he wished the globe of the sun or moon, and of the other bodies called planets, to be each termed worlds. Nay, even that pre-eminent globe itself which they call the non-wandering (*aplançç*), they nevertheless desire to have properly called world. Finally, they summon the book of Baruch the prophet to bear witness to this assertion, because in it the seven worlds or heavens are more clearly pointed out.

Nevertheless, above that sphere which they call non-wandering (*aplançç*), they will have another sphere to exist, which they say, exactly as our heaven contains all things which are under it, comprehends by its immense size and indescribable extent the spaces of all the spheres together within its more magnificent circumference; so that all things are within it, as this earth of ours is under heaven. And this also is believed to be called in the holy Scriptures the good land, and the land of the living, having its own heaven, which is higher, and in which the names of the saints are said to be written, or to have been written, by the Saviour; by which heaven that earth is confined and shut in, which the Saviour in the Gospel promises to the meek and merciful. For they would have this earth of ours, which formerly was named "Dry," to have derived its appellation from the name of that earth, as this heaven also was named firmament from the title of that heaven. But we have treated at greater length of such opinions in the place where we had to inquire into the meaning of the declaration, that in the beginning "God made the heavens and the earth." For another heaven and another earth are shown to exist besides that "firmament" which is said to have been made after the second day, or that "dry land" which was afterwards called "earth."

Certainly, what some say of this world, that it is corruptible because it was made, and yet is not corrupted, because the will of God, who made it and holds it together lest corruption should rule over it, is stronger and more powerful than corruption, may more correctly be supposed of that world which we have called above a "non-wandering "sphere, since by the will of God it is not at all subject to corruption, for the reason that it has not admired any causes of corruption, seeing it is the world of the saints and of the thoroughly purified, and not of the wicked, like that world of ours.

We must see, moreover, lest perhaps it is with reference to this that the apostle says, "While we look not at the things which are seen, but at the things which are not seen; for the things which are seen are temporal, but the things which are unseen are eternal. For we know that if our earthly house of this tabernacle were dissolved, we have a building of God, an house not made with hands, eternal in the heavens." And when he says elsewhere, "Because I shall see the heavens, the works of Thy fingers," and when God said, regarding all things visible, by the mouth of His prophet, "My hand has formed all these things," He declares that that eternal house in the heavens which He promises to His saints was not made with hands, pointing out, doubtless, the difference of creation in things which are seen and in those which are not seen. For the same thing is not to be understood by the expressions, "those things which are not seen," and "those things which are invisible." For those things which are invisible are not only not seen, but do not even possess the property of visibility, being what the Greeks call *asômata*, i.e., incorporeal; whereas those of which Paul says, "They are not seen," possess indeed the property of being seen, but, as he explains, are not yet beheld by those to whom they are promised.

Origen *Contra Celsum*, Book I

Chapter XIX

After these statements, Celsus, from a secret desire to cast discredit upon the Mosaic account of the creation, which teaches that the world is not yet ten thousand years old, but very much under that, while concealing his wish, intimates his agreement with those who hold that the world is uncreated. For, maintaining that there have been, from all eternity, many conflagrations and many deluges, and that the flood which lately took place in the time of Deucalion is comparatively modern, he clearly demonstrates to those who are able to understand him, that, in his opinion, the world was uncreated. But let this assailant of the Christian faith tell us by what arguments he was compelled to accept the statement that there have been many conflagrations and many cataclysms, and that the flood which occurred in the time of Deucalion, and the conflagration in that of Phaethon, were more recent than any others. And if he should put forward the dialogues of Plato (as evidence) on these subjects, we shall say to him that it is allowable for us also to believe that there resided in the pure and pious soul of Moses, who ascended above all created things, and united himself to the Creator of the universe, and who made known divine things with far greater clearness than Plato, or those other wise men (who lived) among the Greeks and Romans, a spirit which was divine. And if he demands of us our reasons for such a belief, let him first give grounds for his own unsupported assertions, and then we shall show that this view of ours is the correct one.

Chapter XX

And yet, against his will, Celsus is entangled into testifying that the world is comparatively modern, and not yet ten thousand years old, when he says that the Greeks consider those things as ancient, because, owing to the deluges and conflagrations, they have not beheld or received any memorials of older events. But let Celsus have, as his authorities for the myth regarding the conflagrations and inundations, those persons who, in his opinion, are the most learned of the Egyptians, traces of whose wisdom are to be found in the worship of irrational animals, and in arguments which prove that such a worship of God is in conformity with reason, and of a secret and mysterious character. The Egyptians, then, when they boastfully give their own account of the divinity of animals, are to be considered wise; but if any Jew, who has signified his adherence to the law and the lawgiver, refer everything to the Creator of the universe, and the only God, he is, in the opinion of Celsus and those like him, deemed inferior to him who degrades the Divinity not only to the level of rational and mortal animals, but even to that of irrational also! – a view which goes far beyond the mythical doctrine of transmigration, according to which the soul falls down from the summit of heaven, and enters into the body of brute beasts, both tame and savage! And if the Egyptians related fables of this kind, they are believed to convey a philosophical meaning by their enigmas and mysteries; but if Moses compose and leave behind him histories and laws for an entire nation, they are to be considered as empty fables, the language of which admits of no allegorical meaning!

Chapter XXI

The following is the view of Celsus and the Epicureans: "Moses having," he says, "learned the doctrine which is to be found existing among wise nations and eloquent men, obtained the reputation of divinity." Now, in answer to this we have to say, that it may be allowed him that. Moses did indeed hear a somewhat ancient doctrine, and transmitted the same to the Hebrews; that if the doctrine which he heard was false, and neither pious nor venerable, and if notwithstanding, he received it and handed it down to those under his authority, he is liable to censure; but if, as you assert, he gave his adherence to opinions that were wise and true, and educated his people by means of them, what, pray, has he done deserving of condemnation? Would, indeed, that not only Epicurus, but Aristotle, whose sentiments regarding providence are not so impious (as those of the former), and the Stoics, who assert that God is a body, had heard such a doctrine! Then the world would not have been filled with opinions which either disallow or enfeeble the action of providence, or introduce a corrupt corporeal principle, according to which the god of the Stoics is a body, with respect to whom they are not afraid to say that he is capable of change, and may be altered and transformed in all his parts, and, generally, that he is capable of corruption, if there be any one to corrupt him, but that he has the good fortune to escape corruption, because there is none to corrupt. Whereas the doctrine of the Jews and Christians, which preserves the immutability and unalterableness of the divine nature, is stigmatized as impious, because it does not partake of the profanity of those whose notions of God are marked by impiety, but because it says in the supplication addressed to the Divinity, "Thou art the same," it being, moreover, an article of faith that God has said, "I change not."

Chapter XXIII

After this, Celsus next asserts that "Those herdsmen and shepherds who followed Moses as their leader, had their minds deluded by vulgar deceits, and so supposed that there was one God." Let him show, then, how, after this irrational departure, as he regards it, of the herdsmen and shepherds from the worship of many gods, he himself is able to establish the multiplicity of deities that are found amongst the Greeks, or among those other nations that are called Barbarian. Let him establish, therefore, the existence of Mnemosyne, the mother of the Muses by Zeus; or of Themis, the parent of the Hours; or let him prove that the ever naked Graces can have a real, substantial existence. But he will not be able to show, from any actions of theirs, that these fictitious representations of the Greeks, which have the appearance of being invested with bodies, are (really) gods. And why should the fables of the Greeks regarding the gods be true, any more than those of the Egyptians for example, who in their language know nothing of a Mnemosyne, mother of the nine Muses; nor of a Themis, parent of the Hours; nor of a Euphrosyne, one of the Graces; nor of any other of these names? How much more manifest (and how much better than all these inventions!) is it that, convinced by what we see, in the admirable order of the world, we should worship the Maker of it as the one Author of one effect, and which, as being wholly in harmony with itself, cannot on that account have been the work of many makers; and that we should believe that the whole heaven is not held together by the movements of many souls, for one is enough, which bears the whole of the non-wandering sphere from east to west, and embraces within it all things which the world requires, and which are not self-existing! For all are parts of the world, while God is no part of the whole. But God cannot be imperfect, as a part is imperfect. And perhaps profounder consideration will show, that as God is not a part, so neither is He properly the whole, since the whole is composed of parts; and reason will not allow us to believe that the God who is over all is composed of parts, each one of which cannot do what all the other parts, can.

Origen *Contra Celsum*, Book VI

Chapter XLIX

Let us notice now what follows, where, expressing in a single word his opinion regarding the Mosaic cosmogony, without offering, however, a single argument in its support, he finds fault with it, saying: "Moreover, their cosmogony is extremely silly." Now, if he had produced some credible proofs of its silly character, we should have endeavoured to answer them; but it does not appear to me reasonable that I should be called upon to demonstrate, in answer to his mere assertion, that it is not "silly." If any one, however, wishes to see the reasons which led us to accept the Mosaic account, and the arguments by which it may be defended, he may read what we have written upon Genesis, from the beginning of the book up to the passage, "And this is the book of the generation of men," where we have tried to show from the holy Scriptures themselves what the "heaven" was which was created in the beginning; and what the "earth," and the "invisible part of the earth," and that which was "without form; " and what the "deep" was, and the "darkness" that was upon it; and what the "water" was, and the "Spirit of God" which was "borne over it; "and what the "light" which was created, and what the "firmament," as distinct from the "heaven" which was created in the beginning; and so on with the other subjects that follow.

Celsus has also expressed his opinion that the narrative of the creation of man is "exceedingly silly," without stating any proofs, or endeavouring to answer our arguments; for he had no evidence, in my judgment, which was fitted to overthrow the statement that "man has been made in the image of God." He does not even understand the meaning of the "Paradise" that was planted by God, and of the life which man first led in it; and of that which resulted from accident, when man was cast forth on account of his sin, and was settled opposite the Paradise of delight. Now, as he asserts that these are silly statements, let him turn his attention not merely to each one of them (in general), but to this in particular, "He placed the cherubim, and the flaming sword, which turned every way, to keep the way of the tree of life," and say whether Moses wrote these words with no serious object in view, but in the spirit of the writers of the old Comedy, who have sportively related that "Proetus slew Bellerophon," and that "Pegasus came from Arcadia." Now their object was to create laughter in composing such stories; whereas it is incredible that he who left behind him laws for a whole nation, regarding which he wished to persuade his subjects that they were given by God, should have written words so little to the purpose, and have said without any meaning, "He placed the cherubim, and the flaming sword, which turned every way, to keep the way of the tree of life," or made any other statement regarding the creation of man, which is the subject of philosophic investigation by the Hebrew sages.

Chapter L

In the next place, Celsus, after heaping together, simply as mere assertions, the varying opinions of some of the ancients regarding the world, and the origin of man, alleges that "Moses and the prophets, who have left to us our books, not knowing at all what the nature of the world is, and of man, have woven together a web of sheer nonsense." If he had shown, now, how it appeared to him that the holy Scriptures contained "sheer nonsense," we should have tried to demolish the arguments which appeared to him to establish their nonsensical character; but on the present occasion, following his own example, we also sportively give it as our opinion that Celsus, knowing nothing at all about the nature of the meaning and language of the prophets, composed a work which contained "sheer nonsense," and boastfully gave it the title of a "true discourse."

And since he makes the statements about the "days of creation" ground of accusation – as if he understood them clearly and correctly, some of which elapsed before the creation of light and heaven, and sun, and moon, and stars, and some of them after the creation of these – we shall only make this observation, that Moses must then have forgotten that he had said a little before, "that in six days the creation of the world had been finished," and that in consequence of this act of forgetfulness he subjoins to these words the following: "This is the book of the creation of man, in the day when God made the heaven and the earth!" But it is not in the least credible, that after what he had said respecting, the six days, Moses should immediately add, without a special meaning, the words, "in the day that God made the heavens and the earth; "and if any one thinks that these words may be referred to the statement, "In the beginning God made the heaven and the earth," let him observe that before the words, "Let there be light, and there was light," and these, "God called the light day," it has been stated that "in the beginning God made the heaven and the earth."

Chapter LI

On the present occasion, however, it is not our object to enter into an explanation of the subject of intelligent and sensible beings, nor of the manner in which the different kinds of days were allotted to both sorts, nor to investigate the details which belong to the subject, for we should need whole treatises for the exposition of the Mosaic cosmogony; and that work we had already performed, to the best of our ability, a considerable time before the commencement of this answer to Celsus, when we discussed with such measure of capacity as we then possessed the question of the Mosaic cosmogony of the six days.

We must keep in mind, however, that the Word promises to the righteous through the mouth of Isaiah, that days will come when not the sun, but the Lord Himself, will be to them an everlasting light, and God will be their glory. And it is from misunderstanding, I think, some pestilent heresy which gave an erroneous interpretation to the words, "Let there be light," as if they were the expression of a wish merely on the part of the Creator, that Celsus made the remark: "The Creator did not borrow light from above, like those persons who kindle their lamps at those of their neighbours." Misunderstanding, moreover, another impious heresy, he has said: "If, indeed, there did exist an accursed god opposed to the great God, who did this contrary to his approval, why did he lend him the light?" So far are we from offering a defence of such puerilities, that we desire, on the contrary, distinctly to arraign the statements of these heretics as erroneous, and to undertake to refute, not those of their opinions with which we are unacquainted, as Celsus does, but those of which we have attained an accurate knowledge, derived in part from the statements of their own adherents, and partly from a careful perusal of their writings.

Chapter LII

Celsus proceeds as follows: "With regard to the origin of the world and its destruction, whether it is to be regarded as uncreated and indestructible, or as created indeed, but not destructible, or the reverse, I at present say nothing." For this reason we too say nothing on these points, as the work in hand does not require it. Nor do we allege that the Spirit of the universal God mingled itself in things here below as in things alien to itself, as might appear from the expression, "The Spirit of God moved upon the water;" nor do we assert that certain wicked devices directed against His Spirit as if by a different creator from the great God, and which were tolerated by the Supreme Divinity, needed to be completely frustrated.

And, accordingly, I have nothing further to say to those who utter such absurdities; nor to Celsus, who does not refute them with ability. For he ought either not to have mentioned such matters at all, or else, in keeping with that character for philanthropy which he assumes, have carefully set them forth, and then endeavoured to rebut these impious assertions.

Nor have we ever heard that the great God, after giving his spirit to the creator, demands it back again. Proceeding next foolishly to assail these impious assertions, he asks: "What god gives anything with the intention of demanding it back? For it is the mark of a needy person to demand back (what he has given), whereas God stands in need of nothing." To this he adds, as if saying something clever against certain parties: "Why, when he lent (his spirit), was he ignorant that he was lending it to an evil being? "He asks, further: "Why does he pass without notice a wicked creator who was counter-working his purposes? "

Chapter LIII

In the next place, mixing up together various heresies, and not observing that some statements are the utterances of one heretical sect, and others of a different one, he brings forward the objections which we raised against Marcion. And, probably, having heard them from some paltry and ignorant individuals, he assails the very arguments which combat them, but not in a way that Shows much intelligence.

Quoting then our arguments against Marcion, and not observing that it is against Marcion that he is speaking, he asks: "Why does he send secretly, and destroy the works which he has created? Why does he secretly employ force, and persuasion, and deceit? Why does he allure those who, as ye assert, have been condemned or accused by him, and carry them away like a slave-dealer? Why does he teach them to steal away from their Lord? Why to flee from their father? Why does he claim them for himself against the father's will? Why does he profess to be the father of strange children?"

To these questions he subjoins the following remark, as if by way of expressing his surprise: "Venerable, indeed, is the god who desires to be the father of those sinners who are condemned by another (god), and of the needy, and, as themselves say, of the very offscourings (of men), and who is unable to capture and punish his messenger, who escaped from him!" After this, as if addressing us who acknowledge that this world is not the work of a different and strange god, he continues in the following strain: "If these are his works, how is it that God created evil? And how is it that he cannot persuade and admonish (men)? And how is it that he repents on account of the ingratitude and wickedness of men? He finds fault, moreover, with his own handwork, and hates, and threatens, and destroys his own offspring? Whither can he transport them out of this world, which he himself has made?"

Now it does not appear to me that by these remarks he makes clear what "evil" is; and although there have been among the Greeks many sects who differ as to the nature of good and evil, he hastily concludes, as if it were a consequence of our maintaining that this world also is a work of the universal God, that in our judgment God is the author of evil. Let it be, however, regarding evil as it may –

whether created by God or not – it nevertheless follows only as a result when you compare the principal design. And I am greatly surprised if the inference regarding God's authorship of evil, which he thinks follows from our maintaining that this world also is the work of the universal God, does not follow too from his own statements. For one might say to Celsus: "If these are His works, how is it that God created evil? And, how is it that He cannot persuade and admonish men?" It is indeed the greatest error in reasoning to accuse those who are of different opinions of holding unsound doctrines, when the accuser himself is much more liable to the same charge with regard to his own.

Chapter LIV

Let us see, then, briefly what holy Scripture has to say regarding good and evil, and what answer we are to return to the questions, "How is it that God created evil?" and, "How is He incapable of persuading and admonishing men?" Now, according to holy Scripture, properly speaking, virtues and virtuous actions are good, as, properly speaking, the reverse of these are evil. We shall be satisfied with quoting on the present occasion some verses from the Psalms 34, to the following effect: "They that seek the Lord shall not want any good thing. Come, ye children, hearken unto me; I will teach you the fear of the Lord. What man is he that desireth life, and loveth many days, that he may see good? Keep thy tongue from evil, and thy lips from speaking guile. Depart from evil, and do good."

Now, the injunctions to "depart from evil, and to do good," do not refer either to corporeal evils or corporeal blessings, as they are termed by some, nor to external things at all, but to blessings and evils of a spiritual kind; since he who departs from such evils, and performs such virtuous actions, will, as one who desires the true life, come to the enjoyment of it; and as one loving to see "good days," in which the word of righteousness will be the Sun, he will see them, God taking him away from this "present evil world," and from those evil days concerning which Paul said: "Redeeming the time, because the days are evil."

Chapter LV

Passages, indeed, might be found where corporeal and external (benefits) are improperly called "good," – those things, viz., which contribute to the natural life, while those which do the reverse are termed "evil." It is in this sense that Job says to his wife: "If we have received good at the hand of the Lord, shall we not also receive evil!"

Since, then, there is found in the sacred Scriptures, in a certain passage, this statement put into the mouth of God, "I make peace, and create evil;" and again another, where it is said of Him that "evil came down from the Lord to the gate of Jerusalem, the noise of chariots and horsemen," – passages which have disturbed many readers of Scripture, who are unable to see what Scripture means by "good" and "evil," – it is probable that Celsus, being perplexed thereby, gave utterance to the question, "How is it that God created evil?" Or, perhaps, having heard some one discussing the matters relating to it in an ignorant manner, he made this statement which we have noticed.

We, on the other hand, maintain that "evil," or "wickedness," and the actions which proceed from it, were not created by God. For if God created that which is really evil, how was it possible that the proclamation regarding (the last) judgment should be confidently announced, which informs us that the wicked are to be punished for their evil deeds in proportion to the amount of their wickedness, while those who have lived a virtuous life, or performed virtuous actions, will be in the enjoyment of blessedness, and will receive rewards from God?

I am well aware that those who would daringly assert that these evils were created by God will quote certain expressions of Scripture (in their support), because we are not able to show one consistent series of passages; for although Scripture (generally) blames the wicked and approves of the righteous, it nevertheless contains some statements which, although comparatively few in number, seem to disturb the minds of ignorant readers of holy Scripture. I have not, however, deemed it appropriate to my present treatise to quote on the present occasion those discordant statements, which are many in number, and their explanations, which would require a long array of proofs. Evils, then, if those be meant which are properly so called, were not created by God; but some, although few in comparison with the order of the whole world, have resulted from His principal works, as there follow from the chief works of the carpenter such things as spiral shavings and sawdust, or as architects might appear to be the cause of the rubbish which lies around their buildings in the form of the filth which drops from the stones and the plaster.

Chapter LVI

If we speak, however, of what are called "corporeal" and "external" evils – which are improperly so termed – then it may be granted that there are occasions when some of these have been called into existence by God, in order that by their means the conversion of certain individuals might be effected. And what absurdity would follow from such a course? For as, if we should hear those sufferings improperly termed "evils" which are inflicted by fathers, and instructors, and pedagogues upon those who are under their care, or upon patients who are operated upon or cauterized by the surgeons in order to effect a cure, we were to say that a father was ill-treating his son, or pedagogues and instructors their pupils, or physicians their patients, no blame would be laid upon the operators or chastisers; so, in the same way, if God is said to bring upon men such evils for the conversion and cure of those who need this discipline, there would be no absurdity in the view, nor would "evils come down from the Lord upon the gates of Jerusalem," – which evils consist of the punishments inflicted upon the Israelites by their enemies with a view to their conversion; nor would one visit "with a rod the transgressions of those who forsake the law of the Lord, and their iniquities with stripes;" nor could it be said, "Thou hast coals of fire to set upon them; they shall be to thee a help."

In the same way also we explain the expressions, "I, who make peace, and create evil;" for He calls into existence "corporeal" or "external" evils, while purifying and training those who would not be disciplined by the word and sound doctrine. This, then, is our answer to the question, "How is it that God created evil? "

Chapter LIX

Celsus, in the next place, suspecting, or perhaps seeing clearly enough, the answer which might be returned by those who defend the destruction of men by the deluge, continues: "But if he does not destroy his own offspring, whither does he convey them out of this world which he himself created?" To this we reply, that God by no means removes out of the whole world, consisting of heaven and earth, those who suffered death by the deluge, but removes them from a life in the flesh, and, having set them free from their bodies, liberates them at the same time from an existence upon earth, which in many parts of Scripture it is usual to call the "world."

In the Gospel according to John especially, we may frequently find the regions of earth termed "world," as in the passage, "He was the true Light, which lighteneth every man that cometh into the 'world;'" as also in this, "In the world ye shall have tribulation; but be of good cheer, I have overcome the world." If, then, we understand by "removing out of the world" a transference from "regions on earth," there is nothing absurd in the expression.

If, on the contrary, the system of things which consists of heaven and earth be termed "world," then those who perished in the deluge are by no means removed out of the so-called "world." And yet, indeed, if we have regard to the words, "Looking not at the things which are seen, but at the things which are not seen;" and also to these, "For the invisible things of Him from the creation of the world are clearly seen, being understood by the things that are made," – we might say that he who dwells amid the "invisible" things, and what are called generally "things not seen," is gone out of the world, the Word having removed him hence, and transported him to the heavenly regions, in order to behold all beautiful things.

Chapter LX

But after this investigation of his assertions, as if his object were to swell his book by many words, he repeats, in different language, the same charges which we have examined a little ago, saying: "By far the most silly thing is the distribution of the creation of the world over certain days, before days existed: for, as the heaven was not yet created, nor the foundation of the earth yet laid, nor the sun yet revolving, how could there be days?" Now, what difference is there between these words and the following: "Moreover, taking and looking at these things from the beginning, would it not be absurd in the first and greatest God to issue the command, Let this (first thing) come into existence, and this second thing, and this (third); and after accomplishing so much on the first day, to do so much more again on the second, and third, and fourth, and fifth, and sixth?" We answered to the best of our ability this objection to God's "commanding this first, second, and third thing to be created," when we quoted the words, "He said, and it was done; He commanded, and all things stood fast;" remarking that the immediate Creator, and, as it were, very Maker of the world was the Word, the Son of God; while the Father of the Word, by commanding His own Son – the Word – to create the world, is primarily Creator.

And with regard to the creation of the light upon the first day, and of the firmament upon the second, and of the gathering together of the waters that are under the heaven into their several reservoirs on the third (the earth thus causing to sprout forth those (fruits) which are under the control of nature alone, and of the (great) lights and stars upon the fourth, and of aquatic animals upon the fifth, and of land animals and man upon the sixth, we have treated to the best of our ability in our notes upon Genesis, as well as in the foregoing pages, when we found fault with those who, taking the words in their apparent signification, said that the time of six days was occupied in the creation of the world, and quoted the words: "These are the generations of the heavens and of the earth when they were created, in the day that the Lord God made the earth and the heavens."

Chapter LXI

Again, not understanding the meaning of the words, "And God ended on the sixth day His works which He had made, and ceased on the seventh day from all His works which He had made: and God blessed the seventh day, and hollowed it, because on it He had ceased from all His works which He had begun to make;" and imagining the expression, "He ceased on the seventh day," to be the same as this, "He rested on the seventh day," he makes the remark: "After this, indeed, he is weary, like a very bad workman, who stands in need of rest to refresh himself!" For he knows nothing of the day of the Sabbath and rest of God, which follows the completion of the world's creation, and which lasts during the duration of the world, and in which all those will keep festival with God who have done all their works in their six days, and who, because they have omitted none of their duties, will ascend to the contemplation (of celestial things), and to the assembly of righteous and blessed beings.

In the next place, as if either the Scriptures made such a statement, or as if we ourselves so spoke of God as having rested from fatigue, he continues: "It is not in keeping with the fitness of things that the first God should feel fatigue, or work with His hands, or give forth commands." Celsus says, that "it is not in keeping with the fitness of things that the first God should feel fatigue."

Now we would say that neither does God the Word feel fatigue, nor any of those beings who belong to a better and diviner order of things, because the sensation of fatigue is peculiar to those who are in the body. You can examine whether this is true of those who possess a body of any kind, or of those who have an earthly body, or one a little better than this. But "neither is it consistent with the fitness of things that the first God should work with His own hands." If you understand the words "work with His own hands" literally, then neither are they applicable to the second God, nor to any other being partaking of divinity.

But suppose that they are spoken in an improper and figurative sense, so that we may translate the following expressions, "And the firmament showeth forth His handywork," and "the heavens are the work of Thy hands," and any other similar phrases, in a figurative manner, so far as respects the "hands" and "limbs" of Deity, where is the absurdity in the words, "God thus working with His own hands?" And as there is no absurdity in God thus working, so neither is there in His issuing "commands;" so that what is done at His bidding should be beautiful and praiseworthy, because it was God who commanded it to be performed.

Chapter LXII

Celsus, again, having perhaps misunderstood the words, "For the mouth of the Lord hath spoken it," or perhaps because some ignorant individuals had rashly ventured upon the explanation of such things, and not understanding, moreover, on what principles parts called after the names of the bodily members are assigned to the attributes of God, asserts: "He has neither mouth nor voice."

Truly, indeed, God can have no voice, if the voice is a concussion of the air, or a stroke on the air, or a species of air, or any other definition which may be given to the voice by those who are skilled in such matters; but what is called the "voice of God" is said to be seen as "God's voice" by the people in the passage; "And all the people saw the voice of God;" the word "saw" being taken, agreeably to the custom of Scripture, in a spiritual sense.

Moreover, he alleges that "God possesses nothing else of which we have any knowledge; "but of what things we have knowledge he gives no indication. If he means "limbs," we agree with him, understanding the things "of which we have knowledge" to be those called corporeal, and pretty generally so termed. But if we are to understand the words "of which we have knowledge" in a universal sense, then there are many things of which we have knowledge, (and which may be attributed to God); for He possesses virtue, and blessedness, and divinity.

If we, however, put a higher meaning upon the words, "of which we have knowledge," since all that we know is less than God, there is no absurdity in our also admitting that God possesses none of those things "of which we have knowledge." For the attributes which belong to God are far superior to all things with which not merely the nature of man is acquainted, but even that of those who have risen far above it. And if he had read the writings of the prophets, David on the one hand saying, "But Thou art the same," and Malachi on the other, "I am (the Lord), and change not," he would have observed that none of us assert that there is any change in God, either in act or thought. For abiding the same, He administers mutable things according to their nature, and His word elects to undertake their administration.

Origen *Commentary on the Gospel of John*, Book 1

16. Meaning of "Beginning" (1) in Space

"In the beginning was the Word." It is not only the Greeks who consider the word "beginning" to have many meanings. Let any one collect the Scripture passages in which the word occurs, and with a view to an accurate interpretation of it note what it stands for in each passage, and he will find that the word has many meanings in sacred discourse also.

We speak of a beginning in reference to a transition. Here it has to do with a road and with length. This appears in the saying: "The beginning of a good way is to do justice." For since the good way is long, there have first to be considered in reference to it the question connected with action, and this side is presented in the words "to do justice;" the contemplative side comes up for consideration afterwards. In the latter the end of it comes to rest at last in the so-called restoration of all things, since no enemy is left them to fight against, if that be true which is said: "For He must reign until He have placed His enemies under His feet. But the last enemy to be destroyed is death." For then but one activity will be left for those who have come to God on account of His word which is with Him, that, namely, of knowing God, so that, being found by the knowledge of the Father, they may all be His Son, as now no one but the Son knows the Father.

For should any one enquire carefully at what time those are to know the Father to whom He who knows the Father reveals Him, and should he consider how a man now sees only through a glass and in a riddle, never having learned to know as he ought to know, he would be justified in saying that no one, no apostle even, and no prophet had known the Father, but when he became one with Him as a son and a father are one.

And if any one says that it is a digression which has led us to this point, our consideration of that one meaning of the word beginning, we must show that the digression is necessary and useful for the end we have in view. For if we speak of a beginning in the case of a transition, and of a way and its length, and if we are told that the beginning of a good way is to do justice, then it concerns us to know in what manner every good way has for its beginning to do justice, and how after such beginning it arrives at contemplation, and in what manner it thus arrives at contemplation.

17. (2) in Time – The Beginning of Creation

Again, there is a beginning in a matter of origin, as might appear in the saying: "In the beginning God made the heaven and the earth." This meaning, however, appears more plainly in the Book of Job in the passage: "This is the beginning of God's creation, made for His angels to mock at." One would suppose that the heavens and the earth were made first, of all that was made at the creation of the world. But the second passage suggests a better view, namely, that as many beings were framed with a body, the first made of these was the creature called dragon, but called in another passage the great whale (leviathan) which the Lord tamed.

We must ask about this; whether, when the saints were living a blessed life apart from matter and from any body, the dragon, falling from the pure life, became fit to be bound in matter and in a body, so that the Lord could say, speaking through storm and clouds, "This is the beginning of the creation of God, made for His angels to mock at." It is possible, however, that the dragon is not positively the beginning of the creation of the Lord, but that there were many creatures made with a body for the angels to mock at, and that the dragon was the first of these, while others could subsist in a body without such reproach. But it is not so. For the soul of the sun is placed in a body, and the whole creation, of which the Apostle says: "The whole creation groaneth and travaileth in pain together until now," and perhaps the following is about the same: "The creation was made subject to vanity, not willingly, but on account of Him who subjected it for hope; "so that bodies might be in vanity, and doing the things of the body, as he who is in the body must... One who is in the body does the things of the body, though unwillingly.

Wherefore the creation was made subject to vanity, not willingly, but he who does unwillingly the things of the body does what he does for the sake of hope, as if we should say that Paul desired to remain in the flesh, not willingly, but on account of hope. For though he thought it better to be dissolved and to be with Christ, it was not unreasonable that he should wish to remain in the flesh for the sake of the benefit to others and of advancement in the things hoped for, not only by him, but also by those benefited by him.

This meaning of the term "beginning," as of origin, will serve us also in the passage in which Wisdom speaks in the Proverbs. "God," we read, "created me the beginning of His ways, for His works." Here the term could be interpreted as in the first application we spoke of, that of a way: "The Lord," it says, "created me the beginning of His ways." One might assert, and with reason, that God Himself is the beginning of all things, and might go on to say, as is plain, that the Father is the beginning of the Son; and the demiurge the beginning of the works of the demiurge, and that God in a word is the beginning of all that exists. This view is supported by our: "In the beginning was the Word." In the Word one may see the Son, and because He is in the Father He may be said to be in the beginning.

18. (3) of Substance

In the third place a beginning may be that out of which a thing comes, the underlying matter from which things are formed. This, however, is the view of those who hold matter itself to be uncreated, a view which we believers cannot share, since we believe God to have made the things that are out of the things which are not, as the mother of the seven martyrs in the Maccabees teaches, and as the angel of repentance in the Shepherd inculcated.

19. (4) of Type and Copy

In addition to these meanings there is that in which we speak of an arche, according to form; thus if the first-born of every creature is the image of the invisible God, then the Father is his arche. In the same way Christ is the arche of those who are made according to the image of God. For if men are according to the image, but the image according to the Father; in the first case the Father is the arche of Christ, and in the other Christ is the arche of men, and men are made, not according to that of which he is the image, but according to the image. With this example our passage will agree: "In the arche was the Word."

20. (5) of Elements and What is Formed from Them

There is also an arche in a matter of learning, as when we say that the letters are the arche of grammar. The Apostle accordingly says: "When by reason of the time you ought to be teachers, you have need again that some one teach you what are the elements of the arche of the oracles of God." Now the arche spoken of in connection with learning is twofold; first in respect of its nature, secondly in its relation to us; as we might say of Christ, that by nature His arche is deity, but that in relation to us who cannot, for its very greatness, command the whole truth about Him, His arche is His manhood, as He is preached to babes, "Jesus Christ and Him crucified." In this view, then, Christ is the arche of learning in His own nature, because He is the wisdom and power of God; but for us, the Word was made flesh, that He might tabernacle among us who could only thus at first receive Him. And perhaps this is the reason why He is not only the firstborn of all creation, but is also designated the man, Adam. For Paul says He is Adam: "The last Adam was made a life-giving spirit."

21. (6) of Design and Execution

Again we speak of the arche of an action, in which there is a design which appears after the beginning. It may be considered whether wisdom is to be regarded as the arche of the works of God because it is in this way the principle of them.

22. The Word Was in the Beginning, i.e., in Wisdom, Which Contained All Things in Idea, Before They Existed. Christ's Character as Wisdom is Prior to His Other Characters

So many meanings occur to us at once of the word arche. We have now to ask which of them we should adopt for our text, "In the beginning was the Word." It is plain that we may at once dismiss the meaning which connects it with transition or with a road and its length. Nor, it is pretty plain, will the meaning connected with an origin serve our purpose.

One might, however, think of the sense in which it points to the author, to that which brings about the effect, if, as we read, "God commanded and they were created." For Christ is, in a manner, the demiurge, to whom the Father says, "Let there be light," and "Let there be a firmament." But Christ is demiurge as a beginning (arche), inasmuch as He is wisdom. It is in virtue of His being wisdom that He is called arche. For Wisdom says in Solomon: "God created me the beginning of His ways, for His works," so that the Word might be in an arche, namely, in wisdom. Considered in relation to the structure of contemplation and thoughts about the whole of things, it is regarded as wisdom; but in relation to that side of the objects of thought, in which reasonable beings apprehend them, it is considered as the Word. And there is no wonder, since, as we have said before, the Saviour is many good things, if He comprises in Himself thoughts of the first order, and of the second, and of the third. This is what John suggested when he said about the Word: "That which was made was life in Him." Life then came in the Word. And on the one side the Word is no other than the Christ, the Word, He who was with the Father, by whom all things were made; while, on the other side, the Life is no other than the Son of God, who says: "I am the way and the truth and the life."

As, then, life came into being in the Word, so the Word in the arche. Consider, however, if we are at liberty to take this meaning of arche for our text: "In the beginning was the Word," so as to obtain the meaning that all things came into being according to wisdom and according to the models of the system which are present in his thoughts. For I consider that as a house or a ship is built and fashioned in accordance with the sketches of the builder or designer, the house or the ship having their beginning (arche) in the sketches and reckonings in his mind, so all things came into being in accordance with the designs of what was to be, clearly laid down by God in wisdom. And we should add that having created, so to speak, ensouled wisdom, He left her to hand over, from the types which were in her, to things existing and to matter, the actual emergence of them, their moulding and their forms. But I consider, if it be permitted to say this, that the beginning (arche) of real existence was the Son of God, saying: "I am the beginning and the end, the A and the Ω, the first and the last."

We must, however, remember that He is not the arche in respect of every name which is applied to Him. For how can He be the beginning in respect of His being life, when life came in the Word, and the Word is manifestly the arche of life? It is also tolerably evident that He cannot be the arche in respect of His being the first-born from the dead. And if we go through all His titles carefully we find that He is the arche only in respect of His being wisdom. Not even as the Word is He the arche, for the Word was in the arche. And so one might venture to say that wisdom is anterior to all the thoughts that are expressed in the titles of the first-born of every creature.

Now God is altogether one and simple; but our Saviour, for many reasons, since God set Him forth a propitiation and a first fruits of the whole creation, is made many things, or perhaps all these things; the whole creation, so far as capable of redemption, stands in need of Him. And, hence, He is made the light of men, because men, being darkened by wickedness, need the light that shines in darkness, and is not overtaken by the darkness; had not men been in darkness, He would not have become the light of men.

The same thing may be observed in respect of His being the first-born of the dead. For supposing the woman had not been deceived, and Adam had not fallen, and man created for incorruption had obtained it, then He would not have descended into the grave, nor would He have died, there being no sin, nor would His love of men have required that He should die, and if He had not died, He could not have been the first-born of the dead. We may also ask whether He would ever have become a shepherd, had man not been thrown together with the beasts which are devoid of reason, and made like to them. For if God saves man and beasts, He saves those beasts which He does save, by giving them a shepherd, since they cannot have a king.

Thus if we collect the titles of Jesus, the question arises which of them were conferred on Him later, and would never have assumed such importance if the saints had begun and had also persevered in blessedness. Perhaps Wisdom would be the only remaining one, or perhaps the Word would remain too, or perhaps the Life, or perhaps the Truth, not the others, which He took for our sake. And happy indeed are those who in their need for the Son of God have yet become such persons as not to need Him in His character as a physician healing the sick, nor in that of a shepherd, nor in that of redemption, but only in His characters as wisdom, as the word and righteousness, or if there be any other title suitable for those who are so perfect as to receive Him in His fairest characters. So much for the phrase "In the beginning."

Lactantius

Lactantius (c. 240 – c. 320) was a Latin apologist. Emperor Diocletian appointed him as a teacher of Latin rhetoric in Nicomedia, but he was deprived of that post when he converted to Christianity in 303. He was later appointed by Emperor Constantine as a tutor for his eldest son (c. 313).

In the Middle Ages, Western humanists thought so highly of his rhetorical abilities that they referred to him as the "Christian Cicero." Lactantius consciously modeled himself on Cicero and thought that Christianity needed to be presented with appeal and charm if it was to be taken seriously by the learned and to find a place in the educational curriculum.

In his main work, *The Divine Institutes*, Lactantius attempts to refute pagan errors and to confirm the true Faith. His theology is pre-Nicene, showing the influence of Origen in subordinating the Son to the Father (contrary to subsequent Trinitarian theology). Lactantius is not the profoundest of theologians, but his work is of interest for its engagement with pagan learning. He often quotes philosophers and poets and draws on them while refuting their perceived errors. Thus, he regards as true the myth of Prometheus, in which humanity is formed from clay; only the poets got the name of the Creator wrong. The true story, as given by Moses, was distorted in oral transmission.

Lactantius affirms creation out of nothing against poets and philosophers who hold opposing views. He considers that each animal kind was created as a male-female pair, which then populated the earth through reproduction. He takes as a general principle that "nothing can exist in the world which does not continue permanent as it began." He then uses this anti-evolutionary principle to refute Lucretius, who held that animals were initially born out of the soil and only later developed the power of generation.

For Lactantius, God did not need to create the world nor did He make it for His own sake; rather, He made it for the sake of living things, and especially for humans.

Lactantius *The Divine Institutes*, Book II

Chapter IX – Of the Devil, the World, God, Providence, Man, and His Wisdom

I will therefore set forth the method of all these things, that difficult and obscure subjects may be more easily understood; and I will bring to light all these deceptions of the pretended deity, led by which men have departed very far from the way of truth. But I will retrace the matter far back from its source; that if any, unacquainted with the truth and ignorant, shall apply himself to the reading of this book, he may be instructed, and may understand what can in truth be "the source and origin of these evils;" and having received light, may perceive his own errors and those of the whole human race.

Since God was possessed of the greatest foresight for planning, and of the greatest skill for carrying out in action, before He commenced this business of the world – inasmuch as there was in Him, and always is, the fountain of full and most complete goodness – in order that goodness might spring as a stream from Him, and might flow forth afar, He produced a Spirit like to Himself, who might be endowed with the perfections of God the Father. But how He willed that, I will endeavour to show in the fourth book.

Then He made another being, in whom the disposition of the divine origin did not remain. Therefore he was infected with his own envy as with poison, and passed from good to evil; and at his own will, which had been given to him by God unfettered, he acquired for himself a contrary name. From which it appears that the source of all evils is envy. For he envied his predecessor, who through his stedfastness is acceptable and dear to God the Father. This being, who from good became evil by his own act, is called by the Greeks diabolus: we call him accuser, because he reports to God the faults to which he himself entices us.

God, therefore, when He began the fabric of the world, set over the whole work that first and greatest Son, and used Him at the same time as a counsellor and artificer, in planning, arranging, and accomplishing, since He is complete both in knowledge, and judgment, and power; concerning whom I now speak more sparingly, because in another place both His excellence, and His name, and His nature must be related by us.

Let no one inquire of what materials God made these works so great and wonderful: for He made all things out of nothing. Nor are the poets to be listened to, who say that in the beginning was a chaos, that is, a confusion of matter and the elements; but that God afterwards divided all that mass, and having separated each object from the confused heap, and arranged them in order, He constructed and adorned the world.

Now it is easy to reply to these persons, who do not understand the power of God: for they believe that He can produce nothing, except out of materials already existing and prepared; in which error philosophers also were involved. For Cicero, while discussing the nature of the gods, thus speaks: "first of all, therefore, it is not probable that the matter from which all things arose was made by divine providence, but that it has, and has had, a force and nature of its own. As therefore the builder, when he is about to erect any building, does not himself make the materials, but uses those which are already prepared, and the statuary also uses the wax; so that divine providence ought to have had materials at hand, not of its own production, but already prepared for use. But if matter was not made by God, then neither was the earth, and water, and air, and fire, made by God."

Oh, how many faults there are in these ten lines first, that he who in almost all his other disputations and books was a maintainer of the divine providence, and who used very acute arguments in assailing those who denied the existence of a providence, now himself, as a traitor or deserter, endeavoured to take away providence; in whose case, if you wish to oppose him, neither consideration nor labour is required: it is only necessary to remind him of his own words. For it will be impossible for Cicero to be more strongly refuted by any one than by Cicero himself.

But let us make this concession to the custom and practice of the Academics, that men are permitted to speak with great freedom, and to entertain what sentiments they may wish. Let us examine the sentiments themselves. It is not probable, he says, that matter was made by God. By what arguments do you prove this? For you gave no reason for its being improbable. Therefore, on the contrary, it appears to me exceedingly probable; nor does it appear so without reason, when I reflect that there is something more in God, whom you verily reduce to the weakness of man, to whom you allow nothing else but the mere workmanship.

In what respect, then, will that divine power differ from man, if God also, as man does, stands in need of the assistance of another? But He does stand in need of it, if He can construct nothing unless He is furnished with materials by another. But if this is the case, it is plain that His power is imperfect, and he who prepared the material must be judged more powerful. By what name, therefore, shall he be called who excels God in power? – since it is greater to make that which is one's own, than to arrange those things which are another's. But if it is impossible that anything should be more powerful than God, who must necessarily be of perfect strength, power, and intelligence, it follows that He who made the things which are composed of matter, made matter also. For it was neither possible nor befitting that anything should exist without the exercise of God's power, or against His will.

But it is probable, he says, that matter has, and always has had, a force and nature of its own. What force could it have, without any one to give it? What nature, without any one to produce it? If it had force, it took that force from some one. But from whom could it take it, unless it were from God? Moreover, if it had a nature, which plainly is so called from being produced, it must have been produced. But from whom could it have derived its existence, except God? For nature, from which you say that all things had their origin, if it has no understanding, can make nothing. But if it has the power of producing and making, then it has understanding, and must be God. For that force can be called by no other name, in which there is both the foresight to plan, and the skill and power to carry into effect.

Therefore Seneca, the most intelligent of all the Stoics, says better, who saw "that nature was nothing else but God." Therefore he says, "Shall we not praise God, who possesses natural excellence?" For He did not learn it from any one. Yes, truly, we will praise Him; for although it is natural to Him, He gave it to Himself, since God Himself is nature. When, therefore, you assign the origin of all things to nature, and take it from God, you are in the same difficulty – "You pay your debt by borrowing, Geta." For while simply changing the name, you clearly admit that it was made by the same person by whom you deny that it was made.

There follows a most senseless comparison. "As the builder," he says, "when he is about to erect any building, does not himself make the materials, but uses those which are already prepared, and the statuary also the wax; so that divine providence ought to have had materials at hand, not of its own production, but already prepared for use." Nay rather it ought not; for God will have less power if He makes from materials already provided, which is the part of man.

The builder will erect nothing without wood, for he cannot make the wood itself; and not to be able to do this is the part of human weakness. But God Himself makes the materials for Himself, because He has the power. For to have the power is the property of God; for if He is not able, He is not God. Man produces his works out of that which already exists, because through his mortality he is weak, and through his weakness his power is limited and moderate; but God produces His works out of that which has no existence, because through His eternity He is strong, and through His strength His power is immense, which has no end or limit, like the life of the Maker Himself.

What wonder, then, if God, when He was about to make the world, first prepared the material from which to make it, and prepared it out of that which had no existence? Because it is impossible for God to borrow anything from another source, inasmuch as all things are in Himself and from Himself. For if there is anything before Him, and if anything has been made, but not by Him, He will therefore lose both the power and the name of God. But it may be said matter was never made, like God, who out of matter made this world.

In that case, it follows that two eternal principles are established, and those indeed opposed to one another, which cannot happen without discord and destruction. For those things which have a contrary force and method must of necessity come into collision. In this manner it will be impossible that both should be eternal, if they are opposed to one another, because one must overpower the other. Therefore the nature of that which is eternal cannot be otherwise than simple, so that all things descended from that source as from a fountain. Therefore either God proceeded from matter, or matter from God. Which of these is more true, is easily understood. For of these two, one is endued with sensibility, the other is insensible. The power of making anything cannot exist, except in that which has sensibility, intelligence, reflection, and the power of motion. Nor can anything be begun, or made, or completed, unless it shall have been foreseen by reason how it shall be made before it exists, and how it shall endure after it has been made. In short, he only makes anything who has the will to make it, and hands to complete that which he has willed. But that which is insensible always lies inactive and torpid; nothing can originate in that source where there is no voluntary motion. For if every animal is possessed of reason, it is certain that it cannot be produced from that which is destitute of reason, nor can that which is not present in the original source be received from any other quarter.

Nor, however, let it disturb any one, that certain animals appear to be born from the earth. For the earth does not give birth to these of itself, but the Spirit of God, without which nothing is produced. Therefore God did not arise from matter, because a being endued with sensibility can never spring from one that is insensible, a wise one from one that is irrational, one that is incapable of suffering from one that can suffer, an incorporeal being from a corporeal one; but matter is rather from God. For whatever consists of a body solid, and capable of being handled, admits of an external force. That which admits of force is capable of dissolution; that which is dissolved perishes; that which perishes must necessarily have had an origin; that which had an origin had a source from which it originated, that is, some maker, who is intelligent, foreseeing, and skilled in making.

There is one assuredly, and that no other than God. And since He is possessed of sensibility, intelligence, providence, power, and vigour, He is able to create and make both animated and inanimate objects, because He has the means of making everything. But matter cannot always have existed, for if it had existed it would be incapable of change. For that which always was, does not cease always to be; and that which had no beginning must of necessity be without an end. Moreover, it is easier for that which had a beginning to be without an end, than for that which had no beginning to have an end.

Therefore if matter was not made, nothing can be made from it. But if nothing can be made from it, then matter itself can have no existence. For matter is that out of which something is made. But everything out of which anything is made, inasmuch as it has received the hand of the artificer, is destroyed, and begins to be some other thing. Therefore, since matter had an end, at the time when the world was made out of it, it also had a beginning. For that which is destroyed was previously built up; that which is loosened was previously bound up; that which is brought to an end was begun.

If, then, it is inferred from its change and end, that matter had a beginning, from whom could that beginning have been, except from God? God, therefore, is the only being who was not made; and therefore He can destroy other things, but He Himself cannot be destroyed. That which was in Him will always be permanent, because He has not been produced or sprung from any other source; nor does His birth depend on any other object, which being changed may cause His dissolution. He is of Himself, as we said in the first book; and therefore He is such as He willed that He should be, incapable of suffering, unchangeable, incorruptible, blessed, and eternal.

But now the conclusion, with which Tully finished the sentiment, is much more absurd. "But if matter," he says, "was not made by God, the earth indeed, and water, and air, and fire, were not made by God." How skilfully he avoided the danger! For he stated the former point as though it required no proof, whereas it was much more uncertain than that on account of which the statement was made.

If matter, he says, was not made by God, the world was not made by God. He preferred to draw a false inference from that which is false, than a true one from that which is true. And though uncertain things ought to be proved from those which are certain, he drew a proof from an uncertainty, to overthrow that which was certain. For, that the world was made by divine providence (not to mention Trismegistus, who proclaims this; not to mention the verses of the Sibyls, who make the same announcement; not to mention the prophets, who with one impulse and with harmonious voice. bear witness that the world was made, and that it was the workmanship of God), even the philosophers almost universally agree; for this is the opinion of the Pythagoreans, the Stoics, and the Peripatetics, who are the chief of every sect.

In short, from those first seven wise men, even to Socrates and Plato, it was held as an acknowledged and undoubted fact; until many ages afterwards the crazy Epicurus lived, who alone ventured to deny that which is most evident, doubtless through the desire of discovering novelties, that he might found a sect in his own name. And because he could find out nothing new, that he might still appear to disagree with the others, he wished to overthrow old opinions. But in this all the philosophers who snarled around him, refuted him.

It is more certain, therefore, that the world was arranged by providence, than that matter was collected by providence. Wherefore he ought not to have supposed that the world was not made by divine providence, because its matter was not made by divine providence; but because the world was made by divine providence, he ought to have concluded that matter also was made by the Deity. For it is more credible that matter was made by God, because He is all-powerful, than that the world was not made by God, because nothing can be made without mind, intelligence, and design.

But this is not the fault of Cicero, but of the sect. For when he had undertaken a disputation, by which he might take away the nature of the gods, respecting which philosophers prated, in his ignorance of the truth he imagined that the Deity must altogether be taken away. He was able therefore to take away the gods, for they had no existence. But when he attempted to overthrow the divine providence, which is in the one God, because he had begun to strive against the truth, his arguments failed, and he necessarily fell into this pitfall, from which he was unable to withdraw himself. Here, then, I hold him firmly fixed; I hold him fastened to the spot, since Lucilius, who disputed on the other side, was silent.

Here, then, is the turning-point; on this everything depends. Let Cotta disentangle himself, if he can, from this difficulty; let him bring forward arguments by which he may prove that matter has always existed, which no providence made. Let him show how anything ponderous and heavy either could exist without an author or could be changed, and how that which always was ceased to be, so that that which never was might begin to be. And if he shall prove these things, then, and not till then, will I admit that the world itself was not established by divine providence, and yet in making this admission I shall hold him fast by another snare. For he will turn round again to the same point, to which he will be unwilling to return, so as to say that both the matter of which the world consists, and the world which consists of matter, existed by nature; though I contend that nature itself is God. For no one can make wonderful things, that is, things existing with the greatest order, except one who has intelligence, foresight, and power. And thus it will come to be seen that God made all things, and that nothing at all can exist which did not derive its origin from God.

But the same, as often as he follows the Epicureans, and does not admit that the world was made by God, is wont to inquire by what hands by what machines, by what levers, by what contrivance, He made this work of such magnitude. He might see, if he could have lived at that time in which God made it. But, that man might not look into the works of God, He was unwilling to bring him into this world until all things were completed. But he could not be brought in: for how could he exist while the heaven above was being built, and the foundations of the earth beneath were being laid; when humid things, perchance, either benumbed with excessive stiffness were becoming congealed, or seethed with fiery heat and rendered solid were growing hard? Or how could he live when the sun was not yet established, and neither corn nor animals were produced? Therefore it was necessary that man should be last made, when the finishing hand had now been applied to the world and to all other things.

Finally, the sacred writings teach that man was the last work of God, and that he was brought into this world as into a house prepared and made ready; for all things were made on his account. The poets also acknowledge the same. Ovid, having described the completion of the world, and the formation of the other animals, added: "An animal more sacred than these, and more capacious of a lofty mind, was yet wanting, and which might exercise dominion over the rest. Man was produced."

So impious must we think it to search into those things which God wished to be kept secret! But his inquiries were not made through a desire of hearing or learning, but of refuting; for he was confident that no one could assert that. As though, in truth, it were to be supposed that these things were not made by God, because it cannot be plainly seen in what manner they were created!

If you had been brought up in a well-built and ornamented house, and had never seen a workshop, would you have supposed that that house was not built by man, because you did not know how it was built? You would assuredly ask the same question about the house which you now ask about the world – by what hands, with what implements, man had contrived such great works; and especially if you should see large stones, immense blocks, vast columns, the whole work lofty and elevated, would not these things appear to you to exceed the measure of human strength, because you would not know that these things were made not so much by strength as by skill and ingenuity?

But if man, in whom nothing is perfect, nevertheless effects more by skill than his feeble strength would permit, what reason is there why it should appear to you incredible, when it is alleged that the world was made by God, in whom, since He is perfect, wisdom can have no limit, and strength no measure? His works are seen by the eyes; but how He made them is not seen even by the mind, because, as Hermes says, the mortal cannot draw nigh to (that is, approach nearer, and follow up with the understanding) the immortal, the temporal to the eternal, the corruptible to the incorruptible. And on this account the earthly animal is as yet incapable of perceiving heavenly things, because it is shut in and held as it were in custody by the body, so that it cannot discern all things with free and unrestrained perception. Let him know, therefore, how foolishly he acts, who inquires into things which are indescribable. For this is to pass the limits of one's own condition, and not to understand how far it is permitted man to approach.

In short, when God revealed the truth to man, He wished us only to know those things which it concerned man to know for the attainment of life; but as to the things which related to a profane and eager curiosity He was silent, that they might be secret. Why, then, do you inquire into things which you cannot know, and if you knew them you would not be happier. It is perfect wisdom in man, if he knows that there is but one God, and that all things were made by Him.

Chapter X – Of the World, and Its Parts, the Elements and Seasons

Now, having refitted those who entertain false sentiments respecting the world and God its Maker, let us return to the divine workmanship of the world, concerning which we are informed in the sacred writings of our holy religion. Therefore, first of all, God made the heaven, and suspended it on high, that it might be the seat of God Himself, the Creator. Then He founded the earth, and placed it under the heaven, as a dwelling place for man, with the other races of animals. He willed that it should be surrounded and held together by water. But He adorned and filled His own dwelling place with bright lights; He decked it with the sun, and the shining orb of the moon, and with the glittering signs of the twinkling stars; but He placed on the earth the darkness, which is contrary to these. For of itself the earth contains no light, unless it receives it from the heaven, in which He placed perpetual light, and the gods above, and eternal life; and, on the contrary, He placed on the earth darkness, and the inhabitants of the lower regions, and death. For these things are as far removed from the former ones, as evil things are from good, and vices from virtues.

He also established two parts of the earth itself opposite to one another, and of a different character – namely, the east and the west; and of these the east is assigned to God, because He Himself is the fountain of light, and the enlightener of all things, and because He makes us rise to eternal life. But the west is ascribed to that disturbed and depraved mind, because it conceals the light, because it always brings on darkness, and because it makes men die and perish in their sins. For as light belongs to the east, and the whole course of life depends upon the light, so darkness belongs to the west: but death and destruction are contained in darkness.

Then He measured out in the same way the other parts – namely, the south and the north, which parts are closely united with the two former. For that which is more glowing with the warmth of the sun, is nearest to and closely united with the east; but that which is torpid with colds and perpetual ice belongs to the same division as the extreme west. For as darkness is opposed to light, so is cold to heat. As, therefore, heat is nearest to light, so is the south to the east; and as cold is nearest to darkness, so is the northern region to the west.

And He assigned to each of these parts its own time – namely, the spring to the east, the summer to the southern region, the autumn belongs to the west, and the winter to the north. In these two parts also, the southern and the northern, is contained a figure of life and death, because life consists in heat, death in cold. And as heat arises from fire, so does cold from water.

And according to the division of these parts He also made day and night, to complete by alternate succession with each other the courses and perpetual revolutions of time, which we call years. The day, which the first east supplies, must belong to God, as all things do, which are of a better character. But the night, which the extreme west brings on, belongs, indeed, to him whom we have said to be the rival of God.

And even in the making of these God had regard to the future; for He made them so, that a representation of true religion and of false superstitions might be shown from these. For as the sun, which rises daily, although it is but one – from which Cicero would have it appear that it was called Sol, because the stars are obscured, and it alone is seen – yet, since it is a true light, and of perfect fulness, and of most powerful heat, and enlightens all things with the brightest splendour; so God, although He is one only, is possessed of perfect majesty, and might, and splendour.

But night, which we say is assigned to that depraved adversary of God, shows by a resemblance the many and various superstitions which belong to him. For although innumerable stars appear to glitter and shine, yet, because they are not full and solid lights, and send forth no heat, nor overpower the darkness by their multitude, therefore these two things are found to be of chief importance, which have power differing from and opposed to one another – heat and moisture, which God wonderfully designed for the support and production of all things.

For since the power of God consists in heat and fire, if He had not tempered its ardour and force by mingling matter of moisture and cold, nothing could have been born or have existed, but whatever had begun to exist must immediately have been destroyed by conflagration. From which also some philosophers and poets said that the world was made up of a discordant concord; but they did not thoroughly understand the matter. Heraclitus said that all things were produced from fire Thales of Miletus from water. Each saw something of the truth, and yet each was in error: for if one element only had existed, water could not have been produced from fire, nor, on the other hand, could fire from water; but it is more true that all things were produced from a mingling of the two.

Fire, indeed, cannot be mixed with water, because they are opposed to each other; and if they came into collision, the one which proved superior must destroy the other. But their substances may be mingled. The substance of fire is heat; of water, moisture. Rightly therefore does Ovid say: "For when moisture and heat have become mingled, they conceive, and all things arise from these two. And though fire is at variance with water, moist vapour produces all things, and discordant concord is adapted to production."...

...But from what source or in what manner God lighted up or caused to flow these two principal elements, fire and water, He who made them alone can know.

Chapter XI – Of Living Creatures, of Man; Prometheus, Deucalion, the Parcae

Therefore, having finished the world, He commanded that animals of various kinds and of dissimilar forms should be created, both great and smaller. And they were made in pairs, that is, one of each sex; from the offspring of which both the air and the earth and the seas were filled. And God gave nourishment to all these by their kinds from the earth, that they might be of service to men: some, for instance, were for food, others for clothing; but those which are of great strength He gave, that they might assist in cultivating the earth, whence they were called beasts of burthen.

And thus, when all things had been settled with a wonderful arrangement, He determined to prepare for Himself an eternal kingdom, and to create innumerable souls, on whom He might bestow immortality. Then He made for Himself a figure endowed with perception and intelligence, that is, after the likeness of His own image, than which nothing can be more perfect: He formed man out of the dust of the ground, from which he was called man, because He was made from the earth.

Finally, Plato says that the human form was godlike; as does the Sibyl, who says – "Thou art my image, O man, possessed of right reason." The poets also have not given a different account respecting this formation of man, however they may have corrupted it; for they said that man was made by Prometheus from clay. They were not mistaken in the matter itself, but in the name of the artificer. For they had never come into contact with a line of the truth; but the things which were handed down by the oracles of the prophets, and contained in the sacred book of God; those things collected from fables and obscure opinion, and distorted, as the truth is wont to be corrupted by the multitude when spread abroad by various conversations, everyone adding something to that which he had heard – those things they comprised in their poems; and in this, indeed, they acted foolishly, in that they attributed so wonderful and divine a work to man. For what need was there that man should be formed of clay, when he might he generated in the same way in which Prometheus himself was born from Iapetus? For if he was a man, he was able to beget a man, but not to make one. But his punishment on Mount Caucasus declares that he was not of the gods. But no one reckoned his father Iapetus or his uncle Titan as gods, because the high dignity of the kingdom was in possession of Saturn only, by which he obtained divine honours, together with all his descendants. This invention of the poets admits of refutation by many arguments.

It is agreed by all that the deluge took place for the destruction of wickedness, and for its removal from the earth. Now, both philosophers and poets, and writers of ancient history, assert the same, and in this they especially agree with the language of the prophets. If, therefore, the flood took place for the purpose of destroying wickedness, which had increased through the excessive multitude of men, how was Prometheus the maker of man, when his son Deucalion is said by the same writers to have been the only one who was preserved on account of his righteousness? How could a single descent and a single generation have so quickly filled the world with men? But it is plain that they have corrupted this also, as they did the former account; since they were ignorant both at what time the flood happened on the earth, and who it was that deserved on account of his righteousness to be saved when the human race perished, and how and with whom he was saved: all of which are taught by the inspired writings. It is plain, therefore, that the account which they give respecting the work of Prometheus is false.

But because I had said that the poets are not accustomed to speak that which is altogether untrue, but to wrap up in figures and thus to obscure their accounts, I do not say that; they spoke falsely in this, but that first of all Prometheus made the image of a man of rich and soft clay, and that he first originated the art of making statues and images; inasmuch as he lived in the times of Jupiter, during which temples began to be built, and new modes of worshipping the gods introduced. And thus the truth was corrupted by falsehood; and that which was said to have been made by God began also to be ascribed to man, who imitated the divine work.

But the making of the true and living man from clay is the work of God. And this also is related by Hermes, who not only says that man was made by God, after the image of God, but he even tried to explain in how skilful a manner He formed each limb in the human body, since there is none of them which is not as available for the necessity of use as for beauty. But even the Stoics, when they discuss the subject of providence, attempt to do this; and Tully followed them in many places. But, however, he briefly treats of a subject so copious and fruitful, which I now pass over on this account, because I have lately written a particular book on this subject to my disciple Demetrianus. But I cannot here omit that which some erring philosophers say, that men and the other animals arose from the earth without any author; whence that expression of Virgil: "And the earth-born race of men raised its head from the hard fields."

And this opinion is especially entertained by those who deny the existence of a divine providence. For the Stoics attribute the formation of animals to divine skill. But Aristotle freed himself from labour and trouble, by saying that the world always existed, and therefore that the human race, and the other things which are in it, had no beginning, but always had been, and always would be. But when we see that each animal separately, which had no previous existence, begins to exist, and ceases to exist, it is necessary that the whole race must at some time have begun to exist, and must cease at some time because it had a beginning.

For all things must necessarily be comprised in three periods of time – the past, the present, and the future. The commencement belongs to the past, existence to the present, dissolution to the future. And all these things are seen in the case of men individually: for we begin when we are born; and we exist while we live; and we cease when we die. On which account they would have it that there are three Parcae: one who warps the web of life for men; the second, who weaves it; the third, who cuts and finishes it. But in the whole race of men, because the present time only is seen, yet from it the past also, that is, the commencement, and the future, that is, the dissolution, are inferred. For since it exists, it is evident that at some time it began to exist, for nothing can exist without a beginning; and because it had a beginning, it is evident that it will at some time have an end. For that cannot, as a whole, be immortal, which consists of mortals.

For as we all die individually, it is possible that, by some calamity, all may perish simultaneously: either through the unproductiveness of the earth, which sometimes happens in particular cases; or through the general spread of pestilence, which often desolates separate cities and countries; or by the conflagration of the world, as is said to have happened in the case of Phaethon; or by a deluge, as is reported in the time of Deucalion, when the whole race was destroyed with the exception of one man. And if this deluge happened by chance, it might assuredly have happened that he who was the only survivor should perish. But if he was reserved by the will of divine providence, as it cannot be denied, to recruit mankind, it is evident that the life and the destruction of the human race are in the power of God.

And if it is possible for it to die altogether, because it dies in parts, it is evident that it had an origin at some time; and as the liability to decay bespeaks a beginning, so also it gives proof of an end. And if these things are true, Aristotle will be unable to maintain that the world also itself had no beginning. But if Plato and Epicurus extort this from Aristotle, yet Plato and Aristotle, who thought that the world would be everlasting, will, notwithstanding their eloquence, be deprived of this also by Epicurus, because it follows, that, as it had a beginning, it must also have an end. But we will speak of these things at greater length in the last book. Now let us revert to the origin of man.

Chapter XII – That Animals Were Not Produced Spontaneously, But by a Divine Arrangement, of Which God Would Have Given Us the Knowledge, If It Were Advantageous for Us to Know It

They say that at certain changes of the heaven, and motions of the stars, there existed a kind of maturity for the production of animals; and thus that the new earth, retaining the productive seed, brought forth of itself certain vessels after the likeness of wombs, respecting which Lucretius says – "Wombs grew attached to the earth by roots;" and that these, when they had become mature, being rent by the compulsion of nature, produced tender animals; afterwards, that the earth itself abounded with a kind of moisture which resembled milk, and that animals were supported by this nourishment. How, then, were they able to endure or avoid the force of the cold or of heat, or to be born at all, since the sun would scorch them or the cold contract them? But, they say, at the beginning of the world there was no winter nor summer, but a perpetual spring of an equable temperature. Why, then, do we see that none of these things now happens? Because, they say, it was necessary that it should once happen, that animals might be born; but after they began to exist, and the power of generation was given to them, the earth ceased to bring forth, and the condition of time was changed.

Oh, how easy it is to refute falsehoods! In the first place, nothing can exist in this world which does not continue permanent, as it began. For neither were the sire and moon and stars then uncreated; nor having been created, were they without their motions; nor did that divine government, which manages and rules their courses, fail to begin its exercise together with them. In the next place, if it is as they say, there must of necessity be a providence, and they fall into that very condition which they especially avoid. For while the animals were yet unborn, it is plain that some one provided that they should be born, that the world might not appear gloomy with waste and desolation. But, that they might be produced from the earth without the office of parents, provision must have been made with great judgment; and in the next place, that the moisture condensed from the earth might be formed into the various figures of bodies; and also that, having received from the vessels with which they were covered the power of life and sensation, they might be poured forth, as it were, from the womb of mothers, is a wonderful and indescribable provision.

But let us suppose that this also happened by chance; the circumstances which follow assuredly cannot be by chance – that the earth should at once flow with milk, and that the temperature of the atmosphere should be equable. And if these things plainly happened, that the newly born animals might have nourishment, or be free from danger, it must be that some one provided these things by some divine counsel.

But who is able to make this provision except God? Let us, however, see whether the circumstance itself which they assert could have taken place, that men should be born from the earth. If any one considers during how long a time and in what manner an infant is reared, he will assuredly understand that those earth-born children could not possibly have been reared without some one to bring them up. For they must have lain for many months cast forth, until their sinews were strengthened, so that they had power to move themselves and to change their place, which can scarcely happen within the space of one year. Now see whether an infant could have lain through many months in the same manner and in the same place where it was cast forth, without dying, overwhelmed and corrupted by that moisture of the earth which it supplied for the sake of nourishment, and by the excrements of its own body mixed together. Therefore it is impossible but that it was reared by some one; unless, indeed, all animals are born not in a tender condition, but grown up: and it never came into their mind to say this.

Therefore the whole of that method is impossible and vain; if that can be called method by which it is attempted that there shall be no method. For he who says that all things are produced of their own accord, and attributes nothing to divine providence, he assuredly does not assert, but overthrows method. But if nothing can be done or produced without design, it is plain that there is a divine providence, to which that which is called design peculiarly belongs.

Therefore God, the Contriver of all things, made man. And even Cicero, though ignorant of the sacred writings, saw this, who in his treatise on the Laws, in the first book, handed down the same thing as the prophets; and I add his words: "This animal, foreseeing, sagacious, various, acute, gifted with memory, full of method and design, which we call man, was produced by the supreme Deity under remarkable circumstances; for this alone of so many kinds and natures of animals, partakes of judgment and reflection, when all other animals are destitute of them." Do you see that the man, although far removed from the knowledge of the truth, yet, inasmuch as he held the image of wisdom, understood that man could not be produced except by God?

But, however, there is need of divine testimony, lest that of man should be insufficient. The Sibyl testifies that man is the work of God: "He who is the only God being the invincible Creator, He Himself fixed the figure of the form of men, He Himself mixed the nature of all belonging to the generation of life." The sacred writings contain statements to the same effect. Therefore God discharged the office of a true father. He Himself formed the body; He Himself infused the soul with which we breathe. Whatever we are, it is altogether His work. In what manner He effected this He would have taught us, if it were right for us to know; as He taught us other things, which have conveyed to us the knowledge both of ancient error and of true light.

Lactantius *Divine Institutes*, Book VII

Chapter I – Of the World, and Those Who are About to Believe, and Those Who are Not; And in This the Censure of the Faithless

It is well: the foundations are laid, as the illustrious orator says. But we have not only laid the foundations, which might be firth and suitable for the support of the work; but we have raised the entire edifice, with great and strong buildings, almost to the summit. There remains, a matter which is much easier, either to cover or adorn it; without which, however, the former works are both useless and displeasing. For of what avail is it, either to be freed from false religions or to understand the true one? Of what avail, either to see the vanity of false wisdom, or to know what is true? Of what avail is it, I say, to defend that heavenly justice? Of what avail to hold the worship of God with great difficulties, which is the greatest virtue, unless the divine reward of everlasting blessedness attends it? Of which subject we must speak in this book, lest all that is gone before should appear vain and unprofitable: if we should leave this, on account of which they were undertaken, in uncertainty, lest any one should by chance think that such great labours are undertaken in vain; while he distrusts their heavenly reward, which God has appointed for him who shall have despised the present sweet enjoyments of earth in comparison of solitary and unrewarded virtue. Let us satisfy this part of our subject also, both by the testimonies of the sacred writings and also by probable arguments, that it may be equally manifest that future things are to be preferred to those which are present; heavenly things to earthly: and eternal things to those which are temporal: since the rewards of vices are temporal, those of virtues are eternal.

I will therefore set forth the system of the world, that it may easily be understood both when and how it was made by God; which Plato, who discoursed about the making of the world, could neither know nor explain, inasmuch as he was ignorant of the heavenly mystery, which is not learned except by the teaching of prophets and God; and therefore he said that it was created for eternity. Whereas the case is far different, since whatever is of a solid and heavy body, as it received a beginning at some time, so it must needs have an end. For Aristotle, when he did not see how so great a magnitude of things could perish, and wished to escape this objection, said that the world always had existed, and always would exist. He did not at all see, that whatever material thing exists must at some time have had a beginning, and that nothing can exist at all unless it bad a beginning. For when we see that earth, and water, and fire perish, are consumed, and extinguished, which are clearly parts of the world, it is understood that that is altogether mortal the members of which are mortal.

Thus it comes to pass, that whatever is liable to destruction must have been produced. But everything which comes within the sight of the eyes must of necessity be material, and capable of dissolution. Therefore Epicurus alone, following the authority of Democritus, spoke truly in this matter, who said that it had a beginning at some time, and that it would at some time perish. Nor, however, was he able to assign any reason, either through what causes or at what time this work of such magnitude should be destroyed. But since God has revealed this to us, and we do not arrive at it by conjectures, but by instruction from heaven, we will carefully teach it, that it may at length be evident to those who are desirous of the truth, that the philosophers did not see nor comprehend the truth; but that they had so slight a knowledge of it, that they by no means perceived from what source that fragrance of wisdom, which was so pleasant and agreeable, breathed upon them.

In the meantime, I think it necessary to admonish those who are about to read this, that depraved and vicious minds, since the acuteness of their mind is blunted by earthly passions, which weigh down all the perceptions and render them weak, will either altogether fail to understand these things which we relate, or, even if they shall understand them, they will dissemble and be unwilling for them to be true: because they are drawn away by vices, and they knowingly favour their own evils, by the pleasantness of which they are captivated, and they desert the way of virtue, by the bitterness of which they are offended. For they who are inflamed with avarice and a certain insatiable thirst for riches – because, when they have sold or squandered the things in which they delight, they are unable to live in a simple style – undoubtedly prefer that by which they are compelled to renounce their eager desires.

Also, they who, urged on by the incitements of lusts, as the poet says, "Rush into madness and fire," say that we bring forward things plainly incredible; because the precepts about self-restraint wound their ears, which restrain them from their pleasures, to which they have given up their soul, together with their body. But those who, swollen with ambition or inflamed with the love of power, have bestowed all their efforts on the acquisition of honours, will not, even if we should bear the sun himself in our hands, believe that teaching which commands them to despise all power and honour, and to live in humility, and in such humility that they may be able to receive an injury, and if they have received one, be unwilling to return it.

These are the men who cry out in any way against the truth with closed eyes. But they who are or shall be of sound mind, that is, not so immersed in vices as to be incurable, will both believe these things, and will readily approach them; and whatever things we say, they will appear to them open, and plain, and simple, and that which is chiefly necessary, true and unassailable...

Chapter II – Of the Error of the Philosophers, and of the Divine Wisdom, and of the Golden Age

Now let us instruct those who are ignorant of the truth. It has been so determined by the arrangement of the Most High God, that this unrighteous age, having run the course of its appointed times, should come to an end; and all wickedness being immediately extinguished, and the souls of the righteous being recalled to a happy life, a quiet, tranquil, peaceful, in short, golden age, as the poets call it, should flourish, under the rule of God Himself. This was especially the cause of all the errors of the philosophers, that they did not comprehend the system of the world, which comprises the whole of wisdom. But it cannot be comprehended by our own perception and innate intelligence, which they wished to do by themselves without a teacher.

Therefore they fell into various and ofttimes contradictory opinions, out of which they had no way of escape, "And they remained fixed in the same mire," as the comic writer says, since their conclusion does not correspond with their assumptions; inasmuch as they had assumed things to be true which could not be affirmed, and proved without the knowledge of the truth and of heavenly things. And this knowledge, as I have often said already, cannot exist in a man unless it is derived from the teaching of God. For if a man is able to understand divine things, he will be able also to perform them; for to understand is, as it were, to follow in their track.

But he is not able to do the things which God does, because he is clothed with a mortal body; therefore he cannot even understand those things which God does. And whether this is possible is easy for every one to measure, from the immensity of the divine actions and works. For if you will contemplate the world, with all the things which it contains, you will assuredly understand how much the work of God surpasses the works of men. Thus, as great as is the difference between divine and human works, so great must be the distance between the wisdom of God and man. For because God is incorruptible and immortal, and therefore perfect because He is everlasting, His wisdom also is perfect, as He Himself is; nor can anything oppose it, because God Himself is subject to nothing.

But because man is subject to passion, his wisdom also is subject to error; and as many things hinder the life of man, so that it cannot be perpetual, so also his wisdom must be hindered by many things: so that it is not perfect in entirely perceiving the truth. Therefore there is no human wisdom, if it strives by itself to attain to the conception and knowledge of the truth; inasmuch as the mind of man, being bound up with a frail body, and enclosed in a dark abode, is neither able to wander at large, nor clearly to perceive the truth, the knowledge of which belongs to the divine nature. For His works are known to God alone. But man cannot attain this knowledge by reflection or disputation, but by learning and hearing from Him who alone is able to know and to teach. Therefore Marcus Tullius, borrowing from Plato the sentiment of Socrates, who said that the time had come for himself to depart from life, but that they before whom he was pleading his cause were still alive, says: Which is better is known to the immortal gods; but I think that no man knows. Wherefore all the sects of philosophers must be far removed from the truth, because they who established them were men; nor can those things have any foundation or firmness which are unsupported by any utterances of divine voices.

Chapter III – Of Nature, and of the World; And a Censure of the Stoics and Epicureans

And since we are speaking of the errors of philosophers, the Stoics divide nature into two parts – the one which effects, the other which affords itself tractable for action. They say that in the former is contained all the power of perception, in the latter the material, and that the one cannot act without the other. How can that which handles and that which is handled be one and the same thing? If any one should say that the potter is the same as the clay, or that the clay is the same as the potter, would he not plainly appear to be mad? But these men comprehend under the one name of nature two things which are most widely different, God and the world, the Maker and the work; and say that the one can do nothing without the other, as though God were mixed up in nature with the world.

For sometimes they so mix them together, that God Himself is the mind of the world, and that the world is the body of God; as though the world and God began to exist at the same time, and God did not Himself make the world. And they themselves also confess this at other times, when they say that it was made for the sake of men, and that God could, if He willed it, exist without the world, inasmuch as God is the divine and eternal mind, separate and free from a body. And since they were unable to understand His power and majesty, they mixed Him with the world, that is, with His own work. Whence is that saying of Virgil: "A spirit whose celestial flame Glows in each member of the frame, And stirs the mighty whole."

What, then, becomes of their own saying, that the world was both made and is governed by the divine providence? For if He made the world, it follows that He existed without the world; if He governs it, it is plain that it is not as the mind governs the body, but as a master rules the house, as a pilot the ship, as a charioteer the chariot. Nor, however, are they mixed with those things which they govern. For if all these things which we see are members of God, then God is rendered insensible by them, since the members are without sensibility, and mortal, since we see that the members are mortal.

I can enumerate how often lands shaken by sudden motions have either opened or sunk down precipitously; how often cities and islands have been overwhelmed by waves, and gone into the deep; marshes have inundated fruitful plains, rivers and pools have been dried up; mountains also have either fallen precipitously, or have been levelled with plains. Many districts, and the foundations of many mountains, are laid waste by latent and internal fire. And this is not enough, if God does not spare His own members, unless it is permitted man also to have some power over the body of God. Seas are built up, mountains are cut down, and the innermost bowels of the earth are dug out to draw forth riches. Why, should I say that we cannot even plough without lacerating the divine body? So that we are at once wicked and impious in doing violence to the members of God. Does God, then, suffer His body to be harassed, and endure to weaken Himself, or permit this to be done by man? Unless by chance that divine intelligence which is mixed with the world, and with all parts of the world, abandoned the first outer aspect of the earth, and plunged itself into the lowest depths, that it might be sensible of no pain from continual laceration.

But if this is trifling and absurd, then they themselves were as devoid of intelligence as those are who have not perceived that the divine spirit is everywhere diffused, and that all things are held together by it, not however in such a manner that God, who is incorruptible, should Himself be mixed with heavy and corruptible elements. Therefore that is more correct which they derived from Plato, that the world was made by God, and is also governed by His providence. It was therefore befitting that Plato, and those who held the same opinion, should teach and explain what was the cause, what the reason, for the contriving of so great a work; why or for the sake of whom He made it.

But the Stoics also say the world was made for the sake of men, I hear. But Epicurus is ignorant on what account or who made men themselves. For Lucretius, when he said that the world was not made by the gods, thus spoke: "To say, again, that for the sake of men they have willed to set in order the glorious nature of the world" – then he introduced: "Is sheer folly. For what advantage can our gratitude bestow on immortal and blessed beings, that for our, sake they should take in hand to administer aught?" And with good reason. For they brought forward no reason why the human race was created or established by God.

It is our business to set forth the mystery of the world and man, of which they, being destitute, were able neither to reach nor see the shrine of truth. Therefore, as I said a little before, when they had assumed that which was true, that is, that the world was made by God, and was made for the sake of men, yet, since their argument failed them in the consequences, they were unable to defend that which they had assumed. In fine, Plato, that he might not make the work of God weak and subject to ruin, said that it would remain for ever. If it was made for the sake of men, and so made as to be eternal, why then are not they on whose account it was made eternal? If they are mortal on account of whom it was made, it must also itself be mortal and subject to dissolution, for it is not of more value than those for whose sake it was made. But if his argument were consistent, he would understand that it must perish because it was made, and that nothing can remain for ever except that which cannot be touched.

But he who says that it was not made for the sake of men has no argument. For if he says that the Creator contrived these works of such magnitude on His own account, why then were we produced? Why do we enjoy the world itself? What means the creation of the human race, and of the other living creatures? Why do we intercept the advantages of others? Why, in short, do we grow, decrease, and perish? What reason is implied in our production itself? What in our perpetual succession? Doubtless God wished us to be seen, and to frame, as it were, impressions with various representations of Himself, with which He might delight Himself. Nevertheless, if it were so, He would esteem living creatures as His care, and especially man, to whose command He made all things subject.

But with regard to those who say that the world always existed: I omit that point, that itself cannot exist without some beginning, from which they are unable to extricate themselves; but I say this, if the world always existed, it can have no systematic arrangement. For what could arrangement have effected in that which never had a beginning? For before anything is done or arranged, there is need of counsel that it may be determined how it should be done; nor can anything be done without the foresight of a settled plan. Therefore the plan precedes every work. Therefore that which has not been made has no plan. But the world has a plan by which it both exists and is governed; therefore also it was made: if it was made, it will also be destroyed. Let them therefore assign a reason, I if they can, why it was either made in the beginning or will hereafter be destroyed.

And because Epicurus or Democritus was unable to teach this, he said that it was produced of its own accord, the seeds coming together in all directions; and that when these are again resolved, discord and destruction will follow. Therefore he perverted that which he had correctly seen, and by his ignorance of system entirely overthrew the whole system, and reduced the world, and all things which are done in it, to the likeness of a most trifling dream, if no plan exists in human affairs.

But since the world and all its parts, as we see, are governed by a wonderful plan; since the framing of the heaven, and the course of the stars and of the heavenly bodies, which is harmonious even in variety itself, the constant and wonderful arrangement of the seasons, the varied fruitfulness of the lands, the level plains, the defences and heapings up of mountains, the verdure and productiveness of the woods, the most salubrious bursting forth of fountains, the seasonable overflowings of rivers, the rich and abundant flowing in of the sea, the opposite and useful breathing of the winds, and all things, are fixed with the greatest regularity: who is so blind as to think that they were made without a cause, in which a wonderful disposition of most provident arrangement shines forth? If, therefore, nothing at all exists nor is done without a cause; if the providence of the Supreme God is manifest from the disposition of things, His excellency from their greatness, and His power from their government: therefore they are dull and mad who have said that there is no providence. I should not disapprove if they denied the existence of gods with this object, that they might affirm the existence of one; but when they did it with this intent, that they might say that there is none, he who does not think that they were senseless is himself senseless.

Chapter IV – That All Things Were Created for Some Use, Even Those Things Which Appear Evil; On What Account Man Enjoys Reason in So Frail a Body

But we have spoken sufficiently on the subject of providence in the first book. For if it has any existence, as appears from the wonderful nature of its works, it must be that the same providence created man and the other animals. Let us therefore see what reason there was for the creation of the human race, since it is evident, as the Stoics say, that the world was made for the sake of men, although they make no slight error in this very matter, in saying it was not made for the sake of man, but of men. For the naming of one individual comprehends the whole human race. But this arises from the fact that they are ignorant that one man only was made by God, and they think that men were produced in all lands and fields like mushrooms. But Hermes was not ignorant that man was both made by God and after the likeness of God.

But I return to my subject. There is nothing, as I imagine, which was made on its own account; but whatever is made at all must necessarily be made for some purpose. For who is there either so senseless or so unconcerned as to attempt to do anything at random, from which he expects no utility, no advantage? He who builds a house does not build it merely for this purpose, that it may be a house, but that it may be inhabited. He who builds a ship does not bestow his labour on this account, only that the ship may be visible, but that men may sail in it. Likewise he who designs and forms any vessel does not do it on this account, that he may only appear to have done it, but that the vessel when made may contain something necessary for use. In like manner, other things, whatever are made, are plainly not made superfluously, but for some useful purposes.

It is plain, therefore, that the world was made by God, not on account of the world itself; for since it is without sensibility, it neither needs the warmth of the sun, or light, or the breath of the winds, or the moisture of showers, or the nourishment of fruits. But it cannot even be said that God made the world for His own sake, since He can exist without the world, as He did before it was made; and God Himself does not make use of all those things which are contained in it, and which are produced. It is evident, therefore, that the world was constructed for the sake of living beings, since living beings enjoy those things of which it consists; and that these may live and exist, all things necessary for them are supplied at fixed times. Again, that the other living beings were made for the sake of man, is plain from this, that they are subservient to man, and were given for his protection and service; since, whether they are of the earth or of the water, they do not perceive the system of the world as man does.

We must here reply to the philosophers, and especially to Cicero, who says: "Why should God, when He made all things on our account, make so large a quantity of snakes and vipers? Why should He scatter so many pernicious things by land and by sea?" A very wide subject for discussion, but it must be briefly touched upon, as in passing. Since man is formed of different and opposing elements, soul and body, that is, heaven and earth, that which is slight and that which is perceptible to the senses, that which is eternal and that which is temporal, that which has sensibility and that which is senseless, that which is endued with light and that which is dark, reason itself and necessity require that both good and evil things should be set before man – good things which he may use, and evil things which he may guard against and avoid.

For wisdom has been given to him on this account, that, knowing the nature of good and evil things, he may exercise the force of his reason in seeking the good and avoiding the evil. For because wisdom was not given to the other animals, they were both defended with natural clothing and were armed; but in the place of all these He gave to man that which was most excellent, reason only. Therefore He formed him naked and unarmed, that wisdom might be both his defence and covering. He placed his defence and ornament not without, but within not in the body, but in the heart. Unless, therefore, there were evils which he might guard against, and which he might distinguish from good and useful things, wisdom was not necessary for him. Therefore let Marcus Tullius know that reason was either given to man that he might take fishes on account of his own use, and avoid snakes and vipers for the sake of his own safety; or that good and evil things were set before him on this account, because he had received wisdom, the whole force of which is occupied in distinguishing things good and evil.

Great, therefore, and right, and admirable is the force, and reason, and power of man, for whose sake God made the world itself and all things, as many as exist, and gave him so much honour that He set him over all things, since he alone could admire the works of God. Most excellently, therefore, does our Asclepiades, in discussing the providence of the Supreme God in that book which he wrote to me, say: "And on this account any one may with good reason think that the divine providence gave the place nearest to itself to him who was able to understand its arrangement. For that is the sun: who so beholds it as to understand why it is the sun, and what amount of influence it has upon the other parts of the system? This is the heaven, who looks up to it? This is the earth, who inhabits it? This is the sea, who sails upon it? This is fire, who makes use of it?" Therefore the Supreme God did not arrange these things on account of Himself, because He stands in need of nothing, but on account of man, who might fitly make use of them.

Chapter V – Of the Creation of Man, and of the Arrangement of the World, and of the Chief Good

Let us now assign the reason why He made man himself. For if the philosophers had known this, they would either have maintained those things which they had found to be true, or would not have fallen into the greatest errors. For this is the chief thing; this is the point on which everything turns. And if any one does not possess this, the truth altogether glides away from him. It is this, in short, which causes them to be inconsistent with reason; for if this had shone upon them, if they had known all the mystery of man, the Academy would never have been in entire opposition to their disputations, and to all philosophy. As, therefore, God did not make the world for His own sake, because He does not stand in need of its advantages, but for the sake of man, who has the use of it, so also He made man himself for His own sake.

What advantage is there to God in man, says Epicurus, that He should make him for His own sake? Truly, that there might be one who might understand His works; who might be able both to admire with his understanding, and to express with his voice, the foresight displayed in their arrangement, the order of their creation, the power exerted in their completion. And the sum of all these things is, that he should worship God. For he who understands these things worships Him; he follows Him with due veneration as the Maker of all things, He as his true Father, who measures the excellence of His majesty according to the invention, the commencement, and completion of His works. What more evident argument can be brought forward that God both made the world for the sake of man, and man for His own sake, than that he alone of all living creatures has been so formed that his eyes are directed towards heaven, his face looking towards God, his countenance is in fellowship with his Parent, so that God appears, as it were, with outstretched hand to have raised man from the ground, and to have elevated him to the contemplation of Himself. "What, then," he says, "does the worship paid by man confer on God, who is blessed, and in want of nothing? Or if He gave such honour to man as to create the world for his sake, to furnish him with wisdom, to make him lord of all things living, and to love him as a son, why did He make him subject to death and decay? Why did He expose the object of His love to all evils? When it was befitting that man should be happy, as though closely connected with God, and everlasting as He is, to the worship and contemplation of whom he was formed."

Although we have taught these things for the most part in a scattered manner in the former books, nevertheless, since the subject now specially requires it, because we have undertaken to discuss the subject of a happy life, these things are to be explained by us more carefully and fully, that the arrangement made by God, and His work and will, may be known. Though He was always able by His own immortal Spirit to produce innumerable souls, as He produced the angels, to whom there exists immortality without any danger and fear of evils, yet He devised an unspeakable work, in what manner He might create an infinite multitude of souls, which being at first united with frail and feeble bodies, He might place in the midst between good and evil, that He might set virtue before them composed as they were of both natures; that they might not attain to immortality by a delicate and easy course of life, but might arrive at that unspeakable reward of eternal life with the utmost difficulty and great labours.

Therefore, that He might clothe them with limbs which were heavy and liable to injury, since they were unable to exist in the middle void, the weight and gravity of the body sinking downwards, He determined that an abode and dwelling place should first be built for them. And thus with unspeakable energy and power He contrived the surpassing works of the world; and having suspended the light elements on high, and depressed the heavy ones to the depths below, He strengthened the heavenly things, and established the earthly. It is not necessary at present to follow out each point separately, since we discussed them all together in the second book.

Therefore He placed in the heaven lights, whose regularity, and brightness, and motion, were most suitably proportioned to the advantage of living beings. Moreover, He gave to the earth, which He designed as their dwelling place, fruitfulness for bringing forth and producing various things, that by the abundance of fruits and green herbs it might supply nourishment according to the nature and requirements of each kind. Then, when He had completed all things which belonged to the condition of the world, He formed man from the earth itself, which He prepared for him from the beginning as a habitation; that is, He clothed and covered his spirit with an earthly body, that, being compacted of different and opposing materials, he might be susceptible of good and evil; and as the earth itself is fruitful for the bringing forth of grain, so the body of man, which was taken from the earth, received the power of producing offspring, that, inasmuch as he was formed of a fragile substance, and could not exist for ever, when the space of his temporal life was past, he might depart, and by a perpetual succession renew that which he bore, which was frail and feeble.

Why, then, did He make him frail and mortal, when He had built the world for his sake? First of all, that an infinite number of living beings might be produced, and that He might fill all the earth with a multitude; in the next place, that He might set before man virtue, that is, endurance of evils and labours, by which he might be able to gain the reward of immortality. For since man consists of two parts, body and soul, of which the one is earthly, the other heavenly, two lives have been assigned to man: the one temporal, which is appointed for the body; the other everlasting, which belongs to the soul. We received the former at our birth we attain to the latter by striving, that immortality might not exist to man without any difficulty. That earthly one is as the body, and therefore has an end; but this heavenly one is as the soul, and therefore has no limit. We received the first when we were ignorant of it, this second knowingly; for it is given to virtue, not to nature, because God wished that we should procure life for ourselves in life.

For this reason He has given us this present life, that we may either lose that true and eternal life by our vices, or win it by virtue. The chief good is not contained in this bodily life, since, as it was given to us by divine necessity, so it will again be destroyed by divine necessity. Thus that which has an end does not contain the chief good. But the chief good is contained in that spiritual life which we acquire by ourselves, because it cannot contain evil, or have an end; to which subject nature and the system of the body afford an argument. For other animals incline towards the ground, because they are earthly, and are incapable of immortality, which is from heaven; but man is upright and looks towards heaven, because immortality is proposed to him; which, however, does not come, unless it is given to man by God. For otherwise there would be no difference between the just and the unjust, since every man who is born would become immortal. Immortality, then, is not the consequence of nature, but the reward and recompense of virtue.

Lastly, man does not immediately upon his birth walk upright, but at first on all fours, because the nature of his body and of this present life is common to us with the dumb animals; afterwards, when his strength is confirmed, he raises himself, and his tongue is loosened so that he speaks plainly, and he ceases to be a dumb animal. And this argument teaches that man is born mortal; but that he afterwards becomes immortal, when he begins to live in conformity with the will of God, that is, to follow righteousness, which is comprised in the worship of God, since God raised man to a view of the heaven and of Himself. And this takes place when man, purified in the heavenly laver, lays aside his infancy together with all the pollution of his past life, and having received an increase of divine vigour, becomes a perfect and complete man.

Therefore, because God has set forth virtue before man, although the soul and the body are connected together, yet they are contrary, and oppose one another. The things which are good for the soul are evil to the body, that is, the avoiding of riches, the prohibiting of pleasures, the contempt of pain and death. In like manner, the things which are good for the body are evil to the soul, that is, desire and lust, by which riches are desired, and the enjoyments of various pleasures, by which the soul is weakened and destroyed. Therefore it is necessary, that the just and wise man should be engaged in all evils, since fortitude is victorious over evils; but the unjust in riches, in honours, in power. For these goods relate to the body, and are earthly; and these men also lead an earthly life, nor are they able to attain to immortality because they have given themselves up to pleasures which are the enemies of virtue.

Therefore this temporal life ought to be subject to that eternal life, as the body is to the soul. Whoever, then, prefers the life of the soul must despise the life of the body; nor will he in any other way be able to strive after that which is highest, unless he shall have despised the things which are lowest. But he who shall have embraced the life of the body, and shall have turned his desires downwards to the earth, is unable to attain to that higher life. But he who prefers to live well for eternity, will live badly for a time, and will be subjected to all troubles and labours as long as he shall be on earth, that he may have divine and heavenly consolation. And he who shall prefer to live well for a time, will live ill to eternity; for he will be condemned by the sentence of God to eternal punishment, be cause he has preferred earthly to heavenly goods.

On this account, therefore, God seeks to be worshipped, and to be honoured by man as a Father, that he may have virtue and wisdom, which alone produce' immortality. For because no other but Himself is able to confer that immortality, since He alone possesses it, He will grant to the piety of the man, with which he has honoured God, this reward, to be blessed to all eternity, and to be for ever in the presence of God and in the society of God.

Athanasius

St. Athanasius the Great (c. 296 – 373), Archbishop of Alexandria (328 – 373) suffered through five exiles and great turmoil for defending the Nicene view that the Son is of "one essence" with God the Father. His chief adversaries were the Arians, who taught that "there was a time when the Son was not." Athanasius devoted his life to defending the Christian teaching that Jesus Christ is fully God.

Athanasius addressed the doctrine of creation in several places. In *Against the Gentiles* and *On the Incarnation*, he argued to skeptical Jews and Greeks that it is eminently reasonable for the eternal Son of God to become a man to save humanity. In thus arguing for the Incarnation, Athanasius had to clarify the original and ongoing relation of God to the world in creation and providence. God is transcendent and wholly other, but His transcendence is not compromised by involvement in the world or contact with matter (as Origen, Arius, and Greek philosophers had thought). God created the world out of nothing by His Son, the eternal Wisdom and Word of God, and it is by God's power that the world continues to exist.

Athanasius used a variety of images to describe the universe. One of the most striking is the lyre. The universe is a lyre of many strings. The Wisdom of God plays this lyre, producing harmony. Athanasius conceived of the world in a dynamic relation to God. For him, the universe is an "open system" that God brings into being, organizes, interacts with, and sustains. Contrast this with contemporary cosmologies that see the world as a self-sustaining closed system, a mechanistic world governed by unbroken natural laws.

In his *Second Discourse Against the Arians*, Athanasius analyzes Proverbs 8:22 to explain in what sense wisdom is created by God. The Arians used this passage to assert the creatureliness of the Son, whom they identified with wisdom (writ small). Athanasius, by contrast, sees the "impress of wisdom" in each creature as reflecting a higher uncreated Wisdom, which is the Word of God and which enables all creation to bear witness to God. Because a created reflection of the eternal Wisdom is imprinted in every created thing, the whole creation is full of the knowledge of God.

Athanasius *Contra Gentes*, Part III

35. Creation a Revelation of God; Especially in the Order and Harmony Pervading the Whole

For God, being good and loving to mankind, and caring for the souls made by Him – since He is by nature in visible and incomprehensible, having His being beyond all created existence, for which reason the race of mankind was likely to miss the way to the knowledge of Him, since they are made out of nothing while He is unmade – for this cause God by His own Word gave the Universe the Order it has, in order that since He is by nature invisible, men might be enabled to know Him at any rate by His works. For often the artist even when not seen is known by his works.

2. And as they tell of Phidias the Sculptor that his works of art by their symmetry and by the proportion of their parts betray Phidias to those who see them although he is not there, so by the order of the Universe one ought to perceive God its maker and artificer, even though He be not seen with the bodily eyes. For God did not take His stand upon His invisible nature (let none plead that as an excuse) and leave Himself utterly unknown to men; but as I said above, He so ordered Creation that although He is by nature invisible He may yet be known by His works.

3. And I say this not on my own authority, but on the strength of what I learned from them who have spoken of God, among them Paul, who thus writes to the Romans: "for the invisible things of Him since the creation of the world are clearly seen, being understood by the things that are made;" while to the Lycaonians he speaks out and says: "We also are men of like passions with you, and bring you good tidings, to turn from these vain things unto a Living God, Who made the heaven and the earth and the sea, and all that in them is, Who in the generations gone by suffered all nations to walk in their own ways. And yet He left not Himself without witness, in that lie did good, and gave you from heaven rains and fruitful seasons, filling your hearts with food and gladness."

4. For who that sees the circle of heaven and the course of the sun and the moon, and the positions and movements of the other stars, as they take place in opposite and different directions, while yet in their

difference all with one accord observe a consistent order, can resist the conclusion that these are not ordered by themselves, but have a maker distinct from themselves who orders them? Or who that sees the sun rising by day and the moon shining by night, and waning and waxing without variation exactly according to the same number of days, and some of the stars running their courses and with orbits various and manifold, while others move without wandering, can fail to perceive that they certainly have a creator to guide them?

36. This the More Striking, If We Consider the Opposing Forces Out of Which This Order is Produced

Who that sees things of opposite nature combined, and in concordant harmony, as, for example, fire mingled with cold, and dry with wet, and that not in mutual conflict, but making up a single body, as it were homogeneous, can resist the inference that there is One external to these things that has united them? Who that sees winter giving place to spring and spring to summer and summer to autumn, and that these things contrary by nature (for the one chills, the other burns, the one nourishes the other destroys), yet all make up a balanced result beneficial to mankind – can fail to perceive that there is One higher than they, Who balances and guides them all, even if he see Him not?

2. Who that sees the clouds supported in air, and the weight of the waters bound up in the clouds, can but perceive Him that binds them up and has ordered these things so? Or who that sees the earth, heaviest of all things by nature, fixed upon the waters, and remaining unmoved upon what is by nature mobile, will fail to understand that there is One that has made and ordered it, even God? Who that sees the earth bringing forth fruits in due season, and the rains from heaven, and the flow of rivers, and springing up of wells, and the birth of animals from unlike parents, and that these things take place not at all times but at determinate seasons – and in general, among things mutually unlike and contrary, the balanced and uniform order to which they conform – can resist the inference that there is one Power which orders and administers them, ordaining things well as it thinks fit?

4. For left to themselves they could not subsist or ever be able to appear, on account of their mutual contrariety of nature. For water is by nature heavy, and tends to flow downwards, while the clouds are

light and belong to the class of things which tend to soar and mount upwards. And yet we see water, heavy as it is, borne aloft in the clouds. And again, earth is very heavy, while water on the other hand is relatively light; and yet the heavier is supported upon the lighter, and the earth does not sink, but remains immoveable. And male and female are not the same, while yet they unite in one, and the result is the generation from both of an animal like them. And to cut the matter short, cold is opposite to heat, and wet fights with dry, and yet they come together and are not at variance, but they agree, and produce as their result a single body, and the birth of everything.

37. The Same Subject Continued

Things then of conflicting and opposite nature would not have reconciled themselves, were there not One higher and Lord over them to unite them, to Whom the elements themselves yield obedience as slaves that obey a master. And instead of each having regard to its own nature and fighting with its neighbour, they recognise the Lord Who has united them, and are at concord one with another, being by nature opposed, but at amity by the will of Him that guides them.

2. For if their mingling into one were not due to a higher authority, how could the heavy mingle and combine with the light, the wet with the dry, the round with the straight, fire with cold, or sea with earth, or the sun with the moon, or the stars with the heaven, and the air with the clouds, the nature of each being dissimilar to that of the other? For there would be great strife among them, the one burning, the other giving cold; the heavy dragging downwards, the light in the contrary direction and upwards; the sun giving light while the air diffused darkness: yes, even the stars would have been at discord with one another, since some have their position above, others beneath, and night would have refused to make way for day, but would have persisted in remaining to fight and strive against it.

3. But if this were so, we should consequently see not an ordered universe, but disorder, not arrangement but anarchy, not a system, but everything out of system, not proportion but disproportion. For in the general strife and conflict either all things would be destroyed, or the prevailing principle alone would appear. And even the latter would shew the disorder of the whole, for left alone, and deprived of the

help of the others, it would throw the whole out of gears just as, if a single hand and foot were left alone, that would not preserve the body in its integrity.

4. For what sort of a universe would it be, if only the sun appeared, or only the moon went her course, or there were only night, or always day? Or what sort of harmony would it be, again, if the heaven existed alone without the stars, or the stars without the heaven? Or what benefit would there be if there were only sea, or if the earth were there alone without waters and without the other parts of creation? Or how could man, or any animal, have appeared upon earth, if the elements were mutually at strife, or if there were one that prevailed, and that one insufficient for the composition of bodies. For nothing in the world could have been composed of heat, or cold, or wet, or dry, alone, but all would have been without arrangement or combination. But not even the one element which appeared to prevail would have been able to subsist without the assistance of the rest: for that is how each subsists now.

38. The Unity of God Shewn by the Harmony of the Order of Nature

Since then, there is everywhere not disorder but order, proportion and not disproportion, not disarray but arrangement, and that in an order perfectly harmonious, we needs must infer and be led to perceive the Master that put together and compacted all things, and produced harmony in them. For though He be not seen with the eyes, yet from the order and harmony of things contrary it is possible to perceive their Ruler, Arranger, and King.

2. For in like manner as if we saw a city, consisting of many and diverse people, great and small, rich and poor, old and young, male and female, in an orderly condition, and its inhabitants, while different from one another, yet at unity among themselves, and not the rich set against the poor, the great against the small, nor the young against the old, but all at peace in the enjoyment of equal rights – if we saw this, the inference surely follows that the presence of a ruler enforces concord, even if we do not see him; (for disorder is a sign of absence of rule, while order shews the governing authority: for when we see the mutual harmony of the members in the body, that the eye does not strive with the hearing, nor is the hand at variance with the foot, but that each accomplishes its service without variance, we

perceive from this that certainly there is a soul in the body that governs these members, though we see it not); so in the order and harmony of the Universe, we needs must perceive God the governor of it all, and that He is one and not many.

3. So then this order of its arrangement, and the concordant harmony of all things, shews that the Word, its Ruler and Governor, is not many, but One. For if there were more than one Ruler of Creation, such an universal order would not be maintained, but all things would fall into confusion because of their plurality, each one biasing the whole to his own will, and striving with the other. For just as we said that polytheism was atheism, so it follows that the rule of more than one is the rule of none. For each one would cancel the rule of the other, and none would appear ruler, but there would be anarchy everywhere. But where no ruler is, there disorder follows of course.

4. And conversely, the single order and concord of the many and diverse shews that the ruler too is one. For just as though one were to hear from a distance a lyre, composed of many diverse strings, and marvel at the concord of its symphony, in that its sound is composed neither of low notes exclusively, nor high nor intermediate only, but all combine their sounds in equal balance – and would not fail to perceive from this that the lyre was not playing itself, nor even being struck by more persons than one, but that there was one musician, even if he did not see him, who by his skill combined the sound of each string into the tuneful symphony; so, the order of the whole universe being perfectly harmonious, and there being no strife of the higher against the lower or the lower against the higher, and all things making up one order, it is consistent to think that the Ruler and King of all Creation is one and not many, Who by His own light illumines and gives movement to all.

39. Impossibility of a Plurality of Gods

For we must not think there is more than one ruler and maker of Creation: but it belongs to correct and true religion to believe that its Artificer is one, while Creation herself clearly points to this. For the fact that there is one Universe only and not more is a conclusive proof that its Maker is one. For if there were a plurality of gods, there would necessarily be also more universes than one. For neither were it reasonable for more than one God to make a single universe, nor for the one universe to be made by more than one, because of the absurdities which would result from this.

2. Firstly, if the one universe were made by a plurality of gods, that would mean weakness on the part of those who made it, because many contributed to a single result; which would be a strong proof of the imperfect creative skill of each. For if one were sufficient, the many would not supplement each other's deficiency. But to say that there is any deficiency in God is not only impious, but even beyond all sacrilege. For even among men one would not call a workman perfect if he were unable to finish his work, a single piece, by himself and without the aid of several others.

3. But if, although each one was able to accomplish the whole, yet all worked at it in order to claim a share in the result, we have the laughable conclusion that each worked for reputation, lest he should be suspected of inability. But, once more, it is most grotesque to ascribe vainglory to gods.

4. Again, if each one were sufficient for the creation of the whole, what need of more than one one being self-sufficient for the universe? Moreover it would be evidently impious and grotesque, to make the thing created one, while the creators were many and different, it being a maxim of science that what is one and complete is higher than things that are diverse.

5. And this you must know, that if the universe had been made by a plurality of gods, its movements would be diverse and inconsistent. For having regard to each one of its makers, its movements would be correspondingly different. But such difference again, as was said before, would involve disarray and general disorder; for not even a ship will sail aright if she be steered by many, unless one pilot hold the tiller, nor will a lyre struck by many produce a tuneful sound, unless there be one artist who strikes it.

6. Creation, then, being one, and the Universe one, and its order one, we must perceive that its King and Artificer also is one. For this is why the Artificer Himself made the whole universe one, lest by the coexistence of more than one a plurality of makers should be supposed; but that as the work is one, its Maker also may be believed to be One. Nor does it follow from the unity of the Maker that the Universe must be one, for God might have made others as well. But

because the Universe that has been made is one, it is necessary to believe that its Maker also is one.

40. The Rationality and Order of the Universe Proves that It is the Work of the Reason or Word of God

Who then might this Maker be? for this is a point most necessary to make plain, lest, from ignorance with regard to him, a man should suppose the wrong maker, and fall once more into the same old godless error, but I think no one is really in doubt about it. For if our argument has proved that the gods of the poets are no gods, and has convicted of error those that deify creation, and in general has shewn that the idolatry of the heathen is godlessness and impiety, it strictly follows from the elimination of these that the true religion is with us, and that the God we worship and preach is the only true One, Who is Lord of Creation and Maker of all existence.

2. Who then is this, save the Father of Christ, most holy and above all created existence, Who like an excellent pilot, by His own Wisdom and His own Word, our Lord and Saviour Christ, steers and preserves and orders all things, and does as seems to Him best? But that is best which has been done, and which we see taking place, since that is what He wills; and this a man can hardly refuse to believe.

3. For if the movement of creation were irrational, and the universe were borne along without plan, a man might fairly disbelieve what we say. But if it subsist in reason and wisdom and skill, and is perfectly ordered throughout, it follows that He that is over it and has ordered it is none other than the [reason or] Word of God.

4. But by Word I mean, not that which is involved and inherent in all things created, which some are wont to call the seminal principle, which is without soul and has no power of reason or thought, but only works by external art, according to the skill of him that applies it – nor such a word as belongs to rational beings and which consists of syllables, and has the air as its vehicle of expression – but I mean the living and powerful Word of the good God, the God of the Universe, the very Word which is God, Who while different from things that are made, and from all Creation, is the One own Word of the good Father, Who by His own providence ordered and illumines this Universe.

5. For being the good Word of the Good Father He produced the order of all things, combining one with another things contrary, and reducing them to one harmonious order. He being the Power of God and Wisdom of God causes the heaven to revolve, and has suspended the earth, and made it fast, though resting upon nothing, by His own nod. Illumined by Him, the sun gives light to the world, and the moon has her measured period of shining. By reason of Him the water is suspended in the clouds; the rains shower upon the earth, and the sea is kept within bounds, while the earth bears grasses and is clothed with all manner of plants.

6. And if a man were incredulously to ask, as regards what we are saying, if there be a Word of God at all, such an one would indeed be mad to doubt concerning the Word of God, but yet demonstration is possible from what is seen, because all things subsist by the Word and Wisdom of God, nor would any created thing have had a fixed existence had it not been made by reason, and that reason the Word of God, as we have said.

41. The Presence of the Word in Nature Necessary, Not Only for Its Original Creation, But Also for Its Permanence

But though He is Word, He is not, as we said, after the likeness of human words, composed of syllables; but He is the unchanging Image of His own Father. For men, composed of parts and made out of nothing, have their discourse composite and divisible. But God possesses true existence and is not composite, wherefore His Word also has true Existence and is not composite, but is the one and only-begotten God, Who proceeds in His goodness from the Father as from a good Fountain, and orders all things and holds them together.

2. But the reason why the Word, the Word of God, has united Himself with created things is truly wonderful, and teaches us that the present order of things is none otherwise than is fitting. For the nature of created things, inasmuch as it is brought into being out of nothing, is of a fleeting sort, and weak and mortal, if composed of itself only. But the God of all is good and exceeding noble by nature – and therefore is kind. For one that is good can grudge nothing: for which reason he does not grudge even existence, but desires all to exist, as objects for His loving-kindness.

3. Seeing then all created nature, as far as its own laws were concerned, to be fleeting and subject to dissolution, lest it should

come to this and lest the Universe should be broken up again into nothingness, for this cause He made all things by His own eternal Word, and gave substantive existence to Creation, and moreover did not leave it to be tossed in a tempest in the course of its own nature, lest it should run the risk of once more dropping out of existence; but, because He is good He guides and settles the whole Creation by His own Word, Who is Himself also God, that by the governance and providence and ordering action of the Word, Creation may have light, and be enabled to abide alway securely. For it partakes of the Word Who derives true existence from the Father, and is helped by Him so as to exist, lest that should come to it which would have come but for the maintenance of it by the Word – namely, dissolution – "for He is the Image of the invisible God, the first-born of all Creation, for through Him and in Him all things consist, things visible and things invisible, and He is the Head of the Church" as the ministers of truth teach in their holy writings.

42. This Function of the Word Described at Length

The holy Word of the Father, then, almighty and all-perfect, uniting with the universe and having everywhere unfolded His own powers, and having illumined all, both things seen and things invisible, holds them together and binds them to Himself, having left nothing void of His own power, but on the contrary quickening and sustaining all things everywhere, each severally and all collectively; while He mingles in one the principles of all sensible existence, heat namely and cold and wet and dry, and causes them not to conflict, but to make up one concordant harmony.

2. By reason of Him and His power, fire does not fight with cold nor wet with dry, but principles mutually opposed, as if friendly and brotherly combine together, and give life to the things we see, and form the principles by which bodies exist. Obeying Him, even God the Word, things on earth have life and things in the heaven have their order. By reason of Him all the sea, and the great ocean, move within their proper bounds, while, as we said above, the dry land grows grasses and is clothed with all manner of diverse plants. And, not to spend time in the enumeration of particulars, where the truth is obvious, there is nothing that is and takes place but has been made and

stands by Him and through Him, as also the Divine says, "In the beginning was the Word, and the Word was with God, and the Word was God; all things were made by Him, and without Him was not anything made."

3. For just as though some musician, having tuned a lyre, and by his art adjusted the high notes to the low, and the intermediate notes to the rest, were to produce a single tune as the result, so also the Wisdom of God, handling the Universe as a lyre, and adjusting things in the air to things on the earth, and things in the heaven to things in the air, and combining parts into wholes and moving them all by His beck and will, produces well and fittingly, as the result, the unity of the universe and of its order, Himself remaining unmoved with the Father while He moves all things by His organising action, as seems good for each to His own Father.

4. For what is surprising in His godhead is this, that by one and the same act of will He moves all things simultaneously, and not at intervals, but all collectively, both straight and curved, things above and beneath and intermediate, wet, cold, warm, seen and invisible, and orders them according to their several nature. For simultaneously at His single nod what is straight moves as straight, what is curved also, and what is intermediate, follows its own movement; what is warm receives warmth, what is dry dryness, and all things according to their several nature are quickened and organised by Him, and He produces as the result a marvellous and truly divine harmony.

43. Three Similes to Illustrate the Word's Relation to the Universe

And for so great a matter to be understood by an example, let what we are describing be compared to a great chorus. As then the chorus is composed of different people, children, women again, and old men, and those who are still young, and, when one, namely the conductor, gives the sign, each utters sound according to his nature and power, the man as a man, the child as a child, the old man as an old man, and the young man as a young man, while all make up a single harmony.

2. Or as our soul at one time moves our several senses according to the proper function of each, so that when some one object is present all alike are put in motion, and the eye sees, the ear hears, the hand touches, the smell takes in odour, and the palate tastes – and

often the other parts of the body act too, as for instance if the feet walk.

3. Or, to make our meaning plain by yet a third example, it is as though a very great city were built, and administered under the presence of the ruler and king who has built it; for when he is present and gives orders, and has his eye upon everything, all obey; some busy themselves with agriculture, others hasten for water to the aqueducts, another goes forth to procure provisions – one goes to senate, another enters the assembly, the judge goes to the bench, and the magistrate to his court. The workman likewise settles to his craft, the sailor goes down to the sea, the carpenter to his workshop, the physician to his treatment, the architect to his building; and while one is going to the country, another is returning from the country, and while some walk about the town others are going out of the town and returning to it again: but all this is going on and is organised by the presence of the one Ruler, and by his management.

4. In like manner then we must conceive of the whole of Creation, even though the example be inadequate, yet with an enlarged idea. For with the single impulse of a nod as it were of the Word of God, all things simultaneously fall into order, and each discharge their proper functions, and a single order is made up by them all together.

44. The Similes Applied to the Whole Universe, Seen and Unseen

For by a nod and by the power of the Divine Word of the Father that governs and presides over all, the heaven revolves, the stars move, the sun shines, the moon goes her circuit, and the air receives the sun's light and the æther his heat, and the winds blow: the mountains are reared on high, the sea is rough with waves, and the living things in it grow the earth abides fixed, and bears fruit, and man is formed and lives and dies again, and all things whatever have their life and movement; fire burns, water cools, fountains spring forth, rivers flow, seasons and hours come round, rains descend, clouds are filled, hail is formed, snow and ice congeal, birds fly, creeping things go along, water animals swim, the sea is navigated, the earth is sown and grows crops in due season, plants grow, and some are young, some ripening, others in their growth become old and decay, and while some things are vanishing others are being engendered and are coming to light.

2. But all these things, and more, which for their number we cannot mention, the worker of wonders and marvels, the Word of God, giving light and life, moves and orders by His own nod, making the universe one. Nor does He leave out of Himself even the invisible powers; for including these also in the universe inasmuch as he is their maker also, He holds them together and quickens them by His nod and by His providence. And there can be no excuse for disbelieving this.

3. For as by His own providence bodies grow and the rational soul moves, and possesses life and thought, and this requires little proof, for we see what takes place – so again the same Word of God with one simple nod by His own power moves and holds together both the visible universe and the invisible powers, allotting to each its proper function, so that the divine powers move in a diviner way, while visible things move as they are seen to do. But Himself being over all, both Governor and King and organising power, He does all for the glory and knowledge of His own Father, so that almost by the very works that He brings to pass He teaches us and says, "By the greatness and beauty of the creatures proportionably the maker of them is seen."

45. Conclusion – Doctrine of Scripture on the Subject of Part I

For just as by looking up to the heaven and seeing its order and the light of the stars, it is possible to infer the Word Who ordered these things, so by beholding the Word of God, one needs must behold also God His Father, proceeding from Whom He is rightly called His Father's Interpreter and Messenger.

2. And this one may see from our own experience; for if when a word proceeds from men we infer that the mind is its source, and, by thinking about the word, see with our reason the mind which it reveals, by far greater evidence and incomparably more, seeing the power of the Word, we receive a knowledge also of His good Father, as the Saviour Himself says, "He that hath seen Me hath seen the Father." But this all inspired Scripture also teaches more plainly and with more authority, so that we in our turn write boldy to you as we do, and you, if you refer to them, will be able to verify what we say.

3. For an argument when confirmed by higher authority is irresistibly proved. From the first then the divine Word firmly taught the Jewish people about the abolition of idols when it said: "Thou shalt not make to thyself a graven image, nor the likeness of anything that is in the heaven above or in the earth beneath." But the cause of their abolition another writer declares, saying: "The idols of the heathen are silver and gold, the works of men's hands: a mouth have they and will not speak, eyes have they. and will not see, ears have they and will not: hear, noses have they and will not smell, hands have they and will not handle, feet have they and will not walk." Nor has it passed over in silence the doctrine of creation; but, knowing well its beauty, lest any attending solely to this beauty should worship things as if they were gods, instead of God's works, it teaches men firmly beforehand when it says: "And do not when thou lookest up with thine eyes and seest the sun and moon and all the host of heaven, go astray and worship them, which the Lord thy God hath given to all nations under heaven." But He gave them, not to be their gods, but that by their agency the Gentiles should know, as we have said, God the Maker of them all.

4. For the people of the Jews of old had abundant teaching, in that they had the knowledge of God not only from the works of Creation, but also from the divine Scriptures. And in general to draw men away from the error and irrational imagination of idols, He saith: "Thou shalt have none other gods but Me." Not as if there were other gods does He forbid them to have them, but lest any, turning from the true God, should begin to make himself gods of what were not, such as those who in the poets and writers are called gods, though they are none. And the language itself shews that they are no Gods, when it says, "Thou shalt have none other gods," which refers only to the future. But what is referred to the future does not exist at the time of speaking.

46. Doctrine of Scripture on the Subject of Part 3

Has then the divine teaching, which abolished the godlessness of the heathen or the idols, passed over in silence, and left the race of mankind to go entirely unprovided with the knowledge of God? Not so: rather it anticipates their understanding when it says: "Hear, O

Israel, the Lord thy God is one God;" and again, "Thou shalt love the Lord thy God with all thy heart and with all thy strength;" and again, "Thou shalt worship the Lord thy God, and Him only shalt thou serve, and shalt cleave to Him."

2. But that the providence and ordering power of the Word also, over all and toward all, is attested by all inspired Scripture, this passage suffices to confirm our argument, where men who speak of God say: "Thou hast laid the foundation of the earth and it abideth. The day continueth according to Thine ordinance." And again: "Sing to our God upon the harp, that covereth the heaven with clouds, that prepareth rain for the earth, that bringeth forth grass upon the mountains, and green herb for the service of man, and giveth food to the cattle."

3. But by whom does He give it, save by Him through Whom all things were made? For the providence over all things belongs naturally to Him by Whom they were made; and who is this save the Word of God, concerning Whom in another psalm he says: "By the Word of the Lord were the heavens made, and all the host of them by the Breath of His mouth." For He tells us that all things were made in Him and through Him.

4. Wherefore He also persuades us and says , "He spake and they were made, He commanded and they were created;" as the illustrious Moses also at the beginning of his account of Creation confirms what we say by his narrative, saying: and God said, "let us make man in our image and after our likeness:" for also when He was carrying out the creation of the heaven and earth and all things, the Father said to Him, "Let the heaven be made," and "let the waters be gathered together and let the dry land appear," and "let the earth bring forth herb" and "every green thing:" so that one must convict Jews also of not genuinely attending to the Scriptures.

5. For one might ask them to whom was God speaking, to use the imperative mood? If He were commanding and addressing the things He was creating, the utterance would be redundant, for they were not yet in being, but were about to be made; but no one speaks to what does not exist, nor addresses to what is not yet made a command to be made. For if God were giving a command to the things that were to be, He must have said, "Be modal, heaven, and be made, earth, and come forth, green herb, and be created, O man." But in fact He did not do so; but He gives the command thus: "Let us make man," and

"let the green herb come forth." By which God is proved to be speaking about them to some one at hand: it follows then that some one was with Him to Whom He spoke when He made all things.

6. Who then could it be, save His Word? For to whom could God be said to speak, except His Word? Or who was with Him when He made all created Existence, except His Wisdom, which says: "When He was making the heaven and the earth I was present with Him?" But in the mention of heaven and earth, all created things in heaven and earth are included as well.

7. But being present with Him as His Wisdom and His Word, looking at the Father He fashioned the Universe, and organised it and gave it order; and, as He is the power of the Father, He gave all things strength to be, as the Savionr says: "What things soever I see the Father doing, I also do in like manner." And His holy disciples teach that all things were made "through Him and unto Him."

8. And, being the good Offspring of Him that is good, and true Son, He is the Father's Power and Wisdom and Word, not being so by participation, nor as if these qualities were imparted to Him from without, as they are to those who partake of Him and are made wise by Him, and receive power and reason in Him; but He is the very Wisdom, very Word, and very own Power of the Father, very Light, very Truth, very Righteousness, very Virtue, and in truth His express Image, and Brightness, and Resemblance. And to sum all up, He is the wholly perfect Fruit of the Father, and is alone the Son, and unchanging Image of the Father.

47. Necessity of a Return to the Word If Our Corrupt Nature is to Be Restored

Who then, who can declare the Father by number, so as to discover the powers of His Word? For like as He is the Father's Word and Wisdom, so too condescending to created things, He becomes, to impart the knowledge and apprehension of Him that begot Him, His very Brightness and very Life, and the Door, and the Shepherd, and the Way, and King and Governor, and Saviour over all, and Light, and Giver of Life, and Providence over all. Having then such a Son begotten of Himself, good, and Creator, the Father did not hide Him out of the sight of His creatures, but even day by day reveals Him to all by means of the organisation and life of all things, which is His work.

2. But in and through Him He reveals Himself also, as the Saviour says: "I in the Father and the Father in Me:" so that it follows that the Word is in Him that begat Him, and that He that is begotten lives eternally with the Father. But this being so, and nothing being outside Him, but both heaven and earth and all that in them is being dependent on Him, yet men in their folly have set aside the knowledge and service of Him, and honoured things that are not instead of things that are: and instead of the real and true God deified things that were not, "serving the creature rather than the Creator," thus involving themselves in foolishness and impiety.

3. For it is just as if one were to admire the works more than the workman, and being awestruck at the public works in the city, were to make light of their builder, or as if one were to praise a musical instrument but to despise the man who made and tuned it. Foolish and sadly disabled in eyesight! For how else had they known the building, or ship, or lyre, had not the shipbuilder made it, the architect built it, or the musician fashioned it?

4. As then he that reasons in such a way is mad, and beyond all madness, even so affected in mind, I think, are those who do not recognise God or worship His Word, our Lord Jesus Christ the Saviour of all, through Whom the Father orders, and holds together all things, and exercises providence over the Universe; having faith and piety towards Whom, my Christ-loving friend, be of good cheer and of good hope, because immortality and the kingdom of heaven is the fruit of faith and devotion towards Him, if only the soul be adorned according to His laws. For just as for them who walk after His example, the prize is life everlasting, so for those who walk the opposite way, and not that of virtue, there is great shame, and peril without pardon in the day of judgment, because although they knew the way of truth their acts were contrary to their knowledge.

Athanasius *On the Incarnation of the Word*

II. Erroneous Views of Creation Rejected – (1) Epicurean (Fortuitous Generation) But Diversity of Bodies and Parts Argues a Creating Intellect; (2) Platonists (Pre-Existent Matter) But This Subjects God to Human Limitations, Making Him Not a Creator But a Mechanic; (3) Gnostics (an Alien Demiurge) Rejected from Scripture

1. Of the making of the universe and the creation of all things many have taken different views, and each man has laid down the law just as he pleased. For some say that all things have come into being of themselves, and in a chance fashion; as, for example, the Epicureans, who tell us in their self-contempt, that universal providence does not exist speaking right in the face of obvious fact and experience.

2. For if, as they say, everything has had its beginning of itself, and independently of purpose, it would follow that everything had come into mere being, so as to be alike and not distinct. For it would follow in virtue of the unity of body that everything must be sun or moon, and in the case of men it would follow that the whole must be hand, or eye, or foot. But as it is this is not so. On the contrary, we see a distinction of sun, moon, and earth; and again, in the case of human bodies, of foot, hand, and head. Now, such separate arrangement as this tells us not of their having come into being of themselves, but shews that a cause preceded them; from which cause it is possible to apprehend God also as the Maker and Orderer of all.

3. But others, including Plato, who is in such repute among the Greeks, argue that God has made the world out of matter previously existing and without beginning. For God could have made nothing had not the material existed already; just as the wood must exist ready at hand for the carpenter, to enable him to work at all.

4. But in so saying they know not that they are investing God with weakness. For if He is not Himself the cause of the material, but makes things only of previously existing material, He proves to be weak, because unable to produce anything He makes without the material; just as it is without doubt a weakness of the carpenter not to be able to make anything required without his timber. For, ex hypothesi, had not the material existed, God would not have made anything. And how could He in that case be called Maker and Artificer, if He owes His ability to make to some other source – namely, to the material? So that if this be so, God will be on their theory a Mechanic only, and not a Creator out of nothing; if, that is,

He works at existing material, but is not Himself the cause of the material. For He could not in any sense be called Creator unless He is Creator of the material of which the things created have in their turn been made.

5. But the sectaries imagine to themselves a different artificer of all things, other than the Father of our Lord Jesus Christ, in deep blindness even as to the words they use.

6. For whereas the Lord says to the Jews: "Have ye not read that from the beginning He which created them made them male and female, and said, For this cause shall a man leave his father and mother, and shall cleave to his wife, and they twain shall become one flesh?" and then, referring to the Creator, says, "What, therefore, God hath joined together let not man put asunder:" how come these men to assert that the creation is independent of the Father? Or if, in the words of John, who says, making no exception, "All things were made by Him," and "without Him was not anything made," how could the artificer be another, distinct from the Father of Christ?

III. The True Doctrine – Creation Out of Nothing, of God's Lavish Bounty of Being; Man Created Above the Rest, But Incapable of Independent Perseverance; Hence the Exceptional and Supra-Natural Gift of Being in God's Image, with the Promise of Bliss Conditionally Upon His Perseverance in Grace

Thus do they vainly speculate. But the godly teaching and the faith according to Christ brands their foolish language as godlessness. For it knows that it was not spontaneously, because forethought is not absent; nor of existing matter, because God is not weak; but that out of nothing, and without its having any previous existence, God made the universe to exist through His word, as He says firstly through Moses: "In the beginning God created the heaven and the earth;" secondly, in the most edifying book of the Shepherd, "first of all believe that God is one, which created and framed all things, and made them to exist out of nothing."

2. To which also Paul refers when he says, "By faith we understand that the worlds have been framed by the Word of God, so that what is seen hath not been made out of things which do appear."

3. For God is good, or rather is essentially the source of goodness: nor could one that is good be niggardly of anything: whence, grudging existence to none, He has made all things out of nothing by His

own Word, Jesus Christ our Lord. And among these, having taken especial pity, above all things on earth, upon the race of men, and having perceived its inability, by virtue of the condition of its origin, to continue in one stay, He gave them a further gift, and He did not barely create man, as He did all the irrational creatures on the earth, but made them after His own image, giving them a portion even of the power of His own Word; so that having as it were a kind of reflexion of the Word, and being made rational, they might be able to abide ever in blessedness, living the true life which belongs to the saints in paradise.

4. But knowing once more how the will of man could sway to either side, in anticipation He secured the grace given them by a law and by the spot where He placed them. For He brought them into His own garden, and gave them a law: so that, if they kept the grace and remained good, they might still keep the life in paradise without sorrow or pain or care besides having the promise of incorruption in heaven; but that if they transgressed and turned back, and became evil, they might know that they were incurring that corruption in death which was theirs by nature: no longer to live in paradise, but cast out of it from that time forth to die and to abide in death and in corruption.

5. Now this is that of which Holy Writ also gives warning, saying in the Person of God: "Of every tree that is in the garden, eating thou shalt eat: but of the tree of the knowledge of good and evil, ye shall not eat of it, but on the day that ye eat, dying ye shall die." But by "dying ye shall die," what else could be meant than not dying merely, but also abiding ever in the corruption of death?

IV. Our Creation and God's Incarnation Most Intimately Connected; As by the Ward Man Was Called from Non-Existence into Being, and Further Received the Grace of a Divine Life, So by the One Fault Which Forfeited that Life They Again Incurred Corruption and Untold Sin and Misery filled the World

You are wondering, perhaps, for what possible reason, having proposed to speak of the Incarnation of the Word, we are at present treating of the origin of mankind. But this, too, properly belongs to the aim of our treatise.

2. For in speaking of the appearance of the Saviour amongst us, we must needs speak also of the origin of men, that you may know that the reason of His coming down was because of us, and that our transgression called forth the loving-kindness of the Word, that the Lord should both make haste to help us and appear among men.

3. For of His becoming Incarnate we were the object, and for our salvation He dealt so lovingly as to appear and be born even in a human body.

4. Thus, then, God has made man, and willed that he should abide in incorruption; but men, having despised and rejected the contemplation of God, and devised and contrived evil for themselves (as was said in the former treatise), received the condemnation of death with which they had been threatened; and from thenceforth no longer remained as they were made, but were being corrupted according to their devices; and death had the mastery over them as king. For transgression of the commandment was turning them back to their natural state, so that just as they have had their being out of nothing, so also, as might be expected, they might look for corruption into nothing in the course of time.

5. For if, out of a former normal state of nonexistence, they were called into being by the Presence and loving-kindness of the Word, it followed naturally that when men were bereft of the knowledge of God and were turned back to what was not (for what is evil is not, but what is good is), they should, since they derive their being from God who IS, be everlastingly bereft even of being; in other words, that they should be disintegrated and abide in death and corruption.

6. For man is by nature mortal, inasmuch as he is made out of what is not; but by reason of his likeness to Him that is (and if he still preserved this likeness by keeping Him in his knowledge) he would stay his natural corruption, and remain incorrupt; as Wisdom says: "The taking heed to His laws is the assurance of immortality;" but being incorrupt, he would live henceforth as God, to which I suppose the divine Scripture refers, when it says: "I have said ye are gods, and ye are all sons of the most Highest; but ye die like men, and fall as one of the princes."

V. For God has not only made us out of nothing; but He gave us freely, by the Grace of the Word, a life in correspondence with God; But men, having rejected things eternal, and, by counsel of the devil, turned to the things of corruption, became the cause of their own corruption in death, being, as I said before, by nature corruptible, but destined, by the grace following from partaking of the Word, to have escaped their natural state, had they remained good

2. For because of the Word dwelling with them, even their natural corruption did not come near them, as Wisdom also says: "God made man for incorruption, and as an image of His own eternity; but by envy of the devil death came into the world." But when this was come to pass, men began to die, while corruption thence – forward prevailed against them, gaining even more than its natural power over the whole race, inasmuch as it had, owing to the transgression of the commandment, the threat of the Deity as a further advantage against them...

XII. For Though Man Was Created in Grace, God, Foreseeing His Forgetfulness, Provided Also the Works of Creation to Remind Man of Him; Yet Further, He Ordained a Law and Prophets, Whose Ministry Was Meant for All the World; Yet Men Heeded Only Their Own Lusts

For whereas the grace of the Divine Image was in itself sufficient to make known God the Word, and through Him the Father; still God, knowing the weakness of men, made provision even for their carelessness: so that if they cared not to know God of themselves, they might be enabled through the works of creation to avoid ignorance of the Maker.

2. But since men's carelessness, by little and little, descends to lower things, God made provision, once more, even for this weakness of theirs, by sending a law, and prophets, men such as they knew, so that even if they were not ready to look up to heaven and know their Creator, they might have their instruction from those near at hand. For men are able to learn from men more directly about higher things.

3. So it was open to them, by looking into the height of heaven, and perceiving the harmony of creation, to know its Ruler, the Word of the Father, Who, by His own providence over all things makes known the Father to all, and to this end moves all things, that through Him all may know God.

4. Or, if this were too much for them, it was possible for them to meet at least the holy men, and through them to learn of God, the Maker of all things, the Father of Christ; and that the worship of idols is godlessness, and full of all impiety.

5. Or it was open to them, by knowing the law even, to cease from all lawlessness and live a virtuous life. For neither was the law for the Jews alone, nor were the Prophets sent for them only, but, though sent to the Jews and persecuted by the Jews, they were for all the world a holy school of the knowledge of God and the conduct of the soul.

6. God's goodness then and loving-kindness being so great – men nevertheless, overcome by the pleasures of the moment and by the illusions and deceits sent by demons, did not raise their heads toward the truth, but loaded themselves the more with evils and sins, so as no longer to seem rational, but from their ways to be reckoned void of reason.

XLI. Answer to the Greeks – Do they recognise the Logos? If He manifests Himself in the organism of the Universe, why not in one Body? For a human body is part of the same whole

We come now to the unbelief of the Gentiles; and this is indeed a matter for complete astonishment, for they laugh at that which is no fit subject for mockery, yet fail to see the shame and ridiculousness of their own idols. But the arguments on our side do not lack weight, so we will confute them too on reasonable grounds, chiefly from what we ourselves also see.

First of all, what is there in our belief that is unfitting or ridiculous? Is it only that we say that the Word has been manifested in a body? Well, if they themselves really love the truth, they will agree with us that this involved no unfittingness at all. If they deny that there is a Word of God at all, that will be extraordinary, for then they will be ridiculing what they do not know. But suppose they confess that there is a Word of God, that He is the Governor of all things, that in Him the Father wrought the creation, that by His providence the whole receives light and life and being, and that He is King over all, so that He is known by means of the works of His providence, and through Him the Father. Suppose they confess all this, what then? Are they not unknowingly turning the ridicule against themselves?

The Greek philosophers say that the universe is a great body, and they say truly, for we perceive the universe and its parts with our senses. But if the Word of God is in the universe, which is a body, and has entered into it in its every part, what is there surprising or unfitting in our saying that He has entered also into human nature? If it were unfitting for Him to have embodied Himself at all, then it would be unfitting for Him to have entered into the universe, and to be giving light and movement by His providence to all things in it, because the universe, as we have seen, is itself a body. But if it is right and fitting for Him to enter into the universe and to reveal Himself through it, then, because humanity is part of the universe along with the rest, it is no less fitting for Him to appear in a human body, and to enlighten and to work through that. And surely if it were wrong for a part of the universe to have been used to reveal His Divinity to men, it would be much more wrong that He should be so revealed by the whole!

XLII. *His union to the body is based upon His relation to Creation as a whole; He used a human body, since to man it was that He wished to reveal Himself*

Take a parallel case. A man's personality actuates and quickens his whole body. If anyone said it was unsuitable for the man's power to be in the toe, he would be thought silly, because, while granting that a man penetrates and actuates the whole of his body, he denied his presence in the part. Similarly, no one who admits the presence of the Word of God in the universe as a whole should think it unsuitable for a single human body to be by Him actuated and enlightened.

But is it, perhaps, because humanity is a thing created and brought into being out of non-existence that they regard as unfitting the manifestation of the Savior in our nature? If so, it is high time that they spurned Him from creation too; for it, too, has been brought out of non-being into being by the Word. But if, on the other hand, although creation is a thing that has been made, it is not unsuitable for the

Word to be present in it, then neither is it unsuitable for Him to be in man.

Man is a part of the creation, as I said before; and the reasoning which applies to one applies to the other. All things derive from the Word their light and movement and life, as the Gentile authors themselves say, "In Him we live and move and have our being." Very well then. That being so, it is by no means unbecoming that the Word should dwell in man. So if, as we say, the Word has used that in which He is as the means of His self-manifestation, what is there ridiculous in that? He could not have used it had He not been present in it; but we have already admitted that He is present both in the whole and in the parts. What, then, is there incredible in His manifesting Himself through that in which He is?

By His own power He enters completely into each and all, and orders them throughout ungrudgingly; and, had He so willed, He could have revealed Himself and His Father by means of sun or moon or sky or earth or fire or water. Had He done so, no one could rightly have accused Him of acting unbecomingly, for He sustains in one whole all things at once, being present and invisibly revealed not only in the whole, but also in each particular part. This being so, and since, moreover, He has willed to reveal Himself through men, who are part of the whole, there can be nothing ridiculous in His using a human body to manifest the truth and knowledge of the Father.

Does not the mind of man pervade his entire being, and yet find expression through one part only, namely the tongue? Does anybody say on that account that Mind has degraded itself? Of course not. Very well, then, no more is it degrading for the Word, Who pervades all things, to have appeared in a human body. For, as I said before, if it were unfitting for Him thus to indwell the part, it would be equally so for Him to exist within the whole.

XLIII. He came in human rather than in any nobler form, because (1) He came to save, not to impress; (2) man alone of creatures had sinned, As men would not recognise His works in the Universe, He came and worked among them as Man; in the sphere to which they had limited themselves.

Some may then ask, why did He not manifest Himself by means of other and nobler parts of creation, and use some nobler instrument, such as sun or moon or stars or fire or air, instead of mere man? The answer is this. The Lord did not come to make a display. He came to heal and to teach suffering men. For one who wanted to make a display the thing would have been just to appear and dazzle the beholders. But for Him Who came to heal and to teach the way was not merely to dwell here, but to put Himself at the disposal of those who needed Him, and to be manifested according as they could bear it, not vitiating the value of the Divine appearing by exceeding their capacity to receive it.

Moreover, nothing in creation had erred from the path of God's purpose for it, save only man. Sun, moon, heaven, stars, water, air, none of these had swerved from their order, but, knowing the Word as their Maker and their King, remained as they were made. Men alone having rejected what is good, have invented nothings instead of the truth, and have ascribed the honor due to God and the knowledge concerning Him to demons and men in the form of stones. Obviously the Divine goodness could not overlook so grave a matter as this. But men could not recognize Him as ordering and ruling creation as a whole. So what does He do? He takes to Himself for instrument a part of the whole, namely a human body, and enters into that. Thus He ensured that men should recognize Him in the part who could not do so in the whole, and that those who could not lift their eyes to His unseen power might recognize and behold Him in the likeness of themselves. For, being men, they would naturally learn to know His Father more quickly and directly by means of a body that corresponded to their own and by the Divine works done through it; for by comparing His works with their own they would judge His to be not human but Divine.

And if, as they say, it were unsuitable for the Word to reveal Himself through bodily acts, it would be equally so for Him to do so through the works of the universe. His being in creation does not mean that He shares its nature; on the contrary, all created things partake of His power. Similarly, though He used the body as His instrument, He shared nothing of its defect, but rather sanctified it by His indwelling. Does not even Plato, of whom the Greeks think so much, say that the Author of the Universe, seeing it storm-tossed and in danger of sinking into the state of dissolution, takes his seat at the helm of the Life-force of the universe, and comes to the rescue and puts everything right? What, then, is there incredible in our saying that, mankind having gone astray, the Word descended upon it and was manifest as man, so that by His intrinsic goodness and His steersmanship He might save it from the storm?

XLIV. As God made man by a word, why not restore him by a word? But (1) creation out of nothing is different than reparation of what already exists; (2) Man was there with a definite need, calling for a definite remedy; Death was ingrained in man's nature: He then must wind life closely to human nature; Therefore the Word became Incarnate that He might meet and conquer death in His usurped territory (Simile of straw and asbestos)

It may be, however, that, though shamed into agreeing that this objection is void, the Greeks will want to raise another. They will say that, if God wanted to instruct and save mankind, He might have done so, not by His Word's assumption of a body, but, even as He at first created them, by the mere signification of His will. The reasonable reply to that is that the circumstances in the two cases are quite different.

In the beginning, nothing as yet existed at all; all that was needed, therefore, in order to bring all things into being, was that His will to do so should be signified. But once man was in existence, and things that were, not things that were not, demanded to be healed, it followed as a matter of course that the Healer and Savior should align Himself with those things that existed already, in order to heal the existing evil. For that reason, therefore, He was made man, and used the body as His human instrument. If this were not the fitting way, and He willed to use an instrument at all, how otherwise was the Word to come? And whence could He take His instrument, save from among those already in existence and needing His Godhead through One like themselves? It was not things non-existent that needed salvation, for which a bare creative word might have sufficed, but man – man already in existence and already in process of corruption and ruin. It was natural and right, therefore, for the Word to use a human instrument and by that means unfold Himself to all.

You must know, moreover, that the corruption which had set in was not external to the body but established within it. The need, therefore, was that life should cleave to it in corruption's place, so that, just as death was brought into being in the body, life also might be engendered in it. If death had been exterior to the body, life might fittingly have been the same. But if death was within the body, woven into its very substance and dominating it as though completely one with it, the need was for Life to be woven into it instead, so that the body by thus enduing itself with life might cast corruption off.

Suppose the Word had come outside the body instead of in it, He would, of course, have defeated death, because death is powerless against the Life. But the corruption inherent in the body would have remained in it none the less. Naturally, therefore, the Savior assumed a body for Himself, in order that the body, being interwoven as it were with life, should no longer remain a mortal thing, in thrall to death, but as endued with immortality and risen from death, should thenceforth remain immortal. For once having put on corruption, it could not rise, unless it put on life instead; and besides this, death of its very nature could not appear otherwise than in a body. Therefore He put on a body, so that in the body He might find death and blot it out. And, indeed, how could the Lord have been proved to be the Life at all, had He not endued with life that which was subject to death?

Take an illustration. Stubble is a substance naturally destructible by fire; and it still remains stubble, fearing the menace of fire which has the natural property of consuming it, even if fire is kept away from it, so that it is not actually burnt. But suppose that, instead of merely keeping the fire from it somebody soaks the stubble with a quantity of asbestos, the substance which is said to be the antidote to fire. Then the stubble no longer fears the fire, because it has put on that which fire cannot touch, and therefore it is safe. It is just the same with regard to the body and death. Had death been kept from it by a mere command, it would still have remained mortal and corruptible, according to its nature. To prevent this, it put on the incorporeal Word of God, and therefore fears neither death nor corruption any more, for it is clad with Life as with a garment and in it corruption is clean done away.

XLV. Thus once again every part of creation manifests the glory of God; Nature, the witness to her Creator, yields (by miracles) a second testimony to God Incarnate; The witness of

Nature, perverted by man's sin, was thus forced back to truth; If these reasons suffice not, let the Greeks look at facts

The Word of God thus acted consistently in assuming a body and using a human instrument to vitalize the body. He was consistent in working through man to reveal Himself everywhere, as well as through the other parts of His creation, so that nothing was left void of His Divinity and knowledge. For I take up now the point I made before, namely that the Savior did this in order that He might fill all things everywhere with the knowledge of Himself, just as they are already filled with His presence, even as the Divine Scripture says, "The whole universe was filled with the knowledge of the Lord."

If a man looks up to heaven he sees there His ordering; but if he cannot look so high as heaven, but only so far as men, through His works he sees His power, incomparable with human might, and learns from them that He alone among men is God the Word. Or, if a man has gone astray among demons and is in fear of them, he may see this Man drive them out and judge therefrom that He is indeed their Master. Again, if a man has been immersed in the element of water and thinks that it is God – as indeed the Egyptians do worship water – he may see its very nature changed by Him and learn that the Lord is Creator of all. And if a man has gone down even to Hades, and stands awestruck before the heroes who have descended thither, regarding them as gods, still he may see the fact of Christ's resurrection and His victory over death, and reason from it that, of all these, He alone is very Lord and God.

For the Lord touched all parts of creation, and freed and undeceived them all from every deceit. As St. Paul says, "Having put off from Himself the principalities and the powers, He triumphed on the cross," so that no one could possibly be any longer deceived, but everywhere might find the very Word of God. For thus man, enclosed on every side by the works of creation and everywhere – in heaven, in Hades, in men and on the earth, beholding the unfolded Godhead of the Word, is no longer deceived concerning God, but worships Christ alone, and through Him rightly knows the Father.

On these grounds, then, of reason and of principle, we will fairly silence the Gentiles in their turn. But if they think these arguments insufficient to confute them, we will go on in the next chapter to prove our point from facts.

LIV. The Word Incarnate, as is the case with the Invisible God, is known to us by His works; By them we recognise his deifying mission; Let us be content to enumerate a few of them, leaving their dazzling plentitude to him who will behold

As, then, he who desires to see God Who by nature is invisible and not to be beheld, may yet perceive and know Him through His works, so too let him who does not see Christ with his understanding at least consider Him in His bodily works and test whether they be of man or God. If they be of man, then let him scoff; but if they be of God, let him not mock at things which are no fit subject for scorn, but rather let him recognize the fact and marvel that things divine have been revealed to us by such humble means, that through death deathlessness has been made known to us, and through the Incarnation of the Word the Mind whence all things proceed has been declared, and its Agent and Ordainer, the Word of God Himself.

He, indeed, assumed humanity that we might become God. He manifested Himself by means of a body in order that we might perceive the Mind of the unseen Father. He endured shame from men that we might inherit immortality. He Himself was unhurt by this, for He is impassable and incorruptible; but by His own impassability He kept and healed the suffering men on whose account He thus endured. In short, such and so many are the Savior's achievements that follow from His Incarnation, that to try to number them is like gazing at the open sea and trying to count the waves. One cannot see all the waves with one's eyes, for when one tries to do so those that are following on baffle one's senses. Even so, when one wants to take in all the achievements of Christ in the body, one cannot do so, even by reckoning them up, for the things that transcend one's thought are always more than those one thinks that one has grasped.

As we cannot speak adequately about even a part of His work, therefore, it will be better for us not to speak about it as a whole. So we will mention but one thing more, and then leave the whole for you to marvel at. For, indeed, everything about it is marvelous, and wherever a man turns his gaze he sees the Godhead of the Word and is smitten with awe.

Athanasius *Contra Arianos*, Discourse II

Chapter XXII. Text Explained; Sixthly, the context of Proverbs 8:22–30; It is right to interpret the passage by the *Regula fidei*; 'Founded' is used in contrast to superstructure; and it implies, as in the case of stones in building, previous existence; 'Before the world' signifies the divine intention and purpose; Recurrence to Proverbs 8:22, and application of it to created Wisdom as seen in the works; The Son reveals the Father, first by the works, then by the Incarnation

78. Now the Only-begotten and very Wisdom of God is Creator and Framer of all things; for 'in Wisdom hast Thou made them all,' he says, and 'the earth is full of Thy creation.' But that what came into being might not only be, but be good, it pleased God that His own Wisdom should condescend to the creatures, so as to introduce an impress and semblance of Its Image on all in common and on each, that what was made might be manifestly wise works and worthy of God . For as of the Son of God, considered as the Word, our word is an image, so of the same Son considered as Wisdom is the wisdom which is implanted in us an image; in which wisdom we, having the power of knowledge and thought, become recipients of the All-framing Wisdom; and through It we are able to know Its Father. 'For he who hath the Son,' saith He, 'hath the Father also;' and 'he that receiveth Me, receiveth Him that sent Me.'

Such an impress then of Wisdom being created in us, and being in all the works, with reason does the true and framing Wisdom take to Itself what belongs to its own impress, and say, 'The Lord created me for His works;' for what the wisdom in us says, that the Lord Himself speaks as if it were His own; and, whereas He is not Himself created, being Creator, yet because of the image of Him created in the works, He says this as if of Himself. And as the Lord Himself has said, 'He that receiveth you, receiveth Me,' because His impress is in us, so, though He be not among the creatures, yet because His image and impress is created in the works, He says, as if in His own person, 'The Lord created me a beginning of His ways for His works.'

And therefore has this impress of Wisdom in the works been brought into being, that, as I said before, the world might recognise in it its own Creator the Word, and through Him the Father. And this is what Paul said, 'Because that which may be known of God is manifest in them, for God has shewed it unto them: for the invisible things of Him from the creation of the world are clearly seen, being understood by the things that are made.' But if so, the Word is not a creature in essence; but the wisdom which is in us and so called, is spoken of in this passage in the Proverbs.

79. But if this too fails to persuade them [the Arians, ed.], let them tell us themselves, whether there is any wisdom in the creatures or not? If not how is it that the Apostle complains, 'For after that in the Wisdom of God the world by wisdom knew not God?' Or how is it if there is no wisdom, that a 'multitude of wise men' are found in Scripture? For 'a wise man feareth and departeth from evil;' and 'through wisdom is a house builded;' and the Preacher says, 'A man's wisdom maketh his face to shine;' and he blames those who are headstrong thus, 'Say not thou, what is the cause that the former days were better than these? For thou dost not inquire in wisdom concerning this.'

But if, as the Son of Sirach says, 'He poured her out upon all His works; she is with all flesh according to His gift, and He hath given her to them that love Him,' and this outpouring is a note, not of the Essence of the Very Wisdom and Only-begotten, but of that wisdom which is imaged in the world, how is it incredible that the All-framing and true Wisdom Itself, whose impress is the wisdom and knowledge poured out in the world, should say, as I have already explained, as if of Itself, 'The Lord created me for His works?' For the wisdom in the world is not creative, but is that which is created in the works, according to which 'the heavens declare the glory of God, and the firmament sheweth His handywork.' This if men have within them, they will acknowledge the true Wisdom of God; and will know that they are made really after God's Image.

And, as some son of a king, when the father wished to build a city, might cause his own name to be printed upon each of the works that were rising, both to give security to them of the works remaining, by reason of the show of his name on everything, and also to make them remember him and his father from the name, and having finished the city might be asked concerning it, how it was made, and then would answer, 'It is made securely, for according to the will of my father, I am imaged in each work, for my name was made in the works;' but saying this, he does not signify that his own essence is created, but the impress of himself by means of his name; in the same manner, to apply the illustration, to those who admire the wisdom in the creatures, the true Wisdom makes answer, 'The Lord created me for the works,' for my impress is in them; and I have thus condescended for the framing of all things.

80. Moreover, that the Son should be speaking of the impress that is within us as if it were Himself, should not startle any one, considering (for we must not shrink from repetition) that, when Saul was persecuting the Church, in which was His impress and image, He said, as if He were Himself under persecution, 'Saul, why persecutest thou Me?' Therefore (as has been said), as, supposing the impress itself of Wisdom which is in the works had said, 'The Lord created me for the works,' no one would have been startled, so, if He, the True and Framing Wisdom, the Only-begotten Word of God, should use what belongs to His image as about Himself, namely, 'The Lord created me for the works,' let no one, overlooking the wisdom created in the world and in the works, think that 'He created' is said of the Substance of the Very Wisdom, lest, diluting the wine with water, he be judged a defrauder of the truth.

For It is Creative and Framer; but Its impress is created in the works, as the copy of the image. And He says, 'Beginning of ways,' since such wisdom becomes a sort of beginning. and, as it were, rudiments of the knowledge of God; for a man entering, as it were, upon this way first, and keeping it in the fear of God (as Solomon says, 'The fear of the Lord is the beginning of wisdom'), then advancing upwards in his thoughts and perceiving the Framing Wisdom which is in the creation, will perceive in It also Its Father, as the Lord Himself has said, 'He that hath seen Me, hath seen the Father,' and as John writes, 'He who acknowledgeth the Son, hath the Father also.' And He says, 'Before the world He founded me,' since in Its impress the works remain settled and eternal. Then, lest any, hearing concerning the wisdom thus created in the works, should think the true Wisdom, God's Son, to be by nature a creature, He has found it necessary to add, 'Before the mountains, and before the earth, and before the waters, and before all hills He begets me,' that in saying, 'before every creature' (for He includes all the creation under these heads), He may shew that He is not created together with the works according to Essence. For if He was created 'for the works,' yet is before them, it follows that He is in being before He was created. He is not then a creature by nature and essence, but as He Himself has added, an Offspring. But in what differs a creature from an offspring, and how it is distinct by nature, has been shewn in what has gone before.

81. But since He proceeds to say, 'When He prepared the heaven, I was present with Him,' we ought to know that He says not this as if without Wisdom the Father prepared the heaven or the clouds above (for there is no room to doubt that all things are created in Wisdom, and without It was made not even one thing); but this is what He says, 'All things took place in Me and through Me, and when there was need that Wisdom should be created in the works, in My Essence indeed I was with the Father, but by a condescension to things originate, I was disposing over the works My own impress, so that the whole world as being in one body, might not be at variance but in concord with itself.'

All those then who with an upright understanding, according to the wisdom given unto them, come to contemplate the creatures, are able to say for themselves, 'By Thy appointment all things continue;' but they who make light of this must be told, 'Professing themselves to be wise, they became fools;' for 'that which may be known of God is manifest in them; for God has revealed it unto them; for the invisible things of Him from the creation of the world are clearly seen, being perceived by the things that are made, even His eternal Power and Godhead, so that they are without excuse. Because that when they knew God, they glorified Him not as God, but served the creature more than the Creator of all, who is blessed for ever. Amen.' And they will surely be shamed at hearing, 'For, after that in the wisdom of God (in the mode we have explained above), the world by wisdom knew not God, it pleased God by the foolishness of the preaching to save them that believe.' For no longer, as in the former times, God has willed to be known by an image and shadow of wisdom, that namely which is in the creatures, but He has made the true Wisdom Itself to take flesh, and to become man, and to undergo the death of the cross; that by the faith in Him, henceforth all that believe may obtain salvation.

However, it is the same Wisdom of God, which through Its own Image in the creatures (whence also It is said to be created), first manifested Itself, and through Itself Its own Father; and afterwards, being Itself the Word, has 'become flesh,' as John says, and after abolishing death and saving our race, still more revealed Himself and through Him His own Father, saying, 'Grant unto them that they may know Thee the only true God, and Jesus Christ whom Thou hast sent.'

82. Hence the whole earth is filled with the knowledge of Him; for the knowledge of Father through Son and of Son from Father is one and the same, and the Father delights in Him, and in the same joy the Son rejoices in the Father, saying, 'I was by Him, daily His delight, rejoicing always before Him.' And this again proves that the Son is not foreign, but proper to the Father's Essence. For behold, not because of us has He come to be, as the irreligious men say, nor is He out of nothing (for not from without did God procure for Himself a cause of rejoicing), but the words denote what is His own and like.

When then was it, when the Father rejoiced not? But if He ever rejoiced, He was ever, in whom He rejoiced. And in whom does the Father rejoice, except as seeing Himself in His own Image, which is His Word? And though in sons of men also He had delight, on finishing the world, as it is written in these same Proverbs, yet this too has a consistent sense. For even thus He had delight, not because joy was added to Him, but again on seeing the works made after His own Image; so that even this rejoicing of God is on account of His Image. And how too has the Son delight, except as seeing Himself in the Father? For this is the same as saying, 'He that hath seen Me, hath seen the Father,' and 'I am in the Father and the Father in Me.' Vain then is your vaunt as is on all sides shewn, O Christ's enemies, and vainly did ye parade and circulate everywhere your text, 'The Lord created me a beginning of His ways,' perverting its sense, and publishing, not Solomon's meaning, but your own comment. For behold your sense is proved to be but a fantasy; but the passage in the Proverbs, as well as all that is above said, proves that the Son is not a creature in nature and essence, but the proper Offspring of the Father, true Wisdom and Word, by whom 'all things were made,' and 'without Him was made not one thing.'

Ephrem the Syrian

> St. Ephrem the Syrian (306 – 373), though best known as a writer of hymns, also wrote ascetical, dogmatic, polemical, and exegetical works, many of them in verse, and all originally in Syriac. His hymns on the Nativity of Christ discuss the Creation of the world and parallel his commentary on Genesis. At the beginning of that commentary, Ephrem denies that there is anything allegorical in the creation account, which he treats as describing the origin of the physical universe.
>
> Ephrem affirms creation out of nothing, but with a twist. Five created things – heaven, earth, fire, wind, and water – were directly created out of nothing, and everything else was created out of those initial elements. Everything that exists was created in the course of six, twenty-four hour days, and all of it was created for the sake of humans.
>
> Ephrem's "young-earth" literalism entails some counterintuitive consequences, which he fully accepts: light was created on day one and existed for three days before the creation of the sun on day four; plant and animal life were created full-grown, as were humans, and so all these created things were temporally young at their creation but old in the sense of maturity.
>
> He views Genesis 2 as filling in details of the creation that were left out in Genesis 1, much like a newspaper feature story rounds out an adjacent news story. He finds the two accounts in harmony. Ephrem is unique among the Fathers in this collection as the only one who denies that the spirit hovering over the waters at the beginning of creation was the Holy Spirit, though he acknowledges that others hold that view.

Ephrem the Syrian *Commentary on Genesis*

Section I

I. In the beginning God created the heavens and the earth, that is, the substance of the heavens and the substance of the earth. So let no one think that there is anything allegorical in the works of the six days. No one can rightly say that the things that pertain to these days were symbolic, nor can one say that they were meaningless names or that other things were symbolized for us by their names. Rather, let us know in just what manner heaven and earth were created in the beginning. They were truly heaven and earth. There was no other thing signified by the names "heaven" and "earth." The rest of the works and things made that followed were not meaningless significations either, for the substances of their natures correspond to what their names signify.

2. *In the beginning God created heaven and earth.* At this point these comprised the only things that had been made, for there was nothing else created along with heaven and earth. Even the elements that were created on that day had not yet been created. If the elements had been created along with heaven and earth, Moses would have said so. But he did not, lest he give the names of the elements precedence over their substances. Therefore, it is evident that heaven and earth came to be from nothing because neither water nor wind had yet been created, nor had fire, light or darkness been given their natures, for they were younger than heaven and earth. These things were created things that came after heaven and earth and they were not self-subsistent beings for they did not exist before [heaven and earth].

3. After this [Moses] spoke not of the things that were above the firmament, but rather of those things that were between the firmament and the earth which is within [the womb]. [Moses] wrote about [the things within the firmament] for us, although he did not write about everything for us, for he did not record for us the day on which the spiritual beings were created.

(2) [Moses] then goes on to write that *the earth was tohu and bohu,* that is, void and desolation. This is to show that even the void and desolation were older than the elements. I am not saying that the void and desolation were something. Rather [I am saying] that the earth, which does exist, was known [to exist] in something which does not exist, for the earth existed alone without any other thing.

4. After [Moses] spoke about the creation of heaven and earth and showed that the waste and desolation preceded the elements that were created by the length of that moment that followed [their creation], he turned to write about those elements saying, *Darkness was upon the face of the abyss.* For the abyss of waters was created at that time. But how was it created on the day on which it was created? Even though it was created on this day and at this moment, Moses does not tell us here how it was created. For now, we should accept the creation of

the abyss as it is written, while we wait to learn from Moses how it was created.

(2) As for the darkness that was upon the face of the abyss, some posit that it was a cloud of heaven. Now, if the firmament had been created on the first day they would speak rightly. If the upper heavens were similar to the firmament, then there would have been a thick darkness between the two heavens, for the light had not been created nor affixed there to dissipate the darkness by its rays. But if the place between the two heavens is light as Ezekiel (Ez 1:1, 22), Paul (Acts 9:3; 22:6; 26:13), and Stephen (Acts 7:55–56) bear witness, then how could the heavens, which had dissipated the darkness with their lights, spread darkness over the abyss?

5. Because everything that was created was created in those six days, whether it was written down that it was created or not, the clouds must also have been created on the first day, just as fire was created along with wind, although Moses did not write about the fire as he did about the wind. Thus, the clouds were created along with the abyss although Moses did not write that the clouds were created along with the abyss, just as he did not record the creation of fire along with that of the wind when he wrote about the creation of the wind.

(2) It was necessary that everything be known to have its beginning in those six days. The clouds were surely created along with the abyss, for how many times were these brought forth from the abyss? Elijah saw a cloud rising up out of the sea. Solomon also said, *By his knowledge the depths broke forth and the clouds sprinkled down dew*. It was not only because of their substance that they should have been created at this point, but they were created on that first night because they also rendered service on that first night. Just as the clouds covered Egypt for three days and three nights, clouds were spread over all of Creation on the first night and on the first day. If the clouds had been dispersed, light would not have been required on the first day because the brightness of the upper heavens would have been sufficient to fill the place of the light that was created on the first day.

6. After one night and one day were completed, the firmament was created on the second evening and henceforth its shadow rendered service for all subsequent nights. Therefore, heaven and earth were created on the evening of the first night. Along with the abyss

that was created, there were also created those clouds which, when they were spread out, brought about the requisite night. After their shadow had served for twelve hours, light was created beneath them and the light dispersed their shadow that had been spread over the waters all night.

7. After Moses spoke of the darkness that was spread over the face of the abyss, he then said, *the wind of God was hovering over the face of the waters.* Because Moses called it *the wind of God*, and said *it was hovering*, some posit that this is the Holy Spirit and, because of what is written here, associate it with the activity of creation. Nevertheless, the faithful do not make this connection, for these things cannot be so related. Rather, by those things that are truly said about it, they associate it with that element, just as, on the basis of the names employed, they cannot posit the Spirit as maker, for it is said that an evil spirit of God consumed Saul.

(2) It is indeed said that *it was hovering*, but what came forth from the waters on the first day when [the wind] was hovering over the waters? If on the day that it was written that *it was hovering over the waters* nothing came out of the waters, and then on the fifth day when the waters brought forth reptiles and birds, it was not written that the wind *was hovering*, how then can anyone say that this wind took part in the activity of creation? For, although Scripture said *it was hovering*, it did not say that anything came out of the waters on the day that it was hovering.

(3) Just as through the service of the clouds, that is, the shadow of the first night, we infer the creation of the clouds that came to be on the first day, so too through the service of the wind, which is its breeze, Moses wished to make known to us the creation [of the wind]. For just as clouds do not exist without a shadow, neither does wind exist without a breeze. It is in their service then that we infer those things that are not otherwise made apparent to us. Therefore that wind was blowing because it was created for this purpose. After it blew and manifested its creation through its service on the first night, it once again became calm on the first day just as the clouds were once again dispersed on the first day.

8. After [Moses] spoke of heaven and earth, of the darkness, the abyss and the wind that came to be at the beginning of the first night, he then turned to speak about the light that came to be at dawn of the

first day. At the end of the twelve hours of that night, the light was created between the clouds and the waters and it chased away the shadow of the clouds that were overshadowing the waters and making them dark. For Nisan was the first month; in it the number of the hours of day and night were equal.

(2) The light remained a length of twelve hours so that each day might also obtain its [own] hours just as the darkness had obtained a measured length of time. Although the light and the clouds were created in the twinkling of an eye, the day and the night of the first day were each completed m twelve hours.

(3) The light then was like a bright mist over the face of the earth. Whether it was like the dawn or like the pillar that gave light to the people in the wilderness, it is obvious that it would have been unable to chase away the darkness that was spread over the face of everything, unless it had spread out completely over everything, either by its substance or by its brightness. The light was released so that it might spread over everything without being fastened down. It dispersed the darkness that was over everything although it did not move. It was only when [the light] went away and when it came that it moved, for when [the light] went away the rule was given to the night and at [the light's] coming there would be an end to [the night's] rule.

9. After the brightness [of the light] rendered its service for three days, lest, like nothing, it return to nothing, God bore clear witness that the light *was very good.* Although God did not [actually] say that the works that preceded the light were very good, He did [in fact] say it about them, for although He did not say it of them in the beginning when only these things had come into existence out of nothing, He did say it of them after everything else had come into existence; for [Moses] included all that had been made together with all that was created in six days, when he said on the sixth day: *God saw everything that he had made, and behold, it was very good.*

(2) Because that first light was indeed created good, it rendered its service by its brightness for three days and it also served, as we say, for the conception and the birth of everything that the earth brought forth on the third day. The sun was in the firmament in order to ripen whatever had sprouted under that first light. It is said that from this

light, now diffused, and from fire, which were both created on the first day, the sun, which was in the firmament, was fashioned, while the moon and the stars also came to be from that same first light.

(3) Just as the sun, which rules the day by the fact that *it gives light to the earth,* actually causes the fruits of the earth to ripen, so too does the moon, which rules the night and tempers the strength of the night by its brightness, also bring forth, according to its first nature, fruits and vegetation. For Moses speaks in his blessings of *the yield which the moon brought forth* (Deut 33:14), along with the other things on account of which the light was created, although they say that, for the sake of the things that were to come forth, the light was created on the first day. After the earth brought forth everything during the course of the third day, then [the moon] came to be in the manner of the light on the fourth day, so that through the moon, as well as through the light, all fruit would have its beginning, and then through the sun all vegetation would become ripe.

10. Thus, through light and water the earth brought forth everything. While God is able to bring forth everything from the earth without these things, it was His will to show that there was nothing created on earth that was not created for the purpose of mankind or for his service...[on saltiness of waters has been cut].

12. Just as the gathering of the waters did not precede that word which said, *"Let the waters be gathered and let the dry land appear,"* neither did the seas exist until that moment when *God called the gathering of water "seas."* When they received their name they were changed. In their [new] place the [waters] attained that saltiness that had not been theirs [even] outside of their [old] place. For [their place] became deep at that very moment when [God] said, *"Let the waters be gathered into one place."* Then either the land [under] the sea was brought down below the [level of the] earth to receive within it its own waters along with the waters that were above the entire earth, or the waters swallowed each other so that the place might be sufficient for them, or the place of the sea shook and it became a great depth and the waters quickly hastened into that basin. Although the will of God had gathered these waters when the earth was created, a gate was opened for them to be gathered into one place. Just as in the gathering of the first and second waters there was found no gathering place because there was no place from which they might go out, so

now do these waters come down with all the rains and showers and are gathered into seas along paths and roads which had been prepared for them on the first day.

14. Heaven, earth, fire, wind, and water were created from nothing as Scripture bears witness, whereas the light, which came to be on the first day along with the rest of the things that came to be afterwards, came to be from something. For when these other things came to be from nothing, [Moses] said, *God created heaven and earth.* Although it is not written that fire, water, and wind were created, neither is it said that they were made. Therefore, they came to be from nothing just as heaven and earth came to be from nothing.

15. After God began to make [things] from something, Moses wrote, *God said, "Let there be light,"* and so on. Although Moses did say, *God created the great serpents,* nevertheless *"let the waters swarm with swarming things"* had been [said] prior to that. Therefore those five created things were created from nothing and everything else was made from those [five] things that came to be from nothing.

(2) Fire was also created on the first day, although it is not written down that it was created. Since [fire] had no existence in and of itself but existed in something else, it was created together with that thing in which it came to be. It is not possible that a thing which does not exist of itself can precede that thing which is the cause of its existence. That [fire] is in the earth, nature bears witness, but that it was not created together with the earth, Scripture affirms, when it said, *In the beginning God created heaven and earth.* Fire too, then, since it does not exist of itself, will remain in the earth, even if the earth and the waters have been commanded at every moment to bring forth fire from their wombs along with the waters and the wind and the clouds.

16. Darkness, too, is neither a self-subsistent being nor a created thing; it is a shadow, as Scripture makes clear. It was created neither before heaven nor after the clouds, for it was with the clouds and was brought forth from the clouds. [Darkness] also exists in another [thing], for it has no substance of its own. When that in which it exists vanishes, the darkness likewise vanishes with it. For whatever comes to an end along with another thing when it vanishes is without its own existence, because that other thing is the cause of its existence.

(2) So, how could darkness, whose existence is due to the clouds and to the firmament and not to the first light or to the sun, exist of itself? It is [a thing] which one thing brings forth by its cover and another destroys by its brightness. If one thing creates it and causes it to become something while another thing turns it back into nothing, how can it be a self-subsistent being? The clouds and the firmament, which were created at the beginning, bring it forth and the light that was created on the first day brings it to an end. If one created thing can create something and another created thing can destroy it – for subsequent to that, one thing can bring it into visibility at any moment – and another, at that very moment that it itself returns to nothing, turns it back into nothing, it is under the compulsion of that [one thing] which causes it to begin and [that other thing] that causes it to go away. If created things cause it to come into existence and also cause it to vanish then it is a [sic] created from created things. [The darkness then] is but a shadow of the firmament and it vanishes in the presence of another thing, as it disappears before the sun. Some teachings posit that this [darkness], which is at all times subject to created things, is an adversary of creatures, and they make that thing which has no substance of its own a self-existent being.

17. After [Moses] spoke of those things that came to be on the first day, he began to write about those things that came to be on the second day, saying, *And God said, "Let there be a firmament between the waters and let it separate the waters below the firmament from the waters above the firmament."* The firmament between the waters was pressed together from the waters. It was of the same measure as the waters that were spread out over the surface of the earth. Then if, in its origin, [the firmament] was above the earth (for the earth, water, and fire were beneath it, while water, wind, and darkness were above it), how do others posit that this [firmament], which is enveloped like an embryo in the uterus within the womb, is the womb of everything created between everything?

(2) For if the firmament had been created between everything, light, darkness, and wind, which were above the firmament when it was created, would have been confined above the firmament. If the creation [of the firmament] had occurred at night, the darkness and wind would also have remained there together with the waters which remained there. But if the creation [of the firmament] had occurred in

the day, the light and the wind also would have remained there along with the waters. And if they had remained there then the [wind, water, and lights] that are here would be different things. When, then, could they have been created? But if they did not remain there, how did those elements that were above [the firmament] when they were created move down below it?

18. The firmament was created on the evening of the second night, just as the heavens came to be on the evening of the first night. But when the firmament came into existence, the covering of clouds that had served for a night and a day in the place of the firmament dissipated. Because [the firmament] had been created between the light and the darkness, no darkness remained above it, for the shadow of the clouds was dispelled when the clouds themselves were dispelled. Nor did any of this light remain there, for its alotted measure of time had come to an end and so it sank into the waters that were beneath [the firmament].

(2) The wind could not have remained there either because it did not even exist there. For, it was on the first night that [Moses] said *it hovered* and not on the second night. If the firmament had been created on the first night when [the wind] was blowing there could then be some debate. But, since it is not written that [the wind] was blowing when the firmament was created, who would say that the wind was there when Scripture does not say so?

19. After the wind hovered on the first day, manifested its service by its blowing and returned to its stillness, then the firmament came to be. It is evident, therefore, that [the wind] neither remained above nor descended below, for how can one seek in any position or place for something whose very substance only exists at the moment of its service and whose service comes to an end when it ceases to blow? The wind underwent three things on the day of its creation: it was created from nothing, it blew in and through something, and it reverted to being hidden in its stillness.

20. After the wind had undergone these three things, the firmament was created on the evening of the second day. There was then nothing that rose along with it, because there was nothing that remained above it. It made a separation between the waters that it was

commanded to separate, but not between the light, the wind, or darkness, for this had not been commanded.

(2) There was no light, therefore, on the first night. On the night of the second and third day, it sank into the waters beneath the firmament and rose up as we said [above]. But on the fourth day, when the waters were gathered into one place, they say that [the firmament] was formed and that the sun, the moon, and the stars were formed from [the firmament] and from fire, and there were places set apart for the lights. Therefore, the moon would rise in the west of the firmament, the sun in the east, and at that same moment, the stars were dispersed in orderly fashion throughout the entire firmament.

(3) Although God said that the light which came to be on the first day *was very good,* He did not say this about the firmament which came to be on the second day, because the firmament had not yet been finished, neither in its structure nor in its adornment. The Creator delayed until the lights came to be so that when [the firmament] was adorned with the sun and the moon and the stars, and the strength of the darkness that was weakened by the lights that shone from it, He would then say of [the firmament], included with the rest [of creation], that *it was very good.*

21. After [Moses] spoke of the firmament that came to be on the second day, he then turned to write about the gathering of the waters and about the grass and the trees that the earth brought forth on the third day, saying, *And God said, "Let the waters under the heavens be gathered together into one place, and let the dry land appear."* From the fact that He said, *"Let the waters be gathered into one place,"* it is evident that it is the earth that supports the seas and that the abysses beneath the earth do not stand on nothing. Although the waters, by the word of God, were gathered in the night, the surface of the earth still became dry in the twinkling of an eye.

22. After these two things had occurred, God commanded the earth to bring forth at dawn grass and herbs of every kind and all the various fruit-bearing trees. Although the grasses were only a moment old at their creation, they appeared as if they were months old. Likewise, the trees, although only a day old when they sprouted forth, were nevertheless like [trees] years old as they were fully grown and fruits were already budding on their branches.

(2) The grass that would be required as food for the animals who were to be created two days later was [thus] made ready. And the new corn that would be food for Adam and his descendants, who would be thrown out of Paradise four days later, was [thus] prepared.

23. After [Moses] spoke about the gathering of the waters and about the sprouting of the vegetation on the earth on the third day, he turned to write about the lights that were created in the firmament, saying, *And God said, "Let there be lights in the firmament of the heavens to separate the day from the night,"* that is, *"one to rule over the day and the other [to rule] over the night."*

(2) That [God] said, *"Let them be for signs,"* [refers to] measures of time, and *"let them be for seasons,"* clearly indicates summer and winter. *"Let them be for days,"* are measured by the rising and setting of the sun, and *"let them be for years,"* are comprised of the daily cycles of the sun and the monthly cycles of the moon.

(3) Indeed [Moses] said, God made the two great lights, the greater light to rule the day, and the lesser light to rule the night; and [He made] the stars. Although all that was done before the fourth day was begun in the evening, the works on the fourth day were fashioned at dawn. Because the third day had been completed, in that [Moses] said, It was evening and it was morning; day three, God did not create the two lights in the evening lest night be changed into day and morning be given priority over evening.

24. Because the days followed the same order in which the first day was created, the night of the fourth day, like that of the other days, preceded its day. And if its evening preceded its dawn, the lights were not created in the evening, but rather at dawn. But to say that one of them was created in the evening and the other at dawn cannot be allowed for Moses said, *"Let there be lights,"* and *God made the two great lights.* If they were great when they were created and they were created at dawn, then the sun would have stood in the east and the moon opposite it in the west. The sun would have been set very low because it was created in the place where it set out over the earth, whereas the moon would have been set higher because it was created in the place where it stands on the fifteenth day. Indeed, at the moment the sun appears over the earth, the lights see each other and the moon sinks. From the position of the moon, from its size and

from the light it produced, it is clear, then, that it was fifteen days old when it was created.

25. Just as the trees, the vegetation, the animals, the birds, and even mankind were old, so also were they young. They were old according to the appearance of their limbs and their substances, yet they were young because of the hour and moment of their creation. Likewise, the moon was both old and young. It was young, for it was but a moment old, but was also old, for it was full as it is on the fifteenth day.

(2) If the moon had been created a day old or even two, it would have given no light; because of its proximity to the sun, it would not even have been visible. If it had been created about four days old, although it might have been visible, it would still not have given any light. This would have rendered false the verse *God created the two great lights,* as well as *He said, "Let there be lights in heaven to give light upon the earth."* Therefore, the moon had to be fifteen days old. The sun, although it was only one day old, was nevertheless four days old, for it is according to the sun that each day is counted and will be reckoned. Accordingly, those eleven days, by which the moon was older than the sun, that were added to the moon at that first moment are also added to it each year, for these [days] are used in the lunar reckoning.

(3) There was nothing lacking in that year for Adam and his descendants, for any deficiency in the measure of the moon had been filled in when the moon was created. Thus, Adam and his descendants learned from this year that, henceforth, eleven days were to be added to every year. Clearly then, it was not the Chaldeans who arranged the seasons and the years; these things had been arranged before [the creation of] Adam.

26. After Moses spoke about the lights that came to be in the firmament, he turned to write about the swarming things, the birds, and the serpents that were created from the waters on the fifth day, saying, *And God said, "Let the waters cause living things to swarm, and let the birds fly above the earth." And God created the great serpents and every living creature with which the waters swarmed according to their kind.*

(2) When the waters were gathered, which had been ordered on the second day, there appeared rivers as well as springs, lakes, and

ponds. At the word of God these waters dispersed throughout Creation and brought forth swarming things and fish from within them; the serpents were created in the abysses and the birds soared in flocks out of the waves into the air.

(3) As for the great serpents that were created, although the Prophets said that Leviathan dwelt in the sea, Job said that the Behemoth dwelt on dry land. David too, speaking of this beast, said that *on a thousand mountains is Behemoth's pasture land*, that is, *his place of repose*. Perhaps it was after they were created that their places were separated so that Leviathan should dwell in the sea and Behemoth on dry land.

27. After [Moses] spoke about the creation of the swarming things and of the birds and the sea serpents on the fifth day, he turned to write about the creeping things and the animals and the beasts that were created on the sixth day, saying, *And God said, "Let the earth bring forth living creatures according to their kinds: cattle and reptiles and beasts."* Although the entire earth was swarming with swarming things, nevertheless the cattle and the beasts were set along the border of Paradise so that they might dwell near Adam.

(2) Therefore, the entire earth stirred with creeping things as had been commanded. [The earth] also brought forth the beasts of the field as companions to the wild beasts, and it brought forth as many beasts as would be suitable for the service of that one who, on that very day, was to transgress the commandment of his Lord.

28. After [Moses] spoke about the reptiles, the beasts and the cattle that were created on the sixth day, he turned to write about the creation of that man who was fashioned on the sixth day, saying, *"And God said..."* But to whom was God speaking? Here, as in every place where He creates, it is clear that he was speaking to His Son. The Evangelist said about Him that *everything came to be through Him and without Him not one thing came to be*. Paul, too, confirms this when he said, *In Him all things were created, in heaven and on earth, all that is visible and all that is invisible*.

29. *And God said, "Let us make man in our image."* According to what has been the rule until now, namely, if it pleases God He will make it known to us, Moses explains in what way we are the image of

God, when he said *"Let them have dominion over the fish of the sea, and over the birds, and over the cattle, and over all the earth."* It is the dominion that Adam received over the earth and over all that is in it that constitutes the likeness of God who has dominion over the heavenly things and the earthly things.

(2) Then [Moses] said, *male and female He created them,* to make known that Eve was inside Adam, in the rib that was drawn out from him. Although she was not in his mind she was in his body, and she was not only in his body with him, but she was also in soul and spirit with him, for God added nothing to that rib that He took out except the structure and the adornment. If everything that was suitable for Eve, who came to be from the rib, was complete in and from that rib, it is rightly said that *male and female He created them.*

30. And God blessed them and said to them, "Be fruitful and multiply, and fill the earth and subdue it; and have dominion over the fish of the sea, over the birds and over every animal that crawls upon the earth." They were blessed on this earth, as if this dwelling place had been prepared for them before they sinned. Although they had not yet sinned, [God] knew that they were about to sin.

(2) *Be fruitful and multiply and fill,* not Paradise, but *the earth,* and *have dominion over the fish of the sea and the birds and over all the beasts.* But how was Adam to rule over the fish of the sea unless he were to be in proximity to the sea? And how was he to rule over the birds that fly throughout every region unless his descendants were to dwell in every region? And how was Adam to rule over every beast of the earth unless his offspring were to inhabit the entire earth?

31. Although Adam was created and was blessed to rule over the earth and over everything that was created and blessed therein, God had indeed made him to dwell within Paradise. God truly manifested His foreknowledge in His blessing and manifested His grace in the place where He set Adam to dwell. Lest it be said that Paradise was not created for [Adam's] sake, [God] set him there in Paradise to dwell. And lest it be said that God did not know that Adam would sin, He blessed him on this earth. And everything with which God blessed Adam preceded the transgression of the commandment, lest by the transgression of him who had been blessed, the blessings of Him who gave the blessings be withheld and the world be turned back into no-

thing on account of the folly of that one for whose sake everything had been created.

(2) Therefore, God did not bless Adam in Paradise, because that place and all that is in it is blessed. But God blessed him on the earth first so that by that blessing with which [His] grace blessed beforehand, the curse of the earth, which was about to be cursed by [His] justice, might [thus] be diminished. But even though the blessing was one of promise, in that it was fulfilled after his expulsion from Paradise, His grace, nevertheless, was of actuality, for on that same day, [God] set [Adam] in the garden to dwell, clothed him with glory, and made him ruler over all the trees of Paradise.

32. After Moses spoke about the reptiles, the cattle and the beasts, about mankind and about their blessing on the sixth day, he turned to write about God's rest that took place on the seventh day saying, *Thus heaven and earth were finished, and all their host. And God rested on the seventh day from all His work which He had done.*

(2) From what toil did God rest? For the creatures that came to be on the first day came to be by implication, except for the light which came to be through His word. And the rest of the works which came to be afterwards came to be through His word. What toil is there for us when we speak one word, that there should be toil for God due to the one word a day that He spoke? If Moses, who divided the sea by his word and his rod, did not tire and Joshua, son of Nun, who restrained the luminaries by his word, did not tire, then what toil could there have been for God when He created the sea and the luminaries by [His] word?

33. It was not because He rested on [that day] that God, who does not weary, blessed and sanctified the seventh day, nor because He was to give it to that people, who did not understand that since they were freed from their servitude, they were to give rest to their servants and maidservants. He gave it to them so that, even if they had to be coerced, they would rest. For it was given to them in order to depict by a temporal rest, which He gave to a temporal people, the mystery of the true rest which will be given to the eternal people in the eternal world.

(2) Also because a full week as required, God exalted by His word that seventh day which His works had not exalted so that, because of the honor accorded that day, it might be united to its com-

panions, and that the reckoning of the week, which is required for the service of the world, might be completed.

Section II

1. After Moses spoke of the sabbath rest, of how God blessed and sanctified this day, he returned to the account of how the Creation was first fashioned, briefly passing over those things of which he had already spoken, while recounting in detail those things that he had left out. He then began to write about the creation account a second time, saying, *These are the generations of heaven and earth when they were created. In the day that God made heaven and earth, when no tree of the field existed and no vegetation had sprouted – for God had not brought down rain upon the earth and Adam was not there to till the earth; but a spring rose up and watered the whole face of the earth.*

2. Understand, O hearer, that although the days of creation were finished and [God] had blessed the Sabbath day which was sanctified and he had completed [his account], Moses still returned to tell the story of the beginning of Creation even after the days of creation had been finished.

(2) *These are the generations of heaven and earth,* that is, this is the account of the fashioning of heaven and earth on the day when the Lord made heaven and earth for as yet *no tree of the field existed and no vegetation had sprouted.* Even if these things were not actually created on the first day – for they had been made on the third day – still [Moses] did not rashly introduce, on the first day, the report of those things that were created on the third day.

3. For [Moses] said, no trees existed and no vegetation had sprouted – for the Lord had not brought down rain upon the earth; but a spring rose up out of the earth and watered the whole face of the earth. Because everything that has been born and will be born from the earth [will be] through the conjunction of water and earth, [Moses] undertook to show that no tree nor vegetation had been created along with the earth, because the rain had not yet come down. But after the great spring rose up from the great abyss and watered the whole face of the earth, and after the waters had been gathered together on the third day, then the earth brought forth all the vegetation.

(2) These waters, then, over which the darkness had been spread on the first day are the same ones that rose up from the spring and, in

the blink of an eye, covered the entire earth. This was also the [same spring] that was opened in the days of Noah and that covered the surface of all the mountains on the earth. This spring did not rise up from below the earth but out of the earth, for [Moses] said, *the spring rose up* not from below the earth but, *out of the earth.* The earth itself, which bears these waters in its womb, bears witness that these waters were not prior to the earth.

(3) *The spring* then *rose up out of the earth,* as Scripture says, *and watered the whole face of the earth.* Thus [the earth] produced trees, grasses, and plants. It was not that God was unable to bring forth everything from the earth in any other way. Rather, it was His will that [the earth] should bring forth by means of water. [God] began the creation [of the vegetation] this way right from the beginning so that this procedure would be perpetuated until the end of time.

4. After [Moses] spoke about those things that had been omitted and that had not been recounted on the first day, he turned to write about how Adam was fashioned saying, *Adam was not there to till the earth.* Obviously, Adam did not exist in the days that preceded the sixth day, since he was created on the sixth day. *Then, on the sixth day the Lord formed Adam from the dust of the earth and blew into his nostrils the breath of life; and Adam became a living being.* Even though the beasts, the cattle, and the birds were equal [to Adam] in their ability to procreate and in that they had life, God still gave honor to Adam in many ways: first, in that it was said, *God formed him with His own hands and breathed life into him;* God then set him as ruler over Paradise and over all that is outside of Paradise; God clothed Adam in glory; and God gave him reason and thought so that he might perceive the majesty [of God].

5. After Moses spoke of how Adam was so gloriously fashioned, he turned to write about Paradise and Adam's entry therein saying, *The Lord had previously planted Paradise in Eden and there He placed Adam whom He had fashioned.*

(2) Eden is the land of Paradise and [Moses] said *previously* because God had [already] planted it on the third day. He explains this by saying, *the Lord caused every tree that is pleasant to the sight and good for food to sprout forth from the* earth. And to show that he

was talking about Paradise, [Moses] said, *and the tree of life was in the midst of Paradise, and the tree of the knowledge of good and evil.*

7. After [Moses] spoke about Paradise and the rivers that were divided outside of it, he turned to speak about Adam's entry into Paradise and about the law that was laid down for him saying, *The Lord God took Adam and put him in the Paradise of Eden to till it and to guard it.*

(2) But with what did Adam till the garden since he had no tools for tilling? How could he have tilled it since he was not capable of tilling it by himself? What did he have to till since there were no thorns or briars there? Moreover, how could he have guarded it as he could not possibly encompass it? And from what did he guard it since there were no thieves to enter it? Indeed, the fence that was erected after the transgression of the commandment bears witness that as long as Adam kept the commandment, no guard was required.

(3) Adam had nothing to guard then except the law that had been set down for him. Nor was any other "tilling" entrusted to him except to fulfill the commandment that had been commanded him. But if [someone were to say that Adam] had or would have these two things [to perform] along with the commandment, I would not oppose this [interpretation].

8. After he spoke about Adam's entry into Paradise and why he had been put there, [Moses] turned to write about the law that was set down for him, saying, *and the Lord God commanded Adam, saying, "You may eat of every tree that is in Paradise; out of the tree of the knowledge of good and evil you shall not eat, for on the day that you eat of it you shall surely die."*

(2) This commandment was an easy one, for God gave to Adam all of Paradise and withheld from him only one tree. If a single tree were sufficient to provide nourishment for someone and many were withheld, [that single tree] would offer relief from the torment [of hunger] by providing nourishment for one's hunger. But if God gave Adam many trees instead of a single one which would have been sufficient for him, any transgression would be due not to any constraint but to disdain.

(3) [God] withheld from Adam a single tree and set death around it, so that if Adam would not keep the law out of love for the One

who had set down the law, then at least the fear of death that was set around the tree would frighten him away from overstepping the law.

9. After he spoke about Adam's entry into Paradise and about the law that had been set down for him, Moses turned to write about the names that [Adam] gave to the animals saying, *the Lord formed out of the ground every beast of the field and every bird of the sky and brought them to Adam to see what he would call them.*

(2) They were not really *formed,* for the earth brought forth the animals and the water the birds. When he said, *"He formed,"* [Moses] wished to make known that every animal, reptile, beast, and bird comes into being from the conjunction of earth and water.

(3) That [Moses] said, *He brought them to Adam,* is so that God might make known the wisdom of Adam and the harmony that existed between the animals and Adam before he transgressed the commandment. The animals came to Adam as to a loving shepherd. Without fear they passed before him in orderly fashion, by kinds and by species. They were neither afraid of him nor were they afraid of each other. A species of predatory animals would pass by with a species of animal that is preyed upon following safely right behind.

10. Adam thus began his rule over the earth when he became lord over all on that day according to the blessing he was given. The word of the Creator came to pass in actuality and His blessing was indeed fulfilled on the same day that he was made ruler over everything, even though he would soon rebel against the Lord of everything. For God gave Adam not only rule over everything, which had been promised to him, but He also allowed him to bestow names [on the animals], which had not been promised to him. If then God did for Adam even more than he had expected, how could God have deprived Adam of these things unless Adam had sinned?

(2) For someone to give a few names to be remembered is not a great thing, but it is too large and too great a thing for any human being to bestow thousands of names in a single moment, without repeating any. It is possible for someone to bestow many names on many kinds of insects, animals, beasts, and birds, but never to name one kind by the name of another belongs either to God or to someone to whom it has been granted by God.

(3) If God did indeed give Adam ruling authority, make him a participant in creation, clothe him with glory, and give him a garden, what else should God have done that Adam heed the commandment but did not do?

11. After he spoke of the formation of the animals and of the names they received, [Moses] turned to write of Adam's sleep and of the rib that was taken from him and made into a woman, saying, *But for Adam there was not found a helper like him.* Moses called Eve *helper* because even though Adam had helpers among the beasts and animals he still required one like him of his own kind. Inside, Eve was very diligent; she was also attentive to the sheep and cattle, the herds, and droves which were in the fields. She would also help Adam with the buildings, pens, and with any other task that Adam was capable of doing. The animals, even though they were subservient, were not able to help him with these things. For this reason God made for Adam a helper who would be solicitous for everything for which he was [solicitous] and who would indeed help him in many things.

12. *And the Lord cast sleep upon Adam and he slept. God took one of his ribs and closed up its place with flesh. And the Lord fashioned the rib which He had taken from Adam into a woman and brought her to Adam.* That man, awake, anointed with splendor, and who did not yet know sleep, fell on the earth naked and slept. It is likely that Adam saw in his dream what was done to him as if he were awake. After Adam's rib had been taken out in the twinkling of an eye, God closed up the flesh in its place in the blink of an eyelash. After the extracted rib had been fashioned with all sorts of beautiful things to adorn it, God then brought her to Adam, who was both one and two. He was one in that he was Adam and he was two because he had been created male and female.

13. After he spoke of Adam's sleep, of the rib that had been taken out, and of the woman who had been fashioned from it and brought to [Adam], [Moses] wrote that *Adam said, "This time she is bone of my bones and flesh of my flesh. This one shall be called woman because she was taken out of man."*

(2) *This time* – that is, this one who came after the animals was not like them for they were from the earth, but this one is *bone of my bones and flesh of my flesh*. Adam said this either as a prophecy or

because he had seen it and knew it from the vision in his dream, as we just said above.

(3) Just as each animal had received from Adam the name of its species on that day, Adam did not call the rib that was fashioned [into the woman] *Eve,* by her own name but named her *woman,* the name that was set down for all her kind. Then [Adam] said, *Let the man leave his father and his mother and cling to his wife so that they might be joined and the two might become one* without division as they were from the beginning.

14. After these things Moses said, *The two of them were naked and were not ashamed.* That they were not ashamed does not mean that they did not know what shame was. If they were children, as [the pagans] say, [Moses] would neither have said, They were naked and were not ashamed, nor, Adam and his wife, if they had not been young adults. The names that Adam bestowed should be sufficient to convince us of [the level of] his wisdom. And the fact that [Moses] said, *he will till it and keep it,* should make known to us Adam's strength. The law that was set for them testifies to their full maturity and their transgression of the commandment should bear witness to their arrogance.

(2) It was because of the glory with which they were clothed that they were not ashamed. It was when this glory was stripped from them after they had transgressed the commandment that they were ashamed because they were naked. The two of them then hastened to cover themselves with leaves – not their entire bodies but only their shameful members.

Methodius of Olympus

> Little is known about St. Methodius of Olympus (d. c. 311). Methodius was Bishop of Lycia. He wrote many works, which were widely read and highly valued at the time, though few have survived. He was one of Origen's earliest critics. His *Concerning Free will* is written against the Gnostics and their fatalistic views. He criticizes them for attributing the existence of evil to uncreated matter. Instead, he maintains that God created matter out of non-existence and that evil results from a human will that disobeys God. In his *Extracts from the Work on Things Created*, Methodius attempts to refute various views of Origen, such as the universe being co-eternal with God.

Methodius *Concerning Free will*

Orthodoxus. The old man of Ithaca, according to the legend of the Greeks, when he wished to hear the song of the Sirens, on account of the charm of their voluptuous voice, sailed to Sicily in bonds, and stopped up the ears of his companions; not that he grudged them the hearing, or desired to load himself with bonds, but because the consequence of those singers' music to those who heard it was death. For such, in the opinion of the Greeks, are the charms of the Sirens. Now I am not within hearing of any such song as this; nor have I any desire to hear the Sirens who chant men's dirges, and whose silence is more profitable to men than their voice; but I pray to enjoy the pleasure of a divine voice, which, though it be often beard, I long to hear again; not that I am overcome with the charm of a voluptuous voice, bat I am being taught divine mysteries, and expect as the result, not death but eternal salvation. For the singers are not the deadly Sirens of the Greeks, but a divine choir of prophets, with whom there is no need to stop the ears of one's companions, nor to load one's-self [*sic*] with bonds, in fear of the penalty of hearing. For, in the one case, the hearer, with the entrance of the voice, ceases to live; in the other, the more he hears, the better life will he enjoy, being led onwards by a divine Spirit.

Let every one come, then, and hear the divine song without any fear. There are not with us the Sirens from the shore of Sicily, nor the bonds of Ulysses, nor the wax poured melting into men's ears; but a loosening of all bonds, and liberty to listen to every one that approaches. For it is worthy of us to hear such a song as this; and to hear such singers as these, seems to me to be a thing to be prayed for. But if one wishes to hear the choir of the apostles as well, he will find the same harmony of song. For the others sang beforehand the divine plan in a mystical manner; but these sing an interpretation of what has been mystically announced by the former. Oh, concordant harmony, composed by the Divine Spirit! Oh, the comeliness of those who sing of the mysteries of God? Oh, that I also may join in these songs in my prayer. Let us then also sing the like song, and raise the hymn to the Holy Father, glorifying in the Spirit Jesus, who is in His bosom...

Valentinian. As I was walking yesterday evening, my friend, along the shore of the sea, and was gazing on it somewhat intently, I saw an extraordinary instance of divine power, and a work of art produced by wise science, if at least such a thing may be called a work of art. For as that verse of Homer says:

> "As when two adverse winds blowing from Thrace,
> Boreas and Zephyrus, the fishy deep
> Vex sudden, all around, the sable flood
> High curled, flings forth the salt weed on the shore;"

So it seemed to me to have happened yesterday. For I saw waves very like mountain-tops, and, so to speak, reaching up to heaven itself. Whence I expected nothing else but that the whole land would be deluged, and I began to form in my mind a place of escape, and a Noah's ark. But it was not as I thought; for, just as the sea rose to a crest, it broke up again into itself, without overstepping its own limits, having, so to speak, a feeling of awe for a divine decree. And as oftentimes a servant, compelled by his master to do something against his will, obeys the command through fear, while he dares not say a word of what he suffers in his unwillingness to do it, but, full of rage, mutters to himself – somewhat so it appeared to me that the sea, as if enraged and confining its awe within itself, kept itself under, as not willing to let its Master perceive its anger.

On these occurrences I began to gaze in silence, and wished to measure in my mind the heaven and its sphere. I began to inquire whence it rises and where it sets; also what sort of motion it had – whether a progressive one, that is to say, one from place to place, or a revolving one; and, besides, how its movement is continued. And, of a truth, it seemed worth while to inquire also about the sun – what is the manner of his being set in the heaven; also what is the orbit he traverses; also whither it is that, after a short time, he retires; and why it is that even he does not go out of his proper course: but he, too, as one may say, is observing a commandment of a higher power, and appears with us just when he is allowed to do so, and departs as if he were called away.

So, as I was investigating these things, I saw that the sunshine was departing, and the daylight failing, and that immediately darkness came on; and the sun was succeeded by the moon, who, at her first rising, was not of full size, but after advancing in her course presented a larger appearance. And I did not cease inquiring about her also, but examined the cause of her waning and waxing, and why it is that she, too, observes the revolution of days; and it seemed to me from all this that there is a divine government and power controlling the whole, which we may justly call God.

And thereupon I began to praise the Creator, as I saw the earth fast fixed, and living creatures in such variety, and the blossoms of plants with their many hues. But my mind did not rest upon these things alone; but thereupon I began to inquire whence they have their origin – whether from some source eternally co-existent with God, or from Himself alone, none co-existing with Him; for that He has made nothing out of that which has no existence appeared to me the right view to take, unless my reason were altogether untrustworthy. For it is the nature of things which come into being to derive their origin from what is already existing. And it seemed to me that it might be said with equal truth, that nothing is eternally co-existent with God distinct from Himself, but that whatever exists has its origin from Him, and I was persuaded of this also by the undeniable disposition of the elements, and by the orderly arrangement of nature about them.

So, with some such thoughts of the fair order of things, I returned home. But on the day following, that is today, as I came I saw two beings of the same race – I mean men – striking and abusing one another; and another, again, wishing to strip his neighbour. And now some began to venture upon a more terrible deed; for one stripped a corpse, and exposed again to the light of day a body that had been once hidden in the earth, and treated a form like his own with such insult as to leave the corpse to be food for dogs; while another bared his sword, and attacked a man like himself. And he wanted to procure safety by flight; but the other ceased not from pursuing, nor would control his anger. And why should I say more? It is enough that be attacked him, and at once smote him with his sword.

So the wounded man became a suppliant to his fellow, and spread out his hands in supplication, and was willing to give up his clothing, and only made a claim for life. But the other did not subdue his anger, nor pity his fellowman, nor would he see his own image in the being before him; but, like a wild beast, made preparations with his sword for feeding upon him. And now he was even putting his mouth to the body so like his own, such was the extent of his rage. And there was to be seen one man suffering injurious treatment, and another forthwith stripping him, and not even covering with earth the body which he denuded of clothing. But, in addition to these, there was another who, robbing others of their marriage rights, wanted to insult his neighbour's wife, and urged her to turn to unlawful embraces, not wishing her husband to be father to a child of his own.

After that I began to believe the tragedies, and thought that the dinner of Thyestes had really taken place; and believed in the unlawful lust of Oinomaos, nor doubted of the strife in which brother drew the sword on brother. So, after beholding such things as these, I began to inquire whence they arise, and what is their origin, and who is the author of such devices against men, whence came their discovery, and who is the teacher of them. Now to dare to say that God was the author of these things was impossible; for surely it could not even be said that they have from Him their substance, or their existence. For how were it possible to entertain these thoughts of God? For He is good, and the Creator of what is excellent, and to Him belongs nothing bad. Nay, it is His nature to take no pleasure in such things; but He forbids their production, and rejects those who delight in them, but admits into His presence those who avoid them. And how could it be anything but absurd to call God the maker of these things of which He disapproves? For He would not wish them not to be, if He had first been their creator; and He wishes those who approach Him to be imitators of Him.

Wherefore it seemed to me unreasonable to attribute these things to God, or to speak of them as having sprung from Him; though it must certainly be granted that it is possible for something to come into existence out of what has no existence, in case He made what is evil. For He who brought them into existence out of non-existence would not reduce them to the loss of it. And again, it must be said that there was once a time when God took pleasure in evil things, which now is not the case. Wherefore it seems to me impossible to say this of God. For it is unsuitable to His nature to attach this to Him. Wherefore it seemed to me that there is co-existent with Him somewhat which has the name of matter, from which He formed existing things, distinguishing between them with wise art, and arranging them in a fair order, from which also evil things seem to have come into being. For as this matter was without quality or form, and, besides this, was borne about without order, and was untouched by divine art, God bore no grudge against it, nor left it to be continually thus borne about, but began to work upon it, and wished to separate its best parts from its worst, and thus made all that it was fitting for God to make out of it; but so much of it as was like lees, so to speak, this being unfitted for being made into anything, He left as it was, since it was of no use to Him; and from this it seems to me that what is evil has now streamed down among men. This seemed to me the right view to take of these things. But, my friend, if you think that anything I have said is wrong, mention it, for I exceedingly desire to hear about these things.

Orthodoxus. I appreciate your readiness, my friend, and applaud your zeal about the subject; and as for the opinion which you have expressed respecting existing things, to the effect that God made them out of some underlying substance, I do not altogether find fault with it. For, truly, the origin of evil is a subject that has called out opinions from many men. Before you and me, no doubt, there have been many able men who have made the most searching inquiry into the matter. And some of them expressed the same opinion as you did, but others again represented God as the creator of these things, fearing to allow the existence of substance as coeval with Him; while the former, from fear of saying that God was the author of evil, thought fit to represent matter as coeval with Him. And it was the fate of both of these to fail to speak rightly on the subject, in consequence of their fear of God not being in agreement with an accurate knowledge of the truth.

But others declined to inquire about such a question at all, on the ground that such an inquiry is endless. As for me, however, my connection with you in friendship does not allow me to decline the subject of inquiry, especially when you announce your own purpose, that you are not swayed by prejudice – although you had your opinion about the condition of things derived from your conjectures – but say that you are confirmed in a desire of knowing the truth. Wherefore I will willingly turn to the discussion of the question. But I wish this companion of mine here to listen to our conversation. For, indeed, he seems to have much the same opinions about these things as you have, wherefore I wish that you should both have a share in the discussion. For whatever I should say to you, situated as you are, I shall say just as much to him. If, then, you are indulgent enough to think I speak truly on this great subject, give an answer to each question I ask; for the result of this will be that you will gain a knowledge of the truth, and I shall not carry on my discussion with you at random.

Valentinian. I am ready to do as you say; and therefore be quite ready to ask those questions from which you think I may be able to gain an accurate knowledge of this important subject. For the object which I have set before myself is not the base one of gaining a victory, but that of becoming thoroughly acquainted with the truth. Wherefore apply yourself to the rest of the discussion.

Orthodoxus. Well, then, I do not suppose you are ignorant that it is impossible for two uncreated things to exist together, although you seem to have expressed nearly as much as this in an earlier part of the conversation. Assuredly we must of necessity say one of two things: either that God is separate from matter, or, on the other hand, that He is inseparable from it. If, then, one would say that they are united, he will say that that which is uncreated is one only, for each of the things spoken of will be a part of the other; and as they are parts of each other, there will not be two uncreated things, but one composed of different elements. For we do not, because a man has different members, break him up into many beings. But, as the demands of reason require, we say that a single being, man, of many parts, has been created by God. So it is necessary, if God be not separate from matter, to say that that which is uncreated is one only; but if one shall say that He is separate, there must necessarily he something intermediate between the two, which makes their separation evident. For it is impossible to estimate the distance of one thing from another, unless there be something else with which the distance between them may be compared. And this holds good, not only as far as the instance before us, but also to any number of others. For the argument which we advanced in the case of two uncreated things would of necessity be of equal force, were the uncreated things granted to be three in number. For I should ask also respecting them, whether they are separate from each other, or, on the other hand, are united each to its neighbour. For if any one resolve to say that they are united, he will be told the same as before; if, again, that they are separate, he will not escape the necessary existence of that which separates them.

If, then, any one were to say that there is a third account which might fitly be given of uncreated things, namely, that neither is God separate from matter, nor, again, are they united as part of a whole; but that God is locally situate in matter, and matter in God, he must be told as the consequence, that if we say that God is placed in matter, we must of necessity say that He is contained within limits, and circumscribed by matter. But then He must, equally with matter, be carried about without order. And that He rests not, nor remains by Himself, is a necessary result of that in which He is being carried, now this way, and now that. And besides this, we must say that God was in worse case still.

For if matter were once without order, and He, determining to change it for the better, put it into order, there was a time when God was in that which had no order. And I might fairly ask this question also, whether God filled matter completely, or existed in some part of it. For if one resolve to say that God was in some part of matter, how far smaller than matter does he make Him; that is, if a part of it contained God altogether. But if he were to say that He is in all of it, and is extended through the whole of matter, he must tell us how He wrought upon it. For we must say that there was a sort of contraction of God, which being effected, He wrought upon that from which He was withdrawn, or else that He wrought in union with matter, without having a place of withdrawal. But if any one say that matter is in God, there is equal need of inquiry, namely, whether it is by His being separated from Himself, and as creatures exist in the air, by His being divided and parted for the reception of the beings that are in Him; or whether it is locally situated, that is to say, as water in land; for if we were to say, as in the air, we must say that God is divisible; but if, as water in earth – since matter was without order and arrangement, and besides, contained what was evil – we must say, that in God were to be found the disorderly and the evil. Now this seems to me an unbecoming conclusion, nay, more a dangerous one. For you wish for the existence of matter, that you may avoid saying that God is the author of evil; and, determining to avoid this, you say that He is the receptacle of evil.

If, then, under the supposition that matter is separate from created substances, you had said that it is uncreated, I should have said much about it, to prove that it is impossible for it to be uncreated; but since you say that the question of the origin of evil is the cause of this supposition, it therefore seems to me right to proceed to inquire into this. For when it is clearly stated how evil exists, and that it is not possible to say that God is the cause of evil, because of matter being subject to Him, it seems to me to destroy such a supposition, to remark, that if God created the qualities which did not exist, He equally created the substances. Do you say then, that there co-exists with God matter without qualities out of which He formed the beginning of this world?

Valentinian. So I think.

Orthodoxus. If, then, matter had no qualities, and the world were produced by God, and qualities exist in the world, then God is the maker of qualities?

Valentinian. It is so.

Orthodoxus. Now, as I heard you say some time ago that it is impossible for anything to conic into being out of that which has no existence, answer my question: Do you think that the qualities of the world were not produced out of any existing qualities?

Valentinian. I do.

Orthodoxus. And that they are something distinct from substances?

Valentinian. Yes.

Orthodoxus. If, then, qualities were neither made by God out of any ready at hand, nor derive their existence from substances, because they are not substances, we must say that they were produced by God out of what had no existence. Wherefore I thought you spoke extravagantly in saying that it was impossible to suppose that anything was produced by God out of what did not exist.

But let our discussion of this matter stand thus. For truly we see among ourselves men making things out of what does not exist, although they seem for the most part to be making them with something. As, for instance, we may have an example in the case of architects; for they truly do not make cities out of cities, nor in like manner temples out of temples.

But if, because substances underlie these things, you think that the builders make them out of what does exist, you are mistaken in your calculation. For it is not the substance which makes the city or the temples, but art applied to substance. And this art is not produced out of some art which lies in the substances themselves, but from that which is not in them.

But you seem likely to meet me with this argument: that the artificer makes the art which is connected with the substance out of the art which he has. Now I think it is a good reply to this to say, that in man it is not produced from any art lying beneath; for it is not to be granted that substance by itself is art. For art is in the class of accidents, and is one of the things that have an existence only when they are employed about some substance. For man will exist even without the art of building, but it will have no existence unless man be previously in being. Whence we must say that it is in the nature of things for arts to be produced in men out of what has no existence. If, then, we have shown that this is so in the case of men, why was it improper to say that God is able to make not only qualities, but also substances, out of that which has no existence? For as it appears possible for something to be produced out of what exists not, it is evident that this is the case with substances. To return to the question of evil. Do you think evil comes under the head of substances, or of qualities of substances?

Valentinian. Of qualities.

Orthodoxus. But matter was found to be without quality or form?

Valentinian. It was.

Orthodoxus. Well, then, the connection of these names with substance is owing to its accidents. For murder is not a substance, nor is any other evil; but the substance receives a cognate name from putting it into practice. For a man is not (spoken of as) murder, but by committing it he receives the derived name of murderer, without being himself murder; and, to speak concisely, no other evil is a substance; but by practising any evil, it can be called evil. Similarly consider, if you imagine anything else to be the cause of evil to men, that it too is evil by reason of its acting by them, and suggesting the committal of evil. For a man is evil in consequence of his actions. For he is said to be evil, because he is the doer of evil. Now what a man does, is not the man himself, but his activity, and it is from his actions that he receives the title of evil. For if we were to say that he is that which he does, and he commits murders, adulteries, and such – like, he will be all these. Now if he is these, then when they are produced he has an existence, but when they are not, he too ceases to be. Now these things are produced by men. Men then will be the authors of them, and the causes of their existing or not existing. But if each man is evil in consequence of what he practises, and what he practises has an origin, he also made a beginning in evil, and evil too had a beginning. Now if this is the case, no one is without a beginning in evil, nor are evil things without an origin.

Valentinian. Well, my friend, you seem to me to have argued sufficiently against the other side. For you appeared to draw right conclusions from the premises which we granted to the discussion. For truly if matter is without qualities, then God is the maker of qualities; and if evils are qualities, God will be the author of evils. But it seems to me false to say that matter is without qualities; for it cannot be said respecting any substance that it is without qualities. But indeed, in the very act of saying that it is without qualities, you declare that it has a quality, by describing the character of matter, which is a kind of quality. Therefore, if you please, begin the discussion from the beginning; for it seems to me that matter never began to have qualities. For such being the case, I assert, my friend, that evil arises from its emanation.

Orthodoxus. If matter were possessed of qualities from eternity, of what will God be the creator? For if we say substances, we speak of them as pre-existing; if, again, we say qualities, these too are declared to have an existence. Since, then, both substances and qualities exist, it seems to me superfluous to call God a creator. But answer me a question. In what way do you say that God was a creator? Was it by changing the existence of those substances into non-existence, or by changing the qualities while He preserved the substances?

Valentinian. I think that there was no change of the substances, but only of the qualities; and in respect to these we call God a creator. And just as if one might chance to say that a house was made of stones, it cannot be said of them that they do not still continue stones in substance, because they are called a house; for I affirm that the house is made by the quality of construction. So I think that God, while substance remained, produced a change of its qualities, by reason of which I say that this world was made by God.

Orthodoxus. Do you think, too, that evil is among the qualities of substances?

Valentinian. I do.

Orthodoxus. And were these qualities in matter from the first, or had they a beginning?

Valentinian. I say that these qualities were eternally co-existent with matter.

Orthodoxus. But do you not say that God has made a change in the qualities?

Valentinian. I do say this.

Orthodoxus. For the better?

Valentinian. I think so.

Orthodoxus. If, then, evil is among the qualities of matter, and its qualities were changed by God for the better, the inquiry must be made whence evil arose. For either all of them, being evil, underwent a change for the better, or some of them being evil, and some not, the evil ones were not changed for the better; but the rest, as far as they were found superior, were changed by God for the sake of order.

Valentinian. That is the opinion I held from the beginning.

Orthodoxus. How, then, do you say it was that He left the qualities of evil as they were? Was it that He was able to do away with them, or that, though He wished to do so, He was unable? For if you say that

He was able, but disinclined to do so, He must be the author of these things; because, while He had power to bring evil to an end, He allowed it to remain as it was, especially when He had begun to work upon matter. For if He had had nothing at all to do with matter, He would not have been the author of what He allowed to remain. But since He works upon a part of it, and leaves a part of it to itself, while He has power to change it for the better, I think He is the author of evil, since He left part of matter in its vileness. He wrought then for the ruin of a part; and, in this respect, it seems to me that this part was chiefly injured by His arranging it in matter, so that it became partaker of evil. For before matter was put in order, it was without the perception of evil; but now each of its parts has the capacity of perceiving evil.

Now, take an example in the case of man. Previously to becoming a living creature, he was insensible to evil; but from the time when he is fashioned by God into the form of man, he gains the perception of approaching evil. So this act of God, which you say was done for the benefit of matter, is found to have happened to it rather for the worse. But if you say that God was not able to stop evil, does the impossibility result from His being naturally weak, or from His being overcome by fear, and in subjection to some more powerful being? See which of these you would like to attribute to the almighty and good God. But, again, answer me about matter. Is matter simple or compound? For if matter be simple and uniform, and the universe compound, and composed of different substances, it is impossible to say that it is made of matter, because compound things cannot be composed of one pure and simple ingredient. For composition indicates the mixture of several simple things. But if, on the other hand, you say that matter is compound, it has been entirely composed of simple elements, and they were once each separately simple, and by their composition matter was produced; for compound things derive their composition from simple things.

So there was once a time when matter did not exist – that is to say, before the combination of the simple elements. But if there was once a time when matter did not exist, and there was never a time when what is uncreated did not exist, then matter is not uncreated. And from this it follows that there are many things which are uncreated. For if God were uncreated, and the simple elements of which matter was composed were uncreated, the number of the uncreated would be more than two. But to omit inquiring what are the simple elements, matter or form – for this would be followed by many absurdities – let me ask, do you think that nothing that exists is contrary to itself?

Valentinian. I do.

Orthodoxus. Yet water is contrary to fire, and darkness to light, and heat to cold, and moisture to dryness.

Valentinian. I think it is.

Orthodoxus. If, then, nothing that exists is contrary to itself, and these are contrary to one another, they will not be one and the same matter – no, nor formed from one and the same matter. But, again, I wish to ask, do you think that the parts of a thing are not destructive of one another?

Valentinian. I do.

Orthodoxus. And that fire and water, and the rest likewise, are parts of matter?

Valentinian. I hold them to be so.

Orthodoxus. Why, then, do you not think that water is destructive of fire, and light of darkness, and so on with the rest?

Valentinian. I do.

Orthodoxus. Then, if parts of a thing are not destructive of one another, and these are found to be so, they will not be parts of the same thing. But if they are not parts of the same thing, they will not be parts of one and the same matter. And, indeed, they will not be matter either, because nothing that exists is destructive of itself. And this being the case with the contraries, it is shown that they are not matter. This is enough on the subject of matter. Now we must come to the examination of evils, and must necessarily inquire into the evils among men. As to these, are they forms of the principle of evil, or parts of it? If forms, evil will not have a separate existence distinct from them, because the species are to be sought for in the forms, and underlie them. But if this is the case, evil has an origin. For its forms are shown to have an origin – such as murder, and adultery, and the like. But if you will have them to be parts of some principle of evil, and they have an origin, it also must have an origin. For those things whose parts have an origin, are of necessity originated likewise. For the whole consists of parts. And the whole will not exist if the parts do not, though there may be some parts, even if the whole be not there.

Now there is nothing existing of which one part is originated, and another part not. But if I were even to grant this, then there was a time when evil was not complete, namely, before matter was wrought by God. And it attains completeness when man is produced by God; for man is the maker of the parts of evil. And from this it follows that the cause of evil being complete, is God the Creator, which it is impious to say. But if you say that evil is neither of the things supposed, but is the doing of something evil, you declare that it has an origin. For the doing of a thing makes the beginning of its existence. And besides this, you have nothing further to pronounce evil. For what other action have you to point out as such, except what happens among men? Now, it has been already shown that he who acts is not evil according to his being, but in accordance with his evil doing. Because there is nothing evil by nature, but it is by use that evil things become such. So I say, says he, that man was made with a free will, not as if there were already evil in existence, which he had the power of choosing if he wished, but on account of his capacity of obeying or disobeying God. For this was the meaning of the gift of Free will. And man after his creation receives a commandment from God; and from this at once rises evil, for he does not obey the divine command; and this alone is evil, namely, disobedience, which had a beginning.

For man received power, and enslaved himself, not because he was overpowered by the irresistible tendencies of his nature, nor because the capacity with which he was gifted deprived him of what was better for him; for it was for the sake of this that I say he was endowed with it (but he received the power above mentioned), in order that he may obtain an addition to what he already possesses, which accrues to him from the Superior Being in consequence of his obedience, and is demanded as a debt from his Maker. For I say that man was made not for destruction, but for better things. For if he were made as any of the elements, or those things which render a similar service to God, he would cease to receive a reward befitting deliberate choice, and would be like an instrument of the maker; and it would be unreasonable for him to suffer blame for his wrong-doings, for the real author of them is the one by whom he is used. But man did not understand better things, since he did not know the author (of his existence), but only the object for which he was made.

I say therefore that God, purposing thus to honour man, and to grant him an understanding of better things, has given him the power of being able to do what he wishes, and commends the employment of his power for better things; not that He deprives him again of free will, but wishes to deprives him again of free will, but wishes to point out the better way. For the power is present with him, and he receives the commandment; but God exhorts him to turn his power of choice to better things. For as a father exhorts his son, who has power to learn his lessons, to give more attention to them inasmuch as, while he points out this as the better course, he does not deprive his son of the power which he possessed, even if he be not inclined to learn willingly; so I do not think that God, while He urges on man to obey His commands, deprives him of the power of purposing and withholding obedience. For He points out the cause of His giving this advice, in that He does not deprive him of the power. But He gives commands, in order that man may be able to enjoy better things. For this is the consequence of obeying the commands of God. So that He does not give commands in order to take away the power which He has given, but in order that a better gift may be bestowed, as to one worthy of attaining greater things, in return for his having rendered obedience to God, while he had power to withhold it. I say that man was made with free will, not as if there were already existing same evil, which he had the power of choosing if he wished…but that the power of obeying and disobeying God is the only cause.

For this was the object to be obtained by free will. And man after his creation receives a commandment from God, and from this at once rises evil; for he does not obey the divine command, and this alone is evil, namely, disobedience, which had a beginning. For no one has it in his power to say that it is without an origin, when its author had an origin. But you will be sure to ask whence arose this disobedience. It is clearly recorded in Holy Scripture, by which I am enabled to say that man was not made by God in this condition, but that he has come to it by some teaching. For man did not receive such a nature as this. For if it were the case that his nature was such, this would not have come upon him by teaching. Now one says in Holy Writ, that "man has learnt (evil)." I say, then, that disobedience to God is taught. For this alone is evil which is produced in opposition to the purpose of God, for man would not learn evil by itself. He, then, who teaches evil is the Serpent.

For my part, I said that the beginning of evil was envy, and that it arose from man's being distinguished by God with higher honour. Now evil is disobedience to the commandment of God.

Methodius *Extracts from the Work on Things Created*

I.

This selection is made, by way of compendium or synopsis, from the work of the holy martyr and bishop Methodius, concerning things created…[discussion of what it means to cast pearls before swine omitted]

II.

Origen says that what he calls the Centaur is the universe which is co-eternal with the only wise and independent God. For he says, since there is no workman without some work, or maker without something made, so neither is there an Almighty without an object of His power. For the workman must be so called from his work, and the maker from what he makes, and the Almighty Ruler from that which He rules over. And so it must be, that these things were made by God from the beginning, and that there was no time in which they did not exist. For if there was a time when the things that are made did not exist, then, as there were no things which had been made, so there was no maker; which you see to be an impious conclusion. And it will result that the unchangeable and unaltered God has altered and changed. For if He made the universe later, it is clear that He passed from not making to making. But this is absurd in connection with what has been said. It is impossible, therefore, to say that the universe is not unbeginning and co-eternal with God. To whom the saint replies, in the person of another, asking,

"Do you not consider God the beginning and fountain of wisdom and glory, and in short of all virtue in substance and not by acquisition?"

"Certainly," he says.

"And what besides? Is He not by Himself perfect and independent?"

"True; for it is impossible that he who is independent should have his independence from another. For we must say, that all which is full by another is also imperfect. For it is the thing which has its completeness of itself, and in itself alone, which can alone be considered perfect."

"You say most truly. For would you pronounce that which is neither by itself complete, nor its own completeness, to be independent?"

"By no means. For that which is perfect through anything else must needs be in itself imperfect."

"Well, then shall God be considered perfect by Himself, and not by some other?"

"Most rightly."

"Then God is something different from the world, and the world from God?"

"Quite so."

"We must not then say that God is perfect, and Creator, and Almighty, through the world?"

"No; for He must surely by Himself, and not by the world, and that changeable, be found perfect by Himself."

"Quite so."

"But you will say that the rich man is called rich on account of his riches? And that the wise man is called wise not as being wisdom itself, but as being a possessor of substantial wisdom?"

"Yes."

"Well, then, since God is something different from the world, shall He be called on account of the world rich, and beneficent, and Creator?"

"By no means. Away with such a thought!"

"Well, then, He is His own riches, and is by Himself rich and powerful."

"So it seems."

"He was then before the world altogether independent, being Father, and Almighty, and Creator; so that He by Himself, and not by another, was this."

"It must be so."

"Yes; for if He were acknowledged to be Almighty on account of the world, and not of Himself, being distinct from the world – may God forgive the words, which the necessity of the argument requires – He would by Himself be imperfect and have need of these things, through which He is marvellously Almighty and Creator. We must not then admit this pestilent sin of those who say concerning God, that He is. Almighty and Creator by the things which He controls and creates, which are changeable, and that He is not so by Himself."

III.

Now consider it thus: "If, you say, the world was created later, not existing before, then we must change the passionless and unchangeable God; for it must needs be, that he who did nothing before, but afterwards, passes from not doing to doing, changes and is altered." Then I said, "Did God rest from making the world, or not?"

"He rested."

"Because otherwise it would not have been completed."

"True."

"If, then, the act of making, after not making, makes an alteration in God, does not His ceasing to make after making the same?"

"Of necessity."

"But should you say that He is altered as not doing today, from what He was, when He was doing?"

"By no means. There is no necessity for His being changed, when He makes the world from what He was when He was not making it; and neither is there any necessity for saying that the universe must have co-existed with Him, on account of our not being forced to say that He has changed, nor that the universe is co-eternal with Him."

IV.

But speak to me thus: "Should you call that a thing created which had no beginning of its creation?"

"Not at all."

"But if there is no beginning of its creation, it is of necessity uncreated. But if it was created, you will grant that it was created by some cause. For it is altogether impossible that it should have a beginning without a cause."

"It is impossible."

"Shall we say, then, that the world and the things which are in it, having come into existence and formerly not existing, are from any other cause than God?"

"It is plain that they are from God."

"Yes; for it is impossible that that which is limited by an existence which has a beginning should be co-existent with the infinite."

"It is impossible."

"But again, O Centaur, let us consider it from the beginning. Do you say that the things which exist were created by Divine knowledge or not?"

"Oh, begone, they will say; not at all."

"Well, but was it from the elements, or from matter, or the firmaments, or however you choose to name them, for it makes no difference; these things existing beforehand uncreated and borne along in a state of chaos; did God separate them and reduce them all to order, as a good painter who forms one picture out of many colours?"

"No, nor yet this."

For they will quite avoid making a concession against themselves, lest agreeing that there was a beginning of the separation and transformation of matter, they should be forced in consistency to say, that in all things God began the ordering and adorning of matter which hitherto had been without form.

V.

But come now, since by the favour of God we have arrived at this point in our discourse; let us suppose a beautiful statue standing upon its base; and that those who behold it, admiring its harmonious beauty, differ among themselves, some trying to make out that it had been made, others that it had not. I should ask them: For what reason do you say that it was not made? On account of the artist, because he must be considered as never resting from his work? Or on account of the statue itself? If it is on account of the artist, how could it, as not being made, be fashioned by the artist? But if, when it is moulded of brass, it has all that is needed in order that it may receive whatever impression the artist chooses, how can that be said not to be made which submits to and receives his labour? If, again, the statue is declared to be by itself perfect and not made, and to have no need of art, then we must allow, in accordance with that pernicious heresy, that it is self-made.

If perhaps they are unwilling to admit this argument, and reply more inconsistently, that they do not say that the figure was not made, but that it was always made, so that there was no beginning of its being made, so that artist might be said to have this subject of his art without any beginning. Well then, my friends, we will say to them, if no time, nor any age before can be found in the past, when the statue was not perfect, will you tell us what the artist contributed to it, or wrought upon it? For if this statue has need of nothing, and has no beginning of existence, for this reason, according to you, a maker never made it, nor will any maker be found. And so the argument seems to come again to the same conclusion, and we must allow that it is self-made. For if all artificer is said to have moved a statue ever so slightly, he will submit to a beginning, when he began to move and adorn that which was before unadorned and unmoved. But the world neither was nor will be for ever the same.

Now we must compare the artificer to God, and the statue to the world. But how then, O foolish men, can you imagine the creation to be co-eternal with its Artificer, and to have no need of an artificer? For it is of necessity that the co-eternal should never have had a beginning of being, and should be equally uncreated and powerful with Him. But the uncreated appears to be in itself perfect and unchangeable, and it will have need of nothing, and be free from corruption. And if this be so, the world can no longer be, as you say it is, capable of change.

VII.

The saint says: We said there are two kinds of formative power in what we have now acknowledged; the one which works by itself what it chooses, not out of things which already exist, by its bare will, without delay, as soon as it wills. This is the power of the Father. The other which adorns and embellishes, by imitation of the former, the things which already exist. This is the power of the Son, the almighty and powerful hand of the Father, by which, after creating matter not out of things which were already in existence, He adorns it.

VIII.

The saint says that the Book of Job is by Moses. He says, concerning the words, "In the beginning God created the heaven and the earth," that one will not err who says that the "Beginning" is Wisdom. For Wisdom is said by one of the Divine band to speak in this manner concerning herself: "The Lord created me the beginning of His ways for His works: of old He laid my formulation." It was fitting and more seemly that all things which came into existence, should be more recent than Wisdom, since they existed through her. Now consider whether the saying: "In the beginning was the Word, and the Word was with God, and the Word was God. The same was in the beginning with God;" – whether these statements be not in agreement with those. For we must say that the Beginning, out of which the most upright Word came forth, is the Father and Maker of all things, in whom it was. And the words, "The same was in the beginning with God," seem to indicate the position of authority of the Word, which

He had with the Father before the world came into existence; "beginning" signifying His power. And so, after the peculiar unbeginning beginning, who is the Father, He is the beginning of other things, by whom all things are made.

IX.

He says that Origen, after having fabled many things concerning the eternity of the universe, adds this also: Nor yet from Adam, as some say, did man, previously not existing, first take his existence and come into the world. Nor again did the world begin to be made six days before the creation of Adam. But if any one should prefer to differ in these points, let him first say, whether a period of time be not easily reckoned from the creation of the world, according to the Book of Moses, to those who so receive it, the voice of prophecy here proclaiming: "Thou art God from everlasting, and world without end... For a thousand years in Thy sight are but as yesterday: seeing that is past as a watch in the night." For when a thousand years are reckoned as one day in the sight of God, and from the creation of the world to His rest is six days, so also to our time, six days are defined, as those say who are clever arithmeticians. Therefore, they say that an age of six thousand years extends from Adam to our time. For they say that the judgment will come on the seventh day, that is in the seventh thousand years. Therefore, all the days from our time to that which was in the beginning, in which God created the heaven and the earth, are computed to be thirteen days; before which God, because he had as yet created nothing according to their folly, is stripped of His name of Father and Almighty. But if there are thirteen days in the sight of God from the creation of the world, how can Wisdom say, in the Book of the Son of Sirach: "Who can number the sand of the sea, and the drops of rain, and the days of eternity?" This is what Origen says seriously, and mark how he trifles.

Cyril of Jerusalem

> St. Cyril of Jerusalem (315 – 386) was Bishop of Jerusalem from 348. He was exiled three times for his resistance to Arianism. He mistrusted the term *homoousios*. Even though this term was championed by Nicaea and St. Athanasius, Cyril regarded it as a man-made term that failed adequately to capture the relation between the Son and the Father. He took part in the Second Ecumenical Council at Constantinople (381).
>
> Cyril is best known for his *Catechetical Lectures*, from which the texts below are taken. These were lectures instructing catechumens in the essentials of the Christian Faith. They were given during Great Lent in preparation for baptism at Easter. Thus what he writes here regarding creation may be taken as what he considered essential for those about to be received into the Church to confess and believe.
>
> In Lecture 9, Cyril comments on the first article of the Nicene Creed, bolstering it with various Scriptural texts. He affirms that God created earth and heaven, both the visible and the invisible worlds. He writes of God being unknowable and invisible in His essence, but that He can be known from His works, from their beauty and greatness, and from the order of the world. Much of this discourse contemplates the beauty and order of the world in the light of God as its Maker and Sustainer.
>
> The excerpts from Lecture 12 underscore the unique way God created Adam and Eve, a topic of interest for many Fathers.

Cyril of Jerusalem *Catechetical Lectures*

Lecture II – On Repentance and Remission of Sins, and Concerning the Adversary

1. A fearful things is sin, and the sorest disease of the soul is transgression, secretly cutting its sinews, and becoming also the cause of eternal fire; an evil of a man's own choosing, and offspring of the will. For that we sin of our own free will the Prophet says plainly in a certain place: *Yet I planted thee a fruitful vine, wholly true: how art thou turned to bitterness, (and become) the strange vine?* (Jer 2:21) The planting was good, the fruit coming from the will is evil; and

therefore the planter is blameless, but the vine shall be burnt with fire; since it was planted for good, and bore fruit unto evil of its own will. *For God*, according to the Preacher, *made man upright, and they have themselves sought out many inventions.* (Ecc 7:29) *For we are His workmanship*, says the Apostle, *created unto good works, which God afore prepared, that we should walk in them.* (Eph 2:10) So then the Creator, being good, created for good works; but the creature turned of its own free will to wickedness. Sin then is, as we have said, a fearful evil, but not incurable; fearful for him who clings to it, but easy of cure for him who by repentance puts it from him. For suppose that a man is holding fire in his hand; as long as he holds fast the live coal he is sure to be burned, but should he put away the coal, he would have cast away the flame also with it. If however anyone thinks that he is not being burned when sinning, to him the Scripture saith, *Shall a man wrap up fire in his bosom, and not burn his clothes?* (Prov 6:27) For sin burns the sinews of the soul, and breaks the spiritual bones of the mind, and darkens the light of the heart.

Lecture IV – On the Ten Points of Doctrine

4. ...There is then One Only God, the Maker both of souls and bodies: One the creator of heaven and earth, the Maker of Angels and Archangels: of many the Creator, but of One only the Father before all ages – of One only, His Only-begotten Son, our Lord Jesus Christ, by Whom He made *all things visible and invisible.* (John 1:3)

5. This Father of our Lord Jesus Christ is not circumscribed in any place, nor is He less than the heaven; but *the heavens are the works of His fingers* (Ps 8:3), and *the whole earth is held in His grasp* (Is 11:12): He is in all things and around all. Think not that the sun is brighter than He, or equal to Him: for He who at first formed the sun must needs be incomparably greater and brighter. He foreknoweth the things that shall be, and is mightier than all, knowing all things and doing as He will; not being subject to any necessary sequence of events, nor to nativity, nor chance, nor fate; in all things perfect, and equally possessing every absolute form of virtue, neither diminishing nor increasing, but in mode and conditions ever the same; who hath prepared punishment for sinners, and a crown for the righteous.

6. Seeing then that many have gone stray in divers ways from the One God, some having deified the sun, that when the sun sets they may abide in the night season without God; others the moon, to have no God by day; others the other parts of the world; others the arts; others their various kinds of food; others their pleasures; while some, made after women, have set up on high an image of a naked woman, and called it Aphrodite, and worshipped their own lust in a visible form; and others dazzled by the brightness of gold have deified it and the other kinds of matter – whereas if one lay as a first foundation in his heart the doctrine of the unity of God, and trust to Him, he roots out at once the whole crop of the evils of idolatry and of the error of the heretics: lay though, therefore, this first doctrine of religion as a foundation in thy soul by faith.

Lecture VI

9. One He is, everywhere present, beholding all things, perceiving all things, creating all things through Christ: *For all things were made by Him, and without Him was not anything made* (John 1:3)...

Lecture IX – On the Words, Maker of Heaven and Earth, and of All Things Visible and Invisible

> Job XXXVIII. 2–3, "Who is this that hideth counsel from Me, and keepeth words in his heart, and thinketh to hide them from Me?"

1. To look upon God with eyes of flesh is impossible: for the incorporeal cannot be subject to bodily sight: and the Only begotten Son of God Himself hath testified, saying, No man hath seen God at any time. For if according to that which is written in Ezekiel any one should understand that Ezekiel saw Him, yet what saith the Scripture? He saw the likeness of the glory of the Lord; not the Lord Himself, but the likeness of His glory, not the glory itself, as it really is. And when he saw merely the likeness of the glory, and not the glory itself, he fell to the earth from fear. Now if the sight of the likeness of the glory brought fear and distress upon the prophets, any one who should attempt to behold God Himself would to a certainty lose his life, according to the saying, No man shall see My face and live. For this cause God of His great loving-kindness spread out the heaven as a veil of His proper Godhead, that we should not perish. The word is not mine, but the Prophet's. If Thou shalt rend the heavens, trembling

will take hold of the mountains at sight of Thee, and they will flow down. And why dost thou wonder that Ezekiel fell down on seeing the likeness of the glory? when Daniel at the sight of Gabriel, though but a servant of God, straightway shuddered and fell on his face, and, prophet as he was, dared not answer him, until the Angel transformed himself into the likeness of a son of man. Now if the appearing of Gabriel wrought trembling in the Prophets, had God Himself been seen as He is, would not all have perished?

2. The Divine Nature then it is impossible to see with eyes of flesh: but from the works, which are Divine, it is possible to attain to some conception of His power, according to Solomon, who says, For by the greatness and beauty of the creatures proportionably the Maker of them is seen. He said not that from the creatures the Maker is seen, but added proportionably. For God appears the greater to every man in proportion as he has grasped a larger survey of the creatures: and when his heart is uplifted by that larger survey, he gains withal a greater conception of God.

4. These things I say to you because of the following context of the Creed, and because we say, We Believe in One God, the Father Almighty, Maker of Heaven and Earth, and of All Things Visible and Invisible; in order that we may remember that the Father of our Lord Jesus Christ is the same as He that made the heaven and the earth, and that we may make ourselves safe against the wrong paths of the godless heretics, who have dared to speak evil of the All-wise Artificer of all this world, men who see with eyes of flesh, but have the eyes of their understanding blinded.

5. For what fault have they to find with the vast creation of God? – they, who ought to have been struck with amazement on beholding the vaultings of the heavens: they, who ought to have worshipped Him who reared the sky as a dome, who out of the fluid nature of the waters formed the stable substance of the heaven. For God said, Let there be a firmament in the midst of the water. God spake once for all, and it stands fast, and falls not. The heaven is water, and the orbs therein, sun, moon, and stars are of fire: and how do the orbs of fire run their course in the water? But if any one disputes this because of the opposite natures of fire and water, let him remember the fire

which in the time of Moses in Egypt flamed amid the hail, and observe the all-wise workmanship of God. For since there was need of water, because the earth was to be tilled, He made the heaven above of water that when the region of the earth should need watering by showers, the heaven might from its nature be ready for this purpose.

6. But what? Is there not cause to wonder when one looks at the constitution of the sun? For being to the sight as it were a small body he contains a mighty power; appearing from the East, and sending forth his light unto the West: whose rising at dawn the Psalmist described, saying: And he cometh forth out of his chamber as a bridegroom. He was describing the brightness and moderation of his state on first becoming visible unto men: for when he rides at high noon, we often flee from his blaze: but at his rising he is welcome to all as a bridegroom to look on.

Observe also his arrangement (or rather not his, but the arrangement of Him who by an ordinance determined his course), how in summer he rises higher and makes the days longer, giving men good time for their works: but in winter contracts his course, that the period of cold may be increased, and that the nights becoming longer may contribute to men's rest, and contribute also to the fruitfulness of the products of the earth. See also how the days alternately respond each to other in due order, in summer increasing, and in winter diminishing; but in spring and autumn granting equal intervals one to another. And the nights again complete the like courses; so that the Psalmist also says of them, Day unto day uttereth speech, and night unto night proclaimeth knowledge. For to the heretics who have no ears, they all but cry aloud, and by their good order say, that there is none other God save the Creator who hath set them their bounds, and laid out the order of the Universe.

10. What should have been the effect of these wonders? Should the Creator have been blasphemed? Or worshipped rather? And so far I have said noticing of the unseen works of His wisdom. Observe, I pray you, the spring, and the flowers of every kind in all their likeness still diverse one from another; the deepest crimson of the rose, and the purest whiteness of the lily: for these spring from the same rain and the same earth, and who makes them to differ? Who fashions them? Observe, pray, the exact care: from the one substance of the tree there is part for shelter, and part for diverse fruits: and the Artificer is One.

Of the same vine part is for burning, and part for shoots, and part for leaves, and part for tendrils, and part for clusters.

Admire also the great thickness of the knots which run round the reed, as the Artificer hath made them. From one and the same earth come forth creeping things, and wild beasts, and cattle, and trees, and food; and gold, and silver, and brass, and iron, and stone. The nature of the waters is but one, yet from it comes the substance of fishes and of birds; whereby as the former swim in the waters, so the birds fly in the air.

11. This great and wide sea, therein are things creeping innumerable. Who can describe the beauty of the fishes that are therein? Who can describe the greatness of the whales, and the nature of its amphibious animals, how they live both on dry land and in the waters? Who can tell the depth and the breadth of the sea, or the force of its enormous waves? Yet it stays at its bounds, because of Him who said, Hitherto shalt thou come, and no further, but within thyself shall thy waves be broken. Which sea also clearly shews the word of the command imposed upon it, since after it has run up, it leaves upon the beach a visible line made by the waves, shewing, as it were, to those who see it, that it has not passed its appointed bounds.

13. Who among men knows even the names of all wild beasts? Or who can accurately discern the physiology of each? But if of the wild beasts we know not even the mere names, how shall we comprehend the Maker of them? God's command was but one, which said, Let the earth bring forth wild beasts, and cattle, and creeping things, after their kinds and from one earth, by one command, have sprung diverse natures, the gentle sheep and the carnivorous lion, and various instincts of irrational animals, bearing resemblance to the various characters of men; the fox to manifest the craft that is in men, and the snake the venomous treachery of friends, and the neighing horse the wantonness of young men, and the laborious ant, to arouse the sluggish and the dull...

14. Is not then the Artificer worthy the rather to be glorified? For what? If thou knowest not the nature of all things, do the things that have been made forthwith become useless? Canst thou know the efficacy of all herbs? Or canst thou learn all the benefit which pro-

ceeds from every animal? Ere now even from venomous adders have come antidotes for the preservation of men. But thou wilt say to me, "The snake is terrible." Fear thou the Lord, and it shall not be able to hurt thee. "A scorpion stings." Fear the Lord, and it shall not sting thee. "A lion is bloodthirsty." Fear thou the Lord, and he shall lie down beside thee, as by Daniel. But truly wonderful also is the action of the animals: how some, as the scorpion, have the sharpness in a sting; and others have their power in their teeth; and others do battle with their claws; while the basilisk's power is his gaze. So then from this varied workmanship understand the Creator's power.

15. But these things perhaps thou knowest not: thou wouldest have nothing in common with the creatures which are without thee. Enter now into thyself, and from thine own nature consider its Artificer. What is there to find fault with in the framing of thy body? Be master of thyself, and nothing evil shall proceed from any of thy members. Adam was at first without clothing in Paradise with Eve, but it was not because of his members that he deserved to be cast out. The members then are not the cause of sin, but they who use their members amiss; and the Maker thereof is wise. Who prepared the recesses of the womb for child-bearing? Who gave life to the lifeless thing within it? Who knitted us with sinews and bones, and clothed us with skin and flesh, and, as soon as the child was born, brought streams of milk out of the breasts? How grows the babe into a boy, and the boy into a youth, and then into a man; and, still the same, passes again into an old man, while no one notices the exact change from day to day? Of the food, how is one part changed into blood, and another separated for excretion, and another part changed into flesh? Who gives to the heart its unceasing motion? Who wisely guarded the tenderness of the eyes with the fence of the eyelids? For as to the complicated and wonderful contrivance of the eyes, the voluminous books of the physicians hardly give us explanation. Who distributes the one breath to the whole body? Thou seest, O man, the Artificer, thou seest the wise Creator.

16. These points my discourse has now treated at large, having left out many, yea, ten thousand other things, and especially things incorporeal and invisible, that thou mayest abhor those who blaspheme the wise and good Artificer, and from what is spoken and read, and whatever thou canst thyself discover or conceive, from the greatness

and beauty of the creatures mayest proportionably see the maker of them, and bending the knee with godly reverence to the Maker of the worlds, the worlds, I mean, of sense and thought, both visible and invisible, thou mayest with a grateful and holy tongue, with unwearied lips and heart, praise God and say, How wonderful are Thy works, O Lord; in wisdom hast Thou made them all. For to Thee belongeth honour, and glory, and majesty, both now and throughout all ages. Amen.

Lecture XI – On the Words, the Only-Begotten Son of God, Begotten of the Father Very God Before All Ages, by Whom All Things Were Made

21. We believe then "In one Lord Jesus Christ, the Only-begotten Son of God, begotten of His Father very God before all worlds, by whom all things were made." For *whether they be thrones, or dominions, or principalities, or powers, all things were made through Him* (Col 1:16), and of things created none is exempted from His authority. Silenced be every heresy which brings in different creators and makers of the world; silenced the tongue which blasphemes the Christ the Son of God; let them be silenced who say that the sun is the Christ, for He is the sun's Creator, not the sun which we see. Silenced be they who say that the world is the workmanship of Angels, who wish to steal away the dignity of the Only-begotten. For whether visible or invisible, whether thrones or dominions, or anything that is named, all things were made by Christ. He reigns over the things which have been made by Him, not having seized another's spoils, but reigning over His own workmanship, even as the Evangelist John has said, *All things were made by Him, and without Him was not anything made.* All things were made by Him, the Father working by the Son.

22. ...For, as I have said, Angels did not create the world, but the Only-begotten Son, begotten, as I have said, before all ages, *By whom all things were made*, nothing having been excepted from His creation. And let this suffice to have been spoken by us so far, by the grace of Christ.

23. But let us now recur to our profession of the Faith, and so for the present finish our discourse. Christ made all things... Not that the

Father wanted strength to created the works Himself, but because He willed that the Son should reign over His own workmanship, God Himself giving Him the design of the the things to be made...

24. Christ then is the Only-begotten Son of God, and Maker of the world. For *He was in the world, and the world was made by Him* (John 1:10)...And not only of the things which are seen but also of the things which are not seen, is Christ the Maker at the Father's bidding...

Lecture XII – On the words Incarnate, and Made Man

29. These are excellent suggestions of the narratives: but the Jews still contradict, and do not yield to the statements concerning the rod, unless they may be persuaded by similar strange and supernatural births. Question them, therefore, in this way: of whom in the beginning was Eve begotten? What mother conceived her the motherless? But the Scripture saith that she was born out of Adam's side. Is Eve then born out of a man's side without a mother, and is a child not to be born without a father, of a virgin's womb? This debt of gratitude was due to men from womankind: for Eve was begotten of Adam, and not conceived of a mother, but as it were brought forth of man alone. Mary, therefore, paid the debt, of gratitude, when not by man but of herself alone in an immaculate way she conceived of the Holy Ghost by the power of God.

30. But let us take what is yet a greater wonder than this. For that of bodies bodies should be conceived, even if wonderful, is nevertheless possible: but that the dust of the earth should become a man, this is more wonderful. That clay moulded together should assume the coats and splendours of the eyes, this is more wonderful. That out of dust of uniform appearance should be produced both the firmness of bones, and the softness of lungs, and other different kinds of members, this is wonderful. That clay should be animated and travel round the world self moved, and should build houses, this is wonderful. That clay should teach, and talk, and act as carpenter, and as king, this is wonderful. Whence, then, O ye most ignorant Jews, was Adam made? Did not God take dust from the earth, and fashion this wonderful frame? Is then clay changed into an eye, and cannot a virgin bear a son. Does that which for men is more impossible take place, and is that which is possible never to occur?

Gregory Nazianzen

> St. Gregory Nazianzen (329 – 389), or St. Gregory the Theologian (as he is known in the Orthodox Church), was one of the three Cappadocian Fathers (along with St. Basil the Great and St. Gregory of Nyssa). Gregory is best known for his contribution to Trinitarian theology. He defended and elaborated the Nicene Faith in his five Theological Orations and other works. A gifted preacher, he was for a short time Bishop of Constantinople and participated in the Second Ecumenical Council in Constantinople (381).
>
> Influened by Origen, Gregory held that God first created the invisible spiritual or "intelligible" realm, after which He created the visible material or "sensible" realm. Humanity is given free will, and the test of that in the Garden of Eden is central to Christian anthropology. In connection with his Trinitarian theology, Gregory asserts the uniqueness of Adam's creation: Adam was created, but Seth and his other children (as all other humans except Eve) were born. Gregory upheld the fixity of created kinds.
>
> Gregory presents a design argument that rivals William Paley's. Only his is based not on a mechanical device – in Paley's case the watch – but on a musical instrument – for Gregory the lute. Thus Gregory argues that just as a beautifully made lute leads us to infer both a lutemaker and a luteplayer, so our beautifully made cosmos leads us to infer a God who created it and continues to act creatively within it.

Gregory *Orations*

Oration XXVIII – The Second Theological Oration

VI. Now our very eyes and the Law of Nature teach us that God exists and that He is the Efficient and Maintaining Cause of all things: our eyes, because they fall on visible ojects and see them in beautiful stability and progress, immovably moving and revolving if I may so say; natural Law, because through these visible things and their order, it reasons back to their Author. For how could this Universe have come into being or been put together, unless God had called it into existence and held it together? For every one who sees a beautifully made lute, and consideres the skill with which it has been fitted together and arranged, or who hears its melody, would think of none but the lutemaker, or the luteplayer, and would recur to him in mind, though he might not know him by sight. And thus to us also is manifested That which made and moves and preserves all created things, even though He be not comprehended by the mind. And very wanting in sense is he who will not willingly go thus far in following natural proofs…

XVI. …But reason receiving us in our desire for God, and in our sense of the impossibility of being without a leader and guide, and then making us apply ourselves to things visible and meeting with the things which have been since the beginning, doth not stay its course even here. For it was not the part of Wisdom to grant the sovereignty to things which are, as observation tells us, of equal rank. But these then it leads to that which is above these, and by which being is given to these. For what is it which ordered things in heaven and things in earth, and those which pass through air, and those which live in water; or other things which were before these, heaven and earth, air and water? Who mingled these, and who distributed them? What is it that each has in common with the other, and their mutual dependence and agreement? For I commend the man, though he was a heathen, who said, What gave movement to these, and drives their ceaseless and unhindered motion? Is it not the Artificer of them Who implanted reason in them all, in accordance with which the Universe is moved and controlled? Is it not He who made them and brought them into being? For we cannot attribute such a power to the Accidental. For, suppose that its existence is accidental, to what will you let us ascribe its order? And if you like we will grant you this: to what then will you ascribe its preservation and protection in accordance with the terms of its first creation. Do these belong to the Accidental, or to something else? Surely not to the Accidental. And what can this Something Else be but God? Thus reason that proceeds from God, that is implanted in all from the beginning and is the first law in us, and is bound up in all, leads us up to God through visible things. Let us begin again, and reason this out.

XXII. …How is it that species are permanent, and are different in their characteristics, although there are so many that their individual marks cannot be described?…

XXVI. ...How is it that the earth stands solid and unswerving? On what is it supported? What is it that props it up, and on what does that rest? For indeed even reason has nothing to lean upon, but only the Will of God...Is this not the clearest proof of the majestic working of God?

Oration XXIX – The Third Theological Oration; On the Son

XI. They do not however assert this, for these qualities are common also to other beings. But God's Essence is that which belongs to God alone, and is proper to Him. But they, who consider matter and form to be unbegotten, would not allow that to be unbegotten is the property of God alone (for we must cast away even further the darkness of the Manichaeans. But suppose that it is the property of God alone. What of Adam? Was he not alone the direct creature of God? Yes, you will say. Was he then the only human being? By no means. And why, but because humanity does not consist in direct creation? For that which is begotten is also human. Just so neither is He Who is Unbegotten alone God, though He alone is Father. But grant that He Who is Begotten is God; for He is of God, as you must allow, even though you cling to your Unbegotten. Then how do you describe the Essence of God? Not by declaring what it is, but by rejecting what it is not. For your word signifies that He is not begotten; it does not present to you what is the real nature or condition of that which has no generation.

What then is the Essence of God? It is for your infatuation to define this, since you are so anxious about His Generation too; but to us it will be a very great thing, if ever, even in the future, we learn this, when this darkness and dullness is done away for us, as He has promised Who cannot lie. This then may be the thought and hope of those who are purifying themselves with a view to this. Thus much we for our part will be bold to say, that if it is a great thing for the Father to be Unoriginate, it is no less a thing for the Son to have been Begotten of such a Father. For not only would He share the glory of the Unoriginate, since he is of the Unoriginate, but he has the added glory of His Generation, a thing so great and august in the eyes of all those who are not altogether grovelling and material in mind.

Oration XXXVIII – On Theophany, or Birthday of Christ

IX. But since this movement of self-contemplation alone could not satisfy Goodness, but Good must be poured out and go forth beyond Itself to multiply the objects of Its beneficence, for this was essential to the highest Goodness, He first conceived the Heavenly and Angelic Powers. And this conception was a work fulfilled by His Word, and perfected by His Spirit. And so the secondary Splendours came into being, as the Minsters of the Primary Splendour; whether we are to conceive of them as intelligent Spirits, or as fire of an immaterial and incorruptible kind, or as some other nature approaching this as near as may be...

X. Thus, then, and for these reasons, He gave being to the world of thought, as far as I can reason upon these matters, and estimate great things in my own poor language. Then when His first creation was in good order, He conceives a second world, material and visible; and this a system and compound of earth and sky, and all that is in the midst of them – an admirable creation indeed, when we look at the fair form of every part, but yet more worthy of admiration when we consider the harmony and the unison of the whole, and how each part fits in with every other, in fair order, and all with the whole, tending to the perfect completion of the world as a Unit. This was to shew that He could call into being, not only a Nature akin to Himself, but also one altogether alien to Himself. For akin to Deity are those natures which are intellectual, and only to be comprehended by mind; but all of which sense can take cognisance are utterly alien to It; and of these the furthest removed are all those which are entirely destitute of soul and of power of motion. But perhaps some one of those who are too festive and impetuous may say, What has all this to do with us? Spur your horse to the goal. Talk to us about the Festival, and the reasons for our being here today. Yes, this is what I am about to do, although I have begun at a somewhat previous point, being compelled to do so by love, and by the needs of my argument.

XI. Mind, then, and sense, thus distinguished from each other, had remained within their own boundaries, and bore in themselves the magnificence of the Creator-Word, silent praisers and thrilling heralds of His mighty work. Not yet was there any mingling of both, nor any mixtures of these opposites, tokens of a greater Wisdom and Generosity in the creation of natures; nor as yet were the whole riches of

Goodness made known. Now the Creator-Word, determining to exhibit this, and to produce a single living being out of both – the visible and the invisible creations, I mean – fashions Man; and taking a body from already existing matter, and placing in it a Breath taken from Himself which the Word knew to be an intelligent soul and the Image of God, as a sort of second world. He placed him, great in littleness on the earth; a new Angel, a mingled worshipper, fully initiated into the visible creation, but only partially into the intellectual; King of all upon earth, but subject to the King above; earthly and heavenly; temporal and yet immortal; visible and yet intellectual; half-way between greatness and lowliness; in one person combining spirit and flesh; spirit, because of the favour bestowed on him; flesh, because of the height to which he had been raised; the one that he might continue to live and praise his Benefactor, the other that he might suffer, and by suffering be put in remembrance, and corrected if he became proud of his greatness. A living creature trained here, and then moved elsewhere; and, to complete the mystery, deified by its inclination to God. For to this, I think, tends that Light of Truth which we here possess but in measure, that we should both see and experience the Splendour of God, which is worthy of Him Who made us, and will remake us again after a loftier fashion.

XII. This being He placed in Paradise, whatever the Paradise may have been, having honoured him with the gift of Free Will (in order that God might belong to him as the result of his choice, no less than to Him who had implanted the seeds of it), to till the immortal plants, by which is meant perhaps the Divine Conceptions, both the simpler and the more perfect; naked in his simplicity and inartificial life, and without any covering or screen; for it was fitting that he who was from the beginning should be such. Also He gave him a Law, as a material for his Free Will to act upon. This Law was a Commandment as to what plants he might partake of, and which one he might not touch. This latter was the Tree of Knowledge; not, however, because it was evil from the beginning when planted; nor was it forbidden because God grudged it to us...Let not the enemies of God wag their tongues in that direction, or imitate the Serpent...But it would have been good if partaken of at the proper time, for the tree was, according to my theory, Contemplation, upon which it is only safe for those who have reached maturity of habit to enter; but which is not good for those who are still somewhat simple and greedy in their habit; just as solid food is not good for those who are yet tender, and have need of milk. But when through the Devil's malice and the woman's caprice, to which she succumbed as the more tender, and which she brought to bear upon the man, as she was the more apt to persuade, alas for my weakness! (for that of my first father was mine), he forgot the Commandment which had been given to him; he yielded to the baleful fruit; and for his sin he was banished, at once from the Tree of Life, and from Paradise, and from God; and put on the coats of skins...that is, perhaps, the coarser flesh, both mortal and contradictory. This was the first thing that he learnt – his own shame; and he hid himself from God. Yet here too he makes a gain, namely death, and the cutting off of sin, in order that evil may not be immortal. Thus his punishment is changed into a mercy; for it is in mercy, I am persuaded, that God inflicts punishment.

Oration XXXIX – On the Holy Lights

XII. For to us there is but One God, the Father, of Whom are all things, and One Lord Jesus Christ, by Whom are all things; and One Holy Ghost, in Whom are all things; yet these words, of, by, in, whom, do not denote a difference of nature (for if this were the case, the three prepositions, or the order of the three names would never be altered), but they characterize the personalities of a nature which is one and unconfused. And this is proved by the fact that They are again collected into one, if you will read – not carelessly – this other passage of the same Apostle, "Of Him and through Him and to Him are all things; to Him be glory forever, Amen." The Father is Father, and is Unoriginate, for He is of no one; the Son is Son, and is not unoriginate, for He is of the Father. But if you take the word Origin in a temporal sense, He too is Unoriginate, for He is the Maker of Time, and is not subject to Time. The Holy Ghost is truly Spirit, coming forth from the Father indeed, but not after the manner of the Son, for it is not by Generation but by Procession (since I must coin a word for the sake of clearness); for neither did the Father cease to be Unbegotten because of His begetting something, nor the Son to be begotten because He is of the Unbegotten (how could that be?), nor is the Spirit changed into Father or Son because He proceeds, or because He is God – though the ungodly do not believe it. For Personality is unchangeable; else how could Personality remain, if it were changeable, and could be removed from one to another? But they who make "Unbegotten" and "Begotten" natures of equivocal gods would perhaps make Adam and Seth differ in nature, since the former was not born of flesh (for he was created), but the latter was born of Adam and Eve. There is then One God in Three, and These Three are One, as we have said.

Basil the Great

> St. Basil the Great (330 – 379) was one of the three Cappadocian Fathers who helped hammer out the terminology needed to express the doctrine of the Trinity. His *Hexæmeron*, a series of nine sermons on the six days of creation in Genesis, was delivered during Great Lent at the daily morning and evening services. It, perhaps more than any other writing of the Church Fathers, epitomizes their treatment of creation. It is a classic of the Patristic age and is presented here in full.
>
> In this work, Basil assumes Mosaic authorship of Genesis 1 and accords to this text the highest inspiration. He grapples with the science and cosmology of his day as expressed by philosophers and poets. For him, the study and contemplation of the created order yields its greatest benefits when it is connected with humanity's ultimate end of salvation and union with God.
>
> In Basil's view, God created the visible world out of nothing. Before that, He created the intelligible or spiritual world. Everything in the world is created for a reason and has a purpose for being. Study of the world should lead one to perceive and worship the Creator, who displays His power, wisdom, and goodness throughout the created order.

Basil the Great *Hexæmeron*

Homily I – In the Beginning God Made the Heaven and the Earth

1. It is right that any one beginning to narrate the formation of the world should begin with the good order which reigns in visible things. I am about to speak of the creation of heaven and earth, which was not spontaneous, as some have imagined, but drew its origin from God. What ear is worthy to hear such a tale? How earnestly the soul should prepare itself to receive such high lessons! How pure it should be from carnal affections, how unclouded by worldly disquietudes, how active and ardent in its researches, how eager to find in its surroundings an idea of God which may be worthy of Him!...

2. "In the beginning God created the heaven and the earth." I stop struck with admiration at this thought. What shall I first say? Where

shall I begin my story? Shall I show forth the vanity of the Gentiles? Shall I exalt the truth of our faith? The philosophers of Greece have made much ado to explain nature, and not one of their systems has remained firm and unshaken, each being overturned by its successor. It is vain to refute them; they are sufficient in themselves to destroy one another. Those who were too ignorant to rise to a knowledge of a God, could not allow that an intelligent cause presided at the birth of the Universe; a primary error that involved them in sad consequences.

Some had recourse to material principles and attributed the origin of the Universe to the elements of the world. Others imagined that atoms, and indivisible bodies, molecules and ducts, form, by their union, the nature of the visible world. Atoms reuniting or separating, produce births and deaths and the most durable bodies only owe their consistency to the strength of their mutual adhesion: a true spider's web woven by these writers who give to heaven, to earth, and to sea so weak an origin and so little consistency! It is because they knew not how to say "In the beginning God created the heaven and the earth." Deceived by their inherent atheism it appeared to them that nothing governed or ruled the universe, and that was all was given up to chance.

To guard us against this error the writer on the creation, from the very first words, enlightens our understanding with the name of God; "In the beginning God created." What a glorious order! He first establishes a beginning, so that it might not be supposed that the world never had a beginning. Then be adds "Created" to show that which was made was a very small part of the power of the Creator. In the same way that the potter, after having made with equal pains a great number of vessels, has not exhausted either his art or his talent; thus the Maker of the Universe, whose creative power, far from being bounded by one world, could extend to the infinite, needed only the impulse of His will to bring the immensities of the visible world into being. If then the world has a beginning, and if it has been created, enquire who gave it this beginning, and who was the Creator: or rather, in the fear that human reasonings may make you wander from the truth, Moses has anticipated enquiry by engraving in our hearts, as a seal and a safeguard, the awful name of God: "In the beginning God created" – It is He, beneficent Nature, Goodness without measure, a worthy object of love for all beings endowed with reason, the beauty the most to be desired, the origin of all that exists, the source of life, intellectual light, impenetrable wisdom, it is He who "in the beginning created heaven and earth."

3. Do not then imagine, O man! that the visible world is without a beginning; and because the celestial bodies move in a circular course, and it is difficult for our senses to define the point where the circle begins, do not believe that bodies impelled by a circular movement are, from their nature, without a beginning. Without doubt the circle (I mean the plane figure described by a single line) is beyond our perception, and it is impossible for us to find out where it begins or where it ends; but we ought not on this account to believe it to be without a beginning. Although we are not sensible of it, it really begins at some point where the draughtsman has begun to draw it at a certain radius from the centre. Thus seeing that figures which move in a circle always return upon themselves, without for a single instant interrupting the regularity of their course, do not vainly imagine to yourselves that the world has neither beginning nor end. "For the fashion of this world passeth away" and "Heaven and earth shall pass away."

The dogmas of the end, and of the renewing of the world, are announced beforehand in these short words put at the head of the inspired history. "In the beginning God made." That which was begun in time is condemned to come to an end in time. If there has been a beginning do not doubt of the end. Of what use then are geometry – the calculations of arithmetic – the study of solids and far-famed astronomy, this laborious vanity, if those who pursue them imagine that this visible world is co-eternal with the Creator of all things, with God Himself; if they attribute to this limited world, which has a material body, the same glory as to the incomprehensible and invisible nature; if they cannot conceive that a whole, of which the parts are subject to corruption and change, must of necessity end by itself submitting to the fate of its parts? But they have become "vain in their imaginations and their foolish heart was darkened. Professing themselves to be wise, they became fools." Some have affirmed that heaven co-exists with God from all eternity; others that it is God Himself without beginning or end, and the cause of the particular arrangement of all things.

4. One day, doubtless, their terrible condemnation will be the greater for all this worldly wisdom, since, seeing so clearly into vain sciences, they have wilfully shut their eyes to the knowledge of the truth. These men who measure the distances of the stars and describe them, both those of the North, always shining brilliantly in our view, and those of the southern pole visible to the inhabitants of the South, but unknown to us; who divide the Northern zone and the circle of the Zodiac into an infinity of parts, who observe with exactitude the course of the stars, their fixed places, their declensions, their return and the time that each takes to make its revolution; these men, I say, have discovered all except one thing: the fact that God is the Creator of the universe, and the just Judge who rewards all the actions of life according to their merit. They have not known how to raise themselves to the idea of the consummation of all things, the consequence of the doctrine of judgment, and to see that the world must change if souls pass from this life to a new life. In reality, as the nature of the present life presents an affinity to this world, so in the future life our souls will enjoy a lot conformable to their new condition. But they are so far from applying these truths, that they do but laugh when we announce to them the end of all things and the regeneration of the age. Since the beginning naturally precedes that which is derived from it, the writer, of necessity, when speaking to us of things which had their origin in time, puts at the head of his narrative these words – "In the beginning God created."

5. It appears, indeed, that even before this world an order of things existed of which our mind can form an idea, but of which we can say nothing, because it is too lofty a subject for men who are but beginners and are still babes in knowledge. The birth of the world was preceded by a condition of things suitable for the exercise of supernatural powers, outstripping the limits of time, eternal and infinite. The Creator and Demiurge of the universe perfected His works in it, spiritual light for the happiness of all who love the Lord, intellectual and invisible natures, all the orderly arrangement of pure intelligences who are beyond the reach of our mind and of whom we cannot even discover the names. They fill the essence of this invisible world, as Paul teaches us. "For by him were all things created that are in heaven, and that are in earth, visible and invisible whether they be

thrones or dominions or principalities or powers" or virtues or hosts of angels or the dignities of archangels.

To this world at last it was necessary to add a new world, both a school and training place where the souls of men should be taught and a home for beings destined to be born and to die. Thus was created, of a nature analogous to that of this world and the animals and plants which live thereon, the succession of time, for ever pressing on and passing away and never stopping in its course. Is not this the nature of time, where the past is no more, the future does not exist, and the present escapes before being recognised? And such also is the nature of the creature which lives in time – condemned to grow or to perish without rest and without certain stability. It is therefore fit that the bodies of animals and plants, obliged to follow a sort of current, and carried away by the motion which leads them to birth or to death, should live in the midst of surroundings whose nature is in accord with beings subject to change. Thus the writer who wisely tells us of the birth of the Universe does not fail to put these words at the head of the narrative. "In the beginning God created;" that is to say, in the beginning of time. Therefore, if he makes the world appear in the beginning, it is not a proof that its birth has preceded that of all other things that were made. He only wishes to tell us that, after the invisible and intellectual world, the visible world, the world of the senses, began to exist...

6. Such being the different senses of the word beginning, see if we have not all the meanings here. You may know the epoch when the formation of this world began, if, ascending into the past, you endeavour to discover the first day. You will thus find what was the first movement of time; then that the creation of the heavens and of the earth were like the foundation and the groundwork, and afterwards that an intelligent reason, as the word beginning indicates, presided in the order of visible things. You will finally discover that the world was not conceived by *chance* and without *reason*, but for an useful end and for the great advantage of all beings, since it is really the school where reasonable souls exercise themselves, the training ground where they learn to know God; since by the sight of visible and sensible things the mind is led, as by a hand, to the contemplation of invisible things. "For," as the Apostle says, "the invisible things of him from the creation of the world are clearly seen, being understood

by the things that are made." Perhaps these words "In the beginning God created" signify the rapid and imperceptible moment of creation.

The beginning, in effect, is indivisible and instantaneous. The beginning of the road is not yet the road, and that of the house is not yet the house; so the beginning of time is not yet time and not even the least particle of it. If some objector tell us that the beginning is a time, he ought then, as he knows well, to submit it to the division of time – a beginning, a middle and an end. Now it is ridiculous to imagine a beginning of a beginning. Further, if we divide the beginning into two, we make two instead of one, or rather make several, we really make an infinity, for all that which is divided is divisible to the infinite. Thus then, if it is said, "In the beginning God created," it is to teach us that at the will of God the world arose in less than an instant, and it is to convey this meaning more clearly that other interpreters have said: "God made summarily" that is to say all at once and in a moment. But enough concerning the beginning, if only to put a few points out of many.

7. Among arts, some have in view production, some practice, others theory. The object of the last is the exercise of thought, that of the second, the motion of the body. Should it cease, all stops; nothing more is to be seen. Thus dancing and music have nothing behind; they have no object but themselves. In creative arts on the contrary the work lasts after the operation. Such is architecture – such are the arts which work in wood and brass and weaving, all those indeed which, even when the artisan has disappeared, serve to show an industrious intelligence and to cause the architect, the worker in brass or the weaver, to be admired on account of his work. Thus, then, to show that the world is a work of art displayed for the beholding of all people; to make them know Him who created it, Moses does not use another word. "In the beginning," he says "God created." He does not say "God worked," "God formed," but" God created."

Among those who have imagined that the world co-existed with God from all eternity, many have denied that it was created by God, but say that it exists spontaneously, as the shadow of this power. God, they say, is the cause of it, but an involuntary cause, as the body is the cause of the shadow and the flame is the cause of the brightness. It is to correct this error that the prophet states, with so much precision,

"In the beginning God created." *He did not make the thing itself the cause of its existence.* Being good, He made it a useful work. Being wise, He made it everything that was most beautiful. Being powerful He made it very great. Moses almost shows us the finger of the supreme artisan taking possession of the substance of the universe, forming the different parts in one perfect accord, and making a harmonious symphony result from the whole...

8. "In the beginning God created the heaven and the earth." If we were to wish to discover the essence of each of the beings which are offered for our contemplation, or come under our senses, we should be drawn away into long digressions, and the solution of the problem would require more words than I possess, to examine fully the matter. To spend time on such points would not prove to be to the edification of the Church. Upon the essence of the heavens we are contented with what Isaiah says, for, in simple language, he gives us sufficient idea of their nature, "The heaven was made like smoke," that is to say, He created a subtle substance, without solidity or density, from which to form the heavens. As to the form of them we also content ourselves with the language of the same prophet, when praising God "that stretcheth out the heavens as a curtain and spreadeth them out as a tent to dwell in." In the same way, as concerns the earth, let us resolve not to torment ourselves by trying to find out its essence, not to tire our reason by seeking for the substance which it conceals...

If I ask you to leave these vain questions, I will not expect you to try and find out the earth's point of support. The mind would reel on beholding its reasonings losing themselves without end. Do you say that the earth reposes on a bed of air? How, then, can this soft substance, without consistency, resist the enormous weight which presses upon it? How is it that it does not slip away in all directions, to avoid the sinking weight, and to spread itself over the mass which overwhelms it? Do you suppose that water is the foundation of the earth? You will then always have to ask yourself how it is that so heavy and opaque a body does not pass through the water; how a mass of such a weight is held up by a nature weaker than itself. Then you must seek a base for the waters, and you will be in much difficulty to say upon what the water itself rests.

9. Do you suppose that a heavier body prevents the earth from falling into the abyss? Then you must consider that this support needs

itself a support to prevent it from falling. Can we imagine one? Our reason again demands yet another support, and thus we shall fall into the infinite, always imagining a base for the base which we have already found. And the further we advance in this reasoning the greater force we are obliged to give to this base, so that it may be able to support all the mass weighing upon it. Put then a limit to your thought, so that your curiosity in investigating the incomprehensible may not incur the reproaches of Job, and you be not asked by him, "Whereupon are the foundations thereof fastened?" If ever you hear in the Psalms, "I bear up the pillars of it;" see in these pillars the power which sustains it. Because what means this other passage, "He hath founded it upon the sea," if not that the water is spread all around the earth? How then can water, the fluid element which flows down every declivity, remain suspended without ever flowing? You do not reflect that the idea of the earth suspended by itself throws your reason into a like but even greater difficulty, since from its nature it is heavier. But let us admit that the earth rests upon itself, or let us say that it rides the waters, we must still remain faithful to thought of true religion and recognise that all is sustained by the Creator's power. Let us then reply to ourselves, and let us reply to those who ask us upon what support this enormous mass rests, "In His hands are the ends of the earth." It is a doctrine as infallible for our own information as profitable for our hearers.

10. There are inquirers into nature who with a great display of words give reasons for the immobility of the earth. Placed, they say, in the middle of the universe and not being able to incline more to one side than the other because its centre is everywhere the same distance from the surface, it necessarily rests upon itself; since a weight which is everywhere equal cannot lean to either side. It is not, they go on, without reason or by chance that the earth occupies the centre of the universe. It is its natural and necessary position...Do not then be surprised that the world never falls: it occupies the centre of the universe, its natural place. By necessity it is obliged to remain in its place, unless a movement contrary to nature should displace it. If there is anything in this system which might appear probable to you, keep your admiration for the source of such perfect order, for the wisdom of God. Grand phenomena do not strike us the less when we

have discovered something of their wonderful mechanism. Is it otherwise here? At all events let us prefer the simplicity of faith to the demonstrations of reason.

11. We might say the same thing of the heavens. With what a noise of words the sages of this world have discussed their nature! Some have said that heaven is composed of four elements as being tangible and visible, and is made up of earth on account of its power of resistance, with fire because it is striking to the eye, with air and water on account of the mixture. Others have rejected this system as improbable, and introduced into the world, to form the heavens, a fifth element after their own fashioning. There exists, they say, an æthereal body which is neither fire, air, earth, nor water, nor in one word any simple body. These simple bodies have their own natural motion in a straight line, light bodies upwards and heavy bodies downwards; now this motion upwards and downwards is not the same as circular motion; there is the greatest possible difference between straight and circular motion. It therefore follows that bodies whose motion is so various must vary also in their essence. But, it is not even possible to suppose that the heavens should be formed of primitive bodies which we call elements, because the reunion of contrary forces could not produce an even and spontaneous motion, when each of the simple bodies is receiving a different impulse from nature.

Thus it is a labour to maintain composite bodies in continual movement, because it is impossible to put even a single one of their movements in accord and harmony with all those that are in discord; since what is proper to the light particle, is in warfare with that of a heavier one. If we attempt to rise we are stopped by the weight of the terrestrial element; if we throw ourselves down we violate the igneous part of our being in dragging it down contrary to its nature. Now this struggle of the elements effects their dissolution. A body to which violence is done and which is placed in opposition to nature, after a short but energetic resistance, is soon dissolved into as many parts as it had elements, each of the constituent parts returning to its natural place. It is the force of these reasons, say the inventors of the fifth kind of body for the genesis of heaven and the stars, which constrained them to reject the system of their predecessors and to have recourse to their own hypothesis. But yet another fine speaker arises and disperses and destroys this theory to give predominance to an idea of his own invention.

Do not let us undertake to follow them for fear of falling into like frivolities; let them refute each other, and, without disquieting ourselves about essence, let us say with Moses "God created the heavens and the earth." Let us glorify the supreme Artificer for all that was wisely and skillfully made; by the beauty of visible things let us raise ourselves to Him who is above all beauty; by the grandeur of bodies, sensible and limited in their nature, let us conceive of the infinite Being whose immensity and omnipotence surpass all the efforts of the imagination. Because, although we ignore the nature of created things, the objects which on all sides attract our notice are so marvellous, that the most penetrating mind cannot attain to the knowledge of the least of the phenomena of the world, either to give a suitable explanation of it or to render due praise to the Creator, to Whom belong all glory, all honour and all power world without end. Amen.

Homily II – "The Earth Was Invisible and Unfinished"

1. In the few words which have occupied us this morning we have found such a depth of thought that we despair of penetrating further. If such is the fore court of the sanctuary, if the portico of the temple is so grand and magnificent, if the splendour of its beauty thus dazzles the eyes of the soul, what will be the holy of holies? Who will dare to try to gain access to the innermost shrine? Who will look into its secrets? To gaze into it is indeed forbidden us, and language. is powerless to express what the mind conceives. However, since there are rewards, and most desirable ones, reserved by the just Judge for the intention alone of doing good, do not let us hesitate to continue our researches. Although we may not attain to the truth, if, with the help of the Spirit, we do not fall away from the meaning of Holy Scripture we shall not deserve to be rejected, and, with the help of grace, we shall contribute to the edification of the Church of God.

"The earth," says Holy Scripture, "was invisible and unfinished." The heavens and the earth were created without distinction. How then is it that the heavens are perfect whilst the earth is still unformed and incomplete? In one word, what was the unfinished condition of the earth? And for what reason was it invisible? The fertility of the earth is its perfect finishing; growth of all kinds of plants, the upspringing of tall trees, both productive and sterile, flowers' sweet scents and fair colours, and all that which, a little later, at the voice of God came forth from the earth to beautify her, their universal Mother. As nothing of all this yet existed, Scripture is right in calling the earth "without form." We could also say of the heavens that they were still imperfect and had not received their natural adornment, since at that time they did not shine with the glory of the sun and of the moon and were not crowned by the choirs of the stars. These bodies were not yet created. Thus you will not diverge from the truth in saying that the heavens also were "without form."

The earth was invisible for two reasons: it may be because man, the spectator, did not yet exist, or because being submerged under the waters which overflowed the surface, it could not be seen, since the waters had not yet been gathered together into their own places, where God afterwards collected them, and gave them the name of seas. What is invisible? First of all that which our fleshly eye cannot perceive; our mind, for example; then that which, visible in its nature, is hidden by some body which conceals it, like iron in the depths of the earth. It is in this sense, because it was hidden under the waters, that the earth was still invisible. However, as light did not yet exist, and as the earth lay in darkness, because of the obscurity of the air above it, it should not astonish us that for this reason Scripture calls it "invisible."

2. But the corrupters of the truth, who, incapable of submitting their reason to Holy Scripture, distort at will the meaning of the Holy Scriptures, pretend that these words mean matter. For it is matter, they say, which from its nature is without form and invisible – being by the conditions of its existence without quality and without form and figure. The Artificer submitting it to the working of His wisdom clothed it with a form, organized it, and thus gave being to the visible world.

If matter is uncreated, it has a claim to the same honours as God, since it must be of equal rank with Him. Is this not the summit of wickedness, that an extreme deformity, without quality, without form, shape, ugliness without configuration, to use their own expression, should enjoy the same prerogatives with Him, Who is wisdom, power and beauty itself, the Creator and the Demiurge of the universe? This is not all.

If matter is so great as to be capable of being acted on by the whole wisdom of God, it would in a way raise its hypostasis to an equality with the inaccessible power of God, since it would be able to measure by itself all the extent of the divine intelligence. If it is insufficient for the operations of God, then we fall into a more absurd blasphemy, since we condemn God for not being able, on account of the want of matter, to finish His own works. The poverty of human nature has deceived these reasoners. Each of our crafts is exercised upon some special matter – the art of the smith upon iron, that of the carpenter on wood. In all, there is the subject, the form and the work which results from the form. Matter is taken from without – art gives the form – and the work is composed at the same time of form and of matter.

Such is the idea that they make for themselves of the divine work. The form of the world is due to the wisdom of the supreme Artificer; matter came to the Creator from without; and thus the world results from a double origin. It hits received from outside its matter and its essence, and from God its form and figure. They thus come to deny that the mighty God has presided at the formation of the universe, and pretend that He has only brought a crowning contribution to a common work, that He has only contributed some small portion to the genesis of beings: they are incapable from the debasement of their reasonings of raising their glances to the height of truth.

Here below arts are subsequent to matter – introduced into life by the indispensable need of them. Wool existed before weaving made it supply one of nature's imperfections. Wood existed before carpentering took possession of it, and transformed it each day to supply new wants, and made us see all the advantages derived from it, giving the oar to the sailor, the winnowing fan to the labourer, the lance to the soldier. But God, before all those things which now attract our notice existed, after casting about in His mind and determining to bring into being time which had no being, imagined the world such as it ought to be, and created matter in harmony with the forth which He wished to give it. He assigned to the heavens the nature adapted for the heavens, and gave to the earth an essence in accordance with its form. He formed, as He wished, fire, air and water, and gave to each the essence which the object of its existence required. Finally, He welded all the diverse parts of the universe by links of indissoluble attachment and established between them so perfect a fellowship and harmony that the most distant, in spite of their distance, appeared united in one universal sympathy. Let those men therefore renounce their fabulous imaginations, who, in spite of the weakness of their argument, pretend to measure a power as incomprehensible to man's reason as it is unutterable by man's voice.

3. God created the heavens and the earth, but not only half – He created all the heavens and all the earth, creating the essence with the form. For He is not an inventor of figures, but the Creator even of the essence of beings. Further let them tell us how the efficient power of God could deal with the passive nature of matter, the latter furnishing the matter without form, the former possessing the science of the form without matter, both being in need of each other; the Creator in order to display His art, matter in order to cease to be without form and to receive a form. But let us stop here and return to our subject.

"The earth was invisible and unfinished." In saying "In the beginning God created the heavens and the earth," the sacred writer passed over many things in silence, water, air, fire and the results from them, which, all forming in reality the true complement of the world, were, without doubt, made at the same time as the universe. By this silence, history wishes to train the activity of our intelligence, giving it a weak point for starting, to impel it to the discovery of the truth. Thus, we are not told of the creation of water; but, as we are told that the earth was invisible, ask yourself what could have covered it, and prevented it from being seen? Fire could not conceal it. Fire brightens all about it, and spreads light rather than darkness around. No more was it air that enveloped the earth. Air by nature is of little density and transparent. It receives all kinds of visible object, and transmits them to the spectators. Only one supposition remains; that which floated on the surface of the earth was water – the fluid essence which had not yet been confined to its own place. Thus the earth was not only invisible; it was still incomplete. Even today excessive damp is a hindrance to the productiveness of the earth. The same cause at the same time prevents it from being seen, and from being complete, for the proper and natural adornment of the earth is its completion:

corn waving in the valleys – meadows green with grass and rich with many coloured flowers – fertile glades and hill-tops shaded by forests. Of all this nothing was yet produced; the earth was in travail with it in virtue of the power that she had received from the Creator. But she was waiting for the appointed time and the divine order to bring forth.

4. "Darkness was upon the face of the deep." A new source for fables and most impious imaginations if one distorts the sense of these words at the will of one's fancies. By "darkness" these wicked men do not understand what is meant in reality – air not illumined, the shadow produced by the interposition of a body, or finally a place for some reason deprived of light. For them "darkness" is an evil power, or rather the personification of evil, having his origin in himself in opposition to, and in perpetual struggle with, the goodness of God. If God is light, they say, without any doubt the power which struggles against Him must be darkness, "Darkness" not owing its existence to a foreign origin, but an evil existing by itself. "Darkness" is the enemy of souls, the primary cause of death, the adversary of virtue. The words of the Prophet, they say in their error, show that it exists and that it does not proceed from God. From this what perverse and impious dogmas have been imagined! What grievous wolves, tearing the flock of the Lord, have sprung from these words to cast themselves upon souls! Is it not from hence that have come forth Marcions and Valentini, and the detestable heresy of the Manicheans, which you may without going far wrong call the putrid humour of the churches.

O man, why wander thus from the truth, and imagine for thyself that which will cause thy perdition? The word is simple and within the comprehension of all. "The earth was invisible." Why? Because the "deep" was spread over its surface. What is "the deep"? A mass of water of extreme depth. But we know that we can see many bodies through clear and transparent water. How then was it that no part of the earth appeared through the water? Because the air which surrounded it was still without light and in darkness. The rays of the sun, penetrating the water, often allow its to see the pebbles which form the bed of the river, but in a dark night it is impossible for our glance to penetrate under the water. Thus, these words "the earth was invisible" are explained by those that follow; "the deep" covered it and itself was in darkness. Thus, the deep is not a multitude of hostile powers, as has been imagined; nor "darkness" an evil sovereign force in enmity with good. In reality two rival principles of equal power, if engaged without ceasing in a war of mutual attacks, will end in self destruction. But if one should gain the mastery it would completely annihilate the conquered. Thus, to maintain the balance in the struggle between good and evil is to represent them as engaged in a war without end and in perpetual destruction, where the opponents are at the same time conquerors and conquered. If good is the stronger, what is there to prevent evil being completely annihilated? But if that be the case, the very utterance of which is impious, I ask myself how it is that they themselves are not filled with horror to think that they have imagined such abominable blasphemies.

It is equally impious to say that evil has its origin from God; because the contrary cannot proceed from its contrary. Life does not engender death; darkness is not the origin of light; sickness is not the maker of health. In the changes of conditions there are transitions from one condition to the contrary; but in genesis each being proceeds from its like, and not from its contrary. If then evil is neither uncreate nor created by God, from whence comes its nature? Certainly that evil exists, no one living in the world will deny. What shall we say then? Evil is not a living animated essence; it is the condition of the soul opposed to virtue, developed in the careless on account of their falling away from good.

5. Do not then go beyond yourself to seek for evil, and imagine that there is an original nature of wickedness. Each of us, let us acknowledge it, is the first author of his own vice. Among the ordinary events of life, some come naturally, like old age and sickness, others by chance like unforeseen occurrences, of which the origin is beyond ourselves, often sad, sometimes fortunate, as for instance the discovery of a treasure when digging a well, or the meeting of a mad dog when going to the market place. Others depend upon ourselves, such as ruling one's passions, or not putting a bridle on one's pleasures, to be master of our anger, or to raise the hand against him who irritates us, to tell the truth, or to lie, to have a sweet and well-regulated disposition, or to be fierce and swollen and exalted with pride. Here you are the master of your actions. Do not look for the guiding cause beyond yourself, but recognise that evil, rightly so

called, has no other origin than our voluntary falls. If it were involuntary, and did not depend upon ourselves, the laws would not have so much terror for the guilty, and the tribunals would not be so without pity when they condemn wretches according to the measure of their crimes. But enough concerning evil rightly so called. Sickness, poverty, obscurity, death, finally all human afflictions, ought not to be ranked as evils; since we do not count among the greatest boons things which are their opposites. Among these afflictions, some are the effect of nature, others have obviously been for many a source of advantage. Let us then be silent for the moment about these metaphors and allegories, and, simply following without vain curiosity the words of Holy Scripture, let us take from darkness the idea which it gives us.

But reason asks, was darkness created with the world? Is it older than light? Why in spite of its inferiority has it preceded it? Darkness, we reply, did not exist in essence; it is a condition produced in the air by the withdrawal of light. What then is that light which disappeared suddenly from the world, so that darkness should cover the face of the deep? If anything had existed before the formation of this sensible and perishable world, no doubt we conclude it would have been in light. The orders of angels, the heavenly hosts, all intellectual natures named or unnamed, all the ministering spirits, did not live in darkness, but enjoyed a condition fitted for them in light and spiritual joy.

No one will contradict this; least of all he who looks for celestial light as one of the rewards promised to virtues the light which, as Solomon says, is always a light to the righteous, the light which made the Apostle say "Giving thanks unto the Father, which hath made us meet to be partakers of the inheritance of the saints in light." finally, if the condemned are sent into outer darkness evidently those who are made worthy of God's approval, are at rest in heavenly light. When then, according to the order of God, the heaven appeared, enveloping all that its circumference included, a vast and unbroken body separating outer things from those which it enclosed, it necessarily kept the space inside in darkness for want of communication with the outer light. Three things are, indeed, needed to form a shadow, light, a body, a dark place. The shadow of heaven forms the darkness of the world. Understand, I pray you, what I mean, by a simple example; by raising for yourself at mid-day a tent of some compact and impenetrable material, and shutting yourself up in it in sudden darkness. Suppose that original darkness was like this, not subsisting directly by itself, but resulting from some external coasts. If it is said that it rested upon the deep, it is because the extremity of air naturally touches the surface of bodies; and as at that time the water covered everything, we are obliged to say that darkness was upon the face of the deep.

6. And the Spirit of God was borne upon the face of the waters. Does this spirit mean the diffusion of air? The sacred writer wishes to enumerate to you the elements of the world, to tell you that God created the heavens, the earth, water, and air and that the last was now diffused and in motion; or rather, that which is truer and confirmed by the authority of the ancients, by the Spirit of God, he means the Holy Spirit. It is, as has been remarked, the special name, the name above all others that Scripture delights to give to the Holy Spirit, and always by the spirit of God the Holy Spirit is meant, the Spirit which completes the divine and blessed Trinity. You will find it better therefore to take it in this sense. How then did the Spirit of God move upon the waters? The explanation that I am about to give you is not an original one, but that of a Syrian, who was as ignorant in the wisdom of this world as he was versed in the knowledge of the Truth. He said, then, that the Syriac word was more expressive, and that being more analogous to the Hebrew term it was a nearer approach to the scriptural sense. This is the meaning of the word; by "was borne" the Syrians, he says, understand: it cherished the nature of the waters as one sees a bird cover the eggs with her body and impart to them vital force from her own warmth. Such is, as nearly as possible, the meaning of these words – the Spirit was borne: let us understand, that is, prepared the nature of water to produce living beings: a sufficient proof for those who ask if the Holy Spirit took an active part in the creation of the world.

7. And God said, Let there be light. The first word of God created the nature of light; it made darkness vanish, dispelled gloom, illuminated the world, and gave to all beings at the same time a sweet and gracious aspect. The heavens, until then enveloped in darkness, appeared with that beauty which they still present to our eyes. The air was lighted up, or rather made the light circulate mixed with its

substance, and, distributing its splendour rapidly in every direction, so dispersed itself to its extreme limits. Up it sprang to the very æther and heaven. In an instant it lighted up the whole extent of the world, the North and the South, the East and the West. For the æther also is such a subtle substance and so transparent that it needs not the space of a moment for light to pass through it. Just as it carries our sight instantaneously to the object of vision, so without the least interval, with a rapidity that thought cannot conceive, it receives these rays of light in its uttermost limits. With light the æther becomes more pleasing and the waters more limpid. These last, not content with receiving its splendour, return it by the reflection of light and in all directions send forth quivering flashes. The divine word gives every object a more cheerful and a more attractive appearance, just as when men in deep sea pour in oil they make the place about them clear. So, with a single word and in one instant, the Creator of all things gave the boon of light to the world.

Let there be light. The order was itself an operation, and a state of things was brought into being, than which man's mind cannot even imagine a pleasanter one for our enjoyment. It must be well understood that when we speak of the voice, of the word, of the command of God, this divine language does not mean to us a sound which escapes from the organs of speech, a collision of air struck by the tongue; it is a simple sign of the will of God, and, if we give it the form of an order, it is only the better to impress the souls whom we instruct...

8. "And God called the light Day and the darkness he called Night." Since the birth of the sun, the light that it diffuses in the air, when shining on our hemisphere, is day; and the shadow produced by its disappearance is night. But at that time it was not after the movement of the sun, but following this primitive light spread abroad in the air or withdrawn in a measure determined by God, that day came and was followed by night.

"And the evening and the morning were the first day." Evening is then the boundary common to day and night; and in the same way morning constitutes the approach of night to day. It was to give day the privileges of seniority that Scripture put the end of the first day before that of the first night, because night follows day: for, before the creation of light, the world was not in night, but in darkness. It is the opposite of day which was called night, and it did not receive its name until after day. Thus were created the evening and the morning. Scripture means the space of a day and a night, and afterwards no more says day and night, but calls them both under the name of the more important: a custom which you will find throughout Scripture. Everywhere the measure of time is counted by days, without mention of nights. "The days of our years," says the Psalmist. "Few and evil have the days of the years of my life been," said Jacob, and elsewhere "all the days of my life." Thus under the form of history the law is laid down for what is to follow. And the evening and the morning were one day.

Why does Scripture say "one day the first day"? Before speaking to us of the second, the third, and the fourth days, would it not have been more natural to call that one the first which began the series? If it therefore says "one day," it is from a wish to determine the measure of day and night, and to combine the time that they contain. Now twenty-four hours fill up the space of one day – we mean of a day and of a night; and if, at the time of the solstices, they have not both an equal length, the time marked by Scripture does not the less circumscribe their duration. It is as though it said: twenty-four hours measure the space of a day, or that, in reality a day is the time that the heavens starting from one point take to return there. Thus, every time that, in the revolution of the sun, evening and morning occupy the world, their periodical succession never exceeds the space of one day.

But must we believe in a mysterious reason for this? God who made the nature of time measured it out and determined it by intervals of days; and, wishing to give it a week as a measure, he ordered the week to revolve from period to period upon itself, to count the movement of time, forming the week of one day revolving seven times upon itself: a proper circle begins and ends with itself. Such is also the character of eternity, to revolve upon itself and to end nowhere. If then the beginning of time is called "one day" rather than "the first day," it is because Scripture wishes to establish its relationship with eternity. It was, in reality, fit and natural to call "one" the day whose character is to be one wholly separated and isolated from all the others. If Scripture speaks to us of many ages, saying everywhere, "age of age, and ages of ages," we do not see it enumerate them as first, second, and third. It follows that we are hereby shown not so much limits, ends and succession of ages, as distinctions between various states and modes of action.

"The day of the Lord," Scripture says, "is great and very terrible," and elsewhere "Woe unto you that desire the day of the Lord: to what end is it for you? The day of the Lord is darkness and not light." A day of darkness for those who are worthy of darkness. No; this day without evening, without succession and without end is not unknown to Scripture, and it is the day that the Psalmist calls the eighth day, because it is outside this time of weeks. Thus whether you call it day, or whether you call it eternity, you express the same idea. Give this state the name of day; there are not several, but only one. If you call it eternity still it is unique and not manifold. Thus it is in order that you may carry your thoughts forward towards a future life, that Scripture marks by the word "one" the day which is the type of eternity, the first fruits of days, the contemporary of light, the holy Lord's day honoured by the Resurrection of our Lord. And the evening and the morning were one day."...

Homily III – On the Firmament

1. We have now recounted the works of the first day, or rather of one day. Far be it from me indeed, to take from it the privilege it enjoys of having been for the Creator a day apart, a day which is not counted in the same order as the others. Our discussion yesterday treated of the works of this day, and divided the narrative so as to give you food for your souls in the morning, and joy in the evening. Today we pass on to the wonders of the second day. And here I do not wish to speak of the narrator's talent, but of the grace of Scripture, for the narrative is so naturally told that it pleases and delights all the friends of truth. It is this charm of truth which the Psalmist expresses so emphatically when he says, "How sweet are thy words unto my taste. yea, sweeter than honey to my mouth." Yesterday then, as far as we were able, we delighted our souls by conversing about the oracles of God, and now today we are met together again on the second day to contemplate the wonders of the second day....

2. And God said "Let there be a firmament in the midst of the waters, and let it divide the waters from the waters." Yesterday we heard God's decree, "Let there be light." Today it is, "Let there be a

firmament." There appears to be something more in this. The word is not limited to a simple command. It lays down the reason necessitating the structure of the firmament: it is, it is said, to separate the waters from the waters. And first let us ask how God speaks? Is it in our manner? Does His intelligence receive an impression from objects, and, after having conceived them, make them known by particular signs appropriate to each of them? Has He consequently recourse to the organs of voice to convey His thoughts? Is He obliged to strike the air by the articulate movements of the voice, to unveil the thought hidden in His heart? Would it not seem like an idle fable to say that God should need such a circuitous method to manifest His thoughts? And is it not more conformable with true religion to say, that the divine will and the first impetus of divine intelligence are the Word of God?

It is He whom Scripture vaguely represents, to show us that God has not only wished to create the world, but to create it with the help of a co-operator. Scripture might continue the history as it is begun: In the beginning God created the heaven and the earth; afterwards He created light, then He created the firmament. But, by making God command and speak, the Scripture tacitly shows us Him to Whom this order and these words are addressed. It is not that it grudges us the knowledge of the truth, but that it may kindle our desire by showing us some trace and indication of the mystery. We seize with delight, and carefully keep, the fruit of laborious efforts, whilst a possession easily attained is despised. Such is the road and the course which Scripture follows to lead us to the idea of the Only-begotten. And certainly, God's immaterial nature had no need of the material language of voice, since His very thoughts could be transmitted to His fellow-worker. What need then of speech, for those Who by thought alone could communicate their counsels to each other? Voice was made for hearing, and hearing for voice. Where there is neither air, nor tongue, nor ear, nor that winding canal which carries sounds to the seat of sensation in the head, there is no need for words thoughts of the soul are sufficient to transmit the will. As I said then, this language is only a wise and ingenious contrivance to set our minds seeking the Person to whom the words are addressed.

3. In the second place, does the firmament that is called heaven differ from the firmament that God made in the beginning? Are there

two heavens? The philosophers, who discuss heaven, would rather lose their tongues than grant this. There is only one heaven, they pretend; and it is of a nature neither to admit of a second, nor of a third, nor of several others. The essence of the celestial body quite complete constitutes its vast unity. Because, they say, every body which has a circular motion is one and finite. And if this body is used in the construction of the first heaven, there will be nothing left for the creation of a second or a third.

Here we see what those imagine who put under the Creator's hand uncreated matter; a lie that follows from the first fable. But we ask the Greek sages not to mock us before they are agreed among themselves. Because there are among them some who say there are infinite heavens and worlds. When grave demonstrations shall have upset their foolish system, when the laws of geometry shall have established that, according to the nature of heaven, it is impossible that there should be two, we shall only laugh the more at this elaborate scientific trifling. These learned men see not merely one bubble but several bubbles formed by the same cause, and they doubt the power of creative wisdom to bring several heavens into being!

We find, however, if we raise our eyes towards the omnipotence of God, that the strength and grandeur of the heavens differ from the drops of water bubbling on the surface of a fountain. How ridiculous, then, is their argument of impossibility! As for myself, far from not believing in a second, I seek for the third whereon the blessed Paul was found worthy to gaze. And does not the Psalmist in saying "heaven of heavens" give us an idea of their plurality? Is the plurality of heaven stranger than the seven circles through which nearly all the philosophers agree that the seven planets pass – circles which they represent to us as placed in connection with each other like casks fitting the one into the other? These circles, they say, carried away in a direction contrary to that of the world, and striking the rather, make sweet and harmonious sounds, unequalled by the sweetest melody. And if we ask them for the witness of the senses, what do they say? That we, accustomed to this noise from our birth, on account of hearing it always, have lost the sense of it; like then in smithies with their ears incessantly dinned. If I refuted this ingenious frivolity, the untruth of which is evident from the first word, it would seem as though I did not know the value of time and mistrusted the intelligence of such an audience.

But let me leave the vanity of outsiders to those who are without, and return to the theme proper to the Church. If we believe some of those who have preceded us, we have not here the creation of a new heaven, but a new account of the first. The reason they give is, that the earlier narrative briefly described the creation of heaven and earth; while here Scripture relates in greater detail the manner in which each was created. I, however, since Scripture gives to this second heaven another name and its own function, maintain that it is different from the heaven which was made at the beginning; that it is of a stronger nature and of an especial use to the universe.

4. "And God said, let there be a firmament in the midst of the waters, and let it divide the waters front the waters. And God made the firmament, and divided the waters which were under the firmament from the waters which were above the firmament." Before laying hold of the meaning of Scripture let us try to meet objections from other quarters. We are asked how, if the firmament is a spherical body, as it appears to the eye, its convex circumference can contain the water which flows and circulates in higher regions? What shall we answer? One thing only: because the interior of a body presents a perfect concavity it does not necessarily follow that its exterior surface is spherical and smoothly rounded. Look at the stone vaults of baths, and the structure of buildings of cave form; the dome, which forms the interior, does not prevent the roof from having ordinarily a flat surface. Let these unfortunate men cease, then, from tormenting us and themselves about the impossibility of our retaining water in the higher regions.

Now we must say something about the nature of the firmament, and why it received I the order to hold the middle place between the waters. Scripture constantly makes use of the word firmament to express extraordinary strength. "The Lord in firmament and refuge" "I have strengthened the pillars of it" "Praise him in the firmament of his power." The heathen writers thus call a strong body one which is compact and full, to distinguish it from the mathematical body. A mathematical body is a body which exists only in the three dimensions, breadths depth, and height. A firm body, on the contrary, adds resistance to the dimensions. It is the custom of Scripture to call firmament all that is strong and unyielding. It even uses the word to denote the condensation of the air: He, it says, who strengthens the thunder. Scripture means by the strengthening of the thunder, the strength and resistance of the wind, which, enclosed in the hollows of the clouds, produces the noise of thunder when it breaks through with violence.

Here then, according to me, is a firm substance, capable of retaining the fluid and unstable element water; and as, according to the common acceptation, it appears that the firmament owes its origin to water, we must not believe that it resembles frozen water or any other matter produced by the filtration of water; as, for example, rock crystal, which is said to owe its metamorphosis to excessive congelation, or the transparent stone which forms in mines. This pellucid stone, if one finds it in its natural perfection, without cracks inside, or the least spot of corruption, almost rivals the air in clearness. We cannot compare the firmament to one of these substances. To hold such an opinion about celestial bodies would be childish and foolish; and although everything may be in everything, fire in earth, air in water, and of the other elements the one in the other; although none of those which come under our senses are pure and without mixture, either with the element which serves as a medium for it, or with that which is contrary to it; I, nevertheless, dare not affirm that the firmament was formed of one of these simple substances, or of a mixture of them, for I am taught by Scripture not to allow my imagination to wander too far afield.

But do not let us forget to remark that, after these divine words "let there be a firmament," it is not said "and the firmament was made" but, "and God made the firmament, and divided the waters." Hear, O ye deaf! See, O ye blind! – who, then, is deaf? He who does not hear this startling voice of the Holy Spirit. Who is blind? He who does not see such clear proofs of the Only begotten, "Let there be a firmament." It is the voice of the primary and principal Cause. "And God made the firmament." Here is a witness to the active and creative power of God.

5. But let us continue our explanation: "Let it divide the waters from the waters." The mass of waters, which from all directions flowed over the earth, and was suspended in the air, was infinite, so

that there was no proportion between it and the other elements. Thus, as it has been already said, the abyss covered the earth. We give the reason for this abundance of water. None of you assuredly will attack our opinion; not even those who have the most cultivated minds, and whose piercing eye can penetrate this perishable and fleeting nature; you will not accuse me of advancing impossible or imaginary theories, nor will you ask me upon what foundation the fluid element rests. By the same reason which makes them attract the earth, heavier than water, from the extremities of the world to suspend it in the centre, they will grant us without doubt that it is due both to its natural attraction downwards and its general equilibrium, that this immense quantity of water rests motionless upon the earth. Therefore the prodigious mass of waters was spread around the earth; not in proportion with it and infinitely larger, thanks to the foresight of the supreme Artificer, Who, from the beginning, foresaw what was to come, and at the first provided all for the future needs of the world.

But what need was there for this superabundance of water? The essence of fire is necessary for the world, not only in the economy of earthly produce, but for the completion of the universe; for it would be imperfect if the most powerful and the most vital of its elements were lacking. Now fire and water are hostile to and destructive of each other. Fire, if it is the stronger, destroys water, and water, if in greater abundance, destroys fire. As, therefore, it was necessary to avoid an open struggle between these elements, so as not to bring about the dissolution of the universe by the total disappearance of one or the other, the sovereign Disposer created such a quantity of water that in spite of constant diminution from the effects of fire, it could last until the time fixed for the destruction of the world. He who planned all with weight and measure, He who, according to the word of Job, knows the number of the drops of rain, knew how long His work would last, and for how much consumption of fire He ought to allow. This is the reason of the abundance of water at the creation.

Further, there is no one so strange to life as to need to learn the reason why fire is essential to the world. Not only all the arts which support life, the art of weaving, that of shoemaking, of architecture, of agriculture, have need of the help of fire, but the vegetation of trees, the ripening of fruits, the breeding of land and water animals, and their nourishment, all existed from heat from the beginning, and have been since maintained by the action of heat. The creation of heat was then indispensable for the formation and the preservation of beings, and the abundance of waters was no less so in the presence of the constant and inevitable consumption by fire.

6. Survey creation; you will see the power of heat reigning over all that is born and perishes. On account of it comes all the water spread over the earth, as well as that which is beyond our sight and is dispersed in the depths of the earth. On account of it are abundance of fountains, springs or wells, courses of rivers, both mountain torrents and ever flowing streams, for the storing of moisture in many and various reservoirs…Thus the habitable part of our earth is surrounded by water, linked together by vast seas and irrigated by countless perennial rivers, thanks to the ineffable wisdom of Him Who ordered all to prevent this rival clement to fire from being entirely destroyed.

However, a time will come, when all shall be consumed by fire; as Isaiah says of the God of the universe in these words, "That saith to the deep, Be dry, and I will dry up thy rivers." Reject then the foolish wisdom of this world, and receive with me the more simple but infallible doctrine of truth.

7. Therefore we read: "Let there be a firmament in the midst of the waters, and let it divide the waters from the waters." have said what the word firmament in Scripture means. It is not in reality a firm and solid substance which has weight and resistance; this name would otherwise have better suited the earth. But, as the substance of superincumbent bodies is light, without consistency, and cannot be grasped by any one of our senses, it is in comparison with these pure and imperceptible substances that the firmament has received its name. Imagine a place fit to divide the moisture, sending it, if pure and filtered, into higher regions, and making it fall, if it is dense and earthy; to the end that by the gradual withdrawal of the moist particles the same temperature may be preserved from the beginning to the end. You do not believe in this prodigious quantity of water; but you do not take into account the prodigious quantity of heat, less considerable no doubt in bulk, but exceedingly powerful nevertheless, if you consider it as destructive of moisture. It attracts surrounding moisture, as the melon shows us, and consumes it as quickly when attracted, as the flame of the lamp draws to it the fuel supplied by the wick and burns it up.

Who doubts that the æther is an ardent fire? If an impassable limit had not been assigned to it by the Creator, what would prevent it from setting on fire and consuming all that is near it, and absorbing sit the moisture from existing things? The aerial waters which veil the heavens with vapours that are sent forth by rivers, fountains, marshes, lakes, and seas, prevent the æther from invading and burning up the universe. Thus we see even this sun, in the summer season, dry up in a moment a damp and marshy country, and make it perfectly arid. What has become of all the water? Let these masters of omniscience tell us. Is it not plain to every one that it has risen in vapour, and has been consumed by the heat of the sun? They say, none the less, that even the sun is without heat. What time they lose in words! And see what proof they lean upon to resist what is perfectly plain. Its colour is white, and neither reddish nor yellow. It is not then fiery by nature, and its heat results, they say, from the velocity of its rotation. What do they gain? That the sun does not seem to absorb moisture?

I do not, however, reject this statement, although it is false, because it helps my argument. I said that the consumption of heat required this prodigious quantity of water. That the sun owes its heat to its nature, or that heat results from its action, makes no difference, provided that it produces the same effects upon the same matter. If you kindle fire by rubbing two pieces of wood together, or if you light them by holding them to a flame, you will have absolutely the same effect. Besides, we see that the great wisdom of Him who governs all, makes the sun travel from one region to another, for fear that, if it remained always in the same place, its excessive heat would destroy the order of the universe. Now it passes into southern regions about the time of the winter solstice, now it returns to the sign of the equinox; from thence it betakes itself to northern regions during the summer solstice, and keeps up by this imperceptible passage a pleasant temperature throughout all the world.

Let the learned people see if they do not disagree among themselves. The water which the sun consumes is, they say, what prevents the sea from rising and flooding the rivers; the warmth of the sun leaves behind the salts and the bitterness of the waters, and absorbs from them the pure and drinkable particles, thanks to the singular virtue of this planet in attracting all that is light and in allowing to fall, like mud and sediment, all which is thick and earthy. From thence come the bitterness, the salt taste and the power of withering and drying up which are characteristic of the sea. While as is notorious, they hold these views, they shift their ground and say that moisture cannot be lessened by the sun.

8. ...And do not let any one compare with the inquisitive discussions of philosophers upon the heavens, the simple and inartificial character of the utterances of the Spirit; as the beauty of chaste women surpasses that of a harlot, so our arguments are superior to those of our opponents. They only seek to persuade by forced reasoning. With us truth presents itself naked and without artifice. But why torment ourselves to refute the errors of philosophers, when it is sufficient to produce their mutually contradictory books, and, as quiet spectators, to watch the war? For those thinkers are not less numerous, nor less celebrated, nor more sober in speech in fighting their adversaries, who say that the universe is being consumed by fire, and that from the seeds which remain in the ashes of the burnt world all is being brought to life again. Hence in the world there is destruction and palingenesis to infinity. All, equally far from the truth, find each on their side by-ways which lead them to error.

9. But as far as concerns the separation of the waters I am obliged to contest the opinion of certain writers in the Church who, under the shadow of high and sublime conceptions, have launched out into metaphor, and have only seen in the waters a figure to denote spiritual and incorporeal powers. In the higher regions, above the firmament, dwell the better; in the lower regions, earth and matter are the dwelling place of the malignant. So, say they, God is praised by the waters that are above the heaven, that is to say, by the good powers, the purity of whose soul makes them worthy to sing the praises of God. And the waters which are under the heaven represent the wicked spirits, who from their natural height have fallen into the abyss of evil. Turbulent, seditious, agitated by the tumultuous waves of passion, they have received the name of sea, because of the instability and the inconstancy of their movements.

Let us reject these theories as dreams and old women's tales. Let us understand that by water water is meant; for the dividing of the waters by the firmament let us accept the reason which has been given us. Although, however, waters above the heaven are invited to give glory to the Lord of the Universe, do not let us think of them as intelligent beings; the heavens are not alive because they "declare the glory of God," nor the firmament a sensible being because it "sheweth His handiwork." And if they tell you that the heavens mean contemplative powers, and the firmament active powers which produce good, we admire the theory as ingenious without being able to acknowledge the truth of it. For thus dew, the frost, cold and heat, which in Daniel are ordered to praise the Creator of all things, will be intelligent and invisible natures. But this is only a figure, accepted as such by enlightened minds, to complete the glory of the Creator. Besides, the waters above the heavens, these waters privileged by the virtue which they possess in themselves, are not the only waters to celebrate the praises of God. "Praise the Lord from the earth, ye dragons and all deeps." Thus the singer of the Psalms does not reject the deeps which our inventors of allegories rank in the divisions of evil; he admits them to the universal choir of creation, and the deeps sing in their language a harmonious hymn to the glory of the Creator.

10. "And God saw that it was good." God does not judge of the beauty of His work by the charm of the eyes, and He does not form the same idea of beauty that we do. What He esteems beautiful is that which presents in its perfection all the fitness of art, and that which tends to the usefulness of its end. He, then, who proposed to Himself a manifest design in His works, approved each one of them, as fulfilling its end in accordance with His creative purpose. A hand, an eye, or any portion of a statue lying apart from the rest, would look beautiful to no one. But if each be restored to its own place, the beauty of proportion, until now almost unperceived, would strike even the most uncultivated. But the artist, before uniting the parts of his work, distinguishes and recognises the beauty of each of them, thinking of the object that he has in view. It is thus that Scripture depicts to us the Supreme Artist, praising each one of His works; soon, when His work is complete, He will accord well deserved praise to the whole together.

Let me here end my discourse on the second day, to allow my industrious hearers to examine what they have just heard. May their memory retain it for the profit of their soul; may they by careful meditation inwardly digest and benefit by what I say. As for those who live by their work, let me allow them to attend all day to their business, so that they may come, with a soul free from anxiety, to the banquet of my discourse in the evening. May God who, after having made such great things, put such weak words in my mouth, grant you the intelligence of His truth, so that you may raise yourselves from visible things to the invisible Being, and that the grandeur and beauty of creatures may give you a just idea of the Creator. For the visible things of Him from the creation of the world are clearly seen, and His power and divinity are eternal. Thus earth, air, sky, water, day, night, all visible things, remind us of who is our Benefactor. We shall not therefore give occasion to sin, we shall not give place to the enemy within us, if by unbroken recollection we keep God ever dwelling in our hearts, to Whom be all glory and all adoration, now and for ever, world without end. Amen.

Homily IV – Upon the Gathering Together of the Waters

1. ...And shall we, whom the Lord, the great worker of marvels, calls to the contemplation of His own works, tire of looking at them, or be slow to hear the words of the Holy Spirit? Shall we not rather stand around the vast and varied workshop of divine creation and, carried back in mind to the times of old, shall we not view all the order of creation? Heaven, poised like a dome, to quote the words of the prophet; earth, this immense mass which rests upon itself; the air around it, of a soft and fluid nature, a true and continual nourishment for all who breathe it, of such tenuity that it yields and opens at the least movement of the body, opposing no resistance to our motions, while, in a moment, it streams back to its place, behind those who cleave it; water, finally, that supplies drink for man, or may be designed for our other needs, and the marvellous gathering together of it into definite places which have been assigned to it: such is the spectacle which the words which I have just read will show you.

2. "And God said, Let the waters under the heaven be gathered together unto one place, and let the dry land appear, and it was so." And the water which was under the heaven gathered together unto one place; "And God called the dry land earth and the gathering together of the waters called He seas." What trouble you have given me in my previous discourses by asking me why the earth was invisible, why all bodies are naturally endued with colour, and why all colour comes under the sense of sight. And, perhaps, my reason did

not appear sufficient to you, when I said that the earth, without being naturally invisible, was so to us, because of the mass of water that entirely covered it. Hear then how Scripture explains itself. "Let the waters be gathered together, and let the dry land appear." The veil is lifted and allows the earth, hitherto invisible, to be seen.

Perhaps you will ask me new questions. And first, is it not a law of nature that water flows downwards? Why, then, does Scripture refer this to the fiat of the Creator? As long as water is spread over a level surface, it does not flow; it is immovable. But when it finds any slope, immediately the foremost portion falls, then the one that follows takes its place, and that one is itself replaced by a third. Thus incessantly they flow, pressing the one on the other, and the rapidity of their course is in proportion to the mass of water that is being carried, and the declivity down which it is borne. If such is the nature of water, it was supererogatory to command it to gather into one place. It was bound, on account of its natural instability, to fall into the most hollow part of the earth and not to stop until the levelling of its surface. We see how there is nothing so level as the surface of water. Besides, they add, how did the waters receive an order to gather into one place, when we see several seas, separated from each other by the greatest distances?

To the first question I reply: Since God's command, you know perfectly well the motion of water; you know that it is unsteady and unstable and fails naturally over declivities and into hollow places. But what was its nature before this command made it take its course? You do not know yourself, and you have heard from no eyewitness. Think, in reality, that a word of God makes the nature, and that this order is for the creature a direction for its future course. There was only one creation of day and night, and since that moment they have incessantly succeeded each other and divided time into equal parts.

3. "Let the waters be gathered together." It was ordered that it should be the natural property of water to flow, and in obedience to this order, the waters are never weary in their course. In speaking thus, I have only in view the flowing property of waters. Some flow of their own accord like springs and rivers, others are collected and stationary. But I speak now of flowing waters. "Let the waters be gathered together unto one place." Have you never thought, when standing near a spring which is sending forth water abundantly, Who

makes this water spring from the bowels of the earth? Who forced it up? Where are the store-houses which send it forth? To what place is it hastening? How is it that it is never exhausted here, and never overflows there? All this comes from that first command; it was for the waters a signal for their course.

In all the story of the waters remember this first order, "let the waters be gathered together." To take their assigned places they were obliged to flow, and, once arrived there, to remain in their place and not to go farther. Thus in the language of Ecclesiastes, "All the waters run into the sea; yet the sea is not full." Waters flow in virtue of God's order, and the sea is enclosed in limits according to this first law, "Let the waters be gathered together unto one place." For fear the water should spread beyond its bed, and in its successive invasions cover one by one all countries, and end by flooding the whole earth, it received the order to gather unto one place. Thus we often see the furious sea raising mighty waves to the heaven, and, when once it has touched the shore, break its impetuosity in foam and retire. "Fear ye not me, saith the Lord...which have placed the sand for the bound of the sea." A grain of sand, the weakest tiring possible, curbs the violence of the ocean...

I report this fact to make you understand the full force of the command, "Let the waters be gathered unto one place"; that is to say, let there be no other gathering, and, once gathered, let them not disperse.

4. To say that the waters were gathered in one place indicates that previously they were scattered in many places. The mountains, intersected by deep ravines, accumulated water in their valleys, when from every direction the waters betook themselves to the one gathering place. What vast plains, in their extent resembling wide seas, what valleys, what cavities hollowed in many different ways, at that time full of water, must have been emptied by the command of God! But we must not therefore say, that if the water covered the face of the earth, all the basins which have since received the sea were originally full. Where can the gathering of the waters have come from if the basins were already full? These basins, we reply, were only prepared at the moment when the water had to unite in a single mass. At that time the sea which is beyond Gadeira and the vast ocean, so dreaded by navigators, which surrounds the isle of Britain and western Spain,

did not exist. But, all of a sudden, God created this vast space, and the mass of waters flowed in...

5. And God said: "Let the waters be gathered together unto one place and let the dry land appear." He did not say let the earth appear, so as not to show itself again without form, mud-like, and in combination with the water, nor yet endued with proper form and virtue. At the same time, lest we should attribute the drying of the earth to the sun, the Creator shows it to us dried before the creation of the sun. Let us follow the thought Scripture gives us. Not only the water which was covering the earth flowed off from it, but all that which had filtered into its depths withdrew in obedience to the irresistible order of the sovereign Master. And it was so. This is quite enough to show that the Creator's voice had effect: however, in several editions, there is added "And the water which was under the heavens gathered itself unto one place and the dry land was seen;" words that other interpreters have not given, and which do not appear conformable to Hebrew usage. In fact, after the assertion, "and it was so," it is superfluous to repeat exactly the same thing. In accurate copies these words are marked with an obelus, which is the sign of rejection...

6. "And God saw that it was good." Scripture does not merely wish to say that a pleasing aspect of the sea presented itself to God. It is not with eyes that the Creator views the beauty of His works. He contemplates them in His ineffable wisdom. A fair sight is the sea all bright in a settled calm; fair too, when, ruffled by a light breeze of wind, its surface shows tints of purple and azure – when, instead of lashing with violence the neighbouring shores, it seems to kiss them with peaceful caresses. However, it is not in this that Scripture makes God find the goodness and charm of the sea. Here it is the purpose of the work which makes the goodness...

Homily V – The Germination of the Earth

1. "And God said Let the earth bring forth grass, the herb yielding seed, and the fruit tree yielding fruit after his kind, whose seed is in itself." It was deep wisdom that commanded the earth, when it rested after discharging the weight of the waters, first to bring forth grass, then wood as we see it doing still at this time. For the voice that was then heard and this command were as a natural and permanent law for it; it gave fertility and the power to produce fruit for all ages to come;

"Let the earth bring forth." The production of vegetables shows first germination. When the germs begin to sprout they form grass; this develops and becomes a plant, which insensibly receives its different articulations, and reaches its maturity in the seed. Thus all things which sprout and are green are developed. "Let the earth bring forth green grass." Let the earth bring forth by itself without having any need of help from without.

Some consider the sun as the source of all productiveness on the earth. It is, they say, the action of the sun's heat which attracts the vital force from the centre of the earth to the surface. The reason why the adornment of the earth was before the sun is the following; that those who worship the sun, as the source of life, may renounce their error. If they be well persuaded that the earth was adorned before the genesis of the sun, they will retract their unbounded admiration for it, because they see grass and plants vegetate before it rose. If then the food for the flocks was prepared, did our race appear less worthy of a like solicitude? He, who provided pasture for horses and cattle, thought before all of your riches and pleasures. If he fed your cattle, it was to provide for all the needs of your life. And what object was there in the bringing forth of grain, if not for your subsistence? Moreover, many grasses and vegetables serve for the food of man.

2. "Let the earth bring forth grass yielding seed after his kind." So that although some kind of grass is of service to animals, even their gain is our gain too, and seeds are especially designed for our use. Such is the true meaning of the words that I have quoted. "Let the earth bring forth grass, the herb yielding seed after his kind." In this manner we can re-establish the order of the words, of which the construction seems faulty in the actual version, and the economy of nature will be rigorously observed. In fact, first comes germination, then verdure, then the growth of the plant, which alter having attained its full growth arrives at perfection in seed.

...Nothing then is truer than that each plant produces its seed or contains some seminal virtue; this is what is meant by "after its kind." So that the shoot of a reed does not produce an olive tree, but from a reed grows another reed, and from one sort of seed a plant of the same sort always germinates. Thus, all which sprang from the earth, in its first bringing forth, is kept the same to our time, thanks to the constant reproduction of kind.

"Let the earth bring forth." See how, at this short word, at this brief command, the cold and sterile earth travailed and hastened to bring forth its fruit, as it cast away its sad and dismal covering to clothe itself in a more brilliant robe, proud of its proper adornment and displaying the infinite variety of plants.

I want creation to penetrate you with so much admiration that everywhere, wherever you may be, the least plant may bring to you the clear remembrance of the Creator. If you see the grass of the fields, think of human nature, and remember the comparison of the wise Isaiah. "All flesh is grass, and all the goodliness thereof is as the flower of the field." Truly the rapid flow of life, the short gratification and pleasure that an instant of happiness gives a man, all wonderfully suit the comparison of the prophet. Today he is vigorous in body, fattened by luxury, and in the prime of life, with complexion fair like the flowers, strong and powerful and of irresistible energy; tomorrow and he will be an object of pity, withered by age or exhausted by sickness. Another shines in all the splendour of a brilliant fortune. and around him are a multitude of flatterers, an escort of false friends on the track of his good graces; a crowd of kinsfolk, but of no true kin; a swarm of servants who crowd after him to provide for his food and for all his needs; and in his comings and goings this innumerable suite, which he drags after him, excites the envy of all whom he meets. To fortune may be added power in the State, honours bestowed by the imperial throne, the government of a province, or the command of armies; a herald who precedes him is crying in a loud voice; lictors right and left also fill his subjects with awe, blows, confiscations, banishments, imprisonments, and all the means by which he strikes intolerable terror into all whom he has to rule. And what then? One night, a fever, a pleurisy, or an inflammation of the lungs, snatches away this man from the midst of men, stripped in a moment of all his stage accessories, and all this, his glory, is proved a mere dream. Therefore the Prophet has compared human glory to the weakest flower.

3. Up to this point, the order in which plants shoot bears witness to their first arrangement. Every herb, every plant proceeds from a germ... A single plant, a blade of grass is sufficient to occupy all your

intelligence in the contemplation of the skill which produced it. Why is the wheat stalk better with joints? Are they not like fastenings, which help it to bear easily the weight of the ear, when it is swollen with fruit and bends towards the earth? Thus, whilst oats, which have no weight to bear at the top, are without these supports, nature has provided them for wheat. It has hidden the grain in a case, so that it may not be exposed to birds' pillage, and has furnished it with a rampart of barbs, which, like darts, protect it against the attacks of tiny creatures.

4. What shall I say? What shall I leave unsaid? In the rich treasures of creation it is difficult to select what is most precious; the loss of what is omitted is too severe. "Let the earth bring forth grass;" and instantly, with useful plants, appear noxious plants; with corn, hemlock; with the other nutritious plants, hellebore, monkshood, mandrake and the juice of the poppy. What then? Shall we show no gratitude for so many beneficial gifts, and reproach the Creator for those which may be harmful to our life? And shall we not reflect that all has not been created in view of the wants of our bellies?

The nourishing plants, which are destined for our use, are close at hand, and known by all the world. But in creation nothing exists without a reason. The blood of the bull is a poison: ought this animal then, whose strength is so serviceable to man, not to have been created, or, if created, to have been bloodless? But you have sense enough in yourself to keep you free from deadly things. What! Sheep and goats know how to turn away from what threatens their life, discerning danger by instinct alone: and you, who have reason and the art of medicine to supply what you need, and the experience of your forebears to tell you to avoid all that is dangerous, you tell me that you find it difficult to keep yourself from poisons! But not a single thing has been created without reason, not a single thing is useless. One serves as food to some animal; medicine has found in another a relief for one of our maladies... These plants, then, instead of making you accuse the Creator, give you a new subject for gratitude.

5. "Let the earth bring forth grass." What spontaneous provision is included in these words – that which is present in the root, in the plant itself, and in the fruit, as well as that which our labour and husbandry add! God did not command the earth immediately to give forth seed

and fruit, but to produce germs, to grow green, and to arrive at maturity in the seed; so that this first command teaches nature what she has to do in the course of ages. But, they ask, is it true that the earth produces seed after his kind, when often, after having sown wheat, we gather black grain? This is not a change of kind, but an alteration, a disease of the grain. It has not ceased to be wheat; it is on account of having been burnt that it is black, as one can learn from its name. If a severe frost had burnt it, it would have had another colour and a different flavour. They even pretend that, if it could find suitable earth and moderate temperature, it might return to its first form. Thus, you find nothing in nature contrary to the divine command.

As to the darnel and all those bastard grains which mix themselves with the harvest, the tares of Scripture, far from being a variety of corn, have their own origin and their own kind; image of those who alter the doctrine of the Lord and, not being rightly instructed in the word, but, corrupted by the teaching of the evil one, mix themselves with the sound body of the Church to spread their pernicious errors secretly among purer souls. The Lord thus compares the perfection of those who believe in Him to the growth of seed, "as if a man should cast seed into the ground; and should sleep and rise, night and day, and the seed should spring and grow up, he knoweth not how. For the earth bringeth forth fruit of herself; first the blade, then the ear, after that the full corn in the ear."

"Let the earth bring forth grass." In a moment earth began by germination to obey the laws of the Creator, completed every stage of growth, and brought germs to perfection. The meadows were covered with deep grass, the fertile plains quivered with harvests, and the movement of the corn was like the waving of the sea. Every plant, every herb, the smallest shrub, the least vegetable, arose from the earth in all its luxuriance. There was no failure in this first vegetation: no husbandman's inexperience, no inclemency of the weather, nothing could injure it; then the sentence of condemnation was not fettering the earth's fertility. All this was before the sin which condemned us to eat our bread by the sweat of our brow.

6. "Let the earth," the Creator adds, "bring forth the fruit tree yielding fruit after his kind, whose seed is in itself." At this command every copse was thickly planted; all the trees, fir, cedar, cypress, pine, rose to their greatest height, the shrubs were straightway clothed with

thick foliage. The plants called crown-plants, roses, myrtles, laurels, did not exist; in one moment they came into being, each one with its distinctive peculiarities. Most marked differences separated them from other plants, and each one was distinguished by a character of its own. But then the rose was without thorns; since then the thorn has been added to its beauty, to make us feel that sorrow is very near to pleasure, and to remind us of our sin, which condemned the earth to produce thorns and caltrops…

8. Plants reproduce themselves in so many different ways, that we can only touch upon the chief among them. As to fruits themselves, who could review their varieties, their forms, their colours, the peculiar flavour, and the use of each of them?…Nothing has been done without motive, nothing by chance. All shows ineffable wisdom.

9. …"Let the earth bring forth the fruit tree yielding fruit." Immediately the tops of the mountains were covered with foliage: paradises were artfully laid out, and an infinitude of plants embellished the banks of the rivers. Some were for the adornment of man's table; some to nourish animals with their fruits and their leaves; some to provide medicinal help by giving us their sap, their juice, their chips, their bark or their fruit. In a word, the experience of ages, profiting from every chance, has not been able to discover anything useful, which the penetrating foresight of the Creator did not first perceive and call into existence…

10. "Let the earth bring forth." This short command was in a moment a vast nature, an elaborate system. Swifter than thought it produced the countless qualities of plants. It is this command which, still at this day, is imposed on the earth, and in the course of each year displays all the strength of its power to produce herbs, seeds and trees. Like tops, which after the first impulse, continue their evolutions, turning upon themselves when once fixed in their centre; thus nature, receiving the impulse of this first command, follows without interruption the course of ages, until the consummation of all things. Let us all hasten to attain to it, full of fruit and of good works; and thus, planted in the house of the Lord we shall flourish in the court of our God, in our Lord Jesus Christ, to whom be glory and power for ever and ever. Amen.

Homily VI – The Creation of Luminous Bodies

1. At the shows in the circus the spectator must join in the efforts of the athletes. This the laws of the show indicate, for they prescribe that all should have the head uncovered when present at the stadium. The object of this, in my opinion, is that each one there should not only be a spectator of the athletes, but be, in a certain measure, a true athlete himself. Thus, to investigate the great and prodigious show of creation, to understand supreme and ineffable wisdom, you must bring personal light for the contemplation of the wonders which I spread before your eyes, and help me, according to your power, in this struggle, where you are not so much judges as fellow combatants, for fear lest the truth might escape you, and lest my error might turn to your common prejudice.

Why these words? It is because we propose to study the world as a whole, and to consider the universe, not by the light of worldly wisdom, but by that with which God wills to enlighten His servant, when He speaks to him in person and without enigmas. It is because it is absolutely necessary that all lovers of great and grand shows should bring a mind well prepared to study them. If sometimes, on a bright night, whilst gazing with watchful eyes on the inexpressible beauty of the stars, you have thought of the Creator of all things; if you have asked yourself who it is that has dotted heaven with such flowers, and why visible things are even more useful than beautiful; if sometimes, in the day, you have studied the marvels of light, if you have raised yourself by visible things to the invisible Being, then you are a well prepared auditor, and you can take your place in this august and blessed amphitheatre.

Come in the same way that any one not knowing a town is taken by the hand and led through it; thus I am going to lead you, like strangers, through the mysterious marvels of this great city of the universe. Our first country was in this great city, whence the murderous daemon whose enticements seduced man to slavery expelled us. There you will see man's first origin and his immediate seizure by death, brought forth by sin, the first born of the evil spirit. You will know that you are formed of earth, but the work of God's hands; much weaker than the brute, but ordained to command beings without reason and soul; inferior as regards natural advantages, but, thanks to the privilege of reason, capable of raising yourself to heaven.

If we are penetrated by these truths, we shall know ourselves, we shall know God, we shall adore our Creator, we shall serve our Master, we shall glorify our Father, we shall love our Sustainer, we shall bless our Benefactor, we shall not cease to honour the Prince of present and future life, Who, by the riches that He showers upon us in this world, makes us believe in His promises and uses present good things to strengthen our expectation of the future. Truly, if such are the good things of time, what will be those of eternity? If such is the beauty of visible things, what shall we think of invisible things? If the grandeur of heaven exceeds the measure of human intelligence, what mind shall be able to trace the nature of the everlasting? If the sun, subject to corruption, is so beautiful, so grand, so rapid in its movement, so invariable in its course; if its grandeur is in such perfect harmony with and due proportion to the universe: if, by the beauty of its nature, it shines like a brilliant eye in the middle of creation; if finally, one cannot tire of contemplating it, what will be the beauty of the Sun of Righteousness? If the blind man suffers from not seeing the material sun, what a deprivation is it for the sinner not to enjoy the true light!

2. "And God said, Let there be lights in the firmament of the heaven to give light upon the earth, and to divide the day from the night." Heaven and earth were the first; after them was created light; the day had been distinguished from the night, then had appeared the firmament and the dry element. The water had been gathered into the reservoir assigned to it, the earth displayed its productions, it had caused many kinds of herbs to germinate and it was adorned with all kinds of plants. However, the sun and the moon did not yet exist, in order that those who live in ignorance of God may not consider the sun as the origin and the father of light, or as the maker of all that grows out of the earth. That is why there was a fourth day, and then God said: "Let there be lights in the firmament of the heaven."

When once you have learnt Who spoke, think immediately of the hearer. God said, "Let there be lights...and God made two great lights." Who spoke? And Who made? Do you not see a double person? Everywhere, in mystic language, history is sown with the dogmas of theology.

The motive follows which caused the lights to be created. It was to illuminate the earth. Already light was created; why therefore say that the sun was created to give light? And, first, do not laugh at the strangeness of this expression. We do not follow your nicety about words, and we trouble ourselves but little to give them a harmonious turn. Our writers do not amuse themselves by polishing their periods, and everywhere we prefer clearness of words to sonorous expressions. See then if by this expression "to light up," the sacred writer sufficiently made his thought understood. He has put "to give light" instead of "illumination." Now there is nothing here contradictory to what has been said of light. Then the actual nature of light was produced: now the sun's body is constructed to be a vehicle for that original light. A lamp is not fire. Fire has the property of illuminating, and we have invented the lamp to light us in darkness. In the same way, the luminous bodies have been fashioned as a vehicle for that pure, clear, and immaterial light. The Apostle speaks to us of certain lights which shine in the world without being confounded with the true light of the world, the possession of which made the saints luminaries of the souls which they instructed and drew from the darkness of ignorance. This is why the Creator of all things, made the sun in addition to that glorious light, and placed it shining in the heavens.

7. ...If the origin of our virtues and of our vices is not in ourselves, but is the fatal consequence of our birth, it is useless for legislators to prescribe for us what we ought to do, and what we ought to avoid; it is useless for judges to honour virtue and to punish vice. The guilt is not in the robber, not in the assassin: it was willed for him; it was impossible for him to hold back his hand, urged to evil by inevitable necessity. Those who laboriously cultivate the arts are the maddest of men. The labourer will make an abundant harvest without sowing seed and without sharpening his sickle. Whether he wishes it or not, the merchant will make his fortune, and will be flooded with riches by fate. As for us Christians, we shall see our great hopes vanish, since from the moment that man does not act with freedom, there is neither reward for justice, nor punishment for sin. Under the reign of necessity and of fatality there is no place for merit, the first condition of all righteous judgment. But let us stop. You who are sound in yourselves have no need to hear more, and time does not

allow us to make attacks without limit against these unhappy men [astrologers].

8. Let its return to the words which follow. "Let them be for signs and for seasons and for days and years." We have spoken about signs. By times, we understand the succession of seasons, winter, spring, summer and autumn, which we see follow each other in so regular a course, thanks to the regularity of the movement of the luminaries...

...I have entered into these details, to show you the grandeur of the luminaries, and to make you see that, in the inspired words, there is not one idle syllable. And yet my sermon has scarcely touched on any important point; there are many other discoveries about the size and distance of the sun and moon to which any one who will make a serious study of their action and of their characteristics may arrive by the aid of reason. Let me then ingenuously make an avowal of my weakness, for fear that you should measure the mighty works of the Creator by my words. The little that I have said ought the rather to make you conjecture the marvels on which I have omitted to dwell. We must not then measure the moon with the eye, but with the reason. Reason, for the discovery of truth, is much surer than the eye...

But enough on the greatness of the sun and moon. May He Who has given us intelligence to recognise in the smallest objects of creation the great wisdom of the Contriver make us find in great bodies a still higher idea of their Creator. However, compared with their Author, the sun and moon are but a fly and an ant. The whole universe cannot give us a right idea of the greatness of God; and it is only by signs, weak and slight in themselves, often by the help of the smallest insects and of the least plants, that we raise ourselves to Him. Content with these words let us offer our thanks, I to Him who has given me the ministry of the Word, you to Him who feeds you with spiritual food; Who, even at this moment, makes you find in my weak voice the strength of barley bread. May He feed you for ever, and in proportion to your faith grant you the manifestation of the Spirit in Jesus Christ our Lord, to whom be glory and power for ever and ever. Amen.

Homily VII – The Creation of Moving Creatures

1. "And God said, Let the waters bring forth abundantly the moving creature that hath life" after their kind, "and fowl that may fly above the earth" after their kind. After the creation of the luminaries the waters are now filled with living beings and its own adornment is given to this part of the world. Earth had received hers from her own plants, the heavens had received the flowers of the stars, and, like two eyes, the great luminaries beautified them in concert. It still retained for the waters to receive their adornment. The command was given, and immediately the rivers and lakes becoming fruitful brought forth their natural broods; the sea travailed with all kinds of swimming creatures; not even in mud and marshes did the water remain idle; it took its part in creation. Everywhere from its ebullition frogs, gnats and flies came forth. For that which we see today is the sign of the past. Thus everywhere the water hastened to obey the Creator's command. Who could count the species which the great and ineffable power of God caused to be suddenly seen living and moving, when this command had empowered the waters to bring forth life? Let the waters bring forth moving creatures that have life. Then for the first time is made a being with life and feeling. For though plants and trees be said to live, seeing that they share the power of being nourished and growing; nevertheless they are neither living beings, nor have they life. To create these last God said, "Let the water produce moving creatures."

Every creature that swims, whether it skims on the surface of the waters, or cleaves the depths, is of the nature of a moving creature, since it drags itself on the body of the water. Certain aquatic animals have feet and walk; especially amphibia, such as seals, crabs, crocodiles, river horses and frogs; but they are above all gifted with the power of swimming. Thus it is said, Let the waters produce moving creatures. In these few words what species is omitted? Which is not included in the command of the Creator? Do we not see viviparous animals, seals, dolphins, rays and all cartilaginous animals? Do we not see oviparous animals comprising every sort of fish, those which have a skin and those which have scales, those which have fins and those which have not? This command has only required one word, even less than a word, a sign, a motion of the divine will, and it has such a wide sense that it includes all the varieties and all the families of fish. To review them all would be to undertake to count the waves of the ocean or to measure its waters in the hollow of the hand. "Let the waters produce moving creatures." That is to say, those which people the high seas and those which love the shores; those which inhabit the depths and those which attach themselves to rocks; those which are gregarious and those which live dispersed, the cetaceous, the huge, and the tiny. It is from the same power, the same command, that all, small and great receive their existence. "Let the waters bring forth."...

2. "Let the waters bring forth moving creatures after their kind." God caused to be born the firstlings of each species to serve as seeds for nature. Their multitudinous numbers are kept up in subsequent succession, when it is necessary for them to grow and multiply...

3. ...Instances have, however, been known of migratory fish, who, as if common deliberation transported them into strange regions, all start on their march at a given sign. When the time marked for breeding arrives, they, as if awakened by a common law of nature, migrate from gulf to gulf, directing their course toward the North Sea. And at the epoch of their return you may see all these fish streaming like a torrent across the Propontis towards the Euxine Sea. Who puts them in marching array? Where is the prince's order? Has an edict affixed in the public place indicated to them their day of departure? Who serves them as a guide? See how the divine order embraces all and extends to the smallest object. A fish does not resist God's law, and we men cannot endure His precepts of salvation! Do not despise fish because they are dumb and quite unreasoning; rather fear lest, in your resistance to the disposition of the Creator, you have even less reason than they.

Listen to the fish, who by their actions all but speak and say: it is for the perpetuation of our race that we undertake this long voyage. They have not the gift of reason, but they have the law of nature firmly seated within them, to show them what they have to do. Let us go, they say, to the North Sea. Its water is sweeter than that of the rest of the sea; for the sun does not remain long there, and its rays do not draw up all the drinkable portions. Even sea creatures love fresh water. Thus one often sees them enter into rivers and swim far up them from the sea. This is the reason which makes them prefer the

Euxine Sea to other gulfs, as the most fit for breeding and for bringing up their young. When they have obtained their object the whole tribe returns home. Let us hear these dumb creatures tell us the reason. The Northern sea, they say, is shallow and its surface is exposed to the violence of the wind, and it has few shores and retreats. Thus the winds easily agitate it to its bottom and mingle the sands of its bed with its waves. Besides, it is cold in winter, filled as it is from all directions by large rivers. Wherefore after a moderate enjoyment of its waters, during the summer, when the winter comes they hasten to reach warmer depths and places heated by the sun, and after fleeing froth the stormy tracts of the North, they seek a haven in less agitated seas.

5. I myself have seen these marvels, and I have admired the wisdom of God in all things. If beings deprived of reason are capable of thinking and of providing for their own preservation; if a fish knows what it ought to seek and what to shun, what shall we say, who are honoured with reason, instructed by law, encouraged by the promises, made wise by the Spirit, and are nevertheless less reasonable about our own affairs than the fish? They know how to provide for the future, but we renounce our hope of the future and spend our life in brutal indulgence. A fish traverses the extent of the sea to find what is good for it; what will you say then – you who live in idleness, the mother of all vices? Do not let any one make his ignorance an excuse. There has been implanted in us natural reason which tells us to identify ourselves with good, and to avoid all that is harmful...God has foreseen all, He has neglected nothing. His eye, which never sleeps, watches over all. He is present everywhere and gives to each being the means of preservation. If God has not left the sea urchin outside His providence, is He without care for you?

Homily VIII – The Creation of Fowl and Water Animals

1. And God said "Let the earth bring forth the living creature after his kind, cattle and creeping things, and beast of the earth after his kind; and it was so." The command of God advanced step by step and earth thus received her adornment. Yesterday it was said, "Let the waters produce moving things," and today "let the earth bring forth the living creature." Is the earth then alive? And are the mad-minded Manichaeans right in giving it a soul? At these words "Let the earth

bring forth," it did not produce a germ contained in it, but He who gave the order at the same time gifted it with the grace and power to bring forth. When the earth had heard this command "Let the earth bring forth grass and the tree yielding fruit," it was not grass that it had hidden in it that it caused to spring forth, it did not bring to the surface a palm tree, an oak, a cypress, hitherto kept back in its depths. It is the word of God which forms the nature of things created. "Let the earth bring forth;" that is to say not that she may bring forth that which she has but that she may acquire that which she lacks, when God gives her the power. Even so now, "Let the earth bring forth the living creature," not the living creature that is contained in herself, but that which the command of God gives her. Further, the Manichaeans contradict themselves, because if the earth has brought forth the life, she has left herself despoiled of life. Their execrable doctrine needs no demonstration...

2. "Let the earth bring forth a living soul." Why did the earth produce a living soul? So that you may make a difference between the soul of cattle and that of man. You will soon learn how the human soul was formed; hear now about the soul of creatures devoid of reason. Since, according to Scripture, "the life of every creature is in the blood," as the blood when thickened changes into flesh, and flesh when corrupted decomposes into earth, so the soul of beasts is naturally an earthy substance. "Let the earth bring forth a living soul." See the affinity of the soul with blood, of blood with flesh, of flesh with earth; and remounting in an inverse sense from the earth to the flesh, from the flesh to the blood, from the blood to the soul, you will find that the soul of beasts is earth. Do not suppose that it is older than the essence of their body, nor that it survives the dissolution of the flesh; avoid the nonsense of those arrogant philosophers who do not blush to liken their soul to that of a dog; who say that they have been formerly themselves women, shrubs, fish. Have they ever been fish? I do not know; but I do not fear to affirm that in their writings they show less sense than fish.

"Let the earth bring forth the living creature." Perhaps many of you ask why there is such a long silence in the middle of the rapid rush of my discourse. The more studious among my auditors will not be ignorant of the reason why words fail me. What! Have I not seen them look at each other, and make signs to make me look at them, and to remind me of what I have passed over? I have forgotten a part of the creation, and that one of the most considerable, and my discourse was almost finished without touching upon it. "Let the waters bring forth abundantly the moving creature that hath life and fowl that may fly above the earth in the open firmament, of heaven." I spoke of fish as long as eventide allowed: today we have passed to the examination of terrestrial animals; between the two, birds have escaped us. We are forgetful like travellers who unmindful of some important object, are obliged, although they be far on their road, to retrace their steps, punished for their negligence by the weariness of the journey. So we have to turn back. That which we have omitted is not to be despised. It is the third part of the animal creation, if indeed there are three kinds of animals, land, winged and water.

"Let the waters" it is said "bring forth abundantly moving creature that hath life and fowl that may fly above the earth in the open firmament of heaven." Why do the waters give birth also to birds? Because there is, so to say, a family link between the creatures that fly and those that swim. In the same way that fish cut the waters, using their fins to carry them forward and their tails to direct their movements round and round and straightforward, so we see birds float in the air by the help of their wings. Both endowed with the property of swimming, their common derivation from the waters has made them of one family.

At the same time no bird is without feet, because finding all its food upon the earth it cannot do without their service. Rapacious birds have pointed claws to enable them to close on their prey; to the rest has been given the indispensable ministry of feet to seek their food and to provide for the other needs of life. There are a few who walk badly, whose feet are neither suitable for walking nor for preying. Among this number are swallows, incapable of walking and seeking their prey, and the birds called swifts who live on little insects carried about by the air. As to the swallow, its flight, which grazes the earth, fulfils the function of feet.

4. What a variety, I have said, in the actions and lives of flying creatures. Some of these unreasoning creatures even have a government, if the feature of government is to make the activity of all the individuals centre in one common end. This may be observed in bees.

They have a common dwelling place; they fly in the air together, they work at the same work together...The book of Proverbs has given the bee the most honourable and the best praise by calling her wise and industrious. How much activity she exerts in gathering this precious nourishment, by which both kings and men of low degree are brought to health! How great is the art and cunning she displays in the construction of the store houses which are destined to receive the honey! After having spread the wax like a thin membrane, she distributes it in contiguous compartments which, weak though they are, by their number and by their mass, sustain the whole edifice. Each cell in fact holds to the one next to it, and is separated by a thin partition; we thus see two or three galleries of cells built one upon the other. The bee takes care not to make one vast cavity, for fear it might break trader the weight of the liquid, and allow it to escape. See how the discoveries of geometry are mere by-works to the wise bee!

The rows of honey-comb are all hexagonal with equal sides. They do not bear on each other in straight lines, lest the supports should press on empty spaces between and give way; but the angles of the lower hexagons serve as foundations and bases to those which rise above, so as to furnish a sure support to the lower mass, and so that each cell may securely keep the liquid honey.

5. How shall we make an exact review of all the peculiarities of the life of birds?...If divine Providence has established these marvellous laws in favour of creatures devoid of reason, it is to induce you to ask for your salvation from God. Is there a wonder which He will not perform for you – you have been made in His image, when for so little a bird, the great, the fearful sea is held in check and is commanded in the midst of winter to be calm.

7. "Let the waters bring forth the moving creatures that have life, and fowl that may fly above the earth in the open firmament of heaven." They received the command to fly above the earth because earth provides them with nourishment. "In the firmament of heaven," that is to say, as we have said before, in that part of the air called *ouranos*, heaven, from the word *horan*, which means to see; called firmament, because the air which extends over our heads, compared to the æther, has greater density, and is thickened by the vapours which exhale from the earth. You have then heaven adorned, earth beauti-

fied, the sea peopled with its own creatures, the air filled with birds which scour it in every direction. Studious listener, think of all these creations which God has drawn out of nothing, think of all those which my speech has left out, to avoid tediousness, and not to exceed my limits; recognise everywhere the wisdom of God; never cease to wonder, and, through, every creature, to glorify the Creator.

...Our God has created nothing unnecessarily and has omitted nothing that is necessary.

8. If we simply read the words of Scripture we find only a few short syllables. "Let the waters bring forth fowl that may fly above the earth in the open firmament of heaven," but if we enquire into the meaning of these words, then the great wonder of the wisdom of the Creator appears. What a difference He has foreseen among winged creatures! How He has divided them by kinds! How He has characterized each one of them by distinct qualities! But the day will not suffice me to recount the wonders of the air. Earth is calling me to describe wild beasts, reptiles and cattle, ready to show us in her turn sights rivalling those of plants, fish, and birds. "Let the earth bring forth the living soul" of domestic animals, of wild beasts, and of reptiles after their kind...

...May He who has filled all with the works of His creation and has left everywhere visible memorials of His wonders, fill your hearts with all spiritual joys in Jesus Christ, our Lord, to whom belong glory and power, world without end. Amen.

Homily IX – The Creation of Terrestrial Animals

1. ...I know the laws of allegory, though less by myself than from the works of others. There are those truly, who do not admit the common sense of the Scriptures, for whom water is not water, but some other nature, who see in a plant, in a fish, what their fancy wishes, who change the nature of reptiles and of wild beasts to suit their allegories, like the interpreters of dreams who explain visions in sleep to make them serve their own ends. For me grass is grass; plant, fish, wild beast, domestic animal, I take all in the literal sense. "For I am not ashamed of the gospel."

Those who have written about the nature of the universe have discussed at length the shape of the earth. If it be spherical or cylindrical, if it resemble a disc and is equally rounded in all parts, or if it has the forth of a winnowing basket and is hollow in the middle; all these conjectures have been suggested by cosmographers, each one upsetting that of his predecessor. It will not lead me to give less importance to the creation of the universe, that the servant of God, Moses, is silent as to shapes; he has not said that the earth is a hundred and eighty thousand furlongs in circumference; he has not measured into what extent of air its shadow projects itself whilst the sun revolves around it, nor stated how this shadow, casting itself upon the moon, produces eclipses. He has passed over in silence, as useless, all that is unimportant for us.

Shall I then prefer foolish wisdom to the oracles of the Holy Spirit? Shall I not rather exalt Him who, not wishing to fill our minds with these vanities, has regulated all the economy of Scripture in view of the edification and the making perfect of our souls? It is this which those seem to me not to have understood, who, giving themselves up to the distorted meaning of allegory, have undertaken to give a majesty of their own invention to Scripture. It is to believe themselves wiser than the Holy Spirit, and to bring forth their own ideas under a pretext of exegesis. Let us hear Scripture as it has been written.

2. "Let the earth bring forth thee living creature." *Behold the word of God pervading creation, beginning even then the efficacy which is seen displayed to-day*, and will be displayed to the end of the world! As a ball, which one pushes, if it meet a declivity, descends, carried by its form and the nature of the ground and does not stop until it has reached a level surface; so nature, once put in motion by the Divine command, traverses creation with an equal step, through birth and death, and keeps up the succession of kinds through resemblance, to the last. Nature always makes a horse succeed to a horse, a lion to a lion, an eagle to an eagle, and preserving each animal by these uninterrupted successions she transmits it to the end of all things. Animals do not see their peculiarities destroyed or effaced by any length of time; their nature, as though it had been just constituted, follows the course of ages, for ever young.

"Let the earth bring forth the living creature." This command has continued and earth does not cease to obey the Creator. For, if there are creatures which are successively produced by their predecessors, there are others that even today we see born from the earth itself. In wet weather she brings forth grasshoppers and an immense number of insects which fly in the air and have no names because they are so small; she also produces mice and frogs. In the environs of Thebes in Egypt, after abundant rain in hot weather, the country is covered with field mice. We see mud alone produce eels; they do not proceed from an egg, nor in any other manner; it is the earth alone which gives them birth. "Let the earth produce a living creature."

Cattle are terrestrial and bent towards the earth. Man, a celestial growth, rises superior to them as much by the mould of his bodily conformation as by the dignity of his soul. What is the form of quadrupeds? Their head is bent towards the earth and looks towards their belly, and only pursues their belly's good. Thy head, O man! is turned towards heaven; thy eyes look up. When therefore thou degradest thyself by the passions of the flesh, slave of thy belly, and thy lowest parts, thou approachest animals without reason and becomest like one of them. Thou art called' to more noble cares; "seek those things which are above where Christ sitteth." Raise thy soul above the earth; draw from its natural conformation the rule of thy conduct; fix thy conversation in heaven. Thy true country is the heavenly Jerusalem; thy fellow-citizens and thy compatriots are "the first-born which are written in heaven."

3. "Let the earth bring forth the living creature." Thus when the soul of brutes appeared it was not concealed in the earth, but it was born by the command of God. Brutes have one and the same soul of which the common characteristic is absence of reason. But each animal is distinguished by peculiar qualities. The ox is steady, the ass is lazy, the horse has strong passions, the wolf cannot be tamed, the fox is deceitful, the stag timid, the ant industrious, the dog grateful and faithful in his friendships. As each animal was created the distinctive character of his nature appeared in him in due measure...

What language can attain to the marvels of the Creator? What ear could understand them? And what time would be sufficient to relate them? Let us say, then, with the prophet, "O Lord, how manifold are thy works! In wisdom hast thou made them all." [Ps 104] We shall not be able to say in self-justification, that we have learnt useful knowledge in books, since the untaught law of nature makes us choose that which is advantageous to us. Do you know what good you ought to do your neighbour? The good that you expect from him yourself. Do you know what is evil? That which you would not wish another to do to you. Neither botanical researches nor the experience of simples have made animals discover those which are useful to them; but each knows naturally what is salutary and marvellously appropriates what suits its nature.

4. Virtues exist in us also by nature, and the soul has affinity with them not by education, but by nature herself. We do not need lessons to hate illness, but by ourselves we repel what afflicts us, the soul has no need of a master to teach us to avoid vice. Now all vice is a sickness of the soul as virtue is its health. Thus those have defined health well who have called it a regularity in the discharge of natural functions; a definition that can be applied without fear to the good condition of the soul. Thus, without having need of lessons, the soul can attain by herself to what is fit and conformable to nature. Hence it comes that temperance everywhere is praised, justice is in honour, courage admired, and prudence the object of all aims; virtues which concern the soul more than health concerns the body. Children love your parents, and you, "parents provoke not your children to wrath." Does not nature say the same? Paul teaches us nothing new; he only tightens the links of nature. If the lioness loves her cubs, if the she wolf fights to defend her little ones, what shall man say who is unfaithful to the precept and violates nature herself; or the son who insults the old age of his father; or the father whose second marriage has made him forget his first children?

With animals invincible affection unites parents with children. It is the Creator, God Himself, who substitutes the strength of feeling for reason in them. From whence it comes that a lamb as it bounds from the fold, in the midst of a thousand sheep recognises the colour and the voice of its mother, runs to her, and seeks its own sources of milk. If its mother's udders are dry, it is content, and, without stopping, passes by more abundant ones. And how does the mother recognise it among the many lambs? All have the same voice, the same colour, the same smell, as far at least as regards our sense of smell. Yet there is in these animals a more subtle sense than our perception which makes them recognise their own. The little dog has as yet no teeth, nevertheless he defends himself with his mouth against any one who teases him. The calf has as yet no horns, nevertheless he already knows where his weapons will grow. Here we have evident proof that the instinct of animals is innate, and that in all beings there is nothing disorderly, nothing unforeseen. All bear the marks of the wisdom of the Creator, and show that they have come to life with the means of assuring their preservation.

The dog is not gifted with a share of reason; but with him instinct has the power of reason. The dog has learnt by nature the secret of elaborate inferences, which sages of the world, after long years of study, have hardly been able to disentangle. When the dog is on the track of game, if he sees it divide in different directions, he examines these different paths, and speech alone fails him to announce his reasoning. The creature, he says, is gone here or there or in another direction. It is neither here nor there; it is therefore in the third direction. And thus, neglecting the false tracks, he discovers the true one. What more is done by those who, gravely occupied in demonstrating theories, trace lines upon the dust and reject two propositions to show that the third is the true one?...

5. But let us return to the spectacle of creation. The easiest animals to catch are the most productive. It is on account of this that hares and wild goats produce many little ones, and that wild sheep have twins, for fear lest these species should disappear, consumed by carnivorous animals. Beasts of prey, on the contrary, produce only a few and a lioness with difficulty gives birth to one lion; because, if they say truly, the cub issues from its mother by tearing her with its claws; and vipers are only born by gnawing through the womb, inflicting a proper punishment on their mother. Thus in nature all has been foreseen, all is the object of continual care. If you examine the members even of animals, you will find that the Creator has given them nothing superfluous, that He has omitted nothing that is necessary. To carnivorous animals He has given pointed teeth which their nature requires for their support. Those that are only half furnished with teeth have received several distinct receptacles for their food. As it is not broken up enough in the first, they are gifted with the power of returning it after it has been swallowed, and it does not assimilate until it has been crushed by rumination. The first, second, third, and fourth stomachs of ruminating animals do not remain idle; each one of them fulfils a necessary function. The neck of the camel is long so that it may lower it to its feet and reach the grass on which it feeds.

Bears, lions, tigers, all animals of this sort, have short necks buried in their shoulders; it is because they do not live upon grass and have no need to bend down to the earth; they are carnivorous and eat the animals upon whom they prey.

6. Beasts bear witness to the faith. Hast thou confidence in the Lord? "Thou shalt walk upon the asp and the basilisk and thou shalt trample under feet the lion and the dragon." With faith thou hast the power to walk upon serpents and scorpions. Do you not see that the viper which attached itself to the hand of Paul, whilst he gathered sticks, did not injure him, because it found the saint full of faith? If you have not faith, do not fear beasts so much as your faithlessness, which renders you susceptible of all corruption. But I see that for a long time you have been asking me for an account of the creation of man, and I think I can hear you all cry in your hearts. We are being taught the nature of our belongings, but we are ignorant of ourselves. Let me then speak of it, since it is necessary, and let me put an end to my hesitation.

In truth the most difficult of sciences is to know one's self. Not only our eye, from which nothing outside us escapes, cannot see itself; but our mind, so piercing to discover the sins of others, is slow to recognise its own faults. Thus my speech, after eagerly investigating what is external to myself, is slow and hesitating in exploring my own nature. Yet the beholding of heaven and earth does not make us know God better than the attentive study of our being does; I am, says the Prophet, fearfully and wonderfully made; that is to say,in observing myself I have known Thy infinite wisdom. And God said "Let us make man." Does not the light of theology shine, in these words, as through windows; and does not the second Person show Himself in a mystical way, without yet manifesting Himself until the great day? Where is the Jew who resisted the truth and pretended that God was speaking to Himself? It is He who spoke, it is said, and it is He who made. "Let there be light and there was light."

But then their words contain a manifest absurdity. Where is the smith, the carpenter, the shoemaker, who, without help and alone before the instruments of his trade, would say to himself; let us make the sword, let us put together the plough, let us make the boot? Does he not perform the work of his craft in silence? Strange folly, to say that any one has seated himself to command himself, to watch over himself, to constrain himself, to hurry himself, with the tones of a master! But the unhappy creatures are not afraid to calumniate the Lord Himself. What will they not say with a tongue so well practised in lying?

Here, however, words stop their mouth; "And God said let us make man." Tell me; is there then only one Person? It is not written "Let man be made," but, "Let us make man." The preaching of theology remains enveloped in shadow before the appearance of him who was to be instructed, but, now, the creation of man is expected, that faith unveils herself and the dogma of truth appears in all its light. "Let us make man." "O enemy of Christ, hear God speaking to His Co-operator, to Him by Whom also He made the worlds, Who upholds all things by the word of His power. But He does not leave the voice of true religion without answer. Thus the Jews, race hostile to truth, when they find themselves pressed, act like beasts enraged against man, who roar at the bars of their cage and show the cruelty and the ferocity of their nature, without being able to assuage their fury. God, they say, addresses Himself to several persons; it is to the angels before Him that He says, "Let us make man."

Jewish fiction! A fable whose frivolity shows whence it has come. To reject one person, they admit many. To reject the Son, they raise servants to the dignity of counsellors; they make of our fellow slaves the agents in our creation. The perfect man attains the dignity of an angel; but what creature can be like the Creator? Listen to the continuation. "In our image." What have you to reply? Is there one image of God and the angels? Father and Son have by absolute necessity the same form, but the form is here understood as becomes the divine, not in bodily shape, but in the proper qualities of Godhead.

Hear also, you who belong to the new concision and who, under the appearance of Christianity, strengthen the error of the Jews. To Whom does He say, "in our image," to whom if it is not to Him who is "the brightness of His glory and the express image of His person," "the image of the invisible God"? It is then to His living image, to Him Who has said "I and my Father are one," "He that hath seen me hath seen the Father," that God says "Let us make man in our image." Where is the unlikeness in these Beings who have only one image? "So God created man," It is not "They made." Here Scripture avoids the plurality of the Persons. After having enlightened the Jew, it dissipates the error of the Gentiles in putting itself under the shelter of unity, to make you understand that the Son is with the Father, and guarding you from the danger of polytheism. He created him in the image of God. God still shows us His co-operator, because He does not say, in His image, but in the image of God.

If God permits, we will say later in what way man was created in the image of God, and how he shares this resemblance. Today we say but only one word. If there is one image, from whence comes the intolerable blasphemy of pretending that the Son is unlike the Father? What ingratitude! You have yourself received this likeness and you refuse it to your Benefactor! You pretend to keep personally that which is in you a gift of grace, and you do not wish that the Son should keep His natural likeness to Him who begat Him.

But evening, which long ago sent the sun to the west, imposes silence upon me. Here, then, let me be content with what I have said, and put my discourse to bed. I have told you enough up to this point to excite your zeal; with the help of the Holy Spirit I will make for you a deeper investigation into the truths which follow. Retire, then, I beg you, with joy, O Christ-loving congregation, and, instead of sumptuous dishes of various delicacies, adorn and sanctify your tables with the remembrance of my words. May the Anomoean be confounded, the Jew covered with shame, the faithful exultant in the dogmas of truth, and the Lord glorified, the Lord to Whom be glory and power, world without end. Amen.

Gregory of Nyssa

> St. Gregory of Nyssa (c. 335 – c. 395) was a younger brother of St. Basil the Great and one of the Cappadocian Fathers. He became bishop of Nyssa (372) and attended the Second Ecumenical Council in Constantinople (381). His ideas about humans achieving union with God not as a one-time event but as a constant dynamic progress deeply influenced Christian soteriology.
>
> Gregory composed a work in defense of Basil's *Hexæmeron* (*Explicatio Apologetica in Hexæmeron*), which has yet to be translated. His *On the Making of Man*, portions of which are presented here, is a long treatise that attempts to fill out Basil's limited treatment of humanity's creation. (Basil had only focused on the first creation story, Genesis 1:1 – 2:3, which covers humanity's creation briefly; the second creation story, Genesis 2:4ff., focuses on humanity at greater length.)
>
> The short passages presented here from *Against Eunomius* not only affirm the uniqueness of Adam and Eve's origin but also make a Trinitarian argument: just as Adam and his descendents are of one nature though of different origins (Adam having no natural parents), so too Father and Son are of one nature though the Father is unbegotten and the Son is begotten.

Gregory of Nyssa *On the Making of Man*

Gregory, Bishop of Nyssa, to his Brother Peter, The Servant of God.

I. Wherein is a Partial Inquiry into the Nature of the World; and a More Minute Exposition of the Things Which Preceded the Genesis of Man

2. These [heaven and earth], moreover, were first framed before other things, according to the Divine wisdom, to be as it were a beginning of the whole machine, the great Moses indicating, I suppose, where he says that the heaven and the earth were made by God "in the beginning" that all things that are seen in the creation are the offspring of rest and motion, brought into being by the Divine will. Now the heaven and the earth being diametrically opposed to each other in their operations, the creation which lies between the op-

posites, and has in part a share in what is adjacent to it, itself acts as a mean between the extremes, so that there is manifestly a mutual contact of the opposites through the mean...

4. But to speak strictly, one should rather say that the very nature of the contraries themselves is not entirely without mixture of properties, each with the other, so that, as I think, all that we see in the world mutually agree, and the creation, though discovered in properties of contrary natures, is yet at union with itself. For as motion is not conceived merely as local shifting, but is also contemplated in change and alteration, and on the other hand the immovable nature does not admit motion by way of alteration, the wisdom of God has transposed these properties, and wrought unchangeableness in that which is ever moving, and change in that which is immovable; doing this, it may be, by a providential dispensation, so that that property of nature which constitutes its immutability and immobility might not, when viewed in any created object, cause the creature to be accounted as God; for that which may happen to move or change would cease to admit of the conception of Godhead. Hence the earth is stable without being immutable, while the heaven, on the contrary, as it has no mutability, so has not stability either, that the Divine power, by interweaving change in the stable nature and motion with that which is not subject to change, might, by the interchange of attributes, at once join them both closely to each other, and make them alien from the conception of Deity; for as has been said, neither of these (neither that which is unstable, nor that which is mutable) can be considered to belong to the more Divine nature.

5. Now all things were already arrived at their own end: "the heaven and the earth," as Moses says, "were finished," and all things that lie between them, and the particular things were adorned with their appropriate beauty; the heaven with the rays of the stars, the sea and air with the living creatures that swim and fly, and the earth with all varieties of plants and animals, to all which, empowered by the Divine will, it gave birth together; the earth was full, too, of her produce, bringing forth fruits at the same time with flowers; the meadows were full of all that grows therein, and all the mountain ridges, and summits, and every hillside, and slope, and hollow, were crowned with young grass, and with the varied produce of the trees, just risen

from the ground, yet shot up at once into their perfect beauty; and all the beasts that had come into life at God's command were rejoicing, we may suppose, and skipping about, running to and for in the thickets in herds according to their kind, while every sheltered and shady spot was ringing with the chants of the songbirds. And at sea, we may suppose, the sight to be seen was of the like kind, as it had just settled to quiet and calm in the gathering together of its depths, where havens and harbours spontaneously hollowed out on the coasts made the sea reconciled with the land; and the gentle motion of the waves vied in beauty with the meadows, rippling delicately with light and harmless breezes that skimmed the surface; and all the wealth of creation by land and sea was ready, and none was there to share it.

II. Why Man Appeared Last, After the Creation

1. For not as yet had that great and precious thing, man, come into the world of being; it was not to be looked for that the ruler should appear before the subjects of his rule; but when his dominion was prepared, the next step was that the king should be manifested. When, then the Maker of all had prepared beforehand, as it were, a royal lodging for the future king (and this was the land, and islands, and sea, and the heaven arching like a roof over them), and when all kinds of wealth had been stored in this palace (and by wealth I mean the whole creation, all that is in plants and trees, and all that has sense, and breath, and life; and – if we are to account materials also as wealth – all that for their beauty are reckoned precious in the eyes of men, as gold and silver, and the substances of your jewels which men delight in – having concealed, I say, abundance of all these also in the bosom of the earth as in a royal treasure-house), he thus manifests man in the world, to be the beholder of some of the wonders therein, and the lord of others; that by his enjoyment he might have knowledge of the Giver, and by the beauty and majesty of the things he saw might trace out that power of the Maker which is beyond speech and language.

2. For this reason man was brought into the world last after the creation, not being rejected to the last as worthless, but as one whom it behoved to be king over his subjects at his very birth. And as a good host does not bring his guest to his house before the preparation of his feast, but, when he has made all due preparation, and decked with

their proper adornments his house, his couches, his table, brings his guest home when things suitable for his refreshment are in readiness, rain the same manner the rich and munificent Entertainer of our nature, when He had decked the habitation with beauties of every kind, and prepared this great and varied banquet, then introduced man, assigning to him as his task not the acquiring of what was not there, but the enjoyment of the things which were there; and for this reason He gives him as foundations the instincts of a twofold organization, blending the Divine with the earthy, that by means of both he may be naturally and properly disposed to each enjoyment, enjoying God by means of his more divine nature, and the good things of earth by the sense that is akin to them.

III. That the Nature of Man is More Precious Than All the Visible Creation

1. But it is right that we should not leave this point without consideration, that while the world, great as it is, and its parts, are laid as an elemental foundation for the formation of the universe, the creation is, so to say, made offhand by the Divine power, existing at once on His command, while counsel precedes the making of man; and that which is to be is foreshown by the Maker in verbal description, and of what kind it is fitting that it should be, and to what archetype it is fitting that it should bear a likeness, and for what it shall be made, and what its operation shall be when it is made, and of what it shall be the ruler, wall these things the saying examines beforehand, so that he has a rank assigned him before his genesis, and possesses rule over the things that are before his coming into being; for it says, "God said, Let us make man in our image, after our likeness, and let them have dominion over the fish of the sea, and the beasts of the earth, and the fowls of the heaven, and the cattle, and all the earth."

V. That Man is a Likeness of the Divine Sovereignty

1. It is true, indeed, that the Divine beauty is not adorned with any shape or endowment of form, by any beauty of colour, but is contemplated as excellence in unspeakable bliss. As then painters transfer human forms to their pictures by the means of certain colours, laying on their copy the proper and corresponding tints, so that the beauty of

the original may be accurately transferred to the likeness, so I would have you understand that our Maker also, painting the portrait to resemble His own beauty, by the addition of virtues, as it were with colours, shows in us His own sovereignty: and manifold and varied are the tints, so to say, by which His true form is portrayed: not red, or white, or the blending of these, whatever it may be called, nor a touch of black that paints the eyebrow and the eye, and shades, by some combination, the depressions in the figure, and all such arts which the hands of painters contrive, but instead of these, purity, freedom from passion, blessedness, alienation from all evil, and all those attributes of the like kind which help to form in men the likeness of God: with such hues as these did the Maker of His own image mark our nature.

2. And if you were to examine the other points also by which the Divine beauty is expressed, you will find that to them too the likeness in the image which we present is perfectly preserved. The Godhead is mind and word: for "in the beginning was the Word" and the followers of Paul "have the mind of Christ" which "speaks" in them: humanity too is not far removed from these: you see in yourself word and understanding, an imitation of the very Mind and Word. Again, God is love, and the fount of love: for this the great John declares, that "love is of God," and "God is love": the Fashioner of our nature has made this to be our feature too: for "hereby," He says, "shall all men know that ye are my disciples, if ye love one another": thus, if this be absent, the whole stamp of the likeness is transformed. The Deity beholds and hears all things, and searches all things out: you too have the power of apprehension of things by means of sight and hearing, and the understanding that inquires into things and searches them out.

VII. Why Man is Destitute of Natural Weapons and Covering

1. But what means the uprightness of his figure? And why is it that those powers which aid life do not naturally belong to his body? But man is brought into life bare of natural covering, an unarmed and poor being, destitute of all things useful, worthy, according to appearances, of pity rather than of admiration, not armed with prominent horns or sharp claws, nor with hoofs nor with teeth, nor possessing by nature any deadly venom in a sting – things such as most animals have in their own power for defence against those who do them harm:

his body is not protected with a covering of hair: and yet possibly it was to be expected that he who was promoted to rule over the rest of the creatures should be defended by nature with arms of his own so that he might not need assistance from others for his own security. Now, however, the lion, the boar, the tiger, the leopard, and all the like have natural power sufficient for their safety: and the bull has his horn, the hare his speed, the deer his leap and the certainty of his sight, and another beast has bulk, others a proboscis, the birds have their wings, and the bee her sting, and generally in all there is some protective power implanted by nature: but man alone of all is slower than the beasts that are swift of foot, smaller than those that are of great bulk, more defenceless than those that are protected by natural arms; and how, one will say, has such a being obtained the sovereignty over all things?

2. Well, I think it would not be at all hard to show that what seems to be a deficiency of our nature is a means for our obtaining dominion over the subject creatures. For if man had had such power as to be able to outrun the horse in swiftness, and to have a foot that, from its solidity, could not be worn out, but was strengthened by hoofs or claws of some kind, and to carry upon him horns and stings and claws, he would be, to begin with, a wild-looking and formidable creature, if such things grew with his body: and moreover he would have neglected his rule over the other creatures if he had no need of the co-operation of his subjects; whereas now, the needful services of our life are divided among the individual animals that are under our sway, for this reason – to make our dominion over them necessary.

3. It was the slowness and difficult motion of our body that brought the horse to supply our need, and tamed him: it was the nakedness of our body that made necessary our management of sheep, which supplies the deficiency of our nature by its yearly produce of wool: it was the fact that we import from others the supplies for our living which subjected beasts of burden to such service: furthermore, it was the fact that we cannot eat grass like cattle which brought the ox to render service to our life, who makes our living easy for us by his own labour; and because we needed teeth and biting power to subdue some of the other animals by grip of teeth, the dog gave, together with his swiftness, his own jaw to supply our need, becoming like a

live sword for man; and there has been discovered by men iron, stronger and more penetrating than prominent horns or sharp claws, not, as those things do with the beasts, always growing naturally with us, but entering into alliance with us for the time, and for the rest abiding by itself: and to compensate for the crocodile's scaly hide, one may make that very hide serve as armour, by putting it on his skin upon occasion: or, failing that, art fashions iron for this purpose too, which, when it has served him for a time for war, leaves the man-at-arms once more free from the burden in time of peace: and the wing of the birds, too, ministers to our life, so that by aid of contrivance we are not left behind even by the speed of wings: for some of them become tame and are of service to those who catch birds, and by their means others are by contrivance subdued to serve our needs: moreover art contrives to make our arrows feathered, and by means of the bow gives us for our needs the speed of wings: while the fact that our feet are easily hurt and worn in travelling makes necessary the aid which is given by the subject animals: for hence it comes that we fit shoes to our feet.

VIII. Why Man's Form is Upright; And that Hands Were Given Him Because of Reason; Wherein Also is a Speculation on the Difference of Souls

8. Now since man is a rational animal, the instrument of his body must be made suitable for the use of reason; as you may see musicians producing their music according to the form of their instruments, and not piping with harps nor harping upon flutes, so it must needs be that the organization of these instruments of ours should be adapted for reason, that when struck by the vocal organs it might be able to sound properly for the use of words. For this reason the hands were attached to the body; for though we can count up very many uses in daily life for which these skilfully contrived and helpful instruments, our hands, that easily follow every art and every operation, alike in war and peace, are serviceable, yet nature added them to our body pre-eminently for the sake of reason. For if man were destitute of hands, the various parts of his face would certainly have been arranged like those of the quadrupeds, to suit the purpose of his feeding: so that its form would have been lengthened out and pointed towards the nostrils, and his lips would have projected from his mouth, lumpy, and stiff, and thick, fitted for taking up the grass, and

his tongue would either have lain between his teeth, of a kind to match his lips, fleshy, and hard, and rough, assisting his teeth to deal with what came under his grinder, or it would have been moist and hanging out at the side like that of dogs and other carnivorous beasts, projecting through the gaps in his jagged row of teeth. If, then, our body had no hands, how could articulate sound have been implanted in it, seeing that the form of the parts of the mouth would not have had the configuration proper for the use of speech, so that man must of necessity have either bleated, or "baaed," or barked, or neighed, or bellowed like oxen or asses, or uttered some bestial sound? But now, as the hand is made part of the body, the mouth is at leisure for the service of the reason. Thus the hands are shown to be the property of the rational nature, the Creator having thus devised by their means a special advantage for reason.

XVI. A Contemplation of the Divine Utterance Which Said – "Let Us Make Man After Our Image and Likeness;" Wherein is Examined What is the Definition of the Image, and How the Passible and Mortal is Like to the Blessed and Impassible, and How in the Image There are Male and Female, Seeing These are Not in the Prototype

1. Let us now resume our consideration of the Divine word, "Let us make man in our image, after our likeness." How mean and how unworthy of the majesty of man are the fancies of some heathen writers, who magnify humanity, as they supposed, by their comparison of it to this world! for they say that man is a little world, composed of the same elements with the universe. Those who bestow on human nature such praise as this by a high-sounding name, forget that they are dignifying man with the attributes of the gnat and the mouse: for they too are composed of these four elements – because assuredly about the animated nature of every existing thing we behold a part, greater or less, of those elements without which it is not natural that any sensitive being should exist. What great thing is there, then, in man's being accounted a representation and likeness of the world – of the heaven that passes away, of the earth that changes, of all things that they contain, which pass away with the departure of that which compasses them round?

2. In what then does the greatness of man consist, according to the doctrine of the Church? Not in his likeness to the created world, but in his being in the image of the nature of the Creator.

3. What therefore, you will perhaps say, is the definition of the image? How is the incorporeal likened to body? How is the temporal like the eternal? That which is mutable by change like to the immutable? That which is subject to passion and corruption to the impassible and incorruptible? That which constantly dwells with evil, and grows up with it, to that which is absolutely free from evil? There is a great difference between that which is conceived in the archetype, and a thing which has been made in its image: for the image is properly so called if it keeps its resemblance to the prototype; but if the imitation be perverted from its subject, the thing is something else, and no longer an image of the subject.

4. How then is man, this mortal, passible, shortlived being, the image of that nature which is immortal, pure, and everlasting? The true answer to this question, indeed, perhaps only the very Truth knows: but this is what we, tracing out the truth so far as we are capable by conjectures and inferences, apprehend concerning the matter. Neither does the word of God lie when it says that man was made in the image of God, nor is the pitiable suffering of man's nature like to the blessedness of the impassible Life: for if any one were to compare our nature with God, one of two things must needs be allowed in order that the definition of the likeness may be apprehended in both cases in the same terms – either that the Deity is passible, or that humanity is impassible: but if neither the Deity is passible nor our nature free from passion, what other account remains whereby we may say that the word of God speaks truly, which says that man was made in the image of God?

7. We must, then, examine the words carefully: for we find, if we do so, that that which was made "in the image" is one thing, and that which is now manifested in wretchedness is another. "God created man," it says; "in the image of God created He him." There is an end of the creation of that which was made "in the image": then it makes a resumption of the account of creation, and says, "male and female created He them." I presume that every one knows that this is a departure from the Prototype: for "in Christ Jesus," as the apostle says,

"there is neither male nor female." Yet the phrase declares that man is thus divided.

8. Thus the creation of our nature is in a sense twofold: one made like to God, one divided according to this distinction: for something like this the passage darkly conveys by its arrangement, where it first says, "God created man, in the image of God created He him," and then, adding to what has been said, "male and female created He them," – a thing which is alien from our conceptions of God.

9. I think that by these words Holy Scripture conveys to us a great and lofty doctrine; and the doctrine is this. While two natures – the Divine and incorporeal nature, and the irrational life of brutes – are separated from each other as extremes, human nature is the mean between them: for in the compound nature of man we may behold a part of each of the natures I have mentioned – of the Divine, the rational and intelligent element, which does not admit the distinction of male and female; of the irrational, our bodily form and structure, divided into male and female: for each of these elements is certainly to be found in all that partakes of human life. That the intellectual element, however, precedes the other, we learn as from one who gives in order an account of the making of man; and we learn also that his community and kindred with the irrational is for man a provision for reproduction. For he says first that "God created man in the image of God" (showing by these words, as the Apostle says, that in such a being there is no male or female): then he adds the peculiar attributes of human nature, "male and female created He them."

10. What, then, do we learn from this? Let no one, I pray, be indignant if I bring from far an argument to bear upon the present subject. God is in His own nature all that which our mind can conceive of good – rather, transcending all good that we can conceive or comprehend. He creates man for no other reason than that He is good; and being such, and having this as His reason for entering upon the creation of our nature, He would not exhibit the power of His goodness in an imperfect form, giving our nature some one of the things at His disposal, and grudging it a share in another: but the perfect form of goodness is here to be seen by His both bringing man into being from nothing, and fully supplying him with all good gifts: but since

the list of individual good gifts is a long one, it is out of the question to apprehend it numerically. The language of Scripture therefore expresses it concisely by a comprehensive phrase, in saying that man was made "in the image of God": for this is the same as to say that He made human nature participant in all good; for if the Deity is the fulness of good, and this is His image, then the image finds its resemblance to the Archetype in being filled with all good.

11. Thus there is in us the principle of all excellence, all virtue and wisdom, and every higher thing that we conceive: but pre-eminent among all is the fact that we are free from necessity, and not in bondage to any natural power, but have decision in our own power as we please; for virtue is a voluntary thing, subject to no dominion: that which is the result of compulsion and force cannot be virtue.

12. Now as the image bears in all points the semblance of the archetypal excellence, if it had not a difference in some respect, being absolutely without divergence it would no longer be a likeness, but will in that case manifestly be absolutely identical with the Prototype. What difference then do we discern between the Divine and that which has been made like to the Divine? We find it in the fact that the former is uncreate, while the latter has its being from creation: and this distinction of property brings with it a train of other properties; for it is very certainly acknowledged that the uncreated nature is also immutable, and always remains the same, while the created nature cannot exist without change; for its very passage from nonexistence to existence is a certain motion and change of the non-existent transmuted by the Divine purpose into being.

13. As the Gospel calls the stamp upon the coin "the image of Caesar," whereby we learn that in that which was fashioned to resemble Caesar there was resemblance as to outward look, but difference as to material, so also in the present saying, when we consider the attributes contemplated both in the Divine and human nature, in which the likeness consists, to be in the place of the features, we find in what underlies them the difference which we behold in the uncreated and in the created nature.

14. Now as the former always remains the same, while that which came into being by creation had the beginning of its existence from change, and has a kindred connection with the like mutation, for this

reason He Who, as the prophetical writing says, "knoweth all things before they be," following out, or rather perceiving beforehand by His power of foreknowledge what, in a state of independence and freedom, is the tendency of the motion of man's will – as He saw, I say, what would be, He devised for His image the distinction of male and female, which has no reference to the Divine Archetype, but, as we have said, is an approximation to the less rational nature.

15. The cause, indeed, of this device, only those can know who were eye-witnesses of the truth and ministers of the Word; but we, imagining the truth, as far as we can, by means of conjectures and similitudes, do not set forth that which occurs to our mind authoritatively, but will place it in the form of a theoretical speculation before our kindly hearers.

16. What is it then which we understand concerning these matters? In saying that "God created man" the text indicates, by the indefinite character of the term, all mankind; for was not Adam here named together with the creation, as the history tells us in what follows? yet the name given to the man created is not the particular, but the general name: thus we are led by the employment of the general name of our nature to some such view as this – that in the Divine foreknowledge and power all humanity is included in the first creation; for it is fitting for God not to regard any of the things made by Him as indeterminate, but that each existing thing should have some limit and measure prescribed by the wisdom of its Maker.

17. Now just as any particular man is limited by his bodily dimensions, and the peculiar size which is conjoined with the superficies of his body is the measure of his separate existence, so I think that the entire plenitude of humanity was included by the God of all, by His power of foreknowledge, as it were in one body, and that this is what the text teaches us which says, "God created man, in the image of God created He him." For the image is not in part of our nature, nor is the grace in any one of the things found in that nature, but this power extends equally to all the race: and a sign of this is that mind is implanted alike in all: for all have the power of understanding and deliberating, and of all else whereby the Divine nature finds its image in that which was made according to it: the man that was mani-

fested at the first creation of the world, and he that shall be after the consummation of all, are alike: they equally bear in themselves the Divine image.

18. For this reason the whole race was spoken of as one man, namely, that to God's power nothing is either past or future, but even that which we expect is comprehended, equally with what is at present existing, by the all-sustaining energy. Our whole nature, then, extending from the first to the last, is, so to say, one image of Him Who is; but the distinction of kind in male and female was added to His work last as I suppose, for the reason which follows.

XXI. That the Resurrection is Looked for as a Consequence, Not So Much from the Declaration of Scripture as from the Very Necessity of Things

1. Wickedness, however, is not so strong as to prevail over the power of good; nor is the folly of our nature more powerful and more abiding than the wisdom of God: for it is impossible that that which is always mutable and variable should be more firm and more abiding than that which always remains the same and is firmly fixed in goodness: but it is absolutely certain that the Divine counsel possesses immutability, while the changeableness of our nature does not remain settled even in evil.

2. Now that which is always in motion, if its progress be to good, will never cease moving onwards to what lies before it, by reason of the infinity of the course to be traversed: for it will not find any limit of its object such that when it has apprehended it, it will at last cease its motion: but if its bias be in the opposite direction, when it has finished the course of wickedness and reached the extreme limit of evil, then that which is ever moving, finding no halting point for its impulse natural to itself when it has run through the lengths that can be run in wickedness, of necessity turns its motion towards good: for as evil does not extend to infinity, but is comprehended by necessary limits, it would appear that good once more follows in succession upon the limit of evil; and thus, as we have said, the ever-moving character of our nature comes to run its course at the last once more back towards good, being taught the lesson of prudence by the memory of its former misfortunes, to the end that it may never again be in like case.

3. Our course, then, will once more lie in what is good, by reason of the fact that the nature of evil is bounded by necessary limits. For just as those skilled in astronomy tell us that the whole universe is full of light, and that darkness is made to cast its shadow by the interposition of the body formed by the earth; and that this darkness is shut off from the rays of the sun, in the shape of a cone, according to the figure of the sphere-shaped body, and behind it; while the sun, exceeding the earth by a size many times as great as its own, enfolding it round about on all sides with its rays, unites at the limit of the cone the concurrent streams of light; so that if (to suppose the case) any one had the power of passing beyond the measure to which the shadow extends, he would certainly find himself in light unbroken by darkness – even so I think that we ought to understand about ourselves, that on passing the limit of wickedness we shall again have our conversation in light, as the nature of good, when compared with the measure of wickedness, is incalculably superabundant.

XXIII. That He Who Confesses the Beginning of the World's Existence Must Necessarily Also Agree as to Its End

1. But if some one, beholding the present course of the world, by which intervals of time are marked, going on in a certain order, should say that it is not possible that the predicted stoppage of these moving things should take place, such a man clearly also does not believe that in the beginning the heaven and the earth were made by God; for he who admits a beginning, of motion surely does not doubt as to its also having an end; and he who does not allow its end, does not admit its beginning either; but as it is by believing that "we understand that the worlds were framed by the word of God," as the apostle says, "so that things which are seen were not made of things which do appear," we must use the same faith as to the word of God when He foretells the necessary stoppage of existing things.

2. The question of the "how" must, however, be put beyond the reach of our meddling; for even in the case mentioned it was "by faith" that we admitted that the thing seen was framed from things not yet apparent, omitting the search into things beyond our reach. And yet our reason suggests difficulties on many points, offering no small occasions for doubt as to the things which we believe.

3. For in that case too, argumentative men might by plausible reasoning upset our faith, so that we should not think that statement true which Holy Scripture delivers concerning the material creation, when it asserts that all existing things have their beginning of being from God. For those who abide by the contrary view maintain that matter is co-eternal with God, and employ in support of their own doctrine some such arguments as these. If God is in His nature simple and immaterial, without quantity, or size, or combination, and removed from the idea of circumscription by way of figure, while all matter is apprehended in extension measured by intervals, and does not escape the apprehension of our senses, but becomes known to us in colour, and figure, and bulk, and size, and resistance, and the other attributes belonging to it, none of which it is possible to conceive in the Divine nature – what method is there for the production of matter from the immaterial, or of the nature that has dimensions from that which is unextended? For if these things are believed to have their existence from that source, they clearly come into existence after being in Him in some mysterious way; but if material existence was in Him, how can He be immaterial while including matter in Himself? And similarly with all the other marks by which the material nature is differentiated; if quantity exists in God, how is God without quantity? If the compound nature exists in Him, how is He simple, without parts and without combination? So that the argument forces us to think either that He is material, because matter has its existence from Him as a source; or, if one avoids this, it is necessary to suppose that matter was imported by Him ab extra for the making of the universe.

4. If, then, it was external to God, something else surely existed besides God, conceived, in respect of eternity, together with Him Who exists ungenerately; so that the argument supposes two eternal and unbegotten existences, having their being concurrently with each other – that of Him Who operates as an artificer, and that of the thing which admits this skilled operation; and if any one under pressure of this argument should assume a material substratum for the Creator of all things, what a support will the Manichaean find for his special doctrine, who opposes by virtue of ungenerateness a material existence to a Good Being. Yet we do believe that all things are of God, as we hear the Scripture say so; and as to the question how they were in God, a question beyond our reason, we do not seek to pry into it,

believing that all things are within the capacity of God's power – both to give existence to what is not, and to implant qualities at His pleasure in what is.

5. Consequently, as we suppose the power of the Divine will to be a sufficient cause to the things that are, for their coming into existence out of nothing, so too we shall not repose our belief on anything beyond probability in referring the World – Reformation to the same power. Moreover, it might perhaps be possible, by some skill in the use of words, to persuade those who raise frivolous objections on the subject of matter not to think that they can make an unanswerable attack on our statement.

XXVIII. To Those Who Say that Souls Existed Before Bodies, or that Bodies Were Formed Before Souls; Wherein There is Also a Refutation of the Fables Concerning Transmigration of Souls

1. For it is perhaps not beyond our present subject to discuss the question which has been raised in the churches touching soul and body. Some of those before our time who have dealt with the question of "principles" think it right to say that souls have a previous existence as a people in a society of their own, and that among them also there are standards of vice and of virtue, and that the soul there, which abides in goodness, remains without experience of conjunction with the body; but if it does depart from its communion with good, it falls down to this lower life, and so comes to be in a body. Others, on the contrary, marking the order of the making of man as stated by Moses, say, that the soul second to the body in order of time, since God first took dust from the earth and formed man, and then animated the being thus formed by His breath: and by this argument they prove that the flesh is more noble than the soul; that which was previously formed than that which was afterwards infused into it: for they say that the soul was made for the body, that the thing formed might not be without breath and motion; and that everything that is made for something else is surely less precious than that for which it is made, as the Gospel tells us that "the soul is more than meat and the body than raiment," because the latter things exist for the sake of the former – for the soul was not made for meat nor our bodies for

raiment, but when the former things were already in being the latter were provided for their needs.

2. Since then the doctrine involved in both these theories is open to criticism – the doctrine alike of those who ascribe to souls a fabulous pre-existence in a special state, and of those who think they were created at a later time than the bodies, it is perhaps necessary to leave none of the statements contained in the doctrines without examination: yet to engage and wrestle with the doctrines on each side completely, and to reveal all the absurdities involved in the theories, would need a large expenditure both of argument and of time; we shall, however, briefly survey as best we can each of the views mentioned, and then resume our subject...

XXIX. An Establishment of the Doctrine that the Cause of the Existence of Soul and Body is One and the Same

1. Nor again are we in our doctrine to begin by making up man like a clay figure, and to say that the soul came into being for the sake of this; for surely in that case the intellectual nature would be shown to be less precious than the clay figure. But as man is one, the being consisting of soul and body, we are to suppose that the beginning of his existence is one, common to both parts, so that he should not be found to be antecedent and posterior to himself, if the bodily element were first in point of time, and the other were a later addition; but we are to say that in the power of God's foreknowledge (according to the doctrine laid down a little earlier in our discourse), all the fulness of human nature had pre-existence (and to this the prophetic writing bears witness, which says that God "knoweth all things before they be"), and in the creation of individuals not to place the one element before the other, neither the soul before the body, nor the contrary, that man may not be at strife against himself, by being divided by the difference in point of time.

2. For as our nature is conceived as twofold, according to the apostolic teaching, made up of the visible man and the hidden man, if the one came first and the other supervened, the power of Him that made us will be shown to be in some way imperfect, as not being completely sufficient for the whole task at once, but dividing the work, and busying itself with each of the halves in turn.

3. But just as we say that in wheat, or in any other grain, the whole form of the plant is potentially included – the leaves, the stalk, the joints, the grain, the beard – and do not say in our account of its nature that any of these things has pre-existence, or comes into being before the others, but that the power abiding in the seed is manifested in a certain natural order, not by any means that another nature is infused into it – in the same way we suppose the human germ to possess the potentiality of its nature, sown with it at the first start of its existence, and that it is unfolded and manifested by a natural sequence as it proceeds to its perfect state, not employing anything external to itself as a stepping-stone to perfection, but itself advancing its own self in due course to the perfect state; so that it is not true to say either that the soul exists before the body, or that the body exists without the soul, but that there is one beginning of both, which according to the heavenly view was laid as their foundation in the original will of God; according to the other, came into existence on the occasion of generation...

Gregory of Nyssa *Against Eunomius*, Book I

34 – The Passage where he attacks the *homoousios*, and the contention in answer to it

The first man, and the man born from him, received their being in a different way; the latter by copulation, the former from the moulding of Christ Himself; and yet, though they are thus believed to be two, they are inseparable in the definition of their being, and are not considered as two beings, without beginning or cause, running parallel to each other; nor can the existing one be said to be generated by the existing one, or the two be ever thought of as one in the monstrous sense that each is his own father, and his own son; but it is because the one and the other was a man that the two have the same definition of being; each was mortal, reasoning, capable of intuition and of science. If, then, the idea of humanity in Adam and Abel does not vary with the difference of their origin, neither the order nor the manner of their coming into existence making any difference in their nature, which is the same in both, according to the testimony of every one in his senses, and no one, not greatly needing treatment for insanity, would deny it; what necessity is there that against the divine nature we should admit this strange thought?

Having heard of Father and Son from the Truth, we are taught in those two subjects the oneness of their nature; their natural relation to each other expressed by those names indicates that nature; and so do Our Lord's own words. For when He said, "I and My Father are one," He conveys by that confession of a Father exactly the truth that He Himself is not a first cause, at the same time that He asserts by His union with the Father their common nature; so that these words of His secure our faith from the taint of heretical error on either side: for Sabellius has no ground for his confusion of the individuality of each Person, when the Only-begotten has so distinctly marked Himself off from the Father in those words, "I and My Father;" and Arius finds no confirmation of his doctrine of the strangeness of either nature to the other, since this oneness of both cannot admit distinction in nature. For that which is signified in these words by the oneness of Father and Son is nothing else but what belongs to them on the score of their actual being; all the other moral excellences which are to be observed in them as over and above their nature may without error be set down as shared in by all created beings...

John Chrysostom

> St. John Chrysostom (c. 347 – 407), the "golden-mouthed," was archbishop of Constantinople from 398. He died in exile after falling afoul the Empress Eudoxia. Earlier, he had lived in Antioch and served as a deacon from 381 and then as a priest from 386. Many of his sermons date from this period in Antioch, including the ones on Genesis below.
>
> Chrysostom's sermons on Genesis were preached during Great Lent, and significant portions treat Lenten themes such as fasting and repentance. A representative of the so-called "Antiochian school," his exegesis of Scripture tended to minimize allegory. Rather than constantly try to apply the message of Scripture to the lives of its hearers, his greater concern was to elucidate what Scripture actually teaches. For Chrysostom, Scripture is God's vehicle for communicating vital truths to humanity, which it accomplishes by accommodating our limited capacity for understanding.
>
> Regarding creation, Chrysostom maintains that Scripture gives a precise account of what happened and in what order. God created all things out of non-existence. All was created in wisdom and out of love for humanity. God initially created the earth formless and without shape lest anyone give misplaced respect to the earth as the source of life rather than to God. The sun's creation on the fourth day after the earth was formed and covered with vegetation counteracts humanity's tendency to worship the sun by showing that it is not the source of life. Chrysostom treats Genesis 1 and 2 as complementary. For him, the image of God in humans signifies the control that God gave them over creation.

John Chrysostom *Homilies on John*

Homily V – John 1:3

"All things were made by Him; and without Him was not anything made that was made."

1. Moses in the beginning of the history and writings of the Old Testament speaks to us of the objects of sense, and enumerates them to us at length. For, "In the beginning," he says, "God made the heaven and the earth," and then he adds, that light was created, and a

second heaven and the stars, the various kinds of living creatures, and, that we may not delay by going through particulars, everything else. But this Evangelist, cutting all short, includes both these things and the things which are above these in a single sentence; with reason, because they were known to his hearers, and because he is hastening to a greater subject, and has instituted all his treatise, that he might speak not of the works but of the Creator, and Him who produced them all. And therefore Moses, though he has selected the smaller portion of the creation, (for he has spoken nothing to us concerning the invisible powers), dwells on these things; while John, as hastening to ascend to the Creator Himself, runs by both these things, and those on which Moses was silent, having comprised them in one little saying, "All things were made by Him." And that you may not think that he merely speaks of all the things mentioned by Moses, he adds, that "without Him was not anything made that was made." That is to say, that of created things, not one, whether it be visible or intelligible was brought into being without the power of the Son...

2. ...What (the Evangelist) says is this, "Without Him was not anything made that was made"; whatever created thing was made, says he, was not made without Him. See you how by this short addition he has rectified all the besetting difficulties; for the saying, that "without Him was not anything made," and then the adding, "which was made," includes things cognizable by the intellect, but excludes the Spirit. For after he had said that "all things were made by Him," and "without Him was not anything made," he needed this addition, lest some one should say, "If all things were made by Him, then the Spirit also was made." "I," he replies, "asserted that whatever was made was made by Him, even though it be invisible, or incorporeal, or in the heavens. For this reason, I did not say absolutely, 'all things,' but 'whatever was made,' that is, 'created things,' but the Spirit is uncreated."

Do you see the precision of his teaching? He has alluded to the creation of material things, (for concerning these Moses had taught before him), and after bringing us to advance from thence to higher things, I mean the immaterial and the invisible, he excepts the Holy Spirit from all creation. And so Paul, inspired by the same grace, said, "For by Him were all things created." (Col 1:16). Observe too here again the same exactness. For the same Spirit moved this soul also.

That no one should except any created things from the works of God because of their being invisible, nor yet should confound the Comforter with them, after running through the objects of sense which are known to all, he enumerates also things in the heavens, saying, "Whether they be thrones, or dominions, or principalities, or powers"; for the expression "whether" subjoined to each, shows to us nothing else but this, that "by Him all things were made, and without Him was not anything made that was made."

But if you think that the expression "by" is a mark of inferiority, (as making Christ an instrument), hear him say, "Thou, Lord, in the beginning, hast laid the foundation of the earth, and the heavens are the work of Thy hands." (Ps. 102:25). He says of the Son what is said of the Father in His character of Creator; which he would not have said, unless he had deemed of Him as of a Creator, and yet not subservient to any. And if the expression "by Him" is here used, it is put for no other reason but to prevent any one from supposing the Son to be Unbegotten. For that in respect of the title of Creator He is nothing inferior to the Father; hear from Himself, where He saith, "As the Father raiseth up the dead and quickeneth them, even so the Son quickeneth whom He will." (John 5:21).

If now in the Old Testament it is said of the Son, "Thou, Lord, in the beginning hast laid the foundation of the earth," His title of Creator is plain. But if you say that the Prophet spoke this of the Father, and that Paul attributed to the Son what was said of the Father, even so the conclusion is the same. For Paul would not have decided that the same expression suited the Son, unless he had been very confident that between Father and Son there was an equality of honor; since it would have been an act of extremest rashness to refer what suited an incomparable Nature to a nature inferior to, and falling short of it. But the Son is not inferior to, nor falls short of, the Essence of the Father; and therefore Paul has not only dared to use these expressions concerning Him, but also others like them. For the expression "from Whom," which you decide to belong properly to the Father alone, he uses also concerning the Son, when he says, "from which all the body by joints and bands having nourishment ministered, and knit together, increaseth with the increase of God." (Col. 2:19).

3. And he is not content with this only, he stops your mouths in another way also, by applying to the Father the expression "by whom," which you say is a mark of inferiority. For he says, "God is faithful, by whom ye were called unto the fellowship of His Son" (1 Cor. 1:9): and again, "By His will" (1 Cor. 1:1 & c.); and in another place, "For of Him, and through Him, and to Him, are all things." (Rom. 11:26). Neither is the expression "from whom," assigned to the Son only, but also to the Spirit; for the angel said to Joseph, "Fear not to take unto thee Mary thy wife, for that which is conceived in her is of the Holy Ghost." (Matt. 1:20). As also the Prophet does not deem it improper to apply to the Father the expression "in whom," which belongs to the Spirit, when he says, "In God we shall do valiantly." (Ps. 60:12). And Paul, "Making request, if by any means now at length I might have a prosperous journey, in the will of God, to come unto you." (Rom. 1:10). And again he uses it of Christ, saying, "In Christ Jesus." (Rom. 6:11, 23 & c.). In short, we may often and continually find these expressions interchanged; now this would not have taken place, had not the same Essence been in every instance their subject. And that you may not imagine that the words, "All things were made by Him," are in this case used concerning His miracles, (for the other Evangelists have discoursed concerning these;) he farther goes on to say, "He was in the world, and the world was made by Him"; (but not the Spirit, for This is not of the number of created things, but of those above all creation).

Let us now attend to what follows. John having spoken of the work of creation, that "All things were made by Him, and without Him was not anything made that was made," goes on to speak concerning His Providence, where he saith, "In Him was Life." That no one may doubt how so many and so great things were "made by Him," he adds, that "In Him was Life." For as with the fountain which is the mother of the great deeps, however much you take away you nothing lessen the fountain; so with the energy of the Only-Begotten, however much you believe has been produced and made by it, it has become no whit the less.

Or, to use a more familiar example, I will instance that of light, which the Apostle himself added immediately, saying, "And the Life was the Light." As then light, however many myriads it may enlighten, suffers no diminution of its own brightness; so also God, before commencing His work and after completing it, remains alike indefectible, nothing diminished, nor wearied by the greatness of the creation. Nay, if need were that ten thousand, or even an infinite number of such worlds be created, He remains the same, sufficient for them all not merely to produce, but also to control them after their creation. For the word "Life" here refers not merely to the act of creation, but also to the providence (engaged) about the permanence of the things created; it also lays down beforehand the doctrine of the resurrection, and is the beginning of these marvelous good tidings. Since when "life" has come to be with us, the power of death is dissolved; and when "light" has shone upon us, there is no longer darkness, but life ever abides within us, and death cannot overcome it. So that what is asserted of the Father might be asserted absolutely of Him (Christ) also, that "In Him we live and move and have our being." (Col. 1:16, Col 1:17). As Paul has shown when he says, "By Him were all things created," and "by Him all things consist"; for which reason He has been called also "Root" and "Foundation."...

John Chrysostom *Homilies on Romans*

Homily III – On Romans 1:18

> *"For the wrath of God is revealed from Heaven against all ungodliness and unrighteousness of men, who hold down the truth in unrighteousness."*

Ver. 19 – "Because that which may be known of God is manifest in them, for God hath showed it unto them."

...The knowledge of Himself God placed in men from the beginning. But this knowledge they invested stocks and stones with, and so dealt unrighteously to the truth, as far at least as they might. For it abideth unchanged, having its own glory immutable. "And whence is it plain that He placed in them this knowledge, O Paul?" "Because," saith he, "that which may be known of Him is manifest in them." This, however, is an assertion, not a proof. But do thou make it good, and show me that the knowledge of God was plain to them, and that they willingly turned aside. Whence was it plain then? Did He send them a voice from above? By no means. But what was able to draw them to Him more than a voice, that He did, by putting before them the Creation, so that both wise, and unlearned, and Scythian, and barbarian, having through sight learned the beauty of the things which were seen, might mount up to God. Wherefore he says,

Ver. 20 – "For the invisible things of Him from the Creation of the world are clearly seen, being understood by the things which are made."

Which also the prophet said, "The heavens declare the glory of God." (Ps. 19:1). For what will the Greeks (i.e. Heathen) say in that day? That "we were ignorant of Thee?" Did ye then not hear the heaven sending forth a voice by the sight, while the well-ordered harmony of all things spake out more clearly than a trumpet? Did ye not see the hours of night and day abiding unmoved continually, the goodly order of winter, spring, and the other seasons remaining both sure and unmoved, the tractableness (*eugnômosunçn*) of the sea amid all its turbulence and waves? All things abiding in order and by their beauty and their grandeur, preaching aloud of the Creator? For all these things and more than these doth Paul sum up in saying, "The invisible things of Him from the creation of the world are clearly seen, being understood by the things which are made, even His eternal Power and Godhead; so that they are without excuse." And yet it is not for this God hath made these things, even if this came of it. For it was not to bereave them of all excuse, that He set before them so great a system of teaching, but that they might come to know Him. But by not having recognized Him they deprived themselves of every excuse...

John Chrysostom *Homilies on Hebrews*

Homily XXII – Hebrews 11:3, 4

> *"Through faith we understand that the worlds were framed by the word of God; so that things which are seen were not made of things which do appear. By faith Abel offered unto God a more excellent sacrifice than Cain, by which he obtained witness that he was righteous, God testifying of his gifts: and by it he being dead yet speaketh."*

1. Faith needs a generous and vigorous soul, and one rising above all things of sense, and passing beyond the weakness of human rea-

sonings. For it is not possible to become a believer, otherwise than by raising one's self above the common customs [of the world].

Inasmuch then as the souls of the Hebrews were thoroughly weakened, and though they had begun from faith, yet from circumstances, I mean sufferings, afflictions, they had afterwards become faint-hearted, and of little spirit, and were shaken from [their position], he encouraged them first indeed from these very things, saying, "Call to remembrance the former days" (Heb. 10:32); next from the Scripture saying, "But the just shall live by faith" (Heb. 10:38); afterwards from arguments, saying, "But Faith is the substance of things hoped for, the evidence of things not seen." (Heb. 11:1). And now again from their forefathers, those great and admirable men, as much as saying; If where the good things were close at hand, all were saved by faith, much more are we.

For when a soul finds one that shares the same sufferings with itself, it is refreshed and recovers breath. This we may see both in the case of Faith, and in the case of affliction: "that there may be comfort for you it is said through our mutual faith." (Rom. 1:12.) For mankind are very distrustful, and cannot place confidence in themselves, are fearful about whatever things they think they possess, and have great regard for the opinion of the many.

2. What then does Paul do? He encourages them by the fathers; and before that by the common notions [of mankind]. For tell me, he says, since Faith is calumniated as being a thing without demonstration and rather a matter of deceit, therefore he shows that the greatest things are attained through faith and not through reasonings. And how does he show this, tell me? It is manifest, he saith, that God made the things which are, out of things which are not, things which appear, out of things which appear not, things which subsist, out of things which subsist not. But whence [is it shown] that He did this even "by a Word"? For reason suggests nothing of this kind; but on the contrary, that the things which appear are [formed] out of things which appear.

Therefore the philosophers expressly say that 'nothing comes out of things that are not' being "sensual" (Jude 19), and trusting nothing to Faith And yet these same men, when they happen to say anything great and noble, are caught entrusting it to Faith. For instance, that

"God is without beginning, and unborn"; for reason does not suggest this, but the contrary. And consider, I beseech you, their great folly. They say that God is without beginning; and yet this is far more wonderful than the [creation] out of things that are not. For to say, that He is without beginning, that He is unborn, neither begotten by Himself nor by another is more full of difficulties, than to say that God made the things which are, out of things which are not. For here there are many things uncertain: as, that some one made it, that what was made had a beginning, that, in a word, it was made. But in the other case, what? He is self-existing, unborn, He neither had beginning nor time; tell me, do not these things require faith? But he did not assert this, which was far greater, but the lesser.

Whence [does it appear], he would say, that God made these things? Reason does not suggest it; no one was present when it was done. Whence is it shown? It is plainly the result of faith. "Through faith we understand that the worlds were made." Why "through faith"? Because "the things that are seen were not made of things which do appear." For this is Faith.

3. Having thus stated the general [principle], he afterwards tests it by individuals. For a man of note is equivalent to the world. This at all events he afterwards hinted. For when he had matched it against one or two hundred persons, and then saw the smallness of the number, he afterwards says, "by whom the world was outweighed in worth." (Heb. 11:38).

John Chrysostom *Homilies on Genesis 1 – 17*

Homily 2 – On the beginning of creation: "In the beginning God created heaven and earth."

(4) Do you see, dearly beloved, from these introductory words the efficacy of fasting? Accordingly, I address myself to you with greater enthusiasm today than before, in the knowledge that I am casting seed upon rich and fertile soil, capable of yielding to us in rapid time an abundant return of what was sown. So let us learn, if you would, the force of what has been read to you today from the words of blessed Moses. Attend carefully, I ask you, to what is said by us; they are not our words that we are uttering, after all, but what the love of God provides for the sake of your salvation. What are they? "In the beginning

God made heaven and earth." It is in order to pose the question here: why did this blessed author, born many generations later, put this to us? Not idly or without good reason. You see, when God formed human beings in the beginning, he used to speak to them personally, in a way that was possible for human beings to understand him. This was the way, for example, that he came to Adam, the way he upbraided Cain, the way he conversed with Noah, the way he accepted Abraham's hospitality. And even when all humankind fell into evil ways, the creator of all did not abandon the human race. Instead, when they then proved unworthy of his converse with them, he wanted to renew his love for them; he sent them letters as you do to people far away from you, and this drew all humankind back again to him. It was God who sent them letters, Moses who delivered them. What do the letters say? "In the beginning God made heaven and earth."

(5) Notice this remarkable author, dearly beloved, and the particular gift he had. I mean, while all the other inspired authors told either what would happen after a long time or what was going to take place immediately, this blessed author, being born many generations after the event, was guided by the deity on high and judged worthy to narrate what had been created by the Lord of all from the very beginning. Accordingly, he began with these words: "In the beginning God created heaven and earth." He well nigh bellows at us all and says, "Is it by human beings I am taught in uttering these things? It is the one who brought being from nothing who stirred my tongue in narrating them." Since we therefore listen to these words not as the words of Moses but as the words of the God of all things coming to us through the tongue of Moses, so, I beg you, let us heed what is said and part company with our own reasoning. Scripture, after all, says: "The thoughts of mortals are deceptive, and their thinking unreliable." Let us accept what is said with much gratitude, not overstepping the proper limit nor busying ourselves with matters beyond us; this is the besetting weakness of enemies of the truth, wishing as they do to assign every matter to their own reasoning, and lacking the realization that it is beyond the capacity of human nature to plumb God's creation.

(6) But why mention God's creation? Even human arts germane to them are beyond them. Tell me, for instance, how the substance of gold takes shape through the art of mining? Or how the purity of glass comes from sand? You can't tell. So if it's impossible to fathom what lies before your very eyes and the things which human wisdom devises, thanks to God's loving kindness, why busy yourself, mere mortal, about the things created by God? What sort of excuse would you manage to adduce? And what defense would you invent for contemplating what lies beyond your natural powers? I mean, to say that existing things came to be from underlying matter, and not to admit that the Creator of all produced them from non-existence, would be a mark of utter stupidity. Accordingly, this blessed author, when he was on the point of beginning the book, stopped the mouths of such idiots, by beginning like this: "In the beginning God made heaven and earth." When you hear "He made," concern yourself no further, but with head bowed believe what is said. For God it is who makes and transforms all things, and refashions all things according to his will.

(7) See the great extent of the considerateness in this statement; there is no mention of unseen powers, nor does it say, In the beginning God made the angels, or the archangels. It was not idly or without purpose that he took this line in his teaching. I mean, since he was talking to Jews, people quite wrapped up in the world about them and incapable of forming any spiritual notion, he led them along for the time being from visible realities to the creator of all things, so that from created things they might come to learn the architect of all and adore their maker, not stopping short at creatures. You see, despite the creation of the world they had not avoided the error of making gods out of creatures, offering worship to the vilest of brutes; so what madness would they not have fallen into if such considerateness had not been shown them?

(8) Don't be surprised, dearly beloved, if Moses followed this procedure speaking as he was at the beginning in the early stages to very down-to-earth Jews, when even Paul in the age of grace, when proclamation of the good news had advanced so much, was able, in the speech he was on the point of delivering to the Athenians, to base his teaching to them on visible realities, in these words: "God made the world and everything in it; being Lord and maker of heaven and earth, he does not dwell in man-made temples, nor can human hands

pay him due worship." I mean, he could see that kind of approach suited them, so he followed that line; that is to say, he was guided by the Spirit to direct his teaching to the ones who would receive what he had to give them. To learn that his basis for deciding this was the difference in his audience and the materialism of his listeners, listen to his words. In addressing his letter to the people of Colossae he did not keep to that approach, but addressed them differently, in these words: "In him were created all things – those in the heaven and on earth, the visible and the invisible, whether thrones, dominations, principalities, powers – all were created by him and with him in mind." John, the Son of Thunder, by contrast shouted aloud, "Everything was made through him, and without him no single thing was made."

(9) Moses, however, did not speak like that, as you'd expect; after all, it wasn't logical that those still requiring to be fed on milk be given solid food instead. To take another example: whereas teachers who have been entrusted by parents with the education of their children give them the fundamentals of learning, those who receive the children from them at the next stage take them through more developed stages of learning. This same pattern was followed by blessed Moses, by the teacher of the Gentiles, and the son of thunder. When Moses, remember, in the beginning took on the instruction of the human race, he taught his listeners the elements, whereas Paul and John, taking over from Moses, could at that later stage transmit more developed notions.

(10) Hence we discover the reason for the considerateness shown to date, namely, that under the guidance of the Spirit he was speaking in a manner appropriate to his hearers as he outlined everything. At the same time he uprooted all the heresies springing up like weeds in the Church by his words, "In the beginning God made heaven and earth." Even if Mani accosts you saying matter preexisted, or Marcion, or Valentinus, or pagans, tell them directly: "In the beginning God made heaven and earth." But what if the person does not believe in the Scriptures? Leave him to his own devices, like an utter madman; for what allowance can you make for a person who does not believe the creator of all things, who treats the truth as falsehood? People of that ilk sport false colors: while wearing the appearance of sweet reasonableness, they are in fact wolves in sheep's clothing.

Don't you be taken in; on the contrary, spurn this behavior all the more for the reason that, while they pretend an obsequiousness towards you though simply your peer, towards God the Lord of all they wage open warfare and do not perceive that they are running from salvation. Let us, on the other hand, cling to the unshakeable rock and keep coming back to the beginning, "In the beginning God made heaven and earth."

(11) Notice how the divine nature shines out of the very manner of creation, how he executes his creation in a way contrary to human procedures, first stretching out the heavens and then laying Out the earth beneath, first the roof and then the foundation. Who has ever seen the like? Who has ever heard of it? No matter what human beings produce, this could never have happened – whereas when God decides, everything yields to his will and becomes possible. So don't pry too closely with human reasoning into the works of God; instead, let the works lead you to marvel at their maker. Scripture says, remember, "What the eye cannot see in him has come into view from the creation of the world and are understood through the things he has made."

If the enemies of truth insist on saying it is impossible for something to be produced from nothing, let us ask them. The first human being – was he made from the earth, or did he come from somewhere else? To a man they'll say from the earth, and make no bones about it. So let them tell us how the substance of flesh came into existence from the earth. I mean, from the earth you get clay, and bricks, and pottery, and potsherds so how would you get the substance of flesh? How would you get bones and nerves and arteries, fat and skin, nails and hair, and all the qualities of different substances from one underlying material? They wouldn't be able to open their mouth in reply. Yet why do I confine my remarks to the body? Let them tell us about the bread we eat daily, how it is changed into blood, gall, bile, and various humors while being one in composition. Bread often has the color of grain, whereas blood is reel or black.

So, if they can't tell about these things that are before our eyes day in and day out, they would hardly tell us about all the other things created by God. If, however, despite such an embarrassment of proofs they want to insist on reinforcing their own obstinacy, let us likewise keep throwing back in their teeth the words, "In the beginning God made heaven and earth." This single sentence, after all, is enough to overthrow all the defenses of our adversaries, and to tear up all their human reasonings, roots and all; and should they ever want eventually to abjure their polemics, it would be possible through this verse for them to be led to the path of truth.

(12) The text proceeds: "The earth was invisible and lacking all shape." For what reason, tell me, did he create the sky bright and finished, but let the earth appear formless? This too was not done without purpose; his intention was that you would learn about his craftsmanship from the better part of creation, and so have no further doubts or think that it all happened out of a lack of power. For a quite different purpose he produced the earth in a formless condition. The earth, you know, is our mother and provider; to it we owe our beginning and our growth; this is homeland and grave for us all alike; to the earth we come back in the end, and through it we lay hold of countless benefits. So in case human beings might through the pressure of necessity treat the earth with a respect beyond its due, he shows it to you first formless and imperfect so that you would not attribute the earth's gifts to it but to the one who brought it into existence from nothing. For this reason the text reads: "The earth was invisible and lacking all shape."

Homily 3 – Further comment on the verse, "In the beginning God made heaven and earth," up to the verse, "Evening came and morning came: one day"

(3) But in order that the sermon may be clearer to you, let us remind you in your goodness of some details of what was said yesterday so as to fit together, as into one whole, what is to be said today with what was said yesterday. We showed you yesterday, as you will recall, how blessed Moses explained to us the creation of these visible elements in saying that in the beginning God made heaven and earth, the land was invisible and lacking all shape." And we taught you why he left the land unshaped and unpeopled, and I think you remember it all precisely, so today we must proceed to what follows in the text. You see, when he says, "The land was invisible and lacking all shape," he teaches us precisely how it came to be invisible and lacking all shape, adding, "Darkness was over the deep, and the Spirit of

God moved over the water." Notice in this case, I ask you, the economy of the blessed author, how he does not describe all created things individually, but teaches us which items were produced together by mentioning heaven and earth and passing over the rest. I mean, he had made no mention of the creation of the waters, but then said, "Darkness was over the deep, and the Spirit of God moved over the water" this, you see, was covering the face of the earth, darkness I mean, and the depths of water. From this we learned that all that could be seen was depths of water, covered in darkness and having need of the wise creator to remove all this shapelessness and bring everything to a condition of order.

(4) "Darkness," the text says, "was over the deep, and the Spirit of Cod moved over the water." What is meant by that part of the text, "The Spirit of God moved over the water"? It seems to me to mean this, that some lifegiving force was present in the waters: it wasn't simply water that was stationary and immobile, but moving and possessed of some vital power. I mean, what doesn't move is quite useless, whereas what moves is capable of many things. So, to teach us that this water, great and cumbersome as it was, had some vital power, he says, "The Spirit of God moved over the water." It is not without reason that Sacred Scripture makes this early comment. Instead, it intends later to describe to us that creatures in these waters were produced by command of the creator of all things, and so at this point it teaches the listener that water was not idly formed, but was moving, and shifting, and flowing over everything.

(5) So, when the shapeless mass of all that could be seen lay about on all sides, God the mighty artificer issued his command and the shapeless mass took on form, the surpassing beauty of this blinding light appeared and dissipated the palpable gloom, illuminating everything. "God said," the text reads, "'Let light be created,' and light was created." He spoke: it was created; he gave his command: darkness was scattered and light produced. See his ineffable power? Yet there are those who ignore the sequence of the text, caught up as they are in their error, and who pay no heed to the words of blessed Moses, "In the beginning God made heaven and earth," and the following verse, "The land was invisible and lacking all shape" On account of its being obscured by the darkness and the waters, the Lord having decided (you see) to create it in the beginning like this. These people say that

matter was the basis for creation, and that darkness preexisted. What could be worse than this madness? You heard that "in the beginning God made heaven and earth," and that from nothing things were created, and do you say that matter was the basis for creation? Who in their right minds would come up with such idiocy? Surely the creator is not human, needing some basis for creation so as to reveal his artistry? God it is to whom all things respond as he creates them by word and command. Remember how he merely spoke, and light was created and darkness dissipated.

(6) "God separated light from darkness." What is meant by "He separated"? He gave each its own place and defined its appropriate time. And when this had been done, he then gave each its proper name. The text goes on, you see: "God called the light day, and the darkness night." Do you see the excellent distinction and the wonderful craftsmanship, surpassing all comment, happening by a single word and command? Do you see the degree of considerateness employed by the blessed author, or rather the loving God through the tongue of the author, instructing the race of men to know the plan of created things, and who was the creator of all, and how each came into being?

(7) I mean, since mankind was yet untutored and could not understand more elaborate matters, the Holy Spirit accordingly explained everything to us by moving the author's tongue in such a way as to take account of the limitations of the listeners. To be convinced that it was on account of the incompleteness of our understanding that he employed such considerateness in his explanation, compare the approach of the Son of Thunder: when humankind had advanced along the path to perfection, no longer did he have them move by this lower way, but led his listeners to a loftier teaching. "In the beginning was the Word," he said, you remember, "the Word was with God, and the Word was God," and added, "He was the true Light, which enlightened everyone coming into the world." In other words, just as in our text this visible light, produced by command of the Lord, removed the darkness from our vision, in like manner the light coming to our minds dissipated the darkness of error, and led those in error to the truth.

(8) So let us receive the teachings of Sacred Scripture with deep gratitude, not resisting the truth nor persisting in darkness, but hastening towards the light and performing actions proper to the light and the day. That is what Paul recommends to us when he says, "Let us walk becomingly as the light of day suggests" and not perform actions proper to the dark.

(9) The text goes on: "God called the light day, and he called the darkness night." Now, a detail that almost escaped us we need to pick up again. I mean, when it said, "'Let light be created,' and light was created," it added, "God saw that the light was good." See there, dearly beloved, the extent of the considerateness in the language. What is the point of the remark? Is it that before the light comes into being he does not know it is beautiful, whereas after its appearance the sight of it shows its creator the beauty of what appears? What sort of sense would that make? I mean, it a man works at some piece of craftsmanship, and before he completes the thing he is making and puts final touches to it he sees the use to which he will put the thing he is making, how much more the creator of all, who by his word brings into being everything from non-being, sees that the light is good before he creates it. So why did he use this expression?

(10) This blessed author spoke this way out of considerateness for the way human beings speak. And just as people work on something with great care, and when they bring their efforts to completion they parade what they have made for scrutiny and commendation, so Sacred Scripture speaks in that way, showing considerateness for the limitations of our hearing when it said, "God saw that the light was good," and added, "God separated light from darkness; he called the light day, and he called the darkness night," allotting to each its own particular area and establishing limits for each right from the beginning so that they could keep to them permanently without interference. Everyone in his right mind can understand this, how from that time till this the light has not surpassed its limits, nor has darkness exceeded its due order, resulting in confusion and disruption. Really, this fact alone should suffice to oblige people obdurate in their lack of response to come to faith and obedience to the words of Sacred Scripture so as to imitate the order in the elements, respecting as they do their course uninterruptedly, and not overstep their own limitations but rather recognize the extent of their own nature.

(11) Then, when he had assigned to each its own name, he linked the two together in the words, "Evening came, and morning came: one day." He made a point of speaking of the end of the day and the end of the night as one, so as to grasp a certain order and sequence in visible things and avoid any impression of confusion.

(12) Now, we are in a position to learn from the Holy Spirit, through the tongue of this blessed author, what things were created on the first day and what things on the other days. This itself is a mark of the considerateness of the loving God. I mean, his all-powerful hand and boundless wisdom were not at a loss even to create everything in one day. Why say 'one day'? Even in a brief moment. Yet it was not because of its utility to him that he produced anything that exists, since being self-sufficient he is in need of nothing. It was rather out of his loving kindness and goodness that he created everything; accordingly he created things in sequence and provided us with a clear instruction about created things through the tongue of the blessed author, so that we might learn about them precisely and not fall into the error of those led by purely human reasoning. You see, if there are still those, despite this manner of creation, will say that things get existence from themselves, what would these people not have been rash enough to invent in their anxiety to say and do everything against their own welfare, had not God employed such considerateness and instruction?

(13) After all, what could be more pitiful and more stupid than people coming up with arguments like this, claiming that beings get existence of themselves, and withdrawing all creation from God's providence? How could you have the idea, I ask you, that so many elements and such great arrangements were being guided without anyone to supervise and control it all? Surely no ship ever managed to navigate the waves of the sea without a pilot, or soldier do brave deed with no general in command, or house stand firm with no householder in charge – whereas this immense universe and the design of all these elements could happen simply by chance without anyone present with the power to guide it all, controlling and maintaining all things in existence from his innate wisdom is this feasible?

Homily 4 – "God said, 'Let a firmament be made in the middle of the water, and let it keep one body of water from the other.' This is what happened."

(5) ...Having thus completed the account of the first day, and having said after the creation of light, "Evening came, and morning came: one day," he says further, "And God said 'Let a firmament be made in the middle of the water, and let it keep one body of water separate from the other.'" Notice here, clearly beloved, the sequence of the teaching. What I mean is that he first brought to our attention, after the creation of heaven and earth, the fact that "the earth was invisible and lacking all shape," and supplied the explanation for it – namely, it was invisible because it was concealed by darkness and water (you recall that everything consisted of darkness and water, and nothing else). Then, at the command of the Lord, light was created and a separation made between light and darkness; one received the name day and the other night. His intention once again is to teach us that just as by producing the light God could cleave the darkness and assigned to each its appropriate name, so by his command he made a division in the mass of water.

(6) Take note of such ineffable power, which surpasses all human imagining. I mean, he simply commands, and one element comes into being while another gives way to it. "God said, 'Let a firmament be made in the middle of the water, and let it keep one body of water separate from the other.'" What does that mean, "Let a firmament be made"? As if someone were to say in human language, Let there be some sort of barrier and division to come between them and make a separation. And, so that you may learn the extraordinary obedience of the elements and the exceeding power of the Creator, he adds, "This is what happened." God had only to speak, and the effect followed immediately.

(7) The text goes on: "God made the firmament, and God divided the water which was below the firmament from the water which was above the firmament." That is to say, once the firmament existed, he ordered some of the water to go below the firmament, and some to be on top of the firmament. Now, what would you say this means, the firmament? Water that has congealed, or some air that has been compressed, or some other substance? No sensible person would be rash

enough to make a decision on it. Instead, it is better to be quite grateful and ready to accept what is told us and not reach beyond the limits of our own nature by meddling in matters beyond us, but rather to know only the simple fact and keep it within us – namely, that by the Lord's command the firmament was produced, causing division of the waters, keeping some on top of it.

(8) "The Lord called the firmament heaven." Notice how Sacred Scripture here too employs the same sequence of thought. Just as it said yesterday, "Let there be light," and after it was created added, "Let there be separation between light" and darkness, and thus the light was called day, so too today it said, "Let a firmament be made in the middle of the water." Then, as with the light, so too here it taught us the use of the firmament, saying, "for the purpose of keeping one body of water separate from the other." And when it made its use clear to us, as it had imposed a name on the light, so too it put a label on the firmament: "He called the firmament heaven," as we saw. How is it, you will say, some people want to claim many heavens were created? They don't get this teaching from Sacred Scripture, but base it on their own reasoning. I mean, blessed Moses teaches us nothing more than this; that is, he says, "In the beginning God made heaven and earth;" then, having taught us the reason why the earth happened to be invisible – that it was concealed by darkness and the waters of the abyss – he employs a kind of order and sequence by saying after the creation of light, "The Lord said, 'Let a firmament be made.'" He then taught us in a precise manner the purpose of the firmament in saying, "so as to keep one body of water from the other," and next gave the name heaven to this same firmament which caused division of the waters. So after this kind of teaching who could take any notice of the people who want to speak off the cuff from their own imagining and be so bold as to propose many heavens against the evidence of Sacred Scripture? But, they claim, see how blessed David sang the praises of God in words like these: "Praise him, heaven of heavens." Don't worry, dearly beloved, don't think Sacred Scripture ever contradicts itself, learn instead the truth of what it says, hold fast what it teaches in truth, and close your ears to those who speak against it.

(9) To grasp the point I'm trying to make, listen very carefully so as not to be easily upset by people prepared to say the first thing that

comes into their head. All the sacred books of the Old Testament were originally composed in Hebrew; everybody would agree with us on this. Not many years before the coming of Christ, King Ptolemy, who was very keen on collecting books and had collected many other ones of different kinds, felt obliged to add the Old Testament books to his collection as well. So he summoned some of the Jews living in Jerusalem, and ordered them to translate the books into Greek; this was in fact brought to completion for him. The upshot of this work of divine providence was that the benefit of the Old Testament was now available not only to people who knew Hebrew but also to anyone living anywhere in the world. What makes this remarkable and ironic is that the initiative for this was taken not by people with belief in Judaism but by a man devoted to idols and opposed in his beliefs to true religion. You see, everything turns out like this under the providence of our Lord: the principles of truth are always vindicated by the people who oppose them.

(10) It was not without purpose that I told this story to you; rather, it was for you, dearly beloved, to know that the Old Testament books were not composed in this language – ours, I mean – but in Hebrew. Now, those with a precise knowledge of that language tell us that among the Hebrews the word 'heaven' is used in the plural, and those who know the language of the Syrians confirm this. In that language – that is, the language they use – no one would say 'heaven', but 'the heavens'. So it is logical that the words spoken by the blessed David, "the heaven of heavens," have that form, not because there are several heavens (the blessed Moses, remember, taught us that) but because it is idiomatic in Hebrew to use the name of a single thing in the plural; if there were several heavens, the Holy Spirit would not have neglected to teach us through the tongue of this blessed author about the creation of the other ones. Keep a close grasp on these matters, I beg you, so as to be able to curb those people wanting to come up with objections against the Church, and be quite sure in your knowledge of the efficacy of what is contained in the Sacred Scriptures. That, after all, is the reason why you gather here so regularly, and why we provide you with such abundant instruction, so that you may be well prepared for anyone seeking to indoctrinate you.

(11) But let us move on to what follows, it you don't mind. "God called the firmament heaven," the text says; "and God saw that it was

good." Notice the extent of the considerateness of the language to accommodate human limitations. That is to say, just as at the creation of light the text said, "He saw it was good," so too now in the case of heaven – that is, the firmament – it says, "God saw it was good," teaching us in this way its extraordinary beauty. I mean, who could fail to be utterly amazed that the firmament in all this period has kept its beauty unimpaired, and that the more time passes, so much the more this beauty increases. After all, what could be more beautiful than the thing that gains commendation from the Creator? I mean, if we see a human being's work brought to completion and marvel at its design, its position, its beauty, its proportion, its symmetry, and everything else about it, how could anyone adequately praise what God has produced, particularly when it has won the praise of the Lord himself? You see, this is said out of considerateness for us, and you will notice the same words used in the case of each created thing, refuting in anticipation the temerity of those who later will be disposed to sharpen their tongue against God's creation and raise the question, why did this and that come into being? So, to check those people ahead of time in their endeavours to voice that opinion, the text says, "God saw that it was good." When you hear that God "saw" and God "praised", take the word in a sense proper to God. That is to say, the Creator knew the beauty of the created thing before he created it, whereas we are human beings and encompassed with such limitations that we cannot understand it in any other way; accordingly, he directed the tongue of the blessed author to make use of the clumsiness of these words for the instruction of the human race.

(12) So, whenever you raise your eyes and admire the beauty of heaven, its immensity, its usefulness to us, then move from there to its Creator, as a wise man has said: "From the magnitude and beauty of creatures we can by comparison see the Creator." [Wisdom 13:5] See too the Lord's power, how great it is, even from the creation of these elements. I mean, any right-minded person who is prepared to scan visible things each day – but why say created things each day? If you only consider carefully your own makeup, you will see through these details God's ineffable power beyond all description. If these visible things suffice to teach us the magnitude of the Creator's power, and if you attain to the unseen powers, and raise your mind to the hosts of

the angels, the archangels, the powers above, the thrones, the dominations, the principalities, the powers, the cherubim, the seraphim – what understanding, what description is of any avail to unfold his greatness? Remember the blessed author David: if in studying the order of visible things he cried out, "How your works are magnified, O Lord; you have made everything in wisdom" [Ps.104:24] – David, a man endowed so generously with the Spirit and deemed worthy to know the obscure and hidden things of the Lord's wisdom – what could we say, dust and ashes that we are, obliged constantly to move with head bowed, and to gape at the unspeakable love of the Lord of all? And why do I quote the psalmist? I mean, blessed Paul, that spirit soaring to heaven, clad in a body yet contending with disembodied powers, treading the earth yet scouring the heavens in his enthusiasm, falling in with one part of God's design (I mean that to do with Jews and Gentiles, rejected by the former and taken possession of by the latter) – Paul it was who cried out in utter bewilderment and stupor, "O the depth of the wealth of God's wisdom and knowledge: how inscrutable his judgements and unsearchable his ways" [Rom 11:33].

Homily 5 – "God said: 'Let the water under heaven be gathered together into one mass, and let dry land appear.'"

(8) But enough of such introductions; let us now listen, if you don't mind, to what it is the grace of the Spirit wants to teach us today as well through Moses' tongue. The text goes on: "God said, 'Let the water under heaven be gathered together into one mass, and let dry land appear.' This is what happened." Notice here, I ask you, dearly beloved, the order and wonderful sequence. I mean, it said in the beginning that "the earth was invisible and lacking all shape" for the reason that it was concealed by the darkness and the waters; then on the second day he ordered the firmament to be made, and caused the separation of the waters, calling the firmament heaven. Now he further teaches us that on the third day he directed that the water under heaven, that is, under the firmament – should come together into one mass, should make room, and the dry land should appear; that is what happened. In other words, since everything was filled with water, he orders the immensity of waters to come together into one mass, so that there would be a way for the dry land to appear.

(9) Note how he sets out for us in detail the orderly arrangement and beauty of it all. "That is what happened," it says. How? In the way the Lord directed. He simply spoke, and the work followed. You see, this is God's way: created things are governed by his will. "The water under heaven was gathered together into its masses, and the dry land appeared." Just as in the case of the light, when darkness was everywhere, he ordered the creation of the light, and caused a division between the light and the darkness, so as to assign one to the day and the other to the night, and likewise in the case of the waters he created the firmament, and bade one lot take the upper place and the other lot be below the firmament, so too in this case he orders this second lot of water which was under the firmament to run together into one mass so that the dry land may appear and he may then give it its own name, as with the light and the darkness. The text says, remember, "The waters were gathered together into their masses, and the dry land appeared; God called the dry land earth." Do you see, dearly beloved, how the earth, which was previously invisible and lacking all shape through being hidden by the waters as though under covers, he unveils, as it were, and shows its face at long last, giving it its own name.

(10) The text goes on: "The masses of the waters he called seas." Notice that the waters also got their own name. To make a comparison: when a first-rate craftsman plans to fashion a vessel from his own skill, he doesn't give it a name until he has brought his creation to completion. Just so, the loving Lord does not give names to the elements until he assigns them to their own place through his own arrangement. So after the earth received its own name and took its own shape, the waters too being now gathered together were in their turn ready to receive their own name. The text says, remember, "The masses of the waters he called seas," and then added, "God saw that it was good." You see, since human nature is limited and is not capable of adequately praising the works of God, Sacred Scripture anticipates by telling us of the praise given by the Creator himself. So, when you learn that created things appeared good to the Creator himself, you have further grounds for wonder without being able any better to apply praise and eulogy. This, after all, is the kind of Lord you have: he does the kinds of things that surpass the bounds of praise by us. I

mean, how could human nature adequately praise God's works or celebrate them at all?

(11) Recognize further, I ask you, in the evidence assembled here the ineffable wisdom of God the artificer. That is to say, after making visible to us the face of the earth, he further bestows upon it by his own design a pleasing aspect, beautifying its face with a profusion of seeds. "God said," the text goes on, "'Let the earth put forth a crop of vegetation, plants yielding seed, each according to its kind and likeness, and fruit trees bearing fruit with seed inside, each according to its kind upon the earth.' This is what happened." What does that mean, "This is what happened"? According to the text, the Lord gave directions and at once the earth went into labor and adorned itself with its own crop of seeds. "The earth brought forth," the text goes on, "a crop of vegetation, plants yielding seed, each according to its kind and likeness, and fruit trees bearing fruit with seed inside, each according to its kind upon the earth."

(12) Consider here, I ask you, dearly beloved, how everything came into being on the earth by the word of the Lord. I mean, it was no man who was the cause, or plough, or help from oxen, or effort towards it from any other source – simply that everything heard the command, and at once sprang from the earth into view. From this we learn that at present likewise what provides us with the harvest of fruits is not the effort of the farmers, or their toil, or the other labors put into farming, but before all these it is the word of God, the same as was directed to it from the beginning. For the particular purpose of correcting later human folly, Sacred Scripture gives us a precise description of everything according to the order of creation so as to offset the absurdities of people speaking idly from their own reasoning in an endeavor to assert that the assistance of the sun is responsible for the germination of the crops.

(13) There are some people who try to ascribe these things to some of the stars. For this reason the Holy Spirit teaches us that before the creation of these elements the earth heard his word and command and brought forth the plants, with no need of anything else by way of assistance. In other words, in place of anything else the earth had need only of that word that was spoken, "Let the earth put forth a crop of vegetation." So, taking our lead from Sacred Scripture, let us never tolerate those who lightly propound contrary views. I

mean, even if human beings till the earth, even if they get assistance from brute beasts, and bestow great attention on the earth, even if the weather is kind, and everything goes according to plan, it will be all to no avail unless the Lord wills; all the toil and trouble will be fruitless unless the hand from on high takes part and brings to fruition these efforts. Who could fail to be absolutely astonished at the thought of how the word uttered by the Lord, "'Let the earth put forth a crop of vegetation,'" penetrated to the very bowels of the earth and, as though with a veil, adorned the face of the earth with a variety of flowers? In an instant you could see the earth, which just before had been shapeless and unkempt, take on such beauty as almost to defy comparison with heaven. I mean, just as heaven would shortly be adorned with a variety of stars, so too the earth was beautified with a range of flowers to such an extent that even the Creator was moved to commendation: "God saw," the text says, remember, "that it was good."

Homily 6 – "God said: 'Let lights be made in the firmament of heaven for lighting up the earth, to separate day from night; let them act as signs and indicate days, seasons and years.'"

(9) However, dear people, to convince you that we have been led to say this out of a heartfelt grief arising from affection and concern and through grave fear for your salvation – come now, let us once more nourish ourselves on sound hopes by proposing to you the customary instruction, so as to demonstrate to you the fatherly regard we have for you. For your part, I beg you, attend to what is said with close attention so as to gain further good and thus return home. I feel the need, dear people, to repeat these words we have read before: "God said, 'Let lights be created in the firmament of heaven for lighting up the earth, so as to separate day from night; let them act as signs and indicate days, seasons and years. Let them provide light in the firmament of heaven, to shine upon the earth.' This is what happened." You see, since the blessed Moses taught us yesterday how the Creator of all beautified the shapelessness of the earth with vegetation, the variety of flowers and the growth of crops, today he switches his description to the arrangement of heaven. In other words, just as the earth was beautified by the things produced from it, in like

manner he caused heaven, which was already visible, to be more conspicuous and bright by lending it the variety that comes from a range of stars and from the creation of the two huge lights, namely, the sun and the moon. "God made," the text goes on, "the two huge lights, the greater light for governing the day, and the lesser light for governing the night and the stars."

(10) Do you see the wisdom of the Creator? He merely spoke, and this marvellous body came into being, namely, the sun. You see, it calls this light great and says it was brought into existence for governing the day. In other words, the sun renders the day brighter, shedding its rays like flashing lights and day by day revealing its own beauty in full bloom: as soon as it appears at dawn, it awakes the whole human race to the discharge of their respective duties. This beauty the blessed author reveals when he says: "The sun beams, like a bridegroom emerging from his chamber, like a giant in the running of his course; its span extends from one corner of heaven right to the other corner of heaven." Do you see how he revealed to us both the sun's beauty and its speed of movement? That is, in saying, "Its span extends from one corner of heaven right to the other corner of heaven," it indicated to us how in one moment of time it traverses the whole world and scatters its rays from end to end, making its great resources available: it not only supplies heat to the earth but also dries it up, and not only dries it up but enkindles it, and supplies us with many different resources, so marvellous a body is it, quite beyond one's power to describe adequately.

(11) I mention this to you and sing the praises of this heavenly body so that you may not stop short there, dearly beloved, but proceed further and transfer your admiration to the Creator of the heavenly body. After all, the greater the sun is shown to be, so much the more marvellous is the revelation of the Creator.

(12) Pagan peoples, however, in their wonder and stupor at this heavenly body were unable to look beyond it to praise its Creator; instead, they sang its praises and treated it as a deity. Hence the reason for the blessed Paul's saying, "They worshipped and served the creature instead of its Creator." [Rom. 1:25] What could be more stupid than people failing to recognize the Creator from the creature and being caught up in such error as to put creature and artefact on the same level as their Creator? So then, foreseeing the inclination of

slothful people to error, Sacred Scripture teaches us that the creation of this heavenly body took place three days later, after the growth of all the plants from the earth, after the earth's taking its own form, so that afterwards no one could say that without this force these things would not have been brought forth from the earth. Hence it shows you everything completed before the creation of this body lest you attribute the production of the crops to it instead of to the Creator of all things, the one who said from the beginning, "Let the earth bring forth a crop of vegetation."

(13) But if they were to say that the sun's virtue also contributes to the ripening of the crops, I would not gainsay them. After all, it's similar to the case of the farmer: in saying he contributes to the processes of the soil, I don't ascribe everything to him: even if thousands of farmers did their best, their efforts would be fruitless unless the One initiating the process through his own design from the beginning willed to put in train the very creation of the crops. In exactly the same way, I say, even if after the farmer's work there is assistance from the work of the sun, and the moon and the mildness of the climate, this would likewise be to no effect unless the hand from above did not play its part; once, however, this mighty hand is ready, the work of the elements makes its most efficacious contribution.

(14) Give close attention to this so as to bridle those still intent on deceiving themselves, and have nothing to do with assigning to creatures the honor due to the Creator. Accordingly, Sacred Scripture not only shows us the sun's beauty, and immensity and usefulness in the words, "It beams like a bridegroom, like a giant in running its course," but also its limitations and powerlessness: listen to what it says elsewhere, "What could provide more light than the sun? Yet even it fails." [Sirach 17:31] Don't be deceived by appearances, it tells us: unless the Creator willed so to direct, it would disappear as though it had never existed. If pagan peoples had understood this, they would not have fallen victim to such deception, but would properly have seen that from contemplation of created things one should move on to the Creator. Accordingly, he created it on the fourth day lest you think it is the cause of the day. In other words, what we said about the plants we will say also about the day, namely, that three days occurred before the creation of the sun. The Lord wanted to

make daylight more brilliant by means of this heavenly body also – something we would say is true in the case of the lesser light as well, by which I mean the moon; after all, three nights occurred before its creation. Still, once created, the moon makes its own contribution, banishing the gloom of the night and accomplishing (you could almost say) the same things the sun does in other respects.

(15) I mean, the sun was designed "for governing the day," the moon "for governing the night." What is meant by "for governing the day" and "for governing the night"? The text implies the sun took control of the day and the moon of the night, so that the sun should render the day brighter with its rays, and the moon should dissipate the gloom and with its light provide the human race with the possibility of discharging their duties. I mean, by this arrangement the traveller travels the path in confidence, the sailor steers the boat and navigates the seas, and everyone conducting personal affairs can without any concern follow the dictates of individual intuition.

(16) Then, after teaching us the usefulness of these lights, the text goes on: "And the stars: God placed them in the firmament of heaven to shine on the earth for governing the day and the night and to separate the light from the darkness." Notice how he made clear to us their usefulness also: "He placed them in the firmament of heaven," it says. What is the meaning of, "He placed"? As though to say "He fixed"? By no means; after all, we often see them traverse a mighty span in the twinkling of an eye, never standing still in one place but following their own course which they have been directed to run by the Lord. So what does "He placed" mean? It is equivalent to saying he directed them to be in heaven. You can, in fact, see Scripture leading up to this when it says elsewhere, "He placed Adam in paradise," not because he had fixed him in paradise but because he directed him to be in paradise. By the same token, about the stars we would say that he directed them to be in the firmament of heaven and shed their light on the earth. I mean, dearly beloved, consider this: would it not be more pleasing to see heaven studded with stars at midnight than any number of fields and gardens, the sky adorned with a range of stars as though with flowers, and the stars themselves shedding light on the earth? This, after all, is what they were designed for, shining on the earth and governing the day and the night, which is generally true of the great lights also. Remember, when it taught us the creation

of the two lights and the stars, it used these words in common about them all: "For governing the day and the night, and separating the light from the darkness." You see, just as you can't spy the stars moving in the sky during the day (the sun, of course, concealing their strength with its great brilliance), so too during the night the sun would never be visible, since the moon is sufficient with its light to dispel the gloom of night; each of the heavenly bodies keeps to its own boundaries and never oversteps its due measure, but rather maintains the Lord's design and fulfils its proper purpose.

(17) Who could tell all the other advantages conferred on the human race through the usefulness of these lights and the stars? The text says, remember, "'Let them act as signs, and indicate days, seasons and years.'" What is meant by 'act as signs, and indicate days, seasons and years'? Sacred Scripture wants to teach us that the movement of these bodies conveys to us the knowledge of times, the changing of solstices, the number of the days, and the course of the year, and from these facts we can fathom everything. The navigator, for example, with his eyes on the path of these bodies, gazing intently at the sky and studying all these signs carefully, is thus able to hold his course and cross the sea; though the night is often black, he can steer by the sight of the stars, and through his own skill bring safety to his company. The farmer, too, knows how to learn from these signs when he must sow the seed, till the soil, do the ploughing, and when sharpen the sickle and set about harvesting the crops. Not a few aids for our daily living are contributed to us by the knowledge of times, the number of the days, and the cycle of the year; and you would find many advantages for human existence stemming from these created things, which it would be impossible to enumerate fully in a precise manner. Hence the need to learn from these few details how to estimate the usefulness of the heavenly bodies, to marvel at their creation and adore and praise their Creator, to be aghast at his ineffable love shown to human beings; for humanity alone and for no other reason did he create everything, intending a little later to place them like some king or ruler over other things created by him.

(18) The text goes on: "God saw that it was good." Do you see how each day Sacred Scripture shows him satisfied with his creatures so as to undercut a pretext of people daring to find fault with the

things created by him? I mean, for the reason that Sacred Scripture with this purpose in mind registers the same point in every case, it becomes clear by dint of repetition. After all, it would have been enough following all the acts of creation to say once that everything he had made was very good; but knowing the extent of the limitations of our reasoning, he repeats the process each time, to teach us that everything was created with a certain inventive wisdom and ineffable love.

(19) "Evening came," the text goes on, "and morning came: a fourth day." In other words, when he had completed the arrangement of heaven; beautifying it with the stars and creating those two great lights, he brought the day to a close: "Evening came, and morning: a fourth day," says Scripture. Notice how it speaks in this way in the case of each day, wanting to rivet the sacred truths in our mind by the repetition in the teaching.

(20) Accordingly, let us carve these truths across our heart and hold fast to them, let us shake off all sloth, let us cling carefully to these salutary truths and with all forbearance instruct people ensnared in pagan error not to confuse this order by deserting the Creator to worship the creatures that have been created for our welfare and utility. I mean, even if pagans shout and scream a thousand times, I will proclaim it from the housetops that all these things were created for the human race, since the Creator is sufficient of himself and needed none of them; instead, it was to show his love for us that he created them all, demonstrating the great regard he has for the human race, and it was for us to move from these creatures to bring to him a proper adoration.

(21) After all, how great would be the folly of stumbling over the beauty of these creatures and remaining at their level, instead of raising the eyes of our minds to their Creator and believing the words of blessed Paul: "From the creation of the world what is invisible to our eyes in God has through created things become perceptible to our understanding." What do you mean, O human being? Do you see the sky and marvel at its beauty, at the variety of the stars, at their utter brilliance? Don't stop there, but lead your mind on to their Creator. Again, the sun's light astonishes you, and the sight of the great usefulness it has stirs you to amazement, and when you see its rays shining on your eyes, you marvel at the beauty of this heavenly body.

But don't stop there, either: consider instead that if the creature is so wonderful and incredible, surpassing all human understanding, what on earth can he be like who creates this merely by a word of command? Consider the very same in the case of the earth too: when you see the earth adorned with flowers like some multicolored garment, the foliage of plants enveloping it all over, don't think this is due spontaneously to the earth's power, or to the energy of the sun, or the moon; realize instead, as wisdom suggests, that for the creation of these things he simply spoke the word, "'Let the earth put forth a crop of vegetation,'" and forthwith the whole face of the earth was brilliant color.

Homily 7 – "God said: 'Let the waters produce reptiles with living souls, and on the earth winged creatures flying across the firmament of heaven.' This is what happened. God made the huge sea monsters, and every single living reptile of various kinds produced by the waters."

(7) But so much by way of introduction. Come now, let us spread a spiritual table before you by laying out before you, dear people, what has been read, and let us see if we can learn what it is today, too, the blessed Moses wants to teach us – or rather the Holy Spirit through his tongue. So what does the text say? "God said, 'Let the waters produce reptiles with living souls, and on the earth winged creatures flying across the firmament of heaven.' This is what happened." See the Lord's loving-kindness, how by a certain order and sequence he teaches us about every created thing. First he taught us how at his command he awakened the earth to produce fruits; then he taught us about the creation of the two lights; he added also the range of stars, through which the beauty of heaven was made more brilliant.

(8) Today finally he switches to the waters and shows us from them living beings coming at his word and command. The text says, remember, "'Let the waters produce reptiles with living souls, and on the earth winged creatures flying across the firmament of heaven.'" What words, tell us, can do justice to that marvel? What tongue can measure up to the praise of the Creator? He simply said, "'Let the earth put forth,'" and immediately he awakened it to birth pangs; now he says, "'Let the waters produce.'" See how his directions cor-

respond: in one case, the text says, "'Let it put forth,'" in this case, "'Let the waters produce reptiles with living souls.'" You see, just as in the case of the earth he simply said, "'Let it put forth,'" and there appeared a wide-ranging variety of flowers and plants and seeds, all created by one word, so too in this case he said, "'Let the waters produce reptiles with living souls,'" and there were created on the earth winged creatures flying across the firmament of heaven (and all of a sudden such kinds of reptiles and such variety of birds as to beggar counting.)

(9) While it was one word, and a short one, the kinds of living things were many and varied. But don't be astonished, dearly beloved; after all, it was God's word, and his word endowed those creatures with life. Do you see how he brings everything from non-being to being? Did you see the precision of the teaching? Did you see the considerateness of the Lord, and how far he demonstrates it in regard to our human race? I mean, how would we have been able to know these things precisely had not he in his really unspeakable love deemed it proper to teach humanity through the tongue of the biblical author, so that we might know the order of created things and the power of the Creator, and how his word took effect, and his utterance endowed creatures with life and the way to existence?

(10) Yet there are some stupid people who, despite this kind of teaching, are rash enough to withhold belief, and do not admit that these visible things have a creator. Some of them hold they came into existence by themselves, others that they were formed from some underlying matter. See the extent of the devil's wiles, how he exploits the facile thinking of people in the thrall of error. For that reason the blessed Moses, inspired by the divine Spirit, teaches us with great precision, lest we fall victim to the same things as they, instead of being able to know clearly both the sequence of created things and how each thing was created. You see, if God in his care for our salvation had not directed the tongue of the biblical author in this way, it would have been sufficient to say that God made heaven and earth, the sea and living things, and not add the order of the days, nor what was created first and what later. But, lest he leave any grounds for excuse to those bent on folly, he explains in this way both the order of created things and the number of the days, and he teaches us everything with great considerateness so that we may learn the whole truth

and not turn our minds to the error of those uttering all these ideas from their own reasoning. But we are able to know the ineffable power of our creator.

(11) "This is what happened," the text says. He said: "'Let the waters produce reptiles with living souls, and on the earth winged creatures flying across the firmament of heaven,'" and the elements obeyed, and carried out what was commanded. "It happened," the text goes on, "just as the Lord commanded. God made the huge sea monsters and every single living reptile which the waters produced in a range of kinds, and every winged creature according to kind. God saw that they were good, and God blessed them in these words: 'Increase and multiply and fill the waters in the seas, and let birds multiply on the earth.'" Notice here again, I ask you, the extent of the Spirit's wisdom. I mean, the blessed Moses, after saying, "This is what happened," teaches us by adding one detail at a time in the words, "God made the huge sea monsters, and every single living reptile which the waters produced in a range of kinds, and every winged creature according to kind. God saw that they were good."

Here once more he takes the ground from under those rash enough to speak always heedlessly. That is, lest anyone be able to say, Why did he make the sea monsters? What good are they to us? What is the advantage of their creation? Of set purpose he first said, "God made the huge sea monsters, and every single living reptile, and the birds," and immediately added, "God saw that they were good." In other words, he is saying, although you stand in ignorance of the reason for the created things, don't presume to find fault with their creation. Having heard the Lord give his approval and declare them good, how can you be so demented as to dare to ask, Why were they made? Are you scorning their creation as pointless? I mean, if you were well disposed you would be able from the creation of these things to get an insight into the power of your Lord and his ineffable love – his power, for the reason that he caused living beings like this to be created from the waters by his word and command, and his love, for the reason that in creating them he gave each of them a particular place, and assigned them a boundless area of the sea so that they might not hinder one another but dwell in the waters and provide an example to teach us the Creator's extraordinary power and cause no harm to the human race.

(12) Do you think that it is an insignificant mark of love that a twofold benefit comes to you from these creatures? They do, after all, lead those of us willing to think aright, to the knowledge of God and cause us to be amazed at the greatness of his loving kindness in freeing the human race from the harm brought on itself. You see, it was not simply for our use that everything was created by him, but on account of his great prodigality: while some things were created for our use, others had this purpose – that the power of their Creator might be proclaimed. So, when you hear that "God saw that it was good," presume no longer to contradict Sacred Scripture, nor bury your head in idle speculation with questions why this or that was made. "God blessed them," the text says, "and said, 'Increase and multiply and fill the waters in the seas, and let the birds multiply on the earth.'" This is the blessing, that they should grow to a great number. You see, since the creatures he made had life in them, he wanted their life to be lasting. Hence the text added: "God blessed them and said, 'Increase and multiply.'" That word, you know, influences them right up to the present, and has spanned such an extent of time without one of those species being diminished. After all, God's blessing and the form of words, "'Increase and multiply,'" bestowed on them life and permanence.

(13) "Evening came and morning came: a fifth day." Do you see how Sacred Scripture taught us also the living things created on the fifth day? Well, just wait a while and you will see once again the loving kindness of your Lord. I mean, he not merely quickened the waters to birth of living things, but also directed land creatures in their turn to be produced from the earth. In other words, today it is hardly inappropriate to arrive at the things made on the sixth day as well. The text says: "God said: 'Let the earth bring forth living things in their various kinds, four-footed creatures, reptiles, wild beasts on the earth, cattle and all the reptiles of the earth in their various kinds.'" And it was so done. See the earth also for a second time producing twofold fruit, and doing the Lord's bidding. On the first occasion, remember, it brought forth a crop of seeds, but on this occasion living beings, four-footed creatures, reptiles, wild beasts and cattle. Notice that this instance demonstrates what I told you in ad-

vance, that it wasn't simply for our use that he produced all these things; instead, it was also for our benefit in the sense that we might see the overflowing abundance of his creatures and be overwhelmed at the Creator's power, and be in a position to know that all these things were produced by a certain wisdom and ineffable love out of regard for the human being that was destined to come into being.

(14) "God made the wild beasts of the earth in their various kinds," the text says, "cattle in their various kinds, and all the reptiles in their various kinds. God saw that they were good." Where now are those people rash enough to ask, What's the point of wild beasts? Of reptiles? Let them listen to the words of Sacred Scripture: "God saw that they were good." Tell me, the Creator himself commends the created things, and do you dare to call them in question. Would this attitude stop short at any madness? Admittedly, in the case of the seeds and the plants the earth has produced not only fruitbearing trees but also those giving no fruit, and brings forth not only crops that are profitless but also some that are strange to us and ones that are in many cases harmful. But no one will presume to find fault with their creation on that account; after all, they have not been produced without rhyme or reason. I mean, they would not have received commendation from the Lord had they not been created to serve some need. So the comparison is clear: in the case of the trees not all are fruitbearing; many bear no fruit and yet even they provide no less a remarkable service to us and contribute to our well-being; we make our houses from them and gain many other advantages contributing to our well-being. So, by and large, there is nothing which has been created without some reason, even if human nature is incapable of knowing precisely the reason for them all.

(15) In like manner, therefore, as with the trees, so too with the wild beasts: some are useful for our food, others for serving us. The species of wild beasts and reptiles, too, are of no little help to us, and if somebody is prepared to study them in a right mind, he will find even now, when control over them has been wrested from us owing to the disobedience of the first human creature, that the benefit is great that comes to us from them. I mean, physicians get from them many things which they employ as medications capable of promoting the health of our bodies. Otherwise, what great harm would have come

from the creation of the wild beasts at a time when they, like domestic animals, were intended to come under the control of the creature soon to be created. In fact, it is time I spoke about this.

(16) Now, with a view to your learning the surpassing love of the Lord of all displayed in regard to our human race, consider the way he stretched out heaven, unfolded the earth, created the firmament like a dividing wall making a separation in the waters, then directed the joining of the waters to happen, called one part seas and the dry part earth, next he beautified the latter with the proliferation of seeds and later with crops. Further, he went on to the creation of the two great lights and the variety of stars through which he added to the beauty of heaven. Then he produced from the waters the living beings and on the earth winged creatures flying across the firmament of heaven; and after completing the number of five days, since it was necessary for living beings to be created from the earth, he directed these to be brought forth, some suitable for food, others useful for our service, as well as wild beasts and reptiles. Then finally, after arranging everything in order, by imposing an appropriate order and design on all visible things, preparing a lavish table filled with rich and varied viands, laden with wealth and abundance, and making what might be called kingdoms above and below, conspicuous from all points and gleaming with variety – then finally he creates the being meant to enjoy all these things, giving this creature power over all these visible things. And as a demonstration of the degree to which this creature about to be fashioned is more elevated than all the other creatures, he bids everything he has made come under this creature's authority and supervision.

(17) Lest, however, we draw out the sermon to a great length, let us be content with what we have said and postpone to the next occasion what has to do with the fashioning of this wonderful being graced with reason and spirit – I mean, the human being. Now we will address to you the customary exhortation so as to preserve the remembrance of the things said, and also, through all the things seen, to stir ourselves to praise of the Lord. The fact that we do not attain this, nor manage to grasp the meaning of 'created things,' should not become for us grounds for unbelief but rather an occasion of praise. You see, when reasoning fails and the intellect proves inadequate, call to your mind the greatness of the Lord, especially from the fact that

his power is such that we fail to understand precisely the meaning of the things made by him. This is the attitude of sensible minds and sober hearts.

(18) When the pagans in this regard fell into error by entrusting everything to their own reasoning and refusing to acknowledge the limitations of their own nature, they let their imagination run riot, exceeded the measure of their own capabilities, and lost the sense of the status they could lay claim to. In other words, though they were elevated by the gift of reason and received such a pre-eminence from the Lord, outranking all other visible creatures in esteem, these people were cast into such stupidity as to worship dogs, monkeys, crocodiles and lowlier animals than these. Why mention brute beasts? Many of them fell into such folly and stupidity as to worship even onions and more worthless things than that. Hence the biblical author had these people in mind when he said: "He was likened to the brute beasts and resembled them." The one who was dignified with the gift of reason, it means, and endowed with such great wisdom has become like the brutes, and even worse. That is to say, those beasts, being without the gift of reason, are not liable to punishment, whereas the creature dignified with reason and yet taking on their condition of irrationality will properly incur heavy penalties for being ungrateful for such liberality. Following this extreme they went on to call sticks and stones gods, and divinized all the visible elements; once, you see, they strayed from the right path, they tell headlong and were cast into the very depths of wickedness.

(19) Let us, however, not give up hope of their salvation; on the contrary, let us bring to the fore what we have to offer and converse with them in a spirit of great zeal and long-suffering, showing them also the absurdity of their behavior and the enormity of its harmfulness. Let us never despair of their salvation. In fact, it is likely that with the passage of time they will be convinced, especially if we live in such a way as to offer them no scandal. I mean, when many of them see some of our associates who bear the name of Christian and lay claim to it, playing the robber like themselves, being guilty of avarice and envy, plotting and scheming, committing all sorts of crimes, victims of luxury and gluttony, no longer do they heed the advice from our lips: they consider all we have to offer is deception,

and that everyone is guilty of the same faults. So think carefully, I beg you, of the severity of the punishments such people have become liable to in not only heaping burning coals on their own heads but also being responsible for the fact that others are stuck fast in error and block their ears to instruction in virtue, as well as putting in the devil's way people in quest of virtue, and – what is worse than everything – being responsible for blasphemy against the Lord by these people. Do you see the extent of the harm caused by this evil? Do you see how people render themselves liable not to normal punishment but to extreme severity, especially as they are fated to bear the guilt of all, not only for their own damnation, but for the scandal caused to those in error, the condemnation of people bent on virtue, and the blasphemies directed against God?

(20) So then, let us keep all this in mind and not neglect our own salvation; let us give careful attention to living a life of God's wanting, in the knowledge that on the basis of this most of all will we be either condemned or judged worthy of loving kindness at his hands. Accordingly, let us so perform every action as to pass our lives with a good conscience and lead towards the truth by means of our godly life-style those people still in error. Then all the others associated with us may because of us enjoy a good name, our Lord may be glorified above all and may take closer care of us. You see, when, at the sight of us, people are edified and give praise to God, we enjoy greater favor in his sight. After all, what could be more blessed than the person who lives in such a fashion that all who witness it are amazed and declare, "Glory to you, O God! What marvellous people Christians are! What wonderful philosophy they give evidence of! How low their esteem for the things of this world! how insubstantial all things are considered to be by them – like shadows and dreams – and how little attached they are to anything in this visible world, treating everything like people living in exile, longing each day for release from this world!" What great recompense do you think these words bring to people living in this fashion, even here and now from God? Actually, the really remarkable thing is that even those who have this opinion of us will desist from their error and come back to the truth. It is quite clear how much encouragement this provides for the kind of people in that situation.

(21) Accordingly, knowing as we do that we are responsible both for the salvation of our neighbors and their loss, let us so regulate our life as not only to be sufficient for ourselves but also to prove an occasion of instruction to others, so that we may draw down on us here and now favor from God, and may in the future enjoy God's loving kindness in generous measure, thanks to the grace and mercy of his only-begotten Son, to whom with the Father and the Holy Spirit be glory, power and honor, now and forever, for ages of ages. Amen.

Homily 8 – "God said: 'Let us make a human being in our image and likeness. Let them have control of the fish of the sea and the birds of heaven, the cattle and the wild beasts, all the earth and all the reptiles creeping upon the earth.'"

(3) Since, therefore, this exercise proves an occasion of greater wealth and abundance for us, and you are insatiable in regard to this spiritual nourishment, come now, let us see what it is today also blessed Moses is teaching us through the text we've read, or rather what the grace of the Spirit has to say to us all through his tongue. "God said," the text goes on, "'Let us make a human being in our image and likeness.'" Let us not rush idly by what is said, dearly beloved; instead, let us investigate each expression, get right to the depth of its meaning, and divine the force concealed in these brief phrases. I mean, although the words may be few, immense is the treasure concealed in them; we must remain alert and vigilant and not stop short at the surface. Likewise with people endeavoring to dig up this material treasure: they don't simply dig around on the ground or study the surface; instead, they go right to the bottom and penetrate to the bowels of the earth, and thus separate the gold from the soil through their own skill, and despite much toil and sweat manage to find just a few nuggets. In our case it is nothing like that: the effort is small, the yield beyond telling. Such, you see, are all spiritual realities.

(4) Accordingly, let us not be found wanting by comparison with those who get excited about material things; let us in our turn search diligently for this spiritual treasure stored up in these words. Let us see first what is the new and surprising element in the words, and why the blessed author employed such a novel turn of phrase – or rather

the loving God through the speech of the author. The text says: "'Let us make a human being in our image and likeness.'" A little time before, remember, we heard him saying, after the creation of heaven and earth, "'Let light be made'" and "'Let a firmament be made in the middle of the water;'" and again, "'Let the water be gathered together into one mass, and let the dry land appear,'" and "'Let lights be made,'" and "'Let the waters produce reptiles with living souls.'" Did you see the whole of creation made in those five days merely by word and command? Notice today how great the difference in the words. That is, no longer does it say, Let a human being be created. Instead, what? "'Let us make a human being in our image and likeness.'" What is new in this? What is strange? Who on earth is this creature now being made whose making required in the Creator such planning and care? Don't be surprised, dearly beloved. I mean, the human being is the creature more important than all the other visible beings, and for this creature all the others have been produced – sky, earth, sea, sun, moon, stars, the reptiles, the cattle, all the brute beasts.

(5) Why is it, you ask, that if this creature is more important than all these, it is brought forth after them? A good question. Let me draw a comparison with a king on the point of entering a city on a visit: his bodyguard has to be sent on ahead to have the palace in readiness, and thus the king may enter his palace. Well now, in just the same way in this case the Creator, as though on the point of installing some king and ruler over everything on earth, first erected the whole of this scenery, and then brought forth the one destined to preside over it, showing us through the created things themselves what importance he gave to this creature.

(6) But let us put a question to a few, and see what he says to that verse, "'Let us make a human being in our image.'" The words, after all, are from Moses, whom they claim to believe, but in fact do not believe. As Christ says, "'If you believed Moses, you would believe me.'" While, however, the words remain with them, their true meaning remains with us. So to whom is the phrase addressed, "'Let us make a human being,'" and to whom does the Lord propose this plan? Not because he has need of plan and consideration – perish the thought; instead, he intends through the pretext of words to indicate the surpassing importance which he demonstrates in regard to the human creature. What then do they say, these people who still have a

veil lying over their hearts and refuse to understand what is contained in these words?

(7) O what stupidity! What idiocy! What reason do you have for saying, human being that you are, that an angel is party to the counsels of the Lord, creatures sharing the Creator's thought? Not for angels is it to be party to the counsels of the Lord, but to stand in waiting and fulfil sacred ministry. To grasp this, listen to Isaiah, most articulate of the prophets, when he says about the angelic powers above that "I saw the Cherubim and the Seraphim standing at God's right hand; they kept covering their faces and feet with their wings." From which it is obvious that they could not bear the radiance beaming from that source, but stood in great fear and trembling. To stand in waiting before the Lord is, after all, proper to creatures. These people, however, who understand nothing of what is contained in the words, idly say the first thing that comes into their head. Hence it falls to us to refute their stupidity and teach the children of the Church the truth of the words.

(8) So who is this to whom he says, "'Let us make a human being'"? Who else is it than the Angel of Great Counsel, Wonderful Counsellor, figure of Authority, Prince of Peace, Father of the age to come, Only-begotten Son of God, like the Father in being, through whom all things were created? To him is said, "'Let us make a human being in our image and likeness.'" This text also deals a mortal blow to those entertaining the position of Arius. I mean, he did not say by way of command, Make such a creature, as though to a subordinate or to one inferior in being, but "'Let us make'" with great deference to an equal. And what follows shows us further the equality in being; it says, you see, "'Let us make a human being in our image and likeness.'" Here again, however, other heretics arise assailing the dogmas of the Church; they say, Look: he said, "'In our image'" – and from these words they want to speak of the divine in human terms, which is the ultimate example of error, namely, to cast in human form him who is without shape, without appearance, without change, and to attribute limbs and forms to the One who has no body. What could match this madness, people not simply refusing to derive any profit from the teaching of the inspired [*theopneustos*] Scriptures, but even incurring severe harm from them? I mean, they are in a

similar predicament to people who are ill and suffering impairment of their bodily vision: just as the latter have a revulsion for the sunlight on account of their weakness of vision and invalids turn away from the healthier foods, so too those ailing in spirit and handicapped in their mind's vision have lost the power to look directly at the light of truth.

(9) So let us do for them what lies in our power and offer them a helping hand, conversing with them in a spirit of great kindness. Blessed Paul, after all, encouraged us to do this when he said, "Instruct your adversaries with gentleness, in the hope that God will grant them a change of heart leading to knowledge of truth, and they may return to a sober mind and escape from the snare of the devil, by whom they were held as captives at his pleasure." Do you see how he declared in the words he chose that they were overcome, as it were, by some drunken stupor? To say, "return to a sober mind," after all, suggested they were in a state of intoxication. Likewise he says, "held captive by the devil," as though to say they are ensnared in traps. What is required of us is much kindness and tolerance so as to be able to rescue them and lead them out of the devil's snares. So let us say to them, Make your escape slowly but surely, look towards the light of righteousness, study the precision of the words. You see, in saying, "'Let us make a human being in our image and likeness,'" he did not stop there, but through the following verse made clear to us what was the reason for choosing the word "image." What in fact does the text go on to say? "'Let them have control of the fish of the sea, the birds of heaven, and all the reptiles creeping on the earth.'" So "image" refers to the matter of control, not anything else, in other words, God created the human being as having control of everything on earth, and nothing on earth is greater than the human being, under whose authority everything falls.

(10) Yet if, despite such great precision in terms, there are still those spoiling for a fight who would want to say "image" is used in terms of form, we will say to them: that means he is not only man but also woman, for both have the same form. But this would make no sense. I mean, listen to Paul's words: "It is not proper for a man to cover his head, being image and glory of God, whereas the woman is man's glory." One is in command, the other is subordinate, just as God had also said to woman from the beginning, "your yearning will

be for your husband, and he will be your master." You see, since it is on the basis of command that the image was received and not on the basis of form, man commands everything whereas woman is subservient – hence Paul's words about man, that he is constituted God's image and glory, whereas woman is man's glory. If, however, he had been speaking about form, he would not have distinguished between them, man and woman being identical in type, after all.

(11) Do you see the full truth of it, how he left us no grounds for defense on the part of those bent on being brazen? All the same, even if this is the situation, let us not desist from our patience in dealing with these people, "in the hope that God will grant them a change of heart leading to knowledge of truth." So let us not slacken in our efforts to show great kindness, in the expectation of being able to wrest them from the devil's deceit; and let us, if we think fit, propose to them blessed Paul's words addressed to the citizens of Athens: "We ought not think the deity is like gold, silver, or stone, or carving from man's skill or imagination." Do you notice the wise teacher, with how much precision he disposes of every error of theirs? I mean, he says not only that the deity is to be distinguished from bodily figure but that human imagining could not shape anything of the kind.

(12) Argue the point with them constantly on these matters and don't desist from bringing them to their attention in the hope that they may yield, in the hope that they may agree to look at the full face of truth. And while not desisting from debate with them in a spirit of great kindness and certainty, hold fast yourselves, I urge you, to the dogmas of the Church with close attention, without confusing the drift of the expression. Instead, argue the point in friendly exchange with Jews, on the one hand, showing them the words have reference not to some one of the ministering powers but to the only-begotten Son of God himself; to those holding Arian views, on the other hand, prove from this text the Son's equality with the Father; and to those imagining the deity has human form bring into play the words of blessed Paul. Root out those noxious ailments springing up like weeds among the dogmas of the Church, and at the same time see to it that religious teachings are strengthened in them.

Homily 9 – On what follows the verse, "'Let us make a human being in our image,'" and against those who ask, Why were the wild beasts created? And, What good comes from their being made? And to prove that this most of all shows regard for the human being and God's unspeakable love

(3) Accordingly, dearly beloved, knowing this as you do, purify your thinking of the affairs of this life, open wide the horizons of your mind, welcome with great enthusiasm what the Spirit furnishes us with, so that like rich and fruitful soil you may produce a crop in excess of what is sown – in one case a hundredfold, in another sixtyfold, in another thirtyfold. You heard on the previous days of the ineffable wisdom of the artificer of all visible realities, and how he produced everything solely by his word and desire. He said, remember, "'Let it be made,'" and it was made, and immediately all the elements were produced; his word sufficed for the sustenance of all created things, not simply because it was a word but because it was God's word.

(4) You recall the arguments we brought to bear against those saying that existing things came into being from underlying matter and substituting their own folly for the dogmas of the Church. You learnt why, on the one hand, he produced the sky in finished form, but left the earth shapeless and incomplete. We gave you, remember, at that point two reasons for this: firstly, so that you might learn the power of the Lord from the more complete thing and not waver in your reasoning with the thought that it was created out of lack of power; and secondly, since the earth has been created as mother and nurse for us, and from it we are nourished and enjoy all other things, and to it we return in the end, being as it is for us all both homeland and tomb, he shows it to us shapeless from the beginning in case the very pressure of necessity, it nothing else, should lead us to conjure up some grandiose ideas about it, instead of learning even through these very things that all the above-mentioned advantages are to be attributed no longer to the nature of the earth but to the power of the Creator. Again, you learnt how he effected the separation of the waters by providing for the creation of this visible firmament; you saw the living beings arising both from the waters and from the earth.

Homily 10 – An exhortation to those ashamed to attend the evening congregation after eating; and from the verse, "'Let us make a human being in our image and likeness,'" up to the verse, "God made the human being; in God's image he made them; male and female he made them."

(7) You are quite well aware, of course, and recall to mind that we began to talk about the shaping of the human being, but were pressed for time and could not complete the whole lecture; instead we finished the instruction to do with the account of the wild beasts, showing that at first the human being had control over them and then lost it through the sin of disobedience. Hence today we want to complete the balance for you, and thus send you off. For the purpose of making the story clear to you, however, you need to recall where it was we broke off our teaching, so that we can begin from that point and thus complete the rest. So where did we interrupt our sermon? We were speaking on the verse, "'Let us make a human being in our image and likeness, and let them have control over the fish of the sea and the birds of heaven;'" the sermon developed into great length and a vast sea of thoughts arose before us, so that it was possible for us to proceed no further, but we stopped short at that point and reached onto none of what follows.

Sacred Scripture, in any case, directly added the following: "God made the human being; in God's image he made them; male and female he made them. God blessed them with the words, 'Increase and multiply, fill the earth and gain dominion over it; have control of the fish of the sea, the birds of heaven and all the cattle, the whole earth and all the reptiles creeping on the earth.'" The words are brief, but the treasure concealed in the brief words is great. You see, speaking through the Spirit this blessed author wants at this point to teach us something kept from human hearing. When he said, remember, "'Let us make a human being,'" the Creator of all applied his will, as it were, and his thought in demonstrating through this shape the importance given to the creature in process of formation, something he began to teach us before the process began.

He also demonstrated the greatness of the control he was entrusting to the being in process of creation; hence, to his words, "'Let us make a human being in our image and likeness,'" he added, "'Let them have control of the fish of the sea.'" See how he reveals to us from the beginning the treasure hidden there. I mean, the biblical author, speaking through the divine Spirit, sees as subsisting and brought into being things not yet subsisting. So why, tell me, after his words, "'Let us make a human being,'" does he now say, "'Let *them* have control'"? Evidently he is already revealing to us at this point some mystery lying hidden. Who are to have control? Quite clearly he has spoken this way to hint at the formation of woman. Do you see how there is nothing in Sacred Scripture which is contained there idly or to no purpose?" Instead, even the chance word has treasure stored up in it.

(8) Don't be surprised, dearly beloved, at what I've said. Such, after all, is the way with all the biblical authors, to speak of things not yet created as though already created. You see, since they perceive with the eyes of the spirit things due to happen after a great number of years, and accordingly view things as though already laid out in front of their very eyes, they describe everything in this way. To gain a clear understanding of this, listen to the words of blessed David prophesying in loud tones the events of Christ's crucifixion so many generations before the event: "They pierced my hands and my feet," and again, "They divided up my garments among themselves." Do you see how ahead of time he announces, as though already happened, things due to take place much later?

In this way, too, our blessed author gives us a hint about the formation of woman when he says cryptically, "'Let them have control of the fish of the sea.'" Then, going on, he says further in a clearer way, "God made the human being; in God's image he made them; male and female he made them." Notice how much precision he employs, saying the same thing once and again so that the words could be riveted in the minds of the listeners. You see, if this had not been an object of concern for him, it would have been enough to say, "God made the human being;" but he adds as well, "In God's image he made them." In other words, after teaching us through the previous verses what was the meaning of "in God's image," accordingly again at this point he repeats the very same notion by saying, "In God's image he made them." Lest he should leave some brazen pretext of controversy to those intent on contesting the Church's dogmas, he presses on a little further and teaches the same things again, that God employed the word "image" in the sense of controlling and having all creatures under subjection.

Finally let us see what he is saying in this verse, "God made the human being; in God's image he made them; male and female he made them." What he hinted at above when saying, "'Let them have control,'" here he says more clearly, though he still teaches us this cryptically, since after all he has not yet taught us about the manner of formation or told us where woman comes from. He says, "Male and female he made them." Do you see how he describes what is not yet created as though already created? That's the way, you see, with the eyes of the spirit; I mean, these bodily eyes cannot see visible things in the same way that the eyes of the spirit can see things that are not visible and things that have no subsistence.

(9) So, after saying, "Male and female he made them" as though to bestow a blessing on each of them, he goes on, "God blessed them in the words, 'Increase and multiply, fill the earth and gain dominion over it, and have control of the fish of the sea.'" Behold the remarkable character of the blessing! I mean, those words, "'Increase and multiply and fill the Barth,'" anyone could see are said of the brute beasts and the reptiles alike, whereas "'Gain dominion and have control'" are directed to the man and woman. See the Lord's loving-kindness: even before creating her he makes her sharer in this control and bestows on her the blessing. "'Have control,'" the text says, "'of the fish of the sea, the birds of heaven and all the cattle, the whole earth and all the reptiles creeping on the earth.'" Did you notice the ineffable authority? Did you notice all created things placed under this being's control? No longer entertain casual impressions of this rational being, but rather realize the extent of the esteem and the Lord's benignity towards it, and be amazed at his love beyond all telling.

(10) "God said: 'Lo, I have given you every crop upon all the earth bearing seed fit for sowing, and every tree containing fruit with seed fit for sowing; they are for your food. And for all the beasts of the earth, all the birds of heaven and every reptile creeping on the earth – whatever has a spirit of life in it – I have given every green crop for food.' This is what happened." See, I ask you, dearly beloved, the precision of the words and the Lord's ineffable love, and do not pass heedlessly by anything of what is said. "God said," the text reads, "'Lo, I have given you every crop for sowing,'" as though the

remark – even this one – is addressed to two people, despite the fact the woman is not yet produced. Then, in order that you may learn his surpassing goodness, see how the signs of his love do not stop short at the man and the woman still to be produced but reach to the very beasts: after saying to the human beings, "'They are for your food,'" he added, "'And for all the beasts of the earth.'"

(11) See again further depths of his loving-kindness: he showed concern not only for the tame beasts that meet our needs for food and service but also for the wild beasts. Who could adequately arrive at the extent of this boundless goodness? "'They are for your food,'" the text says. "'And for all the beasts of the earth, all the birds of heaven and every reptile creeping on the earth – whatever has a spirit of life in it – I have given every green crop for food.'" The Lord's care for the human being created by him emerges in all its fulness. I mean, after producing; him and entrusting him with complete control of creation, the good Lord took steps to prevent his being distressed at once from the outset by the sight of the vast number of beasts through a feeling of being powerless to provide adequately for the nourishment of so many animals: before any such thought came to him about this, the Lord comforted him, so to say, by showing him that he along with all the brute beasts had plenty to eat, as the earth provided for their nourishment thanks to the Lord's direction. So, after saying, "'They are for your food,'" he immediately added, "'And for all the beasts of the earth, all the birds of heaven and every reptile creeping on the earth – whatever has a spirit of life in it I have given every green crop for food.' This is what happened."

(12) Whatever the Lord commanded, the text says, took effect, and he established everything in proper order – hence he immediately added, "God saw everything he had made, and behold, it was very good." Who could adequately extol the precision of Sacred Scripture? I mean, behold here, too, how by speaking one phrase, "God saw everything he had made," it curbed the tongue of all those endeavoring, despite all this evidence, to gainsay it. "God saw everything he had made," the text says, "and behold, it was very good." You see, after saying in the case of each of the created things, "God saw that it was good," at this point when everything was completed and the works of the sixth day had reached finality, and the being destined to enjoy all the created things had been brought forth in their midst, the

text says: "God saw everything he had made, and behold, it was very good."

Notice how by gathering all the created things together under this one word, "everything," it confers commendation on each of them. I mean, it didn't just say "everything" and stop there, but added "that he had made;" nor did it conclude at that point, but said, "And behold it was good," even "very good" – that is to say, "completely good." So when the Lord, the one bringing things from non-being to being, declares creatures to be good and completely good, who would dare, even if bursting with arrogant folly, to open his mouth and gainsay the words uttered by God? After all, amongst the visible creatures it was not only light that was created but also darkness in opposition to light, and not only day but also night in opposition to day. Amongst the growth springing up from the earth it was not only plants that are useful but also those that are harmful, and not only trees that bear fruit but also those that bear none; and not only tame animals but also wild and unruly ones. Amongst the creatures emerging from the waters it was not only fish but also sea monsters and other fierce creatures. It was not only inhabited land but also the unpeopled; not only level plains but also mountains and woods. Amongst birds it was not only tame ones and those suitable for our food but also wild and unclean ones, hawks and vultures and many others of that kind. Amongst the creatures produced from the earth it was not only tame animals but also snakes, vipers, serpents, lions and leopards. In the sky it was not only showers and kindly breezes but also hail and snow. And if anyone had a mind to examine the list in detail, you would find in each case not only things considered not useful to us but even harmful, so that no one would be free after this to survey created things and find fault with their origins, saying, What's the purpose of this one? What's the use of this one? This one's well made, but this other one not so. Hence, Sacred Scripture checks those people endeavoring to show ingratitude, you might say, by adding after the creation of everything on the sixth day, "God saw everything he had made, and behold, it was very good."

(13) What could match this for reliable comment, when the Creator of all gives the verdict in person and says that everything created is good, and even very good? So, whenever you see someone

moved by his own reasoning and intent on gainsaying Sacred Scripture, shun him like a lunatic; or better, don't shun him, but out of pity for his ignorance quote the words from Sacred Scripture and say that "God saw everything he had made" and said "'behold, it is very good,'" and perhaps you will be able to check his unruly tongue. After all, take the case of human affairs. When we see people of good reputation giving their opinion of things that happen, we don't contradict them, but rather fall in with their opinion and often prefer their opinion to our own. So much the more in the case of the God of all things, the Creator of everything we can see, should we do likewise: we should learn his judgement on things, subdue our own reasonings, and instead of presuming further we should be content with the knowledge that everything has been produced by a word coming from him and by his loving kindness, and that nothing has been created idly or to no purpose. Even if, through the limitations of our own reasoning, we should be in ignorance of created things, he himself in his own wisdom and thoughtful love produced all things.

(14) "Evening came," the text goes on, "and morning came: a sixth day." At the close of the sixth day he also brought to a close all his creating – hence the addition of the words, "Heaven and earth and all their array were completed.'" Notice the character of Sacred Scripture, nothing superfluous, nothing idle. Having mentioned the elements that were brought forth together, it goes into no further detail in mentioning the rest but simply says, "Heaven and earth and all their array were completed," referring by this means to everything on earth and in heaven.

(15) The earth's array, you see, is what is produced from it, the growth of plants, the harvest of fruits, the fruits of the trees, and all other things with which the Creator arrayed it; likewise the heaven's array is sun, moon, the variety of the stars, and everything else created in its midst. Hence, Sacred Scripture in mentioning heaven and earth included the whole of creation under those elements. "God completed on the sixth day," the text says, "the works he had done." Notice how it says the same thing twice over so that we might learn all the works of creation were done up to the sixth day. The text says, remember, "He completed on the sixth day the works he had done, and on the seventh day he rested from all the works he had done."

(16) What is the meaning of that verse, "On the seventh day he rested from all the works he had done"? Notice how Sacred Scripture narrates everything in human fashion even out of considerateness to us. I mean, it would not have been possible for us in any other way to understand anything of what was said had not such considerateness been thought fitting. The text says, remember, "On the seventh day God rested from all the works he had done." It says he stopped creating and bringing from non-being into being; he had produced everything he had to, after all, and had created the being destined to enjoy it. "God blessed the seventh day and sanctified it for the reason that on that day he rested from all the works God had begun to do." You see, when he stopped creating, he had out of his own loving kindness brought forth at his own command everything he had intended, and had brought creation to a close on the sixth day; there was nothing else he intended to produce on the seventh day for the reason that everything he intended had been fulfilled.

(17) Hence, in order that this day too might have some distinction and not seem to bear some inferiority through the fact that nothing was created then, he conferred a blessing on it. "God blessed the seventh day," the text says, "and sanctified it." So what does that mean – the rest were not blessed? Of course they were, the text says, but for them it was enough, instead of any blessing, to have created things brought forth each time; hence, whereas in their case it did not say, "He blessed them," in the case of the seventh alone it did say so and added, "and sanctified it." What is the meaning of "He sanctified it"? He set it apart. Then, to teach us the reason for saying "He sanctified it," Sacred Scripture added, "for the reason that on that day he rested from all the works God had begun to do." Already at this point from the outset God provides us with instruction in a cryptic manner, teaching us that he set aside the whole of one day in the cycle of the week and marked it off for the performance of spiritual works.

(18) In other words, this is the reason why the Lord, after completing all the works of creation in six days, bestowed blessing on the seventh and consecrated it – for the reason of his resting on that day from his works which he had begun to do. But once again at this stage I detect a mighty swell of ideas overwhelming you, and I have no wish to pass them by thoughtlessly. Instead, I want to make you

too sharers in these spiritual riches. What, then, is the question that arises for us at this point? While Sacred Scripture in this passage says that God rested from his works, in the Gospels Christ says, "My Father is at work up until now and I am at work." Does there not seem from the sequence of the expressions to be some contradiction in what is said? Perish the thought: there is nothing contradictory in the contents of Sacred Scripture You see, in saying at this point that God rested from his works, Scripture teaches us that he ceased creating and bringing from non-being into being on the seventh day, whereas Christ, in saying that "my father is at work up until now and I am at work," reveals his unceasing care for us: he calls "work" the maintenance of created things, bestowal of permanence on them, and governing of them through all time. If this wasn't so, after all, how would everything have subsisted, without the guiding hand above directing all visible things and the human race as well? It anyone in a spirit of great gratitude has a mind to survey everything, detail by detail, done for our benefit each day by the Creator of all things, you would find an abyss of loving kindness. I mean, what reasoning or what imagination would arrive at the unspeakable goodness which he displays for the race of human beings, making the sun rise on the evil and the good, sending rain upon just and unjust, and bestowing every other kind of good?

Homily 12 – On the sequel to creation: "This is the book about the origins of heaven and earth when they were created, on the day God made heaven and earth."

(3) The text says: "This is the book about the origins of heaven and earth when they were created, on the day God made heaven and earth, before any grass of the field appeared on the earth or any crop of the field sprouted. God, you see, had not sent rain on the earth, and there was no human being to till the soil; a spring used to flow out of the ground and water the whole face of the earth." Notice again, I ask you, the insight of this remarkable author, or rather the teaching of the Holy Spirit. I mean, after narrating to us detail by detail all the items of creation and going through the works of the six days, the creation of human beings and the authority granted them over all visible things, now he sums them all up in the words, "This is the book about the origins of heaven and earth when they were created." It is worth enquiring at this point why it is he calls it the book of heaven and

earth in view of the fact that the book contains many other things and teaches us about a greater number of matters – about the virtue of good people, about God's loving kindness and the considerateness he demonstrated in regard both to the first-formed human being and to the whole human race, and about a lot of other things it would be impossible to list right now. Don't be surprised, dearly beloved; after all, it is the custom with Holy Scripture not to describe everything to us in detail in every case but rather to begin with a summary of related items and to leave further detail to be considered by right-minded listeners as they take in what is said.

(4) So that you may learn this is the case, I will make it clear from the very verses just now read. What I refer to is this: notice Sacred Scripture taught us in detail in the preceding verses the creation of everything, but now, instead of mentioning them all, it says: "This is the book about the origins of heaven and earth when they were created, on the day God made heaven and earth," and so on. Do you see how it continues the whole account to heaven and earth, leaving us to get from them a sweeping view of all the other things? I mean, when it said heaven and earth, it included everything together in those words, both things on earth and things in heaven. So, just as in its account of created things it doesn't mention them all one by one but gives a summary of related items and makes no further attempt to describe them to us, so too it called the whole book the book about the origins of heaven and earth, even though it contains many other things, evidently leaving us to work out from the reference to these two that all visible things are of necessity contained in this book, both those in heaven and those on earth.

(5) "On the day God made heaven and earth," the text goes on, "before any grass of the field appeared on the earth or any crop of the field sprouted, since God, you see, had not sent rain on the earth, and there was no human being to till the soil; a spring used to flow out of the ground and water the whole face of the earth." Great is the treasure concealed in these brief words – hence the need for us to unfold the meaning of the text with great sagacity, under the guidance of God's grace, and to lead you to share in this spiritual wealth. The Holy Spirit, after all, in his foreknowledge of future events wishes to prevent anyone's being able to engage in controversy later on, and in

opposition to Sacred Scripture to set notions from their own reasoning against the dogmas of the Church; so now again, after teaching us the order of created things – what was created first and what second – and the fact that from the earth in compliance with the Lord's word and direction the earth produced plants and was stirred into pangs of fertility, without depending on the sun for assistance (how could it, after all, the sun not yet being created?) nor on the moisture from showers, nor on human labor (human beings, after all, not having been brought forth), accordingly once again he makes mention of all the items one by one so as to stop the unbridled tongue of people spoiling to make a show of their shamelessness.

(6) What in fact does he say? "On the day God made heaven and earth before any grass of the field appeared on the earth or any crop of the field sprouted. God, you see, had not sent rain on the earth, and there was no human being to till the soil; a spring used to flow out of the ground and water the whole face of the earth." He intends to convey the fact that by his word and direction things not existing previously were brought into existence, and what had not been, came into view all of a sudden. "Crop" means what springs from the soil: when it says "crop" it means plants of all kinds. And in teaching us about showers, again Sacred Scripture added, "God, you see, had not sent rain on the earth" – that is to say no showers had so far been sent from on high. And after this it finally shows us that there was no dependence on human labor either: "There was no human being," it says, remember, "to till the soil" – as if to shout aloud and tell everyone coming later: Listen to this and learn how everything springing from the earth was produced, and don't think it was all due to the care of people working the soil, nor attribute its birth pangs of fertility to them but to the word and direction given it from the beginning by the Creator. All this happens that you may learn that there was no dependence on the assistance of the other elements for the growth of its plants; instead, what was required was the direction of the Creator.

(7) What is really remarkable and surprising is that the one who now by his own word awakens the earth to germination of so many plants and demonstrates his own power surpassing human reasoning, this same earth, heavy as it is and supporting such a huge universe on its back, he rested on the waters as foundation, as the inspired author says, "He who rests the earth on the waters as foundation." What

human reasoning could arrive at this design? I mean, when people build their houses and have in mind to sink foundations, they first dig a hole: if on reaching some depth they see a trace of dampness, they take every step to remove it all and only then sink the foundations. By comparison with this the Creator of all creates everything in a way contrary to humankind so that you may learn even from this his ineffable power and the fact that, when he wishes, the very elements can be seen to perform in a way contrary to their own abilities in compliance with the Creator's wishes.

(8) To make this subject clearer to you let us make you familiar with the preceding point and then pass on to the next. You see, it is contrary to the nature of the waters to carry a heavy body in this way; and, again, it is foreign to the earth to take its position on such a foundation. Why do you marvel at this? After all, if you take it into your head to study each created thing, you will encounter the infinite power of the Creator and the fact that by his own will he governs all visible things. This, in fact, can be seen happening also in the case of fire: though it has the capacity to burn up, and it prevails over everything, consuming all material of stone, wood, iron and other bodies with ease, yet when the Creator so directed, it left untouched delicate and perishable bodies and, in fact, kept the children unharmed in the middle of the furnace. Don't be surprised if it left these bodies untouched and if, in tact, this irrational element demonstrated the kind of restraint that cannot be described. You see, it did not so much as harm their hair; instead, it formed a circle around them and kept them inside it; the substance of the fire, as it were, responded in obedience, and in compliance with the Lord's direction it kept those excellent children safe and sound, so that they moved about in the furnace with such ease as though strolling through a meadow or garden. And, lest anyone think that what they saw was not a fire at work, the loving Lord for that purpose did not hamper its efficacy; instead, he allowed its burning qualities to remain active, rendering his servants proof against its harmful effect but ensuring that those who thrust them in might learn the extent of the power of the Lord of all: the fire showed its force against them, burning and consuming them as they stood outside the furnace while at the same time encircling the children inside.

(9) Do you see how, whenever the Lord wishes, each of the elements changes its properties into the very opposite? The Lord, you see, is also Creator, and he governs everything according to his own will. Do you want to see this very thing happening also in the case of the waters? Well, just as in the present case the fire refrained from harming the people right inside it, on the one hand, neglecting to exercise its own power, while, on the other hand, it exercised that power in the case of those who happened to be outside it, in like manner we will see the waters drowning some but giving way before others so that they crossed over in safety. Remember in this connection, I ask you, Pharaoh and the Egyptians, and the people of the Hebrews, how the latter by the Lord's command and under the leadership of the great Moses crossed the Red Sea in this way as though across dry land, whereas the Egyptians with Pharaoh wanted to go the same way as the Hebrews, but were submerged and drowned. Thus even the elements know how to respect the Lord's servants and to keep in check their own impulse.

(11) But I don's know how I strayed from the thread of the sermon onto these matters. Come now, let us return at this late stage to the preceding point, and let us see what else this blessed author wants to teach us today. You see, after saying, "This is the book about the origins of heaven and earth," he presses on and describes further for us with great detail the creation of the human being. Since he had briefly said above, "God made the human being; in God's image he made them," he now says, "God shaped the human being from the dust of the earth, and breathed into him a breath of life; the human being became alive." A mighty saying, giving rise to great wonderment, and beyond the limits of human understanding: "God shaped the human being," it says, "taking dust from the earth." Just as in the case of all the visible creatures I kept saying that the Creator of all performs everything in a manner contrary to human nature so as to demonstrate his ineffable power through this as well, so too in the case of the formation of the human being we will find this taking place. I mean, notice how he rested the earth on the waters, something human reasoning does not without faith succeed in accepting, and that whenever he wishes he succeeds in converting the properties of all things to their opposite, as we have shown. Well, this very same thing Sacred Scripture now reveals to us happening in the case of the

formation of the human being as well: "God shaped the human being," it says, "taking dust from the earth."

(12) What is that you say? Taking dust from the earth he shaped the human being? Yes, it says; it did not simply say "earth" but "dust," something more lowly and substantial even than earth, so to say. You think the saying amazing and incredible; but if you recall who is the creator in this case, you will no longer withhold faith in the event but marvel at the Creator's power and bow your knee to it. If, on the other hand, you chanced to put your mind to these matters in light of the limitations of your powers of reason, you would likely get this strange idea into your head, namely, that a body could never be made from earth – a brick or a pot, yes, but never could such a body be made. Do you see that unless we take into account the Creator's power and suppress our own reasoning which betrays such limitations, we will be unable to accept the sublimity of the message? After all, the words require the eyes of faith, spoken as they are with such great considerateness and with our limitations in mind. You see, that very remark, "God shaped the human being, and breathed," is properly inapplicable to God; yet because of us and our limitations Sacred Scripture expresses it in that way, showing considerateness to us, so that, having been thought worthy of the considerateness, we might be enabled to arrive at that sublime level of thought.

(13) "God shaped the human being," it says, "taking dust from the earth." Finally, from these words spring no little instruction in humility, as long as we are prepared to be alert to it. I mean, whenever we consider where our nature derived the beginning of its subsistence, even if we put our brains to it thousands of times, we are humbled and chastened, and in our efforts to plumb our being we learn to respect proper limits. For this reason, God, caring for our salvation, thus directed the tongue of the sacred writer for our instruction. You see, when Sacred Scripture said in its previous statement, "God made the human being; in God's image he made them," he gave him complete control of visible things lest out of ignorance of the composition of his own being he might conjure up inflated notions of his own importance and transgress the limits proper to him.

(14) Hence, when Scripture comes back to the point it teaches us also the manner of our composition and the beginning of our creation, and whence the first human being was produced and how it was produced. After all, into what depths of madness would we not have tumbled if, despite this teaching and despite the knowledge that the human being takes the beginning of its composition from the earth as do the plants and the irrational beings (though its formation and the bodiless being of the soul has given it a marked superiority, thanks to God's loving-kindness, this constituting after all the basis of its rationality and its endowment with control over all creation), – if then with this knowledge this creature shaped from the earth had conjured up the notion of its equality with God owing to the serpent's deceit, and if the blessed author had been content with his first account and had not repeated himself in teaching us everything with precision, into what depths of madness would we not have tumbled?

(15) The result is that we gain the greatest possible degree of instruction in philosophy from learning whence we derive the composition of our being from the very outset. "God shaped the human being," the text says, "taking dust from the earth, and breathed into him a breath of life." Since it was explaining to human beings who were unable to understand in any way other than we ourselves can understand, it employs this kind of concreteness of expression, and intends also to teach us that the Lord's loving-kindness intended that this creature shaped from the earth should have also a rational being by reason of a soul, by means of which this living thing emerged complete and perfect. "He breathed into him a breath of life," the text says; the creature shaped from the earth, it means, was endowed with this breath as a vital force, and this became the origin of the soul's being. At any rate, the text added: "The human being became alive." That shaped thing, that creature from the dust, received the breathing of the breath of life, and "it became alive," the text says. What is the meaning of "became alive"? Enjoying vital force, having limbs to its body that respond to this vital force and obey its will.

(16) But I have no idea how we upset that arrangement, and how such an onset of evil occurred as to oblige it to follow the bidding of the flesh, so that what should in the manner of a queen have presided and exercised rule we have unseated from her throne and forced to obey the pleasures of the flesh, ignorant as we are of its nobility and

the degree of preeminence it has the good fortune to be accorded. I mean, think of the order of its formation, I ask you, and consider what this shaped thing was before the Lord's breathing which meant a breath of life for it and resulted in its becoming alive. Simply a lifeless shell, without vital force, and useful for nothing, so that its total make-up and its succession to such great esteem all stems from that action of breathing made upon it by God. Lest you think this happened from things already created at that time instead of from something that happens each day at the present time, consider, I ask you, how after the departure of the soul this body appears odious and unpleasant? How repulsive, how much reeking with stench, how marked by complete deformity this creature that previously when it had the soul to conduct it was bright, graceful, marked by beauty of form, abounding with intelligence, enjoying great aptitude for the performance of good deeds.

(17) So, with this in mind, and realizing the nobility of our soul, let us be guilty of no behavior unworthy of it nor defile it with unfitting actions, subjecting it to the thrall of the flesh and showing so little appreciation and regard for what is so noble and endowed with such pre-eminence. After all, because of the soul's being, we who are intertwined with a body can, if we wish and under the influence of God's grace, strive against disembodied powers, can walk on earth as though coursing across heaven, and pass our lives in this manner, suffering no inferiority. How that can be, I will tell you. You see, when people prove, despite entanglement with a mortal body, to live the same life as those supernal powers, how will they not be deemed worthy of grace from God for keeping untarnished the soul's nobility, though subject to the body's necessities.

Augustine of Hippo

St. Augustine of Hippo (354 – 430) is the greatest of the Western Fathers. Trained as an orator, he converted to Christianity after being deeply influenced by Manichaeism and Neoplatonism. He was bishop of Hippo for over thirty years until his death during the siege of Hippo by the Vandals. His views on predestination and election molded the Protestant Reformation. His influence can be felt to this day in every aspect of theology.

In *The City of God*, Augustine affirms that time and the world were created and had a beginning – they have not existed eternally. The days of creation were not days as we know them now, but of what sort they were, we cannot say. The earth itself was initially created in a formless, chaotic state. Evil has no existence of its own, but is the loss of positive good. Concerning the age of the earth, Augustine affirms that by the reckoning of Scripture (the Septuagint translation), no more than 6000 years could have passed since the creation to his day. The whole human race, including the first woman, derives from one man, Adam. Augustine refutes a number of Origen's views, sometimes explicitly citing him by name.

Augustine's *The Literal Meaning of Genesis* is, contrary to the title, quite speculative. In it, he considers many possible interpretations of the text. Interpretations need to be consistent with essential doctrinal affirmations of the Christian Faith. Augustine thereby allows considerable latitude in interpretation. Still, he urges that Christians avoid producing interpretations of Scripture that are ridiculous in the light of true scientific knowledge. Such interpretations only discredit the Scriptures in the eyes of unbelievers and thus hinder their salvation. Uncompromising stands in matters of interpretation should as much as possible be avoided. According to Augustine, one must always bear in mind that the primary purpose of Scripture is to nourish the soul and lead it to salvation.

Augustine *The Literal Meaning of Genesis*,

Book One – The Work of the First Day

Chapter I – The interpretation of Scripture; The meaning of heaven and earth

1. Sacred Scripture, taken as a whole, is divided into two parts, as our Lord intimates when He says: A *scribe instructed in the kingdom of God is like a householder who brings forth from his storeroom things new and old.'* These new and old things are also called testaments.

In all the sacred books, we should consider the eternal truths that are taught, the facts that are narrated, the future events that are predicted, and the precepts or counsels that are given. In the case of a narrative of events, the question arises as to whether everything must be taken according to the figurative sense only, or whether it must be expounded and defended also as a faithful record of what happened. No Christian will dare say that the narrative must not be taken in a figurative sense. For St. Paul says: *Now all these things that happened to them were symbolic.* And he explains the statement in Genesis, *And they shall be two in one flesh,* as a great mystery in reference to Christ and to the Church.

2. If, then, Scripture is to be explained under both aspects, what meaning other than the allegorical have the words: *In the beginning God created heaven and earth?* Were heaven and earth made in the beginning of time, or first of all in creation, or in the Beginning who is the Word, the only-begotten Son of God? And how can it be demonstrated that God, without any change in Himself, produces effects subject to change and measured by time? And what is meant by the phrase "heaven and earth"?

Chapter 3 – What is the light which God created?

7. What is the light itself which was created? Is it something spiritual or material? If it is spiritual, it may be the first work of creation, now made perfect by this utterance, and previously called heaven in the words, *In the 6eginning God created heaven and earth.*

In this supposition, we must understand that when God said, *Let there 6e light,* and light was made, the creature, called by its Creator to Himself, underwent a conversion and illumination.

8. Why, moreover, is it stated, *In the 6eginning God created heaven and earth,* and not, "In the beginning God said, 'Let there be heaven and earth,' and heaven and earth were made"? For in the case of light, the words are: *God said: "Let there 6e light, "and light was made.* Are we to understand that by the expression, *heaven and earth,* all that God made is to be included and brought to mind first in a general way, and that then the manner of creation is to be worked out in detail, as for each object the words *God said* occur? For whatever God made He made through His Word.

Chapter 4 – The formation of a formless being

9. But perhaps there is another reason why the expression, *God said, "Let there be...,"* could not be used in reference to the creation of formless matter, whether spiritual or material. God in His eternity says all through His Word, not by the sound of a voice, nor by a thinking process that measures out its speech, but by the light of Divine Wisdom, coeternal with Himself and born of Himself. Now an imperfect being which, in contrast to the Supreme Being and first Cause, tends to nothingness because of its formless state, does not imitate the exemplar in the Word, who is inseparably united to the Father. But it does imitate the exemplar in the Word, who exists forever in immutable union with the Father, when in view of its own appropriate conversion to the true and eternal Being, namely, the Creator of its own substance, it also receives its proper form and becomes a perfect creature.

And so, when Scripture declares, *God said, "Let there be..."* we may understand this as an immaterial utterance of God in His eternal Word, as the Word recalls His imperfect creature to Himself, so that it may not be formless but may be formed according to the various works of creation which He produces in due order. In this conversion and formation the creature in its own way imitates the Divine Word, the Son of God, who is eternally united with the Father in the perfect likeness and equal essence by which He and the Father are one. But it does not imitate this exemplar in the Word if it is turned from its Creator and remains formless and imperfect. Hence, when Scripture says, *In the beginning God created heaven and earth,* mention of the Son is made not because He is the Word, but only because He is the Beginning; for here the origin of created being is indicated still in its imperfect and formless state.

But there is mention of the Son, who is also the Word, where Scripture declares: *God said, "Let there be..."* Thus, in Him who is the Beginning, Holy Scripture places the origin of created being, which exists through Him but still in an imperfect state. But it shows that to Him as the Word belongs the perfecting of created being, which is called back to Him to be formed by a union with its Creator and by an imitation, in its own way, of the Divine Exemplar, who, eternally and unchangeably united with the Father, is of necessity identical in nature with Him.

Chapter 10 – How can we explain the light and darkness mentioned in v.4?

18. Since the divine utterance was spoken without the limitations of time, because the Word, being coeternal with the Father, is not subject to time, was the work produced by the utterance also made independently of time? This is a question that might be asked. But how can such a theory be accepted? It is said that light was made and separated from the darkness, the names "Day" and "Night" being given to them, and Scripture declares, *Evening was made and morning made, one day.* Hence it seems that this work of God was done in the space of a day, at the end of which evening came on, which is the beginning of night. Moreover, when the night was spent, a full day was completed, and the morning belonged to a second day, in which God then performed another work.

37. In matters that are obscure and far beyond our vision, even in such as we may find treated in Holy Scripture, different interpretations are sometimes possible without prejudice to the faith we have received. In such a case, we should not rush in headlong and so firmly take our stand on one side that, if further progress in the search of truth justly undermines this position, we too fall with it. That would be to battle not for the teaching of Holy Scripture but for our own, wishing its teaching to conform to ours, whereas we ought to wish ours to conform to that of Sacred Scripture.

Chapter 19 – On interpreting the mind of the sacred writer; Christians should not talk nonsense to unbelievers

38. Let us suppose that in explaining the words, *And God said, "Let there be light," and light was made,* one man thinks that it was material light that was made, and another that it was spiritual. As to the actual existence of spiritual light in a spiritual creature, our faith leaves no doubt; as to the existence of material light, celestial or supercelestial, even existing before the heavens, a light which could have been followed by night, there will be nothing in such a supposition contrary to the faith until unerring truth gives the lie to it. And if that should happen, this teaching was never in Holy Scripture but was an opinion proposed by man in his ignorance. On the other hand, if reason should prove that this opinion is unquestionably true, it will still be uncertain whether this sense was intended by the sacred writer when he used the words quoted above, or whether he meant something else no less true. And if the general drift of the passage shows that the sacred writer did not intend this teaching, the other, which he did intend, will not thereby be false; indeed, it will be true and more worth knowing. On the other hand, if the tenor of the words of Scripture does not militate against our taking this teaching as the mind of the writer, we shall still have to enquire whether he could not have meant something else besides. And if we find that he could have meant something else also, it will not be clear which of the two meanings he intended. And there is no difficulty if he is thought to have wished both interpretations if both are supported by clear indications in the context.

39. Usually, even a non-Christian knows something about the earth, the heavens, and the other elements of this world, about the motion and orbit of the stars and even their size and relative positions, about the predictable eclipses of the sun and moon, the cycles of the years and the seasons, about the kinds of animals, shrubs, stones, and so forth, and this knowledge he holds to as being certain from reason and experience. Now, it is a disgraceful and dangerous thing for an infidel to hear a Christian, presumably giving the meaning of Holy Scripture, talking nonsense on these topics; and we should take all means to prevent such an embarrassing situation, in which people show up vast ignorance in a Christian and laugh it to scorn. The shame is not so much that an ignorant individual is derided, but that

people outside the household of the faith think our sacred writers held such opinions, and, to the great loss of those for whose salvation we toil, the writers of our Scripture are criticized and rejected as unlearned men. If they find a Christian mistaken in a field which they themselves know well and hear him maintaining his foolish opinions about our books, how are they going to believe those books in matters concerning the resurrection of the dead, the hope of eternal life, and the kingdom of heaven, when they think their pages are full of falsehoods on facts which they themselves have learnt from experience and the light of reason? Reckless and incompetent expounders of Holy Scripture bring untold trouble and sorrow on their wiser brethren when they are caught in one of their mischievous false opinions and are taken to task by those who are not bound by the authority of our sacred books. For then, to defend their utterly foolish and obviously untrue statements, they will try to call upon Holy Scripture for proof and even recite from memory many passages which they think support their position, although *they understand neither what they say nor the things about which they make assertion.*

Chapter 20 – We should remember that Scripture, even in its obscure passages, has been written to nourish our souls

40. With these facts in mind, I have worked out and presented the statements of the Book of Genesis in a variety of ways according to my ability; and, in interpreting words that have been written obscurely for the purpose of stimulating our thought, I have not rashly taken my stand on one side against a rival interpretation which might possibly be better. I have thought that each one, in keeping with his powers of understanding, should choose the interpretation that he can grasp. Where he cannot understand Holy Scripture, let him glorify God and fear for himself. But since the words of Scripture that I have treated are explained in so many senses, critics full of worldly learning should restrain themselves from attacking as ignorant and uncultured these utterances that have been made to nourish all devout souls. Such critics are like wingless creatures that crawl upon the earth and, while soaring no higher than the leap of a frog, mock the birds in their nests above.

But more dangerous is the error of certain weak brethren who faint away when they hear these irreligious critics learnedly and eloquently discoursing on the theories of astronomy or on any of the questions relating to the elements of this universe. With a sigh, they esteem these teachers as superior to themselves, looking upon them as great men; and they return with disdain to the books which were written for the good of their souls; and, although they ought to drink from these books with relish, they can scarcely bear to take them up. Turning away in disgust from the unattractive wheat field, they long for the blossoms on the thorn. For they are not free to see how sweet is the Lord, and they have no hunger on the Sabbath. And thus they are idle, though they have permission from the Lord to pluck the ears of grain and to work them in their hands and grind them and winnow them until they arrive at the nourishing kernel.

Chapter 21 – The advantage of studying Scripture even when the meaning of the author cannot be found for certain

41. Someone will say: "What have you brought out with all the threshing of this treatise? What kernel have you revealed? What have you winnowed? Why does everything seem to lie hidden under questions? Adopt one of the many interpretations which you maintained were possible." To such a one my answer is that I have arrived at a nourishing kernel in that I have learnt that a man is not in any difficulty in making a reply according to his faith which he ought to make to those who try to defame our Holy Scripture. When they are able, from reliable evidence, to prove some fact of physical science, we shall show that it is not contrary to our Scripture. But when they produce from any of their books a theory contrary to Scripture, and therefore contrary to the Catholic faith, either we shall have some ability to demonstrate that it is absolutely false, or at least we ourselves will hold it so without any shadow of a doubt. And we will so cling to our Mediator, *in whom are hidden all the treasures of wisdom and knowledge,* that we will not be led astray by the glib talk of false philosophy or frightened by the superstition of false religion. When we read the inspired books in the light of this wide variety of true doctrines which are drawn from a few words and founded on the firm basis of Catholic belief, let us choose that one which appears as certainly the meaning intended by the author. But if this is not clear, then at least we should choose an interpretation in keeping with the

context of Scripture and in harmony with our faith. But if the meaning cannot be studied and judged by the context of Scripture, at least we should choose only that which our faith demands. For it is one thing to fail to recognize the primary meaning of the writer, and another to depart from the norms of religious belief. If both these difficulties are avoided, the reader gets full profit from his reading. Failing that, even though the writer's intention is uncertain, one will find it useful to extract an interpretation in harmony with our faith.

Book Two – The Works of the Second, Third, and Fourth Days

Chapter 1 – The firmament in the midst of the waters

1. *And God said, "Let there be a firmament in the midst of the waters, and let it divide the water from the water." And so it was done. And God made the firmament, and God divided the water that was below the firmament from the water that was above the firmament. And God called the firmament heaven. And God saw that it was good. And there was evening and there was morning, the second day.*

Concerning the divine utterance by which God said, *Let there be a firmanent,* and so forth, concerning the satisfaction with which He saw that it was good, and concerning the evening and the morning, there is no need here to repeat the explanations given in the first book. Hence, in what follows, whenever these words occur again, let them for the time being be weighed according to the interpretations already suggested. But what is the firmament? Is it that heaven which extends beyond all the realm of air and above the air's farthest heights, where the lights and the stars are set on the fourth day? Or is the air itself called the firmament? This is the question that must concern us here.

2. Many hold that the waters mentioned in this place cannot be above the starry heaven, maintaining that they would be compelled by their weight to flow down upon the earth or would move in a vaporous state in the air near the earth. No one should argue against this theory by appealing to the power of God, to whom all is possible, and saying that all ought to believe that water, even though it had the same weight as the water we know by experience, was poured forth

over the region of the heavens in which the stars are set. For now it is our business to seek in the account of Holy Scripture how God made the universe, not what He might produce in nature or from nature by His miraculous power. If God ever wished oil to remain under water, it would do so. But we should not thereby be ignorant of the nature of oil: we should still know that it is so constituted as to tend towards its proper place and, even when poured under water, to make its way up and settle on the surface. Now we are seeking to know whether the Creator, who has *ordered all things in measure, and number, and weight,* has assigned to the mass of waters not just one proper place around the earth, but another also above the heavens, a region which has been spread around and established beyond the limits of the air.

3. Those who deny this theory base their argument on the weights of the elements. Surely, they say, there is no solid heaven laid out above like a pavement to serve as a support for the mass of water. Such a solid body, they argue, cannot exist except on the earth, and whatever is so constituted is earth, not heaven. They go on to show that the elements are distinguished not by their locations only but also by their qualities, and that each is assigned its place in keeping with its particular qualities. Water is over earth; and if it rests or flows beneath the earth, as it does in recesses of grottoes and caverns, it is not held by the earth that is above it, but rather by that below. For if a piece of earth drops from above, it does not remain on the surface of the water, but, breaking through, it sinks and falls to the earth. There it comes to rest, for it is in its place: the water is above and the earth below. From this it is clear that while it was above the waters, it was not supported by the waters but was held up by the solid earth that forms the chambers of caverns.

4. Here it will not be out of place to caution the reader against the error about which I warned him in the first book. Let no one think that, because the Psalmist says, *He established the earth above the wafer,* we must use this testimony of Holy Scripture against these people who engage in learned discussions about the weights of the elements. They are not bound by the authority of our Bible; and, ignorant of the sense of these words, they will more readily scorn our sacred books than disavow the knowledge they have acquired by unassailable arguments or proved by the evidence of experience.

The statement of the Psalmist can with good reason be understood figuratively. Since the terms "heaven" and "earth" often mean spiritual and carnal persons in the Church, he indicates that the "heavens" refer to the tranquil understanding of truth when he says, *Who made the heavens in understanding.* *"Earth,"* on the other hand, as the Psalmist shows, refers to the simple faith of children, not a doubtful and deceitful thing based on mythological speculations, but an unshakeable assent founded on the teaching of the prophets and the Gospels, the faith that is made firm by baptism; and so the Psalmist adds, *He established the earth above the water.*

But if anyone insists on a literal interpretation of this verse, he might plausibly understand the earth above the water to be the promontories that tower over the water, whether on continents or on islands; or again, the roofs of caverns that rest on solid supports and overhang the waters below. Accordingly, even in a literal interpretation, one cannot take the words, *He established the earth above the water,* to mean that in nature a mass of water was placed underneath a mass of earth to support it.

Book Four – Reflections on the Days of Creation and God's Rest

Chapter 26 – The meaning of day in the creation narrative

43. All creation, then, was finished by the sixfold recurrence of this day whose evening and morning we may interpret as explained above. And there was the morning that terminated the sixth day at which time there was the beginning of the seventh, which would have no evening, since God's rest is not a creature. For creatures, when they were being produced on the other days, were known to the angels not only in God, the Truth by which they were to be made, but also in themselves as things actually made. This latter knowledge, being a kind of faded likeness of the other, constituted evening. Hence, we can no longer take "day" to mean the form of the work created end "evening" its completion and "morning" the beginning of another work in the account of creation. Otherwise we might be forced to say, against the evidence of Scripture, that beyond the works of the six days a creature was made on the seventh day, or that the

seventh day itself was not a creature. But that day, which God has made, recurs in connection with His works not by a material passage of time but by spiritual knowledge, when the blessed company of angels contemplate from the beginning in the Word of God the divine decree to create. And thus the work is first produced in their knowledge as indicated in the words, *And so it was made.* After that they know the creature itself in itself, and this is revealed to us where it is said that there was evening. Finally, they refer this knowledge of the creature to the praise of eternal Truth, where they had beheld the form of the work to be produced, and this is the meaning of the statement that it was morning.

Thus, in all the days of creation there is one day, and it is not to be taken in the sense of our day, which we reckon by the course of the sun; but it must have another meaning, applicable to the three days mentioned before the creation of the heavenly bodies. This special meaning of "day" must not be maintained just for the first three days, with the understanding that after the third day we take the word "day" in its ordinary sense. But we must keep the same meaning even to the sixth and seventh days. Hence, "day" and "night," which God divided, must be interpreted quite differently from the familiar "day" and "night," which God decreed the lights that He created in the firmament should divide when He said, *And let them divide day and night.* For it was by this latter act that He created our day, creating the sun whose presence makes the day. But that other day which was originally made had already repeated itself three times when, at its fourth recurrence, these lights of the firmament were created.

Chapter 27 – Days familiar to us are quite different from the days of creation

44. That day in the account of creation, or those days that are numbered according to its recurrence, are beyond the experience and knowledge of us mortal earthbound men. And if we are able to make any effort towards an understanding of the meaning of those days, we ought not to rush forward with an ill-considered opinion, as if no other reasonable and plausible interpretation could be offered. Seven days by our reckoning, after the model of the days of creation, make up a week. By the passage of such weeks time rolls on, and in these weeks one day is constituted by the course of the sun from its rising to

its setting; but we must bear in mind that these days indeed recall the days of creation, but without in any way being really similar to them.

Chapter 28 – The interpretation given for "day" is not allegorical

45. I have spoken about spiritual light, about the creation of day in angelic spirits, about their contemplation of the Word of God, about their knowledge of creatures in themselves, and about their referring this to the praise of immutable Truth, where from the first they beheld the forms of creatures yet to be before they knew these creatures as actually produced. Now it must not be thought that these interpretations are applicable to "day" and "evening" and "morning" not literally but only in some figurative and allegorical way. These interpretations, of course, are different from our ordinary understanding of light in the material sense. But it is not true that material light is literally "light," and light referred to in Genesis is metaphorical "light." For where light is more excellent and unfailing, there day also exists in a truer sense. Why, then, should that day not have a truer evening and a truer morning? For if in the days with which we are familiar the light wanes as the day declines, and we call this evening, and if it rises again at daybreak, and we call this morning, why should we not say that there is also evening when angels after contemplating the Creator gaze down upon a creature, and that there is also morning when they rise from a knowledge of a creature to the praise of the Creator? Christ Himself is not called the Light in the same way as He is called a stone: He is literally the Light but metaphorically a stone.

Whoever, then, does not accept the meaning that my limited powers have been able to discover or conjecture but seeks in the enumeration of the days of creation a different meaning, which might be understood not in a prophetical or figurative sense, but literally and more aptly, in interpreting the works of creation, let him search and find a solution with God's help. I myself may possibly discover some other meaning more in harmony with the words of Scripture. I certainly do not advance the interpretation given above in such a way as to imply that no better one can ever be found, although I do maintain that Sacred Scripture does not tell us that God rested after feeling weariness and fatigue.

Chapter 33 – God created all things simultaneously

51. But if the angelic mind can grasp simultaneously all that the sacred text sets down separately in an ordered arrangement according to causal connection, were not all these things also made simultaneously, the firmament itself, the waters gathered together and the bare land that appeared, the plants and tress that sprang forth, the lights and stars that were established, the living creatures in the water and on the earth? Or were they rather created at different times on appointed days?

Perhaps we ought not to think of these creatures at the moment they were produced as subject to the processes of nature which we now observe in them, but rather as under the wonderful and unutterable power of the Wisdom of God, which *reaches from end to end mightily and governs all graciously* [Wisd. 8:1]. For this power of Divine Wisdom does not reach by stages or arrive by steps. It was just as easy, then, for God to create everything as it is for Wisdom to exercise this mighty power. For through Wisdom all things were made, and the motion we now see in creatures, measured by the lapse of time, as each one fulfills its proper function, comes to creatures from those causal reasons implanted in them, which God scattered as seeds at the moment of creation when *He spoke and they were made, He commanded and they were created* [Ps. 32:9].

52. Creation, therefore, did not take place slowly in order that a slow development might be implanted in those things that are slow by nature; nor were the ages established at the plodding pace at which they now pass. Time brings about the development of these creatures according to the laws of their numbers, but there was no passage of time when they received these laws at creation. Otherwise, if we think that, when they were first created by the Word of God, there were the processes of nature with the normal duration of days that we know, those creatures that shoot forth roots and clothe the earth would need not one day but many to germinate beneath the ground, and then a certain number of days, according to their natures, to come forth from the ground; and the creation of vegetation, which Scripture places on one day, namely the third, would have been a gradual process.

And then how many days were necessary for birds to fly, if they proceeded form the earliest stages through the periods of natural growth to the sprouting of feathers and wings? Or perhaps were eggs only created, when on the fifth day, according the scriptural narrative, the waters brought forth every winged bird according to its kind?...

In this narrative of creation Holy Scripture has said of the Creator that He completed His works in six days; and elsewhere, without contradicting this, it has been written of the same Creator that He created all things together. It follows, therefore, that He, who created all things together, simultaneously created these six days, or seven, or rather the one day six or seven times repeated. Why, then, was there any need for six distinct days to be set forth in the narrative one after the other? The reason is that those who cannot understand the meaning of the text, *He created all things together*, cannot arrive at the meaning of Scripture unless the narrative proceeds slowly step by step.

Chapter 34 – All things were made both simultaneously and in six days

53. How, then, can we say that the light was repeated six times in the knowledge of the angels from evening to morning? It was enough for them just once to have day and evening and morning together when, in the primordial and immutable forms by which creatures were made, they contemplated the whole of creation together, as it was made together, thus beholding day; and when, in things existing in their own proper nature, they knew creation, thus beholding evening; and when, recognizing this knowledge as inferior, they praised the Creator, thus beholding morning. How did morning come first, so that the angels would know in the Word what God was to make next, and afterwards know this very thing itself in the evening, if no "before" or "after" was made, because all things were made together?

As a matter of fact, the creatures mentioned in the narrative of creation were made according to a "before" and "after" during the six days, and they were also all made together. For this Scripture text that narrates the works of God according to the days mentioned above, and that Scripture text that says God created all things together, are both true. And the two are one, because Sacred Scripture was written under the inspiration of the one Spirit of truth.

54. In this sort of thing there is no lapse of time to show what is before and what after. We might say that the creation of things took place all at once and also that there was a "before" and "after," but it is more readily understood as happening all at once than in sequence. Thus also, when we look at the sun rising, it is certainly evident that our gaze could not reach it without passing over the whole expanse of air and sky that lies between. And who can calculate this distance? Now this gaze of ours or this ray from our eyes would not be able to traverse the air above the sea unless it first passed over the air above the land as we look out from any inland site towards the seashore.

And then if our gaze, turned in the same direction, meets land again across the sea, it cannot pass through the air above that distant land unless it first travels through the air above the sea that lies between. And let us suppose that beyond this land across the sea only ocean remains. Can our gaze pass through the air spread out over the ocean unless it first penetrates the air over the land on this side of the ocean? The expanse of the ocean is said to be greater than anything we know; but however vast it may be, it is necessary for the rays of our eyes first to pass through the air above it, and afterwards to pass through whatever is beyond, and then finally to come to the sun that we behold.

In describing this experience, I have used the words "first" and "afterwards" several times, but in so speaking I am not denying that our gaze passes over all this space at once with a single glance of the eye. If we close our eyes and turn towards the sun, as soon as we open them we shall have the feeling that our gaze has touched the sun without our being aware that we have stretched it out to that point; and there will seem to be no lapse of time between the moment we open our eyes and the moment our gaze meets its object. Now this is certainly a ray of material light that shines forth from our eyes and touches objects so remote with such speed that it cannot be calculated or equalled. It is quite obvious, then, that all those measureless spaces are traversed at one time in a single glance; and at the same time it is also certain what part of these spaces is passed first and what part later.

55. It was only right that when St. Paul wished to express the speed with which we should rise from the dead, he said it would happen *in the twinkling of an eye.* Surely nothing swifter can be found in the movements and impulses of bodies. Now, if vision in the eyes of the body is capable of such speed, what cannot intellectual vision do, even in the case of men, and much more in the case of angels? And what can we say of the speed of the supreme Wisdom of God Himself, which penetrates everywhere by reason of Its purity, and which no stain ever sullies?

In such actions, therefore, which happen simultaneously, no one sees what must have occurred "first" or "later," unless he beholds it in that Wisdom by which all things were made in due order simultaneously

Chapter 35 – There is no "before" or "after" in God but there is in creatures

56. If, therefore, the day that God first made is the company of spiritual and rational creatures called supercelestial angels and virtues, it was made present to all the works of God to see them in that order in which angelic knowledge foreknows in the Word of God creatures that are to be made and knows in themselves creatures already made. There are no intervals of time here; but one can speak of "before" and "after" in the relationships of creatures, although all is simultaneous in the creative act of God. For God made the creatures that were to be in the future in such a way that without Himself being subject to time He made them subject to time. Thus time when made by Him would run its course.

The seven days, therefore, with which we are familiar, which the light of a heavenly body unfolds and folds in its course, are like a shadow and a sign reminding us to seek those days wherein created spiritual light was able to be made present to all the works of God by the perfection of the number six. We are reminded also that the seventh day, the day on which God rested, has a morning but no evening, and that He rested on this day not because He needed the seventh day for rest, but because He rested in the sight of His angels from all the works He had made, resting only in Himself, who was not made. In other words, the angels that God created were made present to all His works, knowing them in Him and in themselves, as day along with evening; and after all the works of God, which were very good, there was nothing better for them to know than that God Himself was resting in Himself from all His works, needing none of them to add to His beatitude.

Book Five – The Two Narratives and the Causal Reasons

Chapter 1 – God made heaven and earth on one day six times repeated

1. *This is the book of the creation of heaven and earth when day was made. God made heaven and earth and every green thing of the field before it appeared above the earth, and all the grass of the field before it sprang forth. For God had not rained upon the earth, and there was not a man to till the earth. But a spring rose out of the earth and watered all the face of the earth* [Gen. 2:4–6].

Now, certainly, further weight is added to the opinion that holds that God made one day, and that six or seven days could be numbered by reason of the repetition of this one. For Holy Scripture now states the matter more clearly, summing up in general terms all that it had said from the beginning up to this point, when it declares, *This is the book of the creation* (or *making) of heaven and earth when day was made.*

No one is going to say that the words "heaven" and "earth" are here intended in the sense that they had earlier in the narrative before day was said to have been made, *In the beginning God created heaven and earth.* That text seems to mean that God made something apart from any day, before He made day. The interpretation that might be put upon this I have set forth above in its proper place, without, however, denying to others the right of proposing a better explanation.

But now the sacred writer says, *This is the book of the creation of heaven and earth when day was made,* thus making it quite clear. I believe, that here he does not speak of heaven and earth in the sense in which he used these words in the beginning before mentioning the creation of day, *when darkness was over the abyss.* Now he is speaking of the creation of heaven and earth when day was made, that is, when all parts of the world had been made distinct and all classes of things had been already formed, and thus the whole of creation, fittingly arranged, presented the appearance of what we call the universe.

2. Here, therefore, the sacred writer speaks of that heaven (along with all that is in it) which God called the firmament when He created it, and of that earth (along with everything in it) which together with the abyss occupies the lowest region. For he goes on to add, *God made heaven and earth;* and thus, by mentioning heaven and earth before mentioning the creation of day, and then repeating these words after mention of the creation of day, he makes it impossible for us to suppose that "heaven" and "earth" here have the same meaning that they have in the beginning before the creation of day. He states the matter as follows: *This is the book of the creation of heaven and earth when day was made. God made heaven and earth.* Hence, if anyone wishes to understand the words *the book of the creation of heaven and earth* in the sense in which it is said, *In the beginning God created heaven and earth,* before the creation of day, because in both places heaven and earth are mentioned before day was made, he ought to be corrected by the words that follow, because again, after it is said that day was made, the terms "heaven" and "earth" are once more used.

3. Now the word "when" and the statement that goes with it, *day was made,* should compel the most obstinate adversary to admit that no other interpretation is possible. For if the matter were stated thus: "This is the book of the creation of heaven and earth; day was made; God made heaven and earth," one might perhaps think that the book of the creation of heaven and earth was spoken of in the same sense as heaven and earth in the beginning before day was created. And then it might be supposed that the sacred writer added, *Day was made,* in the sense in which he previously had said that God made the day, and that he said immediately once again, *God made heaven and earth,* wishing them to be understood as they exist after the creation of day. But since Scripture says, *when day was made,* whether you connect this clause with the words preceding, so that you read this as one sentence, *This is the book of the creation of heaven and earth when day was made,* or whether you connect it with the following words, so that you have this sentence, *When day was made, God made heaven and earth,* the

sacred text surely compels us to understand heaven and earth as they exist after day had been made Then, after saying, *God made heaven and earth,* the sacred writer adds, *and every green thing of the field;* and this was obviously made on the third day. It is, therefore, abundantly clear that it is one and the same day that God made, and that by the repetition of it the second day was made, and the third, and the rest up to the seventh.

Chapter 2 – The day God made is different from days that we know

4. Since by the terms "heaven" and "earth" the sacred writer, in conformity with the language of Scripture, wished us to understand here the whole of creation, we might ask why he added, *and every green thing of the field.* I believe that he put the matter in this way in order to emphasize what day he spoke of when he said, *When day was made.* One might easily think that this day was a day made up of a material light by whose circuit the hours of day and night are brought to us. But when we recall the order in which creatures were made, we find that *all the grass of the field* was created on the third day, before the sun was made (for it was made on the fourth day), and it is by the presence of the sun that the day with which we are familiar is constituted. When, therefore, we hear, *When day was made, God made heaven and earth, and all the grass of the field,* we are admonished to think of that day which may perhaps be a corporeal thing consisting in some sort of light unknown to us, or a spiritual thing made up of the united company of angels. But at least we know that it is different from the ordinary day with which we are familiar; and we are attempting to discover its true nature.

Chapter 3 – All things were created simultaneously on the day which was seven times repeated

5. There is another consideration that may not be irrelevant. The sacred writer might have said, "This is the book of the creation of heaven and earth, when God made heaven and earth," giving us to understand by "heaven and earth" everything that is in them. This would be in keeping with the language of Scripture, where very frequently by the terms "heaven" and "earth" (sometimes with the addition of "sea") the sacred writer means the whole creation, occasionally adding the phrase, *and all things that are in them.* In this

case, if he had stated the matter in some such form as this, we should understand day to be present also, either the day God first made or our day, which is constituted by the presence of the sun. Now, the sacred writer did not put the matter thus but introduced the word "day" in the clause, *When day was made.*

Scripture, furthermore, does not say, "This is the book of the creation of day and heaven and earth," as if things were actually created in that order; nor does it say, "This is the book of the creation of heaven and earth, when day and heaven and earth were made, when God made heaven and earth and every green thing of the field." And again it does not say, "This is the book of the creation of heaven and earth, when God made day and heaven and earth and every green thing of the field." Finally, it does not say, "This is the book of the creation of heaven and earth; God made day and heaven and earth and every green thing of the field."

The usual way of saying things called for these forms of expression; but actually Scripture says, This is the book of the creation of heaven and earth. When day was made, God made heaven and earth and every green thing of the field. Thus it indicates that after day had been made, then God made heaven and earth and every green thing of the field.

6. Furthermore, the earlier narrative reveals that day was first made, and it reckons this as one day. After this a second day is added, and on this day the firmament was made; and then a third day, on which earth and sea were separated, and the earth brought forth trees and herbs. Now perhaps we have here a confirmation of what we tried to show in the previous book, that God created everything at one time. The earlier narrative stated that all things were created and finished on six successive days, but now to one day everything is assigned, under the terms "heaven" and "earth," with the addition also of "plants." If, therefore, as I have already said, "day" were understood in its ordinary sense, the reader would be corrected when he recalled that God had ordered the earth to produce the green things of the field before the establishment of that day that is marked by the sun. Hence, I do not now appeal to another book of Holy Scripture to prove that God *created all things together.* But the very next page following the first narrative of creation testifies to this when it tells us, *When day was*

made, God made heaven and earth and every green thing of the field. Hence, you must understand that this day was seven times repeated, to make up the seven days. And when you hear that all things were made after day was made, you may possibly understand this sixfold or sevenfold repetition which took place without lapse of time. If you cannot yet understand it, you should leave the matter for the consideration of those who can; and, since Scripture does not abandon you in your infirmity, but with a mother's love accompanies your slower steps, you will make progress. Holy Scripture, indeed, speaks in such a way as to mock proud readers with its heights, terrify the attentive with its depths, feed great souls with its truth, and nourish little ones with sweetness.

Chapter 4 – Genesis 1:12 means that earth received the power of bringing forth crops and trees

7. What, then, is the meaning of the words that follow? The text reads thus: When day was made, God made heaven and earth and every green thing of the field before it appeared above the earth, and all the grass of the field before it sprang forth.

What are we to make of this? Must we not ask where God made these things before they appeared above the earth and before they sprang forth? One might be much more inclined to believe that God made them at the time when they sprang forth, not before they sprang forth, were we not informed by the sacred text that it was before they sprang forth that God made them. As a result, if the reader cannot discover where they were made, he will nevertheless believe that they were made before they sprang forth, if he piously believes Holy Scripture. It is impious, of course, not to believe it.

8. What, then, shall we say? Shall we follow the opinion of those who say that it was in the Word of God that all things were made before they sprang forth on the earth? But if this is the way they were created, it was not when day was made but before the making of day that they were created. Scripture says quite plainly, *When day was made, God made heaven and earth and every green thing of the field before it appeared above the earth, and all the grass of the field before it sprang forth.* If, therefore, this was *when day was made,* it was surely not before day was made. Hence, it was not in the Word, who is coeternal with the Father before day or anything else was

made, but it was only when day was made. For those things that are in the Word of God before all creation were certainly not made; but they were made when day was made, as the words of Scripture declare, although this took place before they appeared above the earth and before they sprang forth, as Scripture says concerning the green things and the grass of the field.

9. Where, then, were they? Were they in the earth in the "reasons" or causes from which they would spring, as all things already exist in their seeds before they evolve in one form or another and grow into their proper kinds in the course of time? But these seeds that we see are already above the earth and have already sprung forth. Or shall we say that they were not above the earth but within the earth, and that, therefore, before they sprang forth they were made, because they only sprang forth when their seeds germinated and with the process of growth burst up above the ground? For this is what we see happening in due course of time in the case of each plant. Were the seeds, therefore, made when day was made, and in them was there every green thing of the field and all the grass, not with the appearance they have when they have sprung forth above the earth, but with the power they have in the formative principles of the seeds? Did earth, then, first produce the seeds?

But that is not the way Scripture put the matter when it said, And the earth brought forth the nourishing crops (or grain), scattering the seeds according to their kind and their likeness, and the fruit tree bearing its fruit, containing within itself its seed according to its kind upon the earth. From these words it appears rather that the seeds sprang from the crops and the trees, and that the crops and trees themselves came forth not from seeds but from the earth. This is what the word of God itself declares. For it does not say, "Let the seeds in the earth bring forth the grain and the fruit-bearing tree"; but it says, Let the earth bring forth the grain scattering its seed. It thus reveals that the seed is from the crops, not the crops from the seed. And thus it was done, and the earth brought them forth. That is to say, it was thus done first in the knowledge of the Day mentioned above, and earth now brought these creatures forth, so that they would now be made also in themselves in the created world.

10. How, then, was this done before they appeared above the earth and before they sprang forth? On the one hand, they were made with heaven and earth when that day transcending our knowledge and experience was made, which God first made; and on the other hand, they sprang forth above the earth, a thing that could not happen except on days marked by the course of the sun after the proper lapse of time for each kind. Are these two things, then, distinct? If this is so, and if that day is the society of supercelestial angels and powers united together, then God's creatures are undoubtedly known to angels with a knowledge far different from ours. Apart from the fact that they know creatures in the Word of God, through whom all things have been made, I believe that their knowledge of creatures in themselves is far different from ours. They have what we might call a primordial or original knowledge of the creatures God first made before He rested from His works, not creating anything further. Our knowledge, on the other hand, is dependent upon the governance of creatures already made, as this takes place in time, inasmuch as God, in the unfolding of His creatures according to the perfection of the number six, is working still.

11. It is, therefore, causally *(causaliter)* that Scripture has said that earth brought forth the crops and the trees, in the sense that it received the power of bringing them forth. In the earth from the beginning, in what I might call the roots of time, God created what was to be in times to come. For God later planted a paradise in the East, and there *from the earth He made every tree to grow, beautiful to the sight and good for food.* But we must not say that He then added to creation something He had not previously made, something that was afterwards to be added to the completeness in which He had finished all that was very good on the sixth day. All the plants and trees had already been made in the first creation, and God rested from that creation, moving and governing in the course of history the things which He created before resting from His creation. It is in this sense that He planted not only Paradise but even now all that earth brings forth. For who now creates these things unless it is He who is working even now? But He now creates from what already exists, whereas in the beginning creatures were made by Him when none of them existed at all. It was then that the day was created which is not to be identified with Him but rather with the spiritual and intellectual creation.

Chapter 5 – Time began with creation; Unformed matter was prior not in time but in the order of causality

12. With the motion of creatures, time began to run its course It is idle to look for time before creation, as if time can be found before time. If there were no motion of either a spiritual or corporeal creature, by which the future moving through the present would succeed the past, there would be no time at all. A creature could not move if it did not exist. We should, therefore, say that time began with creation rather than that creation began with time. But both are from God. For from Him and through Him and in Him are all things.

The statement, "Time began with creation," should not be taken to mean that time is not a creature. It is, in fact, the motion of creatures from one state to another as they succeed one another according to the decree of God, who governs all that He has created. Hence, when we think of the first creation of things, that is, of the works from which God rested on the seventh day, we should not think of those days as solar days, nor of that work of God as if it were the same as His working now in time. Rather, He made that which gave time its beginning, as He made all things together, disposing them in an order based not on intervals of time but on causal connections; and thus the creatures which were made all at once could be shown in their perfection by the sixfold repetition of the "day" of creation.

13. It is not in the order of time but in the order of causality that matter unformed and formable, both spiritual and corporeal, came first in creation. It was the substratum of what was to be made, although it did not exist before it was created. It was created by none other than the sovereign and true God from whom are all things. This unformed matter has been called heaven and earth, which God made in the beginning before that one day which He made, and it is so designated because from it heaven and earth were made. It is also called invisible and formless earth and dark abyss. I his interpretation I have explained in the first book.

14. Among those beings which were formed from formlessness and are clearly said to be created, made, or established, the first made was day. For it was fitting that the primacy in creation should be held by that being which could know the creature through the Creator, not

the Creator through the creature. In the second place there was the firmament, with which the creation of the corporeal world begins. In the third place are sea and earth, and in the earth potentially are plants and trees. For thus the earth at God's word produced these things before they sprang forth, receiving all the numbers of those beings which it would bring forth in their kinds through the ages. Then, after this domicile, as it were, of creatures had been established, on the fourth day the lights and stars were created, so that first the higher part of the universe would be adorned with the visible bodies that move within the universe. On the fifth day the waters, being joined to sky and air, at God's command brought forth their inhabitants, all the fishes and birds; and they produced them potentially in the numbers which would come forth under appropriate influences in the course of time. On the sixth day the animals of the earth were made, the last beings from the last element of the world. They too were created potentially, for time would bring them into view in the ages to come.

15. The first day created knew the whole array of creatures arranged in hierarchical order. Through this knowledge creation was revealed to it as if in six steps called days, and thus was unfolded all that was created; but in reality there was only one day. That day knew creation first in the Creator and then in the creatures themselves; yet it remained not in them, but directing this latter knowledge to the love of God, it brought about in all the works of creation an evening, a morning, and a mid-day, not involving any intervals of time but rather an order in creation. Finally, made aware of the repose of its Creator, who rested from all His works in rest that has no evening, the day thereby deserved to be blessed and sanctified. Scripture, therefore, as the Church has recognized, extols the number seven and presents it as consecrated in a sense to the Holy Spirit.

16. This, then, is *the book of the creation of heaven and earth.* For *in the beginning God made heaven and earth* in the sense that He made what we might call formable matter, which was to be formed subsequently by His word. This formable matter, however, was prior to its formation not in time but in origin. When it received a form, that was when day was first made. *When day was made, God made heaven and earth and every green thing of the field before it appeared above the earth, and all the grass of the field before it sprang forth.* This is

my explanation, unless someone can propose an interpretation that is clearer and more in keeping with the text.

Chapter 6 – The meaning of Genesis 2:5

17. Scripture then says, *For God had not rained upon the earth, and there was not a man to till the earth.* It is difficult to determine what these words mean and what they are intended to suggest. One might say that God made the grass of the field before it came forth from the earth because He had not yet rained upon the earth, since if He had made the grass after the rain, it would seem to have come forth because of the rain rather than to have been made by Him. But does this make sense? Could the vegetation coming forth after the rain be made by any other than God?

And why was there not a man to till the earth? On the sixth day God had already made man, and on the seventh He had rested from all His works. Perhaps this is a summary in which the author recalls that when God made every green thing of the field and all the grass, He had not yet rained upon the earth, and there was not yet any man. For on the third day He made the grass, and on the sixth day man. But when God made all the grass and every green thing of the field before it came forth from the earth, there was lacking not only man to till the earth but also the grass upon the earth, for it was said to have been made before it came forth. Did God make the grass on the third day precisely because there was not yet a man to produce it by tilling the earth? We surely cannot say that the many different trees and the many kinds of plants could come forth from the earth only by the work of man.

Book Six – The Creation of the Man's Body

Chapter 1 – The creation of man, Gen. 2:7; How is this account related to that in Gen. 1:27?

1. *And God formed man of dust from the earth and breathed into his face the breath of life; and man was made a living being.* Here we must see whether this is a restatement intended to describe the manner in which man was made, for we have read already that he was made on the sixth day. On the other hand, when God made all things to-

gether, did He make man among them in some hidden form, as He made the grass of the field before it sprang forth? In this latter supposition, man would have been already made in another manner in the hidden recesses of nature, as were the beings which God created together when day was made; and later, with the passage of time, he would be made in a second manner according to the visible form in which he now lives his life for good or ill. He would then be like the grass of the field, which was made before it sprang forth on the earth, but in the course of time, when a spring watered the land, it came forth and appeared upon the earth.

2. Let us first try to understand the text under consideration as a restatement. Perhaps man was made on the sixth day as day itself was originally made, and the firmament, and land and sea. These creatures are not said to have been first made and hidden away in some primordial causes and then with the unfolding of time to have come forth into the light with the visible features that shape the universe. But from the beginning of the ages, when day was made, the world is said to have been formed, and in its elements at the same time there were laid away the creatures that would later spring forth with the passage of time, plants and animals, each according to its kind.

For we cannot believe that even the stars were made in primordial causes in the elements of the world so as to come forth later with the passage of time and to shine in the radiant forms which now glow in the heavens. Rather, all these beings were created at the same time according to the perfection of the number six when day was made. Was man also, therefore, made in the form and substance in which he now exists and lives his life for good or ill? Or was he made in a hidden form, like the grass of the field before it sprang forth, so that his appearance in due course of time would be accomplished when God would make him from the dust?

Chapter 2 – First hypothesis: man was created on the sixth day in the visible shape familiar to us; the narrative in Gen. 2:7 is a recapitulation

3. Let us assume, then, that man was formed on the sixth day in the clear and visible shape familiar to us, but that in the earlier narrative no mention was made of the details which are given in the

recapitulation. Let us see whether Scripture agrees with this hypothesis.

This is the account in the narrative of the works on the sixth day: And God said, "Let Us make mankind in Our image and likeness; and let them have dominion over the fish of the sea, the birds of the air, all the cattle, all the earth, and all the creatures that crawl on the earth." And God made man, to the image of God He made him: male and female He made them. And God blessed them and said: "Increase and multiply and fill the earth and subdue it, and have dominion over the fish of the sea, the birds of the air, all the cattle, all the earth, and all the creatures that crawl on the earth" [Gen. 1:26–28].

Man, therefore, had already been formed from the slime, and while he slept a woman had been made for him from his side; but in the earlier narrative no mention was made of the details now given in the recapitulation. We are not told that on the sixth day the male was made and later the female in due time. But Scripture says, *He made him; male and female He made them, and He blessed them.* How, then, was it that man was already placed in Paradise when a woman was made for him? Does the sacred writer recall this after passing it over originally? For Paradise was already planted on that sixth day and man was placed in it; and then he was put to sleep so that Eve might be formed, after which he awoke and gave her a name. But these events could happen only in successive periods of time. They could not, therefore, have come about in the manner in which all things were created together.

Chapter 3 – Difficulties inherent in this hypothesis; Gen. 2:7–9 is more than a recapitulation

4. However exalted man recognizes that power to be by which God made these things simultaneously with the others, we surely know that the words of man cannot be uttered by his voice except within a period of time. For we heard the words of man when he gave names to the animals and a name to the woman, and immediately after that when he said, *Therefore a man shall leave his father and mother and cleave to his wife, and they shall be two in one flesh.* Whatever syllables were used in speaking these words, no two syllables of the utterance could have sounded together. It is, then, all the

more impossible that all this could have happened simultaneously with the creation of those beings which were created together.

Consequently, we are faced with a dilemma. On the one hand, we might say that all those creatures were not made together at the dawn of the ages but were made in successive periods of time, and the day first made did not have morning and evening in a spiritual but in a corporeal nature, and morning and evening were made by some sort of revolving motion of light or by a diffusion and contraction of light. On the other hand, if we take into account all that I have discussed earlier in this commentary, we have good reason to conclude that the spiritual day, mysteriously made in the beginning, was called day in so far as it was in a sense the light of wisdom. I have argued that this day was made present to the works created by God, and that this was done in knowledge revealed according to a scheme designated by the number six. The words of Scripture seem to support this interpretation, for after the six days are done it says: *When day was made, God made heaven and earth and every green thing of the field before it appeared above the earth, and all the grass of the field before it sprang forth.* And there is the further testimony of Scripture where it is said, *He who lives forever created all things together.* There can be no doubt, then, that the work whereby man was formed from the slime of the earth and a wife fashioned for him from his side belongs not to that creation by which all things were made together, after completing which God rested, but to that work of God which takes place with the unfolding of the ages as He works even now.

5. We must consider the exact words by which it is told how God planted Paradise, placed in it the man whom He had made, and brought before him the animals for him to name, and how He then formed a woman for him out of a rib taken from him, since no helper like man had been found. The narration of these facts makes it clear that these events do not belong to that work of God from which He rested on the seventh day, but rather to that work by which He works through the course of time even to this moment. For this is what the author says when he tells how Paradise was planted: *And God planted a garden in Eden in the East, and there He put the man whom He had formed. And again from the earth God made to grow every tree that is pleasant to the sight and good for food.*

Chapter 4 – Further reasons why the narrative in Gen. 2:7–9 goes beyond what was stated in the work of the six days

When the author says, *Again from the earth He made to grow every tree that is pleasant to the sight,* he surely makes it clear that the statement about God now bringing forth trees from the earth refers to something different from what was said previously about the earth on the third day bringing forth the nourishing crops scattering their seed according to their kind and the fruit tree according to its kind. This explains the expression, *Again He made to grow (Eiecit adhuc).* This is over and above what God had already made to grow. In the first instance God had created things in potency and in their causes in that work in which He had created all things together, and from which, after they were finished, He rested on the seventh day. But in the second instance He created visible things in the work which belongs to the passage of time, even as He is at work to the present moment.

6. It might be objected that not every kind of tree was created on the third day, but that some kinds were postponed and created on the sixth day, when man was made and placed in Paradise. But Scripture clearly tells what creatures were made on the sixth day: the living creatures, each according to its kind, quadrupeds and creeping things and beasts, and man himself, male and female, made to the image of God.

Accordingly, the author was able to omit saying how man was made (although he narrated the fact of his creation on the sixth day), so that restating the matter later he might also give the manner of his creation by telling how the man was made from the dust of the earth and the woman from his side. On the other hand, he could not omit any kind of creature, either at the moment when God said, *Let there be (fiat)* or *Let Us make (Faciamus),* or when he himself says, *So it was done (Sic est factum)* or *God made (Fecit Deus).* Otherwise it would be to no avail that everything was systematically arranged with such great care throughout the different days if there could be any suggestion that the days were confused, so that after the assignment of plants and trees to the third day we should believe that on the sixth day certain trees were created which Scripture does not mention on the sixth day.

Chapter 5 – Second hypothesis: in the first creation of the six days God created all living beings, including Adam and Eve, potentially and in their causes. From these causes God later created them in their visible forms

7. Finally, what shall we say about the beasts of the field and the birds of heaven which God brought to Adam to see what he would call them? This is what the text says: *And the Lord God said: "It is not good that the man should 6e alone. Let Us make for him a helper like himself" And again God formed from the earth all the beasts of the field and all the birds of heaven and brought them to Adam to see what he would call them. And whatever Adam called a living creature, that is its name. And Adam gave names to all the cattle and to all the birds of heaven and to all the beasts of the field. But for Adam there was not found a helper like himself And God cast Adam into a trance, and as Adam slept, God took one of his ribs and in its place put flesh, and the Lord God made the rib which He took from Adam into a woman.*

Since, therefore, a helper like the man was not found among the cattle and beasts of the field and birds of heaven, God made him a helper of like nature from a rib taken from his side. Now, this was done when God had again formed these same beasts of the field and birds of heaven from the earth and had brought them to the man. But how can this be understood as happening on the sixth day, since on that day the earth produced living creatures at the word of God, whereas on the fifth day the waters produced the birds also at the word of God? It would not be said here, *And again God formed from the earth all the beasts of the field and all the birds of heaven,* unless the earth had already produced all the beasts of the field on the sixth day, and the water all the birds of heaven on the fifth day.

In accordance, therefore, with the original work of creation, in which God made all things together, He created potentially and in their causes works from which He rested on the seventh day. But He works in a different manner now, as we see in those beings which He creates in the course of time, working even yet. Consequently, it was in days as we know them with their corporeal light caused by the sun moving in the sky that Eve was made from the side of her husband. For it was then that God again formed the beasts and birds from the earth, and since among them no helper was found for Adam similar to him, Eve was formed. It was, therefore, in such days as these that God also formed Adam from the slime of the earth.

8. It cannot be said that the male was made on the sixth day and the female in the course of days following. On the sixth day it is explicitly said, *Male and female He made them, and He blessed them,* and so forth, and these words are said about both and to both. The original creation, therefore, of the two was different from their later creation. First they were created in potency through the word of God and inserted seminally into the world when He created all things together, after which He rested from these works on the seventh day. From these creatures all things are made, each at its own proper time throughout the course of history. Later the man and the woman were created in accordance with God's creative activity as it is at work throughout the ages and with which He works even now; and thus it was ordained that in time Adam would be made from the slime of the earth and the woman from the side of her husband.

Chapter 6 – A further explanation; The difference between material seeds and primordial reasons

9. According to the division of the works of God described above, some works belonged to the invisible days in which He created all things simultaneously, and others belong to the days in which He daily fashions whatever evolves in the course of time from what I might call the primordial wrappers. In this interpretation I hope I have not given a misguided or absurd explanation of the words of Scripture which have led me to assume this division. And since an understanding of these matters is somewhat difficult and beyond the grasp of an uneducated reader, I must take care that I am not thought to hold or say anything that I know I do not hold or say. For although I prepared the reader to understand my meaning as far as I was able in the foregoing commentary, nevertheless I suppose that many are not enlightened by my explanations and think that man existed in the original work of God by which He made everything simultaneously so as to have some form of life and to perceive, believe, and understand as addressed to himself the words which God spoke when He said, *See, I have given you every seed-bearing plant.* Whoever thinks this should know that this is not what I have thought or what I have said.

10. But, again, if I say that in the original creation by which God created everything simultaneously man was not there as a man, neither in the maturity of adult life nor in the form of an infant, not as a fetus in a mother's womb nor even as a visible seed of man, someone will think he did not exist at all. Let such a one, then, go back to Scripture. He will find that on the sixth day man was made to the image of God and that he was made male and female. Let him see, then, when the woman was made: he will find that it was outside of the six days. For she was made when God formed from the earth again the beasts of the field and the birds of heaven, not when the waters brought forth the birds, and earth brought forth living creatures, among which were the beasts.

Then, in the first creation, man was made, male and female. This happened, therefore, both then and later. It cannot be then and not later, nor can it be later and not then. Nor were there different persons later, but there were the very same ones in one way then and in another way later. One will ask me how. I shall reply: "Later visibly, in the form of the human body familiar to us; not, however, generated by parents, but the man formed from the slime and the woman formed from his rib." One will ask how they were created originally on the sixth day. I shall reply: "Invisibly, potentially, in their causes, as things that will be in the future are made, yet not made in actuality now."

11. My critic perhaps will not understand this. All that is familiar to him is taken away, including the material dimension of seeds. For man was nothing of the sort when he was made in the first creation of the six days. There is indeed in seeds some likeness to what I am describing because of the future developments stored up in them. Nevertheless, before all visible seeds there are the causes; but he does not understand. What, then, shall I do except to give him a salutary admonition, as far as I can, to believe Holy Scripture and to accept its teaching that man was made when God, at the making of day, made heaven and earth, concerning which Scripture elsewhere says, *He who lives for ever created all things together?* And then creating all things not together but each in its own time, God formed the man from the slime of the earth and the woman from a bone taken out of the man. Scripture does not permit us to understand that in this manner the man

and woman were made on the sixth day, and yet it does not allow us to assume that they were not made on the sixth day at all.

Chapter 7 – It cannot be said that Gen. 1:27 refers only to the creation of the souls of man and woman

12. One might suggest that it was the souls of the man and woman that God created on the sixth day. It is certainly in the spiritual and intellectual part of man that the image of God is understood to be. Their bodies, then, would be formed later.

But Scripture does not allow us to accept such an interpretation first of all, we are told that God finished His work on the sixth day, and I do not see how we can understand this statement if there was lacking something then, which was not made in its causes, to be visibly formed later. Furthermore, the distinction between male and female can exist only in bodies. But if anyone suggests that in intellect and action both sexes were somehow to be understood as in the one soul, what will he make of the food God gave from the fruit trees on the sixth day? Food is needed by man only when he has a body. Finally, if anyone wishes to interpret this food in a figurative sense, he will be departing from the literal interpretation of the facts which should first be established in commenting on a narrative of this kind.

Chapter 8 – In what sense God spoke the words attributed to Him in Gen. 1:27–29

13. How, then, my critic asks, did God speak to those who did not yet hear or understand, since there was no one there to catch the words? I might reply that God spoke to them in the way Christ spoke to us when we were not yet born and were destined to come into being only after a long time, and as He spoke not only to us but also to all who would come to be after us. For it was to all who He knew would be His own that He said, *Behold I am with you until the end of the world.* In a similar way God knew the prophet to whom He said, *Before I formed you in the womb, I knew you;* and Levi paid tithes when he was in the loins of Abraham. Why, then, could not Abraham have been in Adam in a similar manner, and Adam himself in the first works of the world, which God created simultaneously?

But the words of the Lord in the flesh spoken by His mouth, as well as the words of God spoken by the mouths of prophets, are uttered in time by a voice coming from a body, and such words with all their syllables require and fill out corresponding intervals of time. But when God said, *Let Us make mankind in Our image and likeness; and let him have dominion over the fish of the sea, the birds of the air, all the cattle, all the earth, and all the creatures that crawl on the earth;* and, *Increase and multiply and fill the earth and subdue it and have dominion over the fish of the sea, the birds of the air, all the cattle, all the earth, and all the creatures that crawl on the earth;* and, *See, I have given you every seed-bearing plant bearing its seed over all the earth, and every tree that has seed-bearing fruit; these will be food for you;* these words of God, spoken before there were any sound vibrations in air and before any voice coming from man or from cloud existed, were uttered in His supreme Wisdom, through which all things were made. They were not like sounds that strike human ears, but they implanted in things made the causes of things yet to be made. Thus, God by His almighty power made what would appear in the future; and when He who is before the ages created the beginning of the ages, in what we might call the germ or root of time, He created man to be formed later in due time.

Some creatures, indeed, precede others either by reason of time or by reason of causality. But God precedes all that He made not only by reason of His superiority as the Author of all, even of causes, but also by reason of His eternity. But this topic should perhaps be more fully discussed in connection with other passages of Scripture relating more directly to it.

Chapter 9 – God knows us before we are born, but no one is personally responsible for any good or evil before his birth

14. This must conclude what I undertook to say about man. In expressing my views, I have tried to observe moderation so as to show a persevering spirit of enquiry rather than a dogged desire to maintain my opinions in exploring the profound meaning of Scripture.

Now, there is no doubt that God knew Jeremiah before He formed him in the womb, for He says quite clearly, *Before I formed you in the womb, I knew you.* But it is difficult, if not impossible, for our limited understanding to know where God knew him before forming him. Was it in some proximate causes, as in the case of Levi, who paid tithes when he was in the loins of Abraham? Was it in Adam himself, in whom the whole human race had its roots? And if in Adam, was it when he had been formed from the slime, or was it when he had been made in his causes in the works which God created simultaneously? Was it before all creation, inasmuch as God has elected and predestined His saints before the foundation of the world? Or was it rather in all of these causes, whether those I have mentioned or those I have not mentioned, before Jeremiah was formed in the womb?

Whatever the case may be, I do not think it necessary to carry on a more searching enquiry, provided that it is evident to us that from the moment Jeremiah was brought into this world by his parents he led his own life and, as he grew in years, was able to choose to live it well or badly, whereas before that he had no such choice, whether before he was formed in the womb or after he was formed there but before he was born. We are left with no hesitation on this point by St. Paul's view concerning the twins in the womb of Rebecca, who up to that point had done no good or evil.

15. Not in vain, however, does Scripture say that even an infant is not free from sin if he has spent one day of life on earth. The Psalmist says, *In iniquity I was conceived, and in sin my mother nourished me in her womb.* St. Paul says that all die in Adam, *in whom all have sinned.* But let us hold for certain that, whatever merits go from parents to their offspring and whatever grace of God sanctifies anyone before birth, there is no injustice in God, and no one before birth does any good or evil for which he is personally responsible. Some hold that in another life souls have sinned to a greater or lesser degree and that they have been sent into different bodies in accordance with what they deserve because of their sins; but that does not agree with the teaching of St. Paul, who has said quite clearly that those not yet born have done nothing good or evil.

16. We must, therefore, ask ourselves again at the proper time what the whole human race contracted from the sin of our first parents, who were the only ones to commit the sin. There is no doubt, however, that man could have had no such guilt before he was fashioned from the dust of the earth and before he was living his own life. Esau and Jacob, who according to St. Paul did no good or evil before birth, could not be said to have received some merit from their

parents if their parents had done no good or evil, nor could the human race be said to have sinned in Adam if Adam himself had not sinned; and Adam would not have sinned unless he were living his own life, in which he could live either well or badly.

It is idle, therefore, to look for either a sin or a good deed of Adam at the time when he was made in causes in the things simultaneously created but was not yet living his own life nor existing in parents so living. For in that first creation of the world, when God created all things simultaneously, He created man in the sense that He made the man who was to be, that is, the causal principle of man to be created, not the actuality of man already created.

Chapter 10 – Under the influence of the primordial reasons the crops came forth from the earth and then the seeds from the crops

17. Nevertheless, under one aspect these things are in the Word of God, where they are not made but eternally existing; under another aspect they are in the elements of the universe, where all things destined to be were made simultaneously; under another aspect they are in things no longer created simultaneously but rather separately each in its own due time, made according to their causes which were created simultaneously – among which was Adam, formed from the slime and animated by the breath of God, like the grass sprung from the earth; under another aspect they are in seeds, in which they are found again as quasi-primordial causes which derive from creatures that have come forth according to the causes which God first stored up in the world – and thus we have the crops from the earth, and the seed from the crops.

In all these things, beings already created received at their own proper time their manner of being and of acting, which developed into visible forms and natures from the hidden and invisible reasons which are latent in creation as causes. Thus the crops came forth on the earth, and man was made as a living being, and so of the other creatures, whether plants or animals, belonging to the work of God as He works even at this time. But these beings have duplicates of themselves, as it were, carried invisibly within them by reason of the hidden power of reproduction that they possess. They have this power through their primordial causes, in which they were placed in the created world when day was made, before they came forth in the visible shape proper to their kind.

Chapter 11 – Creatures were in one sense completed and in another sense just begun: completed because they were made in their causal reasons, just begun because God subsequently would bring them forth in their visible form

18. Now, if the original works of God, when He created all things simultaneously, were not perfect according to the limits of their nature, no doubt there would later be added the perfections needed to complete their being; and thus the perfection of all the world is made up of what we might call two halves. As they are like parts of a whole, the total universe, whose parts they are, is completed by their union. Moreover, if these creatures attained perfection in the sense that they are perfected when they are brought forth individually, each at its own time, in their visible form and reality, it is surely true that either nothing would come from them later as time unfolds, or God would unceasingly produce from them the effects which in due time have their origin in them.

But these works in a certain sense are already perfected, and in another sense they are just begun. They were made by God when in the beginning He made the world and created simultaneously all things to be unfolded in the ages to follow. They are perfected because in their proper natures by which they fulfill their role in time they have nothing that was not present in them as made in its causes. They are just begun, however, since in them are seeds, as it were, of future perfections to be put forth from their hidden state and made manifest during the ages at the appropriate time.

The words of Scripture make this very clear to anyone who reads the text attentively. For it says that they were both perfected and just begun. Certainly, if they were not perfected, Scripture would not have said, *Thus the heavens and the earth were finished and all their array. And on the sixth day God finished the works He had made...And God blessed the seventh day and made it holy.* On the other hand, unless they had just begun, Scripture would not go on to say that *God rested on that day from all the works He had begun to make.*

19. If someone should ask how God completed His works and at the same time just began them, the answer is clear from what I have said above. For He did not complete some and begin others, but the reference is to the same works from which He rested on the seventh day. We can see that God completed these works when He created all things simultaneously in such a finished state that nothing would have to be created by Him in the temporal order which had not been already created by Him here in the order of causes; and at the same time we understand that God began these works in the sense that what He had originally established here in causes He later fulfilled in effects.

Thus God formed the dust of the earth (or the slime of the earth) into man; that is, He formed man from the dust or slime of the earth. And He breathed (or blew) into his face the breath of life; and man was made a living being. He was not predestined at that time, for that happened before the ages in the foreknowledge of the Creator. Nor was he at that time made in causes, whether begun in a completed state or completed in a beginning state, for that happened with the commencement of the ages in the primordial reasons when all things were created simultaneously. But he was created in time, visibly in the body, invisibly in the soul, being made up of soul and body.

Augustine *City of God*, Book XI

Chapter 3 – Of the Authority of the Canonical Scriptures Composed by the Divine Spirit

This Mediator, having spoken what He judged sufficient first by the prophets, then by His own lips, and afterwards by the apostles, has besides produced the Scripture which is called canonical, which has paramount authority, and to which we yield assent in all matters of which we ought not to be ignorant, and yet cannot know of ourselves. For if we attain the knowledge of present objects by the testimony of our own senses, whether internal or external, then, regarding objects remote from our own senses, we need others to bring their testimony, since we cannot know them by our own, and we credit the persons to whom the objects have been or are sensibly present. Accordingly, as in the case of visible objects which we have not seen, we trust those who have, (and likewise with all sensible objects), so in the case of things which are perceived by the mind and spirit, i.e., which are remote from our own interior sense, it behoves us to trust those who have seen them set in that incorporeal light, or abidingly contemplate them.

Chapter 4 – That the World is Neither Without Beginning, Nor Yet Created by a New Decree of God, by Which He Afterwards Willed What He Had Not Before Willed

Of all visible things, the world is the greatest; of all invisible, the greatest is God. But, that the world is, we see; that God is, we believe. That God made the world, we can believe from no one more safely than from God Himself. But where have we heard Him? Nowhere more distinctly than in the Holy Scriptures, where His prophet said, "In the beginning God created the heavens and the earth." Was the prophet present when God made the heavens and the earth? No; but the wisdom of God, by whom all things were made, was there, and wisdom insinuates itself into holy souls, and makes them the friends of God and His prophets, and noiselessly informs them of His works. They are taught also by the angels of God, who always behold the face of the Father, and announce His will to whom it befits. Of these prophets was he who said and wrote, "In the beginning God created the heavens and the earth." And so fit a witness was he of God, that the same Spirit of God, who revealed these things to him, enabled him also so long before to predict that our faith also would be forthcoming.

But why did God choose then to create the heavens and earth which up to that time He had not made? If they who put this question wish to make out that the world is eternal and without beginning, and that consequently it has not been made by God, they are strangely deceived, and rave in the incurable madness of impiety. For, though the voices of the prophets were silent, the world itself, by its well-ordered changes and movements, and by the fair appearance of all visible things, bears a testimony of its own, both that it has been created, and also that it could not have been created save by God, whose greatness and beauty are unutterable and invisible.

As for those who own, indeed, that it was made by God, and yet ascribe to it not a temporal but only a creational beginning, so that in some scarcely intelligible way the world should always have existed a created world they make an assertion which seems to them to defend God from the charge of arbitrary hastiness, or of suddenly conceiving the idea of creating the world as a quite new idea, or of casually changing His will, though He be unchangeable. But I do not see how this supposition of theirs can stand in other respects, and chiefly in respect of the soul; for if they contend that it is co-eternal with God, they will be quite at a loss to explain whence there has accrued to it new misery, which through a previous eternity had not existed. For if they said that its happiness and misery ceaselessly alternate, they must say, further, that this alternation will continue for ever; whence will result this absurdity, that, though the soul is called blessed, it is not so in this, that it foresees its own misery and disgrace. And yet, if it does not foresee it, and supposes that it will be neither disgraced nor wretched, but always blessed, then it is blessed because it is deceived; and a more foolish statement one cannot make.

But if their idea is that the soul's misery has alternated with its bliss during the ages of the past eternity, but that now, when once the soul, has been set free, it will return henceforth no more to misery, they are nevertheless of opinion that it has never been truly blessed before, but begins at last to enjoy a new and uncertain happiness; that is to say, they must acknowledge that some new thing, and that an important and signal thing, happens to the soul which never in a whole past eternity happened it before. And if they deny that God's eternal purpose included this new experience of the soul, they deny that He is the Author of its blessedness, which is unspeakable impiety. If, on the other hand, they say that the future blessedness of the soul is the result of a new decree of God, how will they show that God is not chargeable with that mutability which displeases them?

Further, if they acknowledge that it was created in time, but will never perish in time – that it has, like number, a beginning but no end, – and that, therefore, having once made trial of misery, and been delivered from it, it will never again return thereto, they will certainly admit that this takes place without any violation of the immutable counsel of God. Let them, then, in like manner believe regarding the world that it too could be made in time, and yet that God, in making it, did not alter His eternal design.

Chapter 5 – That We Ought Not to Seek to Comprehend the Infinite Ages of Time Before the World, Nor the Infinite Realms of Space

Next, we must see what reply can be made to those who agree that God is the Creator of the world, but have difficulties about the time of its creation, and what reply, also, they can make to difficulties we might raise about the place of its creation. For, as they demand why the world was created then and no sooner, we may ask why it was created just here where it is, and not elsewhere. For if they imagine infinite spaces of time before the world, during which God could not have been idle, in like manner they may conceive outside the world infinite realms of space, in which, if any one says that the Omnipotent cannot hold His hand from working, will it not follow that they must adopt Epicurus' dream of innumerable worlds? With this difference only, that he asserts that they are formed and destroyed by the fortuitous movements of atoms, while they will hold that they are made by God's hand, if they maintain that, throughout the boundless immensity of space, stretching interminably in every direction round the world, God cannot rest, and that the worlds which they suppose Him to make cannot be destroyed. For here the question is with those who, with ourselves, believe that God is spiritual, and the Creator of all existences but Himself.

As for others, it is a condescension to dispute with them on a religious question, for they have acquired a reputation only among men who pay divine honors to a number of gods, and have become conspicuous among the other philosophers for no other reason than that, though they are still far from the truth, they are near it in comparison with the rest. While these, then, neither confine in any place, nor limit, nor distribute the divine substance, but, as is worthy of God, own it to be wholly though spiritually present everywhere, will they perchance say that this substance is absent from such immense spaces outside the world, and is occupied in one only, (and that a very little one compared with the infinity beyond), the one, namely, in which is the world? I think they will not proceed to this absurdity. Since they maintain that there is but one world, of vast material bulk, indeed, yet finite, and in its own determinate position, and that this was made by the working of God, let them give the same account of God's resting in the infinite times before the world as they give of His resting in the infinite spaces outside of it.

And as it does not follow that God set the world in the very spot it occupies and no other by accident rather than by divine reason, although no human reason can comprehend why it was so set, and though there was no merit in the spot chosen to give it the precedence of infinite others, so neither does it follow that we should suppose that God was guided by chance when He created the world in that and no earlier time, although previous times had been running by during an infinite past, and though there was no difference by which one time could be chosen in preference to another. But if they say that the thoughts of men are idle when they conceive infinite places, since there is no place beside the world, we reply that, by the same showing, it is vain to conceive of the past times of God's rest, since there is no time before the world.

Chapter 6 – That the World and Time Had Both One Beginning, and the One Did Not Anticipate the Other

For if eternity and time are rightly distinguished by this, that time does not exist without some movement and transition, while in eternity there is no change, who does not see that there could have been no time had not some creature been made, which by some motion could give birth to change – the various parts of which motion and change, as they cannot be simultaneous, succeed one another – and thus, in these shorter or longer intervals of duration, time would begin? Since then, God, in whose eternity is no change at all, is the Creator and Ordainer of time, I do not see how He can be said to have created the world after spaces of time had elapsed, unless it be said that prior to the world there was some creature by whose movement time could pass. And if the sacred and infallible Scriptures say that in the beginning God created the heavens and the earth, in order that it may be understood that He had made nothing previously – for if He had made anything before the rest, this thing would rather be said to have been made "in the beginning," – then assuredly the world was made, not in time, but simultaneously with time. For that which is made in time is made both after and before some time – after that which is past, before that which is future. But none could then be past, for there was no creature by whose movements its duration could be measured. But simultaneously with time the world was made, if in the world's creation change and motion were created, as seems evident from the order of the first six or seven days. For in these days the morning and evening are counted, until, on the sixth day, all things which God then made were finished, and on the seventh the rest of God was mysteriously and sublimely signalized. What kind of days these were it is extremely difficult, or perhaps impossible for us to conceive, and how much more to say!

Chapter 7 – Of the Nature of the First Days, Which are Said to Have Had Morning and Evening, Before There Was a Sun

We see, indeed, that our ordinary days have no evening but by the setting, and no morning but by the rising, of the sun; but the first three days of all were passed without sun, since it is reported to have been made on the fourth day. And first of all, indeed, light was made by the word of God, and God, we read, separated it from the darkness, and called the light Day, and the darkness Night; but what kind of light that was, and by what periodic movement it made evening and morning, is beyond the reach of our senses; neither can we understand how it was, and yet must unhesitatingly believe it. For either it was some material light, whether proceeding from the upper parts of the world, far removed from our sight, or from the spot where the sun was afterwards kindled; or under the name of light the holy city was signified, composed of holy angels and blessed spirits, the city of which the apostle says, "Jerusalem which is above is our eternal mother in heaven;" and in another place, "For ye are all the children of the light, and the children of the day; we are not of the night, nor of darkness."

Yet in some respects we may appropriately speak of a morning and evening of this day also. For the knowledge of the creature is, in comparison of the knowledge of the Creator, but a twilight; and so it dawns and breaks into morning when the creature is drawn to the praise and love of the Creator; and night never falls when the Creator is not forsaken through love of the creature. In fine, Scripture, when it would recount those days in order, never mentions the word night. It never says, "Night was," but "The evening and the morning were the first day." So of the second and the rest. And, indeed, the knowledge of created things contemplated by themselves is, so to speak, more colorless than when they are seen in the wisdom of God, as in the art by which they were made. Therefore evening is a more suitable figure than night; and yet, as I said, morning returns when the creature returns to the praise and love of the Creator. When it does so in the knowledge of itself, that is the first day; when in the knowledge of the firmament, which is the name given to the sky between the waters above and those beneath, that is the second day; when in the knowledge of the earth, and the sea, and all things that grow out of the earth, that is the third day; when in the knowledge of the greater and less luminaries, and all the stars, that is the fourth day; when in the knowledge of all animals that swim in the waters and that fly in the air, that is the fifth day; when in the knowledge of all animals that live on the earth, and of man himself, that is the sixth day.

Chapter 8 – What We are to Understand of God's Resting on the Seventh Day, After the Six Days' Work

When it is said that God rested on the seventh day from all His works, and hallowed it, we are not to conceive of this in a childish fashion, as if work were a toil to God, who "spake and it was done," – spake by the spiritual and eternal, not audible and transitory word. But God's rest signifies the rest of those who rest in God, as the joy of a house means the joy of those in the house who rejoice, though not the house, but something else, causes the joy. How much more intelligible is such phraseology, then, if the house itself, by its own beauty, makes the inhabitants joyful! For in this case we not only call it joyful by that figure of speech in which the thing containing is used for the thing contained (as when we say, "The theatres applaud," "The meadows low," meaning that the men in the one applaud, and the oxen in the other low), but also by that figure in which the cause is spoken of as if it were the effect, as when a letter is said to be joyful, because it makes its readers so. Most appropriately, therefore, the sacred narrative states that God rested, meaning thereby that those rest who are in Him, and whom He makes to rest. And this the prophetic narrative promises also to the men to whom it speaks, and for whom it was written, that they themselves, after those good works which God does in and by them, if they have managed by faith to get near to God in this life, shall enjoy in Him eternal rest. This was prefigured to the ancient people of God by the rest enjoined in their sabbath law, of which, in its own place, I shall speak more at large.

Chapter 9 – What the Scriptures Teach Us to Believe Concerning the Creation of the Angels

At present, since I have undertaken to treat of the origin of the holy city, and first of the holy angels, who constitute a large part of this city, and indeed the more blessed part, since they have never been expatriated, I will give myself to the task of explaining, by God's help, and as far as seems suitable, the Scriptures which relate to this point. Where Scripture speaks of the world's creation, it is not plainly said whether or when the angels were created; but if mention of them is made, it is implicitly under the name of "heaven," when it is said, "In the beginning God created the heavens and the earth," or perhaps rather under the name of "light," of which presently. But that they were wholly omitted, I am unable to believe, because it is written that God on the seventh day rested from all His works which He made; and this very book itself begins, "In the beginning God created the heavens and the earth," so that before heaven and earth God seems to have made nothing.

Since, therefore, He began with the heavens and the earth – and the earth itself, as Scripture adds, was at first invisible and formless, light not being as yet made, and darkness covering the face of the deep (that is to say, covering an undefined chaos of earth and sea, for where light is not, darkness must needs be) – and then when all things, which are recorded to have been completed in six days, were created and arranged, how should the angels be omitted, as if they were not among the works of God, from which on the seventh day He rested?

Yet, though the fact that the angels are the work of God is not omitted here, it is indeed not explicitly mentioned; but elsewhere Holy Scripture asserts it in the clearest manner. For in the Hymn of the Three Children in the Furnace it was said, "O all ye works of the Lord bless ye the Lord;" and among these works mentioned afterwards in detail, the angels are named. And in the psalm it is said, "Praise ye the Lord from the heavens, praise Him in the heights. Praise ye Him, all His angels; praise ye Him, all His hosts. Praise ye Him, sun and moon; praise him, all ye stars of light. Praise Him, ye heaven of heavens; and ye waters that be above the heavens. Let them praise the name of the Lord; for He commanded, and they were created." Here the angels are most expressly and by divine authority said to have been made by God, for of them among the other heavenly things it is said, "He commanded, and they were created."

Who, then, will be bold enough to suggest that the angels were made after the six days' creation? If any one is so foolish, his folly is disposed of by a scripture of like authority, where God says, "When the stars were made, the angels praised me with a loud voice." The angels therefore existed before the stars; and the stars were made the fourth day. Shall we then say that they were made the third day? Far from it; for we know what was made that day. The earth was separated from the water, and each element took its own distinct form, and the earth produced all that grows on it. On the second day, then? Not even on this; for on it the firmament was made between the waters above and beneath, and was called "Heaven," in which firmament the stars were made on the fourth day. There is no question, then, that if the angels are included in the works of God during these six days, they are that light which was called "Day," and whose unity Scripture signalizes by calling that day not the "first day," but "one day." For the second day, the third, and the rest are not other days; but the same "one" day is repeated to complete the number six or seven, so that there should be knowledge both of God's works and of His rest.

For when God said, "Let there be light, and there was light," if we are justified in understanding in this light the creation of the angels, then certainly they were created partakers of the eternal light which is the unchangeable Wisdom of God, by which all things were made, and whom we call the only-begotten Son of God; so that they, being illumined by the Light that created them, might themselves become light and be called "Day," in participation of that unchangeable Light and Day which is the Word of God, by whom both themselves and all else were made. "The true Light, which lighteth every man that cometh into the world," – this Light lighteth also every pure angel, that he may be light not in himself, but in God; from whom if an angel turn away, he becomes impure, as are all those who are called unclean spirits, and are no longer light in the Lord, but darkness in themselves, being deprived of the participation of Light eternal. For evil has no positive nature; but the loss of good has received the name "evil."

Chapter 10 – Of the Simple and Unchangeable Trinity, Father, Son, and Holy Ghost, One God, in Whom Substance and Quality are Identical

...According to this, then, those things which are essentially and truly divine are called simple, because in them quality and substance are identical, and because they are divine, or wise, or blessed in themselves, and without extraneous supplement. In Holy Scripture, it is true, the Spirit of wisdom is called "manifold" because it contains many things in it; but what it contains it also is, and it being one is all these things. For neither are there many wisdoms, but one, in which are untold and infinite treasures of things intellectual, wherein are all invisible and unchangeable reasons of things visible and changeable which were created by it. For God made nothing unwittingly; not even a human workman can be said to do so. But if He knew all that He made, He made only those things which He had known. Whence flows a very striking but true conclusion, that this world could not be known to us unless it existed, but could not have existed unless it had been known to God.

Chapter 16 – Of the Ranks and Differences of the Creatures, Estimated by Their Utility, or According to the Natural Gradations of Being

For, among those beings which exist, and which are not of God the Creator's essence, those which have life are ranked above those which have none; those that have the power of generation, or even of desiring, above those which want this faculty. And, among things that have life, the sentient are higher than those which have no sensation, as animals are ranked above trees. And, among the sentient, the intelligent are above those that have not intelligence – men, e.g., above cattle. And, among the intelligent, the immortal such as the angels, above the mortal, such as men. These are the gradations according to the order of nature; but according to the utility each man finds in a thing, there are various standards of value, so that it comes to pass that we prefer some things that have no sensation to some sentient beings. And so strong is this preference, that, had we the power, we would abolish the latter from nature altogether, whether in ignorance of the place they hold in nature, or, though we know it, sacrificing them to our own convenience. Who, e.g., would not rather have bread in his house than mice, gold than fleas? But there is little to wonder at in this, seeing that even when valued by men themselves (whose nature is certainly of the highest dignity), more is often given for a horse than for a slave, for a jewel than for a maid. Thus the reason of one contemplating nature prompts very different judgments from those dictated by the necessity of the needy, or the desire of the voluptuous; for the former considers what value a thing in itself has in the scale of creation, while necessity considers how it meets its need; reason looks for what the mental light will judge to be true, while pleasure looks for what pleasantly titilates the bodily sense. But of such consequence in rational natures is the weight, so to speak, of will and of love, that though in the order of nature angels rank above men, yet, by the scale of justice, good men are of greater value than bad angels.

Chapter 17 – That the Flaw of Wickedness is Not Nature, But Contrary to Nature, and Has Its Origin, Not in the Creator, But in the Will

It is with reference to the nature, then, and not to the wickedness of the devil, that we are to understand these words, "This is the beginning of God's handiwork;" for, without doubt, wickedness can be a flaw or vice only where the nature previously was not vitiated. Vice, too, is so contrary to nature, that it cannot but damage it. And therefore departure from God would be no vice, unless in a nature whose property it was to abide With God. So that even the wicked will is a strong proof of the goodness of the nature. But God, as He is the supremely good Creator of good natures, so is He of evil wills the most just Ruler; so that, while they make an ill use of good natures, He makes a good use even of evil wills. Accordingly, He caused the devil (good by God's creation, wicked by his own will) to be cast down from his high position, and to become the mockery of His angels – that is, He caused his temptations to benefit those whom he wishes to injure by them. And because God, when He created him, was certainly not ignorant of his future malignity, and foresaw the good which He Himself would bring out of his evil, therefore says the psalm, "This leviathan whom Thou hast made to be a sport therein," that we may see that, even while God in His goodness created him good, He yet had already foreseen and arranged how He would make use of him when he became wicked

Chapter 18 – Of the Beauty of the Universe, Which Becomes, by God's Ordinance, More Brilliant by the Opposition of Contraries

For God would never have created any, I do not say angel, but even man, whose future wickedness He foreknew, unless He had equally known to what uses in behalf of the good He could turn him, thus embellishing, the course of the ages, as it were an exquisite poem set off with antitheses. For what are called antitheses are among the most elegant of the ornaments of speech. They might be called in Latin "oppositions," or, to speak more accurately, "contrapositions;" but this word is not in common use among us, though the Latin, and indeed the languages of all nations, avail themselves of the same ornaments of style. In the Second Epistle to the Corinthians the Apostle Paul also makes a graceful use of antithesis, in that place where he says, "By the armor of righteousness on the right hand and on the left, by honor and dishonor, by evil report and good report: as deceivers, and yet true; as unknown, and yet well known; as dying, and, behold, we live; as chastened, and not killed; as sorrowful, yet always rejoicing; as poor, yet making many rich; as having nothing, and yet possessing all things." As, then, these oppositions of contraries lend beauty to the language, so the beauty of the course of this world is achieved by the opposition of contraries, arranged, as it were, by an eloquence not of words, but of things. This is quite plainly stated in the Book of Ecclesiasticus, in this way: "Good is set against evil, and life against death: so is the sinner against the godly. So look upon all the works of the Most High, and these are two and two, one against another."

Chapter 19 – What, Seemingly, We are to Understand by the Words, "God divided the Light from the Darkness"

Accordingly, though the obscurity of the divine word has certainly this advantage, that it causes many opinions about the truth to be started and discussed, each reader seeing some fresh meaning in it, yet, whatever is said to be meant by an obscure passage should be either confirmed by the testimony of obvious facts, or should be asserted in other and less ambiguous texts. This obscurity is beneficial, whether the sense of the author is at last reached after the discussion of many other interpretations, or whether, though that sense remain concealed, other truths are brought out by the discussion of the obscurity.

To me it does not seem incongruous with the working of God, if we understand that the angels were created when that first light was made, and that a separation was made between the holy and the unclean angels, when, as is said, "God divided the light from the darkness; and God called the light Day, and the darkness He called Night." For He alone could make this discrimination, who was able also before they fell, to foreknow that they would fall, and that, being deprived of the light of truth, they would abide in the darkness of pride. For, so far as regards the day and night, with which we are familiar, He commanded those luminaries of heaven that are obvious to our senses to divide between the light and the darkness. "Let there be," He says, "lights in the firmament of the heaven, to divide the day from the night;" and shortly after He says, "And God made two great lights; the greater light to rule the day, and the lesser light to rule the night: the stars also. And God set them in the firmament of the heaven, to give light upon the earth, and to rule over the day and over the night, and to divide the light from the darkness." But between that light, which is the holy company of the angels spiritually radiant with the illumination of the truth, and that opposing darkness, which is the noisome foulness of the spiritual condition of those angels who are turned away from the light of righteousness, only He Himself could divide, from whom their wickedness (not of nature, but of will), while yet it was future, could not be hidden or uncertain.

Chapter 20 – Of the Words Which Follow the Separation of Light and Darkness, "And God Saw the Light that It Was Good"

Then, we must not pass from this passage of Scripture without noticing that when God said, "Let there be light, and there was light," it was immediately added, "And God saw the light that it was good." No such expression followed the statement that He separated the light from the darkness, and called the light Day and the darkness Night, lest the seal of His approval might seem to be set on such darkness, as well as on the light. For when the darkness was not subject of disapprobation, as when it was divided by the heavenly bodies from this light which our eyes discern, the statement that God saw that it was good is inserted, not before, but after the division is recorded. "And God set them," so runs the passage, "in the firmament of the heaven, to give light upon the earth, and to rule over the day and over the night, and to divide the light from the darkness: and God saw that it was good." For He approved of both, because both were sinless. But where God said, "Let there be light, and there was light; and God saw the light that it was good;" and the narrative goes on, "and God divided the light from the darkness! and God called the light Day, and the darkness He called Night," there was not in this place subjoined the statement, "And God saw that it was good," lest both should be designated good, while one of them was evil, not by nature, but by its own fault. And therefore, in this ease, the light alone received the approbation of the Creator, while the angelic darkness, though it had been ordained, was yet not approved.

Chapter 21 – Of God's Eternal and Unchangeable Knowledge and Will, Whereby All He Has Made Pleased Him in the Eternal Design as Well as in the Actual Result

For what else is to be understood by that invariable refrain, "And God saw that it was good," than the approval of the work in its design, which is the wisdom of God? For certainly God did not in the actual achievement of the work first learn that it was good, but, on the contrary, nothing would have been made had it not been first known by Him. While, therefore, He sees that that is good which, had He not seen it before it was made, would never have been made, it is plain that He is not discovering, but teaching that it is good. Plato, indeed, was bold enough to say that, when the universe was completed, God was, as it were, elated with joy. And Plato was not so foolish as to mean by this that God was rendered more blessed by the novelty of His creation; but he wished thus to indicate that the work now completed met with its Maker's approval, as it had while yet in design.

It is not as if the knowledge of God were of various kinds, knowing in different ways things which as yet are not, things which are, and things which have been. For not in our fashion does He look forward to what is future, nor at what is present, nor back upon what is past; but in a manner quite different and far and profoundly remote from our way of thinking. For He does not pass from this to that by transition of thought, but beholds all things with absolute unchangeableness; so that of those things which emerge in time, the future, indeed, are not yet, and the present are now, and the past no longer are; but all of these are by Him comprehended in His stable and eternal presence. Niether does He see in one fashion by the eye, in another by the mind, for He is not composed of mind and body; nor does His present knowledge differ from that which it ever was or shall be, for those variations of time, past, present, and future, though they alter our knowledge, do not affect His, "with whom is no variableness, neither shadow of turning." Neither is there any growth from thought to thought in the conceptions of Him in whose spiritual vision all things which He knows are at once embraced. For as without any movement that time can measure. He Himself moves all temporal things, so He knows all times with a knowledge that time cannot measure. And therefore He saw that what He had made was good, when He saw that it was good to make it. And when He saw it made, He had not on that account a twofold nor any way increased knowledge of it; as if He had less knowledge before He made what He saw. For certainly He would not be the perfect worker He is, unless His knowledge were so perfect as to receive no addition from His finished works.

Wherefore, if the only object had been to inform us who made the light, it had been enough to say, "God made the light;" and if further information regarding the means by which it was made had been intended, it would have sufficed to say, "And God said, Let there be light, and there was light," that we might know not only that God had made the world, but also that He had made it by the word. But because it was right that three leading truths regarding the creature be intimated to us, viz., who made it, by what means, and why, it is written, "God said, Let there be light, and there was light. And God saw the light that it was good." If, then, we ask who made it, it was "God." If, by what means, He said "Let it be," and it was. If we ask, why He made it, "it was good." Neither is there any author more excellent than God, nor any skill more efficacious than the word of God, nor any cause better than that good might be created by the good God. This also Plato has assigned as the most sufficient reason for the creation of the world, that good works might be made by a good God; whether he read this passage, or, perhaps, was informed of these things by those who had read them, or, by his quick-sighted genius, penetrated to things spiritual and invisible through the things that are created, or was instructed regarding them by those who had discerned them.

Chapter 22 – Of Those Who Do Not Approve of Certain Things Which are a Part of This Good Creation of a Good Creator, and Who Think that There is Some Natural Evil

This cause, however, of a good creation, namely, the goodness of God – this cause, I say, so just and fit, which, when piously and carefully weighed, terminates all the controversies of those who inquire into the origin of the world, has not been recognized by some heretics, because there are, forsooth, many things, such as fire, frost, wild beasts, and so forth, which do not suit but injure this thin blooded and frail mortality of our flesh, which is at present under just punishment. They do not consider how admirable these things are in their own places, how excellent in their own natures, how beautifully adjusted to the rest of creation, and how much grace they contribute to the universe by their own contributions as to a commonwealth; and how serviceable they are even to ourselves, if we use them with a knowledge of their fit adaptations – so that even poisons, which are destructive when used injudiciously, become wholesome and medicinal when used in conformity with their qualities and design; just as, on the other hand, those things which give us pleasure, such as food, drink, and the light of the sun, are found to be hurtful when immoderately or unseasonably used. And thus divine providence admonishes us not foolishly to vituperate things, but to investigate their utility with care; and, where our mental capacity or infirmity is at fault, to believe that there is a utility, though hidden, as we have experienced that there were other things which we all but failed to discover. For this concealment of the use of things is itself either an exercise of our humility or a levelling of our pride; for no nature at all is evil, and this is a name for nothing but the want of good. But from things earthly to things heavenly, from the visible to the invisible, there are some things better than others; and for this purpose are they unequal, in order that they might all exist.

Now God is in such sort a great worker in great things, that He is not less in little things – for these little things are to be measured not by their own greatness (which does not exist), but by the wisdom of their Designer; as, in the visible appearance of a man, if one eyebrow be shaved off, how nearly nothing is taken from the body, but how much from the beauty! – for that is not constituted by bulk, but by the proportion and arrangement of the members. But we do not greatly wonder that persons, who suppose that some evil nature has been generated and propagated by a kind of opposing principle proper to it, refuse to admit that the cause of the creation was this, that the good God produced a good creation. For they believe that He was driven to this enterprise of creation by the urgent necessity of repulsing the evil that warred against Him, and that He mixed His good nature with the evil for the sake of restraining and conquering it; and that this nature of His, being thus shamefully polluted, and most cruelly oppressed and held captive, He labors to cleanse and deliver it, and with all His pains does not wholly succeed; but such part of it as could not be cleansed from that defilement is to serve as a prison and chain of the conquered and incarcerated enemy.

The Manichaeans would not drivel, or rather, rave in such a style as this, if they believed the nature of God to be, as it is, unchangeable and absolutely incorruptible, and subject to no injury; and if, moreover, they held in Christian sobriety, that the soul which has shown itself capable of being altered for the worse by its own will, and of being corrupted by sin, and so, of being deprived of the light of eternal truth – that this soul, I say, is not a part of God, nor of the same nature as God, but is created by Him, and is far different from its Creator.

Chapter 23 – Of the Error in Which the Doctrine of Origen is Involved

But it is much more surprising that some even of those who, with ourselves, believe that there is one only source of all things, and that no nature which is not divine can exist unless originated by that Creator, have yet refused to accept with a good and simple faith this so good and simple a reason of the world's creation, that a good God made it good; and that the things created, being different from God, were inferior to Him, and yet were good, being created by none other than He. But they say that souls, though not, indeed, parts of God, but created by Him, sinned by abandoning God; that, in proportion to their various sins, they merited different degrees of debasement from heaven to earth, and diverse bodies as prison-houses; and that this is the world, and this the cause of its creation, not the production of good things, but the restraining of evil.

Origen is justly blamed for holding this opinion. For in the books which he entitles *peri archôn*, that is, Of Origins, this is his sentiment, this his utterance. And I cannot sufficiently express my astonishment, that a man so erudite and well versed in ecclesiastical literature, should not have observed, in the first place, how opposed this is to the meaning of this authoritative Scripture, which, in recounting all the works of God, regularly adds, "And God saw that it was good;" and, when all were completed, inserts the words, "And God saw everything that He had made, and, behold, it was very good."

Was it not obviously meant to be understood that there was no other cause of the world's creation than that good creatures should be made by a good God? In this creation, had no one sinned, the world would have been filled and beautified with natures good without exception; and though there is sin, all things are not therefore full of sin, for the great majority of the heavenly inhabitants preserve their nature's integrity. And the sinful will though it violated the order of its own nature, did not on that account escape the laws of God, who justly orders all things for good. For as the beauty of a picture is increased by well-managed shadows, so, to the eye that has skill to discern it, the universe is beautified even by sinners, though, considered by themselves, their deformity is a sad blemish.

In the second place, Origen, and all who think with him, ought to have seen that if it were the true opinion that the world was created in order that souls might, for their sins, be accommodated with bodies in which they should be shut up as in houses of correction, the more venial sinners receiving lighter and more ethereal bodies, while the grosser and graver sinners received bodies more crass and grovelling, then it would follow that the devils, who are deepest in wickedness, ought, rather than even wicked men, to have earthly bodies, since these are the grossest and least ethereal of all. But in point of fact, that we might see that the deserts of souls are not to be estimated by the qualities of bodies, the wickedest devil possesses an ethereal body, while man, wicked, it is true, but with a wickedness small and venial in comparison with his, received even before his sin a body of clay.

And what more foolish assertion can be advanced than that God, by this sun of ours, did not design to benefit the material creation, or lend lustre to its loveliness, and therefore created one single sun for this single world, but that it so happened that one soul only had so sinned as to deserve to be enclosed in such a body as it is? On this principle, if it had chanced that not one, but two, yea, or ten, or a hundred had sinned similarly, and with a like degree of guilt, then this world would have one hundred suns. And that such is not the case, is due not to the considerate foresight of the Creator, contriving the safety and beauty of things material, but rather to the fact that so fine a quality of sinning was hit upon by only one soul, so that it alone has merited such a body.

Manifestly persons holding such opinions should aim at confining, not souls of which they know not what they say, but themselves, lest they fall, and deservedly, far indeed from the truth. And as to these three answers which I formerly recommended when in the case of any creature the questions are put, Who made it? By what means? Why? that it should be replied, God, By the Word, Because it was good – as to these three answers, it is very questionable whether the Trinity itself is thus mystically indicated, that is, the Father, the Son, and the Holy Ghost, or whether there is some good reason for this acceptation in this passage of Scripture – this, I say, is questionable, and one can't be expected to explain everything in one volume.

Chapter 29 – Of the Knowledge by Which the Holy Angels Know God in His Essence, and by Which They See the Causes of His Works in the Art of the Worker, Before They See Them in the Works of the Artist

Those holy angels come to the knowledge of God not by audible words, but by the presence to their souls of immutable truth, i.e., of the only-begotten Word of God; and they know this Word Himself, and the Father, and their Holy Spirit, and that this Trinity is indivisible, and that the three persons of it are one substance, and that there are not three Gods but one God; and this they so know that it is better understood by them than we are by ourselves. Thus, too, they know the creature also, not in itself, but by this better way, in the wisdom of God, as if in the art by which it was created; and, consequently, they know themselves better in God than in themselves, though they have also this latter knowledge. For they were created, and are different from their Creator. In Him, therefore, they have, as it were, a noonday knowledge; in themselves, a twilight knowledge, according to our former explanations. For there is a great difference between knowing a thing in the design in conformity to which it was made, and knowing it in itself – e.g., the straightness of lines and correctness of figures is known in one way when mentally conceived, in another when described on paper; and justice is known in one way in the unchangeable truth, in another in the spirit of a just man. So is it with all other things – as, the firmament between the water above and below, which was called the heaven; the gathering of the waters beneath, and the laying bare of the dry land, and the production of plants and trees; the creation of sun, moon, and stars; and of the animals out of the waters, fowls, and fish, and monsters of the deep; and of everything that walks or creeps on the earth, and of man himself, who excels all that is on the earth – all these things are known in one way by the angels in the Word of God, in which they see the eternally abiding causes and reasons according to which they were made, and in another way in themselves: in the former, with a clearer knowledge; in the latter, with a knowledge dimmer, and rather of the bare works than of the design. Yet, when these works are referred to the praise and adoration of the Creator Himself, it is as if morning dawned in the minds of those who contemplate them.

Chapter 30 – Of the Perfection of the Number Six, Which is the first of the Numbers Which is Composed of Its Aliquot Parts

These works are recorded to have been completed in six days (the same day being six times repeated), because six is a perfect number – not because God required a protracted time, as if He could not at once create all things, which then should mark the course of time by the movements proper to them, but because the perfection of the works was signified by the number six. For the number six is the first which is made up of its own parts, i.e., of its sixth, third, and half, which are respectively one, two, and three, and which make a total of six. In this way of looking at a number, those are said to be its parts which exactly divide it, as a half, a third, a fourth, or a fraction with any denominator, e.g., four is a part of nine, but not therefore an aliquot part; but one is, for it is the ninth part; and three is, for it is the third. Yet these two parts, the ninth and the third, or one and three, are far from making its whole sum of nine. So again, in the number ten, four is a part, yet does not divide it; but one is an aliquot part, for it is a tenth; so it has a fifth, which is two; and a half, which is five. But these three parts, a tenth, a fifth, and a half, or one, two, and five, added together, do not make ten, but eight. Of the number twelve, again, the parts added together exceed the whole; for it has a twelfth, that is, one; a sixth, or two; a fourth, which is three; a third, which is four; and a half, which is six. But one, two, three, four, and six make up, not twelve, but more, viz., sixteen. So much I have thought fit to state for the sake of illustrating the perfection of the number six, which is, as I said, the first which is exactly made up of its own parts added together; and in this number of days God finished His work. And, therefore, we must not despise the science of numbers, which, in many passages of holy Scripture, is found to be of eminent service to the careful interpreter. Neither has it been without reason numbered among God's praises, "Thou hast ordered all things in number, and measure, and weight."

Chapter 31 – Of the Seventh Day, in Which Completeness and Repose are Celebrated

But, on the seventh day (i.e., the same day repeated seven times, which number is also a perfect one, though for another reason), the rest of God is set forth, and then, too, we first hear of its being hallowed. So that God did not wish to hallow this day by His works, but by His rest, which has no evening, for it is not a creature; so that, being known in one way in the Word of God, and in another in itself, it should make a twofold knowledge, daylight and dusk (day and evening). Much more might be said about the perfection of the number seven, but this book is already too long, and I fear lest I should seem to catch at an opportunity of airing my little smattering of science more childishly than profitably. I must speak, therefore, in moderation and with dignity, lest, in too keenly following "number," I be accused of forgetting "weight" and "measure."

Suffice it here to say, that three is the first whole number that is odd, four the first that is even, and of these two, seven is composed. On this account it is often put for all numbers together, as, "A just man falleth seven times, and riseth up again," – that is, let him fall never so often, he will not perish (and this was meant to be understood not of sins, but of afflictions conducing to lowliness). Again, "Seven times a day will I praise Thee," which elsewhere is expressed thus, "I will bless the Lord at all times." And many such instances are found in the divine authorities, in which the number seven is, as I said, commonly used to express the whole, or the completeness of anything. And so the Holy Spirit, of whom the Lord says, "He will teach you all truth," is signified by this number. In it is the rest of God, the rest His people find in Him. For rest is in the whole, i.e., in perfect completeness, while in the part there is labor. And thus we labor as long as we know in part; "but when that which is perfect is come, then that which is in part shall be done away." It is even with toil we search into the Scriptures themselves. But the holy angels, towards whose society and assembly we sigh while in this our toilsome pilgrimage, as they already abide in their eternal home, so do they enjoy perfect facility of knowledge and felicity of rest. It is without difficulty that they help us; for their spiritual movements, pure and free, cost them no effort.

Chapter 32 – Of the Opinion that the Angels Were Created Before the World

But if some one oppose our opinion, and say that the holy angels are not referred to when it is said, "Let there be light, and there was light;" if he suppose or teach that some material light, then first created, was meant, and that the angels were created, not only before the firmament dividing the waters and named "the heaven," but also before the time signified in the words, "In the beginning God created the heaven and the earth;" if he allege that this phrase, "In the beginning," does not mean that nothing was made before (for the angels were), but that God made all things by His Wisdom or Word, who is named in Scripture "the Beginning," as He Himself, in the gospel, replied to the Jews when they asked Him who He was, that He was the Beginning; – I will not contest the point, chiefly because it gives me the liveliest satisfaction to find the Trinity celebrated in the very beginning of the book of Genesis. For having said "In the Beginning God created the heaven and the earth," meaning that the Father made them in the Son (as the psalm testifies where it says, "How manifold are Thy works, O Lord! in Wisdom hast Thou made them all," a little afterwards mention is fitly made of the Holy Spirit also. For, when it had been told us what kind of earth God created at first, or what the mass or matter was which God, under the name of "heaven and earth," had provided for the construction of the world, as is told in the additional words, "And the earth was without form, and void; and darkness was upon the face of the deep," then, for the sake of completing the mention of the Trinity, it is immediately added, "And the Spirit of God moved upon the face of the waters."

Let each one, then, take it as he pleases; for it is so profound a passage, that it may well suggest, for the exercise of the reader's tact, many opinions, and none of them widely departing from the rule of faith. At the same time, let none doubt that the holy angels in their heavenly abodes are, though not, indeed, co-eternal with God, yet secure and certain of eternal and true felicity. To their company the Lord teaches that His little ones belong; and not only says, "They shall be equal to the angels of God," but shows, too, what blessed contemplation the angels themselves enjoy, saying, "Take heed that ye despise not one of these little ones: for I say unto you, that in heaven their angels do always behold the face of my Father which is in heaven."

Chapter 33 – Of the Two Different and Dissimilar Communities of Angels, Which are Not Inappropriately Signified by the Names Light and Darkness

That certain angels sinned, and were thrust down to the lowest parts of this world, where they are, as it were, incarcerated till their final damnation in the day of judgment, the Apostle Peter very plainly declares, when he says that "God spared not the angels that sinned, but cast them down to hell, and delivered them into chains of darkness to be reserved into judgment." Who, then, can doubt that God, either in foreknowledge or in act, separated between these and the rest? And who will dispute that the rest are justly called "light?" For even we who are yet living by faith, hoping only and not yet enjoying equality with them, are already called "light" by the apostle: "For ye were sometimes darkness, but now are ye light in the Lord." But as for these apostate angels, all who understand or believe them to be worse than unbelieving men are well aware that they are called "darkness." Wherefore, though light and darkness are to be taken in their literal signification in these passages of Genesis in which it is said, "God said, Let there be light, and there was light," and "God divided the light from the darkness," yet, for our part, we understand these two societies of angels – the one enjoying God, the other swelling with pride; the one to whom it is said, "Praise ye Him, all His angels," the other whose prince says, "All these things will I give Thee if Thou wilt fall down and worship me;" the one blazing with the holy love of God, the other reeking with the unclean lust of self-advancement...

These two angelic communities, then, dissimilar and contrary to one another, the one both by nature good and by will upright, the other also good by nature but by will depraved, as they are exhibited in other and more explicit passages of holy writ, so I think they are spoken of in this book of Genesis under the names of light and darkness; and even if the author perhaps had a different meaning, yet our discussion of the obscure language has not been wasted time; for, though we have been unable to discover his meaning, yet we have adhered to the rule of faith, which is sufficiently ascertained by the faithful from other passages of equal authority. For, though it is the material works of God which are here spoken of, they have certainly a resemblance to the spiritual, so that Paul can say, "Ye are all the children of light, and the children of the day: we are not of the night, nor of darkness."

If, on the other hand, the author of Genesis saw in the words what we see, then our discussion reaches this more satisfactory conclusion, that the man of God, so eminently and divinely wise, or rather, that the Spirit of God who by him recorded God's works which were finished on the sixth day, may be supposed not to have omitted all mention of the angels whether he included them in the words "in the beginning," because He made them first, or, which seems most likely, because He made them in the only-begotten Word. And, under these names heaven and earth, the whole creation is signified, either as divided into spiritual and material, which seems the more likely, or into the two great parts of the world in which all created things are contained, so that, first of all, the creation is presented in sum, and then its parts are enumerated according to the mystic number of the days.

Chapter 34 – Of the Idea that the Angels Were Meant Where the Separation of the Waters by the Firmament is Spoken Of, and of that Other Idea that the Waters Were Not Created

Some, however, have supposed that the angelic hosts are somehow referred to under the name of waters, and that this is what is meant by "Let there be a firmament in the midst of the waters:" that the waters above should be understood of the angels, and those below either of the visible waters, or of the multitude of bad angels, or of the nations of men. If this be so, then it does not here appear when the angels were created, but when they were separated. Though there have not been wanting men foolish and wicked enough a to deny that the waters were made by God, because it is nowhere written, "God said, Let there be waters." With equal folly they might say the same of the earth, for nowhere do we read, "God said, Let the earth be." But, say they, it is written, "In the beginning God created the heaven and the earth." Yes, and there the water is meant, for both are included in one word. For "the sea is His," as the psalm says, "and He made it; and His hands formed the dry land."

But those who would understand the angels by the waters above the skies have a difficulty about the specific gravity of the elements, and fear that the waters, owing to their fluidity and weight, could not be set in the upper parts of the world. So that, if they were to construct a man upon their own principles, they would not put in his head any moist humors, or "phlegm" as the Greeks call it, and which acts the part of water among the elements of our body. But, in God's handiwork, the head is the seat of the phlegm, and surely most fitly; and yet, according to their supposition, so absurdly that if we were not aware of the fact, and were informed by this same record that God had put a moist and cold and therefore heavy humor in the uppermost part of man's body, these world-weighers would refuse belief. And if they were confronted with the authority of Scripture, they would maintain that something else must be meant by the words. But, were we to investigate and discover all the details which are written in this divine book regarding the creation of the world, we should have much to say, and should widely digress from the proposed aim of this work. Since, then, we have now said what seemed needful regarding these two diverse and contrary communities of angels, in which the origin of the two human communities (of which we intend to speak anon) is also found, let us at once bring this book also to a conclusion.

Augustine *City of God*, Book XII

Chapter 10 – Of the Falseness of the History Which Allots Many Thousand Years to the World's Past

Let us, then, omit the conjectures of men who know not what they say, when they speak of the nature and origin of the human race. For some hold the same opinion regarding men that they hold regarding the world itself, that they have always been. Thus Apuleius says when he is describing our race, "Individually they are mortal, but collectively, and as a race, they are immortal." And when they are asked, how, if the human race has always been, they vindicate the truth of their history, which narrates who were the inventors, and what they invented, and who first instituted the liberal studies and the other arts, and who first inhabited this or that region, and this or that island? They reply, that most, if not all lands, were so desolated at intervals by fire and flood, that men were greatly reduced in numbers, and from these, again, the population was restored to its former numbers, and that thus there was at intervals a new beginning made, and though those things which had been interrupted and checked by the severe devastations were only renewed, yet they seemed to be originated then; but that man could not exist at all save as produced by man. But they say what they think, not what they know.

They are deceived, too, by those highly mendacious documents which profess to give the history of many thousand years, though, reckoning by the sacred writings, we find that not 6000 years have yet passed. And, not to spend many words in exposing the baselessness of these documents, in which so many thousands of years are accounted for, nor in proving that their authorities are totally inadequate, let me cite only that letter which Alexander the Great wrote to his mother Olympias, giving her the narrative he had from an Egyptian priest, which he had extracted from their sacred archives, and which gave an account of kingdoms mentioned also by the Greek historians. In this letter of Alexander's a term of upwards of 5000 years is assigned to the kingdom of Assyria; while in the Greek history only 1300 years are reckoned from the reign of Bel himself, whom both Greek and Egyptian agree in counting the first king of Assyria. Then to the empire of the Persians and Macedonians this Egyptian assigned more than 8000 years, counting to the time of Alexander, to whom he was speaking; while among the Greeks, 485 years are assigned to the Macedonians down to the death of Alexander, and to the Persians 233 years, reckoning to the termination of his conquests. Thus these give a much smaller number of years than the Egyptians; and indeed, though multiplied three times, the Greek chronology would still be shorter. For the Egyptians are said to have formerly reckoned only four months to their year; so that one year, according to the fuller and truer computation now in use among them as well as among ourselves, would comprehend three of their old years. But not even thus, as I said, does the Greek history correspond with the Egyptian in its chronology. And therefore the former must receive the greater credit, because it does not exceed the true account of the duration of the world as it is given by our documents, which are truly sacred. Further, if this letter of Alexander, which has become so famous, differs widely in this matter of chronology from the probable credible account, how much less can we believe these documents which, though full of fabulous and fictitious antiquities, they would fain oppose to the authority of our well-known and divine books, which predicted that the whole world would believe them, and which the whole world accordingly has believed; which proved, too, that it had truly narrated past events by its prediction of future events, which have so exactly come to pass!

Chapter 11 – Of Those Who Suppose that This World Indeed is Not Eternal, But that Either There are Numberless Worlds, or that One and the Same World is Perpetually Resolved into Its Elements, and Renewed at the Conclusion of Fixed Cycles

There are some, again, who, though they do not suppose that this world is eternal, are of opinion either that this is not the only world, but that there are numberless worlds or that indeed it is the only one, but that it dies, and is born again at fixed intervals, and this times without number; but they must acknowledge that the human race existed before there were other men to beget them. For they cannot suppose that, if the whole world perish, some men would be left alive in the world, as they might survive in floods and conflagrations, which those other speculators suppose to be partial, and from which they can therefore reasonably argue that a few then survived whose posterity would renew the population; but as they believe that the world itself is renewed out of its own material, so they must believe that out of its elements the human race was produced, and then that the progeny of mortals sprang like that of other animals from their parents.

Chapter 12 – How These Persons are to Be Answered, Who Find Fault with the Creation of Man on the Score of Its Recent Date

As to those who are always asking why man was not created during these countless ages of the infinitely extended past, and came into being so lately that, according to Scripture, less than 6000 years have elapsed since He began to be, I would reply to them regarding the creation of man, just as I replied regarding the origin of the world to those who will not believe that it is not eternal, but had a beginning, which even Plato himself most plainly declares, though some think his statement was not consistent with his real opinion. If it offends them that the time that has elapsed since the creation of man is so short, and his years so few according to our authorities, let them take this into consideration, that nothing that has a limit is long, and that all the ages of time being finite, are very little, or indeed nothing at all, when compared to the interminable eternity. Consequently, if there had elapsed since the creation of man, I do not say five or six, but even sixty or six hundred thousand years, or sixty times as many, or six hundred or six hundred thousand times as many, or this sum multiplied until it could no longer be expressed in numbers, the same question could still be put, Why was he not made before?

For the past and boundless eternity during which God abstained from creating man is so great, that, compare it with what vast and untold number of ages you please, so long as there is a definite conclusion of this term of time, it is not even as if you compared the minutest drop of water with the ocean that everywhere flows around the globe. For of these two, one indeed is very small, the other incomparably vast, yet both are finite; but that space of time which starts from some beginning, and is limited by some termination, be it of what extent it may, if you compare it with that which has no beginning, I know not whether to say we should count it the very minutest thing, or nothing at all. For, take this limited time, and deduct from the end of it, one by one, the briefest moments (as you might take day by day from a man's life, beginning at the day in which he now lives, back to that of his birth), and though the number of moments you must subtract in this backward movement be so great that no word can express it, yet this subtraction will sometime carry you to the beginning. But if you take away from a time which has no beginning, I do not say brief moments one by one, nor yet hours, or days, or months, or years even in quantities, but terms of years so vast that they cannot be named by the most skillful arithmeticians – take away terms of years as vast as that which we have supposed to be gradually consumed by the deduction of moments – and take them away not once and again repeatedly, but always, and what do you effect, what do you make by your deduction, since you never reach the beginning, which has no existence?

Wherefore, that which we now demand after five thousand odd years, our descendants might with like curiosity demand after six hundred thousand years, supposing these dying generations of men continue so long to decay and be renewed, and supposing posterity continues as weak and ignorant as ourselves. The same question might have been asked by those who have lived before us and while man was even newer upon earth. The first man himself in short might the day after or the very day of his creation have asked why he was created no sooner. And no matter at what earlier or later period he had been created, this controversy about the commencement of this world's history would have had precisely the same difficulties as it has now.

Chapter 13 – Of the Revolution of the Ages, Which Some Philosophers Believe Will Bring All Things Round Again, After a Certain Fixed Cycle, to the Same Order and Form as at First

This controversy some philosophers have seen no other approved means of solving than by introducing cycles of time, in which there should be a constant renewal and repetition of the order of nature; and they have therefore asserted that these cycles will ceaselessly recur, one passing away and another coming, though they are not agreed as to whether one permanent world shall pass through all these cycles, or whether the world shall at fixed intervals die out, and be renewed so as to exhibit a recurrence of the same phenomena – the things which have been, and those which are to be, coinciding. And from this fantastic vicissitude they exempt not even the immortal soul that has attained wisdom, consigning it to a ceaseless transmigration between delusive blessedness and real misery. For how can that be truly called blessed which has no assurance of being so eternally, and is either in ignorance of the truth, and blind to the misery that is approaching, or, knowing it, is in misery and fear? Or if it passes to bliss, and leaves miseries forever, then there happens in time a new thing which time shall not end. Why not, then, the world also? Why may not man, too, be a similar thing? So that, by following the straight path of sound doctrine, we escape, I know not what circuitous paths, discovered by deceiving and deceived sages.

Some, too, in advocating these recurring cycles that restore all things to their original cite in favor of their supposition what Solomon says in the book of Ecclesiastes: "What is that which hath been? It is that which shall be. And what is that which is done? It is that which shall be done: and there is no new thing under the sun. Who can speak and say, See, this is new? It hath been already of old time, which was before us." This he said either of those things of which he had just been speaking – the succession of generations, the orbit of the sun, the course of rivers – or else of all kinds of creatures that are born and die. For men were before us, are with us, and shall be after us; and so all living things and all plants. Even monstrous and irregular productions, though differing from one another, and though some are reported as solitary instances, yet resemble one another generally, in so far as they are miraculous and monstrous, and, in this sense, have been, and shall be, and are no new and recent things under the sun.

However, some would understand these words as meaning that in the predestination of God all things have already existed, and that thus, there is no new thing under the sun. At all events, far be it from any true believer to suppose that by these words of Solomon those cycles are meant, in which, according to those philosophers, the same periods and events of time are repeated; as if, for example, the philosopher Plato, having taught in the school at Athens which is called the Academy, so, numberless ages before, at long but certain intervals, this same Plato and the same school, and the same disciples existed, and so also are to be repeated during the countless cycles that are yet to be – far be it, I say, from us to believe this. For once Christ died for our sins; and, rising from the dead, He dieth no more. "Death hath no more dominion over Him;" and we ourselves after the resurrection shall be "ever with the Lord," to whom we now say, as the sacred Psalmist dictates, "Thou shall keep us, O Lord, Thou shall preserve us from this generation." And that too which follows, is, I think, appropriate enough: "The wicked walk in a circle," not because their life is to recur by means of these circles, which these philosophers imagine, but because the path in which their false doctrine now runs is circuitous.

Chapter 14 – Of the Creation of the Human Race in Time, and How This Was Effected Without Any New Design or Change of Purpose on God's Part

What wonder is it if, entangled in these circles, they find neither entrance nor egress? For they know not how the human race, and this mortal condition of ours, took its origin, nor how it will be brought to an end, since they cannot penetrate the inscrutable wisdom of God. For, though Himself eternal, and without beginning, yet He caused time to have a beginning; and man, whom He had not previously made He made in time, not from a new and sudden resolution, but by His unchangeable and eternal design. Who can search out the unsearchable depth of this purpose, who can scrutinize the inscrutable wisdom, wherewith God, without change of will, created man, who had never before been, and gave him an existence in time, and increased the human race from one individual? For the Psalmist himself, when he had first said, "Thou shalt keep us, O Lord, Thou shall preserve us from this generation for ever," and had then rebuked those whose foolish and impious doctrine preserves for the soul no eternal deliverance and blessedness adds immediately, "The wicked walk in a circle." Then, as if it were said to him, "What then do you believe, feel, know? Are we to believe that it suddenly occurred to God to create man, whom He had never before made in a past eternity – God, to whom nothing new can occur, and in whom is no changeableness?" the Psalmist goes on to reply, as if addressing God

Himself, "According to the depth of Thy wisdom Thou hast multiplied the children of men." Let men, he seems to say, fancy what they please, let them conjecture and dispute as seems good to them, but Thou hast multiplied the children of men according to the depth of thy wisdom, which no man can comprehend. For this is a depth indeed, that God always has been, and that man, whom He had never made before, He willed to make in time, and this without changing His design and will.

Chapter 15 – Whether We are to Believe that God, as He Has Always Been Sovereign Lord, Has Always Had Creatures Over Whom He Exercised His Sovereignty; And in What Sense We Can Say that the Creature Has Always Been, and Yet Cannot Say It is Co-Eternal

For my own part, indeed, as I dare not say that there ever was a time when the Lord God was not Lord, so I ought not to doubt that man had no existence before time, and was first created in time. But when I consider what God could be the Lord of, if there was not always some creature, I shrink from making any assertion, remembering my own insignificance, and that it is written, "What man is he that can know the counsel of God? Or who can think what the will of the Lord is? For the thoughts of mortal men are timid, and our devices are but uncertain. For the corruptible body presseth down the soul, and the earthly tabernacle weigheth down the mind that museth upon many things." Many things certainly do I muse upon in this earthly tabernacle, because the one thing which is true among the many, or beyond the many, I cannot find.

If, then, among these many thoughts, I say that there have always been creatures for Him to be Lord of, who is always and ever has been Lord, but that these creatures have not always been the same, but succeeded one another (for we would not seem to say that any is co-eternal with the Creator, an assertion condemned equally by faith and sound reason), I must take care lest I fall into the absurd and ignorant error of maintaining that by these successions and changes mortal creatures have always existed, whereas the immortal creatures had not begun to exist until the date of our own world, when the angels were created; if at least the angels are intended by that light which was first made, or, rather, by that heaven of which it is said, "In the beginning God created the heavens and the earth." The angels, at least did not exist before they were created; for if we say that they have always existed, we shall seem to make them co-eternal with the Creator. Again, if I say that the angels were not created in time, but existed before all times, as those over whom God, who has ever been Sovereign, exercised His sovereignty, then I shall be asked whether, if they were created before all time, they, being creatures, could possibly always exist.

It may perhaps be replied, Why not always, since that which is in all time may very properly be said to be "always?" Now so true is it that these angels have existed in all time that even before time was they were created; if at least time began with the heavens, and the angels existed before the heavens. And if time was even before the heavenly bodies, not indeed marked by hours, days, months, and years – for these measures of time's periods which are commonly and properly called times, did manifestly begin with the motion of the heavenly bodies, and so God said, when He appointed them, "Let them be for signs, and for seasons, and for days, and for years," – if, I say, time was before these heavenly bodies by some changing movement, whose parts succeeded one another and could not exist simultaneously, and if there was some such movement among the angels which necessitated the existence of time, and that they from their very creation should be subject to these temporal changes, then they have existed in all time, for time came into being along with them. And who will say that what was in all time, was not always?

But if I make such a reply, it will be said to me, How, then, are they not co-eternal with the Creator, if He and they always have been? How even can they be said to have been created, if we are to understand that they have always existed? What shall we reply to this? Shall we say that both statements are true? That they always have been, since they have been in all time, they being created along with time, or time along with them, and yet that also they were created? For, similarly, we will not deny that time itself was created, though no one doubts that time has been in all time; for if it has not been in all time, then there was a time when there was no time. But the most foolish person could not make such an assertion. For we can reasonably say there was a time when Rome was not; there was a time when Jerusalem was not; there was a time when Abraham was not;

there was a time when man was not, and so on: in fine, if the world was not made at the commencement of time, but after some time had elapsed, we can say there was a time when the world was not. But to say there was a time when time was not, is as absurd as to say there was a man when there was no man; or, this world was when this world was not. For if we are not referring to the same object, the form of expression may be used, as, there was another man when this man was not. Thus we can reasonably say there was another time when this time was not; but not the merest simpleton could say there was a time when there was no time.

As, then, we say that time was created, though we also say that it always has been, since in all time time has been, so it does not follow that if the angels have always been, they were therefore not created. For we say that they have always been, because they have been in all time; and we say they have been in all time, because time itself could no wise be without them. For where there is no creature whose changing movements admit of succession, there cannot be time at all. And consequently, even if they have always existed, they were created; neither, if they have always existed, are they therefore co-eternal with the Creator. For He has always existed in unchangeable eternity; while they were created, and are said to have been always, because they have been in all time, time being impossible without the creature.

But time passing away by its changefulness, cannot be co-eternal with changeless eternity. And consequently, though the immortality of the angels does not pass in time, does not become past as if now it were not, nor has a future as if it were not yet, still their movements, which are the basis of time, do pass from future to past; and therefore they cannot be co-eternal with the Creator, in whose movement we cannot say that there has been that which now is not, or shall be that which is not yet. Wherefore, if God always has been Lord, He has always had creatures under His dominion – creatures, however, not begotten of Him, but created by Him out of nothing; nor co-eternal with Him, for He was before them though at no time without them, because He preceded them, not by the lapse of time, but by His abiding eternity. But if I make this reply to those who demand how He was always Creator, always Lord, if there were not always a subject creation; or how this was created, and not rather co-eternal with its Creator, if it always was, I fear I may be accused of recklessly affirming what I know not, instead of teaching what I know.

I return, therefore, to that which our Creator has seen fit that we should know; and those things which He has allowed the abler men to know in this life, or has reserved to be known in the next by the perfected saints, I acknowledge to be beyond my capacity. But I have thought it right to discuss these matters without making positive assertions, that they who read may be warned to abstain from hazardous questions, and may not deem themselves fit for everything. Let them rather endeavor to obey the wholesome injunction of the apostle, when he says, "For I say, through the grace given unto me, to every man that is among you, not to think of himself more highly than he ought to think; but to think soberly, according as God hath dealt to every man the measure of faith." For if an infant receive nourishment suited to its strength, it becomes capable, as it grows, of taking more; but if its strength and capacity be overtaxed, it dwines away in place of growing.

Chapter 16 – How We are to Understand God's Promise of Life Eternal, Which Was Uttered Before the "Eternal Times"

I own that I do not know what ages passed before the human race was created, yet I have no doubt that no created thing is co-eternal with the Creator. But even the apostle speaks of time as eternal, and this with reference, not to the future, but, which is more surprising, to the past. For he says, "In hope of eternal life, which God that cannot lie promised before the eternal times, but hath in due times manifested His word." You see he says that in the past there have been eternal times, which, however, were not co-eternal with God. And since God before these eternal times not only existed, but also, "promised" life eternal, which He manifested in its own times (that is to say, in due times), what else is this than His word? For this is life eternal. But then, how did He promise; for the promise was made to men, and yet they had no existence before eternal times? Does this not mean that, in His own eternity, and in His co-eternal word, that which was to be in its own time was already predestined and fixed?

Chapter 17 – What Defence is Made by Sound Faith Regarding God's Unchangeable Counsel and Will, Against the Reasonings of Those Who Hold that the Works of God are

Eternally Repeated in Revolving Cycles that Restore All Things as They Were

Of this, too, I have no doubt, that before the first man was created, there never had been a man at all, neither this same man himself recurring by I know not what cycles, and having made I know not how many revolutions, nor any other of similar nature. From this belief I am not frightened by philosophical arguments, among which that is reckoned the most acute which is founded on the assertion that the infinite cannot be comprehended by any mode of knowledge. Consequently, they argue, God has in his own mind finite conceptions of all finite things which He makes.

Now it cannot be supposed that His goodness was ever idle; for if it were, there should be ascribed to Him an awakening to activity in time, from a past eternity of inactivity, as if He repented of an idleness that had no beginning, and proceeded, therefore, to make a beginning of work. This being the case, they say it must be that the same things are always repeated, and that as they pass, so they are destined always to return, whether amidst all these changes the world remains the same – the world which has always been, and yet was created – or that the world in these revolutions is perpetually dying out and being renewed; otherwise, if we point to a time when the works of God were begun, it would be believed that He considered His past eternal leisure to be inert and indolent, and therefore condemned and altered it as displeasing to Himself. Now if God is supposed to have been indeed always making temporal things, but different from one another, and one after the other, so, that He thus came at last to make man, whom He had never made before, then it may seem that He made man not with knowledge (for they suppose no knowledge can comprehend the infinite succession of creatures), but at the dictate of the hour, as it struck him at the moment, with a sudden and accidental change of mind.

On the other hand, say they, if those cycles be admitted, and if we suppose that the same temporal things are repeated, while the world either remains identical through all these rotations, or else dies away and is renewed, then there is ascribed to God neither the slothful ease of a past eternity, nor a rash and unforeseen creation. And if the same things be not thus repeated in cycles, then they cannot by any science or prescience be comprehended in their endless diversity. Even though reason could not refute, faith would smile at these argumentations, with which the godless endeavor to turn our simple piety from the right way, that we may walk with them "in a circle." But by the help of the Lord our God, even reason, and that readily enough, shatters these revolving circles which conjecture frames. For that which specially leads these men astray to refer their own circles to the straight path of truth, is, that they measure by their own human, changeable, and narrow intellect the divine mind, which is absolutely unchangeable, infinitely capacious, and without succession of thought, counting all things without number. So that saying of the apostle comes true of them, for, "comparing themselves with themselves, they do not understand." For because they do, in virtue of a new purpose, whatever new thing has occurred to them to be done (their minds being changeable), they conclude it is so with God; and thus compare, not God – for they cannot conceive God, but think of one like themselves when they think of Him – not God, but themselves, and not with Him, but with themselves.

For our part, we dare not believe that God is affected in one way when He works, in another when He rests. Indeed, to say that He is affected at all, is an abuse of language, since it implies that there comes to be something in His nature which was not there before. For he who is affected is acted upon, and whatever is acted upon is changeable. His leisure, therefore, is no laziness, indolence, inactivity; as in His work is no labor, effort, industry. He can act while He reposes, and repose while He acts. He can begin a new work with (not a new, but) an eternal design; and what He has not made before, He does not now begin to make because He repents of His former repose. But when one speaks of His former repose and subsequent operation (and I know not how men can understand these things), this "former" and "subsequent" are applied only to the things created, which formerly did not exist, and subsequently came into existence. But in God the former purpose is not altered and obliterated by the subsequent and different purpose, but by one and the same eternal and unchangeable will He effected regarding the things He created, both that formerly, so long as they were not, they should not be, and that subsequently, when they began to be, they should come into existence. And thus, perhaps, He would show, in a very striking way, to those who have eyes for such things, how independent He is of what He makes, and how it is of His own gratuitous goodness He creates, since from eternity He dwelt without creatures in no less perfect a blessedness.

Chapter 18 – Against Those Who Assert that Things that are Infinite Cannot Be Comprehended by the Knowledge of God

As for their other assertion, that God's knowledge cannot comprehend things infinite, it only remains for them to affirm, in order that they may sound the depths of their impiety, that God does not know all numbers. For it is very certain that they are infinite; since, no matter of what number you suppose an end to be made, this number can be, I will not say, increased by the addition of one more, but however great it be, and however vast be the multitude of which it is the rational and scientific expression, it can still be not only doubled, but even multiplied. Moreover, each number is so defined by its own properties, that no two numbers are equal. They are therefore both unequal and different from one another; and while they are simply finite, collectively they are infinite.

Does God, therefore, not know numbers on account of this infinity; and does His knowledge extend only to a certain height in numbers, while of the rest He is ignorant? Who is so left to himself as to say so? Yet they can hardly pretend to put numbers out of the question, or maintain that they have nothing to do with the knowledge of God; for Plato, their great authority, represents God as framing the world on numerical principles: and in our books also it is said to God, "Thou hast ordered all things in number, and measure, and weight." The prophet also says, "Who bringeth out their host by number." And the Saviour says in the Gospel, "The very hairs of your head are all numbered." Far be it, then, from us to doubt that all number is known to Him "whose understanding," according to the Psalmist, "is infinite." The infinity of number, though there be no numbering of infinite numbers, is yet not incomprehensible by Him whose understanding is infinite. And thus, if everything which is comprehended is defined or made finite by the comprehension of him who knows it, then all infinity is in some ineffable way made finite to God, for it is comprehensible by His knowledge.

Wherefore, if the infinity of numbers cannot be infinite to the knowledge of God, by which it is comprehended, what are we poor creatures that we should presume to fix limits to His knowledge, and say that unless the same temporal thing be repeated by the same periodic revolutions, God cannot either foreknow His creatures that He may make them, or know them when He has made them? God, whose knowledge is simply manifold, and uniform in its variety, comprehends all incomprehensibles with so incomprehensible a comprehension, that though He willed always to make His later works novel and unlike what went before them, He could not produce them without order and foresight, nor conceive them suddenly, but by His eternal foreknowledge.

Chapter 19 – Of Worlds Without End, or Ages of Ages

I do not presume to determine whether God does so, and whether these times which are called "ages of ages" are joined together in a continuous series, and succeed one another with a regulated diversity, and leave exempt from their vicissitudes only those who are freed from their misery, and abide without end in a blessed immortality; or whether these are called "ages of ages," that we may understand that the ages remain unchangeable in God's unwavering wisdom, and are the efficient causes, as it were, of those ages which are being spent in time. Possibly "ages" is used for "age," so that nothing else is meant by "ages of ages" than by "age of age," as nothing else is meant by "heavens of heavens" than by "heaven of heaven." For God called the firmament, above which are the waters, "Heaven," and yet the psalm says, "Let the waters that are above the heavens praise the name of the Lord." Which of these two meanings we are to attach to "ages of ages," or whether there is not some other and better meaning still, is a very profound question; and the subject we are at present handling presents no obstacle to our meanwhile deferring the discussion of it, whether we may be able to determine anything about it, or may only be made more cautious by its further treatment, so as to be deterred from making any rash affirmations in a matter of such obscurity. For at present we are disputing the opinion that affirms the existence of those periodic revolutions by which the same things are always recurring at intervals of time.

Now whichever of these suppositions regarding the "ages of ages" be the true one, it avails nothing for the substantiating of those cycles;

for whether the ages of ages be not a repetition of the same world, but different worlds succeeding one another in a regulated connection, the ransomed souls abiding in well-assured bliss without any recurrence of misery, or whether the ages of ages be the eternal causes which rule what shall be and is in time, it equally follows, that those cycles which bring round the same things have no existence; and nothing more thoroughly explodes them than the fact of the eternal life of the saints.

Chapter 20 – Of the Impiety of Those Who Assert that the Souls Which Enjoy True and Perfect Blessedness, Must Yet Again and Again in These Periodic Revolutions Return to Labor and Misery

What pious ears could bear to hear that after a life spent in so many and severe distresses (if, indeed, that should be called a life at all which is rather a death, so utter that the love of this present death makes us fear that death which delivers us from it), that after evils so disastrous, and miseries of all kinds have at length been expiated and finished by the help of true religion and wisdom, and when we have thus attained to the vision of God, and have entered into bliss by the contemplation of spiritual light and participation in His unchangeable immortality, which we burn to attain – that we must at some time lose all this, and that they who do lose it are cast down from that eternity, truth, and felicity to infernal mortality and shameful foolishness, and are involved in accursed woes, in which God is lost, truth held in detestation, and happiness sought in iniquitous impurities? And that this will happen endlessly again and again, recurring at fixed intervals, and in regularly returning periods? And that this everlasting and ceaseless revolution of definite cycles, which remove and restore true misery and deceitful bliss in turn, is contrived in order that God may be able to know His own works, since on the one hand He cannot rest from creating and on the other, cannot know the infinite number of His creatures, if He always makes creatures? Who, I say, can listen to such things? Who can accept or suffer them to be spoken? Were they true, it were not only more prudent to keep silence regarding them, but even (to express myself as best I can) it were the part of wisdom not to know them. For if in the future world we shall not remember these things, and by this oblivion be blessed, why should we now increase our misery, already burdensome enough, by the knowledge of them? If, on the other hand, the knowledge of them will be forced Upon us hereafter, now at least let us remain in ignorance, that in the present expectation we may enjoy a blessedness which the future reality is not to bestow; since in this life we are expecting to obtain life everlasting, but in the world to come are to discover it to be blessed, but not everlasting.

And if they maintain that no one can attain to the blessedness of the world to come, unless in this life he has been indoctrinated in those cycles in which bliss and misery relieve one another, how do they avow that the more a man loves God, the more readily he attains to blessedness – they who teach what paralyzes love itself? For who would not be more remiss and lukewarm in his love for a person whom he thinks he shall be forced to abandon, and whose truth and wisdom he shall come to hate; and this, too, after he has quite attained to the utmost and most blissful knowledge of Him that he is capable of? Can any one be faithful in his love, even to a human friend, if he knows that he is destined to become his enemy? God forbid that there be any truth in an opinion which threatens us with a real misery that is never to end, but is often and endlessly to be interrupted by intervals of fallacious happiness. For what happiness can be more fallacious and false than that in whose blaze of truth we yet remain ignorant that we shall be miserable, or in whose most secure citadel we yet fear that we shall be so? For if, on the one hand, we are to be ignorant of coming calamity, then our present misery is not so short-sighted for it is assured of coming bliss. If, on the other hand, the disaster that threatens is not concealed from us in the world to come, then the time of misery which is to be at last exchanged for a state of blessedness, is spent by the soul more happily than its time of happiness, which is to end in a return to misery. And thus our expectation of unhappiness is happy, but of happiness unhappy. And therefore, as we here suffer present ills, and hereafter fear ills that are imminent, it were truer to say that we shall always be miserable than that we can some time be happy.

But these things are declared to be false by the loud testimony of religion and truth; for religion truthfully promises a true blessedness, of which we shall be eternally assured, and which cannot be interrupted by any disaster. Let us therefore keep to the straight path, which is Christ, and, with Him as our Guide and Saviour, let us turn away in heart and mind from the unreal and futile cycles of the godless. Porphyry, Platonist though he was, abjured the opinion of his school, that in these cycles souls are ceaselessly passing away and returning, either being struck with the extravagance of the idea, or sobered by his knowledge of Christianity. As I mentioned in the tenth book, he preferred saying that the soul, as it had been sent into the world that it might know evil, and be purged and delivered from it, was never again exposed to such an experience after it had once returned to the Father. And if he abjured the tenets of his school, how much more ought we Christians to abominate and avoid an opinion so unfounded and hostile to our faith?

But having disposed of these cycles and escaped out of them, no necessity compels us to suppose that the human race had no beginning in time, on the ground that there is nothing new in nature which, by I know not what cycles, has not at some previous period existed, and is not hereafter to exist again. For if the soul, once delivered, as it never was before, is never to return to misery, then there happens in its experience something which never happened before; and this, indeed, something of the greatest consequence, to wit, the secure entrance into eternal felicity. And if in an immortal nature there can occur a novelty, which never has been, nor ever shall be, reproduced by any cycle, why is it disputed that the same may occur in mortal natures? If they maintain that blessedness is no new experience to the soul, but only a return to that state in which it has been eternally, then at least its deliverance from misery is something new, since, by their own showing, the misery from which it is delivered is itself, too, a new experience. And if this new experience fell out by accident, and was not embraced in the order of things appointed by Divine Providence, then where are those determinate and measured cycles in which no new thing happens, but all things are reproduced as they were before?

If, however, this new experience was embraced in that providential order of nature (whether the soul was exposed to the evil of this world for the sake of discipline, or fell into it by sin), then it is possible for new things to happen which never happened before, and which yet are not extraneous to the order of nature. And if the soul is able by its own imprudence to create for itself a new misery, which was not unforeseen by the Divine Providence, but was provided for in the order of nature along with the deliverance from it, how can we, even with all the rashness of human vanity, presume to deny that God can create new things – new to the world, but not to Him – which He never before created, but yet foresaw from all eternity? If they say that it is indeed true that ransomed souls return no more to misery, but that even so no new thing happens, since there always have been, now are, and ever shall be a succession of ransomed souls, they must at least grant that in this case there are new souls to whom the misery and the deliverance from it are new. For if they maintain that those souls out of which new men are daily being made (from whose bodies, if they have lived wisely, they are so delivered that they never return to misery) are not new, but have existed from eternity, they must logically admit that they are infinite. For however great a finite number of souls there were, that would not have sufficed to make perpetually new men from eternity – men whose souls were to be eternally freed from this mortal state, and never afterwards to return to it. And our philosophers will find it hard to explain how there is an infinite number of souls in an order of nature which they require shall be finite, that it may be known by God.

And now that we have exploded these cycles which were supposed to bring back the soul at fixed periods to the same miseries, what can seem more in accordance with godly reason than to believe that it is possible for God both to create new things never before created, and in doing so, to preserve His will unaltered? But whether the number of eternally redeemed souls can be continually increased or not, let the philosophers themselves decide, who are so subtle in determining where infinity cannot be admitted. For our own part, our reasoning holds in either case. For if the number of souls can be indefinitely increased, what reason is there to deny that what had never before been created, could be created? Since the number of ransomed souls never existed before, and has yet not only been once made, but will never cease to be anew coming into being. If, on the other hand, it be more suitable that the number of eternally ransomed souls be definite, and that this number will never be increased, yet this number, whatever it be, did assuredly never exist before, and it cannot increase, and reach the amount it signifies, without having some beginning; and this beginning never before existed. That this beginning, therefore, might be, the first man was created.

Chapter 21 – That There Was Created at First But One Individual, and that the Human Race Was Created in Him

Now that we have solved, as well as we could, this very difficult question about the eternal God creating new things, without any novelty of will, it is easy to see how much better it is that God was pleased to produce the human race from the one individual whom He created, than if He had originated it in several men. For as to the other animals, He created some solitary, and naturally seeking lonely places – as the eagles, kites, lions, wolves, and such like; others gregarious, which herd together, and prefer to live in company – as pigeons, starlings, stags, and little fallow deer, and the like: but neither class did He cause to be propagated from individuals, but called into being several at once.

Man, on the other hand, whose nature was to be a mean between the angelic and bestial, He created in such sort, that if he remained in subjection to His Creator as his rightful Lord, and piously kept His commandments, he should pass into the company of the angels, and obtain, without the intervention of death, a blessed and endless immortality; but if he offended the Lord his God by a proud and disobedient use of his free will, he should become subject to death, and live as the beasts do – the slave of appetite, and doomed to eternal punishment after death. And therefore God created only one single man, not, certainly, that he might be a solitary, bereft of all society, but that by this means the unity of society and the bond of concord might be more effectually commended to him, men being bound together not only by similarity of nature, but by family affection. And indeed He did not even create the woman that was to be given him as his wife, as he created the man, but created her out of the man, that the whole human race might derive from one man.

Chapter 22 – That God Foreknew that the First Man Would Sin, and that He at the Same Time Foresaw How Large a Multitude of Godly Persons Would by His Grace Be Translated to the Fellowship of the Angels

And God was not ignorant that man would sin, and that, being himself made subject now to death, he would propagate men doomed to die, and that these mortals would run to such enormities in sin, that even the beasts devoid of rational will, and who were created in numbers from the waters and the earth, would live more securely and peaceably with their own kind than men, who had been propagated from one individual for the very purpose of commending concord. For not even lions or dragons have ever waged with their kind such wars as men have waged with one another. But God foresaw also that by His grace a people would be called to adoption, and that they, being justified by the remission of their sins, would be united by the Holy Ghost to the holy angels in eternal peace, the last enemy, death, being destroyed; and He knew that this people would derive profit from the consideration that God had caused all men to be derived from one, for the sake of showing how highly He prizes unity in a multitude.

Chapter 23 – Of the Nature of the Human Soul Created in the Image of God

God, then, made man in His own image. For He created for him a soul endowed with reason and intelligence, so that he might excel all the creatures of earth, air, and sea, which were not so gifted. And when He had formed the man out of the dust of the earth, and had willed that his soul should be such as I have said – whether He had already made it, and now by breathing imparted it to man, or rather made it by breathing, so that that breath which God made by breathing (for what else is "to breathe" than to make breath?) is the soul, – He made also a wife for him, to aid him in the work of generating his kind, and her He formed of a bone taken out of the man's side, working in a divine manner. For we are not to conceive of this work in a carnal fashion, as if God wrought as we commonly see artisans, who use their hands, and material furnished to them, that by their artistic skill they may fashion some material object. God's hand is God's power; and He, working invisibly, effects visible results. But this seems fabulous rather than true to men, who measure by customary and everyday works the power and wisdom of God, whereby He understands and produces without seeds even seeds themselves; and because they cannot understand the things which at the beginning were created, they are sceptical regarding them – as if the very things which they do know about human propagation, conceptions and births, would seem less incredible if told to those who had no experience of them; though these very things, too, are attributed by many rather to physical and natural causes than to the work of the divine mind.

Chapter 25 – That God Alone is the Creator of Every Kind of Creature, Whatever Its Nature or Form

For whereas there is one form which is given from without to every bodily substance – such as the form which is constructed by potters and smiths, and that class of artists who paint and fashion forms like the body of animals – but another and internal form which is not itself constructed, but, as the efficient cause, produces not only the natural bodily forms, but even the life itself of the living creatures, and which proceeds from the secret and hidden choice of an intelligent and living nature – let that first-mentioned form be attributed to every artificer, but this latter to one only, God, the Creator and Originator who made the world itself and the angels, without the help of world or angels. For the same divine and, so to speak, creative energy, which cannot be made, but makes, and which gave to the earth and sky their roundness – this same divine, effective, and creative energy gave their roundness to the eye and to the apple; and the other natural objects which we anywhere see, received also their form, not from without, but from the secret and profound might of the Creator, who said, "Do not I fill heaven and earth?" And whose wisdom it is that "reacheth from one end to another mightily; and sweetly doth she order all things."

Wherefore I know not what kind of aid the angels, themselves created first, afforded to the Creator in making other things. I cannot ascribe to them what perhaps they cannot do, neither ought I to deny them such faculty as they have. But, by their leave, I attribute the creating and originating work which gave being to all natures to God, to whom they themselves thankfully ascribe their existence. We do not call gardeners the creators of their fruits, for we read, "Neither is he that planteth anything, neither he that watereth, but God that giveth the increase." Nay, not even the earth itself do we call a creator, though she seems to be the prolific mother of all things which she aids in germinating and bursting forth from the seed, and which she keeps rooted in her own breast; for we likewise read, "God giveth it a body, as it hath pleased Him, and to every seed his own body." We ought not even to call a woman the creatress of her own offspring; for He rather is its creator who said to His servant, "Before I formed thee in the womb, I knew thee." And although the various mental emotions of a pregnant woman do produce in the fruit of her womb similar qualities – as Jacob with his peeled wands caused piebald sheep to be produced – yet the mother as little creates her offspring as she created herself. Whatever bodily or seminal causes, then, may be used for the production of things, either by the cooperation of angels, men, or the lower animals, or by sexual generation; and whatever power the desires and mental emotions of the mother have to produce in the tender and plastic fetus corresponding lineaments and colors; yet the natures themselves, which are thus variously affected, are the production of none but the most high God.

It is His occult power which pervades all things, and is present in all without being contaminated, which gives being to all that is, and modifies and limits its existence; so that without Him it would not be thus, or thus, nor would have any being at all. If, then, in regard to that outward form which the workman's hand imposes on his work, we do not say that Rome and Alexandria were built by masons and architects, but by the kings by whose will, plan, and resources they were built, so that the one has Romulus, the other Alexander, for its founder; with how much greater reason ought we to say that God alone is the Author of all natures, since He neither uses for His work any material which was not made by Him, nor any workmen who were not also made by Him, and since, if He were, so to speak, to withdraw from created things His creative power, they would straightway relapse into the nothingness in which they were before they were created? "Before," I mean, in respect of eternity, not of time. For what other creator could there be of time, than He who created those things whose movements make time?

Chapter 26 – Of that Opinion of the Platonists, that the Angels Were Themselves Indeed Created by God, But that Afterwards They Created Man's Body

It is obvious, that in attributing the creation of the other animals to those inferior gods who were made by the Supreme, he meant it to be understood that the immortal part was taken from God Himself, and that these minor creators added the mortal part; that is to say, he meant them to be considered the creators of our bodies, but not of our souls. But since Porphyry maintains that if the soul is to be purified all entanglement with a body must be escaped from; and at the same time agrees with Plato and the Platonists in thinking that those who have not spent a temperate and honorable life return to mortal bodies as their punishment (to bodies of brutes in Plato's opinion, to human bodies in Porphyry's); it follows that those whom they would have us worship as our parents and authors, that they may plausibly call them gods, are, after all, but the forgers of our fetters and chains – not our creators, but our jailers and turnkeys, who lock us up in the most bitter and melancholy house of correction.

Let the Platonists, then, either cease menacing us with our bodies as the punishment of our souls, or preaching that we are to worship as gods those whose work upon us they exhort us by all means in our power to avoid and escape from. But, indeed, both opinions are quite false. It is false that souls return again to this life to be punished; and it is false that there is any other creator of anything in heaven or earth, than He who made the heaven and the earth. For if we live in a body only to expiate our sins, how says Plato in another place, that the world could not have been the most beautiful and good, had it not been filled with all kinds of creatures, mortal and immortal? But if our creation even as mortals be a divine benefit, I how is it a punishment to be restored to a body, that is, to a divine benefit? And if God, as Plato continually maintains, embraced in His eternal intelligence the ideas both of the universe and of all the animals, how, then, should He not with His own hand make them all? Could He be unwilling to be the constructor of works, the idea and plan of which called for His ineffable and ineffably to be praised intelligence?

Chapter 27 – That the Whole Plenitude of the Human Race Was Embraced in the First Man, and that God There Saw the Portion of It Which Was to Be Honored and Rewarded, and that Which Was to Be Condemned and Punished

With good cause, therefore, does the true religion recognize and proclaim that the same God who created the universal cosmos, created also all the animals, souls as well as bodies. Among the terrestrial animals man was made by Him in His own image, and, for the reason I have given, was made one individual, though he was not left solitary. For there is nothing so social by nature, so unsocial by its corruption, as this race. And human nature has nothing more appropriate, either for the prevention of discord, or for the healing of it, where it exists, than the remembrance of that first parent of us all, whom God was pleased to create alone, that all men might be derived from one, and that they might thus be admonished to preserve unity among their whole multitude. But from the fact that the woman was made for him from his side, it was plainly meant that we should learn how dear the bond between man and wife should be. These works of God do certainly seem extraordinary, because they are the first works.

They who do not believe them, ought not to believe any prodigies; for these would not be called prodigies did they not happen out of the ordinary course of nature. But, is it possible that anything should happen in vain, however hidden be its cause, in so grand a government of divine providence? One of the sacred Psalmist says, "Come, behold the works of the Lord, what prodigies He hath wrought in the earth." Why God made woman out of man's side, and what this first prodigy prefigured, I shall, with God's help, tell in another place. But at present, since this book must be concluded, let us merely say that in this first man, who was created in the beginning, there was laid the foundation, not in. deed evidently, but in God's foreknowledge, of these two cities or societies, so far as regards the human race. For from that man all men were to be derived – some of them to be associated with the good angels in their reward, others with the wicked in punishment; all being ordered by the secret yet just judgment of God. For since it is written, "All the paths of the Lord are mercy and truth," neither can His grace be unjust, nor His justice cruel.

Maximus

> St. Maximus the Confessor (580 – 663) is one of the great theologians of the Church. Wrongly convicted of heresy for consistently upholding the Chalcedonian two-natures Christology, the rulers of Constantinople cut out his tongue (so that he could no longer speak) and cut off his right hand (so that he could no longer write). Though a simple monk, he was a subtle and sophisticated thinker. He affirmed that the world has a beginning and that reality divides into sensible and intelligible realms. Accordingly, the reality of the created order goes beyond what the senses perceive. To be understood aright, reality must be perceptible to both the senses and the mind. Humans unite both: a human being has a sensible body and an intelligent soul. Though created in time and subject to death, humans are destined for immortality.
>
> The excerpts below emphasize how God can be known through the order of creation and divine providence. God created all things out of nothing and holds them together in existence by His power. Maximus denies that matter is eternal. Nothing is created evil. Evil, rather, comes about when humans misuse their faculties. Evil is a distortion of good. Each created thing has its own *logos*, or principle, which derives from God and makes each thing what it is. Humans can contemplate the *logoi* in creation and thereby attain knowledge of God. These created *logoi* participate in the Divine Logos. They constitute the natural law, the contemplation of which will lead one to God just as the contemplation of Scripture leads one to God. The beauty and order of creation point to God's wisdom and providence.

Maximus *Four Hundred Chapters on Love*

Third Century

3. The vices, whether of the concupiscible, the irascible, or the rational element, come upon us with the misuse of the faculties of the soul. Misuse of the rational faculty is ignorance and folly, of the irascible and concupiscible faculty, hate and intemperance. Their right use is knowledge and prudence. If this is so, nothing created and given existence by God is evil.

21. God knows Himself and the things created by Him. The holy angels also know God and they know, too, the things created by Him. But the holy angels do not know God and the things created by Him as God knows Himself and the things created by Him.

22. God knows Himself of His own sacred essence, and the things created by Him from His wisdom, through which and in which He made all things. The holy angels, however, know God by participation, though He is beyond participation, and they know things created by Him by a perception of what is contemplated in them.

28. When the Greek philosophers affirm that the substance of beings coexisted eternally with God and that they received only their individual qualities from Him, they say that there is nothing contrary to substance but that opposition is found only in the qualities. We maintain, however, that the divine substance alone has no contrary because it is eternal and infinite and bestows eternity on the other substances; furthermore, that nonbeing is the contrary of the substance of beings and that their eternal being or nonbeing lies in the power of the One who properly is being, "and His gifts are not subject to revision." And therefore it both always is and will be sustained by His all-powerful might even though it has nonbeing as its opposite, as was said, since it was brought into being from nonbeing by God and whether it has being or nonbeing depends on His will.

29. Just as evil is the privation of good and ignorance that of knowledge, so is nonbeing the privation of being – but not of being properly so called, for it has no contrary – but of true being by participation. Privations of the former depend on the will of creatures; privation of the latter depends on the will of the Creator, who out of goodness ever wills His creatures to exist and to receive benefits from Him.

Fourth Century

1. The mind is first of all in wonder when it reflects on God's universal infinity and that inaccessible and greatly desired ocean. Next it is amazed at how from nothing He has brought into existence everything that is. But just as, "of His greatness there is no end," so is His wisdom unsearchable.

2. How can one help but marvel when considering that immense ocean of goodness which is beyond astonishment? How can one not be struck when reflecting on how and whence rational and intelligent nature came to be, and also the four elements which make up bodies, when there was no matter at all previous to their existence? And what kind of power is it that moved them to reality and brought them into being? But the pagan Greeks do not admit this and remain in ignorance about the all-powerful goodness and its efficacious wisdom and knowledge which is beyond the mind's powers.

3. Eternally existing as Creator, God creates when He wishes by His consubstantial Word and Spirit out of infinite goodness. But do not object: For what reason did He create at this time, since He was always good? Because, I say in turn, the inscrutable wisdom of the infinite nature is not subject to human knowledge.

4. When He willed it, the Creator gave substance to and produced His eternally preexisting knowledge of beings. It is, of course, absurd to doubt that an omnipotent God can give substance to something when He wishes.

5. Seek the reason why God created, for this is knowledge. But do not seek how and why He only recently created, for that question does not fall under your mind since while some divine things are comprehended by men, others are not. As one of the saints has said, "Unbridled speculation can push you over the precipice."

6. Some say that created things eternally exist with God, which is impossible. For how can what is limited in every way eternally coexist with the wholly infinite? Or how are they really creatures if they are coeternal with the Creator? But this is the theory of the Greeks, who admit God as the Creator not of the substance at all but only of the properties. But we who know the almighty God affirm that He is the Creator not of the properties but of the substance endowed with properties. And if this is true, creatures do not eternally coexist with God.

7. God, along with divine realities, is in one sense knowable and in another sense unknowable: knowable in ideas about Him, unknowable in Himself.

8. Do not search for states and aptitudes in the simple and infinite substance of the Holy Trinity, lest you make it composite like creatures. To have such notions about God is absurd and impious.

9. Only the infinite and all-powerful substance which created all things is simple, of one form, unqualified, peaceful, and undisturbed. Every creature, on the other hand, is a composite of substance and accident and in constant need of divine Providence since it is not free from mutability.

10. Every intellectual and sensitive substance receives from God, when He brings them into existence, powers which allow them to apprehend beings, the intellectual substance through thoughts, and the sensitive substance through sensations.

11. God is participated only; the creature both participates and communicates. He participates in being and in well-being but communicates only in well-being, corporeal substance in one way, incorporeal in another.

12. Incorporeal substance communicates well-being by speaking or acting or by being an object of contemplation. Corporeal substance does so by being and object of contemplation only.

13. Whether the rational and intelligent being has eternal being or nonbeing lies in the will of the one who created all good things. Whether it be good or bad by choice lies in the will of the creatures.

14. Evil is not to be regarded as in the substance of creatures but in its mistaken and irrational movement.

Maximus *Chapters on Knowledge*

First Century

48. Zealous people should look among God's works to know which of them He began to create and which, on the contrary, he did not begin. Indeed, if He has rested from all the works that He began to create, it is clear that He did not rest from those which He did not create. God's works which began in time are all beings which share, for example, the different essences of beings, for they have nonbeing before being. For God was when participated beings were not. The

works of God which did not happen to begin to be in time are participated beings, in which participated beings share according to grace, for example, goodness and all that the term goodness implies, that is, all life, immortality, simplicity, immutability, and infinity and such things which are essentially contemplated in regard to Him; they are also God's works, and yet they did not begin in time. For what does not exist is not older than virtue nor than anything else of what was just listed, even if beings which participate in them in these things began their existence in time. For all virtue is without beginning, not having any time previous to itself. Such things have God alone as the eternal begetter of their being.

66. The mystery of the Incarnation of the Word bears the power of all the hidden meanings and figures of Scripture as well as the knowledge of visible and intelligible creatures. The one who knows the mystery of the cross and the tomb knows the principles of these creatures. And the one who has been initiated into the ineffable power of the Resurrection knows the purpose for which God originally made all things.

70. The whole world is limited by its own principles [*logoi*] and we contribute place and age to whatever it contains. It has modes of thought naturally inherent in it which can produce a partial understanding of God's wisdom over all things. So long as they serve for our understanding, they can not be anything but middle and thus partial understanding. But when what is partial ceases with the appearance of what is perfect, all mirrors and hidden meanings pass away; once the truth arrives face to face, the one who is saved will be above all worlds, ages, and places in which he was once nurtured as a child, and will reach his end in God.

Second Century

76. ...For [God] is known only to a certain extent through His activities. The knowledge of Himself in His essence and personhood remains inaccessible to all angels and men alike and He can in no way be known by anyone. But St. John, initiated as perfectly as humanly possible into the meaning of the Word's incarnation, claims that he

has seen the glory of the Word as flesh, that is, he saw the reason or the plan for which God became man, full of grace and truth...

Maximus *Difficulty 10*

17 – Contemplation of the Transfiguration of the Lord

...Whence in both cases I think it necessarily follows that anyone who wishes may live an upright and blameless life with God, whether through scriptural understanding in the Spirit, or through the natural contemplation of reality in accordance with the Spirit. So the two laws – both the natural law and the written law – are of equal honour and teach the same things; neither is greater or less than the other, which shows, as is right, that the lover of perfect wisdom may become the one who desires wisdom perfectly.

26 – Contemplation that the one who follows Christ transcends law and nature

For the whole nature of reality is divided into the intelligible and the sensible. There is that which is said to be and is eternal, since it receives the beginning of its being in eternity, and that which is temporal, since it is made in time; there is that which is subject to intellection, and that which is subject to the power of sense-perception. The entities on each side of this division are naturally related to each other through an indissoluble power that binds them together. Manifold is the relation between intellects and what they perceive and between the senses and what they experience. Thus the human being, consisting of both soul and sensible body, by means of its natural relationship of belonging to each division of creation, is both circumscribed and circumscribes: through being, it is circumscribed, and through potency, it circumscribes. So in its two parts it is divided between these things, and it draws these things through their own parts into itself in unity. For the human being is circumscribed by both the intelligible and the sensible, since it is soul and body, and it has the natural capacity of circumscribing them, because it can both think and perceive through the senses. God is simply and indefinably beyond all things, both what circumscribes and what is circumscribed and the nature of those [categories] without which none of these could be, I mean, time and eternity and space, by which the universe is enclosed, since He is completely unrelated to anything. Since all this is so, the one who discerns with sagacity how he ought to love God, the transcendent nature, that is beyond reason and knowledge and any kind of relationship whatever, passes without relation through everything sensible and intelligible and all time and eternity and space. Finally he is supernaturally stripped bare of every energy that operates in accordance with sense or reason or mind, and ineffably and unknowably attains the divine delight that is beyond reason and mind, in the form and fashion that God who gives such grace knows and those who are worthy of receiving this form God understand. He no longer bears about with him anything natural or written, since everything that he could read or know is now utterly transcendent and wrapped in silence.

35 – Contemplation of how God is understood from creation

So therefore when the Saints behold the creation, and its fine order and proportion and the need that each part has of the whole, and how all the perfect parts have been fashioned wisely and with providence in accordance with reason that fashioned them, and how what has come to be is found to be not otherwise than good beside what now is, and is in need of no addition or subtraction in order to be otherwise good, they are taught from the things he has made that there is one who fashioned them. So, too, when they see the permanence, the order and position of what has come to be, and its manner of being, in accordance with which each being, according to its proper form, is preserved unconfused and without any disorder; and the course of the stars proceeding in the same way with no alteration of any kind, and the circle of the year proceeding in an orderly manner according to the periodic return of the [heavenly bodies] from and to their own place, and the equal yearly proportion of the nights and days, with their mutual increase and decrease, taking place according to a measure that is neither too small nor too great, they understand that behind everything there is providence, and this they acknowledge as God, the fashioner of all.

36 – Contemplation that the world has a beginning

For who, seeing the beauty and greatness of God's creatures, does not immediately understand that He has brought all this into being, as the beginning and source of beings and their maker? In his understanding he returns to Him alone, leaving behind all these things. For though he cannot accomplish the complete transition with his mind, or receive without intermediary the object of his desires which he knows through the mediation of its effects, he can readily put away the error that the world is without beginning, as he reasons truly that everything that moves must certainly begin to move. No motion is without beginning, since it is not without cause. For motion has a beginning, and a cause from which it is called and an end to which it is drawn....

41 – On the dyad and the monad

But it has been shown that from God, who eternally is, everything has come to be completely and wholly from nothing, not partially or incompletely, as proceeding wisely from a source that is infinitely wise and infinitely powerful, and that everything is held together in it, as protected and supported in an all-powerful foundation, and that everything will return to it, as each to its own goal, as the great Denys the Areopagite has said somewhere.

42 – Contemplation of divine providence

Anyone who is convinced that God exercises providence over the things that are, from which he has learnt that he exists, will judge it right and reasonable that he is none other than the guardian of the things that are and cares for them and that he alone is the fashioner of what is. For the permanence of what is, and its order and position and movement and the consonance of the extremities with the middle, the agreement of the parts with the wholes, and the union throughout of the wholes with the parts, and the unblurred distinction of the parts one from another in accordance with the individuating difference of each, and the unconfused union in accordance with the indistinguishable sameness in the wholes, and the combination and distinction of everything with everything else (not to limit myself to particulars), and the eternally preserved succession of everything and each one according to form, so that the *logos* of each nature is not corrupted by confusion or blurring – all this shows clearly that everything is held together by the providence of the Creator God. For it is not the case that God is good but not beneficent, or beneficent but without providence, and therefore he cares wisely for the things that are and in a way befitting God, so that they are favoured with existence and care.

Providence is, then, according to the God – bearing Fathers, the care that comes from God to the things that are. They also define it thus: providence is the will of God through which everything that is receives suitable direction. If this will is God's, if I may use the very words of my teachers, then it necessarily follows that what happens happens in accordance with right reason, and so no better disposition could be looked for. One who has chosen to take truth as his guide is therefore led to say that providence is either the one who is truly known to be the Creator or is a power exercised by the Creator of all things. And with animals, if we approach them in a rational way we shall find a trace of the intelligible in them which is a not unworthy imitation of what is above reason. For if we look at those beings that naturally care for their offspring, we are encouraged to define for ourselves reverently and with godly boldness that God exercises providence in his sovereign uniqueness over all beings, and not over some beings but not others, as some of the adepts of the "outer learning" have it, but of absolutely everything, in accordance with the one and indistinguishable will of goodness, and indeed of both universals and particulars, for we know that if particulars can perish because they are not within the remit of providence and fitting protection, then universals will perish with them (for universals consist of particulars), in this way propounding a rational demonstration that rightly leads by a reasonable retort to the truth. For if universals consist of particulars, then if the particular examples of any *logos* in accordance with which things exist and consist should perish, then it is quite clear that the corresponding universals will not continue to be. For the parts exist and subsist in the wholes, and the wholes in the parts. No reason can gainsay it. But there are those who are, as it were, unwillingly bound by the truth and betray the power of providence, arguing that it only pervades what is important to them. For they say that only universals are governed by providence, and that particulars are hidden from providence, being led by necessity towards the truth that they are anxious to flee. For if they say that it is because of permanence that universals are worthy of providence, they admit even more strongly that those particulars are worthy, in which the permanence and stability of the universals consist. These are admitted together through the indissoluble natural relationship that they have with each other, and both conserve permanence, nor can one be said to be foreign to the protection of the other, and again if they admit the protection of the one with respect of permanence, they have to grant the other too.

Apart from that there are three ways in which the providence of God is denied. Some say that God does not understand the method of providence, others that he cannot will it, others that he has not the power. But it follows from the common notions that God is good and beyond goodness and eternally wills what is good for everything, and that he is wise and beyond wisdom, or rather the source of all wisdom, and certainly knows everything that is going to happen, and that he is powerful, or rather infinitely powerful, and certainly brings about in a divinely fitting way in everything what is known to him and what he wills for the good and what is fitting. For God is good and wise and powerful, and pervades everything visible and invisible, both universals and particulars, both small and great, indeed everything that possesses existence in any way whatever. He is not diminished by the boundlessness of his goodness and wisdom and power, and conserves everything in accordance with the *logos* of its being, both in relation to themselves and to others, and in accordance with the indissoluble harmony and permanence that relates everything one to another.

Why then can we not understand that nature itself teaches us clearly about the existence of God's providence over everything? For nature itself gives us no small proof that the knowledge of providence is naturally implanted within us, whenever it prepares us to seek salvation through prayers in sudden emergencies, as if pushing us towards God in an untaught way. For seized by necessity, all unawares, without choice, before we have had a chance to think of anything, as if providence itself led us to itself without any thought, faster than any mental power within ourselves, placing before us the divine help as stronger than anything else. Not that nature leads us to the possession of something unnatural. Whatever happens naturally, even if it is obscure to all, possesses the strong and unconquerable power of the demonstration of the truth. If it is the case that the reason for providence as it affects particulars is incomprehensible to us, as in accordance with the verse, *his judgments are unsearchable and his ways past finding out* (Rom. 11:33), then in my view they are not right who say that it shows that there is no such providence. For if the difference and variation between different human beings is great and incomprehensible, in ways of life and customs and opinions and choices and desires, in what they know, and their needs and pursuits, and the almost countless thoughts in their minds, and in everything that happens to them in each day and hour (for this animal, man, is changeable, sharp on occasions and changing with need), it is absolutely necessary that providence, comprehending everything with foresight in the circumscription of its individuality, should be manifest as different and manifold and complex, and should achieve harmony as it extends into the incomprehensibility of the multitudinous, in a way suitable to each individual, whether thing or thought, reaching as far as the least movement of mind or body. If therefore the difference of particulars is incomprehensible, then likewise is the infinite meaning of providence that draws them into harmony, but it should not follow that, since the meaning of particular providence happens to be infinite and unknowable to us, we should make our ignorance a ground for denying the all-wise care for the things that are, but we should receive and hymn all the works of providence, simply and without examination, as divinely fitting and suitable, and believe that what happens happens well, even if the reason is beyond our grasp. And I mean all the works of providence, not what happens by our agency in accordance with our reason, for these are quite different from the *logos* of providence. For the manner indicated by the great teacher of the power and grace of the Saints, according to reason and contemplation, is conjectural rather than categorical (for our mind is very far from truth itself), but trying to act hold of what has been said with the reason, and as it were tracking it down, I have done nothing more than make suggestions.

John of Damascus

St. John of Damascus (c. 650 – c. 749) wrote a compendium of Christian doctrine based on the Greek Fathers titled *An Exact Exposition of the Orthodox Faith*. It is the closest thing to a systematic theology in the Eastern Orthodox Church, where it remains a central text to this day. It influenced Lombard, Aquinas, and others in the West. John also wrote much liturgical poetry, which is still used in Orthodox services.

In Muslim-occupied Damascus, John served as a minister of the Caliph. He resigned about 716 to become a monk and then a priest. He opposed iconoclasm and, protected by the Muslims, he was, ironically, able to write powerfully against it (Islam historically has taken a dim view of representative religious art).

The excerpt below from *An Exact Exposition of the Orthodox Faith* summarizes the Patristic teaching on creation. God created time as well as the universe. John repeats Ephrem in affirming that some elements were created out of nothing while the rest of creation was formed from those first-created elements. All created things are subject to decay and are preserved in existence by God's grace and providence, as in Athanasius.

God commanded the waxing and waning of light on the first three days until He created the sun on the fourth. John understands the "pillars" of the earth as the force that holds it in place. God created all things for humanity's use. Creation *ex nihilo*, providence, and human free will are for John nonnegotiable. Given that the human will is free, John infers that astrology and determinism must be false.

John's flexibility of interpretation in regard to secondary questions of exegesis and teaching – such as *What keeps the earth in place?* – is typical of the Fathers, as is his free use of and engagement with the science of his day. Less an innovator, John was a masterful integrator, drawing together the best thinking of the Patristic age, which he calls to a close.

John of Damascus *An Exact Exposition of the Orthodox Faith*, Book II

Chapter I – Concerning æon or age

He created the ages Who Himself was before the ages, Whom the divine David thus addresses, "From age to age Thou art." The divine apostle also says, "Through Whom He created the ages."

It must then be understood that the word age has various meanings, for it denotes many things. The life of each man is called an age. Again, a period of a thousand years is called an age. Again, the whole course of the present life is called an age: also the future life, the immortal life after the resurrection, is spoken of as an age. Again, the word age is used to denote, not time nor yet a part of time as measured by the movement and course of the sun, that is to say, composed of days and nights, but the sort of temporal motion and interval that is co-extensive with eternity. For age is to things eternal just what time is to things temporal.

Seven ages of this world are spoken of, that is, from the creation of the heaven and earth till the general consummation and resurrection of men. For there is a partial consummation, viz., the death of each man: but there is also a general and complete consummation, when the general resurrection of men will come to pass. And the eighth age is the age to come.

Before the world was formed, when there was as yet no sun dividing day from night, there was not an age such as could be measured, but there was the sort of temporal motion and interval that is co-extensive with eternity. And in this sense there is but one age, and God is spoken of as *aiônios* and *proaiônios*, for the age or æon itself is His creation. For God, Who alone is without beginning, is Himself the Creator of all things, whether age or any other existing thing. And when I say God, it is evident that I mean the Father and His Only begotten Son, our Lord, Jesus Christ, and His all-holy Spirit, our one God.

But we speak also of ages of ages, inasmuch as the seven ages of the present world include many ages in the sense of lives of men, and the one age embraces all the ages, and the present and the future are spoken of as age of age. Further, everlasting (i.e. *aiônios*) life and everlasting punishment prove that the age or neon to come is unending. For time will not be counted by days and nights even after the resurrection, but there will rather be one day with no evening, wherein the Sun of Justice will shine brightly on the just, but for the sinful there will be night profound and limitless. In what way then will the period of one thousand years be counted which, according to Origen, is required for the complete restoration? Of all the ages, therefore, the sole creator is God Who hath also created the universe and Who was before the ages.

Chapter II – Concerning the creation

Since, then, God, Who is good and more than good, did not find satisfaction in self-contemplation, but in His exceeding goodness wished certain things to come into existence which would enjoy His benefits and share in His goodness, He brought all things out of nothing into being and created them, both what is invisible and what is visible. Yea, even man, who is a compound of the visible and the invisible. And it is by thought that He creates, and thought is the basis of the work, the Word filling it and the Spirit perfecting it.

Chapter V – Concerning the visible creation

Our God Himself, Whom we glorify as Three in One, created the heaven and the earth and all that they contain, and brought all things out of nothing into being: some He made out of no pre-existing basis of matter, such as heaven, earth, air, fire, water: and the rest out of these elements that He had created, such as living creatures, plants, seeds. For these are made up of earth, and water, and air, and fire, at the bidding of the Creator.

Chapter VI – Concerning the Heaven

...Others have pictured the heaven as a hemisphere. This idea is suggested by these words of David, the singer of God, Who stretchest out the heavens like a curtain, by which word he clearly means a tent: and by these from the blessed Isaiah, Who hath established the heavens like a vault: and also because when the sun, moon, and stars set they make a circuit round the earth from west to north, and so reach once more the east. Still, whether it is this way or that, all things have been made and established by the divine command, and have the divine will and counsel for a foundation that cannot be moved. For He

Himself spoke and they were made: He Himself commanded and they were created. He hath also established them for ever and ever: He hath made a decree which will not pass...

All things, then, which are brought into existence are subject to corruption according to the law of their nature, and so even the heavens themselves are corruptible. But by the grace of God they are maintained and preserved. Only the Deity, however, is by nature without beginning and without end. Wherefore it has been said, They will perish, but Thou dost endure: nevertheless, the heavens will not be utterly destroyed. For they will wax old and be wound round as a covering, and will be changed, and there will be a new heaven and a new earth...

Chapter VII – Concerning light, fire, the luminaries, sun, moon and stars

Fire is one of the four elements, light and with a greater tendency to ascend than the others. It has the power of burning and also of giving light, and it was made by the Creator on the first day. For the divine Scripture says, "And God said, 'Let there be light,' and there was light." Fire is not a different thing from what light is, as some maintain. Others again hold that this fire of the universe is above the air and call it ether. In the beginning, then, that is to say on the first day, God created light, the ornament and glory of the whole visible creation. For take away light and all things remain in undistinguishable darkness, incapable of displaying their native beauty. And God called the light day, but the darkness He called night. Further, darkness is not any essence, but an accident: for it is simply absence of light. The air, indeed, has not light in its essence. It was, then, this very absence of light from the air that God called darkness: and it is not the essence of air that is darkness, but the absence of light which clearly is rather an accident than an essence. And, indeed, it was not night, but day, that was first named, so that day is first and after that comes night. Night, therefore, follows day. And from the beginning of day till the next day is one complete period of day and night. For the Scripture says, "And the evening and the morning were one day."

When, therefore, in the first three days the light was poured forth and reduced at the divine command, both day and night came to pass.

But on the fourth day God created the great luminary, that is, the sun, to have rule and authority over the day: for it is by it that day is made: for it is day when the sun is above the earth, and the duration of a day is the course of the sun over the earth from its rising till its setting. And He also created the lesser luminaries, that is, the moon and the stars, to have rule and authority over the night, and to give light by night. For it is night when the sun is under the earth, and the duration of night is the course of the sun under the earth from its rising till its setting. The moon, then, and the stars were set to lighten the night: not that they are in the daytime under the earth, for even by day stars are in the heaven over the earth but the sun conceals both the stars and the moon by the greater brilliance of its light and prevents them from being seen.

On these luminaries the Creator bestowed the first-created light: not because He was in need of other light, but that that light might not remain idle. For a luminary is not merely light, but a vessel for containing light...

Now the Greeks declare that all our affairs are controlled by the rising and setting and collision of these stars, viz., the sun and moon: for it is with these matters that astrology has to do. But we hold that we get from them signs of rain and drought, cold and heat, moisture and dryness, and of the various winds, and so forth, but no sign whatever as to our actions. For we have been created with free wills by our Creator and are masters over our own actions. Indeed, if all our actions depend on the courses of the stars, all we do is done of necessity: and necessity precludes either virtue or vice. But if we possess neither virtue nor vice, we do not deserve praise or punishment, and God, too, will turn out to be unjust, since He gives good things to some and afflicts others. Nay, He will no longer continue to guide or provide for His own creatures, if all things are carried and swept along in the grip of necessity. And the faculty of reason will be superfluous to us: for if we are not masters of any of our actions, deliberation is quite superfluous. Reason, indeed, is granted to us solely that we might take counsel, and hence all reason implies freedom of will...

It must be understood, then, that the moon derives its light from the sun; not that God was unable to grant it light of its own, but in order that rhythm and order may be unimpressed upon nature, one part ruling, the other being ruled, and that we might thus be taught to live in community and to share our possessions with one another, and to be under subjection, first to our Maker and Creator, our God and Master, and then also to the rulers set in authority over us by Him: and not to question why this man is ruler and not I myself, but to welcome all that comes from God in a gracious and reasonable spirit.

The sun and the moon, moreover, suffer eclipse, and this demonstrates the folly of those who worship the creature in place of the Creator, and teaches us how changeable and alterable all things are For all things are changeable save God, and whatever is changeable is liable to corruption in accordance with the laws of its own nature.

Now the cause of the eclipse of the sun is that the body of the moon is interposed like a partition-wall and casts a shadow, and prevents the light from being shed down on us: and the extent of the eclipse is proportional to the size of the moon's body that is found to conceal the sun. But do not marvel that the moon's body is the smaller. For many declare that the sun is many times larger even than the earth, and the holy Fathers say that it is equal to the earth: yet often a small cloud, or even a small hill or a wall quite conceals it.

The eclipse of the moon, on the other hand, is due to the shadow the earth casts on it when it is a fifteen days' moon and the sun and moon happen to be at the opposite poles of the highest circle, the sun being under the earth and the moon above the earth. For the earth casts a shadow and the sun's light is prevented from illuminating the moon, and therefore it is then eclipsed.

It should be understood that the moon was made full by the Creator, that is, a fifteen days' moon: for it was fitting that it should be made complete. But on the fourth day, as we said, the sun was created. Therefore the moon was eleven days in advance of the sun, because from the fourth to the fifteenth day there are eleven days. Hence it happens that in each year the twelve months of the moon contain eleven days fewer than the twelve months of the sun. For the twelve months of the sun contain three hundred and sixty-five and a quarter days, and so because the quarter becomes a whole, in four years an extra day is completed, which is called bis-sextile. And that year has three hundred and sixty-six days. The years of the moon, on the other hand, have three hundred and fifty-four days. For the moon wanes from the time of its origin, or renewal, till it is fourteen and three-quarter days' old, and proceeds to wane till the twenty-ninth and a half day, when it is completely void of light. And then when it is once more connected with the sun it is reproduced and renewed, a memorial of our resurrection. Thus in each year the moon gives away eleven days to the sun, and so in three years the intercalary month of the Hebrews arises, and that year comes to consist of thirteen months, owing to the addition of these eleven days.

It is evident that both sun and moon and stars are compound and liable to corruption according to the laws of their various natures. But of their nature we are ignorant. Some, indeed, say that fire when deprived of matter is invisible, and thus, that when it is quenched it vanishes altogether. Others, again, say that when it is quenched it is transformed into air...

Chapter IX – Concerning the waters

Water also is one of the four elements, the most beautiful of God's creations. It is both wet and cold, heavy, and with a tendency to descend, and flows with great readiness. It is this the Holy Scripture has in view when it says, "And darkness was upon the face of the deep. And the Spirit of God moved upon the face of the waters." For the deep is nothing else than a huge quantity of water whose limit man cannot comprehend. In the beginning, indeed, the water lay all over the surface of the earth. And first God created the firmament to divide the water above the firmament from the water below the firmament. For in the midst of the sea of waters the firmament was established at the Master's decree. And out of it God bade the firmament arise, and it arose. Now for what reason was it that God placed water above the firmament? It was because of the intense burning heat of the sun and ether. For immediately under the firmament is spread out the ether, and the sun and moon and stars are in the firmament, and so if water had not been put above it the firmament would have been consumed by the heat.

Next, God bade the waters be gathered together into one mass. But when the Scripture speaks of one mass it evidently does not mean that they were gathered together into one place: for immediately it goes on to say, "And the gatherings of the waters He called seas:" but the words signify that the waters were separated off in a body from the earth into distinct groups. Thus the waters were gathered together into their special collections and the dry land was brought to view.

And hence arose the two seas that surround Egypt, for it lies between two seas. These collections contain various seas and mountains, and islands, and promontories, and harbours, and surround various bays and beaches, and coastlands. For the word beach is used when the nature of the tract is sandy, while coastland signifies that it is rocky and deep close into shore, getting deep all on a sudden. In like manner arose also the sea that lies where the sun rises, the name of which is the Indian Sea: also the northern sea called the Caspian. The lakes also were formed in the same manner...

By the divine decree hollow places are made in the earth, and so into these the waters are gathered. And this is how mountains are formed. God, then, bade the first water produce living breath, since it was to be by water and the Holy Spirit that moved upon the waters in the beginning, that man was to be renewed. For this is what the divine Basilius said: Therefore it produced living creatures, small and big; whales and dragons, fish that swim in the waters, and feathered fowl. The birds form a link between water and earth and air: for they have their origin in the water, they live on the earth and they fly in the air. Water, then, is the most beautiful element and rich in usefulness, and purifies from all filth, and not only from the filth of the body but from that of the soul, if it should have received the grace of the Spirit...

Chapter X – Concerning earth and its products

The earth is one of the four elements, dry, cold, heavy, motionless, brought into being by God, out of nothing on the first day. "For in the beginning," he said, "God created the heaven and the earths:" but the seat and foundation of the earth no man has been able to declare. Some, indeed, hold that its seat is the waters: thus the divine David says, "To Him Who established the earth on the waters." Others place it in the air. Again some other says, "He Who hangeth the earth on nothing." And, again, David, the singer of God, says, as though the representative of God, "I bear up the pillars of it," meaning by "pillars" the force that sustains it. Further, the expression, "He hath founded it upon the seas," shews clearly that the earth is on all hands surrounded with water. But whether we grant that it is established on itself, or on air or on water, or on nothing, we must not turn aside from reverent thought, but must admit that all things are sustained and preserved by the power of the Creator.

In the beginning, then, as the Holy Scripture says, it was hidden beneath the waters, and was unwrought, that is to say, not beautified. But at God's bidding, places to hold the waters appeared, and then the mountains came into existence, and at the divine command the earth received its own proper adornment, and was dressed in all manner of herbs and plants, and on these, by the divine decree, was bestowed the power of growth and nourishment, and of producing seed to generate their like. Moreover, at the bidding of the Creator it produced also all manner of kinds of living creatures, creeping things, and wild beasts, and cattle. All, indeed, are for the seasonable use of man: but of them some are for food, such as stags, sheep, deer, and such like: others for service such as camels, oxen, horses, asses, and such like: and others for enjoyment, such as apes, and among birds, jays and parrots, and such like. Again, amongst plants and herbs some are fruit bearing, others edible, others fragrant and flowery, given to us for our enjoyment, for example, the rose and such like, and others for the healing of disease. For there is not a single animal or plant in which the Creator has not implanted some form of energy capable of being used to satisfy man's needs. For He Who knew all things before they were, saw that in the future man would go forward in the strength of his own will, and would be subject to corruption, and, therefore, He created all things for his seasonable use, alike those in the firmament, and those on the earth, and those in the waters.

Indeed, before the transgression all things were under his power. For God set him as ruler over all things on the earth and in the waters. Even the serpent was accustomed to man, and approached him more readily than it did other living creatures, and held intercourse with him with delightful motions. And hence it was through it that the devil, the prince of evil, made his most wicked suggestion to our first parents. Moreover, the earth of its own accord used to yield fruits, for the benefit of the animals that were obedient to man, and there was neither rain nor tempest on the earth. But after the transgression, when he was compared with the unintelligent cattle and became like to them, after he had contrived that in him irrational desire should have rule over reasoning mind and had become disobedient to the Master's command, the subject creation rose up against him whom the Creator had appointed to be ruler: and it was appointed for him that he should till with sweat the earth from which he had been taken.

But even now wild beasts are not without their uses, for, by the terror they cause, they bring man to the knowledge of his Creator and lead him to call upon His name. And, further, at the transgression the thorn sprung out of the earth in accordance with the Lord's express declaration and was conjoined with the pleasures of the rose, that it might lead us to remember the transgression on account of which the earth was condemned to bring forth for us thorns and prickles.

That this is the case is made worthy of belief from the fact that their endurance is secured by the word of the Lord, saying, "Be fruitful and multiply, and replenish the earth."

Further, some hold that the earth is in the form of a sphere, others that it is in that of a cone. At all events it is much smaller than the heaven, and suspended almost like a point in its midst. And it will pass away and be changed. But blessed is the man who inherits the earth promised to the meek.

For the earth that is to be the possession of the holy is immortal. Who, then, can fitly marvel at the boundless and incomprehensible wisdom of the Creator? Or who can render sufficient thanks to the Giver of so many blessings?...

Chapter XI – Concerning Paradise

Now when God was about to fashion man out of the visible and invisible creation in His own image and likeness to reign as king and ruler over all the earth and all that it contains, He first made for him, so to speak, a kingdom in which he should live a life of happiness and prosperity. And this is the divine paradise, planted in Eden by the hands of God, a very storehouse of joy and gladness of heart (for "Eden" means luxuriousness)...

In its midst God planted the tree of life and the tree of knowledge. The tree of knowledge was for trial, and proof, and exercise of man's obedience and disobedience: and hence it was named the tree of the knowledge of good and evil, or else it was because to those who partook of it was given power to know their own nature. Now this is a good thing for those who are mature, but an evil thing for the immature and those whose appetites are too strong, being like solid food to tender babes still in need of milk. For our Creator, God, did not intend us to be burdened with care and troubled about many things, nor to take thought about, or make provision for, our own life. But this at length was Adam's fate...

Thus, to my thinking, the divine Paradise is twofold, and the God-inspired Fathers handed down a true message, whether they taught this doctrine or that. Indeed, it is possible to understand by every tree the knowledge of the divine power derived from created things. In the words of the divine Apostle, "For the invisible things of Him from the creation of the world are clearly seen, being understood by the things that are made." But of all these thoughts and speculations the sublimest is that dealing with ourselves, that is, with our own composition. As the divine David says, "The knowledge of Thee from me," that is from my constitution, was made a wonder. But for the reasons we have already mentioned, such knowledge was dangerous for Adam who had been so lately created.

The tree of life too may be understood as that more divine thought that has its origin in the world of sense, and the ascent through that to the originating and constructive cause of all. And this was the name He gave to every tree, implying fulness and indivisibility, and conveying only participation in what is good. But by the tree of the knowledge of good and evil, we are to understand that sensible and pleasurable food which, sweet though it seems, in reality brings him who partakes of it into communion with evil. For God says, "Of every tree in Paradise thou mayest freely eat." It is, me-thinks, as if God said, "Through all My creations thou art to ascend to Me thy creator, and of all the fruits thou mayest pluck one, that is, Myself who am the true life: let every thing bear for thee the fruit of life, and let participation in Me be the support of your own being. For in this way than wilt be immortal. But of the tree of the knowledge of good and evil, thou shall not eat of it: for in the day that thou eatest thereof thou shall surely die." For sensible food is by nature for the replenishing of that which gradually wastes away and it passes into the drought and perisheth: and he cannot remain incorruptible who partakes of sensible food.

Chapter XII – Concerning Man

In this way, then, God brought into existence mental essence, by which I mean, angels and all the heavenly orders. For these clearly have a mental and incorporeal nature: "incorporeal" I mean in comparison with the denseness of matter. For the Deity alone in reality is immaterial and incorporeal. But further He created in the same way sensible essence, that is heaven and earth and the intermediate region; and so He created both the kind of being that is of His own nature (for the nature that has to do with reason is related to God, and apprehensible by mind alone), and the kind which, inasmuch as it clearly falls under the province of the senses, is separated from Him by the greatest interval. And it was also fit that there should be a mixture of both kinds of being, as a token of still greater wisdom and of the opulence of the Divine expenditure as regards natures, as Gregorius, the expounder of God's being and ways, puts it, and to be a sort of connecting link between the visible and invisible natures. And by the word "fit" I mean, simply that it was an evidence of the Creator's will, for that will is the law and ordinance most meet, and no one will say to his Maker, "Why hast Thou so fashioned me?" For the potter is able at his will to make vessels of various patterns out of his clay, as a proof of his own wisdom.

Now this being the case, He creates with His own hands man of a visible nature and an invisible, after His own image and likeness: on the one hand man's body He formed of earth, and on the other his reasoning and thinking soul He bestowed upon him by His own in-breathing, and this is what we mean by "after His image." For the phrase "after His image" clearly refers to the side of his nature which consists of mind and free will, whereas "after His likeness" means likeness in virtue so far as that is possible.

Further, body and soul were formed at one and the same time, not first the one and then the other, as Origen so senselessly supposes.

God then made man without evil, upright, virtuous, free from pain and care, glorified with every virtue, adorned with all that is good, like a sort of second microcosm within the great world, another angel capable of worship, compound, surveying the visible creation and initiated into the mysteries of the realm of thought, king over the things of earth, but subject to a higher king, of the earth and of the heaven, temporal and eternal, belonging to the realm of sight and to the realm of thought, midway between greatness and lowliness, spirit and flesh: for he is spirit by grace, but flesh by overweening pride:

spirit that he may abide and glorify his Benefactor, and flesh that he may suffer, and suffering may be admonished and disciplined when he prides himself in his greatness: here, that is, in the present life, his life is ordered as an animal's, but elsewhere, that is, in the age to come, he is changed and – to complete the mystery – becomes deified by merely inclining himself towards God; becoming deified, in the way of participating in the divine glory and not in that of a change into the divine being.

But God made him by nature sinless, and endowed him with free will. By sinless, I mean not that sin could find no place in him (for that is the case with Deity alone), but that sin is the result of the free volition he enjoys rather than an integral part of his nature; that is to say, he has the power to continue and go forward in the path of goodness, by co-operating with the divine grace, and likewise to turn from good and take to wickedness, for God has conceded this by conferring freedom of will upon him. For there is no virtue in what is the result of mere force.

The soul, accordingly, is a living essence, simple, incorporeal, invisible in its proper nature to bodily eyes, immortal, reasoning and intelligent, formless, making use of an organised body, and being the source of its powers of life, and growth, and sensation, and generation, mind being but its purest part and not in any wise alien to it; (for as the eye to the body, so is the mind to the soul); further it enjoys freedom and volition and energy, and is mutable, that is, it is given to change, because it is created. All these qualities according to nature it has received of the grace of the Creator, of which grace it has received both its being and this particular kind of nature...

Chapter XXV – Concerning what is in our own power, that is, concerning Free will

The first enquiry involved in the consideration of free will, that is, of what is in our own power, is whether anything is in our power: for there are many who deny this. The second is, what are the things that are in our power, and over what things do we have authority? The third is, what is the reason for which God Who created us endued us with free will? So then we shall take up the first question, and firstly we shall prove that of those things which even our opponents grant, some are within our power. And let us proceed thus.

Of all the things that happen, the cause is said to be either God, or necessity, or fate, or nature, or chance, or accident. But God's function has to do with essence and providence: necessity deals with the movement of things that ever keep to the same course: fate with the necessary accomplishment of the things it brings to pass (for fate itself implies necessity): nature with birth, growth, destruction, plants and animals; chance with what is rare and unexpected. For chance is defined as the meeting and concurrence of two causes, originating in choice but bringing to pass something other than what is natural: for example, if a man finds a treasure while digging a ditch: for the man who hid the treasure did not do so that the other might find it, nor did the finder dig with the purpose of finding the treasure: but the former hid it that he might take it away when he wished, and the other's aim was to dig the ditch: whereas something happened quite different from what both had in view. Accident again deals with casual occurrences that take place among lifeless or irrational things, apart from nature and art. This then is their doctrine. Under which, then, of these categories are we to bring what happens through the agency of man, if indeed man is not the cause and beginning of action? For it would not be right to ascribe to God actions that are sometimes base and unjust: nor may we ascribe these to necessity, for they are not such as ever continue the same: nor to fate, for fate implies not possibility only but necessity: nor to nature, for nature's province is animals and plants: nor to chance, for the actions of men are not rare and unexpected: nor to accident, for that is used in reference to the casual occurrences that take place in the world of lifeless and irrational things. We are left then with this fact, that the man who acts and makes is himself the author of his own works, and is a creature endowed with free will.

Further, if man is the author of no action, the faculty of deliberation is quite superfluous for to what purpose could deliberation be put if man is the master of none of his actions? For all deliberation is for the sake of action. But to prove that the fairest and most precious of man's endowments is quite superfluous would be the height of absurdity. If then man deliberates, he deliberates with a view to action. For all deliberation is with a view to and on account of action.

Chapter XXVIII – Concerning what is not in our hands

Of things that are not in our hands some have their beginning or cause in those that are in our power, that is to say, the recompenses of our actions both in the present and in the age to come, but all the rest are dependent on the divine will. For the origin of all things is from God, but their destruction has been introduced by our wickedness for our punishment or benefit. For God did not create death, neither does He take delight in the destruction of living things. But death is the work rather of man, that is, its origin is in Adam's transgression, in like manner as all other punishments. But all other things must be referred to God. For our birth is to be referred to His creative power; and our continuance to His conservative power; and our government and safety to His providential power; and the eternal enjoyment of good things by those who preserve the laws of nature in which we are formed is to be ascribed to His goodness. But since some deny the existence of Providence, let us further devote a few words to the discussion of Providence.

Chapter XXIX – Concerning Providence

Providence, then, is the care that God takes over existing things. And again: Providence is the will of God through which all existing things receive their fitting issue. But if Providence is God's will, according to true reasoning all things that come into being through Providence must necessarily be both most fair and most excellent, and such that they cannot be surpassed. For the same person must of necessity be creator of and provider for what exists: for it is not meet nor fitting that the creator of what exists and the provider should be separate persons. For in that case they would both assuredly be deficient, the one in creating, the other in providing. God therefore is both Creator and Provider, and His creative and preserving and providing power is simply His good-will. For, "Whatsoever the Lord pleased that did He in heaven and in earth," and "no one resisted His will." He willed that all things should be and they were. He wills the universe to be framed and it is framed, and all that He wills comes to pass.

That He provides, and that He provides excellently, one can most readily perceive thus. God alone is good and wise by nature. Since then He is good, He provides: for he who does not provide is not good. For even men and creatures without reason provide for their own offspring according to their nature, and he who does not provide is blamed. Again, since He is wise, He takes the best care over what exists.

When, therefore, we give heed to these things we ought to be filled with wonder at all the works of Providence, and praise them all, and accept them all without enquiry, even though they are in the eyes of many unjust, because the Providence of God is beyond our ken and comprehension, while our reasonings and actions and the future are revealed to His eyes alone. And by "all" I mean those that are not in our hands: for those that are in our power are outside the sphere of Providence and within that of our Free will.

Now the works of Providence are partly according to the good-will (of God) and partly according to permission. Works of good-will include all those that are undeniably good, while works of permission are. . .[There are various readings here. Perhaps the best is supplied from *Nemesius, Ch. 44*, which says, "but there are many forms of concession"]. For Providence often permits the just man to encounter misfortune in order that he may reveal to others the virtue that lies concealed within him, as was the case with Job. At other times it allows something strange to be done in order that something great and marvellous might be accomplished through the seemingly-strange act, as when the salvation of men was brought about through the Cross. In another way it allows the pious man to suffer sore trials in order that he may not depart from a right conscience nor lapse into pride on account of the power and grace granted to him, as was the case with Paul.

One man is forsaken for a season with a view to another's restoration, in order that others when they see his state may be taught a lesson, as in the case of Lazarus and the rich man. For it belongs to our nature to be east down when we see persons in distress. Another is deserted by Providence in order that another may be glorified, and not for his own sin or that of his parents, just as the man who was blind from his birth ministered to the glory of the Son of Man. Again another is permitted to suffer in order to stir up emulation in the breasts of others, so that others by magnifying the glory of the sufferer may resolutely welcome suffering in the hope of future glory and the desire for future blessings, as in the case of the martyrs. Another is allowed to fall at times into some act of baseness in order that another worse fault may be thus corrected, as for instance when God allows a man who takes pride in his virtue and righteousness to fall away into fornication in order that he may be brought through this fall into the perception of his own weakness and be humbled and approach and make confession to the Lord.

Moreover, it is to be observed that the choice of what is to be done is in our own hands: but the final issue depends, in the one case when our actions are good, on the cooperation of God, Who in His justice brings help according to His foreknowledge to such as choose the good with a right conscience, and, in the other case when our actions are to evil, on the desertion by God, Who again in His justice stands aloof in accordance with His foreknowledge.

Now there are two forms of desertion: for there is desertion in the matters of guidance and training, and there is complete and hopeless desertion. The former has in view the restoration and safety and glory of the sufferer, or the rousing of feelings of emulation and imitation in others, or the glory of God: but the latter is when man, after God has done all that was possible to save him, remains of his own set purpose blind and uncured, or rather incurable, and then he is handed over to utter destruction, as was Judas. May God be gracious to us, and deliver us from such desertion.

Observe further that the ways of God's providence are many, and they cannot be explained in words nor conceived by the mind.

And remember that all the assaults of dark and evil fortune contribute to the salvation of those who receive them with thankfulness, and are assuredly ambassadors of help.

Also one must bear in mind that God's original wish was that all should be saved and come to His Kingdom. For it was not for punishment that He formed us but to share in His goodness, inasmuch as He is a good God. But inasmuch as He is a just God, His will is that sinners should suffer punishment.

The first then is called God's antecedent will and pleasure, and springs from Himself, while the second is called God's consequent will and permission, and has its origin in us. And the latter is twofold; one part dealing with matters of guidance and training, and having in view our salvation, and the other being hopeless and leading to our utter punishment, as we said above. And this is the case with actions that are not left in our hands.

But of actions that are in our hands the good ones depend on His antecedent goodwill and pleasure, while the wicked ones depend neither on His antecedent nor on His consequent will, but are a concession to free will. For that which is the result of compulsion has neither reason nor virtue in it. God makes provision for all creation and makes all creation the instrument of His help and training, yea often even the demons themselves, as for example in the cases of Job and the swine.

Chapter XXX – Concerning Prescience and Predestination

We ought to understand that while God knows all things beforehand, yet He does not predetermine all things. For He knows beforehand those things that are in our power, but He does not predetermine them. For it is not His will that there should be wickedness nor does He choose to compel virtue. So that predetermination is the work of the divine command based on fore-knowledge. But on the other hand God predetermines those things which are not within our power in accordance with His prescience. For already God in His prescience has prejudged all things in accordance with His goodness and justice.

Bear in mind, too, that virtue is a gift from God implanted in our nature, and that He Himself is the source and cause of all good, and without His co-operation and help we cannot will or do any good thing. But we have it in our power either to abide in virtue and follow God, Who calls us into ways of virtue, or to stray from paths of virtue, which is to dwell in wickedness, and to follow the devil who summons but cannot compel us. For wickedness is nothing else than the withdrawal of goodness, just as darkness is nothing else than the withdrawal of light. While then we abide in the natural state we abide in virtue, but when we deviate from the natural state, that is from virtue, we come into an unnatural state and dwell in wickedness.

Repentance is the returning from the unnatural into the natural state, from the devil to God, through discipline and effort.

Man then the Creator made male, giving him to share in His own divine grace, and bringing him thus into communion with Himself: and thus it was that he gave in the manner of a prophet the names to living flyings, with authority as though they were given to be his slaves. For having been endowed with reason and mind, and free will after the image of God, he was filly entrusted with dominion over earthly things by the common Creator and Master of all.

But since God in His prescience knew that man would transgress and become liable to destruction, He made from him a female to be a help to him like himself; a help, indeed, for the conservation of the race after the transgression from age to age by generation. For the earliest formation is called 'making' and not 'generation.' For 'making' is the original formation at God's hands, while 'generation' is the succession from each Other made necessary by the sentence of death imposed on us on account of the transgression.

This man He placed in Paradise, a home that was alike spiritual and sensible. For he lived in the body on the earth in the realm of sense, while he dwelt in the spirit among the angels, cultivating divine thoughts, and being supported by them: living in naked simplicity a life free from artificiality, and being led up through His creations to the one and only Creator, in Whose contemplation he found joy and gladness.

When therefore He had furnished his nature with free will, He imposed a law on him, not to taste of the tree of knowledge. Concerning this tree, we have said as much as is necessary in the chapter about Paradise, at least as much as it was in our power to say. And with this command He gave the promise that, if he should preserve the dignity of the soul by giving the victory to reason, and acknowledging his Creator and observing His command, he should share eternal blessedness and live to all eternity, proving mightier than death: but if forsooth he should subject the soul to the body, and prefer the delights of the body, comparing himself in ignorance of his true dignity to the senseless beasts, and shaking off His Creator's yoke, and neglecting His divine injunction, he will be liable to death and corruption, and will be compelled to labour throughout a miserable life. For it was no profit to man to obtain incorruption while still untried and unproved, lest he should fall into pride and under the judgment of the devil. For through his incorruption the devil, when he had fallen as the result of his own free choice, was firmly established in wickedness, so that there was no room for repentance and no hope of change: just as, moreover, the angels also, when they had made free choice of virtue became through grace immoveably rooted in goodness.

It was necessary, therefore, that man should first be put to the test (for man untried and unproved would be worth nothing), and being made perfect by the trial through the observance of the command should thus receive incorruption as the prize of his virtue. For being intermediate between God and matter he was destined, if he kept the command, to be delivered from his natural relation to existing things and to be made one with God's estate, and to be immoveably established in goodness, but, if he transgressed and inclined the rather to what was material, and tore his mind from the Author of his being, I mean God, his fate was to be corruption, and he was to become subject to passion instead of passionless, and mortal instead of immortal, and dependent on connection and unsettled generation. And in his desire for life he would cling to pleasures as though they were necessary to maintain it, and would fearlessly abhor those who sought to deprive him of these, and transfer his desire from God to matter, and his anger from the real enemy of his salvation to his own brethren. The envy of the devil then was the reason of man's fall. For that same demon, so full of envy and with such a hatred of good, would not suffer us to enjoy the pleasures of heaven, when he himself was kept below on account of his arrogance, and hence the false one tempts miserable man with the hope of Godhead, and leading him up to as great a height of arrogance as himself, he hurls him down into a pit of destruction just as deep.

An Afterword by Georges Florovsky

> Fr. Georges Florovsky (August 23, 1893 – August 11, 1979) was part of that exodus of Russian intellectuals to the West brought on by the Russian Revolution. A gifted linguist and scholar, he took his first faculty position in the 1920s at St. Sergius Orthodox Theological Institute in Paris. In the 1930s he became an Orthodox priest. After World War II, Florovsky immigrated to the United States, where he held faculty positions at St. Vladimir's Seminary, Harvard, and Princeton. His breadth of erudition and depth of insight mark him as one of the most important Orthodox theologians of the 20th century.
>
> Creation always played a pivotal role in Florovsky's theological reflections. In "Creation and Creaturehood," Florovsky recapitulates the teachings of the Fathers on the doctrine of creation. Two dominant themes emerge in this essay: the freedom of creation and, as he puts it, "the absolute creatureliness and non-self-sufficiency of the world." God creates a world that is free without being autonomous, that is dependent without being enslaved. Florovsky tracks these themes through the various departments of theology including the doctrine of God, Christology, anthropology, and, perhaps most notably, ecclesiology. "Through the Church creaturely efforts are crowned and saved," concludes Florovsky, "and creation is restored to its fulness and reality."

"Creation and Creaturehood"

> Behold, I have graven thee upon the palms of my hands, and thy walls are continually before me... (Isaiah 49:16).

I.

THE WORLD IS CREATED. That means: the world came out of nothing. That means there was no world before it sprang up and came into being. It sprang up and came into being together with time. Because when there was no world, there was no time. Because "time is reckoned from the creation of the heavens and the earth," as St. Maximus the Confessor said.[1] Only the world exists in time – in change, succession, duration. Without the world there is no time. And the genesis of the world is the beginning of time.[2] This beginning, as

St. Basil the Great explains, is not yet time, nor even a fraction of time, just as the beginning of a road is not yet the road itself. It is simple and uncomposite.³ There was no time; and suddenly, all at once, it began. Creation springs, *comes into* being, passes from out of non-being into being. It *begins* to be. As St. Gregory of Nyssa says, "The very subsistence of creation owed its beginning to change,"⁴ "the very transition from non-entity to existence is a change, non-existence being changed by the Divine power into being."⁵ This primordial genesis and beginning of change and duration, this "transition" from void to existence, is inaccessible to human thought. But it becomes comprehensible and imaginable from its opposite.

We always calculate time in an inverse order, back from the present, retreating into the depths of time, going backwards in the temporal sequence; and only secondarily do we think in terms of consecutive reckoning. And going backwards into the past, we stop at some determinate link, one which is calculated and calculable from within the series, with a clear consciousness that we have to stop. The very notion of the beginning of time is this necessity of stopping, is the very impossibility of an infinite regression into the past. It makes no difference whether we can or cannot compute this limit of retreat in terms of centuries or of days. The prohibition itself remains in full force.

A first unit is absolutely postulated in the temporal series, before which there are no other links, no other moments of time, because there was no change, and no sequence whatever. It is not time that precedes time, but "the height of ever-present eternity" transcending duration – *celsitudo semper praesentis aeternitatis*, as St. Augustine used to say. Time began. But there will be a time "when time shall be no more" – ("ὅτι χρόνος οὐκέτι ἔσται" Rev. 10:6). Change will cease. And according to St. John Damascene, "Time, after the resurrection, will no longer be numbered by days and nights; rather, there will be one day without evening."⁶

The temporal sequence will be broken; there will be a last unit in it. But this end and cessation of change does not indicate the abolition of what began with time, of what was and existed in time; it does not suggest a return or relapse into nothingness. There will be no time, but creation will be preserved. The created world can exist even not in time. Creation began, but it will not cease.[7] Time is a kind of line *segment*, with a beginning and an end. And therefore it is incommensurate with eternity, because time has a beginning. And in eternity there is no change, neither a beginning. The whole of temporality does not coincide with eternity. "The fullness of the times" (*omne tempus*) does not necessarily mean "always" (*semper*), as Augustine has pointed out.[8] Infinity or endlessness does not necessarily imply beginninglessness. And creation may be compared to a mathematical "bundle of rays," halves of straight lines extending from their point of origin to infinity. Once brought out of nothingness and non-being, the world has in the creative fiat an immutable and final foundation and support for its existence.

"The creative word is like an adamantine bridge upon which creatures are placed, and they stand under the abyss of the Divine Infinitude, over the abyss of their own nothingness," said Metropolitan Philaret. "Because the word of God must not be imagined as like the spoken word of man, which, when it has been pronounced, straightway desists and vanishes in air. In God there is nothing of cessation, nothing of vanishing: His word proceeds but does not recede: *"The word of the Lord endureth for ever* (1 Peter 1:25).*"*[9] God *"Created all things, that they might have their being"* (Wis. Solomon 1:14). And not for the time being, but for ever did He create: He brought creation into being by His creative word. *"For He hath established the world, so that it shall not be moved"* (Ps. 93:1).

The world exists. But it began to exist. And that means; the world could have not existed. There is no necessity whatsoever for the existence of the world. Creaturely existence is not self-sufficient and is not independent. In the created world itself there is no foundation, no basis for genesis and being. Creation by its very existence witnesses to and proclaims its creaturehood, it proclaims that it has been produced. Speaking in the words of Augustine, "[It] cries out that it has been created – it cries out that it did not create itself: [I] exist because I am created; and I was not before I came to be, and I could not issue from myself..." – *clamant quod facta sunt. Clamant etiam quod seipsa non fecerint: ideo sumus, quia facta sumus; non eramus ante quam essemus, ut fieri possemus a nobis...*[10]

By its very existence creation points beyond its own limits. The cause and foundation of the world is outside the world. The world's being is possible only through the supra-mundane will of the merciful and Almighty God, *"Who calls the things that be not, to be"* (Rom. 4:17). But, unexpectedly it is precisely in its creaturehood and createdness that the stability and substantiality of the world is rooted. Because the origin from out of nothing determines the otherness, the "non-consubstantiality" of the world and of God. It is insufficient and inexact to say that things are created and placed *outside of God*. The *"outside"* itself is posited only in creation, and creation "from out of nothing" [*ex nihilo*] is precisely such a positing of the "outside," the positing of an "other" side by side with God.

Certainly not in the sense of any kind of limitation to the Divine fullness, but in the sense that side by side with God there springs up an *other*, a heterogeneous substance or nature, one different from Him, and in a certain sense an independent and autonomous subject. That which did not exist springs now up and comes forth. In creation something *absolutely new*, an extra-divine *reality* is posited and built up. It is precisely in this that the supremely great and incomprehensible miracle of creation consists – that an "other" springs up, that heterogeneous drops of creation exist side by side with "the illimitable and infinite Ocean of being," as St. Gregory of Nazianzus says of God.[11]

There is an infinite distance between God and creation, and this is a *distance of natures*. All is distant from God, and is *remote* from Him not by place but *by nature* – (οὐ τόπῳ ἀλλὰ φύσει) – as St. John Damascene explains.[12] And this distance is never removed, but is only, as it were, overlapped by immeasurable Divine love. As St. Augustine said, in creation "there is nothing related to the Trinity, except the fact that the Trinity has created it" – *nihilique in ea esse quod ad Trinitatem pertineat, nisi quod Trinitas condidit*...[13] Even on the most exalted heights of prayerful ascent and intimacy there is always an impassable limit, there can always be perceived and revealed the living duality of God and creation. "He is God, and she is non-God," said Macarius "the Great" of the soul. "He is the Lord, and she the handmaid; He the Creator, and she the creation; He the Architect, and she the fabric; and there is nothing in common between Him and her nature."[14]

Any transubstantiation of creaturely nature into the Divine is as impossible as the changing of God into creation, and any "coalescence" and "fusion" of natures is excluded. In the one and only hypostasis and person of Christ – the God-Man – in spite of the completeness of the mutual interpenetration [περιχώρησις εἰς ἀλλήλας] of the two natures, the two natures remain with their unchanged, immutable difference; "without the distinction of natures being taken away by such union, but rather the specific property of each nature being preserved" Οὐδαμοῦ τῆς τῶν φύσεων διαφορᾶς ἀνηρημένες διὰ τὴν ἕνωσιν σωζομένης δὲ μᾶλλον τῆς ἰδιότητος ἑκατέρας φύσεως (the ὅρος of Chalcedon). The vague "out of two natures" the Fathers of Chalcedon replaced by the strong and clear "*in* two natures," and by the confession of the double and bilateral consubstantiality of the God-Man they established an unshakeable and indisputable criterion and rule of faith. The real existence of a created human nature, that is, of an other and second nature outside of God and side by side with Him, is an indispensable prerequisite for the accomplishment of the Incarnation without any change in or transmutation of the Divine nature.

What is created is outside of God, but is united with Him. The Fathers of the fourth century, moved by the Arian controversy to define the concept of creation in a clear and precise manner, stressed above all else the heterogeneity of the created and Creator in counter distinction to the "consubstantiality" of generation; and they corrected this heterogeneity with the dependence of creation upon the will and volition. Everything created, wrote St. Athanasius the Great, "is not in the least like its Creator in substance, but is *outside* of Him," and therefore also could have *not* existed.[15] Creation "comes into being, made up from outside."[16] And there is no similarity between that which bursts forth from nothing and the Creator Who verily *is*, Who brings creatures out of nothing.[17]

Will and volition precede creating. Creating is *an act of will* [ἐκ βουλήματος], and therefore is sharply distinguished from the Divine generation, which is an *act of nature* [γεννᾷ κατὰ φύσιν].[18] A similar interpretation was given by St. Cyril of Alexandria. The generation is out of the substance, (κατὰ Φύσιν). Creating is an act, and is not done out of the creator's own substance; and therefore a creation is heterogeneous to its creator.[19] Summarizing the patristic interpretation, St. John of Damascus gives a following definition: "Begetting means producing from the substance of the begetter an offspring similar in substance to the begetter. Creation, or making, on the other hand, is the bringing into being, from outside and not from the substance of the creator, an actor of something, entirely unlike [by nature]." Generation is accomplished "by a natural power of begetting," [τῆς γοςιμότητος φυσικῆς] and creating is an act of volition and will – (θελήσεως ἔργον).[20] Creaturehood determines the complete dissimilarity of the creation and God, its otherness, and hence its independence and substantiality. The whole section of St. John is actually an elaborate rejoinder to arguments of Origin.

Creation is not a phenomenon but a "substance." The reality and substantiality of created nature is manifested first of all in *creaturely freedom*. Freedom is not exhausted by the possibility of choice, but presupposes it and starts with it. And creaturely freedom is disclosed first of all in the equal possibility of two ways: to God and away from God. This duality of ways is not a mere formal or logical possibility, but a real possibility, dependent on the effectual presence of powers and capacities not only for a choice between, but also for the following of, the two ways. Freedom consists not only in the possibility, but also in the necessity of autonomous choice, the resolution and resoluteness of choice. Without this autonomy, nothing happens in creation. As St. Gregory the Theologian says, "God legislates human self-determination."[21] "He honored man with freedom that good might belong no less to him who chose it than to Him Who planted its seed."[22] Creation must ascend to and unite with God by its own efforts and achievements. And if the way of union requires and presupposes a responsive prevenient movement of Divine Mercy, "the ancient law of human freedom," as St. Irenæus once put it, is not undermined by this.

The way of disunion is not closed to creatures, the way of destruction and death. There is no irresistible grace, creatures can and may lose themselves, are capable, as it were, of "metaphysical suicide." In her primordial and ultimate vocation, creation is destined for union with God, for communion and participation in His life. But this is not a binding necessity of creaturely nature. Of course, outside of God there is no life for creation. But as Augustine happily phrased it, *being and life do not coincide* in creation.[23] And therefore *existence in death* is possible. Of course, creation can realize and establish herself fully only by overcoming her self-isolation, only in God. But even without realizing her true vocation, and even opposing it, thus undoing and losing herself, creation does not cease to exist. The possibility of metaphysical suicide is open to her. But the power of self-annihilation is not given. Creation is indestructible – and not only that creation which is rooted in God as in the source of true being and eternal life, but also that creation which has set herself against God. *"For the fashion of this world passeth away"* (1 Cor. 7:31), and shall pass. But the world itself shall not pass. Because it was created "that it might have being." Its qualities and properties are changeable and mutable, and do change; but its "elements" are immutable. And immutable above all is the microcosm man, and immutable are men's *hypostases*, sealed as they are and brought out of nothing by the creative will of God.

Indeed, the way of rebellion and apostasy is the way of destruction and perdition. But it leads not towards non-being, but to death; and death is not the end of existence, but a *separation* – the separation of soul and body, the separation of creation from God. In fact, evil "is not an entity."[24] Evil has no "substance" – it is ($\dot{\alpha}o\dot{\upsilon}\sigma\iota o\nu$) according to St. John Damascene.[25] Evil has a negative and privative character, it is the absence and privation of true being. And at the same time, as St. Gregory of Nyssa says, "in its very non-being it has its being." – $\dot{\epsilon}\nu \tau\hat{\omega} \mu\dot{\eta} \epsilon\hat{\imath}\nu\alpha\iota \, \ddot{\epsilon}\chi\epsilon\iota$[26] The root and character of evil is delusion and error. Evil, in the incisive phrase of one German theologian, is "a mythopoeic lie" ["eine dichtende Lüge" – F. Staudenmeier]. It is a kind of fiction, but a fiction loaded with enigmatic energy and power.

Evil is active in the world, and in this actuality is real. Evil introduces new qualities into the world, as it were, adding something to the reality created by God, a something not willed and not created by God, although tolerated by Him. And this innovation, in a certain sense "non-being," is in an enigmatic fashion real and powerful, *"For God made not death"* (Wis. Sol. 1:13), and nevertheless the whole creation is become subject to futility, and to the bondage of corruption (Rom. 8:20–21). By sin death spread to all men (Rom. 5:12), and sin, being itself a fictitious innovation in the world, the spawn of the created will and of human devices, creates death and as it were sets up a new law of existence for creation, a kind of anti-law. And in a certain sense, evil is ineradicable. Yet, because the final perdition *in eternal torment* provoked by evil in "the resurrection unto judgment" does not mean total annihilation nor the total suppression of evil beings, it is impossible to ascribe to evil such anti-creative power which would overcome the creative power of God.

By its devastation of being, evil does not wipe out being. And, such a devastated, distorted, deceitful, and false reality is mysteriously received into eternity, even though in the torments of unquenchable fire. The eternity of torments that will come upon the sons of perdition points out with a special urgency and sharpness the reality of creation as a second and extra-divine reality. It is provoked by a persistent though free rebellion, by a self-assertion in evil. Thus, as in becoming, so in dissolution – as in holiness, so in perdition – as in obedience, so in disobedience – creation manifests and witnesses to her own reality as the free object of the divine decrees.

The idea of creation is alien to the "natural" consciousness. Classical, Hellenistic thought did not know it. Modern philosophy has forgotten it. Given in the Bible, it is disclosed and manifested in the living experience of the Church. In the idea of creation are juxtaposed the motif of the immutable, intransitory reality of the world as a free and active subject (more precisely, as a totality of interacting subjects) and the motif of its total non-self-sufficiency, of its ultimate dependence upon another higher principle. And therefore any supposition of the world's beginninglessness, the necessity of its existence, and any admission of its elimination are excluded. Creation is neither self-existent *being*, nor transitory *becoming*; neither eternal *"substance,"* nor illusory *"appearance."* In creaturehood a great wonder is revealed. *The world also might not have existed at all.* And that which might not have existed, for which there are no inevitable causes or bases, does *exist*. This is a riddle, a "foolishness" for "natural" thought. And hence comes the temptation to attenuate and blunt the idea of creation, to replace it by other notions. Only by the contrary approach can the mystery of creation be clarified, by the exclusion and suspension of all evasive speculation and conjecture.

II.

God creates in perfect freedom. This proposition is framed with remarkable precision by the "Subtle Doctor" of the Western middle ages, Duns Scotus: *Procedit autem rerum creatio a Deo, non aliqua necessitate, vel essentiae, vel scientiae, vel voluntatis, sed ex mera libertate, quae non movetir et multo minus necessitatur ab aliquo extra se ad causandum.* "The creation of things is executed by God not out of any necessity, whether of essence or of knowledge or of will, but out of a sheer freedom which is not moved – much less constrained – by anything external that it should have to be a cause."[27] Even so, in defining God's freedom in creation it is not enough to do away with crude conceptions of compulsion, of external necessity. It is obvious that we cannot even speak of any kind of external compulsion, because the very "outside" itself is first posited only in creation. In creation God is determined only by Himself. But it is not so easy to demonstrate the absence of any internal "necessity" in this self-determination, in the revelation of God *ad extra*.

Here, the thought is beset by alluring temptations. The question may be put in this manner: Is the attribute of Creator and Sustainer to be considered as belonging to the essential and formative properties of the Divine Being? The thought of the Divine immutability may prevent us from giving a negative answer. Precisely so did Origen reason in his time. "It is alike impious and absurd to say that God's nature is to be at ease and never to move, or to suppose that there was a time when Goodness did not do good and Omnipotence did not exercise its power."[28] From the perfect extra-temporality and immutability of the Divine Being, Origen, in the words of Bolotov, draws the conclusion "that all His properties and predicates always belong to God in a strict sense – *in actu, in statu quo*."[29] Here, "always" for Origen has the meaning of "extra-temporal eternity," and not only "the whole of temporality." – "Just as nobody can be a father without having a son, nor a lord without holding a possession or a slave," reasons Origen, "so too we cannot even call God Almighty-Pantocrator if there are no creatures over whom he can exercise His power. For if anyone would have it that certain ages, or periods of time, or of Divine Omnipotence – whatever he cares to call them – elapsed during which the present creation did not exist, he would undoubtedly prove that in those ages or periods God was not Almighty but that He became Pantocrator afterward, that He became Almighty from the time when he began to have creatures over whom he could exercise power. Thus God will apparently have experienced a kind of progress, for there can be no doubt that it is better for Him to be Almighty than not to be so.

Now how is it anything but absurd that God should at first not possess something that is appropriate to Him and then should come to possess it? But if there was no time when God was not Almighty, there must always have existed the things in virtue of which He is Almighty; and there must always have existed things under his rule, over which He is their Ruler."[30] In view of the perfect Divine immutability, "it is necessary that the creatures of God should have been created from the beginning, and that there should be no time when they were not." Because it is inadmissible to think that, in time, God "would pass from inaction to action." Hence it is necessary to recognize "that with God all things are without beginning and are co-eternal."[31]

It is not simple or easy to escape from Origen's dialectical nets. In this very problematic there lies an incontestable difficulty. "When I think what God was Lord of from eternity, if creation be not from always," exclaimed Augustine, "I fear to affirm anything." *Cum cogito cuius rei dominus semper fuit, si semper creatura non fuit, affirmare aliquid pertimesco...*[32] Origen complicated his question by his inability to extricate himself completely from time as change.

Together with the sempiternal and immobile eternity of the Divine Being, he imagined an endless flow of ages which had to be filled. Furthermore, any sequence in the Divine predicates appeared to him under the form of real temporal change; and therefore, having excluded change, he was inclined to deny any sequence at all to, or interdependence among, those predicates taken as a whole; he asserted more than the mere "co-eternity" of the world with God; he asserted the necessity of the Divine self-disclosure *ad extra*, the *necessity* of the revelation and out-pouring of Divine goodness upon the "other" from all eternity, the *necessity* of the eternal realization of the fulness and of all the potentialities of Divine power. In other words, in order to comply with the notion of the Divine immutability, Origen had to admit the necessity of a conjointly ever-existent and beginningless "not-I" as a corresponding prerequisite to and correlative of the Divine completeness and life. And here is the ultimate sting of the question. *It was also possible that the world might not have existed at all* – possible in the full sense of the word only granted that *God can also not create*. If, on the other hand, God creates out of necessity, for sake of the completeness of His Being, then the world must exist; then it is not possible that the world might not have existed. Even if one rejects the Origenistic notion of the infinitude of real past time and recognizes the beginning of time, the question remains: Does not *at least the thought of the world* belong to the absolute necessity of the Divine Being?

We may assume that the real world came into being together with time, and that "there was when it was not," when there was no temporal change. But the image of the world, does not *this* remain eternal and everlasting in the Divine knowledge and will, participating immutably and ineluctably in the fulness of the Divine self-knowledge and self-determination? On this point St. Methodius of Olympus had already put his finger, against Origen, stressing that the Divine All-Perfectness cannot depend on anything except God Himself, except on His own nature.[33]

Indeed, God creates solely out of His goodness, and in this Divine goodness lies the only basis of His revelation to the "other," the only basis of the very being of that "other" as recipient and object of this goodness. But should we not think of this revelation as eternal? And if we should – since God lives in eternity and in unchangeable completeness – would not this mean that in the final analysis "the image of the world" was present, and conjointly present, with God unchangingly in eternity, and moreover in the unalterable completeness of all its particular predicates? Is there not a "necessity of knowledge or will?" Does not this mean that God in His eternal self-contemplation also necessarily contemplates even *what He is not*, that which is not He, but other? Is God not bound in His sempiternal self-awareness by the image of His "Non-I" at least as a kind of possibility? And in His self-awareness is He not forced to think of and to contemplate Himself as a creative principle and as the source of the world, and of the world as an object of and participant in His good pleasure? And on the other hand, over the whole world there lies imprinted the Divine seal, a seal of permanence, a reflection of the Divine glory.

The Divine economy of the world, the unchanging and immutable Providence of God, conveys – to our vision – perfect stability and wise harmony – and also a kind of necessity. This vision hinders our understanding and apprehension of the claim that the world also might not have existed. It seems we cannot conceive the world as non-existing without introducing a kind of impious *fortuitousness* or *arbitrariness* in its existence and genesis, either of which is contradictory and derogatory to the Divine Wisdom. Is it not obvious that there must be some kind of sufficient cause for the world, *cur sit potius quam non sit*? And that this cause must consist of the unchangeable and sempiternal will and command of God? Does it not follow that once the world is impossible without God, God also is impossible without the world? Thus the difficulty is only shelved, but not solved, if we limit ourselves to the chronological beginnings of the actual existence of the world, since, in this case, the *possibility* of the world, the *idea* of the world. God's design and will concerning it, still remains eternal and as though con-jointly everlasting with God.

And it must be said at once that any such admission means introducing the world into the ultra-Trinitarian life of the Godhead as a co-determinant principle. And we must firmly and uncompromisingly reject any such notion. The idea of the world, God's design and will concerning the world, is obviously *eternal*, but in some sense *not co-eternal*, and *not conjointly everlasting* with Him, because "distinct and separated," as it were, from His "essence" by His *volition*. One should say rather that the Divine idea of the world is eternal by *another kind* of eternity than the Divine essence. Although paradoxical, this distinction of types and kinds of eternity is necessary for the expression of the incontestable distinction between the *essence* (*nature*) of God and the *will* of God. This distinction would not introduce any kind of separation or split into the Divine Being, but by analogy expresses the distinction between *will* and *nature*, the fundamental distinction made so strikingly explicit by the Fathers of the fourth century.

The idea of the world has its basis *not in the essence, but in the will of God*. God does not so much have as "think up" the idea of creation.[34] And He "thinks it up" in perfect freedom; and it is only by virtue of this wholly free "thinking up" and good pleasure of His that He as it were "becomes" Creator, even though from everlasting. But nevertheless He could also not have created. And any such "refraining" from creation would in no way alter or impoverish the Divine nature, would mean no diminution, Just as the very creation of the world does not enrich the Divine Being. Thus by way of opposites we can come close to an understanding of God's creative freedom. In a sense, it would be "indifferent" to God whether the world exists or not – herein consists the absolute "all-sufficiency" of God, the Divine autarchy. The absence of the world would mean a kind of subtraction of what is finite from the Infinite, which would not affect Divine fulness. And conversely, the creation of the world would mean the addition of what is finite to the Infinite, which in no way affects Divine plenitude. The might of God and the freedom of God must be defined not only as the power to create and to produce but also as the absolute freedom *not to create*.

All these words and presuppositions, obviously, are insufficient and inexact. They all have the character of negations and prohibitions, and not of direct and positive definitions; but they are necessary for the testimony to that experience of faith in which the mystery of Divine freedom is revealed. With a tolerable inexactitude, one could say that God is able to permit and tolerate the absence of anything outside of Himself. By such a presumption the whole immeasurability of the Divine love is not diminished, but on the contrary is thrown into relief. God creates out of the absolute superabundance of His mercies and goodness, and herein His good pleasure and freedom are manifest. And in this sense, one could say that the world is a kind of a surplus. And further, it is a surplus which in no way enriches the Divine fulness; it is, as it were, something "supererogatory" and superadded, something which also could not have existed, and which exists only through the sovereign and all-perfect freedom and unspeakable good pleasure and love of God.

This means that the world is created and is "the work of" God's will, (θελήσεως ἔργον). No outward revelation whatever belongs to the "necessity" of the Divine nature, to the necessary structure of the intra-Divine life. And creative revelation is not something imposed upon God by His goodness. It is executed in perfect freedom, though in eternity also. Therefore it cannot be said that God *began to create*, or "became" Creator, even though "to be Creator" does not belong to those definitions of Divine nature which includes the Trinity of Hypostases. In the everlasting immutability of God's Being there is no origination whatsoever, nor any becoming, nor any sequence. And nevertheless there is a kind of all-perfect harmonic order which is partially knowable and expressible on the level of the Divine names. In this sense St. Athanasius the Great used to say that "to create, for

God, is *secondary*; and to beget, *primary*," that "what is of nature [essence]" is antecedent to "what is of volition."[35]

One has to admit distinctions within the very co-eternity and immutability of the Divine Being. In the wholly simple Divine life there is an absolute rational or logical order [τάξις] of Hypostases, which is irreversible and inexchangeable for the simple reason that there is a "first principle" or "source" of Godhead, and that there is the enumeration of *first, Second,* and *Third* Persons.[36] And likewise it is possible to say that the Trinitarian structure is antecedent to the will and thought of God, because the Divine will is the common and undivided will of the All-Holy Trinity, as it is also antecedent to all the Divine acts and "energies." But even more than this, the Trinity is the internal, self-revelation of the Divine nature.

The properties of God are also revelations of the same sort, but in their particular disclosure God is free. The unchanging will of God freely postulates creation, and even the very idea of creation. It would be a tempting mistake to regard the "thinking up" of the world by God as an "ideal creation," because the idea of the world and the world of ideas are totally *in God*, ἐν τῷ Θεῷ, and in God there is not, and there cannot be, anything of the created. But this ambiguous notion of an "ideal creation" defines with great clarity the complete distinction between the necessity of the Trinitarian Being on the one hand and the freedom of God's design – His good pleasure concerning creation – on the other. There remains an absolute and irremoveable distinction, the denial of which leads to picturing the whole created economy as made up of *essential acts* and conditions which disclose the Divine nature as though of *necessity*, and this leads to raising the world, at least the "intelligible world" [κόσμος νοητός] to an improper height. One might, with permissible boldness, say that in the Divine idea of creation there is a kind of contingency, and that if it is eternal, it is *not an eternity of essence*, but *a free eternity*.

We could clarify the freedom of God's design – His good pleasure – for ourselves by the hypothesis that this idea need not have been postulated at all. Certainly, it is a *casus irrealis*, but there is no inherent contradiction in it. Certainly, once God "thought up" or postulated such an idea, He had sufficient reason for doing so. However, one thinks that Augustine was right in prohibiting any search for "the cause of God's will."[37] But it is bound by nothing and pre-ordained by nothing. The Divine will is not constrained by anything to "think up" the world. From eternity, the Divine Mind, rhapsodized St. Gregory the Theologian, "contemplated the desirable light of His own beauty, the equal and equally-perfect splendor of the triple-rayed Divinity... The world-creating Mind in His vast thoughts also mused upon the patterns of the world which He made up, upon the cosmos which was produced only afterwards, but which for God even then was present. All, with God, lies before His eyes, both what shall be, and what was, and what is now... For God, all flows into one, *and all is held by the arms of the great Divinity*."[38]

"The desirable light" of the Divine beauty would not be enhanced by these "patterns of the world," and the Mind "makes them up" only out of the superabundance of love. They do not belong to the splendor of the Trinity; they are postulated by His will and good pleasure. And these very "patterns of the world" are themselves a surplus and super-added gift or "bonus" of Him Who is All-Blessed Love. In this very good pleasure of His will to create the world the infinite freedom of God is manifest.

So St. Athanasius says, "The Father creates all, by the Word, in the Spirit,"[39] – Creation is a common and indivisible act of the All-Holy Trinity. And God creates by thought, and the thought becomes deed – κτίζει δὲ ἐννοῶν, καὶ τὸ ἐννόημα ἔργου ὑφίσταται, says St. John Damascene.[40] "He contemplated everything from before its being, from eternity pondering it in His mind; hence each thing receives its being at a determinate time according to His timeless and decisive thought, which is predestination, and image, and pattern" – κατὰ τὴν θελητικὴν αὐτοῦ ἄχρονον ἔννοιαν, ἥτις ἐστὶ προορισμὸς καὶ εἰκὼν καὶ παράδειγμα.[41] These patterns and prototypes of things that are to be constitute the *"pre-temporal and unchangeable counsel"* of God, in which everything is given its distinctive character [ἐχαρακτειρίζετο] before its being, everything which is preordained by God in advance and then brought to existence – ἡ βουλὴ αὐτοῦ ἡ προαιώνιος καὶ ἀεὶ ὡσαύτως ἔχουσα.[42]

This "counsel" of God is eternal and unchanging, pre-temporal and without beginning – [ἄναρχος] – since everything Divine is immutable. And this is the *image of God*, the second form of the image, the image turned towards the creation.[43] St. John Damascene is referring to Pseudo-Dionysius. These creative patterns, says the

Areopagite, "are creative foundations pre-existent together in God, and together compose the powers that make being into entities, powers which theology calls 'predestinations,' Divine and 'beneficient,' decisions which are determinative and creative of all things extant, according to which He Who is above being has preordained and produced all that exists" – Παραδείγματα δὲ φάμεν εἶναι τοὺς ἐν Θεῷ τῶν ὄντων οὐσιοποιοὺς καὶ ἑνιαίως προϋφεστῶτας λόγους, οὕς ἡ Θεολογία προορισμοὺς καλεῖ, καὶ Θεῖα καὶ ἀγαθὰ θελήματα, τῶν ὄντων ἀφοριστικὰ καὶ ποιητικά, καθ' οὕς ὁ Ὑπερούσιος τὰ ὄντα πάντα καὶ προώρισε καὶ παρήγαγεν.[44]

According to St. Maximus the Confessor these types and ideas are the Divine all-perfect and everlasting thoughts of the everlasting God, – νοήσεις αὐτοτελεῖς ἀΐδιοι τοῦ ἀϊδίου Θεοῦ.[45] This eternal counsel is God's design and decision concerning the world. It must be rigorously distinguished from the world itself. The Divine idea of creation is not creation itself; it is not the substance of creation; it is not the bearer of the cosmic-process; and the "transition" from "design" [ἐννόημα] to "deed" [ἔργον] is not a process within the Divine idea, but the appearance, formation, and the realization of another substratum, of a multiplicity of created subjects.

The Divine idea remains unchangeable and unchanged, it is not involved in the process of formation. It remains always outside the created world, transcending it. The world is created *according to the idea*, in accordance with the pattern – it is the realization of the pattern – but this pattern is not the subject of becoming. The pattern is a norm and a goal established *in God*. This distinction and distance is never abolished, and therefore the *eternity of the pattern*, which is fixed and is never involved in temporal change, is compatible with temporal beginning, with the entering-into-being of the bearers of the external decrees. "Things before their becoming are as though nonexistent," said Augustine, *utiquae non erant*. And he explains himself: they both were and were not before they originated; "they were in God's knowledge: but were not in their own nature" – *erant in Dei scientia, non erant in sua natura*.[46] According to St. Maximus, created beings *"are images and similes of the Divine ideas,"*[47] in which they are "participants."[48]

In creation, the Creator realizes, "makes substantial" and "discloses" His knowledge, pre-existent everlastingly in Himself.[49] In creation there is projected from out of nothing a new reality which becomes the bearer of the Divine idea, and must realize this idea in its own becoming. In this context the pantheistic tendency of Platonic ideology and of the Stoic theory of "seminal reasons" [σπερματικοί λόγοι] is altogether overcome and avoided. For Platonism the identification of the "essence" of each thing with its Divine idea is characteristic, the endowment of substances with absolute and eternal (beginningless) properties and predicates, as well as the introduction of the "idea" into real things. On the contrary, the *created nucleus* of things must be rigorously distinguished from the *Divine idea* about things. Only in this way is even the most sequacious logical realism freed from a "pantheistic flavor; the reality of the whole will nevertheless be but a created reality. Together with this, pan-logism is also overcome: The thought of a thing and the Divine thought-design concerning a thing are not its "essence" or nucleus, even though the essence itself is characterized by λόγος, [λογικός]. The Divine pattern in things is not their "substance" or "hypostasis;" it is not the vehicle of their qualities and conditions. Rather, it might be called the *truth of a thing, its transcendental entelechy*. But the truth of a thing and the substance of a thing are not identical.[50]

III.

The acceptance of the absolute creatureliness and non-self-sufficiency of the world leads to the distinguishing of two kinds of predicates and acts in God. Indeed, at this point we reach the limit of our understanding, all words become, as it were, mute and inexact, receiving an apophatic, prohibitive, not a cataphatic, indicative sense. Nevertheless, the example of the holy Fathers encourages a speculative confession of faith. As Metropolitan Philaret once said, "We must by no means consider wisdom, even that hidden in a mystery, as alien and beyond us, but with humility should edify our mind towards the contemplation of divine things."[51] Only, in our speculation we must not overstep the boundaries of positive revelation, and must limit ourselves to the interpretation of the experience of faith and of the rule of faith, presuming to do no more than discern and clarify those inherent presuppositions through which the confession of dogmas as intelligible truths becomes possible. And it must be said that the whole structure of the doctrine of faith encourages these distinctions. In essence, they are already given in the ancient and primary distinction between "theology" and "economy." From the very beginning of Christian history, the Fathers and Doctors of the Church endeavored to distinguish clearly and sharply those definitions and names which referred to God on the "theological" plane and those used on the "economical." Behind this stands the distinction between "nature" and "will." And bound up with it is the distinction in God between "essence" [οὐσία] and "that which surrounds the essence," "that which is related to the nature." A distinction, but not a separation.

"What we say about God affirmatively shows us," as St. John Damascene explains, *"not His nature, but only what is related to His nature"* – οὐ τὴν φύσιν, ἀλλὰ τὰ περὶ τὴν φύσιν,[52] "something which accompanies His nature" [τί τῶν παρεπομένων τῇ φύσει].[53] And "what He is by essence and nature, this is unattainable and unknowable."[54] St. John expresses here the basic and constant assumption of all Eastern theology: God's essence is unattainable; only the powers and operations of God are accessible to knowledge.[55] And as matters stand, there is some distinction between them. This distinction is connected with God's relation to the world. God is knowable and attainable only in so far as He turns Himself to the world, only by His revelation to the world, only through His economy or dispensation. The internal Divine life is hedged by "light unapproachable," and is known only on the level of "apophatic" theology, with the exclusion of ambiguous and inadequate definitions and names.

In the literature of the ante-Nicene period, this distinction not seldom had an ambiguous and blurred character. Cosmological motives were often used in the definition of intra-Trinitarian relations, and the Second Hypostasis was often defined from the perspective of God's manifestation or revelation to the world, as the God of revelation, as the Creative Word. And therefore the unknowability and inaccessibility were assigned primarily to the Hypostasis of the Father as being un-revealable and ineffable. God reveals Himself only in the Logos, in "the spoken Word" [λόγος προφορικός], as "in the idea and active power" issuing forth to build creation.[56] Connected with that was the tendency to sub-ordinationism in the ante-Nicene theological interpretation of the Trinitarian dogma.

Only the Fathers of the fourth century obtained in their Trinitarian theology the basis for an adequate formulation of God's relation to the world: the whole entire and undivided "operation" [ἐνέργειαι] of the consubstantial Trinity is revealed in God's acts and deeds. But the single "essence" [οὐσία] of the undivided Trinity remains beyond the reach of knowledge and understanding. His works, as St. Basil the Great explains, reveal the *power and wisdom of God, but not His essence itself.*[57] "We affirm," he wrote to Amphilochius of Iconium, "that we know our God by His energies, but we do not presume that it is possible to approach the essence itself. Because although His energies descend to us, His essence remains inaccessible." And these energies are multiform, yet the essence is simple.[58] The essence of God is unfathomable for men, and is known solely to the Only-begotten Son and to the Holy Spirit.[59]

In the words of St. Gregory the Theologian, the essence of God is "the Holy of Holies, closed even to the Seraphim, and glorified by the three 'Holies' that come together in one 'Lordship' and 'Godhead.'" And the created mind is able, very imperfectly, to "sketch" some small "diagram of the truth" in the infinite ocean of the Divine entity, but based not upon what God is, *but upon what is around* Him [ἐκ τῶν περὶ αὐτόν].[60] "The Divine essence, totally inaccessible and comparable to nothing," says St. Gregory of Nyssa, "is knowable only through His energies."[61] And all our words concerning God denote not His essence but His energies.[62]

The Divine essence is inaccessible, unnameable, and ineffable. The manifold and relative names referring to God do not name His nature or essence but the attributes of God. Yet the *attributes of God* are not just intelligible or knowledgeable signs or marks which constitute our human notion of God; they are not abstractions or conceptual formulae. They *are energies, powers, actions*. They are real, essential, life-giving manifestations of the Divine Life – real images of God's relation to creation, connected with the image of creation in God's eternal knowledge and counsel. And this is "that which may be known of God" – τὸ γνωστὸν τοῦ Θεοῦ – (Rom. 1:19). This is, as it were, the particular domain of the undivided but yet "many-named" Divine Being, "of the Divine radiance and activity," – ἡ Θεία ἐλλαμψις καὶ ἐνέργεια, as St. John Damascene says, following the *Areopagitica*.[63]

According to the Apostolic word, "the invisible things of Him from the creation of the world are clearly seen, being understood by the things that are made, even His *everlasting power and Godhead*" (Rom. 1:20) [– ἥ τε ἀΐδιος αὐτοῦ δύναμις καὶ Θειότης]. And this is the revelation or manifestation of God: *"God hath shewed it unto them"* (Rom. 1:19) [ἐφανέρωσεν]. Bishop Silvester rightly explains in commenting on these Apostolic words: "The invisible things of God, being actually existent and not merely imaginary, become visible not in a kind of illusory way, but certainly, veritably; not as a mere phantom, but in His own eternal power; not merely in the thoughts of men, but in very fact – the reality of His Divinity."[64] They are visible because manifested and revealed. Because God is present everywhere, not phantasmally, not in remoteness, but really present everywhere – "which art in all places, and fillest all things, the Treasury of good things, and Giver of life." This providential ubiquity (different from the "particular" or charismatic presence of God, which is *not everywhere*) is a *particular "form of existence" for God*, distinct from the "form of His existence according to His own nature."[65] And furthermore this form is existentially real or subsistent – it is an actual presence, not merely an *omnipraesentia operativa, sicut agens adest ei in quod agit*. And if we "do not particularly understand" (in the phrase of St. Chrysostom[66]) this mysterious omnipresence, and this form of the Divine Being *ad extra*, nevertheless it is indisputable that God "is everywhere, whole and entirely," "all in all," as St. John Damascene said – ὅλον ὁλικῶς πανταχοῦ ὄν, – ὅλον ἐν πᾶσι.[67]

The life-giving acts of God in the world are God Himself – an assertion which precludes separation but does not abolish distinction.[68] In the doctrine of the Cappadocian fathers concerning "essence" and "energies" we find in an elaborate and systematic form the mysterious author of the *Areopagitica* that was to determine the whole subsequent development of Byzantine theology. Dionysius bases himself on the strict distinction between those "Divine Names" which refer to the intra-Divine and Trinitarian life and those which express the relation of God *ad extra*[69] But both series of names tell of the immutable Divine reality. The intra-Divine life is hidden from our understanding, is known only through negations and prohibitions,[70] and in the phrase of St. Gregory the Theologian "one who by seeing God has understood what he has seen, has not seen Him."[71] And nevertheless God really reveals Himself and acts and is present in creation through His powers and ideas – in "providences and graces which issue from the incommunicable God, which pour out in a flooding stream, and in which all existing things participate,"[72] "in an essence-producing procession," [οὐσιοποιόν πρόοδον], in "a providence that works good things," [ἀγαθοποιόν πρόνοιαν], which are distinguishable but not separable from the Divine entity "which surpasses entity," from God Himself, as St. Maximus the Confessor says in his scholia.[73]

The basis of these "processions" and of the, as it were, procession of God in His providences out of Himself – [ἔξω ἑαυτοῦ γίνεται] – is His goodness and love.[74] These energies do not mix with created things, and are not themselves these things, but are only their basic and life-giving principles; they are the prototypes, the predeterminations, the reasons, the (λόγοι) and Divine decisions respecting them, of which they are participants and ought to be "communicants."[75] They are not only the "principle" and the "cause," but also the "challenge" and beckoning goal which is beyond and above all limits. It would be difficult to express more forcefully both the distinction between and the indivisibility of the Divine Essence and the Divine energies than is done in the *Areopagitica* – τὸ ταυτὸν καὶ τὸ ἕτερον.[76] The divine energies are that aspect of God which is turned towards creation. It is not an aspect imagined by us; it is not what we see and as we see it, but it is the real and living gaze of God Himself, by which He wills and vivifies and preserves all things – the gaze of Almighty Power and Superabundant Love.

The doctrine of the energies of God received its final formulation in the Byzantine theology of the fourteenth century, and above all in St. Gregory Palamas. He bases himself on the distinction between Grace and Essence, "the divine and deifying radiance and grace is not the essence, but the energy of God" – ἡ Θεία καὶ Θεοποιὸς ἔλλαμψις καὶ χάρις οὐκ οὐσία, ἀλλ᾽ ἐνέργεια ἐστὶ Θεοῦ.[77] The notion of the Divine energy received explicit definition in the series of Synods held in the fourteenth century in Constantinople. There is a real distinction, but no separation, between the *essence* or *entity* of God and His *energies*. This distinction is manifest above all in the fact that the Entity is absolutely incommunicable and inaccessible to creatures. The creatures have access to and communicate with the Divine Energies only. But with this participation they enter into a genuine and perfect communion and union with God; they receive "deification."[78] Because this is "the natural and indivisible energy and power of God," – φυσικὴ καὶ ἀχώριστος ἐνέργεια καὶ δύναμις τοῦ Θεοῦ,[79] "it is the common and Divine energy and power of the Tri-Hypostatic God."[80]

The active Divine power does not separate itself from the Essence. This "procession" [προϊέναι] expresses an "ineffable distinction," which in no way disturbs the unity "that surpasses essence."[81] The active Power of God is not the very "substance" of God, but neither is it an "accident" [συμβεβηκός]; because it is immutable and coeternal with God, it exists before creation and it reveals the creative will of God. In God there is not only essence, but also that which is not the essence, although it is not accident – the Divine will and power – His real, existential, essence-producing providence and authority.[82] St. Gregory Palamas emphasizes that any refusal to make a real distinction between the "essence" and "energy" erases and blurs the boundary between generation and creation – both the former and the latter then appear to be acts of essence. And as St. Mark of Ephesus explained, "Being and energy, completely and wholly coincide in equivalent necessity. Distinction between essence and will [θέλησις] is abolished; then God only begets and does not create, and does not exercise His will. Then the difference between foreknowledge and actual making becomes indefinite, and creation seems to be coeternally created."[83]

The essence is God's inherent *self-existence*; and the energy is His relations towards the other [πρὸς ἕτερον]. God *is* Life, and *has* life; *is* Wisdom, and *has* wisdom; and so forth. The first series of expressions refers to the incommunicable essence, the second to the inseparably distinct energies of the one essence, which descend upon creation.[84] None of these energies is hypostatic, nor hypostasis in itself, and their incalculable multiplicity introduces no composition into the Divine Being.[85] The totality of the Divine "energies" constitutes His pre-temporal will, His design – His good pleasure – concerning the "other," His eternal counsel. This is God Himself, not His Essence, but *His will*.⁸⁶ The distinction between "essence" and "energies" – or, it could be said, between "nature" and "grace" [$\phi\acute{u}\sigma\iota\varsigma$ and $\chi\acute{\alpha}\rho\iota\varsigma$] – corresponds to the mysterious distinction in God between "necessity" and "freedom," understood in a proper sense. In His mysterious essence God is, as it were, "necessitated" – not, indeed, by any necessity of constraint, but by a kind of necessity of nature, which is, in the words of St. Athanasius the Great, "above and antecedent to free choice."⁸⁷ And with permissible boldness one may say: God cannot but be the Trinity of persons. The Triad of Hypostases is above the Divine Will, is, as it were, "a necessity" or "law" of the Divine nature. This internal "necessity" is expressed as much in the notion of the "consubstantiality" as in that of the perfect indivisibility of the Three Persons as They co-exist in and intercompenetrate one another.

In the judgment of St. Maximus the Confessor, it would be unfitting and fruitless to introduce the notion of will into the internal life of the Godhead for the sake of defining the relations between the Hypostases, because the Persons of the All-Holy Trinity exist together above any kind of relation and action, and by Their Being determine the relations between Themselves.⁸⁸ The common and undivided "natural" will of God is free. God is free in His operations and acts. And therefore for a dogmatic confession of the reciprocal relations between the Divine Hypostases, expressions must be found such as will exclude any cosmological motives, any relation to created being and its destinies, any relation to creation or re-creation. The ground of Trinitarian being is not in the economy or revelation of God *ad extra*. The mystery of the intra-Divine life should be conceived in total abstraction from the dispensation; and the hypostatic properties of the Persons must be defined apart from all relationship to the existence of creation, and only according to the relationship that subsists between Themselves. The living relationship of God – precisely as a Triad – to the creation is in no way thus obscured; the distinction in the relations of the different Hypostases towards the creation is in no wise obscured.

Rather, a fitting perspective is thus established. The entire meaning of the dogmatic definition of Christ's Divinity as it was interpreted by the Church actually lay in the exclusion of all predicates relative to the Divine condescension which characterize Him as Creator and Redeemer, as Demiurge and Saviour, in order to understand His Divinity in the light of the internal Divine Life and Nature and Essence. The creative relationship of the Word to the world is explicitly confessed in the Nicene Creed – *by Whom all things were made*. And "things" were made not only because the Word is God, but also because the Word is the Word of God, the Divine Word. No one was as emphatic in separating the demiurgical moment in Christ's action from the dogma of the eternal generation of the Word as St. Athanasius the Great. The generation of the Word does not presuppose the being – and not even the design – of the world. Even had the world not been created, the Word would exist in the completeness of His Godhead, because the Word is *Son by nature* [Υίὸς κατὰ φύσιν]. "If it had pleased God not to create any creatures, the Word would nevertheless be with God, and the Father would be in Him," as St. Athanasius said; and this because creatures cannot receive their being otherwise than through the Word.[89]

The creatures are created by the Word and through the Word, "in the image" of the Word, "in the image of the image" of the Father, as St. Methodius of Olympus once expressed it.[90] The creation presupposes the Trinity, and the seal of the Trinity lies over the whole creation; yet one must not therefore introduce cosmological motifs into the definition of the intra-Trinitarian Being. And yet one may say that the natural fulness of the Divine essence is contained within the Trinity, and therefore that the design – His good pleasure – concerning the world is a creative act, an operation of the will – an abundance of Divine love, a gift and a grace. The distinction between the names of "God in Himself," in His eternal being, and those names which describe God in revelation, "economy," action, is not only a subjective distinction of our analytical thinking; it has an objective and ontological meaning, and expresses the absolute freedom of Divine creativity and operation. This includes the "economy" of salvation.

The Divine Counsel concerning salvation and redemption is an eternal and pre-temporal decree, an *"eternal purpose"* (Eph. 3:11), *"the mystery which from the beginning of the world hath been hid in God"* (Eph. 3:9). The Son of God is from everlasting destined to the Incarnation and the Cross, and therefore He is the Lamb *"Who verily was foreordained before the foundation of the world"* (1 Pet. 1:19 –

20), *"The Lamb slain from the foundation of the world"* (Rev. 13:8). But this "purpose" [πρόθεσις] does not belong to the "essential" necessity of the Divine nature; it is not a "work of nature, but the image of economical condescension," as St. John Damascene says.[91] This is an act of Divine love – for God so loved the world ... And therefore the predicates referring to the economy of salvation do not coincide with those predicates by which the Hypostatic Being of the Second Person is defined. In Divine revelation there is no constraint, and this is expressed in the notion of the perfect Divine Beatitude. Revelation is an act of love and freedom, and therefore introduces no change into the Divine nature.[92] It introduces no change simply because there are no "natural" foundations for revelation at all. The sole foundation of the world consists in God's freedom, in the freedom of Love.

IV.

From eternity God "thinks up" the image of the world, and this free good pleasure of His is an *immutable*, unchangeable counsel. But this immutability of the accomplished will does not in the least imply its necessity. The immutability of God's will is rooted in His supreme freedom. And therefore it does not bind His freedom in creation, either. It would be very appropriate here to recall the scholastic distinction between *potentia absoluta and potentia ordinata*.

And in conformity with the design – the good pleasure of God – creation, together with time, is "built up" from out of nothing. Through temporal becoming, creation must advance by its own free ascent according to the standard of the Divine economy respecting it, according to the standard of the pre-temporal image of and pre-destination for it. The Divine image of the world always remains above and beyond creation *by nature*. Creation is bound by it unchangeably and inseparably, is bound even in its very resistance to it. Because this "image" or "idea" of creation is simultaneously the will of God [θελητικὴ ἔννοια] and the power of God by which creation is made and sustained; and the beneficent counsel of the Creator is not made void by the resistance of creation, but through this resistance turns out to be, for rebels, a Judgment, the force of wrath, a consuming fire. In the Divine image and counsel, each creature – i.e., every created hypostasis in its imperishable and irreproducible form – is contained.

Out of eternity God sees and wills, by His good pleasure, each and every being in the completeness of its particular destiny and features, even regarding its future and sin. And if, according to the mystical insight of St. Symeon the New Theologian, in the age to come "Christ will behold all the numberless myriads of Saints, turning His glance away from none, so that to each one of them it will seem that He is looking at him, talking with him, and greeting him," and yet "while remaining unchanged. He will seem different to one and different to another"[93] – so likewise out of eternity, God in the counsel of His good pleasure, beholds all the innumerable myriads of created hypostases, wills them, and to each one of them manifests Himself in a different way. And herein consists the "inseparable distribution" of His grace or energy, "myriadfold hypostatic" in the bold phrase of St. Gregory Palamas,[94] because this grace or energy is beneficently imparted to thousands upon myriads of thousands of hypostases.

Each hypostasis, in its own being and existence, is sealed by a particular ray of the good pleasure of God's love and will. And in this sense, all things are in God – in "image" [$\dot{\varepsilon}\nu$ $\dot{\iota}\delta\dot{\varepsilon}\alpha$ $\kappa\alpha\dot{\iota}$ $\pi\alpha\rho\alpha\delta\varepsilon\dot{\iota}\gamma\mu\alpha\tau\iota$] *but not by nature*, the created "all" being infinitely remote from Uncreated Nature. This remoteness is bridged by Divine love, its impenetrability done away by the Incarnation of the Divine Word. Yet this remoteness remains. *The image of creation* in God transcends created nature and does not coincide with "the image of God" in creation. "Whatever description may be given to the "image of God" in man, it is a characteristic moment of his created nature – *it is created*. It is a "likeness," a mirroring.[95] But above the image the Proto-Image always shines, sometimes with a gladenning, sometimes with a threatening, light. It shines as a call and a norm.

There is in creation a supra-natural challenging goal set above its own nature – the challenging goal, founded on freedom, of a free participation in and union with God. This challenge transcends created nature, but only by responding to it is this nature itself revealed in its completeness. This challenging goal is an aim, an aim that can be realized only through the *self-determination* and efforts of the creature. Therefore the process of created becoming is real in its freedom, and free in its reality, and it is by this becoming that what-was-not reaches fulfilment and is achieved. Because it is guided by the *challenging goal*. In it is room for creation, construction, for reconstruction – not only in the sense of recovering, but also in the sense of generating what is new. The scope of the constructiveness is defined by the contradiction between the *nature* and the *goal*. In a certain sense, this goal itself is "natural" and proper to the one who does the constructive acts, so that the attainment of this goal is somehow also the subject's realization of *himself*. And nevertheless this "I" which is realized and realizable through constructiveness is not the "natural" and empiric "I," inasmuch as any such realization of one's self" is a rupture – a leap from the plane of nature onto the plane of grace, because this realization is the acquisition of the Spirit, is participation in God. Only in this "communion" with God does a man become "himself;" in separation from God and in self-isolation, on the contrary, he falls to a plane lower than himself. But at the same time, he does not realize himself merely *out of himself*.

Because the goal lies beyond nature, it is an invitation to a living and free encounter and union with God. The world is substantially different from God. And therefore God's plan for the world can be realized only by created becoming – because this plan is not a substratum or *substantia* that comes into being and completes itself, but is the standard and crown of the "other's" becoming. On the other hand, the created process is not therefore a development, or not only a development; its meaning does not consist in the mere unfolding and manifestation of innate "natural" ends, or not only in this. Rather, the ultimate and supreme self-determination of created nature emerges in its zealous impulse to outstrip itself in a [κίνησις ὑπερ φύσιν], as St. Maximus says.[96] And an anointing shower of grace responds to this inclination, crowning the efforts of the creatures.

The limit and goal of creaturely striving and becoming is divinisation [θέωσις] or *deification* [θεοποίησις]. But even in this, the immutable, unchangeable gap between natures will remain: any "transubstantiation" of the creature is excluded. It is true that according to a phrase of St. Basil the Great preserved by St. Gregory the Theologian, creation "has been ordered to become God." [97] But this "deification" is only communion with God, *participation* [μετουσία] in His life and gifts, and thereby a kind of acquisition of certain similitude to the Divine Reality. Anointed and sealed by the Spirit, men become conformed to the Divine image or prototype of themselves; and through this they become "conformed to God" [σύμμορφοι Θεῷ].⁹⁸ With the Incarnation of the Word the first fruit of human nature is unalterably grafted into the Divine Life, and hence to all creatures the way to communion with this Life is open, the way of *adoption* by God. In the phrase of St. Athanasius, the Word "became man in order to *deify* [θεοποιήσῃ] us in Himself,"⁹⁹ in order that "the sons of men might become the sons of God." ¹⁰⁰ But this "divinization" is acquired because Christ, the Incarnate Word, has made us "receptive to the Spirit," that He has prepared for us both the ascension and resurrection as well as the indwelling and appropriation of the Holy Spirit."¹⁰¹ Through the "flesh-bearing God" we have become "Spirit-bearing men"; we have become sons "by grace," "sons of God in the likeness of the Son of God."¹⁰² And thus is recovered what had been lost since the original sin, when "the transgression of the commandment turned man into what he was by nature,"¹⁰³ over which he had been elevated in his very first adoption or birth from God, coinciding with his initial creation.¹⁰⁴

The expression so dear to St. Athanasius and to St. Gregory the Theologian, [Θεὸν γενέσθαι],¹⁰⁵ finds its complementary explanation in a saying of two other Cappadocian Saints: [ὁμοίωσις πρὸς τὸν Θεόν].¹⁰⁶ If Macarius the Egyptian dare speak of the "changing" of Spirit-bearing souls "into the Divine nature," of "participation in the Divine nature,"¹⁰⁷ he nevertheless understands this participation as a [κρᾶσις δι᾽ ὅλου], *i.e.*, as a certain "mingling" of the two, preserving the properties and entities of each in particular.¹⁰⁸ But he also stresses that "the Divine Trinity comes to dwell in that soul which, by the cooperation of Divine Grace, keeps herself pure – He comes to dwell *not as He is in Himself*, because He is incontainable by any creature – but according to the measure of the capacity and receptivity of man.¹⁰⁹ Explicit formulae concerning this were not established all at once, but from the very beginning the impassable gulf between the natures was rigorously marked, and the distinction between the notions [κατ᾽ οὐσίαν (or κατὰ φύσιν) and κατὰ μετουσίαν] was rigorously observed and kept.

The concept of "divinization" was crystallized only when the doctrine of God's "energies" had been explicated once and for all. In this regard the teaching of St. Maximus is significant. "The salvation of those who are saved is accomplished *by grace and not by nature*,"[110] and if "in Christ the entire fulness of the Godhead dwelt bodily *according to essence* then in us, on the contrary, there is not the fulness of the Godhead *according to grace.*"[111] The longed-for "divinization" which is to come is a *likeness by grace*, καὶ φανῶμεν αὐτῷ ὅμοιοι κατὰ τὴν ἐκ χάριτος θέωσιν.[112] And even by becoming partakers of Divine Life, "in the unity of love," "by co-inhering totally and entirely with the whole of God," [ὅλος ὅλῳ περιχωρήσας ὁλικῶς τῷ Θεῷ] by appropriating all that is Divine, the creature "nevertheless remains outside the essence of God." – χωρὶς τῆς κατ' οὐσίαν ταυτότητα.[113] And what is most remarkable in this is the fact that St. Maximus directly identifies the deifying grace with the Divine good pleasure as regards creation, with the creative fiat.[114]

In its efforts to acquire the Spirit, the human hypostasis becomes a vehicle and vessel of Grace; it is in a manner imbued with it, so that by it God's creative will is accomplished – the will which has summoned that-which-is-not into being in order *to receive those that will come* into His communion. And the creative good pleasure itself concerning each and every particular is already by itself a descending stream of Grace – but not everyone opens to the Creator and God Who knocks. Human nature must be freely discovered through a responsive movement, by overcoming the self-isolation of its own nature; and by denying the self, as one might say, receive this mysterious, and terrifying, and unspeakable double-naturedness for sake of which the world was made. For it was made to be and to become the Church, the Body of Christ.

The meaning of history consists in this – that the freedom of creation should respond by accepting the pre-temporal counsel of God, that it should respond both in word and in deed. In the promised double-naturedness of the Church the reality of created nature is affirmed at the outset. Creation is the other, another nature willed by God's good pleasure and brought forth from nothing by the Divine freedom for creation's own freedom's sake. It must conform itself freely to that creative standard by which it lives and moves and has its being. Creation is not this standard, and this standard is not creation. In some mysterious way, human freedom becomes a kind of "limitation" on the Divine omnipotence, because it pleased God to save creation not by compulsion, but by freedom alone. Creation is "other," and therefore the process of ascent to God must be accomplished by her own powers – with God's help, to be sure.

Through the Church creaturely efforts are crowned and saved. And creation is restored to its fulness and reality. And the Church follows, or, rather, portrays the mystery and miracle of the two natures. As the Body of Christ, the Church is a kind of "plenitude" of Christ – as Theophan the Recluse says – "Just as the tree is the 'plenitude' of the seed."[115] And the Church is united to Her Head. "Just as we do not ordinarily see iron when it is red-hot, because the iron's qualities are completely concealed by the fire," says Nicholas Cabasilas in his *Commentary on the Divine Liturgy*, "so, if you could see the Church of Christ in Her true form, as She is united to Christ and participates in His flesh, then you would see Her as none other than the Lord's Body alone."[116] In the Church creation is forever confirmed and established, unto all ages, in union with Christ, in the Holy Spirit.

Translated from the Russian
[Translator not listed]

Notes and References for "Creation and Creaturehood"

1. Maximimus the Confessor in *Lib. de div. nomin. schol.*, in V. 8,. *PG* iv, 336.

2. This relationship is vividly elucidated by Augustine, *De Genesi ad lit.* V. 5, *PL* xxxiv, 325: factae itaque creaturae motibus coeperunt currere tempora: unde ante creaturura frustra tempora requiruntur, quasi possint inveniri ante tempora tempora ... potius ergo tempora a creatura, quam creatura coepit a tempore; utrumque autem ex Deo; cf. *de Genesi c. manich.* I. 2 *PL* xxiv, 174, 175; *de Civ. Dei*, XI, t, *PL* xli, 321; quis non videat quod tempora non fuissent, nisi creatura fieret, quae aliquid aliqua mutatione mutaret; c. 322: procul dubio non est mundus factus in tempore, sed cum tempore; *Confess.* XI, 13, *PL* xxxii, 815 – 816 et passim. Cf. P. Duhem, *Le Système du Monde*, II (Paris, 1914), pp. 462 ff.

3. St. Basil the Great in *Hexam.* h. 1, n. 6, *PG* xxix, c. 16.

4. St. Gregory of Nyssa *Or. cath. m.*, c. 6, *PG* xlv, c. 28; cf. St. John Damascene, *De fide orth.* I, 3, *PG* xciv, 796: "for things whose being originated with a change [ἀπὼ τροπῆς] are definitely subject to change, whether it be by corruption or by voluntary alteration."

5. Gregory of Nyssa *De opif. hom.* c. XVI, *PG* xliv, 184; rf. *Or. cath. m.*, c. 21, *PG* xlv, c. 57: ["The very transition from nonentity to existence is a change, non-existence being changed by the Divine power in being"] (Srawley's translation). Since the origin of man comes about "through change," he necessarily has a changeable nature.

6. St. John Damascene *De fide orth.* II, 1, *PG* xciv, c. 864. Οὐδὲ γὰρ μετὰ τὴν ἀνάστασίν ἡμέριας καὶ νιξὶν ὁ χρόνος ἀριθμήσεται, ἔσται δὲ μᾶλλον μία ἡμέρα ἀνέσπ ερος. The whole passage is of interest: Λέγεται πάλιν αἰών, οὐ χρόνος, οὐδὲ χρόνου τι μέρος, ἡλίου φορᾷ καὶ δρόμῳ μερουμένον, ἤγουν δι' ἡμερῶν καὶ νυκτῶν συνιστάμενον, ἀλλὰ τὸ συμπαρεκτινόμενον τοῖς ἀιδίοις συνιστάμενον, ἀλλὰ τὸ συμπαρεκτεινόμενον τοῖς ἀιδίοις, οἱόν χρονικὸν κίνημα, καὶ διάστημα.

7. St. Gregory of Nazianzos, *Or.* 29, *PG* xxxi, 89 – 81: καὶ ἦρκται, οὐ παύτεται.

8. St. Augustine, *De Civ. Dei*, XII, c. xv, *PL* XLI, 363 – 5.

9. The Works of Philaret, Metropolitan of Moscow, "Discourses and Speeches," vol. III (Moscow, 1877), p. 436, "Address on the Occasion of the Recovery of the Relics of Patriarch Alexey," 1830.

10 St. Augustine, *Confessiones*, XI, 4, *PL* xxxii, c. 812.

11. St. Gregory of Nazianzos, *Or.* 38, *In Theoph.*, n. 7, *PG* xxxvi, c. 317.

12. St. John Damascene, *De fide Orth.* I, 13, *PG* xcvi, c. 583 [Russian, I, 183].

13. St. Augustine, *De Genesi ad lit.*, I, imp. c. 2: non de Dei natura, sed a Deo sit facta de nihile... quapropter creaturam universam neque con-substantialem Deo, neque coaeternam fas est dicere, aut credere. *PL* xxxiv, c. 221.

14. St. Macarius of Egypt, *Hom.* XLIX, c. 4, *PG* xxxiv. c. 816.

15. St. Athanasius, *C. arian*, *Or.* 1, n. 20, *PG* xxvi, c. 53.

16. St. Athanasius, *C. arian. Or.* 2, п. 2, *PG* xxvi, c. 152.

17. *Ibid., C. arian. Or.* I, n. 21, c. 56.

18. *Ibid., C. arian. Or.* 3, nfl 60ss., c. 448 squ.

19. St. Cyril of Alexandria, *Thesaurus*, XV, *PG* LXXV, c. 276: τὸ γέννημα... ἐκ τῆς οὐσίας τοῦ γεννῶντος πρόεισι φυσικῶς; – (τὸ κτίσμα) ... ἔξωθέν ἐστίν ὡς ἀλλότριον, ass. xviii, c. 313: τὸ μὲν ποιεῖν ἐνεργείας ἐστι, φύσεως δὲ τὸ γεννᾶν, φύσις δὲ καὶ ἐνέργεια οὐ ταυτόν.

20. St. John Damascene *De fide orth.* I, 8, *PG* xciv, c. 812 – 813; cf. St. Athanasius *C. arian. or.* 2, n. 2, *PG* xxvi. He rebukes the Arians for not recognizing that καρπογόνος ἐστὶν αὐτὴ ἡ θεία οὐσία. The same expression is to be found in St. Cyril's writings.

21. St. Gregory of Nazianzos, *Or. 45 in S. Pascha*, a. 28, *PG* xxxvi, 661.

22. *Ibid.*, n. 8, col. 632.

23. St. Augustine, *De Genesi ad lit.*, I, 5, *PL* xxxiv, c. 250.

24. St. Gregory of Nazianzos, *Or. XL in S. Baptism*, *PG* xxxvi, 424.

25. St. John Damascene, *C. Manich* n. 14, *PG* xciv, c. 1597.

26. St. Gregory of Nyssa, *De anima et resurr.*, *PG* XLVI, 93 B.

27. ...Waddingi, IV, Paris, 1891. This whole discourse of Duns Scotus is notable for its great clarity and profundity. Duns Scotus question disputatae de rerum principio, quaestio IV, articulus I, n. 3 and 4, – *Opera omnia*, editio nova juata editionem.

28. Origen, *De princ.* III, 5, 3. *PG* 327, English translation of G. W. Butterworth.

29. V. V. Bolotov, *Origen's Doctrine of the Holy Trinity*, St. Petersburg, 1879, p. 203.

30. Origen, *De princ.* I, 2, 10, *PG* 138 – 9.

31. *Ibid., Nota ex Methodic Ol. apud Phot. Bibl. cod.*, 235, sub linea, n. (40).

32. St. Augustine, *De Civ. Dei*, XII, 15, *PL* XLI, c. 36.

33. St. Methodius, *De creatis*, apud *Phot. Bibl.* col. 235, *PG* cii, c. 1141.

34. St. Gregory of Nazianzos, *Or.* 45, n. 5, *PG* xxxvi, c. 629: ἐννοεῖ; *Carm.* 4, *theol.* IV, *De mundo*, c. 67 – 68, *PG* xxxv II, 421.

35. St. Athanasius, *C. arian. Or.* 2, π. 2, *PG* xxvi, c. 152 – δεύτερόν ἐστι τὸ δημιουρεῖν τοῦ γεννᾶν τὸν Θεόν, – πολλῷ πρότερον, – τὸ ὑπερκείμενον τῆς βουλήσεως.

36. Of. V. V. Bolotov, "On the filioque Question, III: The significance of the sequence of the Hypostases of the Holy Trinity according to the view of the Eastern Fathers," *Christian Readings* [(Khristianskoe Chtenie) Russian], 1913, Sept., pp. 1046 – 1059.

37. St. Augustine, *De div. quaest.* qu. 28, *PL* XLVI, c. 18: nihil autem majus est voluntatis Dei; non ergo ejus causa quaerenda est.

38. St. Gregory of Nazianzos, *Carm. theol.* IV – *De mundo*, v. 67 – 68, *PG* xxxvii, 421: κόσμοι τύπους ...

39. St. Athanasius, *Ad Serap. Ep. III*, n. 5, *PG* xxvi, c. 632.

40. St. John Damascene, *De fide orth.* I, 2, *PG* xciv, c. 865; St. Gregory of Nazianzos, *Or.* 45 in *S. Pascha*, n. 5, *PG* xxxvi, c. 629.

41. St. John Damascene, *De fide orth.*, I, 9, *PG* xciv, c. 837.

42. St. John Damascene *De imagin.*, I, 10, *PG* xciv, c. 1240 – 1241.

43. *Ibid*; c. 1340: "The second aspect of the image is the thought of God on the subject of that which He will create, that is, His pre-eternal counsel, which always remains equal to itself; for the Divinity remains unchangeable and His counsel is without beginning" [δεύτερος τρόπος εἰκόνος, ἡ ἐν τῷ Θεῷ τῶν ὑπ' αὐτοῦ ἐπομένων ἔννοια, τουτέστιν ἡ προαιώνιος αὐτοῦ βούλησις, ἡ ἀεὶ ὡσαύτως].

44. Dionysius the Areopagite, *De divin. nomin.* V, n. 8, *PG* III, c. 824; cf. c. VII, n. 2, c. 868 – 869.

45. St. Maximus the Confessor, Scholia in liberus de divine nominitus in cap. V 5, – *PG* iv, c. 31; cfr. n. 7... Cf. n. 7, c. 324A: "In the cause of all things, everything is preconstituted [προϋρέστηκεν], as in an idea or prototype;" n. 8, c. 329A – B: ὅτι ποίησιν αὐτοτελῆ ἀΐδιον τοῦ ἀϊδίου Θεοῦ τὴν ἰδέαν, ἤτοι τὸ παράδειγμα φησί. In contrast to Plato, who separated the ideas or God, Dionysius speaks of "images" and "logoi" in God. Cf. A. Brilliantov, *The Influence of Eastern Theology on Western Theology in the Works of Eriugene* (St. Petersburg, 1898), pp. 157 ff, 192 ff.

46. St. Augustine, *De Genesi: ad l.t.*, I, V, c. 18, *PL* xxxiv, c. 334; cf. *De Trin.*, I, IX, c. 6 vel s. n. 9, *PL* XLII, c. 965: alia notitia rei in ipsa se, alia in ipsa aeterna veritate; cf. *ibid.*, I, VIII, c. 4 vel s. n. 7, c. 951 – 952. See also De *div. qu.*, 83, qu. 46, n. 2., *PL* XL, c. 30: ideae igitur latine possumus vel formas vel species dicere . . . Sunt namque ideae principales formae quaedam, vel rationes rerum stabiles atque incommutabiles, quae ipsae formatae non sunt, ac per hoc aeternae ac semper eodem modo sese habentes, quia

in divina mente continentur. Et cum ipsae neque oriantur, neque intereant; secundum cas tamen formari dicitur omne quod oriri et interire potest, et omne quod oritur et interit.

47. St. Maximus the Confessor. *Lib. de div. nom. shol.*, vii, 3, *PG* iv, 352: τὰ γὰρ ὄντα ... εἰκόντες εἰσὶ καὶ ὁμοιώματα τῶν δείων ἰδεῶν ... ὧν εἰκόνες τὰ τῆς κτίσεως ἀποτελέσματα.

48. St. Maximus the Confessor, *Lib. de div. nom. schol.*, V, 5, *PG* iv, 317; ὧν μετέχουσιν.

49. St. Maximus the Confessor. *De charit.*, c. iv, c. 4, *PG* xc, c. 1148: τὴν ἐξ ἀϊδίου ἐν αὐτῷ ὁ Δημιουργὸς τῶν ὄντων προϋπάρχουσαν γνῶσιν, ὅτε ἐβουλήθη, οὐ σίωσε καὶ; *Lib. de div. nom. schol*; IV, 14, *PG*, iv, 265. One must also take into consideration different aspects of the image as described by St. John Damascene, *De imag.* II, 19, *PG* xciv, 1340 – 1341: The first aspect of the image is natural, φυσικός – the Son. The second image is the pre-eternal counsel – ἐν τῷ Θεῷ. The third aspect is man, who is an image by imitation: – ὁ κατὰ μίμησίν ὑπο' Θεοῦ γενόμενος – since one who is created cannot have the same nature as He who is not created. In this passage St. John Damascene perceives the likeness of man to God in the fact that the soul of every man consists of three parts; cf. *Fragm.*, *PG* xcv, 574. By indicating difference of natures in God and in man, the divine nature of the eternal ideas of His counsel is emphasized. The notion of "image" received its final definition only during the Iconoclastic period, especially in the writings of St. Theodore the Studite. He connects the possibility of having icons with the creation of man according to the image of God. "The fact that man is created according to the image and likeness of God indicates that making icons is to some extent a divine occupation" (St. Theod. Stud. *Antirrh*. Ill, c. 2, 5, *PG* xciv. St. Theodore follows here the ideas of *Areopagitica*. In this case it is enough to mention that St. Theodore underscores the indissoluble connection between the "image" and the "proto-image," but makes a sharp distinction between them in essence of nature. Cf. *Antirrh*. III, c. 3, 10, col. 424: "The one is not separate from the other, except in respect to the distinction of essences" [τῆς οὐσίας διάφορον]. Cf. K. Schwartzlose. *Der Bilderstreit* (Gotha, 1890), pp. 174 ff.; the Rev. N. Grossou, *St. Theodore the Stylite, His Times, His Life, His Works* (Kiev, 1908), Russian, pp. 198 ff.; 180 ff.; A. P. Dobroklonsky, *St. Theodore the Studite*, Vol. I (Odessa, 1901 [1914]), Russian.

50. A penetrating and thorough investigation of the problem of ideas is given by a noted Roman Catholic theologian, F. A. Staudenmaier, *Die Philosophic des Christentums*, Bd. I (the only published), "Die Lehre von der Idee" (Gieszen, 1840), and also in his monumental work *Die Christliche Dogmatik*, Bd. Ill, Freiburg im Breisgau 1848 (recently reprinted, 1967).

51. *Discourses and Speeches of a Member of the Holy Synod, Philaret, Metropolitan of Moscow*, part 11, Moscow, 1844, p. 87: "Address on the Occasion of the Recovery of the Relics of Patriarch Alexey" (Russian).

52. St. John Damascene, *De fide orth.*, I, 4, *PG* xciv, 800.

53. *Ibid.*, I, 9, c. 836.

54. *Ibid.*, I, 4, c. 797.

55. For a survey of this question see I. V. Popov, *The Personality and Teachings of the Blessed Augustine*, Vol. I, part 2 (Sergiev Posad, 1916, and *Lichnost' i Uchenie Blazhennago Avgustina*), pp. 350 – 370 ff. (Russian).

56. In the words of Athenagoras, *Legat.* c. 10, *PG* vi, c. 908: ἐν ἰδέᾳ καὶ ἐνεργείᾳ. Cf. Popov, pp. 339 – 41; Bolotov, pp. 41 ff.; A Puech, *Les apologistes grecs du IIe siècle de notre ère* (Paris, 1912). On Origen, see Bolotov, pp. 191 ff. From the formal aspect, the distinction between "essence" and "energies" goes back to Philo and Plotinus. Nevertheless, in their view God receives his own character, even for Himself, only through His inner and necessary self-revelation in the world of ideas, and this "cosmological sphere" in God they named "Word" or "Mind." For a long time the cosmological concepts of Philo and Plotinus retarded the speculative formulation of the Trinitarian mystery. In fact cosmological concepts have no relation to the mystery of God and Trinity. If Cosmological concepts must be discarded, then another problem appears, that of the relationship of God to the world, indeed of a free relationship. The problem is relationship in the conception of the "pre-eternal counsel of God." On Philo see M. D. Muretov, *The Philosophy of Philo of Alexandria in its Relation to the Doctrine of St. John the Theologian on the Logos*, Vol. I (Moscow, 1885); N. N. Gloubokovsky, *St. Paul the Apostle's Preaching of the Glad Tidings in its Origin and Essence*, Vol. II (St. Petersburg, 1910), pp. 23 – 425; V. Ivanitzky, *Philo of Alexandria* (Kiev, 1911); P. J. Lebreton, *Les origines du dogme de la Trinité* (Paris, 1924), pp. 166 – 239, 570 – 581, 590 – 598; cf. excursus A, "On the Energies," pp. 503 – 506. Cf. also F. Dölger, "Sphragis," *Studien zur Geschichte und Kultur des Alterhums*, Bd. V, Hf. 3 – 4 (1911), pp. 65 – 69.

57. St. Basil the Great, *C. Eun.*, I, II, 32, *PG* xxix, 648; cf, St. Athanasius, *De decret.*, n. II, *PG* xxv, c. 441: "God is in all by His goodness and power; and He is outside of all in His own nature" [κατὰ τὴν ἰδίαν φύσιν].

58. St. Basil the Great, *Ad Amphil.*, *PG* xxxii, 869, A – B.

59. St. Basil the Great, *C. Eun.*, I, I, n, 14, *PG* xxix, 544 – 5; cf. St. Gregory of Nazianzos, *Or.* 28, 3, *PG* xxxvi, 29; *Or.* 29, col. 88B.

60. St. Gregory Nazianzos, *Or.* 38, *in Theoph.*, n. 7, *PG* xxxvi, 317.

61. St. Gregory of Nyssa, *Cant. cant.* h. xi, *PG* xlix, 1013 B; *In Phalm.* II, 14, *PG* xliv, 585; cf. V. Nesmelov, *The Dogmatic System of St. Gregory of Nyssa* (Kazan, 1887), pp. 123 ff.; Popov, pp. 344 – 49.

62. St. Gregory of Nyssa, *Quod non sint tres dii*, *PG* xlv, 121B: "We have come to know that the essence of God has no name and it is inexpressible, and we assert that any name, whether it has come to be known through human nature or whether it was handed to us through the Scriptures, is an interpretation of something to be understood of the nature of God, but that it does not contain in itself the meaning of His nature itself... On the contrary, no matter what name we give to the very essence of God, this predicate shows something that has relation to the essence" [τί τῶν περὶ αὐτήν]. Cf. *C. Eunom.* Л, *PG* xlv, c. 524 – 5; *De beatitud.*, *Or.* 6, *PG* xliv, 1268: "The entity of God in itself, in its substance, is above any thought that can comprehend it, being inaccessible to ingenious conjectures, and does not even come close to them. But being such by nature, He who is above all nature and who is unseen and indescribable, can be seen and known in other respects. But no knowledge will be a knowledge of the essence;" *In Ecclesiasten*, h. VII, *PG* xliv, 732: "and the great men speak of the works [ἔργα] of God, but not of God." St. John Chrysostom *Incompreh. Dei natura*, h. III, 3, *PG* xlviii, 722: in the vision of Isaiah (vi, 1 – 2), the angelic hosts contemplated not the "inaccessible essence" but some of the divine "condescension," – "The dogma of the unfathomability of God in His nature and the possibility of knowing Him through His relations towards the world" is presented thoroughly and with penetration in the book of Bishop Sylvester, *Essay on Orthodox Dogmatic Theology*, Vol. I, (Kiev, 1892 – 3), pp. 245 ff.; Vol. II (Kiev, 1892 – 3), pp. 4 ff. Cf. the chapter on negative theology in Father Bulgakov's book, *The Unwaning Light* (Moscow, 1917), pp. 103 ff.

63. St. John Damascene, *De fide orth.*, I, 14, *PG* xciv, 860.

64. Bishop Sylvester, II, 6.

65. Cf. *ibid.*, II, 131.

66. St. John Chrysostom, *In Hebr.* h – 2, n. 1.

67. St. John Damascene, *De fide orth.*, I, 13, *PG* xciv, 852.

68. The Eastern patristic distinction between the essence and energies of God has always remained foreign to Western theology. In Eastern theology it is the basis of the distinction between apophatic and cataphatic theology. St. Augustine decisively rejects it. See Popov, pp. 353 ft.; Cf. Brilliantov, pp. 221 ff.

69. Dionysius Areopagite, *De div. nom.*, II, 5, *PG* iii, 641.

70. Cf., for example, *De coel. hier.*, II, 3, c. 141.

71. *Ep.* I, *ad Caium*, c. 1065A.

72. *De div. nom*; xi, 6, c. 956.

73. Dionysius Areopagite, *De div. nom.*, I, 4, *PG* iii, 589; St. Max. Schol. in V 1; *PG* iv, 309: πρόοδον δὲ τὴν Θείαν ἐνέργειαν λέγει, ἥτις πᾶσαν οὐσίαν παρήγαγε, is contrasted here with αὐτὸς ὁ Θεός.

74. *De div. nom.*, IV, 13, *PG* iii, 712.

75. *De div. nom.*, V, 8, *PG* iii, 824; V, 5 – 6, c. 820; XI, 6, c. 953, ss. Cf. Brilliantov's whole chapter on the *Areopagitica*, pp. 142 – 178; Popov, pp. 349 – 52. The pseudo-epigraphic character of the *Areopagtiica* and their close relationship with Neo-Platonism does not belittle their theological significance, which was acknowledged and testified to by the authority of the Church Fathers. Certainly there is need for a new historical and theological investigation and appraisal of them.

76. Dionysius Areopagite, *De div. nom*; IX, *PG* iii, c. 909.

77. St. Gregory Palamas, *Capit. phys., theol.* etc., *PG* cl, c. 1169.

78. *Ibid.*, cap. 75, *PG* cl, 1173: St. Gregory proceeds from a threefold distinction in God: that of the *essence*, that of the *energy*, and that of the Trinity of the Hypostases. The union with God κατ' οὐσίαν is impossible, for, according to the general opinion of the theologians, in entity, or in His essence. God is *"imparticipable"* [ἀμεθέκτου]. The union according to hypostasis [καθ' ὑπόστασιν] is unique to the Incarnate Word: cap. 78, 1176: the creatures who have made progress are united to God according to His energy; they partake not of His *essence* but of His *energy* [κατ' ἐνέργειαν]: cap. 92, 1168; through the partaking of "God given grace" they are united to God Himself (cap. 93). The radiance of God and the God-given energy, partakers of which become deified, is the grace of God [χάρις] but not the essence of God [φύσις]: cap. 141, 1220; cap. 144, 1221; Theoph. col. 912: 928D: cf – 921, 941. Cf. the Synodikon of the council of 1452 in Bishop Porphyrius [Uspensky]'s book. *History of Mt. Athos*, III, 2 (St. Petersburg, 1902), supplements, p. 784, and in the *Triodion* (Venice, 1820), p. 168. This is the thought of St. Maximus: μθεκτὸς μὲν ὁ Θεὸς κατὰ μεταδόσεις αὐτοῦ, ἀμέθεκτος δὲ κατὰ τὸ μηδὲν μετέχειν τῆς οὐσίας αὐτοῦ, apud Euth. Zyg. Panopl., tit. 3, *PG* cxxx. 132.

79. Bishop Porphyrios, 783.

80. St. Gregory Palamas, *Theoph.*, *PG* cl, 941.

81. *Ibid.*, 940: εἰ καὶ διενήνοχε τῆς φύσεως, οὐ διασπᾶται ταύτης. Cf. *Triodion*, p. 170; and Porphyrius, 784: "Of those who confess one God Almighty, having three Hypostases, in Whom not only the essence and the hypostases are not created, but the very energy also, and of those who say that the divine energy proceeds from the essence of God and proceeds undividedly, and who through the procession designate its unspeakable difference, and who through the undivided procession show its supernatural unity. ..

eternal be the memory." Cf. *ibid.*, p. 169, Porphyrius, 782 – ἕνωσις Θείας οὐσίας καὶ ἐνεργείας ἀσύγχυτον ... καὶ διαφορὰ ἀδιάστατη. See St. Mark Eugen. *Ephes. Cap. Syllog.*, apud W. Gasz, *Die Mystik des N. Cabasilas* (Greiszwald, 1849), App. II, c. 15, p. 221: ἑπομένην ... ἀεὶ καὶ σύδρομον.

82. St. Gregory Palamas, *Cap.*, 127, *PG* cl, 1209: οὔτε γὰρ οὐσία ἐστίν, οὔτε συμβεβηκός, p. 135, 1216: τὸ γὰπ μὴ μόνον οὐκ ἀπογινόμενον, ἀλλ᾽ οὐδ᾽ εὔξησιν ἢ μείωσιν ἥς τινα ὂν ἐπιδεχόμενον, ἢ ἐμποιοῦν, οὐκ ἔσθ᾽ ὅπως ἂν συναριθμοῖτο τοῖς συμβεβηκόσιν ... ἀλλ᾽ ἔστι- καὶ ὡς ἀληθῶς ἐστιν, οὐ συμβεβηκὸς δέ ἐστιν, ἐπειδὴ πα ντάπασις ἀμετάβλητόν ἐστιν, ἀλλ᾽ οὐδὲ οὐσία καὶ γὰρ οὐ τῶν καθ᾽ ἑαυτὸ ὑφεστηκότων ἐστίν, ... ἔχει ἄπα ὁ Θεὸς καὶ ὃ οὐσία, καὶ ὃ μὴ οὐσία κἂν εἰμὴ συμβεβηκὸς καλεῖτο, τὴν Θείαν δηλονότι βουλὴν καὶ ἐνέρ- γειαν, Theoph. p. 298: τὴν δὲ θεατικὴν δύναμίν τε καὶ ἐνέργειαν τοῦ πάντα πρὶν γενέσεως εἰδότος καὶ τὴν αὐτοῦ ἐξουσίαν καὶ τὴν πρόνοιαν, c.f. p. 937, 956.

83. St. Gregory Palamas, *Cap.* 96, *PG* cl, 1181: εἰ ... μηδὲν διαφέρει τῆς Θείας οὐσίας ἡ Θεία ἐνέργεια, καὶ τὸ ποιεῖν, ὅ τῆς ἐνεργείας ἐστι, κατ᾽ οὐδὲν διοίσει τοῦ γεννᾶν καὶ ἐκπορεύειν, ἅ τῆς οὐσίας ἐστιν ... καὶ τὰ ποιήματα κατ᾽ οὐδὲν διοίει τοῦ γεννήματος κ αἱ τοῦ προβλήματος; cf. *Cap.* 97, 98, 100, 102; *Cap.* 103, 1192: οὐδὲ τῷ θέλειν δημιουργεῖ Θεός, ἀλλὰ τὸ πεφυκέναι μόνον, c. 135, 1216: εἰ τῷ βούλεσθαι ποιεῖ ὁ Θεός, ἀλλ᾽ οὐχ᾽ ἁπλῶς τῷ πεφυκέναι, ἄλλο ἄρα τὸ βούλεσθαι, καὶ ἕτερον τὸ πεφυκέναι. S. Mark of Ephesus, apud Gasz., s. 217: ἔτι εἰ ταὐτὸν οὐσία καὶ ἐνέργεια, ταύτη τε καὶ πάντως ἅμα τῷ εἶναι καὶ ἐνεργεῖν τὸν Θεὸν ἀνάγκη συναΐδιος ἄρα τῷ Θεῷ ἡ κτίσις ἐξ ἀϊδίου ἐν- εργοῦντα κατὰ τοὺς ἕλληνας.

84. St. Gregory Palamas, *Cap.* 125, *PG* cl, 1209; St. Mark of Ephesus, apud Gasz., c. 14, s. 220; c. 9, 219: c. 22, 225: εἰ πολυποίκιλος μὲν ἡ τοῦ Θεοῦ σοφία λέγεται τε καὶ ἔστι, πολυποίκιλος δὲ αὐτοῦ ἡ οὐσία οὐκ ἔστιν, ἕτερον ἄρα ἡ αὐτοῦ οὐσία καὶ ἕτερον ἡ σοφία; c. 10, 209.

85. St. Gregory Palamas, *Theoph.*, *PG* cl, 929; 936; 941; St. Mark of Ephesus, apud Gasz., c. 21, s. 223.

86. Byzantine theology concerning the powers and energies of God still awaits monographic treatment, much the more so since the greater part of the works of St. Gregory Palamas are still in MSS. For the general characteristics and theological movements of the times, see Bishop Porphyry's book, *First Journey into the Athonite Monasteries and Sketes*, part II, pp. 358 ff., and by the same author, *History of Mt. Athos*, part III, section 2, pp. 234 ff.; Archimandrite Modestus, *St. Gregory Palamas, Archbishop of Thessalonica* (Kiev, 1860), pp. 58 – 70, 113 – 130; Bishop Alexey, *Byzantine Church Mystics of the XIV Century* (Kazan, 1906), and in the Greek of G. H.

Papamichael, *St. Gregory Palamas, Archbishop of Thessalonica* (St. Petersburg – Alexandria, 1911); cf. the Review of the book by J. Sokolov in the *Journal of the Ministry of Public Education*, 1913, April – July issues. The Eastern distinction between essence and energy met with severe censure from Roman Catholic thelogy. Petavius speaks of it at great length and most harshly, Petavius, *Opus de theologicis*, ed. Thomas, Barri – Ducis (1864), tomus I, I, I, c. 12 – 13, 145 – 160; III, 5, 273 – 6.

87. St. Athanasius, *C. arian. Or.* III, c. 62 – 63, *PG* xxvi.

88. St. Maximus the Confessor, *Ambigu.*, *PG* xci, c. 1261 – 4.

89. St. Athanasius, *C. arian.*, II, 31, *PG* xxvi, c. 212: "It was not for our sake that the Word of God received His being; on the contrary, it is for His sake that we received ours; and all things were created... for Him (Col. i.16). It was not because of our infirmity that He, being powerful, received His being from the One God, that through Him as by some instrument we were created for the Father. Far be it. Such is not the teaching of the truth. Had it been pleasing not to create creatures, nevertheless the *Word was with God*, and in Him was the Father. The creatures could not receive their being without the Word, and that is why they received their being through Him, which is only right. Inasmuch as the Word is, by the nature of His essence, Son of God; inasmuch as the Word is from God and is God, as He Himself has said, even so the creatures could not receive their being but through him."

90. St. Methodius of Olympus, *Conviv.*, VI, I, *PG* xvii, c. 113.

91. St. John Damascene, *C. Jacobitas*, n. 52, *PG* xciv, 144.

92. *Ibid.*, *De fide orth.*, I, 8, c. 812.

93. St. Symeon, Βίβλος τῶν ἠθικῶν, III – St. Symeon le Nouveau Theologien, Traitıs théologiques et Ethiques "Sources Chrétiennes," No. 122 (Paris, 1966), p. 414: Ἔνθεν τοι καὶ βλεπόμενος παρὰ πάντων καὶ πάσας βλέπων αὐτὸς τὰς ἀναριθμήτους μυριάδας καὶ τὸ ἑαυτοῦ ὄμμα ἔχων ἀεὶ ἀτενίζον καὶ ἀμετακινήντων ἱστάμενον, ἕκαστος αὐτῶν δοκεῖ βλέπεσθαι παρ' αὐτοῦ καὶ τῆς ἐκείνου ἀπολαύειν ὁμιλίας καὶ κατασπάζεσθαι ὑπ' αὐτοῦ... ἄλλος ἄλλο τι δεικνύμενος εἶναι καὶ διαιρῶν ἑαυτὸν κατ' ἀξίαν ἑκάστω, καθά τις ἔστιν ἄξιος ...

94. St. Gregory Palamas, *Theoph.*, *PG* cl. 941.

95. Cf. απεικονισμα in St. Gregory of Nyssa, *De hom. opif.*, *PG* xliv, 137. St. Augustine happily distinguishes and contrasts *imago ejusdem substantiae*, man. *August. Quaest. in heptateuch*, I, V, qu. 4, *PL* xxxiv, c. 749. For the most complete catalogue of the opinions of the Church Fathers on the *"image of God"* in Russian, see V. S. Serebrenikov, *The Doctrine of Locke on the Innate Principles of Knowledge and Activity* (St. Petersburgh, 1892), pp. 266 – 330.

96. St. Maximus the Confessor, *Ambigu.*, *PG* xci, c. 1093.

97. St. Gregory of Nazianzos, *Or.* 43, *In laudem Basil. Magni*, *PG* xxxvi, c. 560.

98. St. Amphilochius, *Or.* I *In Christi natalem*, 4.

99. St. Athanasius, *Ad Adelph.*, 4, *PG* xxvi, 1077.

100. *Ibid., De incarn. et c. arian.*, 8, c. 996.

101. *Ibid., C. arian.*, I, 46. 47, c. 108 – 109.

102. *Ibid., De incarn. et c. arian.*, 8, c. 998.

103. *Ibid., De incarn*; 4, c. *PG* xxv, 104: εἰς τὸ κατὰ φύσιν ἐπέστρεπεν.

104. *Ibid; C. arian.*, II, 58 – 59, c. 272 – 3. Cf. N. V. Popov, *The Religious Ideal of St. Athanasius*, Sergiev Posad, 1903.

105. For a summary of citations from St. Gregory see K. Holl, *Amphilochius von Ikonium in seinem Verhältniss zu den grossen Kappa – doziern* (Tübingen and Leipzig, 1904), p. 166; cf. Also N. Popov, "The Idea of Deification in the Ancient Eastern Church" in the journal *Questions in Philosophy and Psychology* (1909, II – 97), pp. 165 – 213.

106. Cf. Holl, 124 – 125, 203 ff.

107. St. Macarius of Egypt, hom. 44, 8, 9, *PG* xxxiv; ἀλλαγῆναι καὶ μεταβληθῆναι ... εἰς ἑτέραν κατάστασιν, καὶ φύσιν θείαν.

108. Cf. Stoffels, *Die mystische Theologie Makarius des Aegyptars* (Bonn, 1900), pp. 58 – 61.

109. St. Macarius of Egypt, *De amore*, 28, *PG* xxxiv, 932: ἐνοικεῖ δὲ οὐ καθ' ὅ ἐστιν.

110. St. Maximus the Confessor, *Cap, theol. et. oecon. cent.*, I, 67, *PG* xci, 1108: κατὰ χάριν γάρ, ἀλλ' οὐ κατὰ φύσιν ἐστὶν ἡ τῶν σωζωμένων σωτηρία.

111. *Ibid., Cent*, II, 21, col. 1133.

112. *Ibid., Ad Ioannem cubic., ep.*, XLII, c. 639; cf. *Div. cap.*, I, 42, *PG* xc, 1193; *De charit.*, c. III, 25, c. 1024: κατὰ μετουσίαν, οὐ κατ' οὐσίαν, κατὰ χάριν, οὐ κατὰ φύσιν, *Ambigu.*, 127[a]: "being deified by the grace of the Incarnate God;" *PG* xci, 1088, 1092.

113. St. Maximus the Confessor, *Ambigu*. 222: The goal of the creature's ascension consists in this – that, having united the created nature with the uncreated by love, in order to show them in their unity and identity – ἕν καὶ ταυτὸν δείξειε – after having acquired grace and integrally and wholly compenetrating with the whole of God to become all that is God – παν ἔι τι πέρ σέτιν ὁ Θεός – *PG* xci, 1038; cf. also Anastasius of Sinai Ὁδηγός, c. 2, *PG* lxxxix, c. 77: "Deification is an ascension towards the better, but it is not an increase or change in nature – οὐ μὴν φύσεως μείωσις, ἡ μετάστασις – neither is it a change of one's own nature."

114. St. Maximus the Confessor, 43 *Ad Ioann. cubic*; *PG* xci, 639; "He has created us for this purpose, that we might become participants of the Divine nature and partakers of eternity's very self, and that we might appear to Him in His likeness, by deification through grace, through which is brought about the coming-into-being [ἡ οὐσίωσις] of all

that exists, and the bringing-into-being and genesis of what does not exist – καὶ ἡ τῶν μὴ ὄρτων παραγωγὴ καὶ γένεσις.

115. Bishop Theophan (the Recluse), *Commentary on the Epistles of Sf. Paul the Apostle to the Ephesians* (Moscow, 1882), in Russian, pp. 112 – 113, to the Ephesians, I, 23.

116. Nicholas Cabasilas, *Stae liturgiae expositio*, cap., 38, *PG* cl., c. 452. (Russian version – *Writings of the Fathers and Doctors of the Church concerning the Divine Services of the Orthodox Church* [St. Petersburg, 1857], p. 385.

LIST OF ABBREVIATIONS

ANF   *The Ante-Nicene Fathers: Translations of the Writings of the Fathers Down to A.D. 325*, ed. Alexander Roberts and James Donaldson. 10 vols. Grand Rapids, MI: Eerdmans, 1988.

NPNF *A Select Library of Nicene and Post-Nicene Fathers of the Christian Church*, ed. Philip Schaff. 14 vols. Grand Rapids, MI: Eerdmans, 1984.

NPNF2 A Select Library of Nicene and Post-Nicene Fathers of the Christian Church, second series, ed. Philip Schaff and Henry Wace. 14 vols. Grand Rapids, MI: Eerdmans, 1984.

BIBLIOGRAPHIC INFORMATION

ANF Series

Athenagoras *A Plea for the Christians*. In *ANF* 2.
Clement of Alexandria *The Instructor*. In *ANF* 2.
_____ *Stromata*. In *ANF* 2.
Irenæus *Against Heresies*. In *ANF* 1.
Justin Martyr *Hortatory Address to the Greeks*. In *ANF* 1.
_____ *The First Apology*. In *ANF* 1.
_____ *The Second Apology*. In *ANF* 1.
Lactantius *The Divine Institutes*. In *ANF* 7.
Methodius *Concerning Free will*. In *ANF* 6.
_____ *Extracts from the Work on Things Created*. In *ANF* 6.
Origen *De Principiis*. In *ANF* 4.
_____ *Contra Celsum*. In *ANF* 4.
_____ *Commentary on the Gospel of John*. In *ANF* 9.
Tertullian *Against Hermogenes*. In *ANF* 3.
_____ *On the Resurrection of the Flesh*. In *ANF* 3.
Theophilus *To Autolycus*. In *ANF* 2.

NPNF Series

Augustine *City of God*. In *NPNF* 2.
John Chrysostom *Homilies on Hebrews*. In *NPNF* 14.
_____ *Homilies on John*. In *NPNF* 14.
_____ *Homilies on Romans*. In *NPNF* 11.

NPNF2 Series

Athanasius *Contra Gentes*. In *NPNF2* 4.
_____ *On the Incarnation*. In *NPNF2* 4.
_____ *Contra Arianos*. In *NPNF2* 4.
Basil the Great *Hexaemeron*. In *NPNF2* 8.
Cyril of Jerusalem *Catechetical Lectures*. In *NPNF2* 7.
Gregory Nazianzen *Orations*. In *NPNF2* 7.
Gregory of Nyssa *Against Eunomius*. In *NPNF2* 5.

_____ *The Making of Man.* In *NPNF2* 5.

John of Damascus *An Exact Exposition of the Orthodox Faith.* In *NPNF2* 9.

Ancient Christian Writers Series

Augustine *The Literal Meaning of Genesis, Vol. 1.* In vol. 41 of *Ancient Christian Writers: The Works of the Fathers in Translation.* Edited by Johannes Quasten, Walter J. Burghardt, and Thomas Comerford Lawler. Translated and annotated by John Hammond Taylor. New York, NY: Newman Press, 1982.

The Fathers of the Church Series

Ephrem the Syrian *Selected Prose Works: Commentary on Genesis, Commentary on Exodus, Homily on Our Lord, Letter to Publius.* In vol. 91 of *The Fathers of the Church.* Edited by Kathleen McVey. Translated by Edward G. Matthews, Jr. and Joseph P. Amar. Washington, DC: The Catholic University of America Press, 1994.

John Chrysostom *Homilies on Genesis (1 – 17).* In vol. 74 of *The Fathers of the Church.* Edited by Thomas P. Halton. Translated by Robert C. Hill. Washington, DC: The Catholic University of America Press. 1986.

Origen *Homilies on Genesis and Exodus.* In vol. 71 of *The Fathers of the Church.* Edited by Hermigild Dressler, O.F.M. Translated by Ronald E. Heine. Washington, DC: The Catholic University of America Press. 1982.

Other Sources for works by Church Fathers

Maximus the Confessor. *Difficulty 10.* In *Maximus the Confessor: The Early Church Fathers* series. By Andrew Louth. London: Routledge, 1996.

_____ *The Four Hundred Chapters on Love.* In *Maximus Confessor: Select Writings,* in the *Classics of Western Spirituality* series. By George C. Berthold. New York: Paulist Press, 1985.

_____ *Chapters on Knowledge.* In *Maximus Confessor: Select Writings,* in the *Classics of Western Spirituality* series. By George C. Berthold. New York: Paulist Press, 1985.

Other

Florovsky, Georges. "Creation and Creaturehood." In *Creation and Redemption: Collected Works of Georges Florovsky, Vol. 3.* Belmont, MS: Nordland Publishing Company, 1976.

SPECIFIC LOCATIONS OF CITED TEXTS

(In order of appearance)

Justin Martyr *Hortatory Appeal to the Greeks* 3–8, 13, 20–23, 26, 30, 33, 36 *ANF* 1; *The First Apology* 10, 20, 59 *ANF* 1; *The Second Apology* 4.2 *ANF* 1. **Athenagoras** *A Plea for the Christians* 2.4, 6, 8, 10, 13, 15, 16, 19, 25 *ANF* 2. **Irenæus** *Against Heresies* 2.2.1–5; 2.3.1–2; 2.9.1–2; 2.10.1–4; 2.14.1–7; 2.25.1–4; 2.26.1–3; 2.27.1–3; 2.28.1–9; 4.14.1–2; 4.20.1–4 *ANF* 1. **Clement of Alexandria** *The Instructor* 1.3 *ANF* 2; *Stromata* 6.16 *ANF* 2. **Tertullian** *Against Hermogenes* 1–3, 8–12, 14–17, 19–22, 26, 29, 31–34, 44–45 *ANF* 3; *On the Resurrection of the Flesh* 5–7 *ANF* 3. **Theophilus** *To Autolycus* 1.4–6; 2.10–13; 2.15–22; 2.24–25; 2.27–28 *ANF* 2. **Origen** *Homilies on Genesis and Exodus* in vol. 71 of *The Fathers of the Church*, pp. 47–71; *De Principiis* 2.1.1–5; 2.2.1–2; 2.3.1–6 *ANF* 4; *Contra Celsum* 1.19–21, 23; 6.49–56, 59–62 *ANF* 4; *Commentary on the Gospel of John* 1.16–22 *ANF* 9. **Lactantius** *The Divine Institutes* 2.9–12; 7.1–5 *ANF* 7. **Athanasius** *Contra Gentes* 3.35–47 *NPNF2* 4; *On the Incarnation* 2.1–6; 3.1–5; 4.1–6; 5.2; 12.1–6; 41–45; 54 *NPNF2* 4; *Contra Arianos* 2.22.78–82 *NPNF2* 4. **Ephrem** *Commentary on Genesis*, in vol. 91 of *The Fathers of the Church*, pp. 74–106. **Methodius** *Concerning Free will* 1 *ANF* 6; *Extracts from the Work on Things Created* 1–9 *ANF* 6. **Cyril** *Catechetical Lectures* 2.1; 4.4–6; 6.9; 9.1–6, 10–11, 13–16; 11.21–24; 12.29–30 *NPNF2* 7. **Gregory Nazianzen** *Orations* 28.6, 16, 22, 26; 29.11; 38.9–12; 39.12 *NPNF2* 7. **Basil** *Hexaemeron* 1.1–11; 2.1–8; 3.1–10; 4.1–6; 5.1–6, 8–10; 6.1–2, 7–8; 7.1–3, 5; 8.1–2, 4, 7–8; 9.1–6 *NPNF2* 8. **Gregory of Nyssa** *Against Eunomius* 1.34 *NPNF2* 5; *The Making of Man* 1.2, 4–5; 2.1–2; 3.1; 5.1–2; 7.1–3; 8.8; 16.1–4, 7–18; 21.1–3; 23.1–5; 28.1–2; 29.1–3 *NPNF2* 5. **John Chrysostom** *Homilies on Hebrews* 22.1–2 *NPNF* 14; *Homilies on John* 5.1–3 *NPNF* 14; *Homilies on Romans* 3.1 *NPNF* 11; *Homilies on Genesis (1–17)*, in vol. 74 of *The Fathers of the Church*, pp. 30–36, 40–45, 53–59, 70–73, 82–89, 95–104, 106–112, 118–119, 131–140, 157–167. **Augustine** *The Literal Meaning of Genesis, Vol. 1*, in vol. 41 of *Ancient Christian Writers*, pp. 19–24, 29–31, 42–48, 133–136, 141–156, 177–191; *City of God* 11.3–10, 16–23, 29–34; 12.10–23, 25–27 *NPNF* 2. **Maximus** *The Four Hundred Chapters on Love*, in *Maximus Confessor: Select Writings*, in the *Classics of Western Spirituality* series, 61–77; *Chapters on Knowledge*, in *Maximus Confessor: Select Writings*, pp. 136–7, 139–140, 164; *Difficulty 10*, in *Maximus the Confessor: The Early Church Fathers*, 94–154. **John of Damascus** *An Exact Exposition of the Orthodox Faith* 2.1–2, 5–7, 9–12, 25, 28–30 *NPNF2* 9. **G. Florovsky** *Creation and Redemption*, pp.43–78, 269–279.

INDEX

1

1 Corinthians, 362, 542
1 Peter, 559

6

6000 years, 418, 481, 483

A

A. See Alpha
Abraham, 109, 367, 451, 453, 488
abyss, 104–5, 107, 226–8, 240, 290, 308, 311, 377, 410, 434–5, 441, 538
accident, 125, 140, 460, 497, 508, 519, 529, 557
Adam, 53, 88, 90, 99–02, 131, 154, 156, 235–45, 267–8, 274, 276–9, 283, 351, 357, 367, 386, 448–9, 451, 453–4, 526, 530
adversary, 105, 112, 168, 232, 297, 435
Aeon(s), 35–38
ages, 92, 131–2, 163, 269, 275, 302, 316, 320–1, 333, 397, 430, 442, 444, 446, 449, 452, 455–8, 467, 483, 486, 490, 494, 509, 517, 543–5, 565
air, 2–6, 15, 20, 25–6, 122, 124, 149, 159, 163, 169, 192–3, 197, 200–1, 214–5, 237, 252, 273, 278, 290, 292, 294, 296–7, 299–01, 304, 307, 313, 330–4, 341, 376, 425, 432, 442, 445, 452, 462, 500, 518–9, 522–3, 538
Alexander of Macedon, 4
Alexander the Great, 481
allegorical, 114, 137, 225, 419, 429
allegorically, 114, 118–20

allegories, 299, 312, 332–3
all-powerful, 164, 375, 506–8
Alpha, 58
Amos, 80
Anaxagoras, 2, 37
Anaximander, 2, 36
angels, 22, 26–33, 50, 54, 104–5, 127, 151–2, 186, 288, 299, 338, 368, 380, 399, 427, 429, 431, 433, 436, 440, 457, 461, 463–8, 474, 477–80, 487–9, 499–01, 504, 506, 509, 526, 534
animals, 23, 30, 37, 82, 92, 97–8, 113–4, 119, 122, 124, 137, 148, 162, 165–6, 169, 171–4, 183–4, 188, 192, 201, 235–7, 243–4, 273–4, 288, 308, 317, 321, 326, 330, 332, 334–6, 341, 344–5, 394–5, 406–7, 422, 442, 444–6, 454, 462, 465, 475, 483, 499–04, 513, 524, 529
Antiphanes, 35
Apostle, 28, 107, 109, 112, 114, 117, 152–3, 221, 269, 282, 288, 299, 324, 349, 362, 467, 478, 526, 570, 576
apostles, 31–2, 40, 63, 83, 109–10, 116–8, 133, 247, 456
Apostle's Creed, i
archangels, 50, 288, 368, 380
archç, 72, 93
arche, 153–5
Aristotle, 3–5, 14, 19–20, 27, 38, 137, 171–2, 176
artificer, iii, iv, 24–6, 158, 162, 169, 191, 195–6, 207–8, 254, 265–6, 271–4, 278, 293–5, 308, 354, 372, 382, 402, 501
ashamed, 50, 245, 332, 402

Athanasius, iv, v, 190–1, 206, 220, 268, 516, 540, 548 550, 558–9, 563, 567–8, 570, 574–5, 578, 580
atheism, 18–9, 23, 195, 285
atheists, 18, 20, 22
Athenians, 8, 14, 18, 123, 368
atoms, 37, 285, 459
Augustine, iii, v, 418–9, 456, 481, 537–41, 545, 559, 551, 566–71, 574, 578–80
Aurelius, Marcus, 1, 18, 90
Ayala, Francisco, iii

B

Basil, iii, 284, 340, 537, 554, 562, 566, 570, 574, 578, 580
Basilius, 523
Basilides, 29, 50, 52
beasts, 75, 78, 97, 113–4, 119–22, 137, 156, 169, 237–44, 273, 329, 332, 337–8, 342–7, 383, 392–8, 402–6, 447–8, 450, 471, 499–00, 524–5, 534
begotten, 11, 50, 59, 99, 198, 205–6, 220–2, 269–70, 275–6, 279, 282, 304, 307, 340, 358, 366, 397–01, 419, 464, 474, 479, 489, 517, 554
Benedict XVI, i, ii
    See also Ratzinger, Cardinal Joseph
birds, 47, 92, 97, 108, 111–4, 119–22, 201, 228, 236–8, 241, 243, 273, 319, 330–2, 345–6, 390–2, 397, 400, 403–7, 423, 431, 442, 445, 448, 450, 452, 523–4
birth, 11, 50, 90, 162, 163, 187–8, 192–3, 229, 285–8, 301, 305, 324, 330, 333–6, 341–2, 389, 392, 412, 452–3, 460, 484, 529–31, 563
book of Maccabees, 126, 153

book of the Shepherd, 126, 166, 171, 183, 208
born again, 96–7, 482
breath of life, 42, 54, 76, 79, 85, 99, 241, 414, 416–7, 443, 456
Bythus, 31, 36, 39
Byzantine theology, 555–6, 573

C

Cain, 120, 364, 367
Cappadocian, iv, 277, 284, 340, 555, 563
carnal, 49, 114, 116, 119, 129, 284, 427, 500
celestial, 30, 106, 127, 134, 148, 179, 286, 299, 305, 307, 334, 422
Celsus, 136–46, 149
changeable, 26, 262–3, 283, 465, 492, 515, 521, 542, 566
chaos, 31, 94, 159, 264, 463
Chaos, 35–6, 77
children of men, 13, 487
choice, 15, 260, 281, 453, 501, 508, 514, 529, 532, 534, 541, 558
Christians, 1, 17–8, 22–4, 60, 90, 138, 324, 396, 418, 422, 497, 578, 580
Chrysostom, 359, 363–4, 366, 571, 578–80
Church, i–v, 8, 32, 59, 60, 103, 108–10, 199, 222, 268, 277, 290, 293, 306, 311, 320, 348, 369, 378, 399, 401–4, 412, 419, 427, 442, 505, 543, 553, 558, 564, 572–80
Church Fathers, i–v
Cicero, 157, 159, 164, 168, 174, 184
clay, 13, 24, 54, 71, 85–8, 109, 157, 169–71, 179, 276, 356, 370, 474, 527
Clement, 57–8, 133–4, 578, 580
co-equal, 62–3

co-eternal, 262, 266, 488–90
co-exist
  coexist, 507
co-existed, 264, 289
co-existent, 61, 70, 248, 250, 256, 264
Colossians, 275, 360–3, 574
co-operator, 304, 338–9
corrupted, 135, 169–70, 174, 210, 320, 329, 472, 512
corruptible, 5, 16, 38, 128–30, 135, 166, 180, 211, 217, 487, 519
corruption, 135, 138, 209–11, 216–7, 266, 286, 307, 323, 337, 348, 504, 519–22, 524, 534–5, 542, 566
Cotta, 164
Cynics, 38
Cyril, 268, 540, 567, 578, 580

D

Damascene, iv, 537–9, 542, 550, 553, 560, 566–71, 574
Daniel, 109, 271, 274, 312
darkness, 16, 23, 77, 79–81, 92–3, 95, 104–5, 109, 113, 139, 155, 167–8, 193, 226–34, 241, 248, 258, 279, 294, 296–03, 324, 353, 363, 372–7, 380–1, 386, 407, 421, 434, 461, 463–4, 468, 478–9, 519, 522, 533
David, 30, 54, 77, 82, 109–10, 150, 237, 377–80, 404, 517–8, 523, 526
death, 11, 13, 16, 66, 83, 90, 100–2, 111, 114, 117, 129–30, 146, 151, 167, 186, 188, 209–11, 216–9, 223–4, 242, 246, 282, 288, 297–9, 322, 333, 363, 467, 482, 495, 499–00, 505, 517, 530, 534, 541
deluge, 131, 146–7, 170, 172
Dembski, William, ii, iv
demiurge, 152, 154

Demiurge, 39, 48, 55, 207, 287, 295, 558
Democritus, 37, 176, 182
demon, 9, 10, 102, 535
  demoniac, 27
  demons, 27
depraved, 33, 167–8, 176, 479
design, 70, 144, 154, 164, 174, 276, 312, 375, 379, 380, 382, 385, 387, 394, 413, 458, 469, 471, 474–5, 486, 492, 547, 549, 551, 557, 560
Deucalion, 136, 169–72
devil, 104, 112, 117, 211, 390, 396, 400–1, 466, 474, 524, 533–5
Devil, 158, 282
Diagoras, 18–9
Dionysius, 550, 555, 568, 571–2
disciple, 30, 133, 171
disobedience, 10, 100–2, 259–61, 393, 403, 525, 543
Divine, 7, 8, 15, 26, 61, 64, 122, 158, 172, 175, 177, 200–1, 209, 211, 215, 218, 247, 264, 266, 271, 281, 333, 340, 341, 343–4, 347, 349, 350–5, 420–1, 430, 456, 497–8, 505, 527, 537, 540–1, 544–8, 550, 553, 556, 560, 562, 564, 566, 575–6, 578, 580
dominion, 63, 98, 114, 118–9, 165, 238, 342–3, 345, 350, 403, 405, 445, 452, 486, 489, 534
  ruling authority, 244
dragon, 102, 105, 112, 151–2, 337
dust, 13, 76, 79, 87, 99, 169, 241, 276, 336, 355, 380, 414–6, 443–4, 447, 453, 456, 500
Dyad, 39

E

Ecclesiastes, 467

Egyptians, 137–8, 218, 414, 482
elements, 2, 3, 23, 25–6, 77, 80, 89, 91, 115, 153, 159, 169, 180, 184, 186, 193–4, 225–6, 233, 248, 251, 257, 260, 264, 285, 292, 300, 307–8, 347, 349, 369, 371, 374–6, 379, 381–2, 385, 391, 395, 402, 408, 412–4, 422, 424, 426, 444, 454, 480, 483, 507, 516–9, 522–3, 542
Empedocles, 3, 37
enemy, 64, 151, 297, 313, 338, 472, 496, 500, 535
Enthymesis, 35
Ephesians, 269, 559
Epicurus, 2–3, 37, 137, 163, 172, 176, 180, 182, 185, 459
   Epicureans, 137, 165, 179, 207
eternal, 6, 9, 11, 18–27, 32, 51, 59, 65–8, 83, 89, 105, 116, 125–6, 135, 161, 163, 166–9, 175, 179, 181, 184–90, 199, 211, 222–3, 239, 246, 261, 264–8, 286–7, 313, 348, 354, 364, 419–20, 423, 428, 457–8, 461–2, 464, 470, 472, 477–8, 482–3, 486–00, 503, 506, 508–10, 517, 527, 530, 534, 542–9, 550, 554, 557, 568–70, 573
eternity, 12, 22, 61, 66, 136, 161, 176, 189, 211, 255, 267, 286, 289, 302–3, 323, 354, 420, 452, 458, 460, 483, 486, 489–93, 495, 498, 502, 506, 510, 517, 534, 537, 543–8, 550, 560–1, 575
Eve, 88, 102, 131, 238, 244–5, 268, 274–7, 283, 445, 448
evil, 9, 59–70, 97, 101, 106, 111–3, 117, 120, 142–6, 158, 167, 182, 184, 186–8, 209–10, 216, 221, 228, 242, 246, 250, 253–61, 268, 271, 274, 281, 297–8, 302, 311–2, 320, 322, 324, 335, 344, 348, 352–3, 367, 396, 410, 416, 418, 452–3, 464–7, 469–73, 497, 505–8, 524–7, 532, 542
   author of evil, 64, 68–70, 143, 250, 253, 257
Ezekiel, 227, 270
ex nihilo, iii

F

faith, 20, 38, 41, 47, 60, 82, 136, 138, 206, 208, 223, 270, 285, 292, 325, 337–8, 353–4, 358, 364–6, 374, 414–5, 421–7, 457, 462, 472, 478–9, 487, 490, 492, 497, 540, 548, 552
fall, 42–6, 52, 82, 99, 101, 132, 173, 195–7, 201, 210, 277, 291, 293, 295, 309–10, 314, 375, 390, 408, 421, 468, 474, 477, 479, 487, 507, 532–5
false, 10, 12, 39, 137, 163, 166, 168, 170, 175, 236, 255, 310, 318, 336, 369, 422–4, 486, 496, 503, 535, 543
fate, 20, 250, 269, 286, 324, 526, 529, 535
female, 35, 118–9, 193–4, 208, 238, 244, 348–52, 403–5, 445, 447–51, 534
fifth day, 97, 112, 228, 236–7, 392, 431, 442, 448, 462
finite, 305, 459, 483, 491, 493, 498, 548
fire, 2–3, 6, 12, 16, 20, 51, 88, 107, 124, 146, 159, 163, 167–9, 176–7, 180, 185, 192–3, 199, 201, 214, 217, 225–7, 230–4, 258, 268, 271, 292, 296, 307–11, 324, 413–4, 471, 481, 518, 519, 522, 543, 560, 565
   fiery, 4, 15, 165, 310
firmament, 13, 75–6, 95, 104–15, 135, 139, 148–9, 154, 221, 226–9, 232–

36, 271, 303–9, 311, 323, 330–2, 376–81, 383, 386, 389, 391, 394, 398, 402, 425, 428, 430, 435, 437, 442, 444, 462, 464, 468–9, 475, 477, 480, 494, 522, 524
first day, 14, 104, 147–8, 227–35, 239–41, 288, 301–3, 375–6, 442, 461, 464, 519, 523
first-begotten, 55
firstborn, 100, 103, 116, 153–5, 199, 334
fish, 92, 97, 184, 273, 442
flesh, 55–6, 77, 79, 83–92, 97, 102, 106, 114–5, 119–20, 147, 152–3, 208, 221–4, 244, 270–1, 274, 281–3, 318, 329, 334, 355, 370, 416–9, 445, 448, 452, 471, 510, 527, 563
flood, 120, 136, 170, 247, 481
   deluge, 136
Florovsky, Georges, iii, 536, 579, 580
foolish, 42, 44–5, 48, 94, 208, 266, 286, 305, 307, 309, 333, 423, 458, 464, 469, 474, 480, 486, 488
foreknowledge, 96, 238, 351, 356, 411, 456, 478, 494, 504, 532, 557
foreseeing, 90, 162, 174, 384
foreseen, 162, 328, 332, 336, 467
foresight, 158, 160, 164, 181, 185, 308, 321, 474, 494, 515
   beforehand, 31, 53, 54, 134, 203, 239, 247, 264, 286, 342, 343, 351, 363, 533
   foresaw, 80, 308, 466, 498, 500
   foretells, 92, 353
forethought, 208
formational economy, iii
foundations, 55, 93, 165, 175, 180, 291, 331, 343, 413, 551, 560
four-footed, 113, 392

fourth day, 96, 109, 230, 234–5, 323, 385, 388, 425, 436, 442, 461–2, 464, 516, 520–1
framed, 20, 57, 151, 208, 340, 353, 364, 530, 543
Framer, 20–5, 220, 222
freedom, 7, 131–2, 159, 324, 344, 351, 520, 528, 541, 543, 547–8, 550, 558, 560, 561, 564
   free will, 123, 131, 259–60, 268–9, 277, 281, 499, 516, 527–9, 533–4
functional integrity, ii

G

garden. *See* Paradise
Genesis
   Gen, 434, 443–5, 447, 451
Gentiles, 190, 203, 212, 218, 285, 339, 369, 380
Godhead, 216, 218–9, 223, 270, 338, 341, 344, 364, 535, 547, 549, 554, 558, 564
godless, 97, 197, 271, 492, 497
goodness, 15, 41, 64, 66, 68, 122, 158, 198, 208, 212, 215–6, 284, 297, 316, 349, 352, 355, 371, 375, 406, 410, 466, 471, 491, 493, 506–7, 509, 513, 518, 528, 530–3, 535, 545–6, 548, 556, 570
grace, 41, 47, 51, 118, 130–2, 209, 211, 238–9, 275, 293, 303, 329, 339, 351, 360, 368, 380, 397, 411, 417, 453, 471, 490, 500, 504, 509–11, 515–6, 519, 523, 527–8, 531, 533, 535, 541, 556, 561, 563, 572, 575
Greek philosophers, 1, 190, 213, 285, 506, 543
   Hellenistic thought, 543
Gregory of Nazianzus, 539

Gregory of Nyssa, 340, 357, 537, 542, 554, 566–7, 571, 574, 578, 580
Gregory Palamas, 556–7, 561, 572–4
Gregory the Theologian, 277, 541, 550, 554, 562

H

Hades, 218
happiness, 87, 126, 131, 287, 318, 458, 495–6, 525
harmonic, 19, 548
harmony, 5, 7, 19, 24, 30, 118, 122–3, 138, 190, 192, 194–5, 199–00, 212, 225, 243, 247, 280, 292, 295, 323, 364, 425, 429, 514, 546
hate, 3, 56, 335, 496, 505
heathen, 32–3, 197, 203, 278, 306, 347
heavenly bodies, 92, 96, 182, 387, 428, 469, 488, 511
Hebrews, 9, 10, 94, 137, 364–6, 378, 414, 522, 578, 580
Heraclitus, 2, 168
heresy, 59, 63, 141, 265, 275, 297
heretics, 30–9, 59, 64, 71, 142, 270–2, 399, 471
heretical, 143, 358
Hermes, 166, 171, 183
Hermogenes, 59–9, 74–85, 90, 578, 580
heterogeneity, 540
heterogeneous, 539–40
Hippasus, 2
His own image. See image of God
His power, 29, 63, 84, 99, 124, 160–1, 179, 182, 199, 215, 218, 261, 267, 271, 284, 313, 338, 351, 544
Holy Ghost, 22, 74–5, 276, 282, 362, 465, 474, 500
Homer, 1, 4, 12–3, 36, 247

human beings, 243, 279, 370, 379, 388, 393–06, 410–6, 510
human reasoning, 370, 375, 412–4
humankind, 367, 373, 413
mankind, 36, 44, 50, 92, 95, 172, 191–2, 203, 210, 216, 225, 230, 236, 239, 351, 365, 373, 445, 452
human nature, 213, 216, 295, 318, 347, 349–50, 356, 367, 381, 393, 414, 504, 540, 563, 571
human race, 17, 55, 158, 170–2, 181, 183, 367, 369, 379, 384–8, 390, 392, 394, 410–1, 418, 453, 481–2, 486, 490, 497, 499, 504
humanity, 213, 219, 279, 344, 347–8, 351, 357, 387, 390
Hypostases, 548–9, 558, 568, 572
hypostasis, 295, 540, 552, 557, 560, 564, 572

I

idolatry, 114, 197, 270
ignorance, 6, 14, 30, 32, 36, 39, 48, 51, 108, 164, 182, 197, 211, 323–4, 328, 391, 408, 415, 422, 465, 485, 496, 505–7, 515, 534
ignorant, 4, 14, 30–1, 36–41, 44, 48–9, 125, 131–2, 142–5, 149, 158, 170, 174, 176–7, 180, 183, 187, 251, 276, 285, 300, 329, 337, 364, 416, 422–3, 426, 456–6, 484, 487, 493, 496, 500, 522
illimitable, 22, 539
image of God, 54, 76, 86, 115–8, 140, 153, 171, 238, 338–9, 348–51, 359, 445, 447, 450–1, 534, 551, 561, 569, 574
immortal, 5–6, 11, 90, 99–01, 115, 129, 166, 172, 178, 180, 186, 188, 217,

281–2, 348, 465, 481, 485, 487, 497, 503, 517, 525–8, 535
immortality, 7, 38, 55, 96, 100–1, 128, 130, 169, 186–9, 206, 210, 217, 219, 489, 494–5, 499, 505, 509
immovable, 314, 341
immoveable, 5, 66, 193
immutability, 138, 341, 352, 509, 544–5, 548, 560
immutable, 341, 348, 350, 363, 420, 429, 431, 458, 474, 538, 540, 542–3, 546, 550, 555, 557, 560, 562
impassable, 133–4, 219, 310, 539, 563
impassible, 21–2, 25, 348
imperishable, 11, 560
Incarnation, 190, 206, 209, 219–20, 509, 540, 559, 561, 563, 578, 580
incomprehensible, 22, 91, 191, 286, 291, 296, 493–4, 514, 525, 539
incorporeal, 115, 126–7, 130, 134, 136, 162, 217, 270, 274, 311, 348–9, 360, 457, 508, 527–8
incorruptible, 66, 115, 129, 163, 166, 178, 180, 219, 280, 348, 472, 526
incorruption, 16, 38, 102, 128–30, 156, 209–11, 534–5
indescribable, 50, 134, 166, 173, 571
indestructible, 3, 6, 142, 542
ineffable, 19, 22, 36, 122, 309, 316, 321–2, 326, 372, 376, 379, 382, 387, 391, 393, 402, 405, 413–4, 493, 503, 509, 553, 557
infallible, 291, 309, 460
infinite, 2, 186–7, 264, 285, 287, 289, 291, 293, 305, 307, 318, 337, 363, 413, 459–60, 465, 491, 493–95, 498, 506–8, 515, 537, 539, 550, 554
infinity, 287, 289, 311, 352, 459, 493–4, 498, 506, 509, 538

injustice, 65, 453
instinct, 22, 92, 319, 336
intelligence, 19, 22, 125, 143, 160, 162, 164, 169, 177, 180, 289, 295–6, 304, 306, 313, 319, 323, 325, 417, 465, 500, 503
intelligences, 287
intelligent, 141, 160, 162, 280–1, 285, 288, 312, 349, 465, 501, 507–8, 528
Intelligent Design (ID), ii–v
invisible, 12, 16, 22, 30, 45, 52, 77–8, 84, 91, 95, 104, 115, 136, 139, 147, 153, 191, 199–02, 219, 221, 223, 237, 268–9, 274–7, 281, 286–8, 293–7, 312–3, 322–3, 338, 360, 364, 369–72, 376–7, 380–1, 388, 441, 449, 454, 457, 463, 465, 471, 514, 518, 522, 525–8, 555
unseen, 135, 215, 219, 272, 368, 379, 571
Irenæus, 28, 53, 541, 578, 580
Isaac, 109
Isaiah, 77–80, 95, 133, 141, 290, 309, 318, 399, 518, 536, 571

J

Jacob, 109, 302, 453, 502
James, 110, 117, 577
Jeremiah, 21, 84, 268, 452, 453
Jesus Christ, 31, 42, 55, 103, 129, 153, 190, 206, 208–9, 224, 269, 271, 275, 282, 321, 325, 332, 517
Christ, 48, 60, 63, 80, 86, 90, 106, 108–11, 116, 118, 121, 129, 131–2, 152–4, 197, 206, 208, 212, 218–9, 224–5, 270, 275–6, 280, 334, 338–9, 344, 348, 357, 361–3, 378, 398, 404, 410, 419, 429, 451,

486, 497, 510, 540, 558–9, 561, 563–5
Jews, 1, 8, 138, 190, 203–4, 208, 212, 276, 338, 368, 378, 380, 401, 477
Job, 112, 145, 151, 237, 266, 270, 291, 308, 531, 533
John, 28, 30, 100, 103, 110, 118, 147, 150, 154, 208, 222, 224, 269–70, 275–6, 344, 359–66, 369, 509, 516–7, 537, 539–42, 550, 553, 560, 566–71, 574, 578–80
John Damascene, 550, 555, 569
John of Damascus, 516–7, 540, 579
Josephus, 8
judgment, 6, 7, 12, 15, 18, 37, 41, 49, 51–2, 65, 111, 140, 143, 145, 158, 173–4, 206, 267, 287, 324, 478, 504, 534, 542, 558
justice, 26, 29, 120, 150–1, 175, 239, 324, 335, 389, 466, 475, 504, 532–3

K

kosmos, 133, 548

L

labour, 43–4, 65, 86, 94, 100–1, 122, 159, 171, 175, 183, 186–9, 265, 292, 319, 345, 534
Lactantius, 157–8, 175, 578, 580
land, 30, 77–8, 96–7, 106–7, 112, 115, 135, 148, 184, 199, 204, 230, 234, 237, 241, 247, 252, 273, 308, 313, 316, 330, 342, 371–2, 380–1, 392, 398, 407, 414, 430, 432, 444, 475, 480, 522
Let us, 85–6, 106, 114–9, 139, 144, 159, 173, 175, 183, 185, 204, 219, 237, 247, 278, 291, 293, 299, 311, 316,

321, 327, 333–4, 337–8, 343, 347, 362, 367, 370, 374, 395–03, 422, 444, 481, 496
logos, 18, 22, 49, 505, 512, 552
Logos, 18–23, 48–9, 212, 505, 553, 570
love, 3, 42, 44, 46–7, 53, 55, 57, 86, 94, 111, 156, 177, 186, 204, 212, 221, 242, 280, 286–7, 323, 327, 335, 344, 359, 366, 380, 387–94, 402, 405, 408, 438, 442, 461, 466, 479, 495–6, 511, 539, 548, 550, 556, 559, 561, 564, 575
loving-kindness, 132, 198, 210, 212, 270, 368, 375, 389, 392, 396–7, 400–1, 405–6, 408–11, 416
Lucilius, 164
luminaries, 92, 520
lust, 94, 111, 121, 188, 249, 270, 479

M

Macarius, 539, 563, 567, 575
Maccabees, 153
Macedonians, 482
Maker, 19–22, 25, 32–3, 41, 65, 73, 86–7, 91, 138, 148, 161, 166, 179, 185, 195–7, 203, 207, 211–2, 215, 259, 266, 268–76, 282, 285, 342–4, 351, 469, 521, 527
Malachi, 54, 150
male, 118–9, 193–4, 208, 238, 244, 347–52, 403–5, 445, 447, 449–51, 533
Manichaeans, 279, 297, 328, 354, 472
manifestation, 125, 213–4, 325, 554, 562
manifested, 132, 212, 215, 219, 224, 228, 233, 238, 278, 342, 348, 352, 357, 490, 541, 543, 555
Marcion, 31, 50, 90, 143, 369

Marcus, 1, 18, 39, 178, 184
Martyr, Justin, iii, v, 1, 2, 15, 17, 578, 580
Mary, 118, 276, 362
Master, 47, 52, 85, 194, 218, 247, 316, 323, 521–4, 534
material, 15, 22, 35, 38, 70–5, 86–8, 127, 130, 160–1, 176, 179, 207–8, 277, 279–81, 285–6, 300, 304, 323, 350, 354, 360, 370, 397, 413, 419–22, 428–9, 432, 436, 449–50, 459, 461, 474, 477, 479, 483, 500, 502, 535
   immaterial, 38, 280, 304, 324, 354, 360, 420, 527
Matthew, 117
Maximus, 505, 508, 510, 536, 551, 556, 558, 562, 564, 568–9, 572, 574–5, 579–8
Methodius, 246, 261, 546, 559, 567, 574, 578, 580
Miletus, 2, 4, 36, 168
moon. *See* sun
mortal, 5–6, 9, 38, 91, 100–1, 128–30, 137, 166, 176, 178–9, 181, 187, 188, 198, 210, 217, 282, 348, 357, 368, 399, 417, 428, 465, 481, 486–7, 497–8, 503, 535
Mosaic, 136, 139, 141
Moses, 1, 7–16, 30, 71, 81, 93, 109, 131, 136–41, 157, 204, 208, 226–45, 266–7, 272, 285, 289–90, 293, 333, 340–1, 355, 359–60, 366–9, 371–2, 377–8, 380, 383, 389–91, 397–8, 414
Mother, 35, 37, 39, 294
motion, 5–6, 20, 25, 91, 162, 187, 200, 248, 274, 278, 280, 288–9, 292, 300, 305, 314, 326, 333, 340–2, 345, 350–5, 422, 430, 441, 446, 460, 488, 512, 517
murder, 254, 259
mystery, 46, 50, 96, 102, 176, 181, 185, 239, 281, 304, 404, 419, 509, 528, 543, 548, 552, 558, 565, 570

N

necessity, 12, 26, 37, 63, 65–70, 90, 98, 126–7, 161–2, 171, 173, 176, 184, 188, 251–2, 259, 263–4, 266, 286–7, 291, 324, 338, 347, 350, 352, 358, 371, 402, 411, 421, 466, 472, 497, 513, 520, 529–30, 537–8, 541, 543–9, 557–8, 560
Nicene Creed, i
Noah, 120, 241, 247, 367
nonbeing, 506, 508
non-existence, 65, 68, 83, 128, 213, 246, 250, 256, 359, 368, 537
non-existing, 546
numbers, 2, 38, 40, 43, 51–2, 327, 430, 442, 476–7, 481, 483, 493–4, 500

O

Oceanus, 36
Old Testament, 73, 80, 90, 359, 361, 378
Omega, 58
oneness, 22, 358
Only-begotten, 275
Origen, 103, 122, 136, 139, 150, 157, 190, 246, 261, 267, 277, 418, 472–3, 518, 527, 544–6, 567, 570, 578–80
origin, 1, 4, 9–10, 25, 35–8, 48–9, 71–2, 74, 82, 86–7, 126, 140, 142, 151–2, 154, 158, 160, 162, 165, 172, 209–10, 225, 232, 248–50, 253, 255, 258–

60, 284–7, 295, 297–8, 307, 320, 322–4, 340, 357, 416, 421, 442, 455, 463, 471, 481, 483, 486, 521, 523, 526, 530, 532, 538–9, 566

P

pagan(s), 1, 57, 90, 157, 245, 369, 385, 388, 395, 507
pain, 101, 128, 152, 180, 188, 209, 527
Pandoros, 38
paradise, 88, 209, 386, 440, 525
Paradise, 10, 98–02, 140, 235–9, 241–3, 274, 281, 440, 445–7, 525–6, 534
passive, 26, 296
Paul, 31, 39, 42, 51, 105, 118, 121, 123, 131–3, 136, 144, 152, 154, 191, 208, 218, 221, 227, 237, 287, 305, 335, 337, 344, 360–5, 368–9, 374, 380, 384, 388, 400–1, 419, 433, 453, 467, 479, 531, 570, 576
   Saul, 222, 228
Paley, William, iv
Pentad, 39
perfection
   imperfect, 42, 60, 119, 139, 160, 196, 262–3, 294, 308, 349, 356, 371, 420–1
   perfect, 3, 23–4, 33, 42, 46, 48, 52, 77, 84, 92, 96, 100, 113, 116, 127, 129, 130, 133–4, 156, 160, 166, 168–9, 178, 188, 196, 199, 205, 262, 265–6, 269, 280–1, 290–6, 306, 323, 333, 338, 342, 349, 357, 416, 419–20, 455, 470, 475–7, 493, 509–11, 535, 543–8, 550–1, 557–8, 560
Peripatetics, 25, 163
perishable, 11, 19, 21, 24–5, 83, 299, 308, 413

permanence, 18, 363, 392, 410, 511–2, 546
Persians, 482
Peter, 110, 340, 478, 538
Phaethon, 136, 172
Phidias, 87, 191
philanthropy, 102, 142
Philo, 8, 570
philosophers, 1–3, 6, 16, 19, 25, 36–8, 44, 60, 62, 83, 94, 96, 157, 159, 163–4, 168, 170–1, 176–9, 184–5, 284–5, 305, 311, 329, 365, 459, 484–5, 498
plants, 4, 92, 96, 99, 198–01, 241, 248, 281, 288, 294, 317–9, 321, 323, 325–6, 332, 341–2, 382, 385, 389–90, 393, 407–8, 412, 416, 430, 437, 440, 442–4, 447, 454, 475, 485, 518, 524, 529
Plato, 1–5, 8, 10–4, 16, 19–20, 24–5, 37, 136, 163, 169, 172, 176, 178, 180–1, 207, 215, 469–70, 483, 486, 493, 503, 568
Platonism, 552, 572
pleasure, 17, 34, 56, 61, 94, 188, 246, 249–50, 318, 321, 355, 400, 466, 471, 532–3, 546–8, 550, 557, 560, 564
Pleroma, 31, 36–9
poets, 1–2, 16–7, 22, 35–6, 38, 94, 99, 157, 159, 165, 168–70, 177, 197, 203, 284
polytheism, 11, 15, 195, 339
   plurality, 10, 15, 195–6, 305, 338
predestination, 485, 550, 560
predestined, 453, 456, 490
predetermination, 70, 533
pre-eminence, 30, 55, 85, 395, 417
   pre-eminently, 35, 346
   pre-eminent, 41, 134, 350

pre-existent, 12–3, 73, 551–2
pre-existing, 59, 255, 518
preordained, 550
pride, 42, 298, 468, 471, 479, 527, 531, 532, 534
principio, 72, 567
principium, 71
process, 29, 36, 89, 128, 216, 385, 388, 403, 420, 430, 439, 551, 562, 565
Process theology, ii
Prometheus, 157, 169–70
prophesy, 51–2, 130
prophet, 13, 16, 30, 49, 75, 93, 95, 110, 123, 134–5, 151, 271, 289–90, 313, 318, 334, 364, 451, 457, 493, 533
Proverbs, 152, 220, 221, 224, 331
providence, 8, 15, 26–7, 43, 86, 90–2, 116, 122, 134, 137, 158–64, 171–4, 179–84, 190, 197, 199, 202, 204, 205–7, 212–3, 328, 331, 362–3, 375, 378, 471, 497–8, 504–5, 508, 511–3, 516, 529–32, 546, 556–7
providential, 18, 21, 125, 341, 497, 530, 555
Psalmist, 504
Psalms, 126, 144, 269, 291, 312, 334, 361-2, 364, 380, 430, 538
Psalmist, 272, 302–5, 426–7, 453, 486, 493
Ptolemaeus, 52
punishment, 10, 16, 65, 101, 170, 189, 269, 282, 324, 336, 395–6, 471, 499, 503–4, 518, 520, 530, 532–3
Pythagoras, 2, 39
Pythagoreans, 19, 38–9, 163

R

Ratzinger, Cardinal Joseph, i

reptiles, 92, 97, 228, 237, 239, 332, 389–94, 397–8, 400, 403, 405
resurrection, 96, 102, 127–8, 218, 363, 423, 486, 517–8, 522, 537, 543, 563
Revelation, 537, 560, 569
Romans, 136, 191, 362–3, 365, 380, 384, 515, 539, 542, 555, 578, 580
Rome, 488, 502
Ruler, 194–5, 201, 212, 261, 466, 545

S

Sabbath
  sabbath, 94, 148, 240, 424
sages, 2–5, 140, 292, 305, 336, 485
saints, 109, 112, 119, 129, 134–5, 152, 156, 209, 299, 324, 453, 490, 495, 507
salvation, 15, 34, 53, 103, 120, 123, 210, 216, 223, 246, 284, 327, 331, 366, 370, 383, 390, 395–7, 415, 423, 514, 531–2, 535, 559, 563
Satan, 102
Saturninus, 50
Savior, 103–4, 116–7, 213, 216–9
Saviour, 38–40, 45, 51, 53, 123, 133–5, 154, 155, 197, 202, 205–6, 210, 493, 497, 558
seas, 23, 77, 92, 96, 106, 169, 230, 234, 294, 309–10, 313–5, 327–8, 381, 386, 391–2, 394, 522–3
seasons, 91–2, 109, 182, 191–2, 201, 235–6, 325, 364, 383, 387, 422, 488
second day, 104–5, 135, 232–4, 236, 303, 312, 380, 421, 425, 436–7, 462, 464
secret, 110, 127, 136–7, 165–6, 336, 501, 504
seed, 4, 23, 37, 39, 71, 74, 77–8, 91, 107–8, 120, 172, 316–7, 319–20,

324, 357, 366, 382, 387, 405, 439,
447, 449–50, 452, 454, 502, 524,
541, 565
self-determination, 541, 544, 546
self-existent, 26, 232, 543
self-existing, 139, 366
self-made, 265
self-subsistent, 226, 231–2
self-sufficiency
  non-self-sufficiency, iii, 536, 543,
  552
self-sufficient, 196, 375, 538
serpent, 102, 416, 524
  Serpent, 261
seventh day, 84, 94, 98, 148, 239, 267,
408–10, 427, 433, 441, 446–9, 455–
6, 462–3, 476
Shepherd, 153, 205
Sige, 36
sin, 55, 57, 98, 100, 102, 117, 120, 129–
30, 132, 140, 156, 218, 238, 263,
268, 274, 282, 313, 320–2, 324, 403,
453–4, 472–4, 497, 500, 528, 531,
542, 561, 563
  sinful, 473, 518
  sins, 57, 97–8, 106, 112, 167, 212,
  337, 453, 473, 477, 486, 500, 503
Sirach, 221, 267, 385
six days, 94, 141, 148, 225, 227, 229,
267, 284, 409–10, 427, 431, 446,
447–8, 450, 463–4, 475, 521
sixth day, 97–8, 148, 229, 237, 239, 241,
392, 406–9, 427, 440, 442–51, 455,
461–2, 479
Socrates, 8, 14, 21, 163, 178
Solomon, 55, 93, 133, 154, 222, 224,
227, 271, 299, 485, 538, 542
  Ecclesiastes, 315, 485

Son, 18, 22, 40, 42, 49–51, 54–5, 59, 86,
99, 121, 126–7, 148, 151–2, 154–8,
190, 205, 220–2, 224, 237, 266–70,
275–6, 279, 282, 338–40, 358, 360–
2, 369, 373, 397, 399, 401, 419–21,
464–5, 474, 478, 517, 531, 554, 559,
563, 569, 574
soul, 5–7, 10, 20, 76, 79, 83, 85–92, 99,
119–23, 129–30, 136–7, 152, 175,
177, 184, 187–9, 195, 197, 200, 202,
206, 212, 238, 268, 270, 280–1, 284,
293, 298, 304, 311–2, 322, 328–9,
332, 334–5, 355–6, 357, 360, 364–5,
416–8, 451, 456, 458, 472, 474, 485–
7, 496–8, 500, 503, 505, 510, 523,
527–8, 534, 539, 542, 563, 569
sovereign, 298, 308, 316, 441, 513, 548
spherical, 21, 24, 306, 332
Spirit, 7, 16, 20, 22, 46, 51, 53–6, 80,
84, 89, 93, 95, 121, 126–7, 139, 142,
158, 162, 186, 225, 228, 246–7, 280,
282, 293, 300, 307, 311, 313, 325,
328, 333, 339, 360, 362, 369, 371–3,
375, 378, 380, 382, 389–91, 397,
402–4, 410–1, 432, 442, 456–7, 465,
474, 477–9, 507, 510, 517–8, 522–3,
550, 554, 562, 565
stars, 6, 20, 23, 43, 77, 82, 91–2, 96,
109, 115, 141, 148, 167–8, 172–3,
182, 191, 193–4, 201–2, 214–5, 230,
234–5, 271, 287, 292, 294, 322, 326,
341, 360, 382, 384, 386–9, 394, 398,
408, 422, 425–6, 430, 442, 444, 462–
4, 468, 475, 511, 518–20, 522
Stoic, 18, 552
Stoics, 16, 20, 25, 38, 60, 83, 138, 160,
163, 171, 179–80, 183
strength, 46, 129, 160–1, 166, 169, 188,
191, 204–5, 230, 234, 245, 276, 285,

INDEX 593

305–6, 319, 321, 325, 335, 387, 490, 524
suffer, 12, 132, 162, 180, 260, 281, 495–6, 521, 528, 531–2, 535
suffering, 162–3, 215, 219, 249, 281, 348, 395, 400, 417, 528, 531
   misery, 458, 485, 494–8
   suffers, 247, 323, 362
sun, 20, 22, 46, 77, 90–1, 96, 108–11, 115, 118, 134, 141, 147, 152, 165, 167–8, 173, 177, 183, 185, 191, 193–4, 198, 201, 203, 207, 214, 225, 229–30, 232, 234–6, 248, 269–72, 275, 294, 297, 301–2, 310, 316–7, 323–7, 333, 339, 353, 382, 384–8, 398, 408, 410, 412, 422, 428, 432, 436–7, 440, 448, 461, 463, 471, 474–5, 485, 516–23
super-celestial, 30, 52, 134

T

temporal, 32, 89, 104, 135, 166, 175, 184, 187, 189, 239, 281–2, 348, 456–7, 470, 488, 491, 494, 510, 517, 527, 537, 544–6, 550, 557, 560, 564
Tertullian, 59, 66, 72, 85, 578, 580
Tetrad, 39
Thales, 2, 4, 36, 168
Theophilus, 59, 90, 92, 94, 99, 578, 580
third day, 90, 106–7, 229–30, 234–5, 240–1, 380, 428, 436–7, 443, 447, 462, 464
this age, 132
throne of God, 124
Timaeus, 10, 12
Titan, 170
transgressed, 98, 209, 243, 245, 535
transgression
   transgress, 97

transgressors, 51, 97
tree of knowledge, 100–1, 281, 525, 534
tree of life, 100, 140, 242, 282, 525–6
Trinity, 18, 96, 127, 284, 300, 465, 474, 478, 508, 539, 548, 550, 554, 558, 563, 567–8, 570, 572
true religion, 3, 15, 168, 195, 197, 291, 304, 338, 378, 495, 504

U

unapproachable, 24, 553
unbegotten, 3, 11, 90, 279, 340, 354
Unbegotten, 279, 282, 361
unborn, 60, 66, 173, 366
unchangeable, 4, 60, 66, 68, 90, 131, 163, 261, 263, 266, 283, 458, 464–5, 472, 475, 486, 489, 492, 494–5, 546, 550, 560, 562, 568
unchangeableness, 341, 470
unchangeably, 47, 421, 560
uncreated, 12, 19–23, 25, 41, 82, 90, 93, 125–6, 136, 142, 153, 173, 246, 251–3, 257, 264, 266, 294, 305, 350, 360, 575
unfashioned, 12
unforeseen, 298, 336, 491, 498
unformed, 1, 15, 77, 78, 293, 441
unjust, 188, 410, 504, 520, 529, 531
unmade, 60, 66, 191
unnatural, 514, 533
unoriginated, 25

V

vacuum, 31, 37
Valentinus, 35, 50, 52, 369
Van Till, Howard, ii, iii
very good, 61, 65–6, 98, 229, 234, 388, 406–7, 434, 440, 473, 550

vice, 298, 324, 335, 355, 466, 520
Virgil, 171, 179
virtue, 63, 65, 83, 88, 150, 154, 175, 177, 186–9, 206–9, 262, 269, 297–8, 310, 312, 315–7, 324, 335, 350, 354–5, 385, 396, 411, 492, 509, 520, 527–8, 531–3, 535, 545, 547
void, 31, 76–8, 93, 186, 199, 212, 216, 218, 226, 478, 522, 537, 560

W

water, 2–4, 6, 13, 23, 26, 30, 36, 45, 71, 76–7, 82, 93, 95, 97, 104–6, 114–5, 122, 124, 139, 142, 159, 163, 167–9, 176, 184, 192, 198, 201, 214, 215, 218, 222, 225–6, 230–3, 240–1, 243, 252, 258, 271, 278, 290–2, 296–7, 300, 305–16, 323, 326–7, 330, 332, 372, 376–7, 380–1, 398, 410–2, 425–7, 430, 448, 464, 475, 480, 483, 518, 522–3
wicked, 16, 94, 102, 135, 142, 145, 180, 297, 311, 466, 473, 480, 486, 504, 524, 533
wickedness, 33, 56, 133, 143, 145, 155, 170, 177, 269, 294, 298, 352–3, 395, 466–8, 473, 528, 530, 533–4
will of God, 17, 29, 58, 97, 102, 135, 188, 230, 289, 301, 357, 362, 513, 530, 542, 547, 549, 557–8, 560
  God's will, 57, 90, 530, 548, 550, 560
  His good pleasure, 549, 559, 561
without form, 76–8, 81, 93, 96, 139, 265, 294, 296, 316, 478

woman, 88, 102, 111, 118, 155, 244, 245, 270, 282, 400, 404–6, 418, 445–51, 499, 502, 504
Word, 28, 30, 36, 41, 46, 49, 50, 53–5, 73, 75, 84–6, 92–3, 95–6, 98–9, 103, 114, 117, 121, 129, 141, 147–56, 190–1, 195, 197–206, 208–20, 222, 224, 266, 280, 304, 325, 344, 351, 365, 373, 419–21, 428–31, 433, 438, 440, 454, 464, 474, 476–7, 479, 507, 509, 518, 550, 553, 559, 561, 563, 570, 572, 574
workmanship, 5, 57, 160, 163, 166, 269, 272, 274–6
world, 1, 7, 16, 17, 19–22, 24–34, 36–7, 39, 43, 46–8, 51–5, 62, 64, 77, 83–4, 87, 89, 90, 93, 94–5, 103–5, 108–9, 114, 122–5, 127, 131–6, 138, 140–8, 151, 157–9, 161–6, 168–73, 176–87, 190–1, 194, 198, 207, 211–2, 220–5, 238–40, 253, 256, 262–8, 270–1, 275–6, 280–1, 284–9, 291–300, 302, 304–5, 308–11, 313, 319, 322–4, 326, 332–3, 336, 339, 341–3, 347–8, 352–3, 362, 364–6, 368, 370, 373, 378, 384, 388, 396, 418, 422, 435, 439, 442, 444, 449, 451, 453–5, 457–61, 463–5, 467, 470–4, 478–85, 487–9, 491, 493, 495–7, 501, 503, 505, 509, 512, 517, 526–7, 529, 536, 538, 542–3, 545–8, 550–3, 559–60, 564, 570–1

Z

Zeus, 4, 20, 138

www.ingramcontent.com/pod-product-compliance
Lightning Source LLC
Chambersburg PA
CBHW030257080526
44584CB00012B/350